Affective, Interactive and Cognitive Methods for E-Learning Design: Creating an Optimal Education Experience

Aimilia Tzanavari
University of Nicosia, Cyprus

Nicolas Tsapatsoulis
Cyprus University of Technology, Cyprus

Information Science REFERENCE

INFORMATION SCIENCE REFERENCE
Hershey · New York

Director of Editorial Content: Kristin Klinger
Director of Book Publications: Julia Mosemann
Development Editor: Joel Gamon
Publishing Assistant: Kurt Smith
Typesetter: Kurt Smith
Quality Control: Jamie Snavely
Cover Design: Lisa Tosheff
Printed at: Yurchak Printing Inc.

Published in the United States of America by
Information Science Reference (an imprint of IGI Global)
701 E. Chocolate Avenue
Hershey PA 17033
Tel: 717-533-8845
Fax: 717-533-8661
E-mail: cust@igi-global.com
Web site: http://www.igi-global.com/reference

Library of Congress Cataloging-in-Publication Data

Affective, interactive, and cognitive methods for e-learning design : creating an optimal education experience / Aimilia Tzanavari and Nicolas Tsapatsoulis, editors.

p. cm.

Includes bibliographical references and index.

Summary: "This book focuses on the study and application of human computer interaction principles in the design of online education"--Provided by publisher.

ISBN 978-1-60566-940-3 (hardcover) -- ISBN 978-1-60566-941-0 (ebook) 1. Internet in education. 2. Instructional systems--Design. 3. Human-computer interaction. I. Tzanavari, Aimilia, 1975- II. Tsapatsoulis, Nicolas, 1969-

LB1044.87.A385 2010

371.33'44678--dc22

2009034904

British Cataloguing in Publication Data
A Cataloguing in Publication record for this book is available from the British Library.

All work contributed to this book is new, previously-unpublished material. The views expressed in this book are those of the authors, but not necessarily of the publisher.

Table of Contents

Detailed Table of Contents

Section 1
Background

Section 1 presents introductory material and deals with the transition from e-learning to e-education. The role of instructors, the development of new learning methodologies, the technological gaps between countries, regions, or segments of the population, and the influence of these gaps on the actual potential of e-learning are investigated.

This chapter aims at setting up the goals and key problems for the transition from early e-learning systems and platforms to an integrated e-education view which examines the technology-enhanced experience from various perspectives and not only from the technological or financial point of view. E-education requires a wider investigation which involves the role of instructors (either of traditional or technology enhanced learning), the development of new learning methodologies, the technological gaps, mainly in Information and Communication Technologies (ICT) between countries and regions, or segments of the population, the influence of these gaps on the actual potential of technology enhanced learning and the role they play in educational institutions and workplace. A look into the learning process and an attempt to relate it to what is known as "Constructivist Learning Theory" is also given in this chapter and the implications of transition of e-learning to e education are discussed.

Section 2
Social Interaction and Collaborative Learning

In Section 2 emphasis is given on collaborative learning and the effects of social interaction within the Web. The Web 2.0 technologies and their usage in e-learning, individual learning in a social interaction environment and interface design for collaborative learning are among the issues covered in this section of the book.

Chapter 2 discusses the transition from "teaching" to "learning" in contemporary education in the context of ICT and the Web. Although the latter had initially a static structure and merely required passive human viewers, this notion is currently changing towards a second generation of dynamic services and communication tools that emphasize on peer-to-peer collaboration, contributing, sharing, both among humans and programs. This revolution, usually known under the collective term Web 2.0, is reviewed from an educational as well as a technological point of view. The issues and controversies arising are backed up by case studies from diverse educational contexts to illustrate the potential of the proposed solutions. The discussion is concluded with even more exciting speculations on the envisaged arrival of Web 3.0 and collaborative content sharing with semantic technologies.

Chapter 3 examines the cognitive processes that allow an individual to learn within learning groups. It addresses the interface between technology and the learner by using cognitive psychology to discuss learning processes in formal and informal groups. It investigates ways to create competent learning groups, and e-learning design methods that facilitate optimal learning by an individual in a group setting. An e-learning design approach which is based on a blend of cognitive and activity theories is presented along with a pilot empirical study that measures the value of e-learning from four constructs derived from the proposed theories. The result of the study suggests that pure virtual learning environments may not always be the best option as some users require some physical contact.

Chapter 4 focuses on the design of social facilities in interfaces that are intended to motivate and sustain the process of communication among students. Although there are design constraints in creating an environment capable of supporting social interaction, previous research findings indicate that social presence is a key factor for social interaction. In addition, previous research has pointed out that social presence is affected by individual, social response and media variables, suggesting that an interface design might enhance social presence. This chapter explores the interface design by investigating how placing an emphasis on interaction facilities and incorporating text, images and animation affects students' experiences of interacting with each other. The overall conclusion is that the interface design can increase the number of interactions and enhance the perceived social presence in e-learning environment.

Section 3
Technology-Enhanced Learning Design

Section 3 composes the main body of the book. It deals with technology-enhanced learning design. Various design approaches are proposed and discussed along with case studies and particular e-learning applications.

The main focus of this chapter is on the exploration of the process-oriented, affective, socio-contextual issues involved in the design of prolonged workflows of e-learning activities. A set of heuristics for designing e-learning experiences that can maintain learners' engagement along the time, and achieve durable, profound educational benefits in the educational context in which they take place are proposed. Furthermore, it is pointed out that involving learners as experience design partners is fundamental for these purposes. The proposed approach is exemplified by widely discussing two case studies that involve different technologies (shared 3D virtual worlds and online collaborative storytelling) in different educational contexts – high and primary schools.

This chapter proposes a new pedagogic pattern model which enables the transcription of blended e-learning practice in a hands-on way to both instructional designers and educational practitioners using e-learning to satisfy the emotional and cognitive needs of learners. This model takes into account the dynamics between technology-bounded determinism of e-learning and users' need to develop their personal emotional and cognitive preferences. Case studies are also presented to demonstrate the proposed approach in simulation-based learning in Human-Computer Interface design, and in writing an online troubleshooting wiki about network computing in English. The study used a qualitative method to evaluate feedback data in the form of tutor self-reports, learners' reports, examination results, and a collective analysis of three experienced tutors-researchers.

Chapter 7 focuses on the design of e-learning applications with students through a particular methodology called We!Design. In years past, many methodological approaches, methods and techniques have been implemented based on the belief that users can and should be involved in the design process of technology products that affect them. We!Design methodology is inspired by the findings of research involving users and particularly students at diverse levels and phases of the design process. It is a student-centered participatory design methodology that assigns students a primary role in the design process. The various phases of the We!Design methodology are presented, and the results of its application are examined in four different design projects: a web-based e-assessment application for tertiary education, a course website, an e-portfolio application, and a tablet-PC-based e-assessment application for secondary education).

Chapter 8 elaborates upon utilization of ontologies for courseware design. The aim is to create teaching strategies for e-learning based on the principles of ontological engineering and cognitive psychology. The proposed framework is targeted at the development of methodologies and related technologies that can scaffold the process of knowledge structuring and orchestrating teaching ontologies for courseware design. The orchestrating procedure is the kernel of ontology development. Ontologies that describe the main concepts of exemplary domains are used both for teaching and assessment techniques. The main stress is put on using visual techniques of mind-mapping and concept mapping as a powerful mind learning tool. Cognitive bias and some results of Gestalt psychology are highlighted as a general guideline. The ideas of balance, clarity, and beauty are applied to the ontology orchestrating procedures. The examples are taken mainly from a course in C-language programming, and in the foundations of intelligent systems development.

Chapter 9 emphasizes on the design of adaptive e-learning systems. One area that can benefit greatly from adaptive e-learning systems is teacher development in the educational uses of computers. In this chapter, the design of PAUL, an adaptive computer-based learning environment for the development of ICT-related pedagogical content knowledge, a unique body of knowledge that teachers need to develop in order to be able to teach with ICT, is discussed. PAUL combines two opposing trends in adapting instruction, namely instruction that is both controlled by the learner and the system. The impact of PAUL is expected to be significant as it will provide a venue for effective teacher professional development situating learning in virtual communities of practice and supporting teacher thinking about the educational uses of ICT in teaching and learning

Chapter 10 presents an application of e-learning design for achieving fluency in foreign languages. It is an interesting topic because it revisits one of the oldest technology enhanced learning methods that of pattern drills (PDs). While being highly regarded in the past, PDs have become unpopular since then, partially because of their rigidity and lack of context (grounding). Despite these shortcomings the virtues of PDs, at least with regard to the acquisition of basic linguistic reflex or skills (automatisms), are still necessary to produce language at a 'normal' rate. However, improvement of PDs is necessary and this chapter deals with this subject in the context of the Web. Unlike tapes or books, computers are open media, allowing for dynamic changes, taking users' performances and preferences into account. A small web-application is presented allowing for these extensions.

The role of multimedia, hypermedia and virtual reality is the subject of Section 4. Both current trends and future directions of multimedia learning design are examined while the role of Virtual Reality in building an immersive e-learning experience is discussed in depth.

Chapter 11 discusses the key factors and new directions of multimedia learning design. It explores specific topics, issues and directions associated with multimedia and hypermedia learning environments. A key aim is to inform researchers, designers, and developers of multimedia learning systems as well as educators who wish to engage students in learning activities rooted in multimedia learning research and design of the critical factors that have had an impact on maximizing learning through multimedia. Strengths and pitfalls of multimedia learning design are discussed through the review of the important conclusions that two generations of multimedia research have contributed to multimedia design. Finally, emerging factors, which are currently formulating a third generation of multimedia design and learning research are presented.

A look into the use of virtual reality in education is given in this chapter. Virtual Reality (VR) is produced by a combination of technologies that are used to visualize and provide interaction with a virtual environment. These environments often depict three-dimensional space which may be realistic or imaginary, macroscopic or microscopic and based on realistic physical laws of dynamics or on imaginary dynamics. The multitude of scenarios that VR might be used makes it broadly applicable to many areas in education. A key feature of VR is that it allows multi-sensory interaction with the space visualized. This chapter looks at how this combination of multi-sensory visualization and interactivity makes VR ideally suited for effective learning and tries to explain this effectiveness in terms of the advantages afforded by active learning from experiences. Some of the applications of VR in education and the drawbacks associated with this technology are also discussed.

Chapter 13 evaluates the educational and motivational value of an augmented reality learning scenario by investigating the transition from usability to user experience. Augmented Reality (AR) is merging real and virtual environments within a single interaction space. This tight integration of computer technologies into a real environment is creating new opportunities and challenges for the designers of e-learning systems as well as a new kind of user experience (UX) for the learner. Recently, AR-based educational systems were developed that are implementing learning scenarios for primary and secondary schools. An important goal of these novel teaching platforms is to enhance the students' motivation to learn. This chapter reports on the perceived educational and motivational value of an AR-based learning scenario for chemistry based on the results of a user-centered formative usability evaluation.

based on the automatic analysis of the learners' emotional state providing different learners' profiles which are built and maintained by "observing" each learner behavior. As a learner is strongly positively affected to the learning procedure in the presence of an agent, the proposed system has adopted an expressive ECA which is adapted to the learner's emotional states in the duration of the learning procedure.

Foreword

To those in the know, it may seem as if e-learning has lost its novelty already. However, if we take human generation time as a yardstick, it has been with us for at most 1 generation only. And in those measly 25 years significant changes have already taken place. Indeed, I am convinced that the pace at which changes thrust themselves upon the educational sector, is too fast for those involved in it to cope with them to the full. In part, this has to do with that same generation time: not everybody is willing to embrace change wholeheartedly; indeed, not everybody is even able to adapt to a changing situation. So, for change to take effect in all the nooks and crannies of the house of education, more time is needed, enough for instance for the baby-boom generation to be replaced by its successor (which, no doubt, will demonstrate the same resistance to pervasive change). But in no insignificant part, it also has to do with the magnitude and depth of the innovation that we are witnessing.

Confronted with the notion of e-learning, or technology-enhanced learning if you like, some will react that there's little news under the sun. Sure, e-learning constitutes an innovation, but hasn't education always been confronted with technology-infused change? Perhaps, for many centuries the apprenticeship system held sway and little changed in the way knowledge about trades and professions was transferred, even if the professions themselves underwent technological progress. However, with the advent of the industrial society and the need to adopt a form of 'broadcasting' in education in order to be able to teach ever growing numbers of labourers, educational innovations have been adopted ever more rapidly. From the slate and pencil, via the blackboard to the white board and smart board; from individual oral exams via hand-marked written exams in classes, to machine-marked multiple-choice exams for the masses. Etc. So, the argument goes, technological innovation has been part and parcel of education at least since the onset of the industrial revolution. And now we are merely witnessing the next step, the incorporation of the computer. But this instrumentalist argument misses the mark in two important ways.

First, it gravely underestimates the extent of change that technological innovations are capable of. Technologies, quite in general, are designed to cope with a particular practical problem, through their design they fulfill a particular function. Thus, a car is a device to transport oneself from A to B. However, philosophers of technology have discovered long since that technologies posses powers of change that go beyond the functions that they were designed for. Wiebe Bijker calls this the 'interpretative flexibility' of technology, Steve Woolgar talks about technology's 'new readings'. And once it is pointed out, it is all too obvious that eventually technological artefacts are always used in ways that transgress their intended functionality. Cars are used for racing on a circuit or for showing of one's wealth, functions that can hardly be seen as transporting people from A to B. Lack of space keeps me from expanding the argument but, really, it is quite simple to find corroborating evidence with most if not all technological devices that our society has brought forth. What goes for cars, goes for blackboards -I vividly remember the beautiful colourful drawings my teacher used to make on the blackboard for her pupils' birthdays; I don't think the inventors of the blackboard had this frivolous use in mind when they designed them, for multiple choice exams - 'objective' comparisons of student achievements can now be made with a push on a button, indeed for almost any educational innovation. In short, then, a technology is never a mere technology as it has the power to shape our culture, including our educational culture.

Second, the computer is a kind of innovation that is not on a par with any of its predecessors. The reason is that a computer is the first genuinely interactive artefact, and it gets ever better at that. Interactivity does not make it human, but it is one of the requirements for being humanlike. Although we are still far removed from the moment a computer could replace a human tutor or teacher (and I am not entirely sure it ever should), it certainly can do so already in some respects. The simplest example is the drill and practice exercises in language or math education. With the computer, the pupil gets instant feedback from a 'teacher' who never tires and always remains patient (unless it has been programmed not to). These are achievements that black boards and their likes can never be capable of. So the sheer impact of the computer as a technological artefact is in a qualitative sense different than anything before it. For sure, then, it is a powerful innovation.

Together, these two arguments make for a potent mixture indeed. Therefore, the introduction of e-learning is not merely yet another technological trick in the teacher's bag, but a foreceful change agent that is going to alter the educational system irreversibly and deeply. Those who stick to a mere instrumentalist view are fooling themselves and their followers; it will not be long before this becomes apparent to each and everyone in education, reluctantly or wholeheartedly. The present volume stands witness to this. Without going into any details, the themes that are discussed - networked collaborative learning, design for e-learning including the use of multimedia and virtual reality, usability and user experiences, and most tellingly perhaps the inclusion of affect in learning - all cry out 'e-learning makes a qualitative difference to learning, learning is never going to be the same anymore'. Not only has the discussion of learning acquired a new depth, we are even beginning to think about education, about learning and teaching along a whole set of new dimensions. The authors and editors are to be congratulated with their achievement.

Prof. Peter B. Sloep
Programme Director Learning Networks for Non-Formal Learning
Co-ordinator for the EU Funded idSpace Project on Distributed, Collaborative Product Innovation
Centre for Learning Sciences and Technologies
Open University of the Netherlands, The Netherlands

Preface

A traditional division of e-learning is that of synchronous – asynchronous. Synchronous e-learning environments try to resample the traditional class-oriented training and put their emphasis on eliminating the distance parameter. The widespread of broadband networks, multimedia streaming technologies and multimedia interactive protocols allows the synchronous e-learning systems to be easily realized and cost effective. Asynchronous e-learning systems, on the other hand, needs to define alternative learning approaches in order, first, to move from training to learning and, second, to get advantage of the availability of learning content anytime, anyplace and anywhere through the Web. These challenges along with the tremendous expansion of Web and web related services and applications put the emphasis of e-learning on the asynchronous mode of operation. In addition, Web-based leaning is considered, nowadays, the basic form of e-learning. In any case, during e-learning the learner spends a significant amount of his/her time online, interacting with web-based applications. This interaction carries tremendous weight in the learning process, because it directly influences the way the learner receives, comprehends and ultimately retains information.

The strong relation of Web and e-learning motivate us to start discussing the possibility to edit a book on e-learning design. There is a lot of work and active research on the design and evaluation of Web-based applications. We consider that specialization and enhancement of this research to technology enhanced learning would be beneficiary to e-learning researchers, academics, policy makers and stakeholders. However, designing successful e-learning is not simple as that. One can find himself/herself confronted with a number of different disciplines, namely, pedagogy, human computer interaction, affective computing, cognitive psychology, multimedia design, just to list a few. Therefore, it is realistic to conclude that e-learning design and in particular designing for creating an optimal educational experience, with the maximum benefits, involves teamwork.

In the past, e-learning was mostly encountered in adult training, frequently limited to teaching primarily technical subjects to company employees. Nowadays technology-enhanced learning can be found everywhere, from K-12 education to training fighter pilots. This expansion has created more complex needs and requirements when designing an e-learning application, course, lesson or material. Being familiar with the use of a particular development tool or system is certainly not enough to lead to effective e-learning. Broad knowledge of the issues involved, in combination with creative and efficient teamwork proves to be the way to designing better educational experiences.

Affective, Interactive and Cognitive Methods for E-Learning Design: Creating an Optimal Education Experience tries to bridge the current gap that exists in e-learning literature. This book gives insight into the most important design and other issues encountered when creating e-learning, helping the reader create better designed, thoughtful e-learning materials, lessons, activities, courses or software. Perspectives from educators, designers, and developers are presented. Theory is complemented with real cases where the reader can see situations, solutions and their results. Open research questions are discussed.

As implied by the title, the book tries to investigate e-learning design along three main axes. The first deals with interaction design and the theories and developments presented in that discipline. Solid theoretical and experimentally evaluated approaches were founded and adopted in e-learning design. Especially the Web-based learning sector has a rich heritage to borrow ideas from. As an example, one may consider the key concept of interaction design: human centered organization. There is no doubt that learner centered design is not only a wish in modern e-learning systems but an absolute necessity. It is anticipated, therefore, that a lot of research in the area of interaction design to be adapted to the peculiarities of Web-based learning. The degree to which this aim can be fulfilled and what are the best practices to push forward is examined in detail in this book.

The second axis of the book examines the cognitive theories and their role in e-learning design. As the years pass more and more constructs of cognitive theory are brought into practical systems: adaptive systems are built to materialize variations on the learning style of learners, the working memory limitations are taken into account, problem based learning is promoted, etc. However, a key challenge is to examine the role of cognitive approaches from a social networking perspective. The emergence of a variety of Web 2.0 applications and the establishment of the, so-called, social Web opened new directions of research on e-learning design as well. Nowadays, the social dimension of Web-based learning is becoming the driving force on e-learning design research. Since learning involves social interactions, or at least takes place in a social environment terms such as collaborative learning and social pedagogy are becoming common. The problem based learning is revisited in a social framework while the situation based learning is becoming a reality.

Affective computing in e-learning design is the third axis. It investigates the effect emotional parameters during the learning process and attempts to combine them with cognitive theories into learning systems that present a significant degree of adaptability to learner characteristics. Affective computing is a new and very challenging area of research. Although very few solid constructs have been achieved so far, some important e-learning applications have been developed and presented in this book.

The basic aim of this book is to present the state of the art work in e-learning design and the influences from interaction design, affective computing and cognitive theories. As a result the intended audience is mainly researchers, academics and educationalists working in the above areas. This does not mean that the book cannot be used as a course book for post graduate students; we organized the material in the book to help preserving this role. The first chapters in each section present introductory material and are appropriate to set the background on research issues on e-learning design. Furthermore, all chapters were carefully selected to ensure smooth readability of the whole; that is the book is not a collection of research papers but it was designed as a single author book presenting the required coherence among all the chapters included therein. In addition to e-learning design researchers and post graduate students this book is expected to be valuable for e-learning system developers. It provides a practical framework for developing e-learning applications based on interactive behavior and pedagogical, cognitive and affective characteristics.

In addition, and based on the fact that e-learning is a strategic goal for future educational policies leads to extensive research by academics as well as by policy makers, the variety on theoretical perspectives presented in this book are anticipated to provide a comprehensive technology enhanced educational background emphasizing on Web-based learning. As a consequence the emergence of affective theories, interaction design and the materialization of a great part of cognitive research into pedagogical approaches is expected to have an important merit in governmentally supported research in e-learning. To that end, one of the targets of this book is to establish a basis of integrating various e-learning design approaches into a wide theoretical framework, as a common ground among diverse directions of research on technology enhanced learning design.

The material in this book is organized into five sections in an effort to give an integrated view of the various disciplines involved in the design of modern technology enhanced learning approaches. Section 1 presents introductory material and deals with the transition from e-learning to e-education. In Section 2 emphasis is given on collaborative learning and the effects of social interaction within the Web. Section 3 composes the main body of the book; it deals with technology-enhanced learning design which is the basic theme of this book. The role of multimedia, hypermedia and virtual reality is the subject of Section 4. There is no doubt that advances in these areas changed dramatically the way we see Web based learning. Finally, Section 5 examines some interesting ideas of affective computing and their utilization in e-learning systems. We should keep into our minds that a really intelligent computer system is the one that exposes some degree of emotion understanding and expressing capabilities.

Despite the organization of the book into these sections, in most cases the material presented in the chapters is cross discipline showing the strong binding between the affective, cognitive and interactive technologies required for creating efficient e-learning environments.

The first chapter of this book aims at setting up the goals and key problems for the transition from early e-learning systems and platforms to an integrated e-education view which examines the technology-enhanced experience from various perspectives and not only from the technological or financial point of view. It is generally accepted that most of the e-learning-related literature looks into technological issues dealing either with content creation, delivery, use and availability or with engineering or technological issues of e-learning systems and structure. The financial facet of distance learning was also examined in detail and to specific sectors (corporate; academia). E-education on the other hand requires a wider investigation which involves the role of instructors (either of traditional or technology enhanced learning), the development of new learning methodologies, the technological gaps, mainly in Information and Communication Technologies (ICT) between countries and regions, or segments of the population, the influence of these gaps on the actual potential of technology enhanced learning and the role they play in educational institutions and workplace. A look into the learning process and an attempt to relate it to what is known as "Constructivist Learning Theory" is also given in this section of the book. Finally, the implications of transition of e-learning to e education are discussed.

The second section of the book begins with Chapter 2 which is entitled "Web Advances in Education: Interactive, Collaborative Learning via Web 2.0". It mainly discusses the transition from "teaching" to "learning" in contemporary education in the context of ICT and the Web. Although the latter had initially a static structure and merely required passive human viewers, this notion is currently changing towards a second generation of dynamic services and communication tools that emphasize on peer-to-peer collaboration, contributing, sharing, both among humans and programs. This revolution, usually known under the collective term Web 2.0, is reviewed from an educational as well as a technological point of view. The issues and controversies arising are backed up by case studies from diverse educational contexts to illustrate the potential of the proposed solutions. The discussion is concluded with even more exciting speculations on the envisaged arrival of Web 3.0 and collaborative content sharing with semantic technologies.

Chapter 3 continues the discussion on collaborative learning by examining the cognitive processes that allow an individual to learn within learning groups. It addresses the interface between technology and the learner by using cognitive psychology to discuss learning processes in formal and informal groups. It investigates ways to create competent learning groups, and e-learning design methods that facilitate optimal learning by an individual in a group setting. An e-learning design approach which is based on a blend of cognitive and activity theories is presented along with a pilot empirical study that measures the value of e-learning from four constructs derived from the proposed theories. The result of the study suggests that pure virtual learning environments may not always be the best option as some users require some physical contact. While e-learning may fill many gaps, it should be perceived as a tool that needs to be attended with emotional and social contact. This conclusion causes a practical issue for the discussion that follows in Sections 4 and 5.

In Chapter 4 interface design for social interaction within e-learning environments is addressed. Discussion focuses on the design of social facilities in interfaces that are intended to motivate and sustain the process of communication among students. Although there are design constraints in creating an environment capable of supporting social interaction, previous research findings indicate that social presence is a key factor for social interaction. In addition, previous research has pointed out that social presence is affected by individual, social response and media variables, suggesting that an interface design might enhance social presence. This chapter explores the interface design by investigating how placing an emphasis on interaction facilities and incorporating text, images and animation affects students' experiences of interacting with each other. The overall conclusion is that the interface design can increase the number of interactions and enhance the perceived social presence in e-learning environment.

Section 3 deals with specific e-learning design methodologies. It begins with chapter 5 which considers technology-enhanced educational activities spanning along a significant period of time, and explores this context from a "quality of experience" perspective. Rather than addressing the design of technology, interface, or interactive contents for learning, the main focus is on the exploration of the process-oriented, affective, socio-contextual issues involved in the design of prolonged workflows of e-learning activities. A set of heuristics for designing e-learning experiences that can maintain learners' engagement along the time, and achieve durable, profound educational benefits in the educational context in which they take place are proposed. Furthermore, it is pointed out that involving learners as experience design partners is fundamental for these purposes. The proposed approach is exemplified by widely discussing two case studies that involve different technologies (shared 3D virtual worlds and online collaborative storytelling) in different educational contexts – high and primary schools.

A pedagogic pattern model of blended e-learning design is presented in Chapter 6. Blended e-learning design based on user feedback is commonly found in grassroots educational practice. After outlining three approaches to understanding blended e-learning, Marcia Bates's informational process approach is used to bring together the design theory of Christopher Alexander and the instructional theory of Jean Houssaye. This results in a new pedagogic pattern model enabling the transcription of blended e-learning practice in a hands-on way to both instructional designers and educational practitioners using e-learning to satisfy the emotional and cognitive needs of learners. This model takes into account the dynamics between technology-bounded determinism of e-learning and users' need to develop their personal emotional and cognitive preferences. Case studies are also presented to demonstrate the proposed approach in simulation-based learning in Human-Computer Interface design, and in writing an online troubleshooting wiki about network computing in English. The study used a qualitative method to evaluate feedback data in the form of tutor self-reports, learners' reports, examination results, and a collective analysis of three experienced tutors-researchers.

Chapter 7 focuses on the design of e-learning applications with students through a particular methodology called We!Design. In years past, many methodological approaches, methods and techniques have been implemented based on the belief that users can and should be involved in the design process of technology products that affect them. We!Design methodology is inspired by the findings of research involving users and particularly students at diverse levels and phases of the design process. It is a student-centered participatory design methodology that assigns students a primary role in the design process. The various phases of the We!Design methodology are presented, and the results of its application are examined in four different design projects: a web-based e-assessment application for tertiary education, a course website, an e-portfolio application, and a tablet-PC-based e-assessment application for secondary education). Participant evaluations indicated that the We!Design methodology was an adequate means for successful elicitation of students' needs and their application in educational software design.

Chapter 8 elaborates upon utilization of ontologies for courseware design. The aim is to create teaching strategies for e-learning based on the principles of ontological engineering and cognitive psychology. The proposed framework is targeted at the development of methodologies and related technologies that can scaffold the process of knowledge structuring and orchestrating teaching ontologies for courseware design. The orchestrating procedure is the kernel of ontology development. Ontologies that describe the main concepts of exemplary domains are used both for teaching and assessment techniques. The main stress is put on using visual techniques of mind-mapping and concept mapping as a powerful mind learning tool. Cognitive bias and some results of Gestalt psychology are highlighted as a general guideline. The ideas of balance, clarity, and beauty are applied to the ontology orchestrating procedures. The examples are taken mainly from a course in C-language programming, and in the foundations of intelligent systems development.

Chapter 9 emphasizes on the design of adaptive e-learning systems. Adaptive e-learning systems can be extremely valuable tools in developing innovative learner-centered environments in any content domain. One area that can benefit greatly from adaptive e-learning systems is teacher development in the educational uses of computers. In this chapter, the design of PAUL, an adaptive computer-based learning environment for the development of ICT-related pedagogical content knowledge, a unique body of knowledge that teachers need to develop in order to be able to teach with ICT, is discussed. PAUL combines two opposing trends in adapting instruction, namely instruction that is both controlled by the learner and the system. The impact of PAUL is expected to be significant as it will provide a venue for effective teacher professional development situating learning in virtual communities of practice and supporting teacher thinking about the educational uses of ICT in teaching and learning.

Section 3 concludes with chapter 10 which presents an application of e-learning design for achieving fluency in foreign languages. It is an interesting topic because it revisits one of the oldest technology enhanced learning methods that of pattern drills. Achieving speaking proficiency in a non-native language is a highly complex process which requires the acquisition of various kinds of knowledge and skills, like the learning of words, rules and patterns and their connection to communicative goals (intentions), the usual starting point. In order to help the learner acquire these skills we propose an electronic version of an age old method: pattern drills (PDs). While being highly regarded in the past, PDs have become unpopular since then, partially because of their rigidity and lack of context (grounding). Despite these shortcomings the virtues of PDs, at least with regard to the acquisition of basic linguistic reflex or skills (automatisms), are still necessary to produce language at a 'normal' rate. However, improvement of PDs is necessary and this chapter deals with this subject in the context of the Web. Unlike tapes or books, computers are open media, allowing for dynamic changes, taking users' performances and preferences into account. A small web-application is presented allowing for these extensions. It is a free, electronic version of PDs, i.e. an open exercise generator, adaptable to the users' ever changing needs.

Section 4 deals with the use multimedia and virtual reality in e-learning. It begins with chapter 11 which discusses the key factors and new directions of multimedia learning design. It explores specific topics, issues and directions associated with multimedia and hypermedia learning environments. A key aim is to inform researchers, designers, and developers of multimedia learning systems as well as educators who wish to engage students in learning activities rooted in multimedia learning research and design of the critical factors that have had an impact on maximizing learning through multimedia. Strengths and pitfalls of multimedia learning design are discussed through the review of the important conclusions that two generations of multimedia research have contributed to multimedia design. Finally, emerging factors, which are currently formulating a third generation of multimedia design and learning research are presented.

A deeper look into the use of virtual reality in education is given in chapter 12. Virtual Reality (VR) is produced by a combination of technologies that are used to visualize and provide interaction with a virtual environment. These environments often depict three-dimensional space which may be realistic or imaginary, macroscopic or microscopic and based on realistic physical laws of dynamics or on imaginary dynamics. The multitude of scenarios that VR might be used makes it broadly applicable to many areas in education. A key feature of VR is that it allows multi-sensory interaction with the space visualized. This chapter looks at how this combination of multi-sensory visualization and interactivity makes VR ideally suited for effective learning and tries to explain this effectiveness in terms of the advantages afforded by active learning from experiences. Some of the applications of VR in education and the drawbacks associated with this technology are also discussed.

Chapter 13 evaluates the educational and motivational value of an augmented reality learning scenario by investigating the transition from usability to user experience. Augmented Reality (AR) is merging real and virtual environments within a single interaction space. This tight integration of computer technologies into a real environment is creating new opportunities and challenges for the designers of e-learning systems as well as a new kind of user experience (UX) for the learner. Recently, AR-based educational systems were developed that are implementing learning scenarios for primary and secondary schools. An important goal of these novel teaching platforms is to enhance the students' motivation to learn. This chapter reports on the perceived educational and motivational value of an AR-based learning scenario for chemistry based on the results of a user-centered formative usability evaluation. Quantitative and qualitative data were collected during two experiments with students from secondary schools. While the comparison between the two types of measure increases confidence in the evaluation results, the qualitative measures also provide a detailed description of the user learning experience.

The last section of the book is composed of two chapters emphasizing on the usage of affective computing in e-learning design. Chapter 14 discusses the potential of affective computing for improving the e-learning experience, both from a theoretical and a practical perspective. The initial focus is on the important role emotions play in the (e-) learning process and on the rationale to include affect in e-learning design. Three trends in the affective computing domain are briefly presented; they represent the core features of a European Union funded project on technology-enhanced learning called "Myself". These trends are: the use of affective Embodied Conversational Agents as virtual tutors; the possibility of automatic recognition of - and adaptation to- the emotional and motivational state of the learner; and the use of 3D simulations for web-based training of emotional competence. Finally, by focusing on the feature of automatic recognition and adaptation, the authors of this chapter present a detailed account of the approach developed within the project and use it as a framework for discussing the main benefits and current limitations to the complex process of integration of affective computing features into e-learning systems.

Chapter 15 explores the incorporation of user expressivity in e-learning environment through a particular example. A learning system adaptive to learner's behavior is considered as an innovative system. The more a learning system exchanges relevant fragments of information about the learner's affective status the more it adapts to it. Following this direction, an integrated learning system taking indo consideration learners' emotional state in order to provide a personalized e-learning system is presented. An extended version of the IEEE Reference Model (WG) LTSA is used for this purpose. The proposed approach is based on the automatic analysis of the learners' emotional state providing different learners' profiles which are built and maintained by "observing" each learner behavior. As a learner is strongly positively affected to the learning procedure in the presence of an agent, the proposed system has adopted an expressive ECA which is adapted to the learner's emotional states in the duration of the learning procedure.

We argue that all of the above chapters contribute to a better understanding of the current and future trends in e-learning design under the prism of the advances achieved in affective computing, social networking, interaction design and cognitive theories. By reading this book an integrated view of the research efforts in the above areas, as far as the e-learning design is concerned, is anticipated. Although social networking parameters seem to dominate modern e-learning systems the prospects of multimedia and virtual reality must not be neglected. These are disciplines already mature to take their role in technology enhanced learning. Affective computing, on the other hand, is definitely a bet for the future. Once establishments of emotion recognition made more efficient and widely applicable affective computing will find its way to future e-learning systems. The current trend is the utilization of emotion expressivity in combination with virtual reality and intelligent agents.

Before concluding we would like to thank the authors of the individual book chapters for their co-operation and willingness to make this book a reality. Finally, we would like to give a special thanks to all the anonymous reviewers for their contribution and help.

We wish you an enjoyable journey through the material of this book!

Aimilia Tzanavari
Nicolas Tsapatsoulis
Editors

Section 1
Background

Section 1 presents introductory material and deals with the transition from e-learning to e-education. The role of instructors, the development of new learning methodologies, the technological gaps between countries, regions, or segments of the population, and the influence of these gaps on the actual potential of e-learning are investigated.

Chapter 1
From e-Learning to e-Education:
Goals, Strategic Assessment and Implications

Zohar Ben-Asher
European Centre for Research & Financing, Israel & ABC Consultants, UK

ABSTRACT

The chapter examines the educational (and schooling) processes as related to the overall social, political and economic processes, so as to set the context within which e-Learning has to be explored and discussed and within which a strategy for it can be forged. Such issues as the economic implications of the educational system, the extent to which economic considerations and realities are actually taken into account in curricula building and in the process of teacher training are discussed, along with the notion of acquisition of knowledge and/or information. The chapter portrays the parameters that are required to create a well balanced strategy for the developing of e-Learning as a major vehicle for the implementation of the overall social goals of education, of which one essential seems to be lacking at times: the preparation of the system's customer, the pupil, as a critical observer of reality and a careful and discriminative customer of the ever developing consumption oriented society.

INTRODUCTION

Much, maybe most, of the e-Learning-related literature looks into technological issues.[1] Very few address content, mainly its use or availability. Platforms on which e-Learning should be developed are not, however, overlooked - with experts examine engineering or technological issues of e-Learning systems and structure (e.g., Gilbert, 2008; Lim, *et al.*, 2005). There is discussion related to financial facet of distance learning (Barmble, 2008), to specific sectors (corporate; academia) and to e-training (Tai, 2008; Kim *et al.*, 2005; Beach, 2002). The role of instructors, the training they should undergo and methodologies (Clark & Mayer, 2008; Marriott & Torres, 2008; Boon *et al.*, 2005) are discussed as well. Technological gaps, mainly in ICT,[2] between countries and regions, or segments of the population are examined. And so their influence on the actual potential of e-Learning and the role they

DOI: 10.4018/978-1-60566-940-3.ch001

play in educational institutions and workplace. Still another facet in the discussion looks into the learning process and attempts to relate it to what is known as "Constructivist Learning Theory." Content, as has been mentioned, receives little, if any, attention. Even Carliner & Shank (2008) present no discussion that even remotely examines educational contents or learning goals.

There are core questions that are evidently absent in much of the body literature on the subject. They concern educational value systems and social and educational goals which are the very *raison d'être* of education as reflected – or should be manifested – in e-Learning. This chapter addresses some of these issues, arranged in a few sub-sections. Starting with examination of educational goals it turns to look at socio-educational aspirations. Exposition and discussion of socio-educational agendas, e.g., conformity, rules, etc. follows. The economic dimension is then presented, as related to the educational process with discussion which is followed by examination of the implications on the student's economic performance, resulting from the practice within the educational arena. Next the relationship between information and knowledge is looked into, as related to the learning process, which is also examined in the context of the classroom in the following section. While examination of various aspects of e-Learning has been done throughout the previous sections as well, the next section focuses on the relationship between learning and e-Learning, leading to the last section which culminates in the call to redefine educational objectives with the development of information society.

COMMONLY PERCEIVED EDUCATIONAL GOALS AND OBJECTIVES

Almost any survey in nearly any society in the world would turn out several cliché responses as to what education is all about. The maxim that education is a social process, aimed at social cohesion (or balance) is hardly ever challenged. Yet, the educational discourse seems to be almost entirely divorced from key social issues. To point at one example, the crucial economic processes (and implications) that shape society and its members are hardly ever addressed in the educational discourse. Still another anomaly stands at the heart of the general socio-educational debate: if education aims to change social values and concepts that have over time become undesirable or unwanted (e.g., discrimination, segregation and other outdated concepts), how can educators, themselves products of the system that encouraged these archaic ideals, be expected to eradicate or change such values, ideas and practice? Can they be true agents for such a desired change?

The concept of "equal opportunity" and its derivatives, "affirmative action" or "positive discrimination", exemplifies this inherent problem. It means equating discriminated groups to those considered to represent the mainstream of society (another problem, of course) through yet another form of discrimination – even if positive and based on good intentions.[3]

Examination of educational systems reveals discrepancy between desired social values and values actually implemented. One reason for this gap is funding. A quick scrutiny of budgets available to education, compared with other items on the national budget, of any country worldwide manifests it.[4] Restricted funding is reflected in budgetary allocations to physical conditions in educational institutions, to state-of-the-art schooling aides and to preparation and training of teachers, their earnings and social status. Budgetary issues also have an impact the pupil's future consumer behavioural patterns. This is also absent from teacher training programs.

Gender imbalances[5] and economic aspects of education occupy a rather modest place in the overall educational debate. It is rather devoted to such questions as whether teaching aims at "what to think?" or "how to think?"[6] This last point will be further discussed later on.

Debates concerning e-Learning, like those of education at large, rarely touch core issues. E-Learning heralds the desired shift towards the learner as the centre. Yet it also harbours some of the more difficult social and educational issues, both in their value-related ethical facets and the economic implications stemming from e-Learning.

The question of access is not just as economic one. Neither is the issue of priority of sectors in introduction to e-Learning. Resolving gaps of computer literacy between regions, sectors and populations is not a mere technical challenge. It goes to the very heart of the socio-educational process. It also touches such issues as equality: "equal opportunity" or otherwise: Is it equality in ownership of assets? Or equality in access to assets, whether social or private? And what should be the normative "objective" (or should it be subjective) measure for equal opportunity, or the threshold for social assistance? And what type of assistance would that be?

Can e-Learning resolve such anomalies and polemics? The *e-Learning Guild* performs annual surveys (Pulichind, 2006) among users, developers, promoters and other interested parties.[7] The results rank desired direction of e-Learning. Number one on the list is "rapid e-Learning design & development," followed by "use of e-Learning to train customers & partners." The list continues to itemise technical subjects down to No. 9, "e-Learning bundled with or embedded in products," and No. 10: "learners assessed on a regular basis." No. 11 goes somewhat beyond technical or practical facets: "use of authoring tools that allow one person to design & produce interactive e-Learning content (instead of differentiated design and production roles)." It is only in No. 12 that we find: "Content management systems," Still a term more technical than content-oriented.

According to the rather wide definition of e-Learning offered by Fallon and Brown (2008:4), e-Learning encompasses "any learning, training or education that is facilitated by the use of well known and proven computer technologies, especially network based on internet technology". It opens endless discussions about myriad technical associated aspects. Other means facilitating learning, training or education, say blackboard and chalk, remain just what they are: means.[8] This calls for examination of the very issues of learning and education. [9]

Since e-Learning came to be, "the field of education has tried to exploit the web as a communications channel to connect distant learners with instructors and a rapidly growing of plethora of learning material". The challenge remains: "to ensure that we develop appropriate theoretical frameworks and formal approaches, which guarantee that we do not stop merely at creating technical solutions" (Mudur, 2005). Notwithstanding, the main models employed in developing e-Learning, tend to obscure this challenge as the body of knowledge is of the smallest concern within the pyramidal working model for e-Learning (Figure 1).

Figure 1. Layered model for e-Learning environment (inspired by Mudur, 2005)

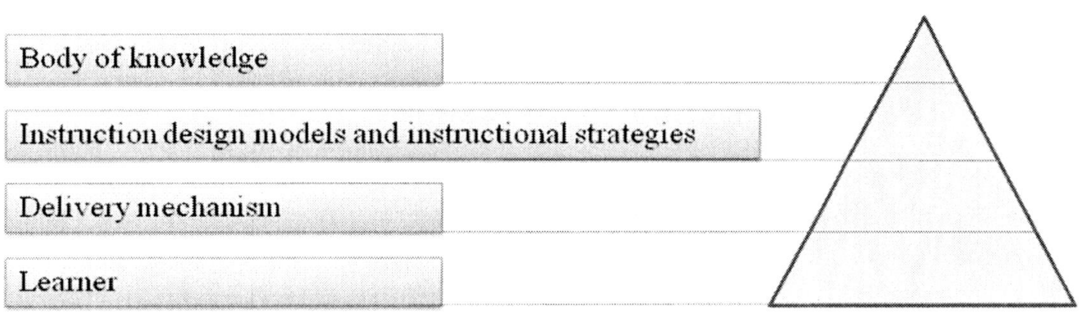

The learner is at the base, being OBJECTIVE, indeed: the object of the entire process, not the SUBJECT. The technical mediating layers dictate the body of knowledge delivered. Directed at the learner, they trigger strategies for instruction to deliver the "body of knowledge". Only a "representation schemes for the body of knowledge" may, or may not, "be such as to permit non-linear access or a strict linear access" (Mudur, 2005).[10]

The bias towards technical and technological and even techno-methodological matters characterises much of the literature in the subject. In the *Handbook of e-Learning* (Brandon, 2008), the word "education" appears about a dozen times, all referring to tools or business or techniques and none relating to educational terms, either pedagogical or philosophical. Shank (2008:34-35) notes that "content-experts… often do not know what content is needed",[11] yet as Bates (2005) points out: "The effectiveness of a technology cannot be judged without making some basic assumptions about what constitutes affective teaching and learning and the goals and purposes of education and training". There is, it seems, an unbridgeable dichotomy between the technical experts whose concern is the medium and educational experts whose domain is the socio-educational philosophy and value system.

SOCIO-EDUCATIONAL ENDS AND ASPIRATIONS: EXPLICIT AND IMPLICIT ISSUES

The gaps between medium, concepts, and goals are far-reaching. Debates regarding educational processes often look into teaching techniques of particular subjects. Or issues like "preparing pupils for life", "instilling" values in youngsters, discipline and order, etc. These are noble issues, but other important questions seem to escape the educational discourse: How such goals coexist with competitive and economic, market life? How can survival in the highly competitive, fast-moving, current market economy be reconciled with deep and thorough research that is still considered to be the most effective practice in gaining and mastering knowledge? How could an atmosphere of quick and pressing decision-making be compatible with a thorough examination of multi-level options for comparative and historical learning and acquisition of knowledge?

These are but a few unanswered questions. They should dominate the development of the "knowledge-based society" and be at the heart of the educational discourse, aimed at the attainment and realisation of the answers, once agreed upon.

Schooling and education are perceived "pure" and "clean", unblemished by the harsh reality of cruel, inhumane competition, rivalry of people and groups, untruth of politicians and marketers, greed and other such social maladies. But is it really so? Are schools and the educational system really divorced (can they be divorced; should they be detached) from life? And if so, how are they supposed to "prepare" students for life and are they really equipped to do it? If schooling is supposed to produce "useful and efficient members of society" it cannot be shun away from real life; from tensions and disparities between various segments of society; from influences of political and economic realities on educational agendas and schooling praxis.

It has long been agreed by most educationalists and social scientists that the main goal of education should be to raise students' awareness of the world around them. It really means that they should become subjects of the world, rather than objects.[12]

Learning, like knowledge, is a social construct or process. The student is supposed to 'make sense' (or meaning) of the world as a result of learning. This cannot be a mechanical process where a collection of facts is deposited in the student's mind and kept "as is" until withdrawn in, say, examination. Such learning only constitutes transference that at best yields machine-like memorisation. Since life is dynamic, knowledge cannot be a stagnant, tradable commodity. Freire (1985; 1987) asserts that teachers should discover how their students develop their understanding of the world as a key to understanding how students learn. Learning, like knowledge, must be contextual and dynamic. Moreover, if knowing is a social process, then learning is the process where knowledge is presented to the learner as raw material to be then formed in experience-related terms into understanding, enhanced by discussion and reflection.

Also, there is the issue of credibility of sources of knowledge. Every social formation has traditional sources, be they religious or other authoritative structures. Maxims originating from these are instilled onto members of society through social institutions concerned with their own self-preservation. Change can come through revolution, collapse of a system, or gradual evolutionary alteration in interpretation, eventually creating a critical mass to effectuate the birth of a new order.

It is only natural that those in charge, in any social formation, are heard best and loudest when preaching changes, having the easiest access to public means of communications. But even if they truly mean it, those whose task is to carry through these change, are still tainted by norms and "true knowledge" of the old system, now challenged and by the values, practice and language that must now be eradicated.

To construct meaning, or understanding of objects, learners must first become thinking subjects. They must be aware of the learning process they undergo so that they can immerse themselves into active and intimate intercourse with their learning process.[13] Such awareness can bring them to gradually know what they did not hitherto. This is very concrete experience; not merely theoretical abstract. Learning, thus, cannot be divorced from previous knowledge. Teaching and learning must relate to (and depend on) content already taught, learnt, and processed. This is true for every level of education. Any attempt to place a "piece" or a "body" of knowledge, independent of prior knowledge of learners, can only result in a temporary knack to mechanically cite some pieces of un-related information.

Previous state of affairs might determine seemingly remote and unrelated issue: "equality of opportunity", twofold appealing concept that lures easy fall in the trap it presents: how either of the terms equality and opportunity, is defined? How can we balance the variance in circumstances (financial, educational, social, cultural, etc.) when we strive for "equality"? Or is it for "opportunity"? Take, at first 'equality': in what? How does equality relate to the uniqueness of each and every person, the most basic premise of humanity? Or is it mere "technical" equality, certain starting point or economic level? And if so, how, if at all, should (or can) unequal pace of advancement of different individuals be equated? And regarding opportunity – where should it begin? What are the criteria for the threshold? How are differences in background, prior accumulated social benefits, personal dispositions and other such considerations be weighed?

Take a person of a second or third generation to formally educated family with their educational performance perfected with experience. It creates enormous advantage, compared with a person who is first generation to family education. This holds true even if the latter is better endowed in terms of talent, IQ or other such measures. The only way to resolve this imbalance is to consider equality in terms of access to social amenities according to self-determined needs. This is not quantifiable. As to opportunity, the problem is even more complex, unless defined in unquantifiable terms and regarded at the personal level of the individual. "Affirmative action" is ill-regarded not only by formal institutions but also by its recipients. Not only in Europe but also in the USA, black, as well as women professionals, argue that affirmative action is discriminatory and that it tint them.[14] The concept of citizenry may provide a key in answering these questions, as it allows access to social amenities while recognising inequalities.

This discussion is thus not devoid of economic, political and social realities operating on the educational process. Nor can it ignore such socio-educational issues or goals of pupil-moulding or what makes the student a useful (and hopefully participating) member of society. Attending to these issues is necessary to achieve coherent compatibility between the educational process and "real life."

HIDDEN AGENDAS: CONFORMITY, ACCEPTANCE, RULES, AND CODES

Behind highly acclaimed educational goals sanctioned by social organisations, there is a harsh historical reality that keeps "haunting" the educational scene until this very day. Consider late 19th century schools. They were mostly established by the Church, often in co-operation with local "well-to-do" and "good hearted" individuals. Some inauguration speeches mentioned how suitable the schools were to the places where their graduates would spend their lives: the manufacturing mill or prison. To this day, more than any other institutions, schools and prisons are so easy to recognise, be it in the USA, Turkey, China or the UK. They all seem to have been planned and built as if inspired by Goffman's analysis of total institutions (1957).[15] While schools are not total institutions, they share many of their characteristics. During the time pupils stay at schools, they are more often than not exposed to such processes as described by Goffman, even if in a milder fashion. Just consider: uniforms (still apparent in many countries, particularly at the elementary level); forms of regimentation; the fact that any staff member has almost endless power over any of the pupils (inmates?); the artificial time setting (lesson duration); and the list goes on.

This is not really surprising. Schools and the educational systems in general, are expected to instil conformity, to assure acceptance of society's demands and enhance adherence to social rules and codes. This had been the case for centuries, although different trends began to emerge in the later part of the 20th century. Freedom of the child to develop unhindered has become a leading slogan, along with the adaptation of a more individually-suited coaching approach. Active and inter-active instruction was supposed to have replaced frontal instruction and study through play had won the day.

Social, political, and economic realities, pressures and interests, apparent and hidden, have been highly influential on the development of the educational systems all over the world (Peters, 2006; Cook, 2002; Quah, 2003; Hildreth & Kimble, 2004). The economic facet of the educational process is substantially accentuated in digital literacy or digital learning. Economic considerations are crucial here as the economic facet is no longer a playground for governments and government budgets alone. Commercial and corporate interests bring forth such measures such as profitability, efficiency, ROI and their like. Commercial entities require that expansion of digital literacy be measured not only in terms of achievement, comprehension or skill nourishment, but also in financial terms. At the same time, political and social demands for better e-inclusion or universal access to education make demands on what they regard as "contribution to society".[16]

However, these realities, pressures and interests escape classrooms and staffrooms debate (and higher level educational forums). They never really appear in the curricula taught in most, maybe all, schools around the world. Even in technologically-related economic issues it is the former rather than the latter that is dealt with.

The story of e-Learning reflects this amalgamation of economic consideration and technological quests. But it also combines other drives, like intellectual curiosity of university professors or interest of human resources professionals. The idea of remote teaching appeals to university officials who wish to expand the studentship body and reach prospective students that cannot (or will not) come to the main campus. This consideration has been valid for institutions of higher education in the west as it has been for, say, African universities.[17] It has not gone unnoticed. For example, Holmes and Gardner (2006:1) begin their work by saying that "e-Learning is 'mission critical' because of globalisation of economy and citizenship and the recognition that the economy must become knowledge-based."[18]

Core educational values are absent in much of the body literature on the subject. It mainly concentrates on systems and structure's engineering or technological issues (Gilbert, 2008; Lim, *et al.*, 2005), financial facet of distance learning (e.g., Barmble, 2008), specific sectors and e-training (Tai, 2008; Kim *et al.*, 2005; Beach, 2002) and instruction or methodologies (Clark & Mayer, 2008; Marriott & Torres, 2008; Boon *et al.*, 2005). Content receives little, if any, attention. Even Carliner & Shank (2008) do not discuss educational contents or learning goals.

Currently, a major concern of the debate about e-Learning revolves around learning environment and, more specifically, its personal aspects and perspectives. Schaffert & Hilzensauer (2008) discuss these attributes of e-Learning while comparing learning management systems (LMS) and personal learning environments (PLE), two technological concepts that allow for pedagogical methods or personal learning strategies while limiting the learning settings.[19] They endorse the transition from "instructing" to "influencing" environments vis-à-vis the learning process so that organisation and adaptation are preserved. In this they accept earlier attempt of Knuth & Cunningham (1993:167), to create constructivist justification for lack of educational value content. This trend has been in the wider educational debate since the 1970s, endorsing slogans like "self-direct learning", where initiative for learning is left solely with the learner, relieving society from its responsibility over education (e.g., Knowles, 1975).

In constructivism, "learners construct knowledge for themselves" but not, indeed, "by themselves." Moreover, they really construct meaning socially, not just individually. Plato suggested that learning equals remembering previously perceived "perfect ideas" (Hein, 1991:1). This social nexus which Hein considers as necessary (even if not sufficient), presents a rather precarious situation for the learner, since it implies that it is really how he or she are guided, how the "fabrication" is made for him or her, that constructs meaning and forms perception.

Constructivists have been aware of this anomaly and therefore also attempted to harness social formations to the educational structure they suggested. Siebert (1998) argued that learning "needs stimuli and challenge from others." Wenger (1998; 2002) developed what is known as the "Community of Practice" approach, whereby learning is thought to happen only in social networks on the basis of shared interest, interaction and a repertoire of tools and resources, namely, social processes. This brings us back to the core of the discussion: what ARE the premises on which education is to be practised and what are the true goals that go beyond any sectarian interest in society?

In the context of e-Learning, its promise must be intertwined with the societal problems associated with the uneven spread of the technique.[20] Clearly, e-Learning manifests the great philosophical, economic and social attributes related to the information and knowledge-based society and more so, to the perennial learning society. Yet these attributes bring back the political issue, in its most acute all-inclusive civic (rather than ideological, party-like) sense. Foremost in this context, with consequences to all other aspects of this discussion, is, again, the economic realm in its widest, societal and civic perspectives.

ECONOMIC PREFERENCES AND REALITIES: THE ECONOMICS OF THE EDUCATIONAL PROCESS

Teaching professionals and students tend to say that economics has nothing to do with education. They are surprised when asked to calculate the size of the market for textbooks alone (ignoring other items like drill books, notebooks, writing instruments and materials, school bags, school activities, trips, etc.). Once assessing it, they fall into total shock, which intensifies when they begin to consider the contents of school textbooks, from publishers' viewpoint. They, naturally, prefer to publish books they think the systems will endorse, which will increase their market share. Pupils must have textbooks, paid for by themselves or by the general school or local authority budget. It is a captive market of hundreds of millions of whatever currency, even in relatively small countries with school population of only one million pupils in twelve grades. Publishers, however righteous, would rather have their books recommended by the system than not. They profit from books. So their primary consideration cannot be the educational contents of their books. It is what would appeal to those deciding that these, not other books, are to be used.

Makers of school uniform, where still customary, consider fashion trends to attract potential customers: students. So do manufacturers of school bags. The list goes on. Huge amount of money revolves within and around the educational system, influencing choices of pupils and parents. This economic reality influences the nature of education and even its contents. It does not result from informed decision-making process based on educational or social considerations. No! The process is driven by market interests.

The economic drive, aiming at financial gain and based on market considerations in the "business" of education, is a legitimate one. It is the estrangement between this and the influence on the system that is baffling; it is the blind eye turned by educational systems towards this factor that reduces its legitimacy. No school devotes even a single class to examine the phenomenon, nor does any teacher training institution make it a topic for its students to ponder and deliberate on.

This is only the tip of the economic and financial iceberg in the world of education. Issues related to budget are even more pressing and cannot be ignored. Since teachers normally constitute the largest body of state employees, each cent added to their individual salaries is translated into many millions in the overall budget. And then there are other expenses: on school buildings and their maintenance, municipal direct and indirect contributions (property tax reliefs, etc.). They seem to be lost on educationalists and education researchers, left to treasury economists.

A glimpse at three lists comprising over 100 research papers specifically focused on economics of education[21] shows that not even a single paper deals with the monetary influences of the economy at large (or any specific aspects of it) on education or on the relationship between these factors and the setting of educational goals. Other absent topics include the financing of educational aids, the relationship between such financing and educational programmes, or the reflection of educational priorities in educational budgets.

UNESCO's list of publications[22] is refreshing in this sense. It contains a few papers that examine the financing of some education systems. However, they focus on the need to define the stakeholders and on ways to inform them of their rights. Some papers also discuss financial and educational issues vis-à-vis involvement of the private sector in education systems, yet their focus remains mainly on aspects of government subsidies (e.g., Pénao, *et al.*, 1997:179-186).

Bray (2007:84) brings illuminating statistics about the involvement of the private sector in the provision of education. He concludes that since "the nature of supplementary tutoring varies; different policies are needed for different societies at different points in time." Consequently, "the range of possible interventions is wide". He observes: "... private supplementary tutoring... is a mechanism through which individuals can expand knowledge and through which societies can accumulate human capital." The shift to e-Learning contributes to the decrease of governmental control in the arena of education, while promoting "social stratification and elitism." Good or bad, says Bray, "in many settings this shift is viewed with ambivalence. Governments may have positive reasons for withdrawing the dominant role that they have played in many countries; but in some societies the rise of private tutoring appears to be social response to inadequacies in government quantitative and qualitative inputs. One result is an exacerbation of social inequalities" (*ibid*: 84-85). Private tutoring is established to cater mainly for clientele characterised by special needs such as religion, language or ethnicity. In tandem, another type of private tutoring emerged in response to excess demand in both developed and developing industrialised societies.[23]

The educational endeavour grows increasingly more complex. Indirect costs and budgetary allocation to education are only part of this complexity. So are costs of developing new mediation techniques or other economic interests. Then there is the political concern about the access to new technology. The same goes for the democratic ideal of participation. The overall globalisation and the spread of inexpensive communications are also a significant factor, both financially and culturally. Just consider the impact of the spread of English as the new "*lingua franca*" of computer and internet age. None of these issues resolve the question of control over education, its related markets, and its content.[24]

The ensuing confusion cannot be too surprising. It is further accentuated in view of the lack of change in teacher training concepts, even if now students type their assignments or submit them electronically. The training curricula did not change. As before, they still do not offer any exposure to economic, bureaucratic, civic, administrative or even communal experiences. The classic works of education are still taught divorced of the new reality of text-messaging dominated by monosyllabic "NewTalk" dictated by cellular communication, so readily available now.

New technologies in the areas of communications and transfer of information have been introduced to daily life and changed it rapidly.[25] This has enormous impact on both people's activities and the way they perceive of these activities. These developments coincided with some other mega-processes, like the collapse of the Soviet bloc, the expansion of the European Union, the development of huge economies as China and India and so forth. Little, if any, time was left for intellectual absorption of these changes. Remote instruction, distance teaching and e-Learning, thus, epitomise, in many ways, the phrase coined by Marshall McLuhan (1964:8): "The medium is the message."[26]

Production and distribution of educational content is mainly dominated by private enterprises. It is "for the most part unregulated, with the exception of copyright regimes" (Downes, 2005). Yet, revenue is drawn mainly from direct public funding, such as school budgets, grants to colleges and universities, library budgets, or grants to museums.[27] Still, digitisation and increased capacity may pose a threat to interested private players, effectuating decrease in demand for commercial educational content and aides. This is not just theoretical figment of the imagination. It is supported by abundance of free online material sponsored by public organisations[28] or educators who publish their content on the net and, of course, the almost limitless amount of private production of content, some of which can certainly be classified as 'learning" material. Downes (2005) suggests that this content affluence may undermine commercial publishers because "the nature of their product has changed into one that can be reproduced for fractions of a cent." Reproduction of learning materials might be prohibited, but not for individually produced and distributed non-commercial material. "Consequently, even if the commercial product remains untouched, it faces increasingly significant competition from the non-commercial sector" (Downes 2005).[29] This may lead to weakening, if not collapse of educational content markets.[30]

Commercial interests (also governments, for other reasons) do not welcome this scenario. It might be because they are afraid that their business might go under and disappear. They respond in heavy lobbying, mounting increasing copyrights defences, offers of sponsorships to colleges and schools and expressed concern with quality-assurance and quality-control issues. They are also apprehensive about royalty-holders within education, marketing and distribution of non-commercial content, etc.

With the appeal of non-commercial content, its acceptability will only increase and spread more widely. Content and content tools become available and cheaper, or free and more user-friendly. It stands to reason that the number of voluntary contributions to the world of content would continue grow. However, traditional authority attributed to educational content would wane gradually. The result can be seen in the development of a secondary technological or technical market of immediate or short-term nature of software tools designed to produce (or re-produce), distribute, manage and display content.

This type of process is not unique to e-Learning or to any other mediating technology. It is characteristic of the e-economy as a whole.[31] The focus of spending on learning shifts from purchasing commercial content towards in-house or self-production of content. Aiming for wide dissemination, it concentrates on the technological aspects of delivery. This represents a challenge in the application of knowledge. With a weak history of cooperation, practitioners and policy-makers should now begin to "direct producers of knowledge in collaboration with researchers" (ECE, 2008:6). With the growing incorporation of e-services, particularly by authorities, more and more content is expected to be distributed freely, available to all. Encouragement, by authorities, of wider distribution of content will eventually be part of the expansion of e-activity. It can then become also a tax item, most likely as tax credit earner.

The business world does not lag in understanding the wave and its direction. Suffice to see how much energy and resources some big corporations allocate to the development of freeware and open sources.[32] Also, content and content-related markets, whether considered as e-Learning or more general education are not really heading towards extinction. To the contrary, various specialising niches are more likely to flourish. A whole range of technologies are now at the core of the developing efforts.[33] Amalgamation of different types of content is also at the height of the technological agenda, e.g., linking textual, audio and video units into seamless sequences of content, which can be analysed as a whole.

These changes allow the educational market to leap sunlight years, from the manufacturing age of production-based economy to the era of maintenance, service and support. Digitisation has allowed consumers to produce their own learning content thus bringing down millennia-old monopolies. Herein lays a true shift in the balance of power, from the authoritative institution to the individual, who now has power, but no knowledge of how to use it. The educational space becomes less regulated, more activity-oriented and self-managed by learners. Many educational officials and governments, local and national, fail to fully grasp this shift.

In economic terms, the *per capita* expenditure on learning is decreasing, allowing for market expansion. This should enable greater variety of contents accessible to more people. Theoretically, this is heaven on earth to governments that can now increase educational opportunities.[34] These realities are well in evidence. But "nature" of education, the "education-ness" of education, to use style coined by Gilbert Ryle's (1949) remains unsettled.[35]

Figure 2. Evidence base for policies in various areas (extrapolated from CESifo, 2007)

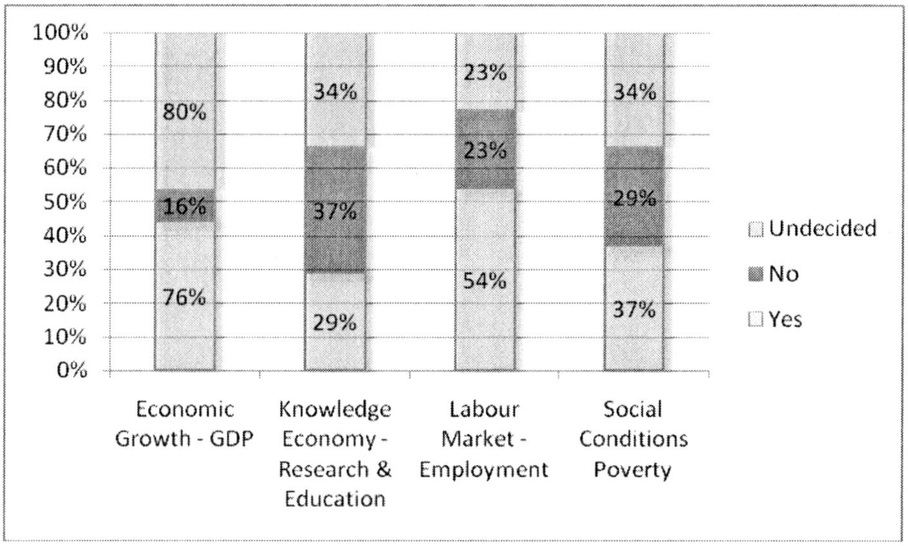

THE STUDENT AS A NON-PARTICULAR CONSUMER/ SHOPPER: PRESENT AND FUTURE

In 2007, a survey was conducted amongst more than 700 economists from over 80 countries attempting to identify the level and strength of evidence on the basis of which, or regardless of which, policies are adopted. Four areas were examined: economic growth (GDP); knowledge economy (research and education); labour market (employment); and social conditions (poverty). The survey measured the extent to which policies are anchored in reality and are based on factual evidence and data (Figure 2).

Policies related to economic growth are fairly considerably based on solid and concrete databases (76%). Labour and employment policies are less substantiated or supported by factual evidence (54%). Policies dealing with social conditions, or poverty, are even less based on fact, rated at only 37%. Knowledge economy policies rate lowest, at 29% only. This is a surprisingly low result in view of the rhetoric around these issues and their seemingly increasing importance in recent years. The combined "undecided" and "no" answers here, at 71%, portray an ominous picture.

Some questions immediately rise. How can people (leaders, teachers, parents, students) take informed decisions if they are not truly informed? How can they draw conclusions if their knowledge base is deficient? How can society be at all a knowledge based one if decisions pertaining education and research are not based on factual evidence and informed contemplation? How could priorities be determined and a developmental path set so that society enters the knowledge era prepared?

It has already been asserted that the educational system does not actually prepare its pupils to successfully participate in economic life; neither as future workers nor as future or current consumers. In the age of instant messaging, multi-channel television and advertisement-infested internet, there is little doubt that it is necessary to train youngsters to become particular and careful consumers. Not only with regard to commercial offers but also non-commercial potential temptations lurking and harbouring risk.

The educational system is perennially under pressure of the political echelon, or the general public, to improve its output. Yet, standard international comparative tests show deterioration in most of the measures, criteria and study subjects tested, like language skills, mathematics and sciences. Some unmeasured aspects are also questionable, like the extent to which the educational system prepares its graduates to real life. It seems, also, that it fails to trains them adequately to tackle economic and market realities; or to live in an atomised society and survive through competition. If such criteria were applied, the failure would have been even greater.

Dissemination of knowledge amongst professionals in the education sector, teachers, is much slower and less profound than in other industries like health (doctors) or planning (engineers).[36] According to OECD studies, the level of expenditure on R&D in education is less than 0.3% of the entire expenditure on it (CERI, 2003:10). Education has "little scientific knowledge to underpin it and not a strong enough body of research evidence about what works to inform it" (Hargreaves, 2000). Knowledge of advances in medicine reaches millions of doctors throughout the world within short period of time. In education, "if practitioners' and policy-makers' learning were as continuous as it is, by and large, for doctors, then they would be able to continually update their knowledge of educational practices so that they could acquire and apply these new techniques as they developed" (Hargreaves, 2000).

This, however, is easier said than done. The low degree of attention spurred on education renders the conditions within the educational sector and possibly also the level of the practitioners in the field not conducive for the creation and development of new content of value and relevance.[37]

It is beyond the scope of this chapter to look into the balance of interests which perpetuates this situation. But the situation itself is the issue here. Absence of informed basis for decision on educational priorities is certainly one reason for the inability of the educational process to prepare its clientele, i.e., the pupils, to be informed and selective customers. It is particularly so in a context of today's highly fast moving, competitive market. The "contexts of knowledge production and use in society are diversifying and new models of research are being developed to respond to these challenges" (Furlong & Oancea, 2005:6). Education cannot be isolated from this process. When considering the level of investment in R&D, this statement becomes clearer. New innovations incorporated into the educational process, such as e-Learning, are born of endeavours that take place beyond the boundaries of the educational discourse that remains neither relevant nor contextually related to real life.

If the educational system is to prepare students to become more particular in their consuming patterns, more informed in their decision-making and more attentive to the various contexts within which they operate, then it must change. The change should be initiated and encouraged by social leaders. As OECD puts it, the links are weak "between research, policy and innovation in education" (CERI, 2003; 2007).

Learning is no longer a monopoly of schools and universities. Life experience is increasingly accepted as a valid source of knowledge-related evidence. However, teachers, hence students "and other practitioners are seldom trained in how to make use of research and evidence and therefore they have a weak capacity to apply evidence-based knowledge" (CEC, 2008:28). There is here a vicious circle. Teacher training requires high level research-based pedagogy and knowledge construction. But this cannot be attained under the prevailing circumstances. Moreover, teachers at school must keep themselves updated on recent developments in the subject matter they teach. They have to be able to "teach different learners in different cultural and societal contexts" and settings (Hargreaves, 2000). With the rapid changes in world economy, technology, social settings and nature of inter-personal relationship, they also need to be well informed about these changes and the powers behind them. They also have to know how to harness and incorporate these changes into their teaching routines. They must also avoid falling into the trap of substituting the medium for the message.

The rapid introduction and deployment of digital technology induces organisational and cultural changes. Modifications occur in internal and external procedures of firms and other subscribers to the ever developing digital world (Castillo-Merino & Sjöberg, 2008:4; Foray, 2004). These include not only means but also management systems and styles, ways of communications, language used, flexible working hours and locations, working environment design and employee involvement schemes, decentralisation and other participatory decision-taking practices; teamwork, knowledge management, work arrangements, compensation schemes and so on (Bates, 2005: 10-12).[38]

None of these happen in the educational system. Even if it does perceive itself to be "digitally aware" sector, it has not adapted to the elements comprising the digital productive culture. It is, therefore, unable to participate in what should have been its "natural" domain, namely, content production and dissemination - particularly for e-Learning. Thus, the educational system is also unable to offer its clientele, its students, a systematic training, supported by experimental space, in how to produce content, judge its validity and assess its effectiveness as educational material.

EXPOSURE TO INFORMATION OR KNOWLEDGE?

Should education guide its customers to acquire further information or should delivery of knowledge result from educational experience? And if so, must knowledge be authoritative final and non-contestable? Answers to these questions reflect the way learning and teaching would be carried out in general as well as through e-Learning. e-Learning is typically associated with the relationship between humans and computers and other means through which information or knowledge are transferred. The question, therefore, is which of the two potential objectives – information or knowledge – (or is it both?) should be at the centre of this human-machine interaction. Also, how should either option be defined in the context of e-Learning process, both in terms of goals and of capabilities?[39]

The subject matter of education is the creation and dissemination of information and the intake of these, which is the learning process. It differs from production and distribution of other commodities. This assertion has led many to think that because of its special nature, educational processes cannot survive, let alone compete successfully, in open market conditions without external, governmental, assistance.

Some experts argue that "information is not a commodity; at least not in the way the term is used in neoclassical economics or understood in industrial society" (Bell, 1980: 513). It is accentuated when compared to industrial commodities, "produced in discrete, identifiable units, exchanged and sold, consumed and used up." When an industrial commodity is sold, or bought, a physical item is exchanged. When information, or knowledge, is sold, it still remains with the producer. Moreover, "It is a collective good in that once it has been created it is by its nature available to all" (*ibid*: 513). This argument is easily refuted, of course, particularly in context of the intellectual property market or that of scientific and technological developments (Walberg & Bast, 2003: 208).

Incentives for production of knowledge or information are as apparent and tenable as they are in the market of tangible commodities. Maybe even more so, if we judge by the amount of money revolving in the "breaking news" market alone. The difference between "announce-able" and tangible commodities is in the consumption end. Value of tangible commodities does not necessarily diminish with repeated use. News of just one hour ago is normally of no value at all or of very limited value.

And yet, unlike educational produced information or knowledge, other types of information are capable of generating huge amounts of money. Even the growing quantities of freeshare available to the public pose no threat. Already in 1999, the value of US market transactions on software and hardware alone was, respectively, $ 157 bn. and $ 800 bn., or total of $ 957 billion.[40] Additional tens of billions of dollars were spent on pharmaceutical R&D.[41] These do not include other knowledge-based industries like biotech, engineering, telecommunications, broadcasting and telecasting etc. Auxiliary and supporting services requiring knowledge base, like law or management are also not considered here. These data show clearly that information, or knowledge, end up as consumable commodities, even if of particular nature.

But the assertion regarding the non consumable nature of information is not entirely baseless. Some information has no market value. Data collected by governments in the course of service provided to citizens: defence, social security, civil registration, educational services and so on. Governments use it for the perceived greater good of society. On the basis of these data and information governments make theoretically informed decisions as to the allocation of resources, regulatory policies, distribution, etc.

The truth is that this information or knowledge can also be priced. Only because of its abundance and because it is not obliterated once used, it is thought to be available to all freely and costless.[42]

Production of information or knowledge can only happen within the constraints of ample investment, organisational structure and competitive environment. Yet, when it comes to schooling, many, including leading scholars, tend to look at this procedure as a metaphor, borrowed from other economic activities rather than reality (McCloskey, 1985: 40-51; Cobb, 1992: 1; Henig, 1994: 13; Fiske & Ladd, 2000: 312).

But schooling is part and parcel of the information industry with all the characteristic of commodity economy. To begin with, in every country in the world, expenditure on education is the largest item on the national budget. Hundreds of millions are spent on K-12 schools alone, mostly on teachers' salaries. There are markets of books and other paraphernalia items associated with schooling. Also, there are financial wavers accorded to school buildings, or activities, by the various authorities.[43] Lastly, providers and consumers in the schooling (or education) market perennially face and have to make decisions and choices between alternatives, in view of limited resources and budgets, like they would do in any other economic activity.

We still have to determine what, if any, is the difference between knowledge and information. We also need to ascertain what is, could be and/or should be, delivered in the educational process in general and through e-Learning (or should it be referred to as e-Education?) in particular.

Information is regarded as related to human participation in the purposeful organisation of raw data. This includes "organised data" (e.g., Saint-Onge, 2002); "data endowed with relevance and purpose" (Drucker, 2001); or "interpreted data" (Probst *et al.*, 2002). Knowledge, on the other hand, is harder to define. The Greek *episteme*, from which the concept derives, means "absolute truth," in itself a difficult concept, dwelt upon already by early philosophers such as Aristotle and Plato. Knowledge can presumably only reside in one's mind, resulting from experience and reflection and based on a set of beliefs shared by individuals and the collective where they belong (Gordon, 2002). Originated and applied within individual minds, knowledge is gained by evaluating and incorporating new experiences and information. It consists of a mix of non-distinct values, experiences, contextual information and intuition: "true and justified belief" (Nonaka & Takeuchi, 1995).

Management of knowledge differs from that of information, albeit the tendency to mix the two. Information is easier to identify, organise and distribute, unlike knowledge, which is inherent in the particular mind of a specific person. Managing knowledge, therefore, is confined to the setting of ample learning environment for individuals. It is done through the use of information, supported by and supportive of individual and social experiencing of the world.[44]

Information, thus, is concerned with answers to questions such as "who", "what", "where", and "when." Knowledge is the domain of questions of "how" (Ackoff, 1989).

If this is the case, then the subject matter of any means of mediation, whether human or electronic, should be information-related and technical. Questions regarding PLE (Personal Learning Environment) vs. LMS (Learning Management Systems) should confine themselves to technical aspects of contents delivery to the e-learner. But can means of transference adapt themselves to educational content, rather than creating a situation whereby content should adapt to means of mediation? Judging from numerous publications, both practitioners and researchers in the field have yet to answer this question.[45] The major attempt in the field is to confine and make pedagogy and even educational philosophy deliverable.

For amassing information, it is enough to collect data to which contextual and relational connection give meaning. But this is not the case for knowledge. Knowledge is not merely the collection of information, nor is it just a process that seeks to create added value of usefulness. Knowledge requires true cognitive and analytical ability. It requires the incorporation of understanding and aptitude, as well as prior or "stored" knowledge, into the mental processes, intellectual and emotional, even just for the answering of questions. Understanding involves an interpolative and probabilistic processes and observational capacities, used mainly in comparative nexus. It is process of distilling and synthesising new knowledge. This is learning; enabling the undertaking of useful actions based on synthesis of new knowledge, now rendered dynamic. Learning, thus, can build on information, knowledge and understanding of new constructions which are not only conceptual, but also capable of inspiring action. This is different from instrumental processes, such as mediation of preset materials, or artificial intelligence and machine learning, which could manipulate digital texts but which cannot change the course of events on the basis of dynamic understanding. Delivery of true e-Learning in this sense is currently lacking.

THE CLASSROOM

In itself, e-Learning eliminates the need for a classroom. However, as the notion of classroom, its physical layout and the activities within it have changed greatly during the last hundred years or so, e-Learning may prompt yet another change while being incorporated into classroom practice. Classrooms are not all evil even if they might be structures that leading powers controlling education may wish to uphold to.

The physical layout of a class can encourage or discourage interaction, thus affecting the process of learning. Eye contact is an essential key in establishing human rapport (Argyle, 1975; Miller, 1967; Ornstein, 1972). It is also an important tool that can be, indeed is, employed by instructors, even if unconsciously.

Consider conventional, or traditional, classroom layout, dominated by rows. It allows the instructor to maintain eye-contact with all the participants.[46] It eases delivery and interaction (e.g., questions and answers). Such layout ensures the instructor's centrality. But participants cannot communicate with one another, exercising eye-contact. They are in rows, looking at the backs of their fellow classmates.

Informal sitting arrangements encourage group exchanges and the formation of relationships. Small-group-atmosphere is also conducive to effective learning. Eye contact encompasses all participants and even if the instructor is still in the centre, the intercourse is all embracing.

The "U"-shape or semi-circle arrangements are typically used in general discussions situations. Such arrangements allow group members to maintain eye-contact and interact among themselves as well as with the instructor without too many difficulties. Tables in such arrangements can create barriers while their absence may bring into play a measure of embarrassment resulting from the removal of "protection" they offer. This might cause participants to feel exposed and vulnerable.

e-Learning set-ups reveal new realms of interaction in a classroom. Even if there is eye-contact in the set-up, it is still mediated, less "threatening" but also less personal.

Thus the physical layout of the place-of-study effectuates the extent to which it is conducive to better and more efficient acquisition of knowledge. Learning efficiency depends also on the level of free flow of interchanges, particularly if moderated. It depends no less on the richness and fullness of knowledge, the subject matter of that flow.[47] But the role of knowledge base eclipses that of the free flow. The strength of the source of knowledge transferred in a learning session is of the utmost importance. We are thus re-directed back to contents, stressing that knowledge transferred must be full and complete, authoritative and standing on a wide and solid basis. It must be transmitted confidently since the human element in the transmission is extremely important: it can encourage or daunt learners.

Within this framework, e-Learning could constitute an essential and, more importantly, natural ingredient of day-to-day classroom activity. However, employing contents as servants of means could only lead to the deterioration in learners' capability to conceptualise and intellectualise whatever subject-matters they are exposed to. The missing element of human contact takes its toll on the learning session. e-Learning tools introduced into classroom, must therefore overcome the alienated nature of the electronic contact. Emphasis must be placed on other components of the learning process; primarily, the knowledge base. Harnessing mediating technologies to the service of the e-Learning process, instead of the other way around, might compensate for the difficulties presented by electronic modes of communications. This can happen if we agree to retain the less glamorous goals of classroom activities, like social conformity, discipline and obedience and, of course, enriching students' knowledge.

INDIVIDUAL LEARNING IN E-LEARNING WORLD: EXCHANGE VS. UNIDIRECTIONAL INSTRUCTION

Learning at large and e-Learning in particular, demand certain attributes of teachers and educators, which are not necessarily part of their training curricula. There are attempts, maybe not enough, to change these curricula.[48]

Historically, education aimed at the training of the students to act in accordance to their standing in society. It helped in maintaining social strata intact. Society could thus resist and fend of all threats, real, potential and imaginary, to prevailing social order. The educational system had to be of highly rigid structure and discipline. Obedience defined success and the transmission of educational contents had to be authoritative and unidirectional. Precision in performance was also demanded.

With changes in the socio-economic realities, corresponding modifications in teaching and learning experiences followed suit. These changed contents but eluded adaptation of new means of mediation. Students were still expected to perform accurately, often in a mechanical way. The overall expectation of society from its educational system was to prepare graduates to be good and useful citizens.

The debates about the role of individuals within society and about individual capacity vs. social expectations of individuals are long standing, starting with Greek philosophers in ancient societies. A renewed interest was actively resumed in later centuries as monarchies were thrown over and democracies emerged. These debates produced insights that characterised the educational thought in the 20th century. Here, the main thrust was that a child should be nourished to develop his or her individual unique capacities while retaining his or her position within the social context and codes. But these debates neglected to catch up with economic and technological developments and changes. A lag developed between the educational system and techno-economical realities. It was only in the last decade or two of the 20th century that the alarm was sounded, as parents became less and less satisfied with the lagging educational system. As a result, ICT were incorporated into the educational system in a hysterical rush. The balance between individual and society no longer mattered. Just as the social interaction no longer scored highly as an educational goal, although deemed necessary to induce efficient learning combined with social awareness.

A ritual of canonisation of ICT developed, succeeding that of individual learning. However, it lacked a thorough inward "soul searching" that could produce or re-define educational values and contents. It also lacked development of curricula that would encourage the understanding of economic and technological realities and explore relationship between these realities, educational values and the student experience. Educational environments cannot be isolated from their educational processes. These cannot be detached from target groups and stakeholders who are part of those environments. Yet this is exactly what happened (Ehlers, 2007).

e-Learning practitioners and researchers were more interested in mechanistic features of means and techniques of delivery and neglected fundamental issues such as content. Where educational content issues tend to be discussed, they are subject-specific, not general.[49]

Learning scenarios should allow for (and adapt to) different contexts. They should also consider personal and environmental conditions. This means that the learning process must assume mode of negotiation (Ehlers, 2007).

One way to overcome the content issue problem is developing "social software" which might "narrow the divide between producers and consumers… through creating and sharing" (Atwell, 2007). This can pave the way for "a new ecology of 'open' content, books, learning materials and multimedia, through learners themselves becoming producers of learning materials". But this attempt to address the difficulties of contents production and availability provides no answer to the questions of values or to how to prepare students to independently understand socio-economical and cultural realities through educational tools.

Technology can and does offer vehicles for exchange and sharing. But it is not clear that they can enrich instruction, let alone contents. Some think that for this reason the "hype about e-Learning will decrease rather than increase in coming years" (Davey, 2007 quoting Prof. Ulrich Hoppe).[50]

There is no doubt, of course, that e-Learning can enhance learning through exchange and even elevate it considerably. However, like every other platform, it is the contents it carries that would render it useful or harmful. Educational scrutiny and approval – helpful as it may be – will not suffice. The real challenge for the next e-Learning developmental endeavours can be defined as follows: Developing new concepts and methods to deliver contents deriving from and shaping educational materials, value systems and understanding of socio-economic and socio-cultural realities and goals.

THE NEED TO RE-DEFINE EDUCATIONAL OBJECTIVES AND THE POTENTIAL OFFERED BY INFORMATION SOCIETY AND INFORMATION TECHNOLOGY

The evidence presented in this chapter clearly shows that educational objectives must be reformed, or redefined, to suit and harness technological developments as e-Learning and economic processes as globalisation. While some changes can already be detected, many are no more than a mere technical adaptation of what might be regarded as more convenient ways to do the same which was done before. Only by addressing the core issues of education and the social expectations and demands of education, could the latter truly enjoy the whole range of benefits that can be found in information technology and the information-based society. Moreover, only in this way can education become part of the overall socio-cultural and socio-economic development warranted by information technology. Educational objectives are the basic goals as set, accepted or agreed by social consensus, which determines where society expects the educational system should bring its graduates. Such objectives go beyond the technical taxonomy, as suggested by Bloom (1956). These objectives are anchored in society's most noble aspirations while also embedded in the socio-economic and socio-cultural realities.

The internet has imposed a wide range of changes on value systems and instigated a lively ongoing debate concerning these issues. Value systems are affected not merely in terms of the internationalisation of culture and the diminishing of local uniqueness, but also in terms of morals and other aspects of the value systems adhered to by various societies. The role of generation gaps, religious gaps, language gaps, and other such cultural attributes is changing, albeit at a different pace in different locations around the world. Notably, there is a call for new definition of participation, of civil and social bonds, of civil and social responsibility and so on.

Clearly, there is a need to formulate afresh concepts of socio-educational goals and a core value system that would define education. e-Learning, if subjected to these concepts, could become a leading vehicle at the service of education.

e-Learning is currently of mediatory nature in the main. It can, however, very well go beyond this role. It can grow and turn into true e-Education. Such a transition, however, is dependent on a transition in social outlook. Only if society enters an ongoing debate, in which all segments of society participate, could such a transformation be achieved. This in itself proposes what might be the first educational objective – to widen e-literacy to the entire population. Such a goal would necessitate changes in the allocation of resources and in the budgeting of education; a change in the mode of communications between governments and their citizens. Within the educational field, such a goal means a radical change in the way teachers are prepared in their various teachers' training institutions. The amended curricula to be pursued in such institutions will, as a matter of course, change the quality and professional (possibly also the psychological) profile of the new teachers. The direction of e-Learning, indeed of education development, would take an upturn signified by the ability to harness ICT to create vivid and viable contacts between basic educational goals as determined by civic society on the one hand and, on the other hand, by socio-economic and socio-cultural, as well as environmental realities (in their widest sense, not just in its natural sense).

REFERENCES

Ackoff, R. L. (1989). From Data to Wisdom. *Journal of Applies Systems Analysis*, *16*, 3–9.

Ala-Mutka, K., & Punie, Y. (2007). Aging Societies, Learning and ICT, *eLearning Papers,* 6 (November), http://www.elearningeuropa.info/files/media/media- 14198.pdf

Argyle, M. (1967). *The Psychology of Interpersonal Relations*. London: Penguin Books.

Argyle, M. (1975). *Bodily Communication*. New York: International Universities Press.

Atwell, G. (2007, January). Personal Learning Environments – the Future of eLearning? *eLearning Papers*, 2. Retrieved from http://www.elearningeuropa.info/files/media/media- 11561.pdf

Aviram, A., Ronen, Y., Somekh, S., Winer, A., & Sarid, A. (2008, July). Self-Regulated Personalised Learning (SRPL): Developing iClass Pedagogical Model. *eLearning Papers*, 4. Retrieved from http://www.elearningeuropa.info/files/media/media15974.pdf

Banyard, P., & Underwood, J. (2008). Understanding the Learning Space. *eLearning Papers*, 4. Retrieved from http://www.elearningeuropa.info/files/media/media15970.pdf

Bates, A. W. (2005). *Technology, E-Learning and Distance Education*. London: Routledge.

Beach, V. (2002). *The E-Learning Industry – Retrospect and Prospect*. Retrieved from http://www.learningcircuits.org/2002/sep2002/beach.html

Beard, C., Wilson, J. P., & McCaster, R. (2007). Towards a Theory of e-Learning: Experimental e-Learning. *Journal of Hospitality, Leisure . Sport and Tourism Education*, *6*(2), 3–15.

Becker, H. S. (2003). The Politics of Presentation: Goffman and Total Institutions. *Caliber . Symbolic Interaction*, *26*(4), 659–669. doi:10.1525/si.2003.26.4.659

Bell, D. (1980). The Social Framework of the Information Society. In T. Forester (Ed.), *The Microelectronics Revolution*. Cambridge, MA: The MIT Press.

Benigno, V., Bocconi, S., & Ott, M. (2007, November). Inclusive education: Helping Teachers to Choose ICT Resources and to Use Them Effectively. *eLearning Papers*, 6. Retrieved from http://www.elearningeuropa.info/files/media/media14199.pdf

Bloom, B. S. (Ed.). (1956). *Taxonomy of Educational Objectives: The Classification of Educational Goals*. New York: Susan Fauer Company.

Boon, J., Ramasundram, V., Van der Klink, M., & Tattersall, C. (2005). Developing a Critical View on e-Learning Trend Reports: Trend Watching or Trend Setting? *International Journal of Training and Development*, *9*(3), 205–211. doi:10.1111/j.1468-2419.2005.00229.x

Borger, R., & Seaborne, A. E. M. (1966). *The Psychology of Learning*. London: Pelican Books.

Bouthillier, F., & Shearer, K. (2002, October). Understanding Knowledge Management and Information Management: the Need for an Empirical Perspective. *Information Research*, 8(1).

Boyle, E., & Crosland, A. (1976). *The Politics of Education (Conversations with M. Kogan) (2nd Ed.)*. Harmondsworth, UK: Penguin Books.

Bramble, W. J. (2008). *Economics of Distance and Online Learning: Theory, Practice and Research*. London & New York: Routledge.

Brandon, B. (Ed.). (2008). *Handbook of e-Learning*. Retrieved from http://www.elearningguild.com/showfile.cfm?id=2509

Brandsford, J. D., Brown, A. L., & Cocking, R. R. (Eds.). (2000). *How People Learn: Brain, Mind, Experience and School*. Washington, DC: National Academies Press.

Bray, M. (2007). The Shadow Education System: Private Tutoring and its Implication for Planners. *Fundamentals of Educational Planning, 61*.

Capuano, N., Marsella, M., & Salerno, S. (2000). ABITS: An agent based intelligent tutoring system for distance learning. In C. Peylo, (Ed.), *Proceedings of the International Workshop on Adaptive and Intelligent Web- Based Educational Systems* (pp. 17–28).

Carliner, S., & Shank, P. (Eds.). (2008). *The e-Learning Handbook: Past Promises, Present Challenges*. San Francisco: Pfeiffer.

Carwile, J. (2007). A Constructivist Approach to Online Teaching and Learning. *Inquiry*, *12*(1), 68–73.

Casacuberta, D. (2007, November). Digital Inclusion: Best Practices from eLearning. *eLearning Papers*, 6. Retrieved from http://www.elearningeuropa.info/files/media/media-14197.pdf

Castillo, D., & Sjöberg, M. (2008). A Theoretical Framework for the Economics of E-Learning in Castillo, D. (ed.), *The Economics of E-Learning*, Monograph, *Revista de Univesidad y Sociedad del Conocimiento*, Vol. 5, No. 1, pp. 1-11, Universitat Oberta de Catalunya, http://www.uoc.edu/rusc/5/1/dt/eng/monograph.pdf

CEC - Commission of European Communities. (2008). *Towards More Knowledge-Based Policy and Practice in Education and Training*, Commission Staff Working Document, http://www.eenee.de/portal/page/portal/EENEEContent/_IMPORT-_TELECENTRUM/DOCS/Commission_eductrain.PDF

Centre for Educational Research and Innovation (CERI). OECD (2003). *New Challenges for Educational Research*. Paris, OECD

Centre for Educational Research and Innovation (CERI). OECD/ (2007) *Evidence in Education: Linking Research and Policy*, Paris, OECD

CESifo. (2007). World Economic Survey, Volume 6, N. 1

Clark, R. C., & Mayer, R. E. (2002). *E-Learning and the Science of Instruction: Proven Guidelines for Consumers and Designers of Multimedia Learning*. San Francisco: Pfeiffer.

Cobb, C. W. (1992). *Responsive Schools, Renewed Communities*. San Francisco: Institute for Contemporary Studies.

Cook, P. (2002). *Knowledge Economics. Clusters, Learning and Cooperative Advantage*. London: Rutledge.

Cosin, B. R. (Ed.). (1972). *Education: Structure and Society*. Hamondsworth, UK: Penguin Books.

Davenport, T., & Prusak, L. (1998). *Working knowledge: how organizations manage what they know*. Cambridge, MA: Harvard Business School Press.

Davey, P. (2007, January). Can Technologies Offer Intelligence in Tutoring? An Interview with Prof. Ulrich Hoppe. *eLearning Papers*, 2. Retrieved from http://www.elearningeuropa.info/files/media/media11562.pdf

Davies, C. (1989, June). Goffman's concept of the total institution: Criticisms and revisions. *Human Studies*, *12*(1-2), 77–95. doi:10.1007/BF00142840

Delrio, C., & Fischer, T. (2007, May). HELIOS: Redefining e-Learning Territories. *eLearning Papers*, 4. Retrieved from http://www.elearningeuropa.info/files/media/media12725.pdf

Dichenz, H. (2001). *E-Learning, A Linguistic, Psychological and Pedagogical Analysis of A Misleading Term.* A Paper Presented at the 20th ICDE World Conference, Düsseldorf, Germany.

Downes, S. (2005). *The Economy of E-Learning*. Retrieved from http://www.downes.ca/cgi-bin/page.cgi?post=5

Drucker, P. (2001). *Management Challenges for the 21st Century*. New York: Harper Business Press.

ECP. (2000, May 24). *EC Policy Document on e-Learning*.

Ehlers, U. D. (2007, January). The 'E' – Empowering Learners: Myths and Realities in Learner-Oriented eLearning Quality. *eLearning Papers,* 2. Retrieved from http://www.elearningeuropa.info/files/media/media11560.pdf

EU. (2001, September). *2001 – Where is e-Learning Headed?* Fallon, C., & Brown, S. (2008). *e-Learning Standards.* Boca Raton, FL: Sage & St. Lucie Press.

Fiske, E. B., & Ladd, H. F. (2000). *When Schools Compete: A Cautionary Tale.* Washington, DC: Brookings Institution Press.

Foray, D. (2004). *Economics of Knowledge.* Cambridge, MA: MIT Press.

Freire, P. (1985). *The Politics of Education - Culture, Power, and Liberation.* (D. Macedo, Trans.). New York: Bergin & Garvey.

Freire, P. (1987). *Pedagogy of the Oppressed.* (M. Bergman Ramos, Trans.). New York: The Continuum Publishing Corporation.

Furlong, J., & Oancea, A. (2005). *Assessing Quality in Applied and Practice-based Educational Research, A Framework for Discussion.* Oxford, UK, The University Department of Educational Studies.

Gilbert, L., & Gale, V. (2008). *Principles of e-Learning Systems Engineering.* Cambridge, UK: Chandos.

Gjøvik, Ø. (2009). Connections between Learning Theory and e-Learning Theory. *Scrib.* Retrieved from http://www.scribd.com/doc/2932693

Godejord, P. A. (2007, November). Perspectives on Project Based Teaching and 'Blended Learning' to Develop Ethical Awareness in Students. *eLearning Papers,* 6. Retrieved from http://www.elearningeuropa.info/files/media/media14200.pdf

Goffman, E. (1957). Characteristics of Total Institutions. In *Symposium on Preventative and Social Psychiatry,* Washington, DC (pp. 43-93).

Gonella, L., & Panto, E. (2008, July). Didactic Architecture and Organisation Models: a Process of Mutual Adaptation. *eLearning Papers,* 9. Retrieved from http://www.elearningeuropa.info/files/media/media15973.pdf

Gordon, C. (2002). *Contributions of Cultural Anthropology and Social Capital Theory to Understandings of Knowledge Management.* Unpublished Doctoral Thesis, Ontario Institute for Studies in Education, University of Toronto.

Halsey, A. H. (1979). Social Mobility and Education, pp. 57-78 in Rubinstein (1979)

Hargreaves, D. H. (2000). The production, Mediation and Use of Professional Knowledge among Teachers and Doctors: a Comparative Analysis. In *CERI 2000.*

Hein, G. E. (1991). Constructivist Learning Theory, the Museum and the Needs of People. In *CECA (International Committee of Museum Educators) Conference,* Jerusalem, Israel, Institute of Inquiry. Retrieved from http://www.exploratorium.edu/ifi/resources/constructivistlearning.html

Henig, J. R. (1994). *Rethinking School Choice: Limits of the Market Metaphor.* Princeton, NJ: Princeton University Press

Hildreth, P., & Kimble, C. (2004). *Knowledge Networks: Innovation through Communities of Practice.* Hershey, PA: Idea Group Publishing.

Holmes, B., & Gardner, J. (2006). *E-Learning, Concepts and Practice.* Thousand Oaks, CA: Page Publications.

Jackson, B., & Marsden, D. (1962). *Education and the Working Class.* Harmondworth, UK: Penguin Books.

Junge, K., & Hadjivassiliou, K. (2007, November). What are the EU and Member States Doing to Address Digital Literacy? *eLearning Papers,* 6. Retrieved from http://www.elearningeuropa.info/files/media/media14196.pdf

Kastis, N. (2007, May). Observing the e-Learning Phenomenon: the Case of School Education. Analysing the Transformative Innovation of e-Learning. *eLearning Papers,* 4. Retrieved from http://www.elearningeuropa.info/files/media/media12729.pdf

Keegan, D. (2002). *The Future of learning: from e-Learning to m-learning*. Institute for Research into Distance Education, Fein University (Hagen, Germany).

Kim, K. J., Bonk, C. J., & Zeng, T. T. (2005, June). Surveying the Future of Workplace e-Learning: the Rise of Blending, Interactivity, and Authentic Learning. *e-Learn Magazine*, 2005(6).

Knowles, M. S. (1975). *Self-Directed Learning, a Guide for Learners and Teachers*, Englewood Cliffs, Prentice Hall/ Cambridge

Knuth, R. A., & Cunningham, D. J. (1993). Tools for Constructivism. In T. M. Duffy, J. Lowyck & D. H. Jonassen (Eds.), *Designing Environment for Constructive Learning* (pp. 163-188). Berlin, Germany: Springer.

Korte, W. B., & Hüsing, T. (2006, January). Benchmarking Access and Use of ICT in European Schools 2006: Results from Head Teacher and a Classroom Teacher Surveys in 27 European countries. *eLearning Papers,* 2. Retrieved from http://www.elearningeuropa.info/files/media/media11563.pdf

Lim, C. C., Yu, M. H., & Jin, J. J. (2005). Generic e-Learning Data Structure and Web Teaching. In *Proceedings of IEEE 2005 the International Conference on e-Technology, e-Commerce and e-Service* (pp. 564-569).

Lyons, J. (2001). *Paulo Freire's Educational Theory*. New Foundations. Retrieved from http://www.newfoundations.com/GALLERY/Freire.html

Mace, C. A. (1932). *The Psychology of Study*. London: Pelican Books.

Marriott, R. de C. V., & Torres, P. L. (Eds.). (2008). *Handbook of Research on e-Learning Methodologies for Language Acquisition*. Hershey, PA: Information Science Reference.

McCloskey, D. N. (1985). *The Rhetoric of Economics*. Madison, WI: University of Wisconsin Press.

McLuhan, M. (1964). *Understanding Media: The Extensions of Man*. New York: Mentor.

Meadow, C. T., Boyce, B. R., & Kraft, D. H. (2000). *Text information retrieval systems* (2nd ed.). San Diego, CA: Academic Press.

Miller, G. A. (1967). *The Psychology of Communication*. London: Penguin Books.

Mitchell, K. D. (2000). Knowledge management: the Next Big Thing. *Public Management, 29*(2), 57–60.

Mudur, S. P. (2005). e-Learning: Prospects and Challenges. *Elel Tech India*. Retrieved from http://elearn.cdac.in/eSikshak/eleltechIndia05/PDF/00-E-Learning%20Prospects%20and%20Challenges-%20SP%20Mudur-00.pdf

Nichols, M. (2003a). Formal Discussion: A Theory for e-Learning. In *International Forum of Educational Technology and Society, March.* Retrieved from http://ifntcs.ieee.org/discussions/discuss_march 2003.html

Nicohls, M. (2003). A Theory for e-Learning. *Educational Technology and Society*, *6*(2), 1–10.

Nonaka, I., & Takeuchi, H. (1995). *The knowledge creating company: how Japanese companies create the dynamics of innovation*. New York: Oxford University Press.

Ornstein, R. E. (1972). *The Psychology of Consciousness*. London: Pelican Books.

Pénao, S., Noumon, R. C., Kitaev, I., & Oulai, D. (1997). Financing and Financial Management of Education. In *Pan African Seminar*, Dakar, Senegal, (pp. 12-14).

Peters, M. A. (2006). Higher Education, Development and the Learning Economy. *Policy Futures in Education*, *4*(3), 279–291. doi:10.2304/pfie.2006.4.3.279

Pharmaceutical Research and Manufacturers Association (PhRMA). (2001). *The Value of Medicines*. Washington, DC.

Probst, G., et al. (2002). *Gestão do conhecimento-os elementos construtivos do sucesso* [Knowledge management-the constructive elements of success]. Porto Alegre, Brasil: Bookman.

Pulichind, J. (2006). *The e-Learning Guild Research: Future Directions in e-Learning*. Retrieved from http://www.elearningguild.com/showfile.cfm?id=1685.

Quah, D. (2003). *Digital Goods and the New Economy*. Centre for Economic Performance, LSE. Retrieved from http://cep. lse.ac.uk/pubs/download/dp0563.pdf

Ravenscorft, A. (2001). Designing e-Learning Interactions in the 21st Century: Revisiting and Rethinking the Role of Theory. *European Journal of Education*, *36*(2), 133–156. doi:10.1111/1467-3435.00056

Rubinstein, D. (1979). *Education & Equality*. Harmondsworth, UK: Penguin Books.

Ryle, G. (1949). *The Concept of the Mind*. Chicago: The University Press.

Saint-Onge, H. (2002). *Linking Knowledge to Strategy.* Presentation at the Strategic Planning for KM Conference, Toronto, May 28-29.

Schaffert, S., & Hilzensauer, W. (2008). On the Way towards Personal Learning Environments: Seven Crucial Aspects. *E-Learning Papers*. Retrieved from http://www.elearningpapers.eu

Siebert, H. (1998). Konstruktivismus. Konsequenzen für Bildungsmanagement und. Seminargestaltung. In *Deutsches Institut für Erwachsenenbildung*, Bonn, Germany. Retrieved from http://www.die-bonn.de/esprid/dokumente/doc-1998/siebert98_01.pdf

Smith, G. (Ed.). (1999). *Goffman and Social Organisation: Studies in a Sociological Legacy*. London: Routledge.

Software Survey. (2001, April 14). The Beast of Complexity. *The Economist*.

Tai, L. (2008). *Corporate e-Learning: an Inside View of IBM's Solutions*. Oxford, UK: The University Press.

Thorndike, E. L. (1931). *Human Learning*. Cambridge, MA: MIT Press.

Tsui, M.-J. (2009). The Model of Strategic e-Learning: Understanding and Evaluating Student e-Learning from Meta-cognitive Perspectives. *Journal of Educational Technology & Society*, *12*(1), 34–38.

Tüker, M. A., & Zingel, S. (2008, July). Formative Interfaces for Scaffolding Self-Regulated Learning in PLEs. *eLearning Papers,* 4. Retrieved from http://www.elearningeuropa.info/files/media/media15975.pdf

Tuparova, D., & Tuparov, G. (2007 May). e-Learning in Bulgaria. *eLearning Papers,* 4. Retrieved from http://www.elearningeuropa.info/files/media/media12735.pdf

Walberg, H. J., & Bast, J. L. (Eds.). (2003). *Education and Capitalism: How Overcoming Our Fear of Markets and Economics Can Improve America's Schools*. New York: The Hoover Press.

Wenger, E. (1998). *Communities of Practice, Learning, Meaning, and Identity*. Cambridge, UK: Cambridge University Press.

Wenger, E., McDermott, R., & Snyder, W. (2002). *Cultivating Communities of Practice, a Guide to Managing Knowledge*. Cambridge, MA: Harvard Business School Press.

Wiig, K. M. (1999). Introducing knowledge management into the Enterprise. In J. Liebowitz (Ed.), *Knowledge Management Handbook*. New York: CRC Press

Wild, F., Mödritscher, F., & Sigurdarson, S. (2008, July). Designing for Change: Mash-up Personal Learning Environment. *eLearning Papers, 9*. Retrieved from http://www.elearningeuropa.info/files/media/media15972.pdf

ENDNOTES

1 For example, PLE (Personal Learning Environment) vs. LMS (Learning Management Systems), attempting to determine which might be more learner-oriented or user-friendly through a study of their characteristics. See also Beard *et al.* (2007:3), Tsui (2009), Gjøvik (2009), Bates (2005), Carwile (2007) and Nichols (2003).

2 Information & Communications Technology

3 This issue has reached the European Court of Justice, which ruled against affirmative action, which is perceived as merely another form of discrimination and is hence illegal. Neither the court not other who debated the issue have been able to determine how to balance between the need to encourage less privileged members of society with the equally important need - to enable other members of society to move on and advance in their own pace.

4 The official EU document on the development of education system aimed at the enhancement of knowledge-based society states: "The challenges relating to the creation of knowledge on education and training are related to concerns about its relevance and quality as well as low levels of funding available for such research. This appears to be more of a concern than in other policy fields, such as social care or employment policy…" (CEC, 2008:6).

5 The issue of gender distribution is, in fact, highly important and goes well beyond the political correctness or the social ethics (which are, of course, also important). Experience shows that whenever a profession undergoes a process of "feminisation" – that is, women become the majority of its occupants, not only do salaries in this profession, or sector, plummet but also, the social status of the profession deteriorates. Those who practise the profession are regarded less and less as primary household "bread winner" and in overall social terms, the clients of this profession no longer enjoy a balanced attitude towards the problems treated by the profession, as half of the population is no longer represented in the profession adequately. This has happened to the teaching profession in most countries and it can now be seen in some other professions, notably in the public domains of the legal services (prosecution services, etc.). Such degradation also occurred in several countries in relation to junior academic appointments. Interestingly enough, "feminized" professions tend to hold feminine majorities only in lower professional levels while the higher echelons of these professions remain masculine at large; yet another facet of the imbalance in gender distribution.

6 This is a most important debate, even if this is not what is meant by most discussants. Indeed it goes beyond the constructivist debate which regards learning mainly in terms of the learner's construction, or reconstruction, of his or her learnt information or knowledge. If a student is taught how to think, the "what" will ensue automatically, since the "how" will always determine the "what". If, on the other hand, it is the "what" which is taught, then the student might be merely brainwashed. It is striking, albeit not surprising, when teacher education is examined, that none of these anomalies – or polemics – is found in their training courses.

7 Including personnel affiliated with higher education comprising (17%), commercial training or educational service (11%), financial services (9%), healthcare (8%), professional business or consulting (6%), insurance and government (5% each), manufacturing (4%), and others.

8 It seems that many tend to ignore that "the effectiveness of a technology cannot be judged without making some basic assumptions about what constitutes affective teaching and learning and the goals and purposes of education and training" (Bates, 2005, 4).

9 Bates (2005: 10) mentions two main roles of e-Learning: a) developing and enhancing new knowledge-based industry; b) serving as a means to improve quality of education & production of technology savvy graduates. According to Keegan (2002: 35), e-Learning definitions address themselves to teaching and information packages delivered electronically. They may contain units of information, self testing batteries and tests for quick (or automatic) evaluation and scoring and placement. He also refers to Dichenz 2001 (p. 91) who argues that E-Learning offers lower level learning goals. Higher order goals like understanding, reasoning and (moral) judging are more difficult to achieve. They require an individualised interactive discourse and can hardly be planned." Keegan agrees and adds that while learners are more and more mobile "learning cannot be mobile" and he adds that **"most definitions [of e- and m-Learning] take technology as the starting point."** (Emphasis added).

10 For years this issue has been widely discussed as a technical issue that warranted technical solutions. See, for example, Capuano *et al.* (2000) as well as others.

11 See also, in this regard, Branson, (2008: 34-35).

12 There are schools of thought, for instance the one adhering to the teachings of Freire (e.g., 1985; 1987), that argue that this goal can only be achieved through what they call 'teaching students to think democratically,' which in turn means provoking students' thinking by perennially posing questions which would help them to make sense – and meaning – from what they learn (Lyons, 2001).

13 The learning process is crucial stage in acquiring knowledge. Learners must be equipped with tools enabling them to read and write properly and effectively. They should also have analytical capabilities and contextual understanding of the world, based on a broad foundation of socially and educationally related subjects, including economics, ethics, scientific know-how, at least to a minimal operable degree, etc. Some add also cultural and cross-cultural studies and literature and comparative text reading aided by literary instruments (e.g., lingual, etymological and philosophical dictionaries, thesauruses, encyclopaedias, etc.). The list could be endless. The lack of such tools is reflected in the poor results of international examinations of reading comprehension, of sciences and of the level of use of native language. Techniques, it turn out, do not suffice.

14 When reaching senior position, they fear it will be looked at as if they got there thanks to some 'affirmative action'.

15 For some illuminating discussions following Goffman's analysis see also Davies (1989), Becker (2003), and Smith (1999).

16 See, for example, Junge & Hadjivassiliou (2007) for the issue of measuring, Casacuberta (2007) and Benigno *et al.* (2007) for the issue of e-inclusion and Ala-Mutka & Punie (2007) for the issue of expansion, particularly in view of the phenomenon of aging society.

17 As was the case in the early years of the current century when institutions such as Kampala International University and other privately owned universities in Eastern Africa established multitude of remote teaching systems in order to increase their income from remote students.

18 Later on they also say: While deriving its underpinning theories from such notable scholars as Plato, Rousseau, Skinner, Dewey, Vygotsky and Piaget, to name but a few, e-Learning is arguably eclipsing their impacts as the most dynamic development in education ever. Even with several decades behind us, there seems no end to the innovation and development that stretches into the future for e-Learning. For now and the foreseeable future, e-Learning remains 'mission critical.' It has emerged as an unparalleled explosion of innovations, creating opportunities for enriched experiences in traditional education for enhancing the breadth of opportunity and content for lifelong learning. The scope for e-Learning future development is so wide that it is with some trepidation that we attempt to paint the picture of the future (Holmes and Gardner 2006: 147). They hope that "future development of e-Learning will be dominated by social and technological dimensions of e-Learning" as "change catalyst." But they also recognise that it could, at best, "improve" learner's awareness of design (149). They dare not hope for an improvement in awareness of values.

19 Bates makes the following observation, which is not unrelated to our debate: "Whenever a new technology emerges in education people in general ignore what has been learned in previous contexts. In most cases thought, many of the lessons learned from previous applications of technology are just as relevant for the new technology application, yet the same mistakes are made. For instance, the need to reorganise and redesign teaching to exploit fully a new technology is often ignored.... The failure to learn from prior experience in distance education has led to many costly disasters in online learning in the last few years." But also: "The effectiveness of a technology cannot be judged without making some basic assumptions about what constitutes affective teaching and learning and the goals and purposes of education and training." (Bates, 2005: 4)

20 Bates says: "... technologies do not roll out evenly and all at once. Even in the more advanced industrial countries, there will be some target groups who will have access only to print, television and possibly the telephone. In developing countries, many of the newer technologies, for instance, the Internet will be beyond the reach of most of the target groups for distance education for many years to come." (2005: 4)

21 One list is published by the Centre for Economics of Education of the London School of Economics and can be found at the following address: http://cee.lse.ac.uk/pubs/default.asp; the other is published by the Centre for Economic Performance also part of the London School of Economics, and can be found at: http://cep. lse.ac.uk/_new/publications/default.asp; the third list examined is that of the Institute of Education

(IoE), University of London, to be found at http://ioewebserver.ioe.ac.uk/ioe/cms/get.asp?cid=11652&11652_0=11659.

22 http://www.unesco.org/iiep/eng/publications/recent/rec8.htm.

23 China might be an interesting case. In the last two decades or so, private education has sprung and grown significantly, as parents decided that they wanted to enable their children to stand out as "different", better cared for, believing that if they paid for their children's education they might indeed receive better tutoring and possibly also richer curricula. In many cases this belief was found justified.

24 Already seven years ago, over 50% of all employees spent up to 50% of their time out of office. More than 75% of al internet viewing is done on wireless platforms. Over 525 million web-enabled phones have been shipped. Mobile commerce market was over $ 200 Bn. and mobile devices outnumber landline PCs. By 2005 there were more than 1 bn. wireless Internet subscribers. (Keegan, 2002: 13-14)

25 Computing technology was introduced into telecommunication in the 1960s with the first public analogue software switchboards of the mid 1970s. These were digitalised almost immediately and were followed by the development of Integrated Services Digitalised Networking (ISDN) in the 1980s. In the 1990s, seamless digitalised connections between fixed and air networks were introduced. The increase in chips speed was crucial here. The replacement of silicon chips by nano-chips aims at further speed increase.

The development of broad band technology (more than 2 Mbits per second over a public switched network) is of vital importance for distant training, because of the needs of extensive bandwidth for picture, audio, video and virtual realities. Interactive multimedia, image processing, data and video are all large consumers of bandwidth.

The electronic revolution of the 1980s enabled face-to-face distance communication, with electronic eye-to-eye contact and distance group teaching.

It is worthy to mentions several currently used protocols: **Bluetooth** (Universal Radio Interface for Wireless Connectivity is improvement on infra-red linked portable devices; **GPRS** (General Packet Radio System is internet connectivity to mobile terminals that gives instant, transparent IP access with no cell set-up time; **WAP** (Wireless Access Protocol is web browser usability of the Internet to mobile terminals, providing data oriented non-voice services anywhere and at any time. (Keegan, 2002: 11-12)

26 McLuhan argued that the medium, regardless of the content it carries, becomes the real message, hence acting as agent of change. Because of its own characteristics it would become a "message" in its own right, since it creates, by its very innovation or use, a "change of scale or pace or pattern" (1964: 8).

27 Other sources include corporations, which use materials for their own learning or training and also some purchases by individual users. Materials purchased are determined almost always by the clientele, that is, educational institutions and corporations (Downes, 2005).

28 For example, *BBC*, *SchoolNet*, NYPL, MIT OpenCourseWare, to name but a few.

29 *Wikipedia* might be the most striking example. Also, consider such products as *Google Maps* and *Google Earth*, or the free content of the *Live 8 videos*. They all show that this impact will be widespread.

30 Downes and other estimate that such a collapse, if not adequately tended to, might happen within a short period of a few years.

[31] Consider, for example, the economy of audio creation and storage technology and how it had so quickly developed into a huge free, open source shared non-commercial market, albeit the tenacious battle waged against it by the various interested parties in the audio related industry, from creators to producers to performers to marketers. Or, consider the blogging market, with the disappearance of sorts of Typepad or Userland which were replaced by free blogging services. This particular market has also implications pertaining to the e-Learning market, certainly in the domain of content.

[32] A case in point is the development of Linux by IBM and its new corporate strategic direction, to leave behind production of hardware or even software and become instead a consulting and integrator service provider. Likewise, consider *Google Maps*, *Google Earth*, or the free content of the *Live 8 videos*.

[33] They include such endeavours as classification, indexing, summarisation and dynamic relational database. Also, in this regard, one should consider the attempt to adopt hand held devices to the learning arena – or to information transferring in general. It requires simplification of the scenarios used. It also shifts the emphasis from textual – or visual – emphasis to the oral capabilities. It must be emphasised that working on the transferring of existing multimedia scenarios for collaborative learning to mobile multimedia scenarios is really more within the technological domain than that of pedagogy. See Keegan (2002: 35). In this regard, WAP based courses should be mentioned. They are supposed to be offered via PDA or Smartphones. Such courses a "keep it simple" attitude, avoiding large amount of data, underlined texts, using selection list for data entries and use short words.

[34] In the business sector, these developments allow SMEs, hitherto unable to bear costs of independent internal educational/training endeavours, to access affordable contents and means to mediate them to employees.

[35] See also the European Commission document on knowledge-based society: "Although the spread of the internet has given us unprecedented access to vast amounts of information, much of this is not subject to quality control. This increases the risk that irrelevant or questionable material may be taken up in the policy-making process and valuable evidence may be lost in the 'noise'" (CEC, 2008: 7).

[36] Note that education is always referred to as "sector" whereas other domains, like health or engineering, are "industries".

[37] To attribute it only to public apathy vis-à-vis education is a gross over-simplification. Also, it is wrong to copy development drivers in ICT or health 'as is' (or even in a "modified" form) into the educational field. The levels of R&D expenditure in high-tech it is very high; in health and medicine it is high to very high level. In education, it is low, or even very low level. R&D quality is high in high-tech, varied in medicine and low in education. Success in knowledge creation is, respectively, very high, high and low and speed of new knowledge mediation is very fast, fast and slow, with speed of implementation of new knowledge is very fast, varied and slow to very slow.
Success in knowledge creation and speed of the implementation of new knowledge are particularly important. The data for the educational sector, low and slow to very slow, might imply that possibly, education is kept at bay deliberately
The issue of content or knowledge creation is crucial, regardless of the medium through which it is transferred. Of course, the less informed are the customers, the less can

they judge its quality or put it to ample use. This means that customers must be trained to understand the terms of consumption before even contemplating consumption. But since speed of knowledge creation and implementation in ICT is so much superior to the educational body of content, ICT knowledge products – the means, the media – become the new content. There might be a wish to bring everyone to ample computer/ ICT literacy, hoping they will be able to look after themselves. But is it really possible?

38 Bates mentions also the growing demand for higher education for many who were unable to obtain it (school leavers, etc.); cost effectiveness of education, particularly where demand exceeds number of available places; geographical distances; commercialisation of education; openness of discussion & learning through the Internet; etc. He does relate it all – as well as the flourishing of e-Learning, the attempt to develop new knowledge-based industry and, at the same time, means to improve quality of education by production of technology savvy graduates. But over all, he also recognises the importance of knowledge-based economics s necessary way to compete with lower-wage economies.

39 Tsui (2009) identifies two major problems associated with online learning and with electronic/web based (or hypertext) environments: 1) unrestricted control by the learner of sequencing; 2) lack of learner's ability to meaningfully integrate unstructured information (which is so readily available on the net).

Also, there the issue of learning how to learn on the Internet: It requires pre-requisites skills, e.g., reflection, planning, study search, application, self evaluation, control, etc. These are not innate, but need to be groomed and nourished. "Inability of students to transfer learning strategies from traditional to online learning environment may result in different performance. Internet-based learning environment may prefer students with mature computer skills and meta-cognitive skills" Tsui (2009).

What is needed to emulate learning and transfer learning into knowledge is a multiple skill set of predispositions: skill, will, self regulation (the way students manage their learning process), planning skills, monitoring capabilities, focusing, self evaluation, ability to facilitate the acquisition, understanding and later the transfer of knowledge and skills Tsui (2009).

40 *The Economist*, 14.4.2001, p. 4 of "Software Survey"

41 $30 in 2001 (PhRMA, 2001:25)

42 This, of course, is not limited to the information collected by governments. Consider television. While there are quite a few programmes based on "pay per view" arrangement, so called "free television" is still the most common way to consume this medium. Yet this "free" watching is entails a numerous expenses, ranging from the purchase of the set through subscription fees to the satellite or cable operator, or the state's television fee or license, etc. and we have not mentioned here the cost of the competition associated with the production of the programmes watched...

43 Including property tax wavers, as well as other tax breaks, VAT wavers, etc.

44 The term "data," denotes at facts serving as a basis for reasoning, discussion, or calculation. "Information" also indicates transferring of knowledge or intelligence. "Knowledge" means the understanding of facts or information retrieved through experience, or the comprehension through reasoning of truth or fact (Bouthillier & Shearer, 2002). Information, it turns out, "carries the connotation of evaluated, validated or useful data." While knowledge implies "a

higher degree of certainty or validity than information," having "the characteristic of information shared and agreed upon within a community" (Meadow, *et al.* 2000: 35, 38).

Other extrapolations make no difference. Information can be regarded as organised facts and data depicting specific state of affairs. Knowledge would then be collection of concepts, perspectives, truths, beliefs, judgments and expectations, organised in a methodological manner based on formerly gained know-how (Wiig, 1999). In other words, information is data that by context-related arrangement becomes meaningful. Knowledge is data that create sense through the reliance on experience (or inference), pertaining to the interaction between actions and their consequences. Thus, it also has the capability to guide (Mitchell, 2000).

Transferring information to knowledge may be achieved by means of "experiential learning" which, in essence, "is the integration of theory and practice. The two are regarded not as independent but as continuous process of interaction between the development of theoretical frameworks and their testing in reality" Ravenscorft, A. (2001: 12).

And also: "The natural order in the acquisition of knowledge is from the vague to the precise, from the rough outline sketch to the detailed picture, from the provisional and inaccurate approximation to the refined and balanced truth. This, too, has practical implications Mace" (1932: 43).

45 For example, Clark and Mayer (2008); Tai (2008): Delrio and Fischer (2007); Kastis (2007); Wild *et al.* (2008), who argue that "learning environments and their construction as well as maintenance make up the most crucial part of the learning process"; Gonella and Panto (2008), who discusses 'e-Learning 2.0' and the incorporation of 2.0 technologies and tools into the new mechanism of LMS, as a major didactic endeavour; Aviram *et al.* (2008), in their discussion of the iClass; Tüker and Zingel (2008); Banyard and Underwood (2008), who examine the relationship between digital technologies and learning mechanisms; and many more.

46 How effective or efficient is such an eye contact – which in order to include all the audience require a gaze and movement at a narrow arc of vision – is beyond this discussion.

47 See, on this subject, discussions in Ryle (1949/1964), Borger & Seaborne (1966/1976); or Thorndike (1931/1968), particularly in regards to the centrality of knowledge base for the conceptualisation process and also the value of freely flowing exchange in the human learning process.

48 See, for example, the discussion with former ministers of education, in Boyle & Crosland (1971); or Jackson & Marsden (1962); Rubinstein (1979), particularly Halsey (1979); Cosin (1972); etc.

49 For example, Godejord (2007); Tuparova & Tuparov (2007); Korte & Hüsing (2007).

50 An interview with Prof. Ulrich Hoppe. While advocating "intelligent tutoring", the mainstream of education-related AI (Artificial Intelligence), Hoppe maintains that it "has more difficult relationship with Computer Support for Collaborative Learning (CSCL)." He also suggests that "a potential conflict may exist between restricting the role of technologies to facilitating human-to-human communication, and Intelligent Tutoring Systems (ITS) that are often seen as active agents to steer human learning."

Section 2
Social Interaction and Collaborative Learning

In Section 2 emphasis is given on collaborative learning and the effects of social interaction within the Web. The Web 2.0 technologies and their usage in e-learning, individual learning in a social interaction environment and interface design for collaborative learning are among the issues covered in this section of the book.

Chapter 2
Web Advances in Education:
Interactive, Collaborative Learning via Web 2.0

Eleni Kaldoudi
Democritus University of Thrace, Greece

Stathis Konstantinidis
Aristotle University of Thessaloniki, Greece

Panagiotis D. Bamidis
Aristotle University of Thessaloniki, Greece

ABSTRACT

The evolving shift from 'teaching' to 'learning' in contemporary education is strongly related to an increasing involvement of information and communication technologies and the Web. Although the latter was initially of a static nature and merely required passive human viewers, this is currently changing towards a second generation of dynamic services and communication tools that emphasize on peer-to-peer collaboration, contributing, and sharing, both among humans and programs. In this chapter, this revolution, usually known under the collective term Web 2.0, is reviewed from an educational as well as a technological point of view. The issues and controversies arising are backed up by case studies from diverse educational contexts to illustrate the potential of the proposed solutions. The discussion is finally concluded with some exciting speculations on the envisaged arrival of Web 3.0 and collaborative content sharing with semantic technologies.

INTRODUCTION

Traditional education requires students at any level to sit through hours of lectures, and read through entire volumes of textbooks. However, advances in the understanding of learning processes suggest that such techniques may be suboptimal, and that learning should evolve from 'learning by acquisition' to 'learning by participation'. Thus alternative learning approaches build on concepts of active learning, defined as the process of having students engage in some activity that makes them reflect upon ideas and how they are using these ideas. Such new educational approaches require students to regularly assess their skills and knowledge at handling real world problems. Some student centered, active

DOI: 10.4018/978-1-60566-940-3.ch002

learning approaches include problem-based or case-based learning, inquiry and discovery based learning, role and game playing based learning, as well as collaborative and interactive learning of all kinds. Such approaches rely on situational learning and are active, self-directed, student-centered, and experiential. Their aim is also to develop problem-processing skills, self-directed learning skills and group competence. Learning is thus regarded to address two types of knowledge: explicit knowledge (conveyed by books, lectures and scientific documents) and tacit knowledge (directly related to experience and practice, as shared by interaction and collaboration).

This evolving shift from 'teaching' to 'learning' in contemporary education is also strongly related to an increasing involvement of information and communication technology. There is currently an international trend to involve computers and the Internet in formal education as well as in continuing life-long learning. This practice is reinforced by active support and funding from bodies such as the European Union and local governments. Specifically, the European Council in its Lisbon meeting in March 2000 set forth the European policy for an information and knowledge-based society, stressing the need to encompass the emerging technological revolution and change in the exchange of knowledge affecting all institutions and various aspects of the society (European Council, 2000).

Like many other cognitive domains, education can be considered in terms of levels of increasing complexity and importance: information (i.e. processed data and simple facts), knowledge (i.e. information with a purpose), and understanding (i.e. conscious knowledge, achievement of explanation and grasp of reasonableness), which leads eventually to ability, competence and professionalism (Ehlers, 2007). Technology has been employed in diverse ways to support different levels of the educational process, and especially conventional instructional teaching. Structuring and organizing information with a particular educational purpose refers to knowledge. On the other hand, understanding implies experience as well as inquiring. Managing and supporting these levels of the educational process is a rather complex issue. Although technology and the Web in particular have been extensively used to support conventional education, new active learning approaches that emphasize on active learning, participation, and competence have been less supported. However, the emerging Web 2.0 paradigm gives the perfect opportunity, because of its mere nature.

Although Web 2.0 emphasizes on participation, in its early days in supporting learning it is still used in the majority of cases to hold and provide content (albeit created dynamically and via peer participation and collaboration) and then systematically deliver it to students. However, there are emergent applications of web 2.0 tools to implement and support active, collaborative educational episodes on the internet, creating virtual places for learners and experts to collaborate and explore and thus create new knowledge and expertise.

This chapter elaborates on the potential of Web 2.0 for active and, potentially, effective learning and reviews current practices and emerging advances in the field. The chapter also presents case studies of how web 2.0 technologies can be used in different educational settings to support conventional instruction and active learning in undergraduate, post-graduate and continuing medical education, as well as, a case study of using web 2.0 technologies to disseminate physics and astronomy to the public. Additionally, discussion addresses open research questions regarding the evaluation of the learner in terms of practical skills gained, e.g. critical searching, critical appraisal of literature, collaboration, etc. Finally, the potential benefit and envisaged merit upon merging with Web 3.0 technologies is also discussed.

BACKGROUND

Before going any further with discussing the issues of concern and proposing the necessary solutions it is wise to summarise important relevant background.

Education and Learning

Training and education draws even more attention with the growing importance of a 'knowledge society', that is a society based on knowledge as a value, not only cultural but also economic. Nowadays, the competitive advantage of a nation is shown by the expertise and the behavior of its human resources. Current innovations in information systems and communication services mark the switch from the "information society", characterized by a mass information seeking and based on the distribution of pre-defined and standardized data, towards a "knowledge society", which emphasizes the cognitive advancement and, consecutively, the active involvement of each individual. The growing use of Internet not only modifies quickly and habitually the way people work but it also leads the race in this educational revolution.

New educational approaches build on concepts of adult education. They rely on situational learning and are active, self-directed, student-centered, and experiential (National Research Council, 1999). Learning is perceived as a qualitative change of one's conception of phenomena and ideas (Marton et al, 1977) and, consequently, knowledge must be actively processed by the student. A fundamental idea is that learning is organized in small student groups, i.e. tutorial groups, and not around lecture meetings. In the tutorial group students actively work with reality-based situations to formulate problems and learning needs that will guide their further studies. The teacher's role is that of facilitating learning rather than transferring knowledge. In the tutorial group, the students discuss and defend their choices and standpoints. Using library resources, text books, databases, laboratory work, field studies, lectures and other forms of faculty resources, they are urged to find answers to and perspectives on their problems and learning needs. The aim is also to develop problem-processing skills, self-directed learning skills and group competences (Ehlers, 2007; Fyrenious, 2005). In response, professional organizations worldwide have called for increased emphasis on training in life-long self-directed learning. The emerging view is of learning as an active, constructive, social, and self-reflective process (Berliner & Calfee, 1996). These basic research findings on learning suggest the need for educational environments that are learner-centered and knowledge-rich, guided by assessment, and situated in a community of learners (Schuable & Glaser, 1996). In higher education, educational programs increasingly include case-based or problem-based learning and other small group instructional models, collaborative organizations to support student-faculty interactions, and technology-enhanced educational tools (Jones et al, 2001).

When new technologies were deployed in education about two decades ago (although experimental attempts date back to 1970s), there was a considerable hype about the emerging electronic teacher, which fortunately soon enough subsided to reveal serious limitations of the computer-to-student educational model (Dertouzos, 1997). In retrospect, it is possible to identify three generations of information technology supported learning, which usually come under the collective term of "e-learning" (literally translated as "electronic learning"). The first generation is based on multimedia technology support, such as videos, CD-ROMs or other stand-alone educational software. The second generation employs telematic technologies and it is basically set up as teaching via the Web, where conventional educational material, as well as entire educational courses, is delivered via the Internet to remote students. The last, emerging generation, is about web based learning, where the Internet is used as a means to create active, context based, personalized learning experiences. This last generation of e-learning shifts the emphasis from 'teaching' to 'learning' and from the notion of technology as a didactic mediator to the notion of sociable, peer-supported, involved learner.

Web and Web 2.0

The Internet and the Web were initially of a static nature with passive viewers. Moreover, they were mainly targeted to human users, with the central role of information distribution; programs had little to do in this environment. Currently the Web is changing towards a second generation of dynamic services and communication tools that emphasize on peer-to-peer collaboration, contributing, sharing, both among humans and programs. This revolution is usually known under the collective term Web 2.0. In Web 2.0 the user is seen as a contributor, rather than a recipient. Content is created by participation and collaboration as an emergent product of human interactions. In the core of Web 2.0 lies an ensemble of standards, protocols, technologies and software development architectures and approaches that enable the seamless communication of third party programs thus creating the communities and networks of services that bring people together. One can argue that a major characteristic of Web 2.0 is the fact that it continually improves and grows in size, function, complexity and approach, thus making the term even more uncertain and difficult to define. An incomplete attempt to summarize what Web 2.0 refers to is given in Figure 1.

Initially, the term was coined by O'Reilly (2005) as an attempt to emphasize the fact that despite the late 90's shortcomings of the '.com' model, the Web still appeared strong and promising new features such as 'social software technologies' were emerging. Web 2.0 is not a program or an upgrade or a single concrete piece of technology; it is rather a more fully implemented Web. It is based on the same infrastructure and standard protocols, and on well-proven technologies and tools of the Internet and the Web. However, the term Web 2.0 encompasses a whole new meaning and a collective emergent behavior of the use of these technologies, tools and applications that create networks and communities of users (both humans and programs) that enhance and promote:

- **Participation:** People of any background, culture, age, etc. can participate without the need to understand the underlying technologies. Participation is perceived equally as accepting and as providing information (including new items as well as commenting and feedback). Core examples: wikis, blogs and personal profiles
- **Collaboration and sharing:** Together with collaboration comes sharing of information and personal attitudes. For example, social bookmarking, where not only links and services are shared, but their collaborative tagging and rating gives a new dimension to information organization
- **Openness:** Information is freely shared among humans and programs, thus promoting the notion that knowledge cannot be owned
- **Reuse:** Content and information is discovered, used and re-used via notions such as content syndication and supporting technologies that allow programs and humans to build their own content aggregates and distribute them
- **Personalization:** Content and service openness and reuse make it easier to customize information, function and their intertwining to create personalized experiences, such as personalized curricula, etc. Dynamically interlacing all this individual contribution, a 'wisdom of crowds' emerges. A striking example is the controversial new form of metadata for the organization of information, coming under

Figure 1. A pictorial summary of what Web 2.0 refers to

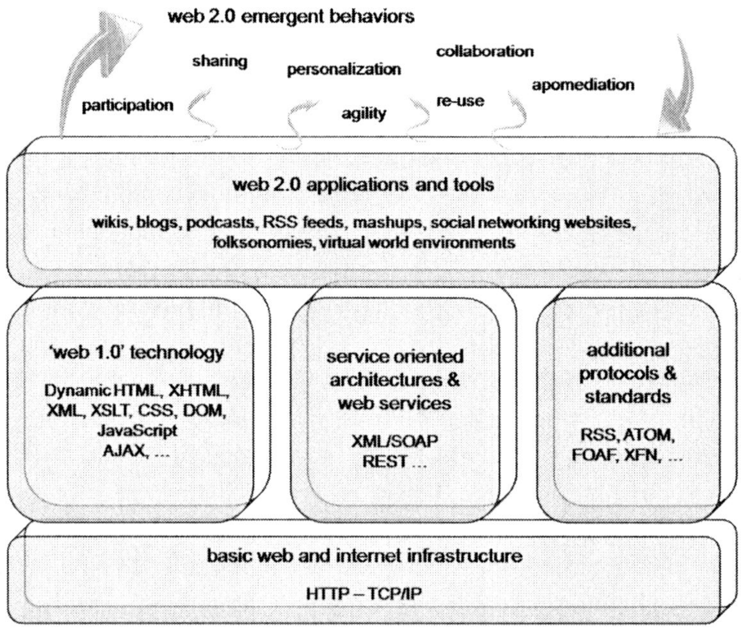

the term 'folksonomies', as opposed to 'taxonomies'

- **Agility:** Function and content from many sources (personalized and third party alike) are combined to create new added value for individuals. This can always be readily shared with others. Mashup applications are a major example
- **Apomediation:** A term coined by Eysenbach (2007) to characterize the third way for users to identify trustworthy and useful information. The first approach is to use some sort of mediation, e.g. a librarian or a teacher, in the case of education. The second approach is to bypass such mediation (commonly referred to as disintermediation), and this has been the basic role of conventional Web, with students seeking autonomously additional information on a variety of web-based information sources. In this third approach, enhanced and realized by Web 2.0, the user seeks information with peer guidance, as a result of networked collaborative filtering processes

All this emergent behaviour that characterizes Web 2.0 is enabled one way or the other by a variety of applications and tools that form the core of Web 2.0, and are empowered by an ensemble of technology, embracing both familiar technologies from the early days of the Web as well as innovations. Among common Web 2.0 tools that are being explored for their possible use in education are wikis, blogs, podcasts, social networking tools and virtual worlds (Alexander, 2006).

Wikis are dynamic, group-developed websites that can be edited, updated or changed by anyone who has access to them (usually any visitor). The current status for wiki technology includes pages with fruitful discussions on each entry and there is always the ability to view the evolving history of any entry and recover previous versions. The most well-known wiki is Wikipedia (www.wikipedia.org), the online editable encyclopedia.

Blogs is a short form of the term Weblogs, because it started as online diaries (logs) written by individuals on the Web. They are basically dated entries in reverse chronological order, and this is where the similarities with a conventional diary end. Blog entries can contain a variety of multimedia material and links to other web resources; can be commented by other users, while information can be organized by user defined and generic tags. An newer form of blog, known as microblogging, restricts the size of each posting, allowing it however to be submitted by a variety of means, e.g. conventional blog entry, instant messaging, email, etc., thus allowing for easy and often updates.

Mashups are web applications that merge data from one or more sources and present it in new ways. In many cases this is made possible by data providers that develop application programming interfaces (APIs) for their data. These APIs follow standard web service protocols and/or generic internet formats to represent data (such as RSS) and can easily be implemented in different programming languages. At the same direction, notification services offer continuous updates of web sites in a standardized form for use in mashups and in a variety of other applications. Usually under the term "RSS feed", which is borrowed from the commonly used data representation standard RSS (meaning Really Simple Syndication or, as renamed, Rich Site Summary), they include summarized text and respective metadata and they can be read either by standalone special purpose software or by software embedded in commonly used Internet tools (e.g. web browsers, mail clients, etc). RSS feeds and similar syndication technology is also used to distribute streams of audio and video data files to personal computers and portable media players – what is known under the term podcasting.

Social networking websites focus on creating online communities of individuals who publish their content and activities while exploring others' content and activities. Such sites cover a variety of topics and provide most of web 2.0 tools and technologies for users to interact. Therefore an astonishing number of simple or more sophisticated social networking sites are currently emerging ranging from mere casual social networking to collaborative web bookmarking and searching, school teacher rating, collaborative document and spreadsheet editing, etc.

Virtual worlds are simulated environments were individual users participate via fictional avatars. Their implementation on the Internet provides a unique way to realize fictional communities for individuals to freely meet others, communicate, and participate in a variety of activities and eventually learn.

Most often Web 2.0 sites combine more than one of the above applications, and have in common a variety of tools and features that enhance participation and collaboration such as search engines, links to other resources, ability for the user to add content and/or comments, tools for organizing content (e.g. tags, extensions by similarity, rating, etc), and signals for updates (McAfee, 2006).

Web 2.0 tools and applications use a range of technologies, mainly based on common Internet and Web technologies, that is the HTTP protocol and the suite of web development technologies, such as all variations of HTML and XHTML and CSS, XML and XSLT, Javascript, etc. Currently the core of this basic suite of technologies comes under the collective term AJAX (Asynchronous Java Script and XML), an interrelated group of web technologies used to develop interactive web pages that process user requests immediately. AJAX brings together data, content and presentation: presentation by XHTML and CSS, interaction with the page by DOM (an interface to allow Java scripts and programs to update content style and structure of documents dynamically), data interchange based on XML and XSLT, and JavaScript, a language that integrates all the above to create dynamic web pages. Applications created with AJAX use an engine that acts as an intermediary between a user's browser and the server from which it is requesting information. Instead of loading a traditional Web page, the user's browser loads the AJAX engine, which displays the page the user sees. The engine continues to run in the background, using JavaScript to communicate with the Web browser. User input or clicking on the page sends a JavaScript call to the Ajax engine, which can respond instantly in many cases. If the engine needs additional data, it requests it from the server, usually using XML, while it is simultaneously updating the page.

However, it can be argued that the real predecessor of Web 2.0 notions and technology is the programming paradigm of web services and service oriented architectures. Web services are a middleware technology for developing service-oriented architectures (SOAs). A SOA refers to a collection of interconnected software entities (services) that provide some capability through exchange of messages, and can be described, discovered and invoked over a network. Web services are loosely defined as self-contained, self-describing, modular applications that can be located and invoked over the Internet. Web services are based on open Internet standards: built on the HyperText Transfer Protocol (HTTP), they use XML for data presentation while messaging is described in an XML-based messaging protocol, SOAP (Simple Object Access Protocol). Web services describe themselves through a standardized Web Service Description Language (WSDL) document, and can be published to one or more Intranet or Internet repositories for potential users to locate through a standard Universal Description, Discovery and Integration (UDDI) registry. A whole suite of additional standards have been developed to formally address issues such as security, reliability, transactions, etc. REST is a technologically simpler approach to web services that bypasses the SOAP communication protocol and concentrates on getting information content of a web page via the HTTP protocol from its published XML file that contains desired information.

This core technology that supports Web 2.0 is continuously evolving and growing, as new specialized formats, standards, and protocols emerge. Examples include the RSS data/metadata XML format, the FOAF (Friend of a Friend) and XFN (XHTML Friends Network) protocols involved in social networking applications.

ISSUES, CONTROVERSIES, PROBLEMS

Initial involvement of the web to support education was based on the metaphor of a virtual classroom, where by the web application follows the model of a real classroom transferring there the conventional lecture, discussion, workshop and other educational activities (Cronje, 2006). About a decade ago, a systematic and critical meta-analysis of more than 330 studies by Russell concluded that there is no significant difference between various learning/teaching methods, the focus being the comparison between technology-enhanced versus conventional education (Russell, 2001). Today, it is widely accepted that this is an inappropriate comparison, as the use of technology not only changes the way education is deployed, but has a profound effect in the pedagogy, as it carries a meaning by itself. So, nowadays the discussion is about how technology, and the Web in particular, can stimulate a new learning culture. In these terms, to make a difference implies harvesting the potential of learning via the web to equip the learner with competences rather than mere subject knowledge (Ehlers, 2007).

Active education towards understanding and competence poses certain requirements that include:

- Communication among peers
- Collaboration among peers
- Ample access to alternative sources of information
- Some sort of reporting and rating of information, to account for information overload and limited quality control
- Potential for different representations of the same content (for people with special needs, with different cultural backgrounds,

different ages, different background)

- Support for content evolution, as knowledge data banks are growing quickly
- Contextual learning, i.e. repurpose content and process initially designed to have a specific meaning and purpose for an intended audience
- Mutated learning, i.e. content and process re-purposed and re-engineered from original design for a different purpose and/or audience, while attaining an acceptable level of validity
- Context based organization of resources and activities

From the list above, it is evident that Web 2.0 behaviors and application seem best suited to support such educational action. However, although Web 2.0 emphasizes on participation, collaboration and meets at least partially all the above requirements, in its early days it is still used in the majority of cases to hold and provide content (albeit created dynamically and via peer participation and collaboration) and then systematically deliver it to students.

Educators are using blogs in various educational settings and in many different ways, but mainly as a replacement of other forms of asynchronous computer mediated communication, merely because of their additional functionality, such as updates via feeds, their notion of ownership, decentralization, tagging, and archiving (Kim, 2008). Blogs in education are mainly used to publish articles and other educational material, as well as to keep track of class activities, often spanning across semesters and years of studies. An alternative approach involves using blogs to create dynamic learning maps and help students find easily and quickly qualified course material (Wang et al, 2008). However, this blog use is still based on the traditional learning environment with the teacher being the primary contributor of resources.

Some preliminary blog uses within the Web 2.0 paradigm, involve personal input from students and teachers in an attempt to create a learning community. An example involves use of blogs to record personal experiences of students and teachers as a reflection of one's own ideas, for feedback from peers or just as a means of communication (Hammond, 2006). Another example involves structured personal student blogs that post course assignments for evaluation and assessment together with participation on a course blog for informal communication and for collaborative story development in creative writing (Armstrong & Retterer, 2008).

Wikis are increasingly used in education, as an ideal tool for collaborative work done by both students and teachers. At first, educational wiki implementations involved the mere development of material in a collaborative manner. Additionally, wikis have been used to allow collaborative data collection for certain educational set ups. Both uses do not really exploit the Web 2.0 paradigm for peer collaboration, engagement and participation. Currently new applications are emerging where wikis are used as a classroom metaphor for students to collaborate on a group report, compile data or share the results of their research, while faculty might use the wiki to collaboratively author the structure and curriculum of a course.

Tonkin argues that different educational uses of wikis can include single-user wiki used more like a blog without the date format to hold and edit over time personal thoughts and output of the educational endeavor, while collaborative wikis can be used along the metaphor of a lab book, collaborative writing assignment, or with the aim to produce a knowledge base (Tonkin, 2005). A comprehensive review of published work supporting the above is given by Parker & Chao (2007). Yet, wikis can find their place in education when used not for substituting the handing in of paper reports or the in-class conventional collaboration, but rather when their potential for distributed peer educational engagement is fully exploited. An interesting example involves using wikis for initial ice-breaking collaboration among students during the initialization phase of a course (Augar et al, 2004). More fully implemented applications employ wikis to support collaborative learning, for example in the case of social learning within communities of practice (Wenger, 2000), that is, networks of individuals and institutions that share common practices, goals and problems about a certain topic. In this case, wikis can act as an evolving knowledge platform where members can share pieces of information, discuss and collaborate (Schaffert et al, 2006). Some more interesting examples are presented in the next chapter.

Podcasting can be used for archiving and distributing lectures in video or audio format. Video and slide sharing websites can be used to publish lectures and conference presentations more widely and as part of a curriculum to enhance mobility in learning (Evans, 2008). It can especially enhance the learning experience in demanding hands-on educational environments such as in medicine as suggested by Boulos, Maramba, and Wheeler (2006). Although such podcasting uses are closer to traditional passive learning and conventional web paradigm, they can free class time to be used for problem-solving, project sessions and other active learning activities (Kurtz et al, 2007). An example of using podcasting to support collaborative and active learning can be found in the initiative of the Duke University, where podcasts are created both by teachers and students, covering not only formal educational material, but discussions as well as feedback comments on assignments, etc. (Belanger, 2005).

Teachers and learners are also turning to video-sharing sites (such as www.teachertube.com) to share educational videos. Social networking sites are also used in various educational settings. Collaborative writing is supported by a number of respective websites that offer tools for collaborative text editing (such as www.thinkfree.com and docs.google.com). A striking example that fully realizes the Web 2.0 paradigm is del.icio.us (http://delicious.com/), a collaborative bookmarking web site, that allows users to share their bookmarks, creating their own tags and organizing dynamically bookmarks (on any possible topic and within any context, including educational subjects and contexts), thus creating a vibrant bookmark folksonomy that evolves over time.

Finally, virtual worlds on the web are increasingly used to create fluid learning communities that can be engaged in real world didactic situations, collaborate to approach solutions to problems, seek knowledge, and communicate and interact with peers; a comprehensive review is given in (De Lucia et al, 2009). Although there is a large number of virtual worlds dedicated to learning, when generic virtual world web environments are used, such as Second Life (http://secondlife.com/) and There (http://www.there.com/), there is the additional advantage of the vast size of the community that participates and can potentially engage in learning activities (Kelton, 2008).

As a final comment, it should be stressed that nowadays most of the above applications and tools are combined and intertwined within the same web site or service to give hybrid added value applications, enhancing the Web 2.0 paradigm and the corresponding emergent behaviors mentioned above.

SOLUTIONS AND RECOMMENDATIONS

Web 2.0 tools have crossed Moore's chasm, easily reached early majority and are currently under rapid development and evolution (Ebner et al, 2007). However, the idea of social learning software itself, especially in educational scenarios, is not as far developed as one may imagine, since too few innovators and early adopters are actually using Web 2.0 technology to enhance existing curricula designs and learning behaviors.

What is also true is that Web 2.0 technologies have led to a flood of new healthcare applications and services, with the potential to revolutionise the entire spectrum of health and medicine (Boulos, 2007). With areas such as consumer-led preventive medicine, public health, home care, telemedicine, clinical care and biomedical research strongly affected and enriched by the use of Web 2.0, it is mandatory that health and medical education should also follow and exploit this media, content and collaboration rich revolution (Bamidis & Pappas, 2008). Thus the following of this chapter will concentrate on specific examples of novel solutions and recommendations of employing Web 2.0 for supporting active learning mainly drawing from the demanding field of medical education. All three levels of medical education are affected, namely, undergraduate, postgraduate and continuing medical education (or profession development). In all three levels the tools to be used may be similar, but the way of using them should be different, so as to conform to the diverse skills and learning outcomes envisaged and mandated by the particular curricula or portfolio designs. For example, in undergraduate medical education emphasis might be placed upon the skill of recognizing information taught in a traditional classroom and attempting its sideways expansion so as to ease comprehension and knowledge acquisition. For postgraduate learners the focus is shifted more towards skills related to analyzing and/or synthesizing different facets of information from contexts of existing formal and/or tacit knowledge. In continuing life long learning or professional development level the need is shifted towards familiarization with new technology and/or new (evidence based) knowledge in a specified area as well as the exchange of peer experiences, activity or practice based training, and point of care or pervasive learning. In public education (or else communicating science to the public) challenges are associated with the wide diversity of the public scientific background and their differences in pursuing knowledge.

Some of the efforts to cover the above needs by exploiting the aforementioned Web 2.0 technologies are presented below. The first three cases may be categorized as "blended learning" examples, since e-learning and Web 2.0 are used in addition to traditional class lectures. In all cases, emphasis is placed on how collaboration is enhanced and learning is enriched with web 2.0 technologies as opposed to conventional web approaches.

Example 1: Undergraduate Medical Education

Medical students at the first semester of their studies at Medical School of Aristotle University of Thessaloniki register with the School's e-learning environment which is based on Moodle (www.moodle.org) learning management system and is facilitated by numerous Web 2.0 tools. The purpose here is to accompany traditional large audience lectures in the amphitheatre, where specific topic discussions and instructor-student interactions are minimal if not absent, with a virtual class example facilitated by a discussion forum. The forum module is a virtual place of knowledge. The instructor poses a topic threaded by a topic taught in the lecture, and the asynchronous discussion is kicked off. In the figure below (Figure 2), a screenshot where a "first week of the semester" discussion is evolved around the "pros and cons of the Computer Science intrusion in the health care sector" is illustrated as part of the School's Medical Informatics Module. Initially some students give short, strict answers/inputs, but as the discussion evolves, at some point students start to argue. In their effort to build these arguments and convince the others about their points, the "pros and cons" are gathered. The instructor intervenes, in order to evaluate the arguments, as well as, to bridge disparate opinions or recap when points are headed away the envisaged goals. In a further expansion, the notion of collaborative learning is enhanced by a "voting" scheme, where in the very same paradigm students "rate" the relative

Figure 2. An illustration of the undergraduate discussion forum on a topic touched upon in the class but virtually discussed though student-student or student-instructor interaction in the discussion forum of the e-learning system

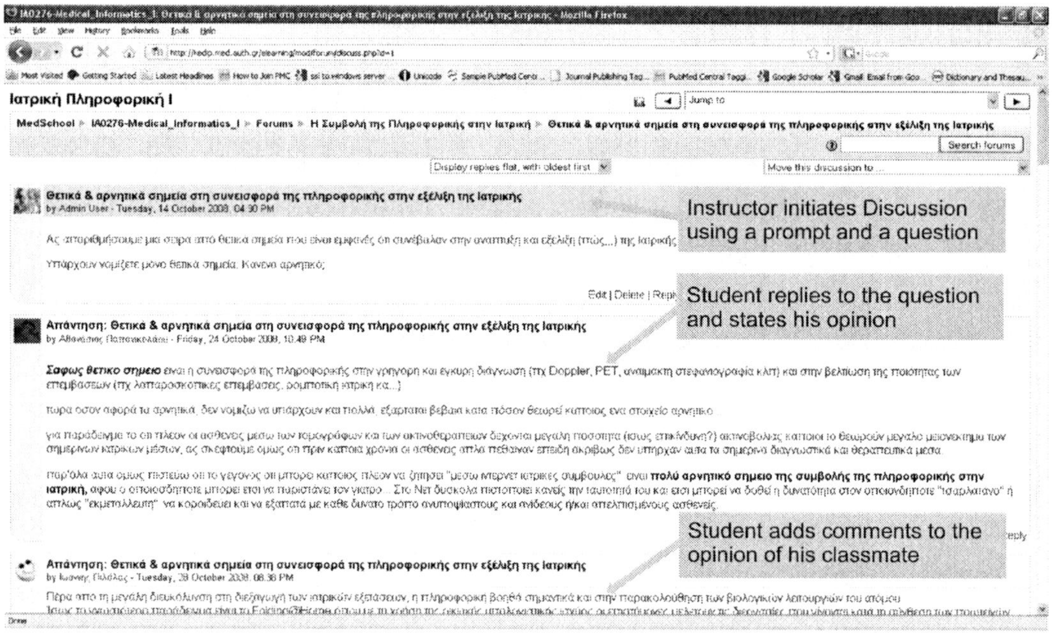

merits of certain technological applications in the health care sector in an effort to materialize any "abstract" points of the on-going and afore described discussion.

In a similar way, another discussion forum is populated by an exercise set (in this case "numerical systems transitions") initially provided by the instructor (Figure 3). Wrong student answers are corrected by other student inputs, while the instructor's role in those forums is merely advisory.

Example 2: Postgraduate Medical Education

Another case is from a course on Medical Informatics taught at a postgraduate level. Emphasis is placed not only in creating and promoting information, but also how to best utilise Web 2.0 as an active support mechanism towards a problem (or case) based learning. In our approach, students and instructors use the web as a virtual place to collaborate and create new knowledge and new educational experiences. Three web 2.0 applications are utilized, namely, discussion forums, collaborative wikis, and blogs. Forums were used in addition to the wiki and several (topic/tag marked) personal blogs within a specific problem related to Electronic Health Records (Bamidis et al, 2008). Every student had to complete each task in their own personal blogs and when they felt the answer was complete, they had to publish it to the wiki. All students were able to see each other's blogs and comment in there. In this way, these tools are not utilized to create, store and provide information, but as active tools to support problem based learning (PBL) in medicine (Figure 4).

The approach is summarized as follows. Instructors collaboratively develop a problem in the wiki. Discussion is initiated via the problem's discussion forum, where students and instructors collaborate to analyse the problem, identify conquered knowledge and argue about possible

Figure 3. An illustration of the undergraduate discussion forum populated by "exercises" solved by the students online and corrected by the evolving inputs

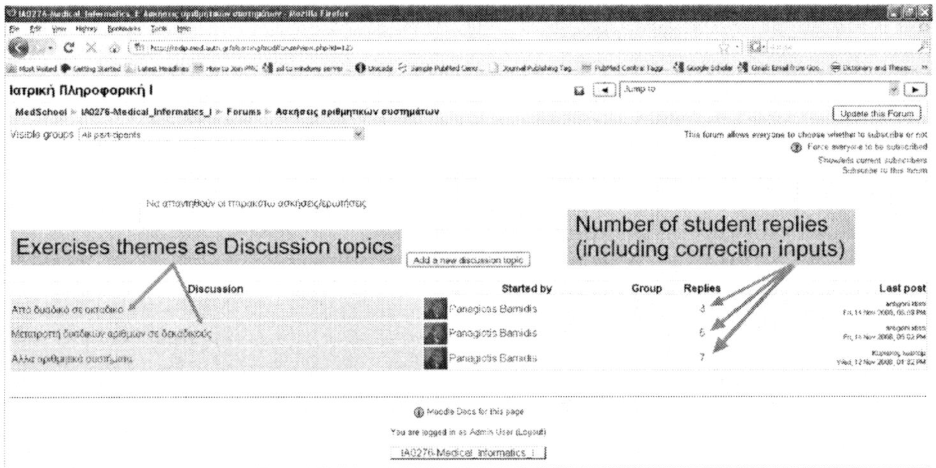

Figure 4. An illustration of the post-graduate PBL setting through use of a wiki. The instructor(s) set the problem and the steps here, while students are expected to update it (once ready) by their replies to the problem question(s). The dynamic nature of the evolving effort is characteristic of the collaborative web 2.0 use of the internet based course, as well as, the active learning approach.

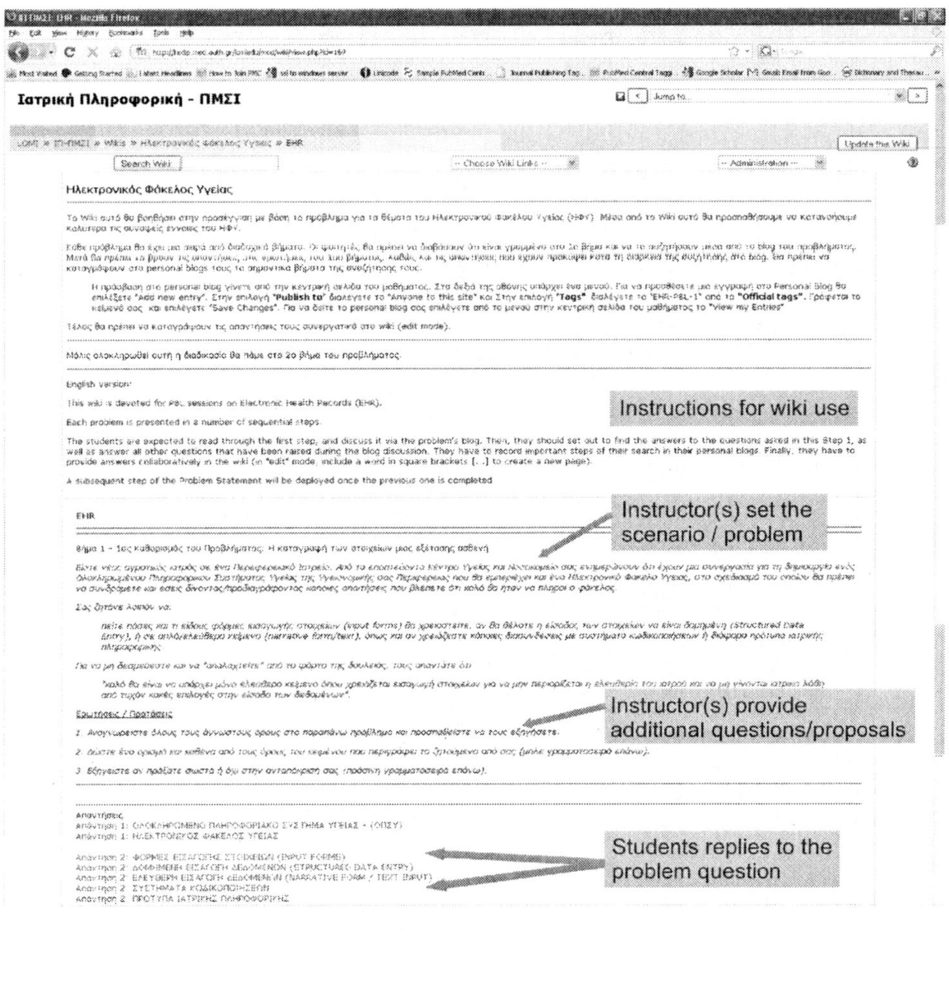

Figure 5. An illustration of the post-graduate student blog entries on the problem originally posed in the course's wiki by the instructor. Students work online and record their activities in these blogs. The evolving effort is not only monitored by the instructor, but also adds "collaborative value" to the acquired skill/knowledge of the students, as these are open to all for inspecting and commenting.

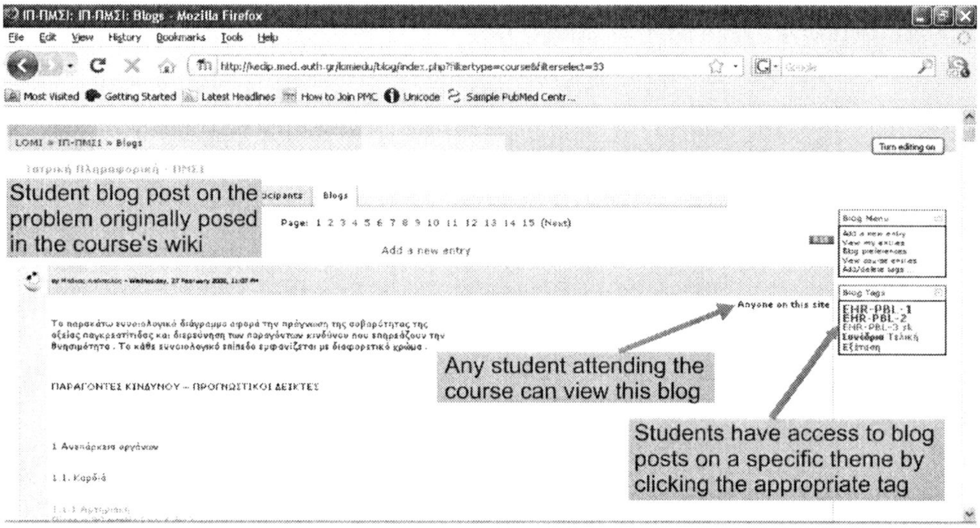

solutions. Then students search and collaborate to solve the case. Student progress and gained experience and competences are recorded, shared and commended on via their personal blogs, while updates of the collaborative class wiki with "each student's final solution" presumably enhance the problem solving capacity and skill acquisition of the students even further (Figure 5).

Example 3: Continuing Medical Education and Professional Development

Similar ideas and tools may be also exploited to enhance Continuing Medical Education (CME) and professional development. In this case an e-learning environment may consist of links to evidence by use of mashup technologies and interlinked content web sites/portals. However, this by itself is a mere advanced compilation of conventional Web functionality, while it fails to exploit the full potential of Web 2.0, and in particular dynamic collaborative content development by a number of distributed contributors and/or educators. A wiki or a blog here may function as medical case repositories. The cases may be initialized by one or more experts but may be continued, updated, corrected, enriched and argued by the same or other experts in an effort to collaboratively seek for the best possible prognosis or diagnosis, treatment plan, or follow up guidelines. Such an effort, taken from a smoking cessation network developed at the Medical School of the Aristotle University of Thessaloniki, Greece, is illustrated in Figure 6. A blog dedicated to a relevant case repository together with a collaborative wiki for defining relevant medical terms, pharmaceuticals, epidemiology techniques etc, accounts for the aforementioned collaborative content development for this specific online learning community.

Example 4: Disseminating Science to the Public

Communicating science to the public is a main concern of contemporary societies and presents the core of numerous initiatives. However, public education presents certain significant challenges: (a) highly specialized scientific knowledge is

Figure 6. A simplistic illustration of the smoking cessation wiki set for use within the Continuing Medical Education scheme for pulmonary experts/residents. The wiki is collaboratively developed by several contributors to account for a medical case encyclopaedia for smoking cessation specialists.

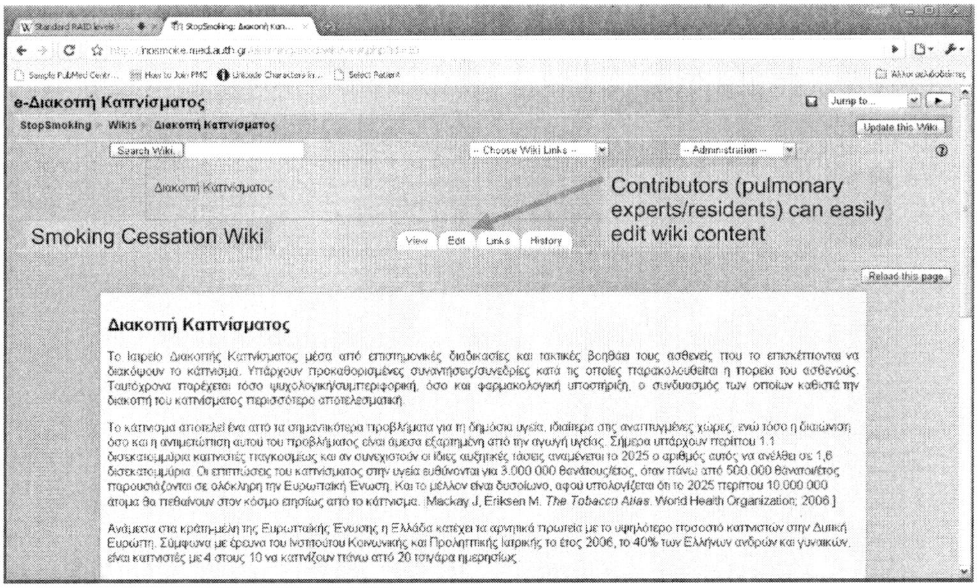

disseminated to an audience of a disperse scientific background, often without extended and/or uniform scientific education and skills; (b) the audience is of a wide age range, preferences and goals regarding their pursuit of professional knowledge; and (c) the audience has a diverse daily time-schedule while scattered over a region considerably larger than a university campus. Most importantly, considering the amateur, sideline nature of this form of education, the whole educational procedure ought to be more of a leisure activity rather than formal learning. Web 2.0 learning paradigm may be the proper way to meet such requirements.

An example is the educational activities at the regional Amateur Astronomy Club of Thrace, Greece, that aim to disseminate the basics of astronomy and related physics to the public and especially the young (Antoniou et al, 2008). Their approach involves the use of wikis and blogs to entirely re-create the process of problem-based learning approach on the internet. Astronomy problems at various levels of difficulty and specialization are deployed on the internet. Problem deployment and presentation is collaboratively performed via the internet by a number of instructors using wiki technology. Participating students and instructors can resolve and discuss the problem via a dedicated blog, while they can record their educational experiences in their personal blogs, thus providing a way for a temporal recording of attitude, experience and skills progress. Problem solution is then performed collaboratively via a wiki. User (student and instructor) satisfaction analysis shows that the endeavour is well accepted.

FUTURE TRENDS

Effective online learning experiences require a successful alignment of the learning approach with the technology used. Such an inherent alignment exists between the notion of active, collaborative learning and the paradigm of Web 2.0 technologies, as they both rely on and emphasize social skills (such as collaboration, interaction and peer activity) as opposed to mere content. Within this framework, it is expected that future work will put emphasis to individual's competences for knowledge management, rather than knowledge itself. Work in progress elaborates on mechanisms to process and analyze the learning procedure as recorded in personal blogs, wikis and social networks so as to extract meaningful information about capturing expert's practical skills competences and share this with the novice (Kaldoudi et al, 2008). The interesting issue is that via web 2.0 tools, tacit knowledge can be recorded, archived and mined, via personal blog entries. Thus, experts and instructors can record interesting and important steps in exploring and appraising information, acquiring knowledge and addressing educational problems, thus implicitly recording their expertise in scientific problem solving. On the other hand, learners can record their own process of tackling information, searching literature, resolving ambiguities etc. These personal or group entries may help evaluate personal progress and especially reveal skills mastered.

Additionally, the current enormous expansion in knowledge (including expert competences and tacit knowledge as well) constitutes a fundamental educational challenge. Higher academic institutions are increasingly required to invest in order to enrich their curricula with courses given by external experts, while experts working within an academic institution often restrict their state-of-the-art knowledge to a very limited audience (Papaioakeim et al, 2006). In order to support the emerging integrative curricula structures and accommodate the over-specialized knowledge available by different experts, Web 2.0 applications can be employed to develop virtual distributed pools of autonomous specialized educational modules and provide the mechanisms for searching, retrieving, evaluating and rating, adapting and revising educational content in medicine and life sciences (Kaldoudi et al, 2008). This is the scope of the European mEducator Best Practice Network (project ECP 2008 EDUCATION 418006, funded under the EU eContePlus2008 program), which aims to enable seamless content sharing in medical formal education (www.meducator.net). Specifically, mEducator addresses a comprehensive collection of different types of health educational material. These include conventional educational content types also used in other areas (e.g. lecture notes, books, exam questions, practicals, graphs, images/videos, algorithms and simulators, etc), educational content types unique in medical education (e.g. teaching files, virtual patients, evidence based medicine forms, clinical guidelines, anatomical atlases, etc,) and alternative educational content types, either reflecting active learning techniques (extensively used in health education) and/or stemming from newly introduced web 2.0 technologies (e.g. problem/case based learning sessions, serious games, web traces, wikis, blogs/discussion forums, etc). Additionally, mEducator focuses on implementing and comparing two alternative solutions for educational content discovery and retrieval on the web. The first solution is based on traditional isolated learning content management systems (LCMS), loosely associated via commonplace web 2.0 technologies, using RSS feeds for notification and updates of newly published content. The second solution is based on a federated architecture which is founded on a reference Semantic Web Service (SWS) architecture for search, interchange and delivery of learning objects.

Such current research focusing on data semantics, ultimately leads to a further interesting advancement that is currently emerging and shows potential to grow into the next Web revolution, what is commonly referred to as Web 3.0. The notion and the prediction of this evolution is attributed to the founders of Web Berners-Lee and colleagues (2001) almost a decade ago. However, the explosion of Web 2.0 has really prepared both technology and users to emerge in the paradigm of semantic networking of information and services, thus the Web 3.0 is currently arising with a promising potential for educational applications (Bratsas et al, 2008). Among other things, Web 3.0 is about making information and services more meaningful to individuals as well as programs. Such an environment is expected to shift focus from 'finding information' to constructing 'meaningful and relevant information maps', leading to personal learning agents that will eventually support individuals in maintaining and administering their personal education and personal learning network (Ohler, 2008). Thus, collaborative, participative learning within Web 2.0 will be transformed to a context based personalized learning shared within a network society. Web 2.0 applications such as wikis, blogs, mashups and RSS feeds will contain context related 'intelligence' and the problem will not be to find relevant information, but to identify information of quality and to learn how to use it best. Last but not least, for the aforementioned developments to be well accommodated within education systems and curricula, the pivoting importance of standardising content sharing should be understood and exploited (Bamidis et al, 2008). In other words, much work will need to be carried along the paths of describing in standard ways the content to be shared and the various learning attributes associated with it (i.e. the context).

To conclude, recent technological advances have shifted the core focus of education towards more active learning approaches. This shift is certainly related with evolutions on the Internet and the Web, and certainly the emergence of Web 2.0, which is being stressed as a promising tool for advanced support of education. However, emphasis with Web 2.0 should be geared along collaboration and participation and not the mere provision of content if it were to play a key role in education. The slow but sure emergence of Web3.0 in combination with Web2.0 creates even greater hopes and anticipations.

ACKNOWLEDGMENT

Work presented in this chapter is funded in part under the project "mEducator: Multi-type Content Repurposing and Sharing in Medical Education", supported by the eContentplus 2008 program, Information Society and Media Directorate-General, European Commission (ECP 2008 EDU 418006)

REFERENCES

Alexander, B. (2006). Web 2.0. A new wave of innovation for teaching and learning? *EDUCAUSE Review*, *41*(2), 32–44.

Antoniou, P., Delidou, E., Aggeioplasti, K., & Kaldoudi, E. (2008). Astronomy Education for the Public via Web 2.0 technologies. In *Proceeding of ICERI2008 – International Conference of Education, Research and Innovation,* Madrid, Spain.

Armstrong, K., & Retterer, O. (2008). Blogging as L2 writing: A case study. *Association for the Advancement of Computing in Education Journal*, *16*(3), 233–251.

Augar, N., Raitman, R., & Zhou, W. (2004). Teaching and learning online with wikis. In R. Atkinson, C. McBeath, D. Jonas-Dwyer & R. Phillips (Eds.), *Beyond the comfort zone: Proceedings of the 21st ASCILITE Conference,* Perth, Australia (pp. 95-104).

Bamidis, P. D., Constantinidis, S., Kaldoudi, E., Maglaveras, N., & Pappas, C. (2008). The use of Web 2.0 in teaching Medical Informatics to postgraduate medical students: first experiences. In G. Eysenbach (Ed.), *Medicine 2.0: Social Networking, Collaboration, Participation, Apomediation, and Openness. J Med Internet Res, 10*(3). Retrieved from http://www.jmir.org/2008/3/e22/

Bamidis, P. D., & Pappas, C. (2008). *Medical Informatics and the Internet in Contemporary Healthcare Services*. Authority of the 3rd Health Region, Thessaloniki, Greece.

Belanger, Y. (2005). *Duke University iPod first year experience final evaluation report*. Durham, NC: Duke University. Retrieved November 14, 2008, from http://www.duke.edu/ddi/ipodfye.html

Berliner, D., & Calfee, R. (Eds.). (1996). *Handbook of educational psychology*. New York: Macmillan.

Berners-Lee, T., Hendler, J., & Lassila, O. (2001). The semantic web. *Scientific American, 184*(5), 34–43. doi:10.1038/scientificamerican0501-34

Boulos, M., Maramba, I., & Wheeler, S. (2006). Wikis, blogs and podcasts: A new generation of web-based tools for virtual collaborative clinical practice and education. *BMC Medical Education, 6*(41).

Boulos, M. K. (2007). *Healthcare on Web 2.0*. Healthcare Information and Management Systems Society. Retrieved on 30 Dec 2007 from http://emea.himss.org/news/expertviews_archive.asp

Bratsas, C., Bamidis, P. D., Kaimakamis, E., & Maglaveras, N. (2008). Usage of Semantic Web Technologies (Web-3.0) Aiming to Facilitate the Utilisation of Computerized Algorithmic Medicine in Clinical Practice. In G. Eysenbach (Ed.), *Medicine 2.0: Social Networking, Collaboration, Participation, Apomediation, and Openness. J Med Internet Res, 10*(3). Retrieved from http://www.jmir.org/2008/3/e22/

Cronje, J. C. (2001). Metaphors and models in internet-based learning. *Computers & Education, 37*(3-4), 241–256. doi:10.1016/S0360-1315(01)00049-5

De Lucia, A., Francese, R., Passero, I., & Tortora, G. (2009). Development and evaluation of a virtual campus on Second Life: The case of Second-DMI. *Computers & Education, 52*(1), 220–233. doi:10.1016/j.compedu.2008.08.001

Dertouzos, M. (1997). *What will be*. London: Judy Piatkus Ltd.

Ebner, M., Holzinger, A., & Maurer, H. (2007). Web 2.0 Technology: Future Interfaces for Technology Enhanced Learning. In C. Stephanidis (Ed.), *Universal Access in HCI, Part III, HCII 2007* (LNCS 4556, pp. 559–568). Berlin: Springer-Verlag. Ehlers, U. (2007). The new pathway for e-learning: From distribution to collaboration and competence in e-learning. *Association for the Advancement of Computing in Education Journal*, 16(2), 187-20.

European Council. (2000). *Employment, economic reforms and social cohesion - towards a Europe based on innovation and knowledge.* Document submitted to Lisbon European Council, official number 5256/00. Lisbon, Portugal: European Council. Retrieved November 4, 2008, from http://ue.eu.int/ueDocs/cms_Data/docs/pressdata/en/misc/05256.en0.html

Evans, C. (2008). The effectiveness of m-learning in the form of podcast revision lectures in higher education. *Computers & Education, 50*(2), 491–498. doi:10.1016/j.compedu.2007.09.016

Eysenbach, G. (2007). From intermediation to disintermediation and apomediation: new models for consumers to access and assess the credibility of health information in the age of Web2.0. *Studies in Health Technology and Informatics, 129*(Pt 1), 162–166.

Fyrenious, A. (2005). Lectures in problem-based learning—Why, when and how? An example of interactive lecturing that stimulates meaningful learning. *Medical Teacher, 27*(1), 61–65. doi:10.1080/01421590400016365

Hammond, M. (2006). Blogging within formal and informal learning contexts: Where are the opportunities and constraints? In *Proceedings of the International Research Conference on Networked Learning 2006*, Lancaster, UK.

Jones, R., Higgs, R., de Angelis, C., & Prideaux, D. (2001). Changing face of medical curricula. *Lancet, 357*(9257), 699–703. doi:10.1016/S0140-6736(00)04134-9

Kaldoudi, E., Bamidis, P. D., Papaioakeim, M., & Vargemezis, V. (2008). Problem-based learning via Web 2.0 technologies. In *Proceedings of CBMS2008: The 21th IEEE International Symposium on Computer-Based Medical Systems, Special Track: Technology Enhanced Learning in Medical Education* (pp. 391-396). Jyväskylä, Finland: IEEE Computer Society.

Kaldoudi, E., Papaioakeim, M., Bamidis, P. M., & Vargemezis, V. (2008). Towards expert content sharing in medical education. In *Proceedings of INTED2008: International Technology, Education and Development Conference*. Valencia, Spain: IATED.

Kelton, A. J. (2008). Virtual worlds: Outlook good. *EDUCAUSE Review, 43*(5), 5–22.

Kim, H. N. (2008). The phenomenon of blogs and theoretical model of blog use in educational contexts. *Computers & Education, 51*(3), 1342–1352. doi:10.1016/j.compedu.2007.12.005

Kurtz, B., Fenwick, J., & Ellsworth, C. (2007). Using podcasts and tablet PCs in computer science. In *Proceedings of 45th ACM South East Conference* (pp. 484 - 489). Winston Salem, NC: ACM.

Marton, F., Dahlgren, L.-O., Svensson, L., & Saljo, R. (1977). *Inlarning och omvarldsuppfattning*. Stockholm, Sweden: Almqvist och Wiksell forlag AB.

McAfee, A. (2006). Enterprise 2.0: The dawn of emergent collaboration. *MIT Sloan Management Review, 47*(3), 21–28.

National Research Council. (1999). *How people learn*. Washington, DC: National Academy Press.

O'Reilly, T. (2005). *What is Web 2.0: Design patterns and business models for the next generation of software*. Retrieved February 1, 2008, from http://www.oreillynet.com/pub/a/oreilly/tim/news/2005/09/30/what-is-web-20.html

Ohler, J. (2008). The semantic web in education. *EDUCAUSE Quarterly, 31*(4), 7–9.

Papaioakeim, M., Kaldoudi, E., Vargemezis, V., & Simopoulos, K. (2006). Confronting the problem of ever expanding core knowledge and the necessity of handling overspecialized disciplines in medical education. In *Proceedings of ITAB 2006: IEEE International Special Topic Conference on Information Technology in Biomedicine*. Ioannina, Greece: IEEE.

Parker, K. R., & Chao, J. T. (2007). Wiki as a teaching tool. *Interdisciplinary Journal of Knowledge and Learning Objects, 3*, 57–72.

Russell, T. L. (2001). *The no significant difference phenomenon*. Montgomery, USA: IDECC.

Schaffert, S., Bischof, D., Buerger, T., Gruber, A., Hilzensauer, W., & Schaffert, S. (2006). Learning with semantic wikis. In *Proceedings of the First Workshop on Semantic Wikis – From Wiki To Semantics (SemWiki2006)*, Budva, Montenegro(pp.109-123).

Schuable, L., & Glaser, R. (Eds.). (1996). *Innovations in learning*. New Jersey, NY: Mahwah.

Tonkin, E. (2005). Making the case for a wiki. *Ariadne*, 42. Retrieved November 14, 2008, from http://www.ariadne.ac.uk/issue42/tonkin/

Wang, K. T., Huang, Y.-M., Jeng, Y.-L., & Wang, T.-I. (2008). A blog-based dynamic learning map. *Computers & Education*, *51*(1), 262–278. doi:10.1016/j.compedu.2007.06.005

Wenger, E. (2000). Communities of practice and social learning systems. *Organization*, *7*(2), 225–246. doi:10.1177/135050840072002

Chapter 3
Individual and Collaborative Approaches in E-Learning Design

Abel Usoro
University of the West of Scotland, UK

Grzegorz Majewski
University of the West of Scotland, UK

Len Bloom
University of Botswana, Botswana

ABSTRACT

There is no doubt that e-learning is not all about technology but includes the human aspect which is often neglected in studies of e-learning. This chapter addresses the interface between technology and the learner by using cognitive psychology to discuss learning processes in formal and informal groups, investigate how to create competent learning groups, and how to design e-learning to facilitate optimal learning by an individual in a group setting. The chapter proposes an e-learning design based on a blend of cognitive and activity theories. It also presents a pilot empirical study that measured the value of e-learning from four constructs derived from the theories. The result of the study suggests that pure virtual learning environments may not always be the best option as some users require some physical contact. While e-learning may fill many gaps, it should be perceived as a tool that needs to be attended with emotional and social contact.

INTRODUCTION

There is no doubt that there is no such thing as pure technology *simpliciter*; technology always interacts with the people who invent and make use of it. Technology, including technologies used for the delivery of on-line learning, cannot be understood and used as though it has an existence distinct from the skills, interests and imaginations of the people who adapt it to their needs and ideas.

This chapter focuses on e-learning as a psycho-socio-technical phenomenon. Its centre of attention will be the learner at individual and group levels and how to address his or her needs at those levels in the

DOI: 10.4018/978-1-60566-940-3.ch003

e-Learning Design Process (eLDP). E-learning design often puts the main focus on technical aspects of e-learning such as on-line content, technical problems (e.g. accessibility, bandwidth, printing facilities) and not taking into account the problems associated with the divide between technology and human. This chapter will provide psychological background will be provided. The most important findings in the cognitive psychology will be reviewed and discussed. Research will go back to Edward C. Tolman's findings in the field of cognitive psychology and to his legacy that exists till today in academic research and disputes. Problems in learning and e-learning from a psychological point of view will be identified and discussed. In general, e-learning will be perceived as a phenomenon starting with people rather than pure technology.

It will also be described how psychologists perceive individuals and their interactions which may lead to the formation of a group. It will be assessed how particular learning processes proceed in formal and informal groups. Group dynamics will be discussed and assessed in the context of time as well as cause and effect relationships and e-learning content. It will be discussed whether and how the course may be structured in a way that is responsive to the learner's needs as they emerge or change throughout the course. The effect of e-learning content, environment and context on learners both at individual and group levels will be examined.

In the next section it will be investigated how to stimulate creation of groups and how to prevent creation of informal groups that could deteriorate learner's experience (cheating, groups that dominate members and limit their own creativity). It will also be answered whether the same methodology may be applied to pure virtual groups. Discussion will be carried out on how to assess groups – their cohesion, sense of community among members, structure and performance. It will be discussed how an individual can fit into a group and benefit from it and to what degree groups are influenced by individuals and their quality.

It will be investigated how to put theory into practice and how to design e-learning content, structure and delivery that would address the learner both at individual and group levels. It will be answered how far it is possible and feasible to go with the customization of content and delivery to suit individuals from different backgrounds and with diverse needs and attitudes. It will be explored whether it is possible to design an e-learning course in such a way as to increase individual creativity of the participants. It will also be considered how to maintain quality in e-learning projects designed from scratch as well as transferred from other media of delivery. Ideas in this section will be supported by findings of a survey distributed among the participants of e-learning courses delivered by the University of the West of Scotland as well as interview with a person responsible for their administration.

BACKGROUND

In order to educate the learner at individual and group levels it is necessary to begin with a consideration of the social psychology of cognition. If cognition is simply our understanding of our world then how we learn to handle and to manipulate that world is to a great or small extent a function of our cognitive awareness. We learn as we understand. Both learning and e-learning fall short of what they can achieve unless individuals enhance their cognitive and intellectual power to explore, question and play with whatever the computer presents and breath life to their imaginations.

Answers to questions are constructed by the joint activities of the computer and of the individual learning to use it. Byrne (2007) goes so far as to argue persuasively that the rational thought of the computer (and one hopes that of the learner and the practitioner) is lacking unless there is room for an attempt to create an imaginative supplement to the computer's inevitably limited reality.

It may be argued further that there are major questions to be asked about the results of the human social life. Has it an influence on individual thinking, skills and learning? What sort of influence has it and conceivably are there limits to that influence? It has been argued that the mind is completely independent from social influences and on the other extreme that it is totally subordinate to social influence. In reality the mind reacts with social influences.

COGNITION: ITS NATURE AND SIGNIFICANCE

Cognition is possibly the most basic of psychological activities. Humans attempt to construct their own meaningful world within which they create order, predictability, a measure of control of many objects and activities some of which are the understanding of and relationships with other individuals. Human beings perceive, imagine, think and reason. Their lives are a striving after meaning (Krech *et al*., 1962, p. 17), a struggle to create an image, a map in human terms of the world within which it is possible to live.

A *caveat* must now be expressed. Although individuals create their own idiosyncratic cognitive worlds derived from their own understanding of a segment of social and physical worlds there is even if only ideally, a cognitive world that all people live within. Humans have in common a neurological-physiological nature, basic wants and needs. It is arguable that there are psychobiological needs that are common to all people, although there are individual and developmental peculiarities.

Krech *et al*. (1962) distinguished three characteristics of cognition, among which are:

1. Individuals develop, during their childhood, individual cognitive worlds out of their experiences and what they need to understand and do in order to survive. Therefore psychology is concerned with "the experience of the individual in relation to the conditions under which the experience goes on" (Mead, 1946, p. 40): both the actual conduct of the individual and the experience, both the social context and individuals' response to it
2. Therefore how and what individuals learn partly depend on the world they live in and partly on their natural aptitudes and interests. Teachers and learners therefore have *frames of reference* which influence their learning and their performance. If my world consists of people, fairies and other fantasies rather than computers or word processors my performance and learning may shape differently, unless my innate skills and interest are otherwise orientated
3. It follows that cognitive change is limited by existing cognitive systems and orientations. For example, does the culture of education favour or discourage change and striving for new skills and orientation? Does the cognitive world favour open-minds that are sensitive and responsive to change or closed-minds which are insensitive and impervious to change?

If cognition means what we learn (in the widest sense) of how we make sense of our world, then learning bare facts (if indeed this be possible) is a poor sort of education. Narrow empirical learning and research rarely leads to understanding and innovation. What is the golden goal of learning and e-learning is to help the learner build their "cognitive world" or rather reconstruct and expand the one they already have.

Neisser (1967) ask: Does the mind work like a computer or like a brain? Do we only process information? Can we only think of one thing at a time? Is it impossible for us to derive sense from fantasy? Is reality real or do we construct elaborate it, and play with it? Neisser regarded cognition as a complex interaction of many psychological, neural and social processes. We do more than use our senses. We also use our imagination to transform, elaborate, store, reject or accept, retrieve accurately (or inaccurately), and turn into useful information what otherwise may only be a passing sensation, need or want.

Processing information therefore often demands that design meaningfully symbolizes or represents what is going on in the real world. We do not directly and unambiguously process information; we transform a symbol of a relevant aspect of the world into a warning, a speed, direction, temperature, a communication ....

CULTURAL AND SOCIAL INFLUENCES

It is mere truism that individuals are unique, yet they are embedded in a social and cultural world. Two kinds of problems therefore arise: (1) What are the influences of a group and individuals on one another? and (2) What distinguished an effective from an ineffective group?

Individuals in the Group

Groups set standards, procedures and goals for their members and the members respond, each in his or her own way. But individual conformity may accurately reflect inner feelings or simulated ones. Individual needs, wishes and fantasies influence the nature and quality of participation in the group. The other members of the group are not identity-less beings defined by the group needs and aims, but are perceived by and therefore related to individual members idiosyncratically. The individual's past shapes his or her own present and therefore the nature and quality of the past and present relationships influence the individual capacity to learn and his or her style of learning. Some authors declare that "no matter how monolithic the structure of the group, no matter how ancient its traditions no group is immune to the changes brought about through the interactions of its members" (Krech *et al.*, 1962, p. 486). Informal groups may evolve their own aims, goals and styles of approaches to satisfying the goals, demands and ethos of the group of which they are part.

A group, like an individual, may be "marginal" – they may exist on the boundaries between two groups and the marginal group feel uncomfortable with their ambiguous status. "Marginal" groups like "marginal" individuals are not merely different from other subgroups but feel that although they belong to the main group they are in some respects in conflict with it. A group, a leader and a committee therefore have the delicate exercise of reducing incompatible aims, styles and practices yet without suppressing subgroup creativity and innovation. Nor must the main group be so little cohesive that the subgroup split off and their contribution is lost. An illustration of such a case is the situation of a 21 years old student named Kitso. He was attending a Java programming course in Southern Africa. There were around one hundred and seventy other participants. During the course a subgroup was formed with around three or four members. They suggested an improved way of teaching and learning the Java programming. This was accepted by the professor and now it is being evaluated.

Let us focus now on the most important factors that influence individual or subgroup to decide whether to stay within the main group (even if they have other goals, etc. different from those of the main group) and contribute to it or split apart. In the situation above, members of the subgroup were recognized by the whole group and respected. They were also not able to quit the group, because they would lose the place at the university and a grant. They would be marked as trouble-makers and it would be difficult to go somewhere else. Thus these formal restrictions imposed by external authorities made the group more cohesive. Generalizing, it is possible to distinguish group-internal factors: reputation of the individual/subgroup members, subgroup members to main group members factors, characters of the individual or subgroup members, group culture, character of the person in "charge" (professor in the situation described previously); and group-external factors: culture of the society, external authorities and powers as well as restrictions imposed by them.

The Group in the Individual

The world is rapidly becoming one, partly merging cultures technologically sophisticated with those less sophisticated. Even so within existing sophisticated cultures such as the USA some children may not have the opportunity to acquire more than the rudiments of electronic know-how during their education. The culture and groups that individuals live in "exist" within the individuals and may be of concern to learning and e-learning process. In other words, individuals approach e-learning with the trappings of their culture and group from which they come.

These problems should not be ignored or made light of. For example: Stevenson, Lee & Graham (1993) compared children in Chinese and Japanese kindergartens, and found that Asian children emphasised group or collective activity, while comparable American children favoured individualism. If an American child had a problem the child and the teacher were likely to consider possible difficulties that are somehow due to the child's individual ability and interests or emotional problems. In the Japanese school such a situation is more likely to be investigated in a different perspective: How do teacher and child interact in the school? Is there something in the way teaching is performed in the school to explain the child's poor performance or unsatisfactory behaviour? Culture and influences of the society could be underlying reasons. Anglo-saxonian and in particular American culture emphasises the individual and his or her rights, while the culture of the Far East Asian countries emphasise team work and collaboration for common good.

The reasons behind existence of such differences may be found in the varied history of both civilizations, demography (cooperation is necessary in a highly populated and congested countries) and economy. Compared with East Asians, Westerners pay more attention to context and situations, and because Asians tend to attend holistically, search for *gestalten*, whereas Westerners are more analytical. These (and many other comparative studies) confirm Hebb's classical hypothesis that "learning at maturity concerns patterns, events, where parts at least are familiar and which already have a number of other associations" (Hebb, 1949, p. 127), so that adult learning is a result of both internal – often neural associations and chains of associations, "surfacing" in the form of psychological associations – and external, environmental associations. One Chinese or Westerner learner is not the same as another!

The problems of an individual may have motivational and idiosyncratic aspects. Manual skills may also play a role as well as the difficulty of the task itself. People perceive the information acquired in a way that is consistent with their way of handling their "cognitive world" and their self-awareness. This is an efficient way of dealing with the abundance of information in our environment. Furthermore our view of self affects the way we construct our learning and work, what tasks and competencies are considered as important, and what we expect from others (Tams 2008, p. 197).

E-LEARNING DESIGN: A PSYCHO-SOCIO-TECHNICAL APPROACH

The design of any software intended for human use should be user-centred and iterative. A designer of an e-learning course has to either gather user requirements or start with a prototype and refine it through iterations after receiving feedback from users. The beginning of this process is the learner both at the individual level as well as group level. It is therefore appropriate that "numerous educators and policy makers are advocating a move away from teacher-centered models of instruction and toward more learner-centered and community-based models" (Barab *et al.* 2004, p. 3). There are hardly any criteria provided by the educational literature on what constitutes a community and in particular a virtual community. In the case of e-learning design it is necessary to ascertain the degree to which it takes into account the issues of sociability: whether it supports (or even makes possible) social interactions among learners.

Theories of learning and cognition seem to evolve from focusing on "individual thinkers and their isolated minds" to including the social nature of cognition. Cognitive and cultural theories centre on the "reciprocal character of the interaction [by] which ... cognition and meaning are considered socially and culturally constructed" (Barab *et al.* 2000, p. 2). In the case of culture it is a more anthropological approach which is emphasised. In the centre of cognitive theory of learning stands the representational theory of the mind with its idea of representational position which states that "knowledge is constituted of symbolic mental representations, and cognitive activity consists of the manipulation of the symbols in these representations" (Barab *et al.* 2000, pp. 4, 5). Learning may be perceived as "acquiring" these symbols, while instruction may be perceived as an activity focusing on finding the best means of making it possible.

Since the very beginning of e-learning numerous on-line learning initiatives have been used. However on average they do not strive to create a truly learning environment. It is comparatively easy to start an online forum or just put some texts from a book on the website and direct learners to it. However attracting and keeping hold of learners may be a considerable accomplishment. Communities have a history, a shared cosmology, a social interdependence, a common cultural and historical heritage, and a reproduction cycle (Barab *et al.* 2004). In the case of e-learning design, as opposed to traditional learning collaborative aspect is much more important. Consequently not only individual needs have to be taken into account, but also the interactions between individual learners and the needs of groups that may form in the process of learning. Usually the process of designing an e-learning environment starts with recognizing what is to be taught and learned. It is necessary to take into account the real world situations in which the activity would occur.

The learning process consists of virtual situations, activities, objectives and experiences that map similar situations from the real world. These virtual experiences have to represent most of the cognitive demands the learner would encounter in the "real world". The learner has to use his or her skills and critical thinking in the virtual setting before being able to apply them in the real situations. Where virtual situations are irrelevant to practice, the result may be the acquisition of knowledge that is difficult to be applied. Ideally it is expected that the learner will be able to use his or her knowledge acquired in virtual settings to real life problems and situations that are similar in some aspects and differ in others from the virtual simulation (Barab *et al.*, 2004, pp. 6, 7). Figure 1 below presents a model for mapping the requirements from the real environment into virtual cognitive world. It illustrates that the content of e-learning course should have an anchor in the real world. It is expected that the on-line course prepares the individual to challenges he or she could face in the present or future work.

At this stage the course should offer the individual learner a content that is appropriate to the cognitive demands and that should be similar to real world situations. During the course, individuals may form groups, and even social networks may come into existence. Good design could facilitate this natural process (by providing collaborative software – e.g. chat, discussion board) and move on-line experience to a social level. There is a significant need to develop more

Figure 1. Mapping real world situations into virtual activities, experiences and objectives

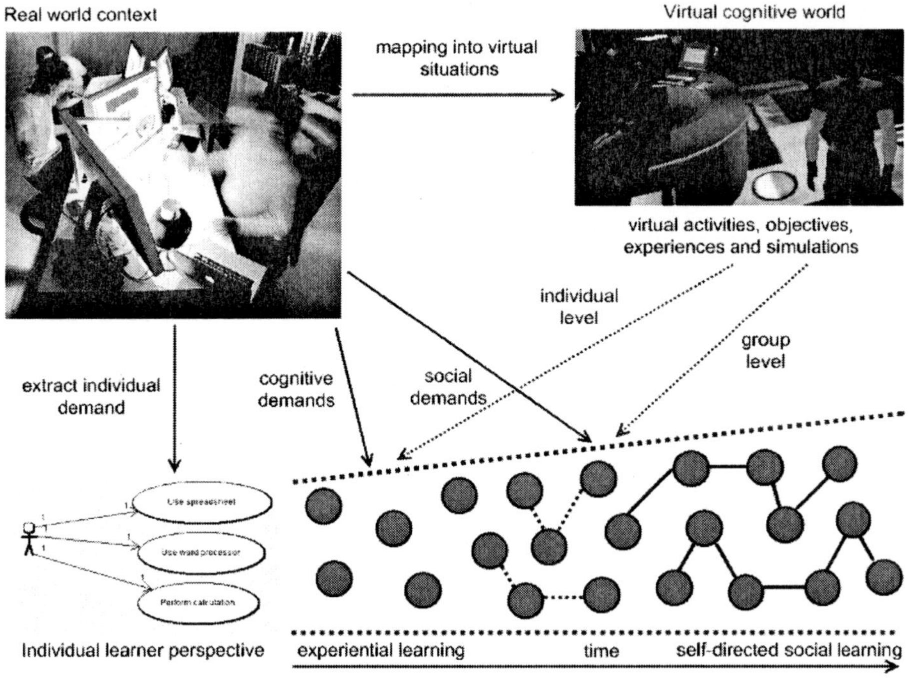

broadly instead of acquiring basic skills. "People need to develop their abilities through ongoing engagement not only with their tasks, but also social environment" (Tams 2008, pp. 196-197). In the first case learners may undergo experiential learning, which involves reflection upon one's activities and expected outcomes. In the latter case it is self-directed social learning that is one of the most suitable. This form of learning is defined as cognitions of the participants by which they reflect upon their environment in order to improve their social abilities and self-efficiency. Social learning takes place whenever the learner observe other participants, asks for advice, as well as seeks guidance or encouragement from their peers, colleagues, supervisors and other people. In the course of such activities, knowledge sharing occurs and people can share their experiences, and learn social requirements and expectations.

Therefore, the design of e-learning courses has to merge methods originating from such domains as software engineering, pedagogy and social networks as they coexist and modernise. The model proposed for e-learning design that takes into account individual and group perspectives as well as the underlying technology was derived from Activity Theory formulated by Russian psychologists, for example, Leont'ev (1978, 1981) and Vygotsky (1931). Activity theory focuses on the technical and cultural mediation of human actions. It describes actions in psycho-socio-technical systems as a set of interdependent components which constitute a conceptual system. Its foundations were laid down by Peirce, who developed a theory of mediation about the idea of a relationship between a sign and an interpretation. The model has evolved since then and has been used for various research purposes, but it was Engeström who applied it first also to learning activities too. These activities play an important role in nearly all human societies.

The outcome or object of learning activities is a social practice or a social life-world (Engeström 1987). It is intangible but measurable. The structure of the learning activity is a dynamic one and evolves in time. Activity theory helps to understand how a social organization and social artefacts mediate social activities. Some of the authors use it as a framework for representing "the structural relationships among a community of practice, individual practices, and professional development projects" (Barab 2004, p. 130). Using Activity Theory as a framework, it is possible to focus on an individual as well as his or her activities and then zoom out to view these activities in a wider context of a larger group or community.

Activity Theory when applied to learning and e-learning in particular focuses on the *learning activities* performed by the *learner(s)* (or subject(s) in the original version of the Activity Theory). Examples of such actions in the context of e-learning could be online searching of materials, conversations and discussions. The learner(s) perform these actions to accomplish a given outcome – *learning objective* or a set of learning objectives. These objectives should be measurable with examples from e-learning practice being assessments, exams or coursework. Activities are performed using tools (technical or cognitive).

In this model technology plays a supportive role in the learning process. Community influences the actions performed by the individuals in different aspects. One of them is the *rules* recognized by the members. Examples of rules that may exist in an e-learning environment are netiquette, language, norms of behaviour, trust and commitment. Within the community may exist less or more sophisticated *division of tasks* (division of labour in original concept) which may be perceived as a natural inclination of people working together to accomplish a common goal. It is achieved by the specialization of roles and allocation of resources and responsibilities. All activities in the scope of interest of the e-learning design process take place in this context (Barab 2004, pp. 130, 131). Other authors go a step further and define an online learning activity as "an education procedure designed to stimulate learning by online experience utilizing online learning systems and tools" (Levy 2006, p. 30). According to this concept online learning activity combines the subjects (learners and instructors) with the learning systems and tools, as well as with the learning actions and operations in order to accomplish the learning outcome(s) (Levy 2008, p. 1666).

E-learning design may be perceived as a process of refining particular components of the framework provided previously individually or in combination with other parts of the system. In particular the combinations of two or three components (triads) should be analysed as they reflect a comprehensive part of the system while maintaining relative easiness of the interpretation. For example if it is necessary to investigate whether the technology enhances collaboration between the individuals and leads to group formation, it is necessary to bring three aspects together: Subject(s)–Community–Tools.

For e-learning courses, technology (hardware and software) must be adapted to learners' needs using appropriate methodologies of software engineering. Which one of them will be employed is the choice of the project manager responsible for this area. In general, iterative and incremental methodologies may function better if there are continual changes to the system. The order of scenarios examined is flexible and dependent on the situation and such factors as course content, participants and goals. Some researchers propose that software evolves through interactions with the community of its users. Thus, it is advisable however to start with the learner(s) and try to grasp all the scenarios involving them in the first place. An interactive learning environment that is not static should enrich the experience of the learners by allowing them to explore information on their own (Stahl 2006, pp 47-8).

Figure 2. Adaptation of Activity Theory constructs to e-learning context

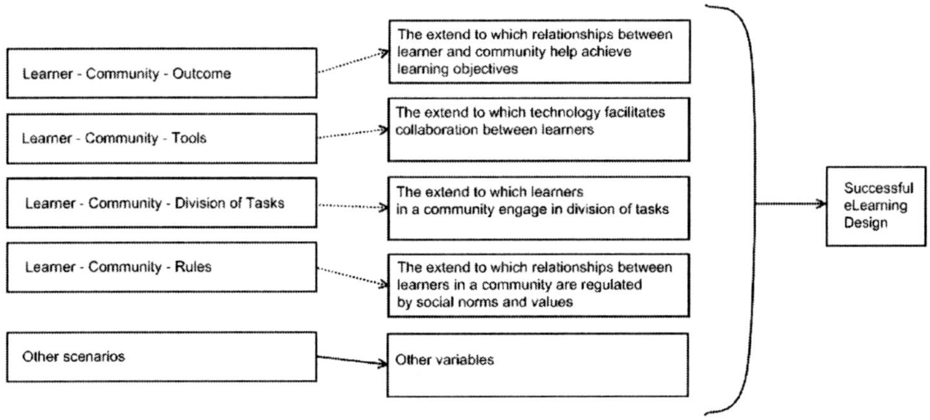

Measuring the Value of the E-Learning Course

After designing an online course it is necessary to evaluate whether it serves the intended purposes. Most of the stakeholders involved in e-learning initiatives focus on the value of e-learning courses in terms of their economical worth (whether it costs less to train an employee using an e-learning course, return on investment, etc.) as well as their objective effectiveness (ability to train more employees and staff in geographically dispersed locations). Although these are very important benefits of e-learning they are outside the scope of this research because the main emphasis is put on the participant at the individual level as well as group level. From the Activity Theory already discussed, we derived the following four constructs:

A. Learner – Community – Outcome
B. Learner – Community – Tools
C. Learner – Community – Division of Tasks
D. Learner – Community – Rules

Focus is put on the relationship between the learner and a community with regards to four triads (lettered "A" to "D" above) that measure social learning. These constructs have been selected as they are most significant in view of the context of this paper. These constructs are then transformed into a set of variables which try to model a successful e-learning design. Figure 2 shows how these aspects have been defined in the context of e-learning. An additional section was added to measure successful e-learning design as a dependent construct. With regards to measure of success of e-learning design, a number of perspectives can be used (Usoro and Abbas, 2008). However, for the scope of this pilot study, we have chosen to use participant satisfaction as a measure of success. A questionnaire based on the definition of all the constructs including participant satisfaction is in Appendix A.

PRIMARY STUDY

Questionnaire and Interview

A self-administered questionnaire was distributed in October 2008 to participants of three on-line courses offered in 2007 by the Centre for the Lifelong Learning at the University of the West of Scotland. An internet link to the questionnaires was sent with a cover letter by email to 220 participants. Five email addresses either turned to be inactive or resulted in delivery failure. After removal of spoiled questionnaire there were 36 usable responses. That represents a response rate of 16.34%. It is not a very good response rate; however, given that the course took place the previous year and most of the students did not have a continuous affiliation with the UWS it is not surprising that only some of them decided to participate (and perhaps some of them no longer use, at least often, their university email accounts). Moreover most of the part-time students have full time jobs and families (as some of them mentioned in the comments section of the survey). The respondents were mainly male (72.22%) with the average age 32 years or above.

Additionally an interview was carried out with the person responsible for the administration and design of some of the content for these courses. The interview was formed according to seven stages of interview investigation (Kvale, 1996). These stages are (1) thematizing phase (formulation of the purpose of an investigation), design phase (planning the design of the study), (2) interviewing (conducting the interview based on an interview guide and with a reflective approach to the knowledge sought), (3) transcribing (preparation of the interview material for analysis), (4) analysing (deciding on appropriate analysis methods and applying them), (5) verifying (establishing the generalizability, reliability and validity of the interview findings) and (6) reporting (communicating the findings of the study and the methods applied in a form that meets the scientific criteria).

The key questions that were addressed at the interview planning stage were: (1) what? (obtaining a pre-knowledge of the subject matter to be investigated), (2) why? (clarifying the purpose of the study) and (3) how? (acquiring a knowledge of different technique of interviewing and analysing, and deciding which to apply to obtain intended knowledge). The purpose of the interview was to evaluate the extent to which e-learning course designers take into account the learner at both individual and group levels. This evaluation was carried out using the four perspectives derived from Activity Theory and explained earlier. Thus the interview helped to buttress the findings of the questionnaire. The interview questions and responses are in Appendix B.

Table 1. Cronbach's coefficient alpha

Reliability Statistics		
Cronbach's Alpha	Cronbach's Alpha Based on Standardized Items	N of Items
.710	.696	20

Reliability

Reliability is a major concern with the positivist research approach and indicates the degree to which a research is repeatable (Golafshani 2003, p. 599). A major reliability measure is internal consistency, which is usually applied to groups of items. Items should measure different perspectives of the same underlying concept (Pallant 2005, p. 95). One of the most commonly used techniques for assessing the internal consistency is Cronbach's alpha coefficient. It is usually expressed as a correlation coefficient and values of 0.70 and above are generally accepted as representing high reliability (Litwin 1995, pp. 24-31). This value from the analysis of our questionnaire is 0.71, which indicates that the set of variables is reliable. In other words it is possible to say that the questions measure the same concept or phenomenon. Results are presented in Table 1.

Validity

Validity is a concept that explains how well a questionnaire or a survey measures what it is meant to measure and provides researchers and the whole scientific society the guarantee that the methods chosen are appropriate for searching the truth (Usoro *et al.* 2007). There are different ways of assuring validity (Litwin 1995, p. 33). For this research construct validity is the most appropriate one. At the first stage it is necessary to ensure that constructs are solidly rooted in theories and concepts in literature.

The next step is to investigate how much weight the questionnaire carries when applied in practice. It usually requires years of experience with questionnaire distributed among people from diverse backgrounds and in various circumstances (Litwin 1995, pp. 33-43). Thus it is not possible to employ this technique given the limited time of the study. Instead a substitutive method of factorial validity was used. In this approach statistical techniques are utilized to describe the construct validity. Some of the most important techniques in the case of the information systems research are Principal Components Analysis (PCA) or Confirmatory Factor Analysis (Straub *et al.* 2004, p. 10). As a relationship between the constructs of social learning and e-learning success (measured by participant satisfaction with the course) has been hypothesised a PCA with Direct Oblimin rotation was selected (Pallant 2005, pp. 179-186). According to this study there should be five factors extracted: four measuring the constructs presented previously and one evaluating different aspects of participants' satisfaction. The results are presented in Table 2.

Table. 2. Factors extracted

Factor Extraction - oblimin					
	Component				
	1	2	3	4	5
Construct A.1[1]	-.159		.754		
Construct A.2			.763		
Construct A.3	.249	.629	.254	-.101	
Construct A.4	.213	.530	.559		
Construct B.1				.195	-.692
Construct B.2		-.598	.314	.451	.492
Construct B.3	.334	-.498	.406	-.302	-.149
Construct B.4	.713	.144		-.128	
Construct C.1	.137	.681			.418
Construct C.2	-.117	.656		.370	
Construct C.3				.895	
Construct C.4	.308	.453	.145	.395	.140
Construct C.5	-.165	.768			-.125
Construct D.1	.651			.359	-.167
Construct D.2	.779	-.112		.226	-.110
Construct D.3	.200		-.367	.489	-.336
Construct D.4	.683		-.304	-.278	
Construct E.1	.174		.101	-.147	-.850
Construct E.2	.478			.300	-.495
Construct E.3	.188	-.116		-.190	-.682

Extraction Method: Principal Component Analysis.
Rotation Method: Oblimin with Kaiser Normalization.
a Rotation converged in 25 iterations.

Items do not always cluster at their expected construct groupings. It is however possible to notice that questions of the first construct seem to group within component 3 (except for question 3) with good values of above 0.5. In the case of the second construct questions correlate with different components and it may be necessary to refine them in future studies. The third construct questions group within component 2 (except for the third question of the construct) with good values. Questions of the fourth construct cluster within component 1, except for the second question which is much better correlated with component 4. It may be necessary to refine this question or move it to a different construct.

The fact that there is some cross loading of the factors (constructs) may suggest that although they are distinct they reinforce each other. This could be an indication that each of the constructs should be considered. The real problem is with the questions measuring the satisfaction of the course participants. They seem not to correlate well with any of the components. Some of the higher values are correlated with component One, but they are not particularly high. It is noteworthy that satisfaction levels for networking issues are greater than those with the e-learning content itself. In order to address this problem it is necessary to evaluate the components and the total variability they explain. This is shown in Table 3.

The five components extracted explain around 65% of the total variability. It seems that the first component, which is explaining above 20% of

Table. 3. Principal component analysis

Total Variance Explained							
Vari-ables[2]	Initial Eigenvalues			Extraction Sums of Squared Loadings			Rotation Sums of Squared Loadings(a)
	Total	% of Variance	Cumulative %	Total	% of Variance	Cumulative %	Total
1	4.162	20.811	20.811	4.162	20.811	20.811	3.259
2	3.468	17.339	38.151	3.468	17.339	38.151	3.221
3	2.093	10.465	48.616	2.093	10.465	48.616	2.089
4	1.801	9.004	57.620	1.801	9.004	57.620	2.294
5	1.455	7.275	64.895	1.455	7.275	64.895	3.036
6	1.251	6.257	71.153				
7	1.126	5.630	76.783				
8	.892	4.459	81.241				
9	.774	3.869	85.110				
10	.609	3.045	88.155				
11	.574	2.868	91.023				
12	.479	2.393	93.416				
13	.390	1.952	95.368				
14	.251	1.256	96.624				
15	.205	1.026	97.650				
16	.177	.883	98.534				
17	.098	.492	99.026				
18	.092	.458	99.483				
19	.065	.324	99.808				
20	.038	.192	100.000				

Extraction Method: Principal Component Analysis.
a When components are correlated, sums of squared loadings cannot be added to obtain a total variance.

the total variability, is a cluster of the variables (questionnaire items) from various sections. This could be the reason behind its correlation with questions measuring the overall satisfaction of the participants with the course.

On the whole, it can be concluded that the questionnaire items do measure the 5 constructs though there are some cross-loadings making it necessary to refine the constructs in future studies.

Qualitative Data

The pilot study sought to establish the importance of group learning activities in participant satisfaction of e-learning. The statistical analysis from the survey provided some support to this thesis. To add some credence to this conclusion, an interview was held with the e-learning coordinator for modules attended by the respondents to the survey questionnaire. The coordinator's role was quite complicated and involved deciding on whether to adapt and use a course from different vendors. Additionally the courses had to be internally validated within the University (of the West of Scotland). The main part of the design was by the course vendors (e.g. Sun and Microsoft) while some parts of the assessment were designed by the coordinator. For tutoring, an external agency was hired. The agency ensured tutors had satisfactory skills, experience and certification. Some of the interview questions were irrelevant to the situation. This is especially in the case of the drop-out rate, as in the case of the CPD (Continual Professional Development) some of the participants only join to get online materials. The assignments were designed by the coordinator with the objective of enhancing the social aspect of learning:

I design and specify coursework assignments where appropriate. This is guided by a methodological approach:

- *where courses that are too focused on technical skills to the exclusion of their usefulness,*
- *a coursework is required that focuses on*
    - *the economic value of the technical skills, and*
    - *professional ability of the technical expert to work with non-technical people such as clients and management.*

Some students found the specification of assignments too vague. However this is similar to the working conditions of the consultants where details are provided while the work is being carried out. Generally, participants are encouraged to do the group work as it could help them in the real world:

I think group work is extremely important and worth the trouble involved in setting it up. Not all modules have group work, however ...

In the computing industry it is an essential part of a graduate's transferable skills to be able to work as a member of a team. We cannot discriminate on grounds of such preferences. We can make adjustments if someone has a particular physical challenge ...

Group work, however, causes most of the problems:

Biggest problem so far is facilitating group assignments. Students who want to undertake the group assignment let me know and I can put them in touch with others, and they will work by email etc. At present 6 students are working in groups on the Webmaster Foundations coursework: some of these are distance students.

It seems that the problem is how to connect students with each other – social network creation. This thesis is also supported by the comments inputted by the participants of an on-line questionnaire:

There was also no real chance for the members of the "class" to meet over a coffee! As regards the course, I personally found it difficult to commit the time to it, with the pressures of work and family life. Whereas, if it were based in the UWS, I would know that I had to attend a class one evening a week. Given this, there would have been the opportunity to meet other people on the course, and become involved in "group" tasks.

FUTURE TRENDS

The most important trends that are emerging are concerned with the user-centred design and the underlying technology. The concept of "cognitive worlds" where learners acquire knowledge individually and in a group could be further investigated together with the progress of the underlying technology. Although most of the on-line courses use some collaborative technology (chat, discussion board) most of these technologies do not adequately and consistently provide emotional and interpersonal support for group learning: social networking, community building, and allocating of tasks.

Cognitive e-learning design may be further enhanced by new trends in the technology such as Second Life. Second Life allows users to be surrogated by artificial computer created persons in a virtual world and was originally made for recreation but now it is used not only for social networking but e-learning in subjects like languages; computing such as games and 3 dimensional objects development; arts and culture.

Another innovative approach is to incorporate Web 2.0 technologies into e-learning rather than keeping solely to the traditional e-learning technologies (Craig, 2007). Some of the Web 2.0 technologies are Face Book and You Tube. A Sky News commentator recently[3] said that use of emails will soon be a thing of the past as people (especially youths) are these days using the social networking tools of Web 2.0 to communicate online through "blogs" etc. While these are often used for leisure, research is afoot to incorporate these technologies into e-learning since it makes it easy for learners to take the initiative in creating and sharing content as well as taking the responsibility of group building and networking.

CONCLUSION

This chapter along with its pilot study tried to connect the fundamental concepts of the cognitive psychology with recent advances in technology with a view to providing both individual and group experience to participants of e-learning courses. On one hand it is possible to see the demands and requirements of the users and other stakeholders, while on the other hand technology seems not to always be a good facilitator. It seems that pure virtual learning environment may not be the best option as some of the users require some physical contact ("meeting over a coffee"). It is noted that in the UK, as opposed to the US, most the successful e-learning programmes are of the blended nature rather than the pure (no face to face contact) approach (Ennew & Fernandez-Young, 2006).

It seems that although e-learning may fill many gaps it is increasingly minimising human contact but not the *need* for such contact. Contact is often a *sine qua non* for effective individual and group learning. It should be recognized in e-learning design, that individuals learn in social context and that learning should take prepare learners for the real world, where they would make meaning of their environments. Therefore simulations of real world in virtual environments should be as realistic as possible. In conclusion, e-learning should be perceived rather as a tool that is very useful and therefore research efforts should continue to explore methods that should maintain, if not increase, ways of humanising rather than dehumanising learners.

REFERENCES

Barab, S. A., & Duffy, T. (2000). From practice fields to communities of practice. In D. Johassen & S. M. Land (Eds.), *Theoretical Foundations of Learning Environments* (pp. 25-56). Mahwah, NJ: Erlbaum.

Barab, S. A., Kling, A., & Gray, J. H. (2004). *Designing for Virtual Communities in the Service of Learning.* Cambridge, UK: Cambridge University Press.

Barton, D., & Tusting, K. (2005). *Beyond Communities of Practice. Language, Power and Social Context.* Cambridge, UK: Cambridge University Press.

Byrne, R. M. J. (2007). *The Rational Imagination: How People Create Alternatives to Reality.* Cambridge, MA: MIT.

Chen, R. S., & Hsiang, C. (2006). A study on the critical success factors for corporations embarking on knowledge community-based e-learning. *Information Sciences, 177*, 570–586. doi:10.1016/j.ins.2006.06.005

Daradoumis, T., Martinez-Monés, A., & Xhafa, F. (2004). An integrated approach for analysing and assessing the performance of virtual learning groups. In *Lecture Notes in Computer Science*. Springer Berlin/Heidelberg

Engeström, Y. (1987). *Learning by expanding: An activity-theoretical approach to developmental research*, Helsinki: Orienta-Konstultit.

Engeström, Y. (1999). Expansive visibilization of work: An activity-theoretical perspective. In *Computer Supported Collaborative Work (CSCW)*. Vol 8, Nos 1 and 2). pp 63-93.

Ennew, C. T., & Fernandez-Young, A. (2006). Weapons of mass instruction? The rhetoric and reality of online learning. *Marketing Intelligence & Planning*, *24*(2), 148–157. doi:10.1108/02634500610654008

Golafshani, N. (2003). Understanding reliability and validity in questionnaire research. *Qualitative Report*, *8*(4), 597–607.

Hebb, D. (1949). *The Organization of Behavior.* New York: Wiley.

Krech, D., Crutchfield, R. S., & Ballachey, E. L. (1962). *Individual in Society*. New York: McGraw Hill.

Kvale, S. (1996). *InterViews. An Introduction to Qualitative Research Interviewing*. Thousand Oaks, CA: Sage Publications.

Leont'ev, A. N. (1978). *Activity, consciousness and personality*. Englewood Cliffs, NJ: Prentice Hall.

Leont'ev, A. N. (1981). *Problems of the development of mind.* Moscow: Progress Press.

Levy, Y. (2006). The top 10 most valuable online learning activities for graduate MS students. *International Journal of Information and Communication Technology Education*, *2*(3), 27–44.

Levy, Y. (2008). An empirical development of critical value factors (CVF) of online learning activities: An application of activity theory and cognitive value theory. *Computers & Education*, *51*, 1664–1675. doi:10.1016/j.compedu.2008.04.003

Litwin, M. S. (1995). *How to Measure Survey Reliability and Validity*. London: Sage Publications.

Neisser, U. (1967). *Cognitive Psychology*. New York: Appleton-Century-Crofts.

Pallant, J. (2005). *SPSS Survival Manual*. Maidenhead, UK: Open University Press.

Saunders, M., Lewis, P., & Thornhill, A. (2007). *Research Methods for Business Students*. Harlow, UK: Financial Times Prentice Hall.

Stahl, G. (2006). *Group Cognition. Computer Support for Building Collaborative Knowledge*. Cambridge, MA: MIT Press.

Stevenson, H. W., Lee, S. Y., & Graham, T. (1993). Chinese and Japanese kindergartens: case study in comparative research. In B. Spodek (Ed.), *Handbook of research on the education of young children* (pp. 519–535). New York: Macmillan.

Straub, D., Boudreau, M., & Gefen, D. (2004). Validation guidelines for IS positivist research. *Communications of the Association for Information Systems*, *13*, 380–427.

Tams, S. (2008). Self-directed social learning: the role of individual differences. *Journal of Management Development*, *27*(2), 196–213. doi:10.1108/02621710810849335

Thompson, T. L., Colla, T., & MacDonald, J. (2005). Community building, emergent design and expecting the unexpected: Creating a quality e-learning experience. *The Internet and Higher Education*, *8*, 233–249. doi:10.1016/j.iheduc.2005.06.004

Tolman, E. C. (1948). Cognitive Maps in Rats and Man. *Psychological Review*, *55*, 189–208. doi:10.1037/h0061626

Tolman, E. C. (1967). *Purposive Behavior in Animals and Men.* New York: Appleton-Century-Crofts.

Usoro, A., & Abid, A. (2008). A conceptual view of quality e-learning in higher education. *E-Learning*, *5*(1), 79–90. doi:10.2304/elea.2008.5.1.75

Usoro, A., & Abid, A. (2008). A conceptual view of quality e-learning in higher education. *E-Learning*, *5*(1), 79–90. doi:10.2304/elea.2008.5.1.75

Usoro, A., Sharratt, M. W., Tsui, E., & Shekhar, S. (2007). Trust as an antecedent to knowledge sharing in virtual communities of practice. *Knowledge Management Research and Practice*, *5*, 199–212. doi:10.1057/palgrave.kmrp.8500143

Vitari, C., & Revarini, A. (2006). Validation of IS positivist research: an application and discussion of the Straub, Boudreau and Gefen's guidelines. In *itAIS Conference*, Venice, Italy.

Vygotsky, L. S. (1931). *Mind and society*. Cambridge, MA: MIT Press.

Wasonga, T. A. (2007). Using technology to enhance collaborative learning. *International Journal of Educational Management*, *21*(7), 585–592. doi:10.1108/09513540710822184

ENDNOTES

1. Refer to Appendix A for the full statement that measure each of the sub-constructs. For example, Construct A.1 refers to the first question in Section A of the Appendix, viz: "1. Do you prefer to work on your own or in a group to achieve your learning objective?"
2. Questionnaire items.
3. In March 2009.
4. Each of the sections refers to a construct of the study. Eg, Section A measures Learner-Community-Outcome.

APPENDIX A

Introductory Details:

1. What is your education level? [Drop down list]
2. What is your age? [Drop down list]
3. What is your gender? [two options]
4. What is your interest in this course? [Descriptive]
5. What is the course you are in? [Descriptive]
6. What are the course objectives? (if any) [Drop down list]

Section[4] A

1. Do you prefer to work on your own or in a group to achieve your learning objective? [5 scale]
2. Do you think that learning in a group helps you in achieving the learning objectives? [5 choice]
3. Do you rate the learning objectives of your course (such as exams, assessments, coursework) as more addressed at an individual or a group? [5 scale]
4. Do you think that the focus of the learning objectives should be put on individual learner or a group? [5 scale]

Section B

1. On average how often do you use collaboration software (e.g. email, discussion board, chat) in your course? [5 scale]
2. Do you prefer to use collaboration software to communicate with other participants or do you prefer face-to-face communication? [5 scale]
3. Do you perceive collaboration software as a limitation in your learning process or as an enhancement? [5 scale]
4. How do you rate collaboration software provided? [5 scale]

Section C

1. What part of your learning activities during the course are group learning? [5 scale]
2. On average do the members of your group perform similar or different learning tasks? [5 scale]
3. In your opinion do you think it is better if the participants of a course perform similar tasks or individually assigned tasks? [5 scale]
4. Do you think that specialization of tasks in a group is a bad or a good thing? [5 scale]
5. On average are the roles of the members of your group uniform or different? (for example an assessor and a doer) [5 scale]

Section D

1. What is the degree to which the behaviour of the participants of your course somehow regulated? [5 scale]

2. What is the degree to which the participants follow the regulations? [5 scale]
3. Do you think it is better to learn in an environment with no regulations or are any regulations needed? [5 scale]
4. Do the participants of you class adhere to basic rules such as netiquette or a proper language? [5 scale]

Section E

1. What is the degree to which you are satisfied with your e-learning course in terms of study related issues (e.g. new skills, knowledge)? [5 scale]
2. What is the degree to which you are satisfied with your e-learning course in terms of other issues (e.g. atmosphere, new friends)? [5 scale]
3. Have you passed the required exams, assessments, coursework for the course you are participating in?

APPENDIX B

Introductory

1. Could you briefly describe your role, duties and responsibilities?

I am module coordinator for a (quite large) number of modules that have recently been offered in a distance learning mode.

These modules are university validated modules that have been derived mainly from external Vendor materials.

I am involved in administration of the courses, and in some aspects of assessment, but not involved either in the course design or direct support to students.

Each CRN (module occurrence) has an experienced online administrator (e.g. Lynn Rowand) and a tutor (e.g. supplied by Elite consulting).

The Tutors

- must be certified in the appropriate subject matter and
- experienced in handling distance students, and
- are appointed according to the University's requirements for part-time teaching staff..

Direct support to students takes place at fixed session times (e.g. 1930-2230 weekly) and by email outside those times.

The distance learning versions of these courses have been produced externally and validated internally as required.

I evaluate these on an ongoing basis, and change suppliers when this becomes appropriate. (E.g. I am currently planning to discontinue using CIW other than for Webmaster foundations and Site Designer, and bringing in a suite of Sun modules).

I deal with entering the results of any assessments that students take into the University Banner system. Assessments take two main forms: online exams taken via the Test Centre and (since the start of this session) assignment/presentations submitted by Blackboard drop box.

I design and specify coursework assignments where appropriate. This is guided by a methodological approach:

- where courses that are too focused on technical skills to the exclusion of their usefulness,
- a coursework is required that focuses on
    - the economic value of the technical skills, and
    - professional ability of the technical expert to work with non-technical people such as clients and management.

The same assignment and mechanisms for presentation are used whether students are distance learning or not.

Students may request a live presentation and this will be done by web conference.

So far only one student has submitted one assignment, and is currently resubmitting it.

2. How long have you been involved in distance learning teaching/administration/design?

I had some distance learning students for some taught modules last session, but really I am quite new to distance learning administration.

3. How many e-learning courses/modules have you supervised so far?

I am scheduled to coordinate 99 CRN's for distance learning this session. A smaller number of these modules have already completed.

4. What are the main problems you have experienced while designing/supervising e-learning courses?

Biggest problem so far is facilitating group assignments. Students who want to undertake the group assignment let me know and I can put them in touch with others, and they will work by email etc. At present 6 students are working in groups on the Webmaster Foundations coursework: some of these are distance students.

5. What is the average drop-out rate of the courses you design/supervise?

It is too soon to say. With CPD courses of this type the concept of drop-out is rather diffuse. Many people join the course in order to get the online materials, and have no interest in taking the assessments.

Section A

1. To what extend did the e-learning courses (CIW Foundations, Site Design, Web Languages) you designed/supervised focused on learner with a view of achieving the course objectives?

My role in relation to module design has been limited to the specification of assignments. Learners have found the assignment specifications rather vague: but this is just like real life, where a consultant gains information about details on an initial visit.

2. Have you applied any particular methodology and/or technique while designing/supervising the e-learning course?

See above: limited to coursework assignments where these have been necessary.

3. Do you think that learning in the group could help an individual achieve learning objectives?

I think group work is extremely important and worth the trouble involved in setting it up. Not all modules have group work, however.

4. While designing/supervising an e-learning course do you usually address learner at individual or a group level? (For example while designing e-learning activities or assigning coursework)

Transparency is important: the same task and mechanism for all students whether distance learning or not.

5. While designing/supervising an e-learning course do you take into account the different types of learners in terms of social activities (some prefer to work on their own and some in a group)?

No. In the computing industry it is an essential part of a graduate's transferable skills to be able to work as a member of a team. We cannot discriminate on grounds of such preferences. We can make adjustments if someone has a particular physical challenge, and I can recall a hard case where we came under pressure to waive a presentation requirement on medical grounds, but I do not regard this as acceptable.

Section B

1. In your opinion did the courses designed/supervised by you enhanced learners experience in the social perspective (e.g. by providing collaborative software, chat, virtual classroom)

We do provide chat rooms in Blackboard and I believe these work well.

2. Do you perceive the technology as a limitation or enhancement of the learning activities?

Some technology helps to make distance learning more effective.

3. Do you prefer to design/supervise "traditional" classroom or e-learning classroom?

I prefer face-to-face teaching (like most people?) but I have conducted classes remotely via Blackboard and in Second Life.

Section C

1. Do you treat learners uniformly or try to differentiate the roles and tasks depending on the learner perceived knowledge and skills?

It is extremely important to treat learners uniformly, and as far as possible overcome any differences caused by different tutors, different locations, daytime vs evening, distance etc.

2. In your opinion is it better if the participants of the course perform similar tasks or individually assigned diversified tasks? (in terms of administration, learning objectives, assessments)

I am comfortable with students following different tracks in a given scenario, using different approaches, taking advantage of looseness in the coursework specification etc.

3. Do you think it is possible to assign group activities with diversified roles in distance learning in the context of some of the learners "not doing their share" (more difficult to enforce it in the e-learning environment)?

It is for the group to allocate roles within the groups, and report on any ensuing difficulties. It is always quite hard, and I don't think distance makes it any harder. Remote working is not a reality for many people.

Section D

1. Was the behaviour of the participants of the courses you have designed/supervised somehow regulated?

Via an acceptable use policy.

2. In your opinion is the influence of the formal rules beneficial or deteriorating to the learning process?

   A loose framework of rules help to provide more stable interactions.

3. Did the participants of the courses you have designed/supervised follow the regulations?

   No complaints so far.

Section E

1. Do you think that introducing the collaboration technique (e.g. Web 2, chat, blogs) into the e-learning course design/supervision could enhance learners' satisfaction and help them achieve learning objectives?

Chat is fine. So far any experiments we have done with blogs have not been very happy. Most students hate writing blogs. I am comfortable with requiring a PDP-related paragraph with each coursework.

2. Do you think that introducing such techniques could decrease the drop-out rate of the learners?

   We use chat.

Chapter 4
Interface Design for Social Interaction in E-Learning Environments

Luciane Maria Fadel
UNOESC Videira, Brazil

Mary C. Dyson
The University of Reading, UK

ABSTRACT

This chapter concerns the contribution of the interface design to social interaction in e-learning environments. More specifically this chapter focuses on the design of social facilities in the interface that are intended to motivate and sustain the process of communication among students. Although there are design constraints in creating an environment capable of supporting social interaction, previous research findings indicate that social presence is a key factor for social interaction. In addition, previous research has pointed out that social presence is affected by individual, social response and media variables, suggesting that an interface design might enhance social presence. This chapter explores the interface design by investigating how placing an emphasis on interaction facilities and incorporating text, images and animation affects students' experiences of interacting with each other. The overall conclusion is that the interface design can increase the number of interactions and enhance the perceived social presence in e-learning environments.

INTRODUCTION

The wide use of computer networks to deliver education and the emergence of people-centred online education have dramatically increased the demand for systems that support social interaction (Anderson, 2003a; McInnerney & Roberts, 2004). Much work has been done to support e-learning successfully by understanding the interdependence of social and technical elements in a design space. Developments in social collaborative-based learning theories (Slavin, 1990; Vygotsky, 1984; Wenger, 1998) have linked the e-learning environments with online communities. By valuing the importance of people's relationships, e-learning environments are now at a new and important stage in design development. Yet much of the effort to enhance the participation and interaction of people has focused

DOI: 10.4018/978-1-60566-940-3.ch004

on tools (e.g., chat tools, bulletin boards, instant messaging) rather than on the interface design that is crucial for the success of any computer application (Jung & Lee, 2000). Without specialised interfaces, acceptance rates of computer applications will remain low, use will be difficult, and gains and benefits will fall short of their potential. Frequently, e-learning environments are little more than web pages. They are based on management tools that provide a means to sequence content and create a manageable structure for instructors (Siemens, 2004). These environments are designed as a management tool and not as a learning environment tool. Therefore the interface is designed to the instructor's needs, and not for what the students want to do.

In particular, the user interfaces of many e-learning systems suffer from their web page origins. The interface design for e-learning applications, however, offers many more challenges than the design of web pages (Kreijns, Kirschner, & Jochems, 2002). The interface must provide information about others to efficiently support social interactions – it must enhance social presence (Lee, Danis, Miller, & Jung, 2001). Social interactions are actions of two or more people with mutual orientation; in other words, people attach meaning to a situation, interpret what others are meaning, and respond accordingly (Argyle, 1976; Wagner, 1994). We define social presence as the extent to which virtual entities that represent others are perceived as real in an e-learning environment. The perception comes through interactions between participants and the virtual representations of others. Interactions use text, and are considered to be messages exchanged between students. In addition, e-learning refers to undergraduate courses delivered through a computer network. Thus, the interface for these courses is conceived not as a transparent layer in the communication process through the computer, but as an active contributor to this process.

In this chapter we explore the design of social facilities that enhance social presence in e-learning applications. Social facilities here refer to interaction facilities, to social information facilities and to the system feedback facility. In this context, interaction facilities refer to chat, forum, web mail and instant mailing. Social information denotes information about the presence, location and connection duration of the online users. The system feedback facility refers to the alerting system for incoming messages and system updates. We assume that the design of the social facilities must involve, engage and motivate the students to explore the e-learning environment by creating opportunities for exploration, discovery, and communication. Thus, to create an optimal education experience, the design of the e-learning environment should consider social presence as an affective factor in e-learning interactions.

The sections below clarify terminology to be used in this chapter and provide background material for those unacquainted with social presence theory. We start by addressing the challenges of defining and measuring social presence.

BACKGROUND

The term social presence was defined by Short, Williams and Christie (1976, p. 65) as 'the degree of salience of the other person in the interaction and the consequent salience of the interpersonal relationships'. They relate social presence to the concepts of intimacy and immediacy. Short, Williams and Christie (1976) hypothesize that individuals are aware of the degree of social presence of the medium, and they may avoid a certain medium depending on the kind of interaction they want to have. In addition, the degree of social presence of the medium depends on how much information it can transmit, and how the person who receives this information perceives it. Variations in social presence may be influenced by the capability of the medium to transmit information about facial expression, gestures, direction of gaze, tone of voice, and much more.

We do not focus on how much information the medium can transmit, but investigate if the degree of social presence depends on how information is transmitted. Other definitions of social presence that emerge from reviewing the literature are briefly discussed below. These include theories about social presence which maximise the power of the medium as a social actor (Lombard & Ditton, 1997) and attempts to qualify social presence in terms of the user's access to it (Biocca, 1997) and community of inquiry (Garrison et al., 2000).

Lombard and Ditton (1997) reviewed several conceptualisations of social presence in an early attempt to explicate the concept. They define social presence as 'the perceptual illusion of non-mediation' (Lombard & Ditton, 1997, p. 10). The overwhelming majority of work cited by Lombard and Ditton, however, deals with broadcast, visual and non-interactive media.

In this chapter we assume that the interface design is studied as the agent that mediates student-student interaction. As such, interface design might contribute to the interaction process, by highlighting the participants' presence, for example. Therefore, we consider that mediation is to be noticed and the degree of social presence might be increased by enhancing some of the features of the mediation, i.e., social facilities.

Biocca's (1997, p.22) definition of social presence is rooted in virtual reality environments. Biocca, Burgeoon, Harms and Stoner (2001) classified and summarized different definitions of social presence into three themes as follows:

1. Co-presence, co-location and mutual awareness, which all express elements of being together
2. The experience of psychological involvement, which includes the concepts of saliency, immediacy, intimacy, and making oneself known
3. Behavioural engagement, which refers to the behavioural interaction through which social presence is realised

In this chapter we are concerned with student-student interaction. Thus, the degree of social presence is always related to perceiving the other students in the environment. As such, this is a problem of co-presence, co-location and mutual awareness.

In the context of a Community of Inquiry, social presence is a core element along with cognitive presence and teacher presence. Community of Inquiry theory is rooted in pragmatism, a tradition of philosophy and social action which views knowledge as emergent, communally constructed, and a melding of creativity and critical thinking. The key description marking out the Community of Inquiry is a group (or social setting) of individuals who use dialogue to solve problems. This group is strongly linked, even in a virtual world, socially and cognitively. The critical analysis and the challenging of assumptions that is inherent in the community are consistent with the premise that an educational learning experience is both collaborative and reflective.

The function of social presence in a Community of Inquiry is to support the cognitive and affective objectives of learning, and is defined by Garrison, Anderson and Archer (2000, p. 94) as 'the ability of participants in a community of inquiry to project themselves socially and emotionally, as "real" people (i.e., their full personality), through the medium of communication being used'. They defined three categories of indicators to analyse social presence. These indicators are the expression of emotions, group cohesion, and open communication.

The expression of emotions is related to the idea that humans continuously communicate through body language. Humour, specifically, has been identified as a factor contributing to social presence and subsequently to learning (Eggins, 1997). Self-disclosure is another important feature that contributes to enhancing social presence. Self-disclosure is described as a sharing of feelings, attitudes, experiences and interests. It encourages others to be more forthcoming and to reciprocate, increasing trust, support, and a sense of belonging. Thus, giving means for the students to interact might create opportunities for them to share feelings and experiences. We explore the impact of the interface design on self-disclosure, where interaction facilities are designed to foster interactions.

The second category of social presence indicators is group cohesion. Building cohesion and a sense of belonging is important for sharing meaning. This category is exemplified by activities that build and sustain a sense of group commitment. Thus, a sense of group commitment might be built by sustaining the sense of belonging, which might be helped by enhancing the visibility of the others. We explore the impact of the interface design on group cohesion, where social information facilities are designed to highlight the presence of the others.

The third category of indicators of social presence is open communication, which is described as reciprocal and respectful exchanges such as mutual awareness and recognition of each other's contributions. Mutual awareness is the evidence that others are present and attending to messages. Because there is a lack of visual cues in a text-based e-learning environment, recognition of each other's contributions can be shown by explicitly expressing appreciation. Thus, students might attend to messages if they are aware of incoming messages. We explore the influence of the interface design on mutual awareness, where feedback facilities are designed to alert students to incoming messages.

As discussed in the introduction, the degree of social presence is defined as the extent to which the virtual entities that represent others are perceived as real. Perceiving others as real fosters interactions among students. Therefore, the design of social facilities that support these interactions might influence the number of interactions, i.e., messages exchanged and how students perceive the others.

The following subsection will discuss the requirements that have to be considered in order to design systems that enhance social presence.

Variables that Affect Social Presence

Previous literature has suggested three types of variables that affect social presence: media variables, individual variables and social response to media variables (Garrison, Anderson & Archer, 2000; Gunawardena & Zittle, 1997; Lee & Nass, 2003; Lombard & Ditton, 1997; Short, Williams & Christie, 1976). Next, these variables are briefly discussed and one characteristic of each is chosen to be enhanced using graphic design.

Media Variables

In the studies reviewed by Lombard and Ditton (1997), media variables are related to:

1. The number of sensory dimensions and channels presented and engaged
2. Image quality and image size
3. Narrative quality
4. Production techniques
5. Sound fidelity
6. The presence of other people in the environment

The presence of other people in the environment may only enhance social presence if interactions with them are considered possible (Schubert, Regenbrecht, & Friedman, 2002). A number of researchers have explored ways of portraying social information in Computer Mediated Communication systems (CMC). Ackerman and Starr (1995) argued for the importance of displaying social activities in CMC systems. Kollock (1996) pointed out that people need to identify each other to interact and cooperate. And many researchers have constructed environments which attempt, in various ways, to provide cues for the presence and activities of their users (Erickson & Kellogg, 2000; Paula et al., 2005; Viegas & Donath, 1999).

Promoting the visibility of people and their activities can encourage people to become active and prolong participation (Erickson & Kellogg, 2000). Promoting the visibility of the students within the e-learning environment establishes a state of being informed which enables students to interpret other's actions and to guide their own actions (Girgensohn & Lee, 2002).

Individual Variables

Willingness to suspend disbelief, gender and a prior exposure to media are some of the individual variables that are suggested by Lombard and Ditton (1997). Prior exposure to media can help the user to feel comfortable with the environment. The text-based format of CMC requires that users possess some level of computer literacy such as typing, reading and writing to avoid communication anxiety (Gunawardena, 1995). Students who feel comfortable might interact more, which contributes to enhanced social presence. This assumption is based on the studies of Garramone, Harris and Anderson (1986). They found there was a significant relationship between social presence and personal satisfaction for participants who interacted more on political bulletin boards. The relationship between social presence and the number of interactions was also studied by Perse, Burton, Kovner, Lears, and Sen (1992). They studied college students' utilisation of email, and concluded that students replied more to e-mails they felt conveyed more presence.

Social Response Variables

Social responses to media occur when individuals unconsciously attribute human characteristics to media. The use of language, voice and interactivity are characteristics of media that affect social response (Lee & Nass, 2003). In this chapter interactivity is considered a primary characteristic of media that may cue social responses to media (Lee & Nass, 2003). Wagner (1994) distinguishes between interaction and interactivity. Interactivity she describes as a characteristic of the technology itself, while interaction may be perceived as an outcome of using such technology. Tu (2002) classifies interactivity as the designs and strategies to stimulate social presence and includes the response time, communication styles, task types, topics and size of groups. The shorter the response time to incoming messages the higher the interactivity. This might be related to the fact that when an expected immediate response is not received a feeling of low interactivity is created, thus diminishing the level of social presence.

Summary of Social Presence Variables

The interface design used in the experiments described in Fadel and Dyson (2006a; 2006b; 2006c; 2007) enhanced three variables that are thought to affect social presence. They were selected prioritising those that could affect the categories of indicators of social presence described by Garrison, Anderson and Archer (2000). The variables are:

1. The number of interactions, which might be related to an individual variable, the prior exposure to media (Garramone et al., 1986; Perse et al., 1992). Increasing the number of interactions could contribute to sharing feelings and experiences which would enhance the expression of emotions, one of the three categories of indicators of social presence (Garrison et al., 2000). Enhancing the visibility of the interaction facilities might increase the number of interactions
2. The presence of other people in the environment, which is a media variable (Erickson & Kellogg, 2000; Paula et al., 2005; Viegas & Donath, 1999). The presence of others might enhance the sense of belonging, which

affects another social presence category of indicators, group cohesion (Garrison et al., 2000)

3. Response time, which is related to interactivity and is a social response to media variable (Tu, 2002). Shortening the response time to incoming messages might enhance mutual awareness and encourage students to attend to messages. Attending to messages affects the third category of indicators of social presence, open communication

In addition, the literature points out how critical social presence is to student performance in learning (Picciano, 2002; Richardson & Swan, 2003). This informs the design of a model for enhancing social presence, where social presence is affected by the number of interactions, the presence of others, and response time, and where enhanced social presence improves performance.

THE EXPERIMENTS

Before we show how to enhance social presence this section discusses the planning of experiments that evaluate the relationship between the interface design and students' interaction and perceptions. This section describes the design of the e-learning environment, the participants, and data collection.

This research adopted field experiments in order to achieve an authentic activity (Breakwell, Hammond, & Fife-Schaw, 2000). To be authentic the students should have genuine reasons to be connected to the learning activity (Leont'ev, 1978). In addition, the students should attain meaningful goals and be intellectually and emotionally engaged in the tasks they carry out. In this case, the activities should promote collaboration and be arranged so that the students could attain goals which are difficult to reach alone. The tutors were instructed, therefore, to develop such activities and the environments created for the experiments described in this chapter should give means of collaboration, such as synchronous and asynchronous communication features. In addition, the learning environment must be able to support the learning experience in an authentic context. In this case, the students were enrolled in a mandatory course offered by the Universidade do Oeste de Santa Catarina Videira (UNOESC VDA) in Brazil. The online courses were designed as a relevant e-learning activity placed within the larger context of the goals of the University.

The intervention was restricted to the mediating tool of the activity, which was the e-learning environment, and the associated synchronous and asynchronous communication tools. The experimental design preserved the authenticity of the actions performed within the e-learning environment while allowing the tool to be investigated.

However, the design of a field experiment needs to deal with unpredictability. This could be caused by technical problems, students dropping out of courses, and the educational policies of the University. For example at UNOESC VDA, students' final grades must have a written text as part as their assessment, which implies a face-to-face meeting. Students also attended other face-to-face courses together. These factors could have implications for the perceived social presence, as will be discussed in the next section. In addition, the experimenter was based in UK while the experiments were carried out in Brazil. This means that no student behaviour could be observed, nor could interviews be carried out without mediation.

We considered both subjective and objective responses, therefore we used data gathered through questionnaires, as well as participants' grades and system logs. In addition, debriefing sessions were carried out with the tutor using chat facility. During these sessions the tutor reported how the students were behaving, his impression about the course and any difficulty he could be facing.

The experimental approach adopted established a control and an experimental group,

Figure 1. Interface interaction model

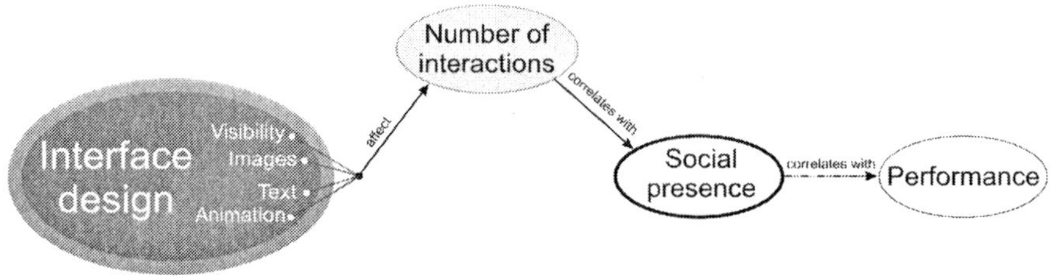

based on changes to the interface. Participants were assigned to use one of the two interfaces such that equal numbers of participants used one or the other interface. The criteria used to assign the students to groups were age, gender and the report from the tutor about each student's previous performance in another course. The aim of assigning students to groups was to ensure that, as far as possible, both groups were equivalent in terms of these factors (age, gender and level of performance).

Enhancing Social Presence

One significant barrier to supporting interaction in current e-learning environments is the low sense of social presence experienced by participants compared with a face-to-face environment. To enhance social presence designers should attempt to build as many features as possible into e-learning environments (Wheeler, 2005). One of the challenges in developing e-learning environments that enhance social presence is therefore the design of the interface to enhance social facilities. This section will begin by discussing the interface interaction model and follow with research studies on the impact of the interface features that were identified in the interface interaction model. The first interface feature is visibility, which is explored in terms of designing for focused attention. The second feature reviewed is the use of images, animation and text to convey information and the third is the use of animation to alert students to incoming messages. In addition, some design requirements and the challenges they entail are discussed. In particular, there are technical restrictions on the amount of visual detail that can be conveyed and on the distraction this information may cause. Enhancing social facilities therefore, entails a potential trade-off between focused and divided attention.

The Interface Interaction Model

We start by assuming a theoretical model which describes means for increasing the number of interactions and for enhancing social presence in an e-learning environment (Figure 1).

This model considers Anderson's model of e-learning (Anderson, 2003a) and the variables indicated in the literature that might enhance social presence (Figure 2). These variables are: number of interactions, presence of others and response times. They were selected prioritising those that could affect the categories of indicators of social presence described by Garrison, Anderson and Archer (2000). The model identifies four interface features that might enhance social facilities: visibility, images, animation and text. Visibility is used to emphasise the interaction facilities to promote students' participation. Images, animation and text are used to portray social information while animation is also used to present system feedback. Three experiments were designed to test and validate the corresponding concepts (Fadel & Dyson, 2006a; 2006b; 2006c; 2007). Research prototypes of e-learning environments were created for these experiments.

Figure 2. Adaptation of Anderson's model of e-learning to study the impact of the interface design on perceived social presence and the number of interactions

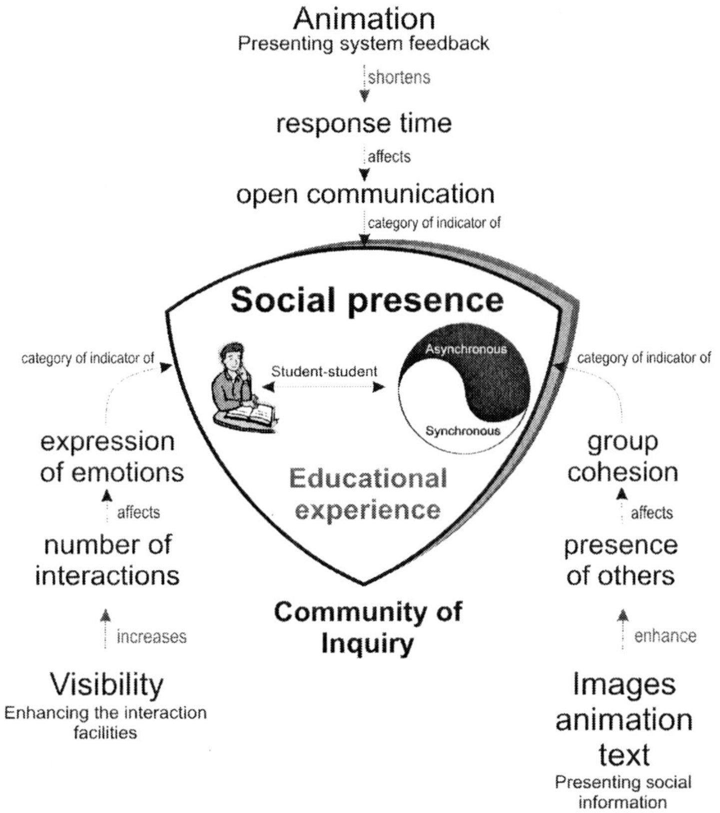

Visibility

Assuming that students will share their feelings and experiences if they have the means to interact, the interface design should foster interactions. Past research about designing visual interfaces would suggest that a well designed interface might attract users' attention and motivate them to interact (Lee & Boling, 1999; Szabo & Kanuka, 1999). Therefore, making the interaction facilities visible within the page structure could foster interactions. The visibility of the interaction facilities can be enhanced using design principles such as simplicity, emphasis, organization and modularity.

Simplicity enhances visibility because simple designs can be rapidly apprehended and are understood well enough to support immediate use (Mullet & Sano, 1995). Simplicity involves a paring down to only the essential elements required to achieve the desired effect and helps to unify the elements in the interface, which are seen as a coherent whole.

Emphasis might attract users' attention (Lohr, 2003). Emphasis provides the basis for visual distinctions, which might drive the users' attention to a specific part of the visual work. Indeed, interface design can support both focusing attention on a single interface object (without distraction from other objects) and dividing attention between multiple objects.

Organization enhances readability by grouping information in subsets that can be processed separately or in parallel. The organization of the elements is balanced when the visual weight of the design elements on either side of the composition is distributed across the centre of balance. Organization might also be used to attract users' attention and thus enhance visibility (Lohr, 2003).

Finally, modularity reduces visual complexity by repeating elements, which might enhance the visibility of the interface.

These design principles were selected as important aspects to improve motivation and hold the user's attention by Lee and Boling (1999). In addition, Szabo and Kanuka (1999) studied the effects of violating these design principles in creating the interface, especially on recall, learning and study time. Szabo and Kanuka found no difference in achievement scores between a group that used the lesson with good design principles and a group that used the lesson with poor design principles. However, the students who used the lesson with good design principles completed the lesson in less time and had a higher completion rate, than those who used the lesson with poor design principles. This might be related to the fact that with a poor interface design more time might be spent inspecting the visual representation without a gain in achievement (Hegarty, Carpenter, & Just, 1991).

Hence an interface design focusing on simplicity, emphasis, organization and modularity might attract users to the interaction facilities and motivate them to interact. An interface design focusing on simplicity, emphasis, organization and modularity could be used to enhance the visibility of the interaction facilities such as chat, web mail and forum, which might result in more frequent use of these facilities, in other words, users would interact more. Interacting more might contribute to sustaining a higher satisfaction with the course and a stronger presence. These ideas were explored in the design of the experiment described in Fadel and Dyson (2006b) and summarized as follows.

Experiment on Visibility

This experiment sought to answer whether the visibility of the menu and the interaction facilities can enhance the perceived social presence. The experiment was conducted using a control group working with the same interface that was used in the University in Brazil (UNOESC), and an experimental group working with a visibility-based interface (Figure 3). Both interfaces had the same functionalities. The design of the visibility-based interface was focused on the simplicity, emphasis, organisation and modularity of the interaction facilities in order to motivate interactions. The results showed that the visibility-based interface group tended to post more messages than the other group. They also spent more time at forum and logged into chat more times than the other group. This suggests that the visibility of the interaction facilities might have motivated students to participate more. In addition, considering all the messages posted by the students combined, the results showed a strong positive correlation between the number of messages posted at forum and the perceived social presence.

IMAGES, ANIMATION AND TEXT

Perception of Images

Having established that social information is important, it would be useful if it could be conveyed rapidly to students. Research has shown that certain types of images are perceived fairly rapidly. The process of abstraction results in simplified forms that are processed and assimilated more rapidly (Dondis, 1973). Abstract forms are perceived without effort and involuntarily because of their perceptual immediacy and generality (Mullet & Sano, 1995). Indeed, abstraction is used to broaden an image's referential representationality (Williams, 1993). This term refers to a scale where the end points are realistic photographs at one extreme and purely alphanumeric information at the other. Images look like their referents while words need to be narrowed by adding modifiers.

Images might transmit social information in a more rapid way than text because the nature of

Figure 3. Home page of the original (upper figure) and visibility-based interface (lower figure)

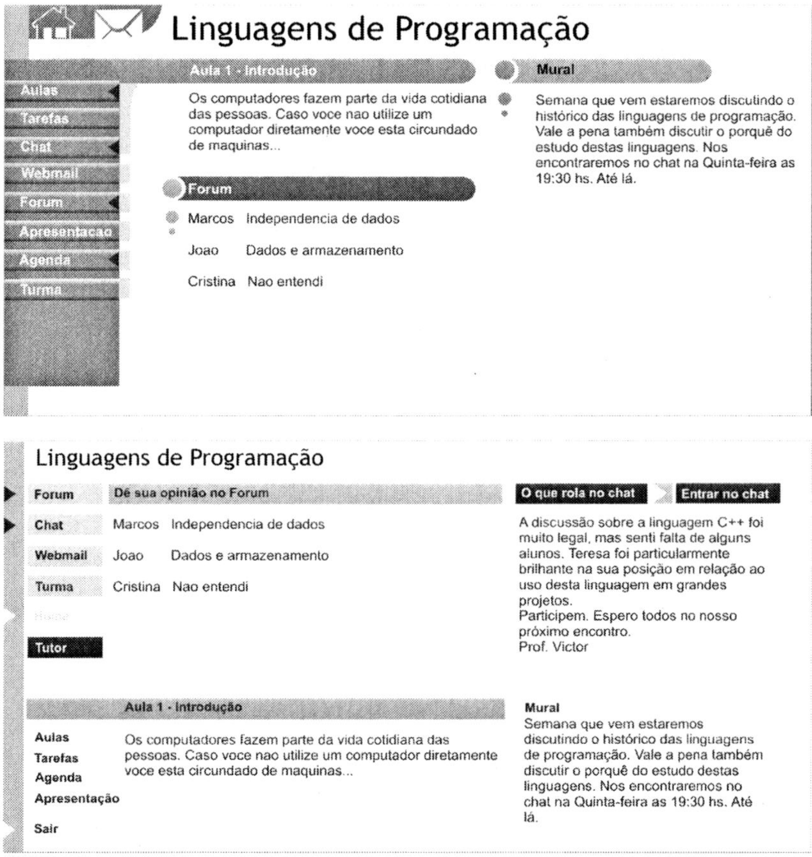

images is amenable to pre-attentive processing. This means that objects within an image are distinguished automatically without any conscious effort. The same thing occurs when first looking at a word. Initially the letters are processed as shapes, and the word is then processed serially under the control of the reader's conscious attention (Williams, 1993). The degree of conscious attention that must be employed in the interpretation of the messages that a text conveys is higher for words than for images. Using abstract images to represent the virtual users might help in grouping them. Grouping might facilitate perception of the online users.

Images might help perceive the relationships among virtual users, their connection duration, and location, because images have the flexibility to inform graphically while words impose a sequential structure on the information, i.e., a list. This means that images might be better able to convey spatial and conceptual relationships.

In addition, based on the idea that memory for images tends to be better than memory for words, abstract images might be remembered long after people see them which might help in group awareness (Paivio, 1979; Shepard, 1967). The majority of studies on text illustration have focused on the effects of images on the retention of the text. These studies indicate that images are capable of affecting the retention of illustrated text (Peeck, 1987). It is also clear that picture memory is extraordinary in both duration and capacity. This result is supported in a study by Shepard (1967). In Shepard's study, the participants were tested for their ability to recognise old stimuli from a set of new ones.

Hence, using images may make it easier and quicker to perceive the constantly changing relationships between user, connection duration and location. Furthermore, the user experience must be enjoyable, which can be achieved by the interplay between words and images.

The Interplay Between Words and Images

The interplay created by integrating words and images might provide a compelling experience to the user. Integrating words and images can be done in five ways as described by Schriver (1997), i.e., redundant, complementary, supplementary, juxtapositional or stage-setting. Complementary refers to the content of text and images. This means that both modes (images and text) are necessary to understand who is online, for how long and where the virtual user is. The challenge for the user in reading different content in distinct modes would also be driven by the amount of conscious attention necessary to interpret the messages the modes convey, as explained earlier.

Images might also arouse interest, create emotion and stimulate curiosity (Peeck, 1987). Peeck grouped these characteristics of images as the affective-motivational role. She investigated this role of images in a study which found that children thought their illustrated booklets more attractive than non-illustrated text. The affective-motivational role of images might be crucial to students' satisfaction with the interface in an online course.

The Social Space

The social space might better be represented using images, because images might suggest a vision of the virtual space using a metaphor. The suggestion of a virtual space is rooted in the association the user might have with their own experience in the physical world (Chen, 1999). In the experiment described in Fadel and Dyson (2006c), the virtual space is created using the social information available. The social space is organized in two-dimensional space. One axis is time, and the other axis is location. The relationship among users, time and location might better be represented using image and text (Williams, 1993). Therefore, the user might read the images as places which would facilitate the perception of the virtual user's location (Mullet & Sano, 1995). This impact of using this combination was evaluated in Fadel and Dyson (2006a; 2006c) and summarized as follows.

Experiment on Images, Animation and Text

The experiment presented in Fadel and Dyson (2006a; 2006c) sought to investigate the impact of images, animation and text on the perception of virtual users in an e-learning environment. The interface created using images, animation and text was referred to as the visual-based interface (Figure 4). In terms of presence, it represented virtual users with image and text; in terms of location, virtual users were located in a pie chart (image); in terms of connection duration, virtual users were animated on the chart to show their connection time. The design rationale for the visual-based interface was to provide a coherent shared sense of place to facilitate a context for interactions. The sense of place in the visual-based interface was based on the concept of a site map, conceived in abstract representation as a 'pie chart'. In this chart the virtual users can be seen in their specific locations. Their presence and location will vary over time.

An abstract avatar was created to represent the user. This avatar is a small dark blue circle labelled with the virtual user's name. In this interface, the distance between the centre of the circle and the centre of the dot (avatar) represents the connection duration. The pie chart is divided into sectors to represent each page of the site. Different colours are used in each of these sectors. Yellows are used

Figure 4. Home page of the text- based (upper figure) and visual-based interface with 4 users online (lower figure)

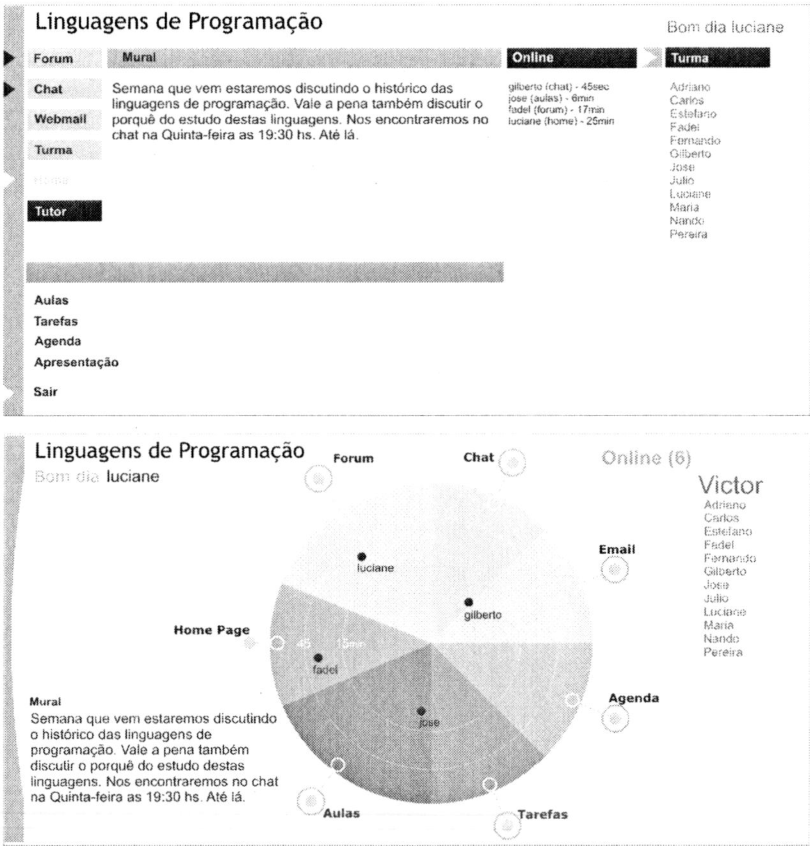

in the sectors associated with pages that support users' interaction like the home page, forum, chat and web mail. Blues are used to paint the sectors that correspond to pages associated with the content of the course like lectures, tasks and agenda. The visual-based interface was compared to another interface referred to as the text-based interface which presented presence, location and connection duration using text alone.

The results showed that the visual-based interface group posted significantly more web mail and instant mail messages than the text-based interface group. The number of messages posted via web mail and instant mail were 36 and 39 respectively for the visual-based interface group. The text-based interface group sent only 1 web mail and 2 instant mail messages. A chi-square test reveals a difference between the two groups in terms of web mail (χ^2=6, 1df, p<0.05) and instant mail messages (χ^2=8.5, 1df, p<0.05). This finding suggests that the use of images, animation and text to portray virtual users encouraged the students to interact through web mail or instant mail features.

It is important to remember that the instant mailing feature is available to send messages only to the online users. Therefore, sending more messages using the instant mailing feature suggests that the visual-based interface group better perceived the online users than the text-based interface group. This result might be associated with the diagrammatic structure used in this experiment to help the perception of relationships among virtual users, and their connection duration and location. In addition, as Dondis (1973) and Mullet & Sano (1995) argued, abstract forms might be perceived without effort and involuntarily which implies faster recognition of the information. Furthermore, the perception of the presence of virtual users might also be enhanced by animation. Indeed, animation linked to a social space suggests presence and activity because it is based on a metaphor of the physical world, as claimed by Chen (1999).

Finally, students' performance correlated positively with perceived social presence (r = 0.55). Although the significance of this correlation could not be tested because there is no evidence that the social presence data follows a normal distribution, there is an indication that the students have interacted to complete the tasks. This might have enhanced their presence and at the same time helped in the learning process.

ANIMATION

The Perception of Animation

Mutual awareness has been identified as crucial for enhancing social presence, so it would be important that students attend to messages. Moreover the feedback about incoming messages should be perceived promptly, as this could encourage a reply. Animation might be used as an alerting system because there is evidence that humans are highly sensitive to motion (Johansson, 1973). Large, Beheshti, Breuleux and Renaud (1996) state that animation helps the understanding of an idea when that idea involves motion. Therefore, students might notice events such as users changing location and connection duration by observing geometric shapes that move in simple ways. Motion is also considered an attribute of a visual object by Limoges, Ware and Knight (1989). This means that motion might be used to group distinct data points. Hence, motion can express certain kinds of relationships in data. Therefore, motion might depict the presence of virtual users. Animation might also be used to represent time, and motion might help users to group the online users. Grouping online users might facilitate the perception of the presence of the others. In this case, the visualisation of people is enhanced by situating them in a social space.

Animation uses the principle that the mind fills in the gaps between frames when a rapid series of still images are presented. The illusion of continuous motion is called apparent motion (Ramachandran & Anstis, 1986). Ramachandran and Anstis (1986) suggest that the visual system applies strategies that limit the number of matches the brain needs to consider to detect which parts of a successive image reflect a single object in motion (correspondence). Among the features that the visual system might attempt to extract from images, Ramachandran and Anstis (1986) found that blotches of brightness and darkness, areas of low spatial frequency, serve as cues for detecting correspondence. In this case, an object animated by altering its brightness might not generate information overload because the visual system is likely to detect correspondence between regions of similar low spatial frequencies before it detects more detailed outlines. Thus, animation based on changing brightness could be used to direct students' attention to a specific point on the interface without generating information overload.

The Effects of Animation

The literature on audio-visual communication contains many references to the effects on learning that occur when animation is used to represent information. Animation may enhance descriptive and procedural text (Large, Beheshti, Breuleux, & Renaud, 1994, 1995; 1996). Large, Beheshti, Breuleux, and Renaud indicated that the presence of animation can help students to understand a text which outlines a series of steps that must be undertaken to achieve a goal. In addition, they suggest that animation is likely to be most effective when combined with text whose content is related to motion. Animation may concentrate attention on those aspects of a text that deal with motion. A similar recommendation is made by Rieber (1990a; 1990b). The experimental evidence brought together by Rieber led him to recommend that animation should be used when visualisation, motion or trajectory are needed for the successful completion of an instructional task. Although the use of animation as an alerting system differs in nature to animation as illustration of text, the idea of motion is implicit; in the case of this research the actual state of the system is altered by an incoming message or update.

Therefore, animation is an important visual attribute that might enhance the perception of other visual information such as system feedback and might contribute to shortening the response time to incoming messages and system updates. An experiment on animation was carried out and described in Fadel and Dyson (2007). The results are summarized as follows.

Experiment on Animation

The experiment on animation sought to extend the work of the experiment on images, animation and text by investigating the impact of animation. This experiment used animation to alert students to incoming messages and system updates, and investigated how this affected the number of interactions and the perceived social presence. The experiment on images, animation and text showed that students interact more if others are visible. However, students limited these interactions to instant mailing and web mail messages. The experiment on animation focused on alerting the students to all new messages. If the students were alerted to new messages they might answer them more promptly thus enhancing interactivity. Therefore, the two interfaces used in the experiment on images, animation and text were modified to present system feedback. In the experiment on animation the text-based interface presented system feedback using text alone, while the animation-based interface presented system feedback using animation (Figure 5).

The findings confirmed the results of the experiment on images, animation and text regarding the number of instant mail messages. There were a total of 240 messages posted using the instant mailing feature for the animation-based interface group against 14 for the text-based interface group. There is a significant difference between the two groups ($\chi^2=9.5$, 1df, $p<0.05$). In addition, the animation-based interface group sent significantly more messages (considering chat, forum, web mail and instant mail features) than the text-based interface group. The text-based interface group sent a total of 158 messages during the course and the animation-based interface group sent a total of 502 messages. A Wilcoxon's Rank-Sum test was carried out to examine the differences between the means and found $W_s=115.5$ ($n_1=n_2=13$, $p<0.05$). The conclusion was that images, animation and text can have a significant positive effect on the number of interactions students make. This effect can be reinforced if animation is used to present system feedback. This finding has implications for interface design that seeks to foster students' participation in e-learning environments. It suggests that social information and feedback design that is based on images, animation and text can motivate students to interact in an e-learning environment.

In addition, there was a positive correlation between the number of instant mail messages sent by the animation-based interface group and the perceived social presence. The significance of this correlation could not be tested because there is no evidence that the social presence data follows a normal distribution. What remains is an indication that a student might have a stronger perception of the presence of others if he/she interacts more. This finding suggests that the use of the instant mailing feature might enhance the presence of virtual users, probably because of its immediacy. The immediacy associated

Figure 5. Home page of the text- based (upper figure) and animation-based interface with 5 users online (lower figure)

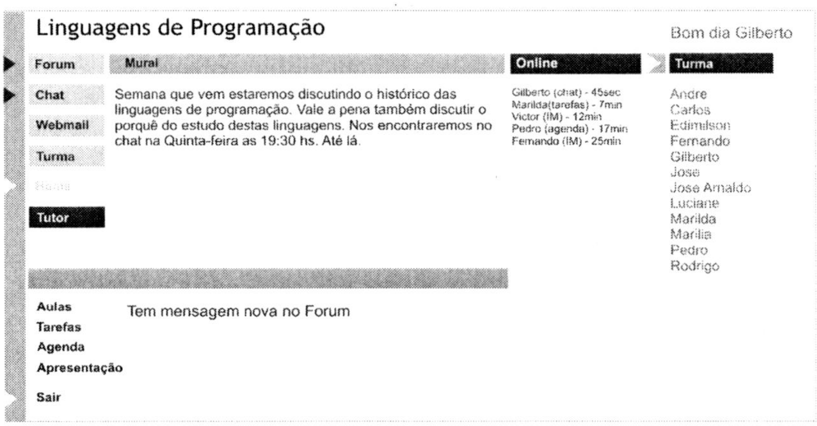

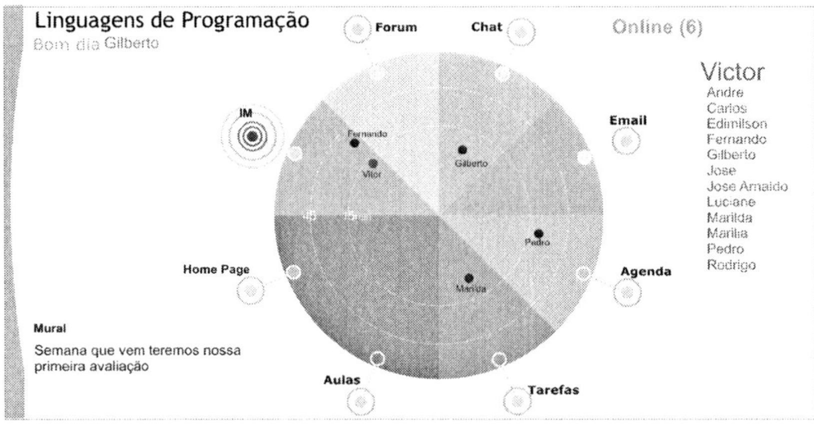

with the instant mailing feature is rooted in an expectation that when messages are posted they will be responded to quickly. In addition, instant mail messages might have contributed to students feeling part of the group, as previously reported by Contreras-Castillo, Favela, Perez-Fragoso and Santamaria-del-Angel (2003). Feeling part of the group enhances group cohesion, one of the social presence categories of indicators pointed out by Garrison, Anderson and Archer (2000). Therefore, the relation between number of interactions and social presence should be further investigated.

Finally, the results suggest that those students who perceived a stronger social presence also performed better, supporting the findings of the experiment on images, animation and text.

FUTURE RESEARCH DIRECTIONS

The findings reported in this chapter indicate that students behave differently using different interfaces. Previous research has indicated that social presence is perceived differently by each user. Potentially research could include approaches towards creating design solutions that are responsive to dynamic changes in information and in the user's intention. Interfaces that are responsive to dynamic changes are called adaptive interfaces.

The argument for investigating adaptive interfaces is that it addresses design solutions that can continuously adapt in response to dynamic changes both in the information itself, in the user's intention or in the perceived social presence. Adaptive interfaces have the potential to correspond to each user's needs individually. Research on adaptive interfaces would entail a multidisciplinary approach because an adaptive interface needs to be modelled on the systems it will interact with (Gajos et al., 2008). The development of systems models involves different knowledge domains like the knowledge of the current user, knowledge of the interaction scheme, knowledge of the problem task and knowledge of the underlying system. At the level of the interaction model, the adaptability of the interface could be driven by design agents. Design agents are artificial intelligent software that can note changes in the environment induced by the actions of the user, and can cooperate with them to maintain a state of dynamic balance for a specified feeling. This feeling could be satisfaction, a sense of belonging, etc. The design agents should be created as a graphic and as a semiotic element of the interface, with artificial intelligence developed through cognitive science and computer-human interactions. The adaptive interface would be sensitive to students' actions and its agents would work to promote social interactions. To promote social interaction it would be necessary to detect the user's social interaction level. With this data the agent could promote the student's participation in the system, motivating them to interact in order to exchange messages, help another user or to do something, etc. This development would entail collaboration amongst a diversity of agents. It is nevertheless, a new and promising way to design interfaces.

CONCLUSION

At present, e-learning environments are used to deliver and manage the online education process. However, they have the potential to extend beyond their present usage to address the practical social interaction needs of geographically dispersed students. A chief attraction of the e-learning environment lies in its ability to provide students with freedom of time and space. The challenge for designing such environments is to support groups of people to collaborate and interact socially in an efficient and enjoyable way, while permitting maximum student freedom.

One key barrier to effective social interaction in current e-learning environments is the lack of social presence as compared to face-to-face communication. However, enhancing the perceived social presence involves significant challenges. Compared to face-to-face communication, e-learning requires a balance between the distraction caused by too much information and the attention required to read the content. Social presence must therefore be traded off against the need to support focused attention. In terms of presentation, the tension between the use of text alone and images, animation and text underlines the difficulty in portraying information. Text alone would entail an unacceptable monotony. On the other hand, images, animation and text, whilst breaking the monotony, can add complexity to the information and may not be desirable in a medium where the students must have control over the process.

Given these constraints, the approach taken in this chapter was to explore the design of the social facilities that support social presence. In other words, this chapter discussed the design of e-learning interfaces that support social interaction and enhance social presence. The overarching goal was to investigate whether placing an emphasis on interaction facilities, incorporating text, images and animation, could affect students' experiences when interacting with each other. The theoretical foundation of social presence and the process of enhancing social presence was analysed through the literature review. The literature presented in this review shows that interactions among students are critical to learning and cognitive development. This is also true in an e-learning experience where a learning community must be established and sustained to reach its educational potential. In this regard, a community of inquiry conceptual model was used to set the stage from an educational perspective. The community of inquiry conceptual model identifies three core elements associated with learning in an online environment: cognitive presence, teacher presence and social presence. Variables associated with media have a direct effect on the perceived social presence, as well as introducing individual and social response variables.

Social presence was considered in terms of three categories of indicators determined by Garrison, Anderson and Archer (2000). These categories are the expression of emotions, group cohesion and open communication. Therefore, three variables that might affect these categories of indicators were chosen: participation, the presence of others and system feedback.

In addition, the relevant factors that influence the interface design enhancing social presence were identified and contributions to the practical realisation and evaluation of these factors were made. In this regard, an interface interaction model was developed. This interface interaction model proposed a set of key interface features that are essential to build e-learning applications with adequate support for social interaction. These features are:

1. The visibility of the interaction facilities
2. The use of images, animation and text to present the presence of others
3. The use of animation to present system feedback

To validate the interface interaction model, three experiments have been carried out under real-life conditions in the context of e-learning. The three experiments were conducted investigating the relationship between the number of interactions and social presence, and these three features of the design of social facilities that support social presence.

To support the expression of emotions, the visibility of the interaction facilities was highlighted in the interface of the e-learning environment. Highlighting the visibility of the interaction facilities promotes their use by the students by creating opportunities for sharing experiences and feelings, which encourages the expression of emotions.

Group cohesion was supported through the use of images, animation and text to present the presence of others, their connection duration, and location in the e-learning environment. This enhanced the perception of the others and sustained the feeling that the students are all part of a group. This sense of belonging fosters group cohesion.

Finally, open communication was supported by adding animation to alert students to incoming messages. Alerted by the arrival of new messages, the students feel encouraged to reply quickly, thus increasing interactivity and mutual awareness. Mutual awareness is also sustained as others attend to messages. Attending to a message, which usually continues a thread as the reply feature is used, gives crucial support and recognition to others' contributions. Thus, students must be informed of the arrival of new messages so that they can reply promptly.

The use of images, animation and text to portray information about the others fosters web mail and instant mail interaction among students. In addition, the use of animation providing system feedback to incoming messages contributes to an increase in the number of interactions. Furthermore, the number of interactions might relate to the perceived social presence although the significance of this relationship could not be tested. Finally, there is a relationship between the perceived social presence and performance.

As Anderson (2003b) pointed out, all the interactions in an e-learning environment are mediated. The interface mediates interaction. This work concluded that the interface design is not passive in student-student interactions but affects the interactions and should be carefully considered in the development of e-learning environments. Students' behaviour may be driven by the interface design, i.e., students might interact more, use a facility more than another, or follow a predetermined path. These findings have implications for designing online course environments where the interface design plays a crucial role in enhancing social presence.

REFERENCES

Ackerman, M., & Starr, B. (1995). Social activity indicators: interface components for CSCW systems. In *8th annual ACM symposium on User interface and software technology*, Pittsburgh, Pennsylvania, United States.

Anderson, T. (2003a). Getting the mix right again: An updated and theoretical rationale for Interaction. *International Review of Research in Open and Distance Learning*, *4*(2).

Anderson, T. (2003b). Modes of interaction in distance education: Recent developments and research questions. In M. Moore (Ed.), *Handbook of Distance Education* (pp. 129-144). Mahwah, NJ: Erlbaum.

Argyle, M. (1976). *Social Interaction*. London: Tavistock.

Biocca, F. (1997). The cyborg's dilemma: progressive embodiment in virtual environments. *Journal of Computer-Mediated Communication*, *3*(2).

Biocca, F., Burgoon, J., Harm, C., & Stoner, M. (2001). *Criteria and scope conditions for a theory and measure of social presence*. Retrieved March 29, 2007, from http://www.temple.edu/ispr/prev_conferences/proceedings/2001/Biocca1.pdf

Breakwell, G. M., Hammond, S., & Fife-Schaw, C. (2000). *Research methods in psychology* (2nd Ed.). London: Sage Publications.

Chen, C. (1999). *Information visualisation and virtual environments*. London: Springer.

Contreras-Castillo, J., Favela, J., Perez-Fragoso, C., & Santamaria-del-Angel, E. (2003). Informal interaction and their implications for online courses. *Computers & Education*, *42*, 149–168. doi:10.1016/S0360-1315(03)00069-1

Dondis, D. A. (1973). *A primer of visual literacy* (7th Ed.). London: The MIT Press.

Eggins, S. (1997). *Analysing casual conversation*. London: Cassell.

Erickson, T., & Kellogg, W. A. (2000). Social translucence: an approach to designing systems that support social processes. *ACM Transactions on Computer-Human Interaction*, *7*(1), 59–83. doi:10.1145/344949.345004

Fadel, L. M., & Dyson, M. C. (2006a). Comparing a text- and visual-based interface presenting social information in an online environment. In *IEEE Symposium on Visual Languages and Human-Centric Computing*, Brighton, UK.

Fadel, L. M., & Dyson, M. C. (2006b). The effect of interface design on the enhancement of social presence in online courses. In *ICL2006*, Villach, Austria.

Fadel, L. M., & Dyson, M. C. (2006c). A Comparison of the perception of social information in text and visual-based interfaces. In *12th International Conference on Technology Supported Learning & Training - Online Educa Berlin*, Berlin, Germany.

Fadel, L. M., & Dyson, M. C. (2007). Enhancing interactivity in an e-learning environment. In *Interact 07 - Socially responsible interaction*, Rio de Janeiro, Brazil.

Gajos, K. Z., Everitt, K., Tan, D. S., Czerwinski, M., & Weld, D. S. (2008). Predictability and Accuracy in Adaptive User Interfaces. In *SIGCHI Conference on Human Factors in Computing Systems* (pp. 1271-1274). ACM Press: Florence, Italy.

Garramone, G. M., Harris, A. C., & Anderson, R. (1986). Uses of political computer bulletin boards. *Journal of Broadcasting & Electronic Media, 30*(3), 325–339.

Garrison, D. R., Anderson, T., & Archer, W. (2000). *Critical inquiry in a text-based environment: Computer conferencing in higher education*. Unpublished manuscript, Edmonton, CA.

Girgensohn, A., & Lee, A. (2002, November). Making web sites be places for social interaction. In *CSCW'02*, New Orleans.

Gunawardena, C. N. (1995). Social presence theory and implications for interactions and collaborative learning in computer conferences. *International Journal of Educational Telecommunications, 1*(2/3), 147–166.

Gunawardena, C. N., & Zittle, F. J. (1997). Social presence as a predictor of satisfaction within a computer-mediated conferencing environment. *American Journal of Distance Education, 11*(3), 8–26. doi:10.1080/08923649709526970

Hegarty, M., Carpenter, P. A., & Just, M. A. (1991). Diagrams in the comprehension of scientific text. In R. Barr, M. L. Kamil, P. B. Mosenthal & P. D. Pearson (Eds.), *Handbook of reading research* (Vol. 2, pp. 641-668). New York: Longman.

Johansson, G. (1973). Visual perception of biological motion and a model for its analysis. *Perception & Psychophysics, 14*(2), 201–211.

Jung, Y., & Lee, A. (2000). Design of social interaction environment for electronic marketplaces. In *DIS'00 - Designing Interactive Systems: Processes, Practices, Methods, Techniques*, New York.

Kollock, P. (1996). *Design principles for online communities.* Harvard Conference on the Internet and Society.

Kreijns, K., Kirschner, P. A., & Jochems, W. (2002). The sociability of computer-supported collaborative learning environments. *Educational Technology & Society, 5*(1), 1–19.

Large, A., Beheshti, J., Breuleux, A., & Renaud, A. (1994). Multimedia and comprehension: a cognitive study. *Journal of the American Society for Information Science American Society for Information Science, 45*(7), 515–528. doi:10.1002/(SICI)1097-4571(199408)45:7<515::AID-ASI6>3.0.CO;2-3

Large, A., Beheshti, J., Breuleux, A., & Renaud, A. (1995). Multimedia and comprehension: the relationship among text, animation, and captions. *Journal of the American Society for Information Science American Society for Information Science, 46*(5), 340–347. doi:10.1002/(SICI)1097-4571(199506)46:5<340::AID-ASI5>3.0.CO;2-S

Large, A., Beheshti, J., Breuleux, A., & Renaud, A. (1996). Effect of animation in enhancing descriptive and procedural texts in a multimedia learning environment. *Journal of the American Society for Information Science American Society for Information Science, 47*(6), 437–448. doi:10.1002/(SICI)1097-4571(199606)47:6<437::AID-ASI4>3.0.CO;2-W

Lee, A., Danis, C., Miller, T., & Jung, Y. (2001). Fostering social interaction in online spaces. In *INTERACT 2001*, Amsterdam.

Lee, K. M., & Nass, C. (2003, April). Designing social presence of social actors in human computer interaction. In *CHI 2003*, Ft. Lauderdale.

Lee, S. H., & Boling, E. (1999). Screen design guidelines for motivation in interactive multimedia instruction: A survey and framework for designers. *Educational Technology, 39*, 19–26.

Leont'ev, A. N. (1978). *Activity, consciousness, and personality. Upper Saddle River,* NJ: Prentice-Hall.

Limoges, S., Ware, C., & Knight, W. (1989, June). Displaying correlations using position, motion, point size or point colour. In *Graphics Interface*, London, Ontario.

Lohr, L. L. (2003). *Creating graphics for learning and performance: Lessons in visual literacy.* Columbus, Ohio: Merrill Prentice Hall.

Lombard, M., & Ditton, T. (1997). At the heart of it all: The concept of presence. *Journal of Computer-Mediated Communication, 3*(2), 1–43.

McInnerney, J. M., & Roberts, T. S. (2004). E-learning: Social interaction and the creation of a sense of community. *Educational Technology & Society, 7*(3), 73–81.

Mullet, K., & Sano, D. (1995). *Designing visual interfaces*. Mountain View: SunSoft Press.

Paivio, A. (1979). *Imagery and verbal processes*. Hillsdale, NJ: Lawrence Erlbaum.

Paula, R. D., Ding, X., Dourish, P., Nies, K., Pillet, B., Redmiles, D., et al. (2005, July 6-8). Two experience designing for effective security. In *Symposium On Usable Privacy and Security (SOUPS)*, Pittsburgh, PA.

Peeck, J. (1987). The role of illustrations in processing and remembering illustrated text. *The Psychology of Illustration, 1*, 115–151.

Perse, E., Burton, P., Kovner, E., Lears, M., & Sen, R. (1992). Predicting computer-mediated communication in a college class. *Communication Research Reports, 9*(2), 161–170. doi:10.1080/08824099209359908

Picciano, A. G. (2002). Beyond student perceptions: issues of interaction, presence, and performance in an online course. *JALN, 6*(1), 21–40.

Ramachandran, V. S., & Anstis, S. M. (1986). The perception of apparent motion. *Scientific American, 254*(6), 80–87.

Richardson, J. C., & Swan, K. (2003). Examining social presence in online courses in relation to students' perceived learning and satisfaction. *JALN, 7*(1), 68–88.

Rieber, L. (1990a). Animation in computer-based instruction. *Educational Technology Research and Development, 38*(1), 77–86. doi:10.1007/BF02298250

Rieber, L. (1990b). Using computer animated graphics in science instruction with children. *Journal of Educational Psychology, 82*, 135–140. doi:10.1037/0022-0663.82.1.135

Schriver, K. A. (1997). *Dynamics in document design: creating text for readers*. New York: Wiley.

Schubert, T., Regenbrecht, H., & Friedman, F. (2002). Real and illusory interaction enhance presence in virtual environments. *Presence: teleoperators and virtual environment, 11*(4), 425-434.

Shepard, R. N. (1967). Recognition memory for words, sentences and pictures. *Journal of Verbal Learning and Verbal Behavior, 6*, 156–163. doi:10.1016/S0022-5371(67)80067-7

Short, J., Williams, E., & Christie, B. (1976). *The social psychology of telecommunications*. London: John Wiley & Sons.

Siemens, G. (2004). *Learning management systems: The wrong place to start learning.* Retrieved December, 26, 2006, from http://Elearnespace.org.

Slavin, R. E. (1990). *Cooperative learning: Theory, research and practice*. London: Allyn and Bacon.

Szabo, M., & Kanuka, H. (1999). Effects of violating screen design principles of balance, unity, and focus on recall learning, study, time, and completion rates. *Journal of Educational Multimedia and Hypermedia, 8*(1), 23–42.

Tu, C.-H. (2002). The impacts of text-based CMC on online social presence. *Journal of Interactive E-learning, 1*(2), 1–24.

Viegas, F. B., & Donath, J. S. (1999, 15-20 May). Chat circles. In *CHI 99*, Pittsburgh, PA.

Vygotsky, L. S. (1984). *A formação social da mente - O desenvolvimento dos processos psicológicos superiores* (6th Ed.). São Paulo: Martins Fontes.

Wagner, E. D. (1994). In support of a functional definition of interaction. *American Journal of Distance Education, 8*(2), 6–29. doi:10.1080/08923649409526852

Wenger, E. (1998). Communities of practice. Learning as a social systems. *Systems Thinker, 9*(5).

Wheeler, S. (2005). *Creating social presence in digital learning environments: A presence of mind?* TAFE, Queensland, Australia.

Williams, T. R. (1993). What's so different about visuals? *Journal of the Society for Technical Communication, 40*, 669–676.

KEY TERMS AND DEFINITIONS

Social Presence: The extent to which virtual entities that represent others are perceived as real in an e-learning environment.

Interactions: Messages exchanged between students.

Interaction Facilities: Chat, web mail and forum.

Interface Design: Graphic project of the interface elements.

Visibility: How well the graphic elements are perceived.

Images: Graphic elements.

Animation: Graphic elements in motion.

Interactivity: The designs and strategies to stimulate social presence.

Interface Interaction Model: Theoretical model which describes means for increasing the number of interactions and for enhancing social presence.

Section 3
Technology-Enhanced Learning Design

Section 3 composes the main body of the book. It deals with technology-enhanced learning design. Various design approaches are proposed and discussed along with case studies and particular e-learning applications.

Chapter 5
E-Learning Design from a "Quality of Experience" Perspective:
Heuristics and Case-Studies

Franca Garzotto
Politecnico di Milano, Italy

ABSTRACT

This chapter considers technology-enhanced educational activities spanning along a significant period of time, and explores this context from a "quality of experience" perspective. Rather than addressing the design of technology, interface, or interactive contents for learning, our main focus is the exploration of the process-oriented, affective, socio-contextual issues involved in the design of prolonged workflows of e-learning activities. We propose a set of heuristics for designing e-learning experiences that can maintain learners' engagement along the time and achieve durable, profound educational benefits in the educational context in which they take place, and are valuable for all involved stakeholders. We also pinpoint that involving learners as experience design partners is fundamental for these purposes. Our approach is exemplified by widely discussing two case studies that involve different technologies (shared 3D virtual worlds and online collaborative storytelling) in different educational contexts – high and primary schools.

INTRODUCTION

Many existing studies that investigate design issues in e-learning from a Human-Computer Interaction perspective focus on how the characteristics of technological tools - i.e., their contents, functionality, interface, or interaction paradigms - affect learning (Clayton et al., 1998).

DOI: 10.4018/978-1-60566-940-3.ch005

Still, e-learning technology per se may have a limited educational impact unless it is included in an epistemologically coherent educational "project" that redefines the teaching-learning, student-student, and student-technology relationships, turning learners (and instructors) into researchers who can experience a stimulating process of discovery and challenge, not only sporadically or episodically but also in the long term. Our work attempts to move beyond asking "How should we design educational e-tools?" and rather explores how we can design *prolonged* e-learning *activities* in all their educational, emotional, socio-contextual characteristics. We propose a shift of focus - from the design of e-learning technology to the design of e-learning *experiences*, which focuses on the *use* of technology in real educational settings. We suggest that these aspects are equally important to be investigated as the actual characteristics of the adopted digital artifacts.

Hence we explore the concept of *quality of e-learning design* in terms of *quality of the e-learning experience,* defined as " how well a set of technology-enhanced activities serve their educational purposes, i.e., support the achievement of durable, profound educational benefits, how well they fits into the educational context in which technology is used, how pleasant and valuable they are for all involved stakeholders – learners, teachers, and families". We propose a set of heuristics for designing e-learning activities that require *prolonged engagement* of learners with technology in order to be educationally effective, and identify a number of factors that may contribute to maintain engagement. In particular, we propose that the participation of *learners as experience design partners* contributes to the quality of e-learning design, since this partnership potentially induces a number educational benefits. This view of learners in relationship to technology is relatively unexplored in HCI and in the e-learning literature, and its investigation represents a further novel contribution of our work.

The different heuristics are exemplified by widely discussing two case studies that involve different technologies (shared 3D virtual worlds and online collaborative storytelling) in two educational contexts – high and primary schools. We will highlight how the different heuristics have been applied in the design of these experiences, and the educational benefits we could measure on learners.

The rest of the paper is organized as follows. In the following section we frame our approach in the contexts of existing works in HCI and e-learning. Then we introduce our heuristics and the case studies. The conclusions pinpoint the critical aspects of our work and outline our future steps.

RATIONALE AND BACKGROUND

The term "*experience*" is associated to a wide range of concepts at different levels of abstraction and no cohesive theory of experience and experience design currently exists.

In Interaction Design, an experience is defined as the set of user-product interactions and all aspects of "experiencing" an interactive product – physical, sensual, emotional, social, and aesthetic (Marcus 2002, Norman 2004, McClennan 2005). A number of works attempt to indentify the factors that contribute to the "quality of experience", broadly defined as " how well a product serves its purposes, how well it fits into the entire context in which it is used, how pleasant and valuable it is for its users" (Alben 1996). Still, most of these works focus on "short experiences", which involve sporadic or episodic interactions for short periods of time. For this kind of experiences, quality is defined in terms of various design attributes, such as aesthetics of the interface (Austin 2000, Dalsgård & Halskov 2006, Desmet 2006, Norman 2004, Alben 1996) and usability of lay-out, information architecture, or task flow (Garret 2002).

Short experiences may be effective to achieve narrow educational benefits, mainly at the knowledge and skill levels in the Bloom taxonomy (Bloom 1964). Still, they can hardly support more profound forms of learning aimed at developing complex attitudes and skills at in the intellectual, emotional, or ethical sphere and at achieving durable educational effects that endures after the digital experience. This form of e-learning, which is the main focus of our educational research, requires time and involves the *use of a digital artifact over a prolonged period of time* (weeks or months) and a (possibly complex) *workflow of activities*. This kind of experiences are oftentimes referred to as *large experiences* in the HCI literature (Forlizzi 2004, Kaptelin et al. 2006).

To enforce quality in large experiences, *engagement* is acknowledged as a fundamental factor; the problem of how to "*design for long term engagement*" has recently received attention in the HCI community (Bickmore 2009), mostly in domains such as wellness applications and games, but is largely unexplored in the e-learning context. Many studies pinpoint that *enjoyment* and *fun* are fundamental to maintain engagement along the time (Bickmore 2009, Norman 2004, Sweetser 2005, Blythe et al. 2004, Csikszentmihalyi 1991, Malone 1982), and is central to any learning activity (DiSessa 2001), as also suggested by various educational theories such as Active Learning (Bonwell & Eison 1991) and Game-based Learning (Prensky 2001). Enjoyment represents a key motivation for engaging learners in proposed activities and is a crucial driver to involve them emotionally and to create an intrinsically rewarding learning experience.

In the educational community, designing e-learning activities for long term instructional units, such as a course or a curriculum, is addressed within the *Instructional Design* (ID) process (Gagne 1992, Heinrich 1983). Still, to our knowledge most of existing researches in ID that consider technology-mediated education do not explicitly investigate the practice of educational activity design from a "quality of the experience" perspective. A number of works (Cobb 2003, Botturi 2003, Heirich 1983,) report case studies that can be regarded as examples of "large experience design", but they do not explore explicitly the process- oriented design characteristics of long term interaction with technology that make it more conducive to learning. They rather tend to investigate how traditional or new theories on learning represent the epistemological underpinnings of different ID solutions for e-learning (Karagiorgi et al Symeou 2005) or focus on models that can be used as conceptual means for structuring a "correct" ID process (Botturi 2008, Gustafson & Branch 1997, Retalis 2002).

With respect to the role of role of learners in the design process, most examples of large experiences reported in the e-learning literature are designed *for* learners but not *with* learners as partners: their design is driven by educators only – usually before the experience takes place. In contrast, we pinpoint that the design of large experiences can be shaped as a fluid, evolving process that may occur during the experience itself, and propose that the active involvement of learners in this process can contributes to the achievement of relevant educational benefits and to increase satisfaction of all involved stakeholders (learners, teachers, and families).

The role of learners in relationship to technology has been investigated in the HCI field, particularly by the Interaction Design and Children community, where it has been classified along four main profiles (Druin 1999, Druin 2002, Hourcade 2006): *user, tester, informant,* and *design partner*. In the role of *users,* children help researchers to understand the impact that an existing technology has on child users, so such technology can be enhanced or future technologies can be designed. In the role of *tester* (Kaplan et al., 2004, Hana et al. 2004), children test prototypes, and testing results are used to improve the product to release. In the role of *informant*, children play a part in the design process at various stages, e.g., they may involved in the elicitation of needs (Druin et al. 2001, Dindler et al. 2005, Scaife et al. 1997, Read et al. 2002), or they may be asked for input on design sketches or low-tech prototypes or for feedback once the technology is developed (Becker 2003, Belly et al. 2006, Jason Li 2007, Hanna 2004). Finally, with the role of *design partner* (Druin et al. 1997, Cassel &Roykoioiai 2001, Garzotto 2008, Guha 2005, Guha 2004, Jensen & Skov 2005, Rossou et al. 2007), children are considered to be equal stakeholders in the design of new technologies, in ways that are appropriate for children and the process. This classification considers children's participation during the process of developing *digital artifacts* - mainly educational games (Verhaegt 2006), storytelling systems (Druin et al. 1997, Antle 2006, Alborzi et at. 2000, Garzotto 2008, Garzotto & Forfori 2007, Stanton et al. 2001, Benford et al. 2000), or learning tools for outdoor or indoor contexts such as schools (Stanton et al. 2001), cultural heritage sites (Rossou et al. 2007), natural environments (Randell et al. 2003). Still, the above classification does not consider youngsters as *stakeholders in experience design*. To our knowledge, only two studies report examples where learners play this role. The research reported in (Clayton 1998) adapts the classical programming walkthrough method for the purpose of designing computer supported educational activities in elementary school science. Still, the methodological interest of this paper, as claimed by its authors, is in the comparison of the walkthrough technique for activity design against its conventional use for interface design, rather than investigating the role of children as experience design partners. This is the subject of the contextual study reported in (Garzotto 2008), which explored the educational benefits of this multigenerational partnership for primary school children and paved the ground for the more general approach discussed in this chapter.

HEURISTIC QUALITY CRITERIA FOR E-LEARNING "LARGE" EXPERIENCES

The quality of a large experience for e-learning is determined by both the intrinsic *educational* characteristics of contents and tasks provided by technology, and the capabilities of involving learners in activities that maintain their *engagement* from a prolonged time. While it might be easy to keep a young person engaged with a system for a short time, having youngsters repeatedly involved in prolonged activities that have "something serious" behind (i.e., are not just pure fun) is a complex task.

The following heuristics define some attributes for large experiences can be useful to design activities in an e-learning large experience in such a way that they foster long term engagement and potentially make the experience particularly conductive to profound forms of learning in the long term. These heuristics are based on the analysis of existing literature in HCI and e-learning (as discussed in the previous section), and on our on-the-field expertise achieved in the context of a wide number of e-learning projects involving hundreds of teachers and thousands of students in real education environments, from primary to high school.

H1: Content-Driven Activities

To foster quality of an e-learning large experience, contents which learner are exposed to should be tailored to the developmental and instructional level of learners and to the educational goals of the context of use. Task completion should draw directly on the knowledge that the activity is designed to foster in its users, and should promote reflection about or application of such knowledge (Garzotto 2007, Fish 2005).

H2: Blended Activities

Learning is facilitated by the effective combination of different kinds of (digital and physical) resources, and different modes of developing knowledge and skills – a paradigm known as *Blended Learning* (Werger 1999). This implies that concepts, topics, and tasks introduced by the different technology-mediated activities should promote off-line reflections and should be appropriate for further off-line exploration and application; the technological experience should be smoothly extensible to, or integrated with, ancillary educational activities occurring in the classroom, at home (e.g., reading, writing, drawing, story-telling, group discussions, ...), or during outdoor experiences (e.g., school trips). This interplay of tasks in the real and the virtual world is not only important from a cognitive perspective, as pinpointed by Blended Learning theories, but also makes learning more "situated" (Sasha 2002, Brown, Collins, & Duguid 1989).

H3: Scaffolding

Within the execution of an activity, proper guidance and feedbacks should be provided to learners by the technological tool or by a (possibly remote and online) tutor in response to incorrect actions or incomplete tasks; such scaffolding should offer an opportunity for learning, exposing learners to educational content and encouraging them to continue the activity (Sweetser 2005).

H4: Structured, Goal-Oriented Activities

As opposed to spontaneous interaction without specific objectives, activities in an e-learning large experience should provide learners with clear goals at appropriate times, to help them concentrate on the educational tasks, develop proper strategies, and finalize their actions. Reflection, constructive discussion, and engagement are more effectively achieved when the workflow is well organized and focused (Sweetser 2005).

H5: Concentration

The activity should keep the learner's concentration through an appropriate work-load and proper stimuli, so that the person's attention is completely absorbed by the activity, and all relevant skills are employed in it (Sweetser 2005, Csikszentmihalyi 1991).

H6: Challenge

For many learners, testing their abilities and overcoming obstacles creates emotions and rewards. From an educational perspective, challenge helps learners to focus attention, inspires creativity, and fosters the development and application of skills or strategies (Fisher 2005). To be "sufficiently" challenging, the required tasks should match the learner skill level without being discouragingly hard or boringly easy; they may progress through a series of challenges requiring a progressive level of skills, unlocking new challenges and opportunities along the way. Challenge can be promoted by means of competition, as discussed in H8.3.

H7: Pure Gaming

As proposed by Game-Based Learning approaches (Presky 2001, Monk 2002, Revelle 2003), games provide emotionally driven situations that foster engagement and support the acquisition of a variety of skills, e.g., learners' ability to collect information from different sources and make decisions quickly, to apply their knowledge for creative problem solving, to develop strategies for overcoming obstacles, to optimize performance within constraints. In the long term, games foster the very attitude we would all like our learners to have: interested, competitive, cooperative, results-oriented, actively seeking information and solutions (Steriner et al. 2006, Desurvivre et al. 2004). "Serious moments" which require cognitive effort or critical reflection on complex concepts at individual or social level, should be interplayed with pure gaming tasks to break the intellectual tension, refresh interest, and stimulate engagement.

H8: Social Interaction

The social basis for learning, particularly in early years and primary education, has been acknowledged since the seminal research of the Russian psychologist L. Vygotsky (Vygotsky 1978) and is the principle underlying the paradigm of *Collaborative Learning*. In the context of e-learning, social interaction represents both a vehicle to learn collaboration attitudes and skills, and a powerful *motivator* to engage in educational content and educational tasks. Various forms of social interaction may promote the educational effectiveness of an e-learning large experience: **connection, cooperation**, and **competition**.

H8.1: Social Interaction: Connection

The experience should create the feeling of being "a member of a group" (community) and promote connection with other people inside or outside the technology mediated experience: these features enhance the sense of social *identity* and enforces the feeling of *self-recognition* without which learning attitudes, in young people, may be weakened (Rogoff 1990, Werger 1999). Activities should include moments to discuss strategies and solutions with others, which is a way "to make thinking visible" and to create a more tangible context for what has been learned, building the conditions for *Situated Learning* (Brown, Collins, & Duguid 1989).

H8.2: Social Interaction: Cooperation

Cooperation can take two forms in a e-learning large experience:

- *Co-located cooperation among shoulder-to-shoulder mates*. In many situations occurring in the conventional classroom, learners learn by interacting with each other in a face-to-face situation. In technology enhanced environments, computers are seldom used individually, but there are typically groups of 2-3 students, each one working together with a single device.
- *Remote cooperation* with distant peers (implicit in multi-user technological environments, e.g., on-line shared worlds), which is less common in conventional school contexts.

In both cases, activities must be structured so that they require the active involvement of *all* group members. For this purpose, activities should have clear *shared* goals that pinpoint the need for more than one person to be involved, and for complementary skills and knowledge. They should support the acknowledgment of the mutual benefits of working together (e.g., through appropriate feedbacks). The need of coordination with others should not impose a suspension of individual activities: learners should not be forced to wait inactively "until others finish something" but should be enabled to continue to experience novel activity details.

H8.3: Social Interaction: Competition

Most young people gain satisfaction from competing against and beating peers. Although competition is in antithesis of cooperation, the need or desire to compete with others is a very common impetus that motivates individuals to cooperate with each other in order to form a stronger competitive force. Competition adds emotions that make the experience more exciting and fun (Vorderer 2003, Ducheneaut 2006, Garzotto & Poggi 2009), and is a powerful motivator for being engaged in educational content, both during technology mediated activities, and before them, e.g., in preparation for the "race".

H8.4: Social Interaction: Scalability

The educational activities supported by technology need to engage *small groups as well larger groups,* enabling multiuser (not necessarily synchronous) interaction. If the use of a digital tool product involves the active participation of few students while the others are totally passive, the latter will become rapidly bored, and will lose interest in the experience. Teachers should be enabled to *scale up* the use of technology to support collaboration and social interaction in a way that can potentially involve both small groups and the whole class.

H9: Flexibility of the Workflow

The workflow of activities, although focused and well structured, should be sufficiently flexible in order to accommodate the needs of different educational contexts, to suit the profile of a class and its different learners, and to meet their specific educational and curricular needs. Flexibility is also a prerequisite to enable the participation of learners as experience co-designers, as discussed below.

H10: Learners as Experience Co-Designers

Children can contribute, with the design team, to define an effective workflow of educational activities with the given technology, and this intergenerational partnership in experience design can lead to creative solutions and unexpected innovations in the way technology can be used in an educational setting (Garzotto 2008). The technology-mediated activities designed to achieve specific educational goals should be interplayed with moments during which learners *document* the experience as it proceeds, and *critically reflect* on it, e.g., on the aspects that have been more difficult or more satisfactory, on the tasks that can be improved or extended, on what has been learned from the overall experience. These moments of reflection and documentation should become *part of the experience itself*, and can support a novel form of *meta-cognition* (Hatman 2001) that plays a critical role in a successful e-learning experience. As a result of this meta-cognition process, learner can develop a *project oriented attitude towards technology* and a critical capability of *reflecting on the role of technology itself* in their life. As pinpointed in (Garzotto & Schelhowe 2008), this attitude is fundamental to overcome the new kind of *digital divide* arising among young generations, which does not result from having no or limited access to ICT, but is produced by "remaining *only a user*" vs. "becoming *a critical actor*" who can exploit technology in order to achieve large scale goals and to increase his or her emotional, cultural, or social capital.

DESIGNING E-LEARNING LARGE EXPERIENCES: CASE STUDIES

The Hypermedia Open Center (HOC) of Politecnico di Milano has been working for over ten years with various national and international institutions to promote the adoption of different types of technological tools in real educational settings and to investigate the actual benefits of e-learning. The characteristics of all these projects is that they have not involved episodic or sporadic use of technology, but have been shaped as large experiences, spanning for weeks or months (in some case, across multiple years). So far, these initiatives have involved over 17.000 students – from primary to high schools, in 4 different continents.

This section describes some examples from our projects that highlight the application of the heuristics introduced in the previous section, and discusses the educational benefits achieved by the students participating in the reported e-learning experiences. The first set of case studies pinpoint the application of heuristics H1-H8, while the last example highlights mainly (but not exclusively) the implementation of the principle of "Learners as experience co-designers" (H10).

E-Learning Large Experiences using 3D Virtual Worlds

We have exploited the use of collaborative 3D virtual environments for teen agers education since 2000, in five different projects. The educational

Figure 1. The typical structure of edutainment activities in our 3D Virtual Worlds

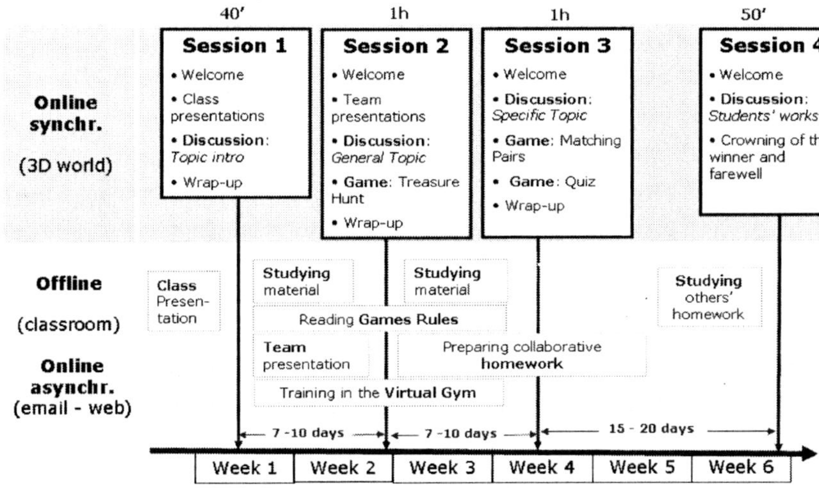

content of these projects is heterogeneous, spanning from Leonardo da Vinci's machines (Virtual Leonardo Project - Barbieri & Paolini 2000) to the Dead Sea Scrolls (Shrine Educational Experience Project - Di Blas et al. 2005), from European Modern history (Learning@Europe Project) (Di Blas & Poggi 2006, Paolini & Di Blas 2006) to Italian Medieval History (Stori@Lombardia Project, Project, Poggi & Torrebruno 2007) and the social value of sports (Learning@SocialSport Project, Di Blas, Paolini, Poggi & Torrebruno 2008). The 3D environments developed in these projects are implemented using WebTalk (Barbieri 2000), a proprietary platform for 3D shared virtual worlds developed at our lab before the advent of Second Life Technology (www.secondlife.com).

Besides transmission of knowledge, one of the main educational benefits that we attempted to achieve in all these projects was the promotion of values and ethical attitudes, such as positive feeling towards people from different countries and backgrounds, respect and curiosity for them, reciprocal trust and accountability, importance of collaboration, and increased interest for the subject matter of the experience and for "school" in general.

All our large experiences in shared 3D virtual worlds have a common experience design "format". Participants are organized in two teams, each one grouping two classes of students from two different geographical locations. As highlighted in Figure 1, the experience is *focused* and *carefully structured*, with a precise set of clearly planned goal-oriented activities to take place within and between each 3D session *(heuristic H4: Structured, Goal Oriented Activities)*.

Remote peers meet in the 3D world for 4 times along about 6 weeks, and in each session are engaged in (a subset of) the following activities:

- Solving an array of knowledge-driven quizzes about educational material they study before online meetings (*Heuristic H1:Content Driven Activities; Heuristic H5: Concentration).* Quiz solution allows "winners" to gain points for their team (*Heuristic H8.3: Social Interaction-Competition)*; the complexity of the quizzes progressively increases as the experience proceeds along the time and the level of students competence about the experience subject evolves (*Heuristic H6: Challenge).* Quiz solution involves synchronous collaboration (via chat) among remote members of the same team (*Heuristic H8.2: Social Interaction-Cooperation*) as well as on-site cooperation of all members of the same class. The systems supports up to eight simultaneous users, but while few students control interaction the others are not passive: they search on printed material and on the Internet information useful to solve the quizzes, discuss and propose solutions (*Heuristic H.,4: Social Interaction-Scalability*).

- Playing team-against-team games of different nature: discovery games (e.g., treasure hunt) and interaction skill games (e.g., moving avatars to overcome obstacles) *(Heuristic H7: Pure Gaming).* Games are designed so that they keep the attention of the whole team attention fully absorbed (*Heuristic H5: Concentration),* both in students who are in control of the interaction and in the rest of the classroom, who can follow what happens in the 3D virtual world from the screen projection on the wall, give hints, and root for their team (*Heuristic H.,4: Social Interaction-Scalability*).
- "Just talking" with remote peers, using the chat tool of the 3D environment in scheduled moments of the 3D session; this increases the sense of "being connected" and promotes the sense of "community" among members of the same team and among all students participating in the same project (*Heuristic H8.1: Social Interaction-Connection*).

Online human tutors from the educational staff of our lab guide the interaction remotely, leading participants from an activity to the other, moderating discussions, refereeing games and awarding points; face-to-face, every group of students is closely followed by one or more on-site educators, who supervise the reading of contents and the preparation of assignments, discussing them with pupils (*Heuristic H3: Scaffolding*).

In addition to 3D sessions, the workflow includes freely scheduled social activities outside the 3D environment (*Heuristic H9: Flexibility of the Workflow*). Students can interact online several times at their own pace, either individually or in small groups, during the intervals between 3D sessions, both synchronously, using a conventional chat tool, and a*synchronously,* using the forum or the email. Synchronous and asynchronous interaction is aimed to complete research assignments in collaboration with remote team partners (*Heuristic H8.2: Social Interaction-Cooperation*) or simply to "connect" (*Heuristic H8.1: Social Interaction: Connection*). Finally, online activities alternate with more "traditional" offline activities (e.g., study of printed material, discussions in the classroom), blending different modes of developing knowledge and promoting values (*Heuristic H2: Blended Activities*).

We shortly exemplify this approach providing some details on *Learning@Europe (L@E)* project. Started in 2004 in collaboration with Accenture International Foundation, L@E targets European high-school students, between 14 and 19 years of age, and aims at promoting values such as awareness of one's own national identity, respect for others' national identities, and development of a common European identity. Since 2004 over 6000 students have been involved in L@E.

Students from 4 different European countries at a time meet in the 3D environment (Figure 2), study and discuss the history of each other's country, present their own national symbols, reflect (via chat, forum, or email) on the historical development of theirs and others' national identities, and find that similarities in national values, as well as in their own lifestyles and interests, are more relevant than differences (Di Blas, Paolini & Poggi 2005, Di Blas, Poggi & Reeves 2006, Di Blas & Poggi 2007).

We could measure (Di Blas & Poggi 2006, Paolini & Di Blas 2006) that students concluded the experience with an improved attitude towards other cultures and nations, a more articulated

Figure 2. Students' avatars in the 3D shared world of Learning@Europe

view of what Europe is, and – often – a sense of surprise at discovering how much their country's history is found interesting and respected by other nations. Surveys to teachers reveal every year high or very high improvements in terms of positive attitudes towards other cultures for 70% to 89% of students; 35-50% of students acknowledge in their surveys a marked change in their opinion of other countries and Europe. Another relevant change of attitude reported by many teachers was the discovery, by the students, of their "Europeanness". A French teacher for example said, during a focus group in 2006: "*before the L@E experience my students felt French; now they feel French and European*".

E-Learning Large Experiences using On-line Storytelling Tools

In 2007 a team from our lab carried on a contextual study in a local primary school for a period of three months, involving two teachers and twenty-four children aged 10-11. Our research goal was to explore how children of this age can contribute to design an effective workflow of educational activities with the given technology *(H10: Learners as Experience Co-designers)* and to identify the educational benefits induced by this co-design process (Garzotto, 2008).

The assignment to learners was to collaboratively build a hypermedia "story" on a history subject using an online tool for cooperative storytelling (*Heuristic H8.2: Social Interaction-Collaboration*). The tool is *1001stories* (a name inspired by the well-know collection of tales "The book of One Thousand and One Nights") and was developed at our laboratory to support the simple and fast creation of multi-channel "hyperstories" (i.e., non linear multimedia narratives), and their delivery on different devices - CD-ROMs, Web, and MP3 player (Bolchini & Garzotto, 2008).

The entire class was organized into eight small groups (three persons each), according to their current practice during computer lab activities. After a preliminary training session, each group focused on the creation, organization, and implementation of the multimedia contents for a specific Topic within the general subject of the hyperstory: "Milan during the Roman Empire Age" – or "Roman Milan" for short. This subject was chosen since it was the subject of a school trip (i.e., the visit to the Roman ruins in downtown Milan) children performed before the experience, during which they took pictures and collected printed material at various archeological sites (*Heuristic H1: Content-driven Activities; Heuristic H2: Blended Activities*).

The entire class mostly worked together in the computer lab. Still, in some cases, a single group of students used the only computer in the classroom during breaks, while the rest of the class was playing in the corridor, to complete their work on the assigned topic (*Heuristics H8.3: Social interaction-Scalability*).

A detailed workflow of the hyperstory development experience was defined by a team of e-learning designers at our lab on the basis of a previous study *(Heuristic H4: Structured, Goal Oriented Activities)*. In 2006, over one hundred of high-schools schools in Italy used 1001stories in the context of a national "hyperstory competition" launched by our university (www.policultura.it). From the questionnaires filled by teacher participants, we identified the "optimal" macro structure of activities that were proposed to teachers of the Roman Milan Project. This structured workflow was composed of the following "phases", each one defined in terms of activities to be carried on with the hyperstory tool, expected timing, and corresponding outputs to be delivered: *Build the Hyperstory Structure, Identify the Source of Contents, Create Digital Contents, Instantiate the Structure.*

Children as Large Experience Design Partners

During the development of the hyperstory, our design team stimulated children to express ideas and suggestions on how to carry on the different phases, giving them a voice on the experience design process. We interplayed development tasks with group discussion and brainstorming on the current activity, on how to perform it in the best way, and on what to do next. We also asked children to give us feedbacks on their work, keeping track of how they cooperated both within the groups and among groups, and documenting their experience during or after the execution of the different activities.

Children gave a very creative contribution to the implementation of the workflow and introduced a number of activities that our design team had not envisioned in our previous projects involving 1001stories (*Heuristic H9: Flexibility of the Workflow*). For example, they had the idea of creating their own visual content for the story to complement the material found on books or on the Internet. They spent a significant amount of time in creating drawings and paintings to be included in their story (see figure 3 and figure 4), thus blending more "traditional" offline activities in the classroom with technology-mediated activities (*Heuristic H2: Blended Activities*). Children found an original way to *engage families in the experience*: They asked parents to visit Milan together during the weekend, and took further pictures of places and monuments related to the Roman period.

These proposals were conceptualized in the definition of the "new" activities "Drawing" and "Visit Milan with family" (see figure 4) within the phase "Create Digital Contents".

Figure 3. Integrating digital and tangible activities

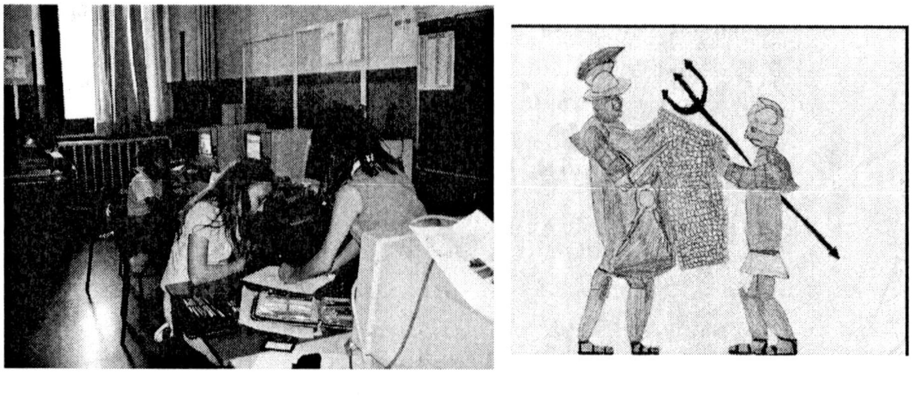

Figure 4. Visit to Roman monuments in town (left) and children's representation of the activity (right)

Figure 5. Audio recording (how it was executed (left), and how children represented it (right))

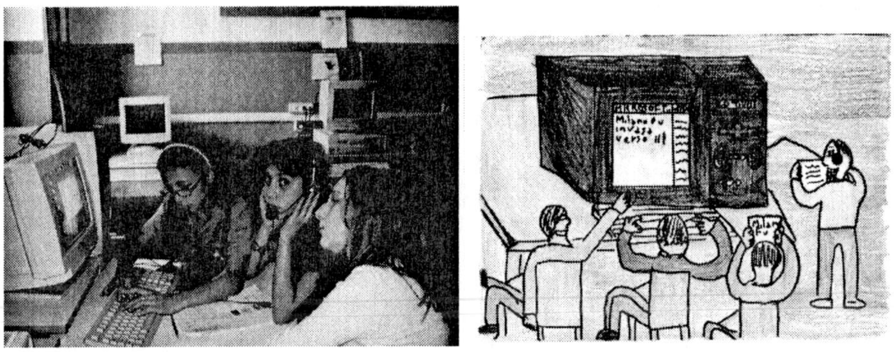

Another example of children's contribution to experience co-design concerns the activity of audio tracks creation. Usually, previous 1001 stories users have a single speaker reading an entire semantic unit of the story. In contrast, our children decided to split each single unit in pieces, and to assign the reading and audio recording of each piece to a different group member (figure 5). This solution was particularly time consuming: Children read and read again each unit many times before being satisfied of the voice and tone of all actors, and spent quite a lot of time to merge the pieces in a single audio track. Still, they were very satisfied of the final effect, which was particularly nice and much more engaging for a story reader than the use of a single voice for each unit.

Children gave an important contribution to shaping the *documentation activity.* Initially, we simply proposed them to take textual notes on a project journal, but they progressively improved and refined this raw technique. Some children asked to use the digital camera to document the work of their group and of the others. Others decided to create drawings (e.g., while they were waiting of their turn to use the computer) to describe what was happening (see figures 4 and 5 – left side). One of the most significant suggestions generated by children was the adoption of *Activity Cards* and *Phase Boxes* as tools for compact documentation and efficient organization of the experience design material (this idea was inspired by a similar "Box and Card" Montessorian

Figure 6. Cards organization (right) and poster creation (center and left)

method of organizing learning material that they adopt in the classroom). Cards represent an activity, using different colors to distinguish different types of works. Boxes represent Phases and were progressively filled in as cards were generated. When the hyperstory was finally built, children created the final presentation of the experience on a large poster composed of the activity cards associated to the most representative image of the activity (a drawing or a camera picture) (see figure 6).

It is interesting to notice that during the whole project, learners expressed a level of attention, discipline, and emotional participation that was surprising for both teachers and us. They seldom moved from their place for reasons that were not functional of their current task, nor talked about subjects other than their story. They were completed absorbed by their work without being distracted by the surroundings e.g., they did not realize when the bell rang and it was break or lunch time (*Heuristic H5: Concentration*). A boy affected by the Tourrette Syndrome (a serious neurological disorder characterized by the presence of multiple motor and phonic tics) was so immersed in what he was doing that none of his symptoms manifested.

When the hyperstory on Roman Milan was completed, children were so engaged in the project, so excited of their results, and so conscious of the value of documenting their experience, that they decided to do some extra work: to tell "their" story of the whole process, and to add it as a new component in their hyperstory. To describe this component, they adopted an original metaphor, presenting the project work as a cook recipe – the "Milan Roman Digital Meal". The content resources needed for the hyperstory were described as "ingredients" for the recipe and the needed activities as to-do steps to prepare and cook "Milan Roman" (see Figure 7). Then they linked the recipe to additional hyperstory units, each one describing the *emotional* perception of the experience by each group. Some groups narrated for example how surprised they were to discover the hidden past of their town, and how much they like to show their story on the Internet to their family at home. Other children invented rhymes or funny songs to describe their feelings. All groups also took new pictures and created new drawings for the purpose of this new section.

Discussion

This case study shows that 10-11 years old children can actively participate in experience design not only as informants but also as co-designers, and that this intergenerational partnership can lead to creative solutions and unexpected innovations in the way technology can be used in an educational setting. Young learners can really represent *the* driving force in designing large experiences around a given technology, introducing novel ways to use it that might not be envisioned by an adult design team.

Another, perhaps more important aspect highlighted by our study is that the involvement of children as experience design partners may promote a number of *educational benefits*.

Figure 7. The "reflection on the project" topic of Roman Milan (recipe on the right)

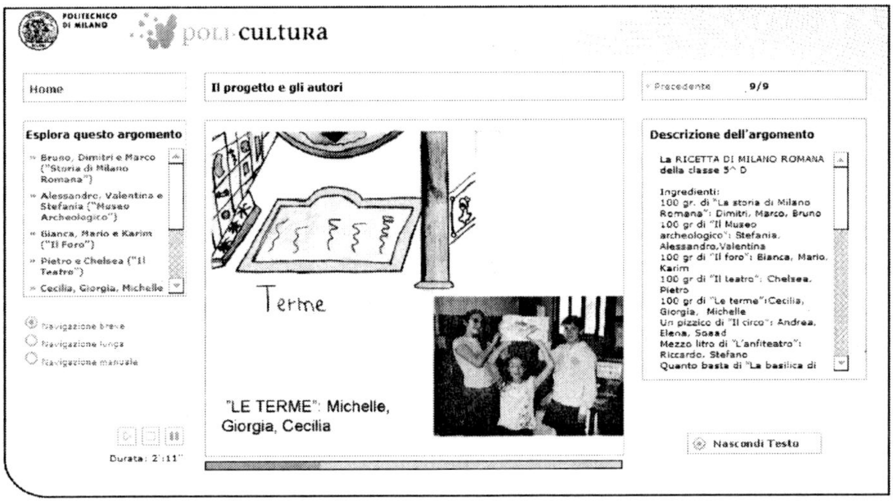

Teachers, interviewed at the end of the overall project, reported that this co-design work stimulated children's *ability of conceptual representation* and improved their *capability of structuring ideas at the level of process* (while typical school activities for students of this age promote structuring capabilities at the level of narrative planning or organization of factual knowledge). Teacher also mentioned that *collaboration skills* were promoted by the group mode of carrying on hyperstory creation *and* the experience design work.

In addition, the experience co-design activities fostered *reflection* on the experience (which continued in the classroom). Reflection was not implemented just as brainstorming and discussion, but *became part of the overall experience.* It was operationalized by means of the same technological tools used for the experience, thus making a *reflexive use of technology*. By creating new hyperstory units about their feelings on project, children brought the unconscious elements of their experience to conscious awareness, and invested time and energy in making such understanding explicit in order to share it with the future readers of their digital artifact.

A number of researches in HCI report critical reflections on values, emotions, attitudes, and ways of looking the world that are induced by a technology (Norman 2004, Friedman 2003); the emerging field of Reflexive Design (or Critical Design) (Sengers et al. 2005) proposes that an analysis of these aspects should be a core principle of the design of digital products. Our children implemented this concept in a fresh, creative, and original way. From a pedagogical perspective, what these children did was quintessentially 'constructionist' (Harel and Papert 1991): they learned through owning and publicizing their learning product, reflected on the process, and organized such constructionist work around a single cohesive theme.

According to teachers, before this project children asked to use the computer in the classroom only for gaming; after this experience they autonomously used it to search for information or for creating representations needed for their ordinary classroom work. Returning to school after the summer holidays, many children asked to use 1001 stories tool again, and to build another hyperstory on a new subject. This can be regarded as the embryonic achievement of a *project oriented attitude towards technology* and a (rudimental) critical capability of reflecting *on its role.*

Finally, this case study highlights that young learners can play as *experience design innovators*; their freshness, imagination, and technology fluency enable them to discover creative forms of using digital artifacts and novel modes of integrating technology in their every day life, in a way that can go beyond the expectations of an adult design team.

CONCLUSION

The main contribution in this chapter is to provide a more comprehensive understanding of how technology can be used in real educational settings, of the gamut of process-oriented, affective, socio-contextual issues involved in e-learning design, and of the variety of benefits that we may achieve in the (meta-)cognitive, emotional, ethical sphere when we adopt a "quality of the experience" approach.

Putting computers in the classroom, supporting well equipped computer labs, providing innovative and engaging systems, may represent only a pre-condition for exploiting the educational potential of ICT at schools. Educational technology per se does not guarantees learning: it is the way it is used, i.e., how we design technological contexts of use, how we engage learners, and how they decide to get engaged, that can either promote or undermine enduring learning benefits (DiSessa 2001).

We believe that the use of technology holds stronger educational value, in terms of development of durable attitudes and competencies related to the cognitive, emotional, and relational spheres, if technology use is carefully shaped as a prolonged workflow of activities. Therefore in this chapter we suggest a number of design principles, or heuristics, for e-learning activities that aim at fostering e-learning design quality from a large experience perspective, exemplifying them by means of two case studies.

Our heuristics pinpoint the need of organizing the use of technology around a well structured set of challenging, content-driven activities that span along a significant period of time, are designed to meet clear goals that require collaboration, and are interplayed with moments of gaming and competition as well as conventional classroom activities.

The most original heuristics we propose is to involve learners as partners in the process of experience design, pinpointing how this participation leads to a number of educational benefits: stronger collaboration skills, goal oriented attitudes, and critical thinking capability. This principle introduces a novel, more holistic perspective to how learners can be considered in relation to technology, broadening the theoretical perspective on what young learners experience when they are exposed to digital artifacts.

It is important to notice that the proposed set of heuristics is not meant to be exhaustive and not all of them must necessary be applied in the design of any large experiences for e-learning. We hope that future studies and contributions from other researchers will extend or refine our approach, which can be regarded as a preliminary step towards a conceptual framework that can support both the design of an optimal e-learning large experience and the evaluation of its effectiveness from a "quality of experience" perspective. Our future work will further test the validity of our heuristics through additional empirical studies in real educational contexts, and will attempt to give them a stronger theoretical foundation.

REFERENCES

Alben, L. (1996). Quality of Experience. *Interaction, 13*(5), 12–15.

Alborzi, H., et al. (2000). Designing StoryRooms: Interactive Storytelling Spaces for Children. In *Proc. DIS'00*. New York: ACM Press.

Antle, A. (2003). *Case Study: The Design of CB-4Kids' Story Builder*. Proc. IDC 2003, Preston, UK, ACM Press, 59-67.

Austin, H. (2000). Design for What? Six Dimensions of Activity. *Interaction*, 17–22.

Barbieri, T. (2000). Networked Virtual Environments for the Web: The WebTalk-I and WebTalk-II Architectures. In *IEEE Computer Multimedia & Expo 2000 (ICME)*, New York, NY.

Barbieri, T., & Paolini, P. (2000). Cooperative Visits to WWW Museum Sites a Year Later: Evaluating the effect. In *Proceeding Museums& Web2000*, Minneapolis, USA.

Bekker, M. (2003). KidReporter: a User Requirements Gathering Technique for Designing with Children. *Interacting with Computers*, *15*, 187–202. doi:10.1016/S0953-5438(03)00007-9

Benford, S., et al. (2000). Designing Storytelling Technologies to Encourage Collaboration Between Young Children. In *Proc. CHI 2000*, The Hague, Netherlands (pp. 236-245).

Bickmore, T., Consolvo, S., & Intille, S. (2009). Engagement by Design. In *CHI 2009 Extended Abstracts*.

Bloom, B. S., Mesia, B. B., & Krathwohl, D. R. (1964). *Taxonomy of Educational Objectives*. New York: David McKay.

Blythe, M., Hassenzahl, M., & Wright, P. (2004). More funology. A special issue. *Interaction*, *11*(5).

Bolchini, D., & Garzotto, F. (2008). Success Factors for Hypermedia Tools in Education. In *Proc. ACM Hypertext 2008*, June 2008, Pittsburgh, USA.

Bonwell, C., & Eison, J. (1991). *Active Learning: Creating Excitement in the Classroom. AEHE-ERIC Higher Education Report No.1*. Washington, DC.

Botturi, L. (2008). E2ML: A Tool for Sketching Instructional Designs. In L. Botturi & T. Stubbs (eds.), *Handbook of Visual Languages in Instructional Design: Theories and Practices* (pp. 112-132). Hershey, PA: Informing Science Reference.

Botturi, L., Inglese, T., & Rozalèn, S. (2003). Design and Trust as Key Factor in E-learning. In *AACE, SITE 2003*, Albuquerque, New Mexico (pp. 1379-1382).

Brown, J. S., Collins, A., & Duguid, P. (1989). Situated cognition and the culture of learning. *Educational Researcher*, *18*(1), 32–42.

Cassel, J., & Ryokoiai, K. (2001). Making space for Voice: Technologies to support Children Fantasy and Storytelling. *Personal and Ubiquitous Computing*, *5*(3). Clayton, L., Brand, C., Cherry, G., & Rader, C. (98). Adapting User Interface Design Methods to the Design of Educational Activities. In *Proc. CHI 98*, Los Angeles, CA, USA (pp. 619-628).

Cobb, P. (2003). Design Experiments in Educational Research. *Educational Researcher*, *32*(1), 9–13. doi:10.3102/0013189X032001009

Collins, A., & Ferguson, W. (2003). Epistemic forms and epistemic games: Structures and strategies to guide inquiry. *Educational Psychologist*, *28*(1), 25–42. doi:10.1207/s15326985ep2801_3

Csikszentmihalyi, M. (1991). *Flow: The Psychology of Optimal Experience*. New York: Harper Perennial.

Dalsgård, P., & Halskov, K. (2006). Real Life Experiences with Experience Design. In *Proc. NordiCHI 2006*, (pp. 331-340).

Desmet, P. M. A. (2008). *Pleasant emotions in product experience*. In P.M.A. Desmet, M.A. Karlsson, & J. van Erp (Eds.), *Design & Emotion Moves*. Cambridge, UK: Cambridge Scholars Publishing.

Desurvire, H., Maplan, M., & Toth, J. A. (2004). Using heuristics to evaluate the playability of games. In *Extended Abstracts of CHI 2004* (pp. 1509-1512).

Di Blas, N., Paolini, P., & Poggi, C. (2005). Educational benefits: testing and evaluation of a collaborative 3d world. In *Proc. ED-MEDIA 2005* (pp. 1002-1011).

Di Blas, N., Paolini, P., Poggi, C., & Torrebruno, A. (2008). 3D Worlds for Learning and Play: 6 years of Experience. In *Proc. E-Learn 2008*, AACE.

Di Blas, N., & Poggi, C. (2006). 3D for Cultural Heritage and Education: Evaluating the Impact. In D. Bearman & J. Trant (Eds.), *Selected Papers from Museums and the Web '06*. Albuquerque, NM: Archives and Museum Informatics.

Di Blas, N., Poggi, C., & Reeves, T. (2006). Collaborative Learning in a 3D Virtual Environment: Design Factors and Evaluation Results. In *Proc. 7th International Conference of the Learning Sciences (ICLS)*, Indiana University, Bloomington, IN (Vol. 1, pp. 127-133).

Dindler, C., et al. (2005), *Mission from Mars-A Method for Exploring User Requirements for Children in a Narrative Space*. In *Proc. IDC 2005*, Boulder, USA.

DiSessa, A. (2001). *Changing minds: computer, learning, and literacy*. Cambridge, MA: MIT Press.

Druin, A. (Ed.). (1999). *The Design of Children's Technology*. San Francisco, CA: Morgan Kaufmann.

Druin, A. (1999). Cooperative Inquiry: Developing New Technologies for Children with Children. In *Proc. ACM CHI '99*, Pittsburgh, PA, USA (pp. 592-599).

Druin, A. (2002). The Child as Learner, Critic, Inventor, and Technology Design Partner. *International Journal of Technology and Design Education, 12*, 189–213. doi:10.1023/A:1020255806645

Druin, A., et al. (1997). KidPad: A Design Collaboration Between Children, Technologists, and Educators. In *Proc. CHI' 97*, Atlanta, GA, USA.

Druin, A., et al. (2001). Designing a Digital Library for Young Children: An Intergenerational Partnership. In *Proc. JCDL'01*, Roanoke, Virginia, USA (pp. 398-405).

Ducheneaut, N., Yee, N., Nickel, E., & Moore, R. (2006). Alone Together: Exploring the social dynamics of massively multiplayer online games. In *Proc. CHI2006*, (pp. 407-416).

Fisch, M. S. (2005). Making Educational Computer Games "Educational." In *Proc. IDC'05*, Boulder, CO, June 2005.

Forlizzi, J., & Battarbee, K. (2004). Understanding Experience in Interactive Systems. In *Proc. DIS2004*, Cambridge, MA, USA (pp. 261-68).

Friedman, B., & Kahn, P. H., Jr. (2003). Human values, ethics, and design. In J. A. Jacko & A. Sears (Eds.), *The human-computer interaction handbook* (pp. 1177-1201). Mahwah, NJ: Lawrence Erlbaum Associates.

Gagné, R., Briggs, R., & Wager, W. (1992). *Principles of Instructional Design*. Houston, TX: HBJ College Publishers.

Garrett, J. J. (2002). The Elements of User Experience: User-Centered Design for the Web. New York: New Riders Publishing.

Garzotto, F. (2007). Investigating the Educational Effectiveness of Multiplayer Online Games for Children. In *Proc. IDC 2007 (Interaction Design and Children)*, June 2007 (pp. 56-59).

Garzotto, F. (2007). Was Vygotsky Right? Evaluating Learning Effects of Social Interaction in Children Internet Games. In *Proc. INTERACT 2007*, Rio de Janeiro (Brazil), Sept. 2007 (pp. 147-151).

Garzotto, F. (2008). Interactive Storytelling, Cooperative e-Learning, and Kids: a Field Study. In *Proc. IDC'05*, Boulder, USA (pp. 121-123).

Garzotto, F. (2008, June). Broadening Children's Involvement as Design Partners: From Technology to Experience. In *Proc. ACM IDC 2008 - Interaction Design and Children 2008*, Chicago, USA.

Garzotto, F., & Forfori, M. (2006). Hyperstories and Social Interaction in 2D and 3D Edutainment Spaces for Children. In *Proc. ACM Hypertext '06*, Odense, Denmark (pp. 46-55).

Garzotto, F., & Poggi, C. (2009). Design Patterns for Collaborative Learning in Shared Virtual Worlds. In P. Goodyear & S. Retalis (Eds.), *Technology-enhanced learning: design patterns and pattern languages*. Hershey, PA: IGI Global.

Garzotto, F., & Rizzo, F. (2005). Interactive Storytelling, Cooperative e-Learning, and Kids: a Field Study. In *Proc. IDC'05*, Boulder, USA (pp. 121-123).

Garzotto, F., & Schelhowe, H. (2008). Marginalized Young People: Inclusion Through ICT. In *Proc. ACM IDC 2008 - Interaction Design and Children 2008*, Chicago, USA.

Guha, M., et al. (2004). Mixing Ideas: A New Technique for Working with Young Children as Design Partners. In *Proc. IDC 2004*, College Park, MD, USA (pp. 35-42).

Guha M. et al. (2005). *Working with Young Children as Technology Design Partners*, CACM Jan. 2005/Vol. 48, No. 1 39, 39-42

Gustafson, K. L., & Branch, R. M. (1997). Revisioning Models of Instructional Development. *Educational Technology Research and Development, 45*(3), 73–89. doi:10.1007/BF02299731

Hanna, L., Neapolitan, D., & Risden, K. (2004). *Evaluating Computer Game Concepts with Children*. In *Proc. IDC 2004*, College Park, Maryland, USA (pp. 49-47).

Harel, I., & Papert, S. (1991). *Constructionism*. New York: Ablex Publishing Corporation.

Hartman, H. J. (2001). *Metacognition in Learning and Instruction: Theory, Research and Practice*. Dordrecht, Netherlands: Kluwer Academic Publishers.

Heinrich, R., Molenda, M., & Russell, J. (1983). *Instructional Media and new Technologies*. New York: Macmillan.

Hourcade, J. P. (2006). *Design for Children*. In G. Salvendy (Ed.), *Handbook of Human Factors and Ergonomics* (3rd ed.) (pp. 1446-1458). New York: Wiley.

Jensen, J., & Skov, M. (2005). A Review of Research methods in Children's Technology Design. In *Proc.IDC 05*, Boulder, USA

Kaptelinin, V., Nardi, B., & Macaulay, C. (1999). The Activity Checklist: A Tool for Representing the "Space" of Context. *Interaction*, 27–30. doi:10.1145/306412.306431

Karagiorgi, Y., & Symeou, L. (2005). Translating Constructivism into Instructional Design: Potential and Limitations. *Educational Technology & Society, 8*(1), 17–27.

Kelly, S. R., et al. (2006). Bluebells: A Design Method for Child-Centred Product Development. In *Proc. NordiCHI 2006* (pp. 362-369)

Li, J., et al. (2007). Comicboarding: Using Comics as Proxies for Participatory Design with Children. In *Proc. CHI 2007*, San Jose, CA (pp. 1371-1375).

Malone, T. W. (1982). Heuristics for Designing Enjoyable User Interfaces: Lessons from Computer Games. In *Proceedings of the 1982 conference on Human factors in computing systems*, Gaithersburg, MD, USA(pp. 63 – 68).

Marcus, A. (2002). The Challenge of User Experience Design. *Interaction*, 29–35.

McClellan, I. (2005). User Experience' Design - A new form of design practice takes shape. In *Proc. CHI'05*, Portland, Oregon, April 2005 (pp. 1097-1097)

Monk, A., Hassenzahl, M., Blythe, M., & Reed, D. (2002). *Funology: designing enjoyment.* In *Proc. CHI'02*, (pp. 2135-145).

Norman, D. A. (2004). *Emotional Design*. New York: Basic Books.

Paolini, P., & Di Blas, N. (2006). Multi-User Virtual Environments for Education: A European Experience. In *Proc. E-Learn 06 Conference*, Honolulu, HI (pp. 1383-1394).

Poggi, C., & Torrebruno, A. (2007). From the Dead Sea Scrolls to Social Sports, passing through European History: an Effective Pedagogical Format Based on 3D Worlds. In *Proceedings of ED-Media 07*, Chesapeake, VA (pp. 4240-4248).

Prensky, M. (2001). *Digital Game-Based Learning*. New York: McGraw-Hill.

Randell, C., Phelps, T., & Rogers, Y. (2003). Ambient Wood: Demonstration of a digitally enhanced field trip for school children. In *Adjunct Proceedings of UbiComp 2003*, Seattle, USA (pp. 100-104).

Read, J. C., Gregory, P., MacFarlane, S. J., McManus, B., Gray, P., & Patel, R. (2002). An Investigation of Participatory Design with Children - Informant, Balanced and Facilitated Design. In *Proc. IDC 2002*, Eindhoven, Netherlands (pp. 56-64).

Retalis, S., Papasalouros, A., & Skordalakis, M. (2002). Towards a Generic Conceptual Design Meta-Model for Web-Based Educational Applications. In *Proc. 2nd IWWOST*, Malaga, Spain.

Revelle, G. (2003). Educating via Entertainment Media: the Sesame Workshop approach. In *ACM Computer and Entertainment, 1*(1), 1-9.

Rogoff, T. (1990). *Apprenticeship in Thinking: Cognitive development in social context*. Oxford, UK: Oxford University Press.

Roussou, M., Kavalieratou, E., & Doulgeridis, M. (2007). Children Designers in the Museum: Applying Participatory Design for the Development of an Art Education Program. In *Proc. IDC '07*, Aalborg, Denmark (pp. 77-80).

Sasha, A. B., & Plucker, J. A. (2002). Smart People or Smart Contexts? Cognition, Ability, and Talent Development in an Age of Situated Approaches to Knowing and Learning. *Educational Psychologist*, *37*(3), 165–182. doi:10.1207/S15326985EP3703_3

Scaife, M., Rogers, Y., Aldrich, F., & Davies, M. (1997). Designing For or Designing With? Informant Design for Interactive Learning Environments. In *Proc. CHI 97,* Atlanta (pp. 235-244).

Sengers, P., Boehner, K., Davod, S., & Kaye, J. (2005). Reflective Design. In *Proc. Critical Computing'05,* (pp. 49 – 58).

Stanton, D., et al. (2001). Classroom Collaboration in the Design of Tangible Interfaces for Storytelling. In *Proc. CHI 2001*, Seattle, USA (pp. 482-489)

Steiner, B., Kaplan, N., & Moulthrop, S. (2006). When play works: Turning game-playing into learning. In *Proc. IDC'2006*, Tampere, Finland.

Sweetser, P., & Wyeth, P. (2005). Game Flow: A Model for Evaluating Player Enjoyment in Games. *ACM Computer and Entertainment*, *3*(3), 1–23. doi:10.1145/1077246.1077248

Verhaegh, J., et al. (2006). On the design of Camelot, an outdoor game for children. In *Proc. IDC '06,* Tampere, Finland (pp. 9-17).

Vorderer, P., Hartmann, T., & Klimmt, C. (2003). Explaining the enjoyment of playing video games: The role of competition. In *Proc. of the 2nd International Conference on Computer Games*, Pittsburgh, PA.

Vygotsky, L. S. (1978). *Mind and Society: The development of higher psychological Process* (M. Cole, V. John Steiner, S. Scribner, & E. Souberman, Eds.). Cambridge, MA: Harvard University Press.

Werger, E. (1999). *Communities of Practice, Learning, Meaning, and Identity.* Cambridge, UK: University Cambridge Press

Chapter 6
A Pedagogics Pattern Model of Blended E-Learning:
A Step Towards Designing Sustainable Simulation-Based Learning

Michel Labour
Univ Lille Nord de France, France & UVHC, LSC, France

Christophe Kolski
Univ Lille Nord de France, France & UVHC, LAMIH-UMR CNRS, France

ABSTRACT

In this chapter, we examine blended e-learning design based on user feedback commonly found in grass-roots educational practice. After outlining three approaches to understanding blended e-learning, we present Marcia Bates's informational process approach to bring together the design theory of Christopher Alexander and the instructional theory of Jean Houssaye. This results in our pedagogics pattern model to transcribe blended e-learning practice in a hands-on way to both instructional designers and educational practitioners using e-learning to satisfy the emotional and cognitive needs of learners. The Model takes into account the dynamics between technology-bounded determinism of e-learning and users' need to develop their personal emotional and cognitive preferences. We present case studies demonstrating the viability of our approach in simulation-based learning in Human-Computer Interface design, and writing an online troubleshooting wiki about network computing in English. The study used a qualitative method to evaluate feedback data in the form of tutor self-reports, learners' reports, examination results, and a collective analysis of three experienced tutors-researchers.

INTRODUCTION

In this chapter we look at how successful grass-roots blended e-learning design can be modelized and communicated to generate e-learning design. With the advances of the Web 2.0, teachers and learners increasingly participate as both users and co-developers of digital resources. This has created a growing awareness of the intricate relationship between design, instructional practices and modelling theories. Indeed, for Steen (2008, p. 526) designing successful e-learning is part art and part science in that it draws from an understanding of instruction

DOI: 10.4018/978-1-60566-940-3.ch006

theory, and the knowledge and skills that users' wish to appropriate. This begs the question, however, of *what to do once blended e-learning has apparently been successfully crafted as a desirable educational experience?* We respond to this question by proposing a hands-on framework for e-learning designers, developers and instructors wishing to transpose a successful experience to different contexts.

Our touchstone is to go beyond the pure technology of e-learning, on the one hand, and blended leaning as a *de facto* "compromise" position, on the other hand. Oliver & Trigwell (2005, p. 21) point out that blended learning is often little more than a compromise position of the dominant features of purely e-learning and face-to-face interaction. We take up this point and redefine blended e-learning based on user feedback "patterns". With this in mind, the chapter is divided in five sections.

The first section (Background) examines three different approaches to blended e-learning, followed by Alexander's "design pattern" movement and Houssaye's included-middle "Pedagogic Triangle" linked together by the informational process perspective of Marcia Bates to create our Model. The second section (Method of our study) presents the rationale of the method used in our study. The third section (*pedagogics pattern* model) lays out the five basic facets of our Model. The fourth section (Applications of the *pedagogics pattern* model) presents the results of our case studies to highlight the operational viability of our Model. The final section (Future Research Directions) discusses the possibilities our Model affords and some research issues it raises.

BACKGROUND

In his article, "Theory construction in design research: criteria, approaches, and methods", Ken Friedman (2003, p.7) argues that design involves solving problems, creating something new, or transforming less desirable situations to targeted situations by studying "why" and "how" things work *via* a theory-drive framework. In doing this, designers can move between individual cases and broad explanatory principles when tackling set problems. We apply this insight by starting with an overview of blended e-learning approaches.

Blended E-Learning

Tutors have been combining educational technologies and face-to-face interaction for at least the last 30 years (cf. Bliuc, Goodyear, & Ellis 2007, p.231). It is around the year 2000, however, that "blended learning" came to the fore (Bliuc *et al.* 2007, p.231). In their well-known article, "Can "blended learning" be redeemed?", Oliver & Trigwell (2005) question the conceptual legitimacy and the exactitude of blended learning as an operational concept by asking what exactly is meant "blended"? To answer this we look at three approaches to blended e-learning.

First, there is the approach portrayed by the emblematic World Bank Institute (WBI). For the WBI blended e-learning is a way of creating an educational experience "cost effectively using a mix of integrated distance learning technologies (...) traditional face-to-face meetings, classroom activities (and) a variety of instructional strategies such as action learning and participatory learning" (WBI 2008). This view of blended e-learning focuses on a Return On Investment logic (cf. Bliuc, Goodyear, & Ellis 2007, p.231-232). Little mention is made of the emotional or affective quality of the learning experience for its learners and tutors (instructors).

The second approach to understanding blended e-learning comes from wishing to make traditional distance learning more attractive. Bliuc *et al.* (2007, p.231-232), and Reiser (2001) suggest that blended e-learning is a response to the failure of pure Computer Assisted Learning. Recent studies, however, show that pure online, and blended e-learning continue to co-exist today without one cannibalising the other (cf. Allen, Seaman & Garrett 2007).

The third approach to blended e-learning considers itself as a domain in its own right. Blended e-learning, in this strong sense, creates its own applicative space. It represents a functional whole with different elements counterbalancing and complementing each other (cf. Aycock, Garnham, Kaleta 2002).

A blended learning design represents a significant departure from either (face-to-face and Internet technology). It represents a fundamental reconceptualization and reorganization of the teaching and learning dynamic, starting with various specific contextual needs and contingencies (e.g. discipline, developmental level, and resources). In this respect, no two blended learning designs are identical (Garrison & Kanuka 2004, p. 3).

This "significant departure" can be found in the work of cognitive scientist Mark Turner when he speaks of "conceptual blending". The blend happens when the integration of at least two domains appear to conflict in their conceptual organizations but result in a "new organizing structure and emergent meaning of its own" (Underhill 2001, para.45). In doing this, the blend does not obliterate the difference between domains, such as face-to-face interactions and online technology. What it does do is create an interstice of "blended space" between the domains, which we call an "inter-domain", in the sense that one speaks of intercultural *i.e.* when two cultures, which simultaneously complement and rival each other meet to create a common "interculture" (Labour 2006). While we do not seek to apply strictly Turner's principles in this chapter, his work does give us a starting point to grasp the phenomena of blended e-learning. It goes beyond assembling the "best" of online and face-to-face worlds, which do not in themselves create an enhanced learning experience (cf. Oliver & Trigwell 2005). It is from this position that we tackle blended e-learning design principles in examining the work of architect, engineer and recognised design theorist, Christopher Alexander.

Alexander's Design Pattern Movement

Underpinning our Model is the idea that sustainable innovation is based on harnessing rules and principles based on user feedback. Such rules (from the Latin, *regula*) attempt to identify perceived regularities of how past successes nurtured further innovation. As argues mathematician Keith Delvin (2000, p.7) life, and certainly intellectual life, is possible because there are certain perceived regularities in the world. In the same vein, in her article, "The science of patterns", in *Science*, Lynn Steen (1988, p.611) states that mathematics is no longer the mere study of number and space but of "relations among patterns and on applications derived from the fit between pattern and observation". In our study, our aim is to clarify and formalise qualitative patterns of the blended e-learning process with its host of emotional, cognitive and social dynamics.

Alexander, Ishikawa, Silverstein, Fiksdahl-King and Angel (1977) produced the pattern language approach to empower people to design and build what they need. At the heart of the design pattern movement is the precept of reusing and categorizing processes that users' feel have successfully satisfied their social, emotional and affective needs. This led Alexander and his team to create an operational concept of "pattern" to resolve recurring problems so "you can use this solution a million times over, without ever doing it the same way twice" (Alexander *et al.* 1977, p. X). The approach is used in object-oriented software development (Gamma 1991, Gamma *et al.*, 1995). It can be used when gathering expertise by identifying elements of "design patterns" practice; agreeing to a shared vocabulary and concepts; solving reoccurring problem in alternative ways; centralizing elements into a catalogue where each model names, explains and evaluates concepts that frequently occur.

Frequent use (reoccurring solution) is not, however, the sole distinguishing trait of a sustainably operational "pattern". It also requires *usability* (how a solution can be used to resolve a problem) and *usefulness* (why it appears to "make sense" for a person). That said, how can one ensure that a given reoccurring solution is in tune with usability and usefulness in satisfying, for example, affective and cognitive needs? The response to this is the three-part rule of "design patterns" where a pattern consists of a rule that establishes a relationship between a system of forces, which arises in a context, and a configuration to enable the "system of forces" satisfy users' deep-felt needs (Alexander 1979 p. 253).

This concept of design pattern has spread to other knowledge domains, such as to the study of instructional processes cf. Fincher (1999); The Pedagogical Patterns Project (2001); Fincher & Utting (2002); Wade (2002). It can also be found in fields like Information Science research, where Marcia Bates defines information as all physical and biological processes that construct emerging patterns of organization "extracted, stored, and used by living beings" (Bates 2005 para. 22). Bates (2005 para. 83) makes a useful formal distinction between this first-order information, which she calls Information 1, and a related, but qualitatively different concept, Information 2. The second-order Information 2 is defined as "some pattern of organization of matter and energy given meaning by a living being (or its constituent parts)" (*ibidum*). In doing this, Bates stresses that apparent patterns of Information 1 are not inherently meaningful. It needs a living being to assign it meaning, as part of a cognitive and emotional process, to help construct a personal knowledge system.

For Bates (2005 para. 83) defines personal knowledge as "information given meaning and integrated with other contents of understanding". In this, she associates Information 2 (*i.e.* Information 1 that has meaning for someone) with acquired personal knowledge ("other contents"). These other contents can be found in Alexander's focus on what users' consider as reoccurring (emotional, cognitive, social) elements deemed useable and useful to resolve a problem, along with Houssaye's theory of presences-absences in the dynamics of teaching/learning (instruction). It is in this way that Bates's meaning-based definition of "patterns of organization" (Information 2) helps us understand the importance of why users consider something as "useful", i.e. why something is emotionally and/or cognitively meaningful, in the instructional process.

Houssaye's Included-Middle Pedagogic Triangle

At face value, instructional theory specialist Jean Houssaye (1992) describes his Triangle as having four basic elements: the knowledge domain, the tutor, the learner, and the all-encompassing background governing body (see Figure 1). We add to this, that it is the perceptions (with its emotional and cognitive aspects) of the rapport between the domains that creates a learning dynamic, rather the mere existence of the elements *per se*. The importance of the Houssaye's Triangle, however, lies in the concept of the included middle[1] (Houssaye 1992, p.236). In practice, this means that the three key elements (knowledge domain, tutor, learner) function in dyadic pairs by rendering absent a third key element as "dead[2]". This is one way of avoiding emotional and cognitive "overload".

The dynamic of the "Dead" constitutes the bedrock of Houssaye's instructional process both from an emotional and social point of view. We created Figure 2 to show how the included-middle approach describes the dynamics of the instructional process, notably through the feedback role of the rebel Madcap[3] as an unplanned, and often disruptive, presence.

It needs to be said that pedagogics pattern is used to emphasise the compound sense of our model. This compound sense is found in the studied blending of the viewpoints of Houssaye (1992), Alexander (1979) and Bates (2005) into one emergent framework. This differs from

Figure 1. The Pedagogic Triangle revisited

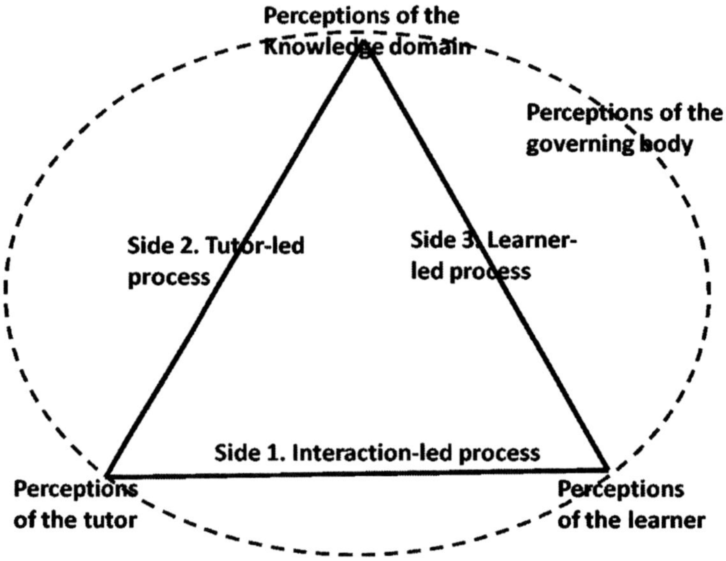

"pedagogical pattern" where "pedagogical" can be understood as one attribute, among others, relating to an overarching "pattern".

METHOD OF OUR STUDY

The purpose of the *pedagogics pattern* model is to put into operation salient elements that come into play when designing blended e-learning taken from successful grassroots practice. To do this, we used a qualitative methodology taking heed of its attendant dangers (cf. Richards & Richards 1994, Becker *et al.* 2005). One major danger is the temptation of over-emphasizing evidence based on personal opinion. To avoid this pitfall, the critical questioning of the data in our study was conducted by confronting the practices of three[4] experienced university tutors-researchers working in different disciplines *i.e.* Human-Computer Interface design, foreign language learning in computer network maintenance, and business

Figure 2. Our synoptic view of Houssaye's included-middle Pedagogic Triangle

	Tutor-led process 	Interaction-led process 	Learner-led process 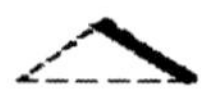
Dyadic *co-presence*	Tutor + Knowledge domain *e.g.* lectures	Tutor + Learner, and Leaner + Learner	Learner + Knowledge domain *e.g.* self-directed activities
Designated third party *absence* (the "Dead")	Learner is requested to be an "onlooker" to the tutor's performance as a "sage on the stage"	Knowledge domain of the tutor as gatekeeper	Tutor as a dominant source of knowledge
Disruptive *presence* ("Madcap" does not play "Dead")	*e.g.* learners become bored, rebellion, inattentive, indifferent, frustrated *etc.* (Madcap #1)	*e.g.* learners fall back on pre-fabricated knowledge domain (Madcap #2)	*e.g.* learners become over dependent on the tutor (Madcap #3)

management. This trans-disciplinary approach implies that the study does not limit itself to one knowledge domain.

The questioning of the heuristic educational practices of each tutor was conducted by submitting self-reports for analysis to the other two colleagues over a 10-month period. This examination involved studying tutors' feedback from students through teaching notes, records of learners' grades and work they handed in. It must be stressed, here, that the *method of feedback is that commonly used by tutors in higher education*. This is a key point given the objective of making our approach accessible to a range of people in a hands-on way that includes tutors, as experts in their field, but though having little technical expertise in computer-generated adaptive learning units, pedagogical agents and such like, they may be heavy users of such technology. Once tutors' mutually examined each other's practice, the results were confronted to the different viewpoints of Alexander, Bates, and Houssaye. From this arose a generic *pedagogics pattern* model (see figures 3 and 4) as a blend of top-down theory and bottom-up grassroots practice.

Each tutor transcribed their enhanced self-reports into case studies guided by the generic *pedagogics pattern* model. Then it was submitted again to the other two researchers for a further round of peer evaluation. The case studies show

Figure 3. Synoptic grid of the pedagogics pattern model

General description and context

Spacio-temporal bondary markers

TØ :
T1 :
T2 :

A1. "Knowledge domain" Pole		
Aims	**Classroom context**	**Discourse community context**
"Initial State"		
"Final state"		

A.2 "Tutor" Pole		
Aims	**Classroom context**	**Discourse community context**
"Initial State"		
"Final state"		

A.3 "Learner" Pole		
Aims	**Classroom context**	**Discourse community context**
"Initial State"		
"Final state"		

Overall action plan of pedagogical techniques and tools used
(insert a figure here)

Group interaction at each Pole of the Pedagogic Triangle

Interaction at the "learner" pole
Interaction between groups of learners:
Interaction within groups of learners:
Interaction with the institution:

Interaction at the "tutor" pole
Interaction between groups of tutors:
Interaction within groups of tutors:
Interaction with the institution:

Interaction at the "knowledge domain" pole
Interaction between knowledge domains:
Interaction within a knowledge domain:
Interaction with the institution:

Feedback
Feedback from the "learner" pole:
Feedback from the "tutor" pole:
Feedback from the "knowledge domain" pole:

Figure 4. Overall action plan underlying the pedagogics pattern model

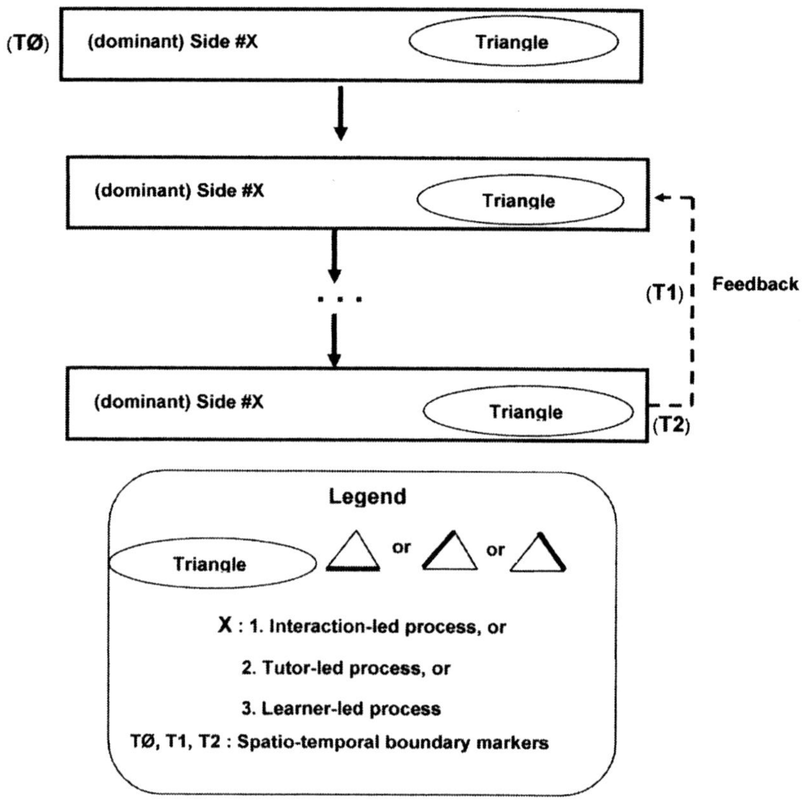

how different observable (surface) pedagogic activities can be guided by a common, though less observable (deep) design as conceived by Alexander's user feedback approach.

What is a case study? Carla Willig (2008, p.88) and Michael Wallace (1998, p.161) see case studies as a way of understanding what is singular in an individual instance (ideographic). This has the advantage of identifying a "*pattern* of influences that is too infrequent to be discernible by traditional statistical analyses" (Bell, Bush, Fox, Goodey & Goulding 1984 p.76, 77). Willig (2007, p.74,86) and Wallace (1998:161) point out that while case studies are not (statistically) generalisable they can be used as evidence to support a theory or, in our case, a model based on a theoretical framework.

Our case studies share three key features. First, they are situated in the same university context. Second, they are based on our Alexander-Bates-Houssaye conceptual framework. Third, each of the case studies study "simulations" (make believe/ fiction coherent worlds) to promote experiential learning and construction of alternative responses to a given problem. Psychologist, Jean-Marie Schaeffer (1999, p.225), a specialist of fiction as a cognitive tool, argues that personal knowledge structures are triggered off when a person is drawn to a universe of "fiction" (*e.g.* a simulation) that momentarily suspends the imperative constraints of a reality of reference ("real" life). Schaeffer (1999, p.166, 319) goes on to say that invariably the person has to forgo the world of fiction to respond to the imperatives of "real life". In short, a simulation affords an in-between immersive fictional universe based on attraction/ rejection dynamics that can help modify a personal knowledge system.

PEDAGOGICS PATTERN MODEL

We postulate that the transfer of experience can be facilitated by identifying elements that "anchor" an activity within a given context. These anchors identify factors such as the objectives, form, and content chosen to resolve a reoccurring problem. Our framework consists of five interdependent anchors (see Figure 3):

1. General description and context
2. Spatio-temporal boundary markers
3. Overall action plan of pedagogical techniques and tools used
4. Group interactions at each pole of the Pedagogic Triangle
5. Feedbacks

General Description and Context

This rubric sets the overall scene of the objectives to be attained to cement different actions and resources into a functional whole. Resources can range from the type of software to be used, and how and when it is to be used, to specifying what face-to-face events and activities are proposed as "systems of forces" (Alexander 1979, p.253) offered by the "context" of the governing institution.

Spatio-Temporal Boundary Markers

The concept of spatial brackets identifies different dimensions of analysis. This can be done by using, what Goffman (1974, p.251) calls, "boundary markers[5]" or "brackets". For the purpose of our model, the temporal markers are threefold (see Figure 4). First, we have the **TØ** marker. This indicates the "Initial state" of the training session for the learner, the tutor, and the researcher. This is followed by the **T1** marker indicating the "Final state" (closure) of the instructional session for the learner and the tutor. Finally, we have the **T2** marker to identify the "End" state" of reflection and analysis of the researcher.

We have identified two basic interrelated dimensions of analysis, the "space" of a classroom, and that of a (scientific, professional) discourse community. The "classroom space" dimension refers to events in a space and time in learner-tutor interactions. While the "discourse community" dimension refers to norms, values, and recognised knowledge domains generated within a given group, of which classroom tutors are members. The influence of the discourse community on the classroom context can determine what is considered as the accepted limits of a "knowledge domain" and the professional behaviour of tutors and students. To provide the link between the two basic levels, the **T2** boundary marker provides an overall cohesive dimension. Figure 3 portrays one way of transposing the principles of the Pedagogic Triangle into, what we call, a *pedagogics pattern* model.

Overall Action Plan

As it stands, Figure 3 explains *what* actions are to be done but not *how* they can be carried out. This can be done is by creating an "action plan" to help learners "solve a problem and to focus on a specific goal… (by) step-by-step actions to be taken to reach the goal" (Champion 2001 p.62). An action plan can thus include operational techniques associated with the scheduling or, in pattern language parlance, "sequencing" *i.e.* deciding which decision comes first, getting it right and then moving to the next decision (Alexander 2001 para.25). We propose a diagrammatic representation of this in Figure 4.

Figure 4 portrays spatio-temporal boundary markers on the left hand side of a "task box" with the appropriate **TØ**, **T1**, or **T2** marker. In each task box the nature of the chosen pedagogic strategy (tutor-driven, interaction-driven, or learner-driven) is displayed by a triangle of which only *one* side is shaded (Figure 2) to designate the Pedagogic Triangle's declared dominant pedagogic process. The task box is then filled with a succinct description of the objective of the task, followed by a downward arrow to indicate the direction of the process. Finally, an upward dotted-line arrow indicates the feedback flow.

Group Interactions at Each Pole of the Pedagogic Triangle

Given that learners cannot do everything at the same time, three types of emotional, socio-cognitive interactions can be identified in the instruction process.

Interactions at the "learner" pole:

- Interaction *between* groups of learners: This refers to learners as participants of a group competing with other groups *e.g.* in a game-led approach of "winners" and "losers".
- Interaction *within* groups of learners: Learners work together within a group *e.g.* peer learning.
- Interaction *with* the institution: The emphasis, here, is on the extent to which the person respects the norms of the governing institution *e.g.* preparing a national examination.

Interactions at the "tutor" pole:

- Interaction *between* groups of tutors: There are situations when tutors co-operate around a common educational task *e.g.* team teaching.
- Interaction *within* groups of tutors: The community to which tutors refers for a set of norms of what is acceptable behaviour and knowledge.
- Interaction *with* the institution: Tutors are often directly accountable to their institution and this can have a direct impact on what they do with learners.

Interactions at the "knowledge domain" pole:

- Interaction *between* knowledge domains: Drawing from different knowledge domains can lead to "win-lose" conflicts, but it can also create an interdisciplinary interstice among knowledge domains (cf. Labour, Useille, & Crévits 2006).
- Interaction *within* a knowledge domain: A constituted knowledge domain has various ways of ensuring that its norms are respected *e.g.* in the selection of articles for publications in journals, indexation of publications in a database.
- Interaction *with* the institution: Different knowledge domains are allocated different status depending on the priorities of a governing body.

Feedback

One of the objectives of harnessing *pedagogics pattern* is to include appropriate feedback about the relevance for users of events staged and tools proposed. It is here that Houssaye's included-middle approach is particularly useful. It can help identify disruptive emotional and cognitive elements in the form of "Madcaps" as feedback indicators of presence and absence of elements in the instructional process (see Figure 2). It is with this feedback that users and designers can fine tune their framework.

APPLICATIONS OF THE PEDAGOGICS PATTERN MODEL

Case Study #1: Human-Computer Interface Design

General Description and Context

We conducted a simulation in Human-Computer Interface (HCI) design course where student engineers played the role of HCI designers in a simulation. The students were in their fourth year of a Bachelor's degree in Electrical Engineering and Industrial Computer Science. The simulation is made up of three basic phases (see Figure 5).

Figure 5. Simulation of the HCI designing phases

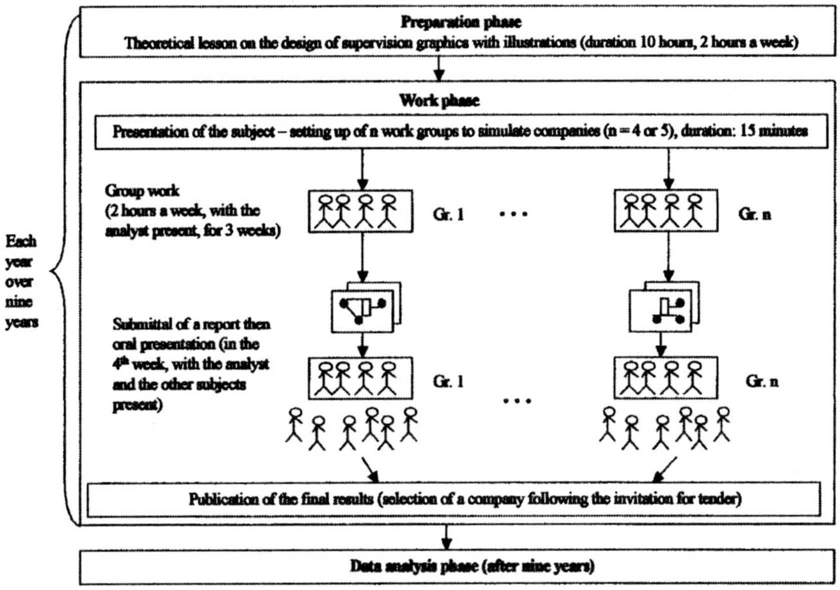

The simulation has been performed over the past nine years with classes of 20 to 25 students.

Phase 1 is the preparation step composed of 10 hours of tutor-directed classes in HCI design used by operators in control rooms, for example, of power plants. The classes were based on works of Rasmussen (1986), Kolski (1997) as well as the tutor's personal professional experience with industrial partners.

In **Phase 2** students attended classes two hours a week for four weeks and were placed in separate groups of four or five to conduct simulations. Each group represented a company that competed against each other when submitting tenders for the design of an HCI for the supervision in a control room of five product-mixing stations. Each station has a control panel with set of dynamic variables (temperatures, pressures…) to be supervised by human operators in a variety of situations. For the first three classes, in this phase, students could question the tutor who represented the organisation that had launched the invitation to tender. In the last session, each group presented their tender in describing the layout of the control room and a human-computer interface.

With **Phase 3** the tutor offered feedback about each student's bid based on a set of evaluation criteria considered as crucial to the HCI field (usability problems, methodological gaps…).

The study of the simulation took into account data from the 63 student dossiers collected over the nine-year period of the simulation (cf. Kolski *et al.* 2004a and 2004b2004b). Besides assessing design errors, students were also asked questions such as:

- What evidence was there that the instruction methods and content (supervision, and control rooms design) had influenced learners' decisions?
- Did learners use knowledge gained in other classes (ergonomics, artificial intelligence, software engineering, etc.) to enhance their design?
- Did learners take into account human factors involved in their design?

Spatio-Temporal Boundary Markers

To validate the usability of this model, we drew up Figure 7.

Action Plan of Pedagogical Techniques and Tools Used

Figure 5 and Figure 7 present the data in a way that they can be contrasted to other instructional contexts, notably case study #2 (below). Figure 7 shows an overall process that goes from TØ to T1 in three different phases of the Pedagogic Triangle. **Phase 1** is a tutor-led process (side #2 of the Pedagogic Triangle). **Phase 2** is a learned-led process (side #3 of the Triangle). **Phase 3** is an interaction-led process (side #1 of the Triangle). All three sides are concerned in this instructional process but at different moments. This is followed by a tutor-led process (side #2 of the Triangle) during which the tutor undertakes a critique of the module. It is here that a loop back of information operates for future classes (see Figure 6). Finally, the tutor-led process (side #2) moves on to a broader analysis as a HCI researcher within a discourse community, to finish at T2. Figure 6 portrays the overall process in a more schematic way, than Figure 7. This is followed by a step-by-step description of what our *pedagogics pattern* affords its user.

The consequences of the *pedagogics pattern* portrayed in Figure 7 and in Figure 8 are made explicit under the concepts of "group interactions" and "feedback" below.

Group Interactions at Each Pole of the Pedagogic Triangle

Interactions at the "learner" pole:

- Interaction between groups of learners: The groups competed as rival "companies". They did not share data with the other groups.
- Interaction within groups of learners: As the work was difficult and long, members of each group had to cooperate. Learners could interact face-to-face, and by email and other forms of electronic messaging.
- Interaction with the institution: There was a low possibility for students to have discussed with students from previous years, or with other tutors. The tutor never noticed

Figure 6. Example of a screen page (given in a specifications dossier)

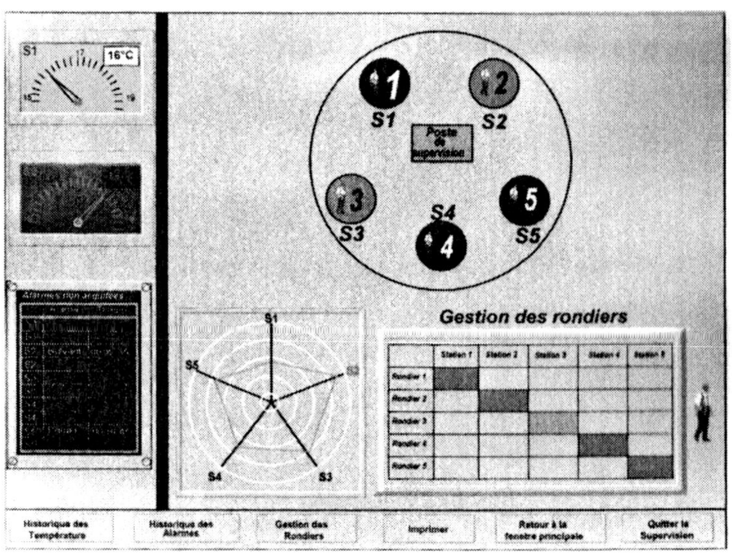

Figure 7. Pedagogics pattern model of case study #1

A.1. Knowledge domain pole of the Pedagogic Triangle:		
	Classroom context	**Discourse community context**
Aims	/	Improving identification of student designers' design errors
"Initial" state	**(at TØ)** Making available to students appropriate texts and explanations	**(at TØ)** Having access to current knowledge and resources given to the students
"Final" state	**(at T1)** The same as TØ plus learners solutions and tutor comments	**(at T2)** The same as TØ plus two scientific papers (Kolski *et al.*, 2004a, 2004b) studying student designers' design errors
A.2. Tutor pole of the Pedagogic Triangle:		
	Classroom context	**Discourse community context**
Aims	To teach HCI	Learning about design errors in HCI
"Initial" state	**(at TØ)** Encouraging students to learn, *viz.* through simulation	**(at TØ)** Collecting data concerning students as potential HCI designers
"Final" state	**(at T1)** Designing HCI by students	**(at T1)** Analyzing the available data
A.3. Learner pole of the Pedagogic Triangle:		
	Classroom context	**Discourse community context**
Aims	Passing an examination	Obtaining a degree to get a job
"Initial" state	**(at TØ)** Acquiring skills to pass exams	**(at TØ)** Acquiring knowledge about HCI specifications
"Final" state	**(at T1)** Producing appropriate skills *via* the production of a quality HCI specification dossier	**(at T1)** Producing real HCI specification dossiers in companies (knowledge transfer)

this type of influence in the nine years of the simulation.

Interactions at the "tutor" pole:

- Interaction between groups of tutors: not applicable as the tutor worked by himself
- Interaction within groups of tutors: not applicable as the tutor worked by himself
- Interaction with the institution: The tutor took into account the fact that students had attended other classes about human-computer interaction.

Interactions at the "knowledge domain" pole:

- Interaction between knowledge domains: The tutor provided appropriate texts while other texts were available from the Internet and the University library.

Figure 8. Overall action plan for case study #1

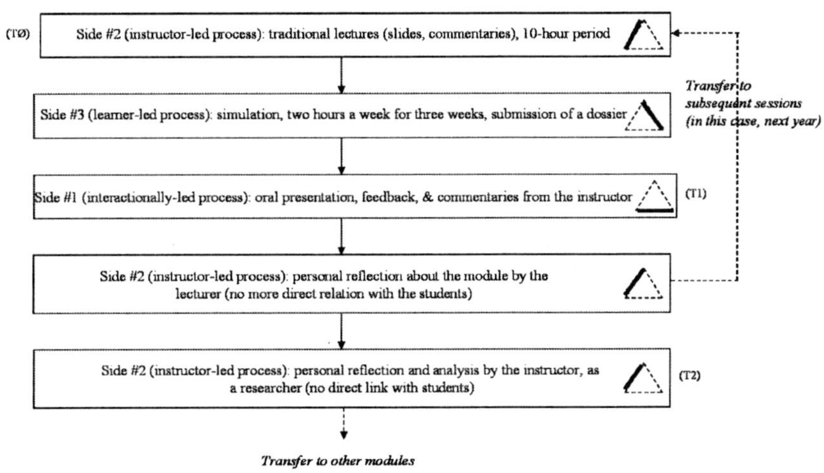

- Interaction within a knowledge domain: In certain groups, they were several students who had acquired knowledge in HCI for supervision of industrial processes during internships. The tutor noticed in such cases, some students tried to share some of their experience with the group.
- Interaction with the institution: Other tutors cold have provided useful knowledge for students who wanted to improve the technical quality of their bid. Apparently, learners did not question other tutors on this subject.

Feedback

Feedback from the "learner" pole:

- In the nine years, each of the groups participated with a high degree of student satisfaction in the simulation as witnessed by the virtual lack of absenteeism to the simulation classes and by the fact that all of the dossiers handed in included many positive aspects found in the evaluation criteria. This was probably due to students feeling they were working on a project that was close to industrial reality. They also appreciated the competitiveness ("gaming") between the groups. In short, there was no visible presence of the Madcap #1 (*e.g.* learner boredom, see Figure 2), or the excessive intrusion of the all-knowing "tutor" (Madcap #3).

Feedback from the "tutor" pole:

- Learners appreciated the simulation as a valuable addition to their formal university instruction. The professional nature of student dossiers and their active participation satisfied the tutor's expectations. Questions from learners during the simulation provided, and ideas and illustrations from learners' dossiers were integrated into the subsequent classes of the tutor. This feedback led to the conclusion that the Madcap #2 (*e.g.* learners fell back on prefabricated knowledge) was not a dominant feature of the simulation.

Feedback from the "knowledge domain" pole:

- The tutor wrote two articles about this novel pedagogical approach for two HCI international congresses. The reactions were globally positive, with many questions asked by the audience, as little work exists in the HCI domain regarding this approach.

Case Study #2: Writing a Troubleshooting Network Computing Journal

General Description and Context

This simulation was conducted with a group of adults enrolled in a two-year, work-study course in computer network maintenance in a *Microsoft* and *Cisco* certified technical college, called ACTIF (Valenciennes, France). The learners have varied academic backgrounds and range from 23 to 40 years old. In our case study, the French learners were in their final year and participated in weekly, three-hour blended-learning workshops of technical English over a 25-week period. One of the aims of the module is to apply the principles of "empowerment" as a feeling of co-authorship that authorises an individual to take control of actions as a participant in a social network (cf. Labour 2006). The approach is inspired from Michel Foucault (1982/2001), for whom "power" is seen as an action guiding other actions. We add to this idea of power, the phenomenon of "feeling" as an implicit form of self-awareness of one's emotions (Damasio 2003, p.83). We argue that utilizing one's "power" includes cognitive skills as well as a feeling, based on emotions, of one's capacity to change things.

In **Phase 1** the tutor briefed learners about the objectives of the workshop and checked learners' expectations and needs in negotiating the dominant theme of the workshop. **Phase 2** saw learners going back and forth from French and English versions of the same text with the help of resources, such as online CISCO instructional modules, electronic dictionaries and translators. The objective of **Phase 3** checked how successful learners were in their trial and error attempts to make sense of texts in resolving computer maintenance problems. Learner did this by creating cloze online texts and crossword puzzles (using the *Hotpotatoes* software) for other learners in the group to learn from. The tutor gave corrective feedback on the learners' productions before publishing it online.

For **Phase 4** learners were asked to write a make-believe online computer troubleshooting journal using a wiki. They were to simulate the role of online hotliners who were replying to questions from fictitious clients. The tutor played the role of the client. Learners worked in mini-groups to offer the most appropriate solution to clients using recently acquired concepts and vocabulary. At the end of the allocated time period (about 75 minutes), the wiki with the most satisfactory solution earned a higher grade than the other mini-groups. In **Phase 5**, there was a debriefing of the previous phases to see if there was any evidence of emerging empowerment by asking:

1. What surprised you in what you did in the workshop today? (identification of learners' cognitive and emotional expectations and preoccupations).
2. What reassured you in today's workshop? (establishing what resources were found to be meaningful).
3. What advice could you give to new students about today's workshop? (extracting the salient operational points of learners' experience).

Figure 9. Pedagogics pattern model of case study #2

A.1. Knowledge domain pole of the Pedagogic Triangle		
	Classroom context	**Discourse community context**
Aims	Access to specialized English texts for computer technicians	Adapting technical English digital texts to empower French computer network technicians
"Initial" state	**(TØ)** Texts written in English for student learners	**(TØ)** Existing legitimate knowledge (online resources, face-to-face expertise) including texts and explanations offered to learners
"End" state	**(T1)** The same as **TØ** with solutions from students and observations from the tutor	**(T2)** Dialogue with colleagues from different knowledge domains
A.2. Tutor pole of the Pedagogic Triangle		
	Classroom context	**Discourse community context**
Aims	Appropriation of language skills for computer maintenance	Identifying sense making words and expressions in English and French associated with computer maintenance
"Initial" state	**(TØ)** Identification of appropriate texts as resources for learners	**(TØ)** Understanding what sense learners make of intra- and extra-textual elements of texts
"End" state	**(T1)** Learners are able to make sense of texts as viable resources	**(T2)** Analyzing learner generated feedback
A.3. Learner pole of the Pedagogic Triangle		
	Classroom context	**Discourse community context**
Aims	To obtain the diploma in passing the institution's State approved examination	Getting a job with skills required for the job market
"Initial" state	**(TØ)** Appropriating course content in the framework given by the tutor	**(TØ)** Acquiring insights about sense making processes when consulting technical texts
"End" state	**(T1)** Feeling empowered to accomplish new tasks *via* texts written in English	**(T2)** Producing sense making texts that help empower users

Spatio-Temporal Boundary Markers

To validate the usability of this model, we drew up Figure 9.

Action Plan of Pedagogical Techniques and Tools Used

Represented as a diagram, the action plan shows how it differs from its counterpart in case study #1 while being recognizably part of the same general *pedagogics pattern* model.

In using a case study approach, we see how the generic figures 3 and 4 are transposed into Figure 9 and Figure 10. Clearly, there is no mechanical transfer from one context to another, but a relative freedom to show how the singularities of an instructional context can be nurtured. As with case study #1 (Figure 7, Figure 8) these singularities do not exclude the possibility of identifying a common underlying pattern found in the generic figures 3 and 4.

In case study # 2 the tutor-led process (side #2 of the Pedagogic Triangle) sets the scene for learners and the tutor. The learned-led process (side #3 of the Triangle) is crucial in that it calls on an active cognitive and emotional involvement from learners wanting to make sense of specialized vocabulary in English.

It is in the interaction-led process (side #1 of the Triangle) of Phase 1 that learners can find mutual support to anchor what they are learning to a tangible reality. This anchoring also provides a framework for learners to experiment and discover different ways of constructing new personal knowledge structures.

The upward-direction of arrows indicates that learner feedback is used to improve future workshops. These improvements are enhanced with the tutor-researcher taking a broader view from his/her local context by consulting specialized literature in the domain.

Group Interactions at Each Pole

Interaction at the "learner" pole:

- Interaction between groups of learners: The groups competed with each other to write

Figure 10. Overall action plan for case study #2

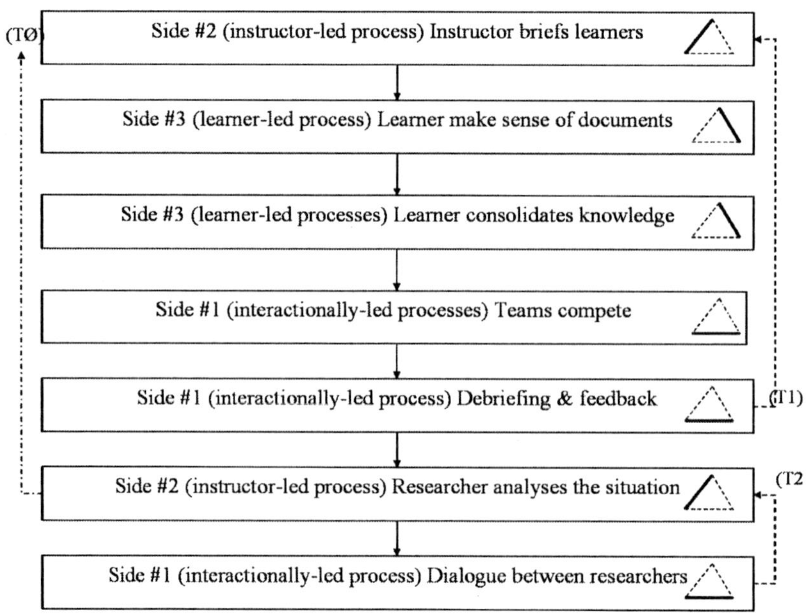

up and then correct a text in applied computer science. The work was done with a *wiki*, an electronic forum, the Internet, and online cross-word and cloze-making software. This meant that learners in different groups, separated in different parts of the classroom, could ask each other for advice without the other groups being aware of the exchanges within the group.

- Interaction within groups of learners: Using the principle of peer learning, learners who were more able in English or computer science helped colleagues in difficulty. The bulk of the interaction was mainly done in French, despite recommendations that English be used as much as possible. Working with in an electronic medium meant that it was possible to identify who tended to be the more active members of the group. This helps the tutor encourage less active learners to participate more in the group. The electronic medium allowed the less "extroverted" or "verbal" learners to share their ideas.
- Interaction with the institution: There was some contact with other tutors who were specialist in various areas of computer science.

Interactions at the "tutor" pole:

- Interaction between groups of tutors: As a specialist in adult education and communication, not computer science, it was necessary for the tutor to ask colleagues to co-validate the project offered to learners.
- Interaction within groups of tutors: This was not in the remit of the simulation.
- Interaction with the institution: The tutor reiterated to learners that they could use their notes from other disciplines.

Interactions at the "knowledge domain" pole:

- Interaction between knowledge domains: The tutor provided learners with appropriate texts, and students used their notes taken during classes. Other texts were retrieved online. The interaction occurred mainly between a book-centred knowledge domain and learner's practical skills acquired at the workface.
- Interaction within a knowledge domain: There was regular transfer of knowledge between French and American approaches to applied computer science.
- Interaction with the institution: Given that learners were being trained to CISCO standards they were able to consult other tutors specialized in their domain.

Feedback

Feedback from the "learner" pole:

- Learners more skilled in English tended to dominate those who had a better knowledge of computer science. In terms of Houssaye's included-middle (Figure 2), the group had to deal with a "Madcap #2" (using unauthorised knowledge of French), and to a lesser extent, "Madcap #3" (as rogue "tutors" giving answers to colleagues, cf. Figure 2).

Feedback from the "tutor" pole:

- In using the *wiki*, it was easy for learners to check the successive modifications of their work once the "general editor" (the tutor) had highlighted errors. Some of the students, however, did not revise the errors highlighted in their initial work. This can be characterised as "Madcap #1" ("rebellion").

Feedback from the "knowledge domain" pole:

- The work done on the *wiki* was presented to the other tutors as a way of showing the usefulness of blended e-learning.

FUTURE RESEARCH DIRECTIONS

The novelty of our reflection lies in providing a user-feedback framework to designing and communicating blended e-learning environments. This can contribute to interdisciplinary exchanges about "good[6]", "best" and "promising" pedagogical practices. We showed that despite the apparent singularities of our case studies, they possess a common patterning of the blended e-learning process. In no way, however, is our Model meant to be used as a recipe ("method") for cataloguing, evaluating or standardizing blended e-learning. The originality of our approach is that it offers an underlying logic in how to design blended e-learning, which can be sufficiently transcribed for communication. In the field of educational management, this can provide a useful means for accountability without rigidly standardizing the instructional process.

One challenge about our Model is the issue of the granularity of its elements. Our Model could have gone further in detailing the processes involved in blended e-learning. Some may say there are already too many details in our Model, while for others that there are not enough. For example, our Model could have transcribed in more detail features like the types of peer learning and tools used (software, books, etc.) in the activities. To do this, however, could have caused two major handicaps.

First, there is a risk of overloading in time, effort, and volume the Model with finer details that it would lose its operational validity. Second, the construct validity of our Model corresponds to tried and tested principles of our Alexander-Bates-Houssaye framework. To highlight more logistic details without a direct correspondence to this conceptual base would undermine the rigour of our Model.

The use of two case studies, rather than, for example, five or nine, could be taken to task. That said, it is important to underline the danger of being flooded by data coming from too many case studies. This point is important, as one of the aims of our study is its operational application and not an exhaustive cataloguing of the instruction processes. In this sense, our two very different case studies satisfy this aspect of operational validity.

Beyond the examples of our case studies, what other evidence is there that the *pedagogics pattern* model has a sufficient level of operational validity? For, if a pattern were simply to identify a context-problem-solution, it could be challenged as being anecdotal. Within the field of software engineering, James O. Coplien (2005 para.10-13) advocates five points to identifying a valid "pattern".

1. **It solves a problem**: Patterns capture solutions, not just abstract principles or strategies
2. **It is a proven concept**: Patterns capture solutions with a track record, not abstract speculation
3. **Its solution is not self-evident**: Many problem-solving techniques, such as software design paradigms or methods, try to derive solutions from first principles, whose applications are not always self-evident
4. **It describes a relationship**: Patterns do not just describe surface level modules, but also describe relationships of deeper system structures and mechanisms
5. **The pattern has a significant human component**: Software serves human comfort, or quality of life explicitly appealling to aesthetics and utility

In terms of Coplien's framework, our Model addresses the problem (Coplien's Point 1) of how to capitalise successful past experience by using the "proven concepts" (Coplien's Point 2) found in the Alexander-Bates-Houssaye framework. At first view, the solution we propose is not "self-evident". One has to look beyond the surface singularity of our case studies to identify its less visible commonalities. The underlying coherence of our model is found in the application of the included-middle logic of the Pedagogic Triangle (Coplien's Point 3). It is this that describes complex emerging relationships of a "deeper system structures and mechanisms" (Coplien's Point 4).

Finally, the *pedagogics pattern*, once identified and written up, can provide a reassuring ("human comfort", Coplien's Point 5) structure to tutors wanting to enhance, and communicate about their practice in harnessing user satisfaction.

Researchers in blended e-learning design can usefully explore Mark Turner's "conceptual blending[7]" to better understand the nature and functions of what is understood as "blended instruction" and how to design for it creatively. Of particular interest is the Turnerian notion of filling in "partial patterns" (Underhill 2001, para. 56) in the selection phase of creating a "blend". This could help understand the nuts and bolts of blending as a dynamic *inter-domain* with its organizing structure and emergent meaning.

Further research into blended e-learning design would benefit from ongoing work like that of Yrjö Engeström's socio-dialogic activity theory. Engeström (1999, p. 31) speaks of the importance of "modelling" the structure and dynamic relations of an activity system. He raises thorny issues, such as, what is the individual's precise role in a learning group? Does it depend on the demands of the activity or are there other factors to be taken into account? To what extent does one need to individualize an activity for learners? To what extent must learners conform to pre-determinned norms? Though not new in themselves, such questions acquire a fertile sense when seen through the reflective experience on which is founded the *pedagogics pattern* model.

Satisfying user needs and satisfaction can also be handled in looking at learning styles and strategies. Coffield, Moseley, Hall & Ecclestone (2004) undertook a major study about learning styles and strategies to show the scientific validity of the learning styles studied. Akkoyunlu & Yılmaz-Soylu (2007, p. 26) support this point of view when they say that careful blending of different models of teaching and styles of learning would give a richer and more accurate sense to the term blended learning. A word of caution is needed at this point. Following the heydays of learning styles in the 1980's and 1990's, time has shown that being aware of one's preferences and habits when learning is not the much hoped for silver bullet (Labour 2002). The danger today is the risk of throwing away the baby with the bath water. To reject naively out of hand all the work done on learning styles and strategies is to ignore, at the very least, the heuristic value of such grassroots practices. Its value is not so much what it seems to shows about a person's "style", but rather the projective sense that the person ascribes to these partial representations of his/her learning "styles" and "strategies". Learning styles and strategies can be used as a mirror to help learners step back from their actions and choices. It is in taking this distance that the process of empowerment can emerge. This is especially important given the growing demands of a type of lifelong learning that expects individuals to fend for themselves following decreasing state-aid to help those less able, for example, to make sense of an information process in terms of their personal knowledge. Philippe Useille (2007), a researcher in information-communication, has shown the fecundity of developing Marcia Bates' Information 1 and Information 2 (Bates 2005) within the field of human sciences. Using an action-research approach, Useille examined the conditions in which blended learning can generate sense making as an informational phenomenon in the personal knowledge construction process. The question can then be asked if a learner's sense making corresponds to how to the person sees his/her own learning preferences and strategies. To put the question in another way, can a clearer understanding of learner's cognitive style and preferences improve how the person makes sense of an information process?

For those working in the area of learning styles and strategies (*e.g.* Labour 2002), there is reason to suppose that knowledge construction patterns operates in a way that can be associated with sense making as a key element of the empowerment process. It is in enhancing learner preferences that relative freedom of choice can be introduced in a technology bounded system. To do this, one would need to individualize our Model to understand better, how individuals, for example, make sense of their actions when engaged in blended e-learning. This individualisation would need to include ways of empowering learners to being aware of the *pedagogics pattern* that could help them construct personalised learning paths in a blended learning way. The key issue here, being that there is no blueprint to acquiring knowledge. Adults face the recurring problems of how to adapt their learning to their personal and social freedoms in a world that is both unpredictable and increasingly connected. This highlights the question of the "opportune moments" in the learning process. At what moment is a synchronic interaction more appropriate than an asynchronic mode, and in what form? Are there critical moments when, for example, face-to-face contacts are more profitable to the learner than other moments? How do we best do this? Laurent Verclyte, a researcher in information-communication science, has developed the concept of "opportune moments" (Verclytte 2002) as a key factor in the informationnal process when using digital texts. Concept such as these could enrich the *pedagogics pattern* model when it comes to sequencing various tasks (see Figure 4) in the different phases of blended instructional. In short, given the technical advances of network computing and social media, and the increasingly heavy demands of lifelong learning, it is important to study the different "opportune moments" in which learners and tutors use the variety of human and digital resources available. It is here that our Model provides a basis for formalising how blended e-learning paths can be set up to better understand interaction processes between learners and tutors in terms of a knowledge domain in a situated context.

CONCLUSION

This chapter started with a presentation of three approaches to blended e-learning (Return On Investment, enriched distance learning, and inter-domain blending). In our study, we consider blended e-learning as an inter-domain that manifests an underlying pattern addressing the age-old question of how to reconcile technology-bounded determinism with users' emotional and cognitive preferences and choices. We outlined our qualitative methodology and looked at the concept of "pattern" as a form of constructed regularity of guiding "rules" that sustains innovation. Based on this, the *pedagogics pattern* model is based on user feedback and refined by design theorist Christopher Alexander's pattern language, and the instructional theory of Jean Houssaye's included-middle Pedagogic Triangle. The informational perspective of Marcia Bates acts as the overall cohesive element that underpins the five anchors of the Model:

1. General description and context
2. Spatio-temporal boundary markers
3. Overall action plan of pedagogical techniques and tools used
4. Group interactions at each pole of the Pedagogic Triangle
5. Feedback

The *pedagogics pattern* model was applied to two different simulation based blended e-learning contexts: Human-Computer Interface design by engineering students, and writing an online troubleshooting journal by computer network technicians. Using these case studies as demonstrations of the viability of our Model, we hope to have convincingly argued for a view of blended e-learning as a more rational and operational framework accessible to instructional designers as well as less technically savvy practitioners using e-learning to satisfy the emotional and cognitive needs of learners in a hands-on way.

ACKNOWLEDGMENT

Concerning the first case study, we thank the *Région Nord-Pas de Calais* (France) and the FEDER (MIAOU and EUCUE European projects) for their support, and colleagues Dr Mouldi Sagar (UVHC) & Professor Pierre Loslever (UVHC) for their contribution, and their help in the data analysis. For the second case study, our thanks go to Samir Haggouchi of the technical college ACTIF for his advice and support. A special thanks goes to the third member of our team, Dr Jacqueline Ducret (UVHC) whose insights were invaluable to this work.

REFERENCES

Akkoyunlu, A., & Yılmaz-Soylu, M. (2008)... *The Internet and Higher Education*, *11*, 26–32. doi:10.1016/j.iheduc.2007.12.006

Alexander, C. (1979). *The Timeless Way of Building*. New York: Oxford University Press.

Alexander, C. (2001). *A Just So Story. How patternlanguage.com got its name.* Retrieved July 22, 2006, from http://www.patternlanguage.com/ leveltwo/patternsframe.htm?/leveltwo/./ history/ ajustsostory6.htm

Alexander, C., Ishikawa, S., Silverstein, M., & Jacobson, M. Fiksdahl-King, & Angel, S. (1977). *A Pattern Language*. New York: Oxford University Press.

Allen, I. E., Seaman, J., & Garrett, R. (2007). *Blending in. The extent and promise of blended education in the United States*. Retrieved on November 5, 2008, from http://www.blendedteaching.org/system/files/Blending_In.pdf

Aycock, A., Garnham, C., & Kaleta, R. (2002). Lessons learned from the hybrid course project. *Teaching with Technology Today, 8*(6). Retrieved November 5, 2008, from http://www.uwsa.edu/ ttt/articles/garnham2.htm

Barrows, H. (1999). *Problem based learning initiative: Generic problem-based learning essentials*. Retrieved November 5, 2008 from http:// www.pbli.org/pbl/generic_pbl.htm

Bates, M. (2005). Fundamental Forms of Information. *Journal of the American Society for Information and Technology*. Retrieved November 5, 2008, from http://www.gseis.ucla.edu/ faculty/ bates/articles/NatRep_info_11m_050514.html

Becker, B., Dawson, P., Devine, K., Hannum, C., Hill, S., Leydens, J., et al. (2005). *Case Studies.* Writing@CSU, Colorado State University Department of English. Retrieved November 5, 2008, from http://writing.colostate.edu/ guides/ research/casestudy/ com4a3.cfm/

Bell, J., Bush, T., Fox, A., Goodey, J., & Goulding, S. (1984). *Conducting Small-Scale Investigations on Educational Management*. London: Paul Chapman Publishing.

Bliuc, A.-M., Goodyear, P., & Ellis, R. A. (2007)... *The Internet and Higher Education*, *10*, 231–244. doi:10.1016/j.iheduc.2007.08.001

Brenner, J. (2005). Knowledge as system: A logic of epistemology. In *6ème Congrès de l'Union européenne de systémique,* Paris, 19-22 September 2005. Retrieved November 5, 2008, from http:// www.autogenesis.ch/brenner.html

Champion, R. (2001). Planning for action, step by step. *Journal of Staff Development.* [NSDC]. *National Staff Development Council, 22*(4), 62–63.

Coffield, F., Moseley, D., Hall, E., & Ecclestone, K. (2004). *Learning styles and pedagogy in post-16 learning. A systematic and critical review*. London: Learning and Skills Research Centre.

Coplien, J. O. (2005). *A Pattern Definition. Software Patterns*. Retrieved November 5, 2008, from http://hillside.net/patterns/definition.html

Damasio, A. R. (2003). *Spinoza avait raison: Joie et tristesse, le cerveau des émotions*. Paris: Odile Jacob.

Deproost, P.-A. (1998). *L'héritage latin. Une culture de l'universel*. Research seminar on L'Europe et la culture des cultures, Council of Europe project EUxIN. University of Louvain, Belgium. Retrieved July 22, 2006 from www.areopage.net/heritage.htm

Devlin, K. (2000). *The Math Gene: How Mathematical Thinking Evolved and Why Numbers Are Like Gossip*. New York: Basic Books.

Engeström, R. Miettinen, & R. Punamaki (Eds.), *Perspectives on Activity theory*. New York: Cambridge University Press.

Engeström, Y. (1999). Activity theory and individual and social transformation. In Y.

Equal. (2004). *Mainstreaming and Creating Impact – A Guide for Development Partnerships*. Sharing Practice from the Equal Programme. Birmingham, UK: Equal Support Unit. Retrieved July 13, 2008 from http://www.equal.ecotec.co.uk/resources/gpg/ gpg/down_doc.asp?file=gpg_mainstreaming.doc

Fincher, S. (1999). Analysis of design: an exploration of patterns and pattern languages for pedagogy. *Journal of Computers in Mathematics and Science Teaching*, *18*(3), 331–348.

Fincher, S., & Utting, I. (2002). Pedagogical patterns: their place in the genre. In *Proceedings of the 7th annual conference, Innovation and technology in computer science education* (pp.199-202). Denmark: Aarhus.

Foucault, M. (2001). Le Sujet du pouvoir. In D. Defert & F. Ewald (Eds.), *Michel Foucault. Dits et Ecrits II* (pp. 1041-1062). Paris: Gallimard.

Friedman, K. (2003). Theory construction in design research: criteria: approaches, and methods. *Design Studies*, *24*, 507–522. doi:10.1016/S0142-694X(03)00039-5

Gamma, E. (1991). *Object-oriented software development based on ET++: Design patterns, class library, tools*. Unpublished Doctoral thesis, University of Zurich, Institut für Informatik.

Gamma, E., Helm, R., Johnson, R., & Vlissides, J. (1995). *Design patterns: elements of reusable object-oriented software*. Boston, MA: Addison-Wesley Longman Publishing.

Garrison, D. R., & Kanuka, H. (2004)... *The Internet and Higher Education*, *7*, 95–105. doi:10.1016/j.iheduc.2004.02.001

Goffman, E. (1991). *Les cadres de l'expérience*. Paris: Editions de Minuit.

Goleman, D., Boyatzis, R., & McKee, A. (2002). *L'intelligence émotionnelle au travail*. Paris: Editions Village Mondial.

Houssaye, J. (1992). *Théorie et pratiques de l'éducation scolaire I: Le triangle pédagogique*. Berne, Switzerland: Peter Lang.

Kolski, C. (1997). *Interfaces homme-machine, application aux systèmes industriels complexes*. Paris: Hermes Science Publishers.

Kolski, C., Sagar, M., & Loslever, P. (2004a). Experiment based on participative ergonomics and performed as part of a supervision engineers' training course. In *Proceedings HAAMAHA'2004. Human and Organisational Issues in the Digital Enterprise*, Galway, Ireland.

Kolski, C., Sagar, M., & Loslever, P. (2004b). Spécification d'IHM dans les systèmes critiques: retour d'expérience sur une pratique en enseignement de l'IHM. In *Proceedings IHM'2004, Interaction Homme-Machine*, Namur, Belgium.

Labour, M. (1998). *Que pense l'apprenant de l'apprentissage guidé de l'anglais ? Un*

Labour, M. (2002). Integrating ICT and learning profiles in an EFL training course for primary school teachers. In *Australian Computers in Education Conference 2002, Linking learners*, Hobart, Australia.

Labour, M. (2006). Recomposer les métiers du multimédia: quel espace pour un *empowerment* coopératif? Cinquième Colloque international. *Formation, Recherche et Métiers des Technologies de l'Information et de la Communication (TIC)*. Invited paper, University Antonine.

Labour, M., Useille, P., & Crévits, I. (2006). Evaluation formative et TIC: quelle résolution d'une problématique interdisciplinaire? In *8e Biennale de l'éducation et de la formation, Débats sur les recherches et les innovations,* Lyon, France. Retrieved June 2, 2006, from http://ateliers.inrp.fr/Biennale/Ateliers/Atelier-2/travaux/DIGOR_Biennale2006.doc

Merriam-Webster Online. (2005). Retrieved November 5, 2008, from http://www.m-w.com/

Nicolescu, B. (2000). Transdisciplinarity and Complexity: Levels of Reality as Source of Indeterminacy. *Bulletin Interactif du Centre International de Recherches et Études transdisciplinaires* n° 15. Centre International de Recherches et Études Transdisciplinaires.

Oliver, M., & Trigwell, K. (2005). Can "blended learning" be redeemed. *E-Learning, 2*(1). Retrieved September 2, 2006 from http://www.wwwords.co.uk/pdf/viewpdf.asp?j=elea&vol=2&issue=1&year= 2005&article=3_Oliver_ELEA_2_1_web&id=86.215.192.54

Panorama des représentations des adultes en formation continue. Unpublished doctoral Thesis, Université de Technologie de Compiègne, France.

Pedagogical Patterns Project. (2001). Retrieved November 5, 2008, from http://www.pedagogicalpatterns.org/

Phipps, R., & Merisotis, R. (1999). *What's the difference? A review of contemporary research on the effectiveness of distance learning in higher education*. The Institute for Higher Education Policy, Washington, DC.

Rasmussen, J. (1986). *Information processing and human-machine interaction, an approach to cognitive engineering*. Amsterdam: Elsevier Science Publishing.

Reiser, R. (2001). A History of Instructional Design and Technology. Part 1: A History of Instructional Media. *Educational Technology Research and Development, 49*(1), 53–64. doi:10.1007/BF02504506

Retrieved from November 5, 2008 http://nicol.club.fr/ciret/bulletin /b15/b15c4.htm.

Richards, L., & Richards, T. (1994). From filing cabinet to computer. In Bryman, A. & Burgess, R.G. (eds.) *Qualitative Data*. 1994. (pp.146-172). New York: Routledge.

Schaeffer, J.-M. (1999). *Pourquoi la fiction?* Paris: Seuil.

Steen, H. L. (2008). Effective elearning design. *MERLOT Journal of Online Learning and Teaching, 4*(4), 526-532. Retrieved March 27, 2009, from http://jolt.merlot.org/ vol4no4/steen_1208.pdf

Steen, L. A. (1988). The science of patterns. *Science, 240*, 611–616. doi:10.1126/science.240.4852.611

Underhill, J. W. (2001). *Meaning, language, and mind: an interview with Mark Turner –Interview.* Northern Illinois University: Gale Group. Retrieved November 5, 2008, from http://findarticles.com/p/articles/mi_m2342/is_4_36/ai_98167920/print?tag= artBody;col1

Useille, P. (2007). *Une approche informationnelle du Document: vers l'émergence du sens formatif.* Unpublished doctoral thesis, University of Valenciennes and Hainaut-Cambrèsis, France.

Verclytte, L. (2002). Vers des documents sur mesure au moment opportun. Application au document d'apprentissage. In *Journées doctorales de la Société Française des Sciences de l'Information de la Communication (SFSIC)*, Paris.

Wade, S. J. (2002). The application of pedagogical design patterns to the development of distance learning materials. *Distance Learning Colloquium*. Organised by LTSN-ICS University of York, UK.

Wallace, M. J. (1998). *Action Research for Language Teachers*. Cambridge, UK: Cambridge University Press Watzlawick, P., Beavin J., & Jackson D. (1967/1972). *Une logique de la communication*. Paris: Seuil.

Willig, C. (2008). *Introducing Qualitative Research in Psychology.* Maidenhead, UK: Open University Press.

ADDITIONAL READING

Alexander, C. (2002). *The Nature of Order. The Phenomenon of Life*. Centre for Environmental Structures: Berkeley, Calif. USA

Carliner, S., & Shank, P. (2008). *The E-learning Handbook: Past Promises, Present Challenges*. San Francisco, CA: Jossey-Bass

Fee, K. *(2009).* Delivering E-learning: A Complete Strategy for Design, Application and Assessment.

London: Kogan Page Leung, E.W.C., Wang, F.L., Miao, L., Zhao, J., & Jifeng, H. (ed.). (2008). *Advances in Blended Learning: Second Workshop on Blended Learning*. Revised Selected Papers. Wbl Jinhua, China. Berlin: Springer-Verlag

Macdonald, J. (2008). *Blended Learning and Online Tutoring: Planning Learner Support and Activity Design.* 2nd revised edition. Aldershot, UK: Gower Publishing

Sears, A., & Jacko, J. A. (Eds.). (2007). *The Human-Computer Interaction Handbook Fundamentals, Evolving Technologies and Emerging Applications*. 2nd Edition. London: CRC Press

Shank, P. (Ed.). (2007). *The Online Learning Idea Book: 95 Proven Ways to Enhance Technology-based and Blended Learning*. San Francisco, CA: Jossey-Bass

Stacey, E., & Gerbic, P. (Eds.). (2009). *Effective Blended Learning Practices: Evidence-based Perspectives in ICT-facilitated Education*. Hershey, PA: Information Science Reference

ENDNOTES

1 The "included middle" principle of modern science challenges a "single level of Reality" (cf. Brenner 2005, Nicolescu 2000) in that there are occasions when apparently "different" qualities simultaneously and necessarily attract/repulse each other. For example, one finds the description in quantum physics when the photon is seen as having simultaneously wave *and* particle properties. The photon thus finds itself in the "middle" of complementary relations involving qualitatively different properties. This leads to a multi-level perception of what is constructed as a given "reality".

2 The **Dead** is the element akin to that of an uninvited guest to a party who accepts the decision of being left out, though not completely forgotten (Houssaye 1992, p. 238).

3 The **Madcap**, taking the metaphor of being invited to a party, represents a gatecrasher (Houssaye 1992, p.43).

4 Dr Jacqueline Ducret (University of Valenciennes and Hainaut-Cambrésis, UVHC) conducted a third case study with her business students in the course of this study. For reasons of space, only two case studies were used to demonstrate the validity of our Model in this chapter.

5 "Activity framed in a particular way – especially collectively organized social activity – is often marked off from the ongoing flow of surrounding events of a conventionalized kind. These occur before and after the activity in time and may be circumscriptive in space, in brief there are temporal and spatial brackets" (Goffman 1974, pp.251-252).

6 The European funded program, *Equal*, defines "good" practice as "approaches that are working well and can be duplicated elsewhere". This differs from "promising" practice (unevaluated practice in the early stages of development), "effective" practice (practice working well under specific conditions), and "best" practice (practice working at the highest standard, better than "good practice") (*Equal* 2004, Section 1.1).

7 Turner's blended space consists of three basic mental operations: 1. *mapping* between "input spaces", involving connections like identity, analogy, similarity, causality, time, space, intentionality, role; 2. *selective projection*, projecting elements from the input spaces to the **blended space**; and 3. *emergent structure*, putting together of elements, filling in of "partial patterns", and developing the blended space according to the above principles (Underhill 2001, para. 52-57).

Chapter 7
Designing E-Learning Applications with Students: The Case of the We!Design Methodology

George N. Triantafyllakos
Aristotle University of Thessaloniki, Greece

George E. Palaigeorgiou
University of Thessaly, Greece

Ioannis A. Tsoukalas
Aristotle University of Thessaloniki, Greece

ABSTRACT

In years past, many methodological approaches, methods and techniques have been implemented based on the belief that users can and should be involved in the design process of technology products that affect them. Inspired by the findings of research involving users and particularly students at diverse levels and phases of the design process of technology products, we have developed the We!Design methodology, a student-centered participatory design methodology that assigns students a primary role in the design process. We present the various phases of the We!Design methodology, examine the results of its application in four different design projects (a web-based e-assessment application for tertiary education, a course website, an e-Portfolio application, and a Tablet-PC-based e-assessment application for secondary education) and elaborate upon our overall experiences with the methodology during the past 3 years. Participant evaluations indicated that the We!Design methodology was an adequate means for successful elicitation of students' needs and their application in educational software design.

INTRODUCTION

The participation of users at diverse levels and phases in the design process of technology products has become common practice within the HCI community. As pointed out by Kay (1990) and further elaborated in the seminal work of Druin (2002)

"...the actual dawn of user interface design first happened when computer designers finally noticed, not just that end-users had functioning minds, but that a better understanding of how

DOI: 10.4018/978-1-60566-940-3.ch007

these minds worked, would completely shift the paradigm of interaction."

In recent years, many methodological approaches, methods and techniques have strived to achieve such a goal. The overarching link between all of these approaches is a commitment to the belief that users can and should be involved in the design process of technology that affects their work or their life (Ehn & Kyng, 1991; Bødker et al., 1991, Muller, 1991). There are only a few exceptions to this rule (Webb, 1996).

Children, and particularly students, comprise a unique group of participants whose perspectives as designers or merely initiators of educational activities in learning environments have not been adequately conveyed. This conclusion is further confirmed by Könings (2007) in a recent study investigating the desirability and feasibility of use of participatory design in education. In one of his questions on whether students convey their ideas about education to teachers, none of the students gave a positive answer. Various reasons are presented as justifying this negative result; namely, the fear that teachers will not use the information given by students, the fear of conflicts with teachers, and the lack of opportunities for students to convey their ideas. However, as shown in the same study, the majority of the students (58.3%) would appreciate the opportunity to engage in the participatory design of their education, while only 20.8% objected to that idea (Könings, 2007).

In this chapter, our objective is to present the main principles and issues governing the idea of the participation of students in the design process of educational technology products. We present the We!Design methodology, a student-centered participatory design methodology which aims at involving students in the design of e-learning applications and we look into the results of its application in four different design projects. Finally, we elaborate upon our overall experiences with the methodology for the past 3 years.

DESIGNING EDUCATIONAL TECHNOLOGY PRODUCTS WITH CHILDREN

While the literature is quite rich in case studies of adult users participating in the design of technology products (e.g. Bødker et al., 1991; Muller, 1991), it is nevertheless limited when it comes to children as participants (Nesset & Large, 2004). There are two main reasons why this is the case. The first and most important reason is that children are an extremely diverse and special user group per se. Markopoulos & Bekker (2003) adopt Akuff and Reiher's four developmental stages to distinguish the following age groups for children: (a) the dependency/exploratory stage (ages birth–2 years), (b) the emerging-autonomy stage (ages 3–7), (c) the rule/role stage (ages 8–12), and (d) early and late adolescence (age 13 upwards). Each age group is characterized by its specific cognitive abilities, social behavior patterns, relations, preferences in technology products and interfaces, and so on. Thus, it is imperative that any team involved in design projects that plans to involve children in the design process should establish beforehand a deep understanding of children's cognitive, social and developmental traits and adapt its methods and techniques to the corresponding age group.

The second reason refers to the nature of technological products being designed by and for children. Any kind of technology designed for children is characterized by its inherent educational nature. Even though a more traditional perspective would suggest that technology for children could be divided into two broad categories, recreational and educational, the "all-learning" disposition of a child (Druin, 2002) gives a more or less evident educational character to all technology products. Typically, they must be conceived and designed in a way that they embody specific and complex learning theories and interface principles that, as a rule, children are aware of. Thus, it is not clear how children can contribute to the design of such products, when neither the domain knowledge which the educational product is concerned with nor the approach by which it should be taught to them is something they know about (Scaife, 1997).

Druin (2002) distinguishes four roles that children can play when involved in the design process. Each role frames a different level of involvement in the design process, either in terms of the phase of the product design life cycle at which children might contribute, or in terms of the empowerment and the opportunities given to the children as designers. The four roles form a continuum of involvement ranging:

- From children as *users* who explore the technology and act more as subjects to be observed in search for future design directions
- To children as *testers* that hold a more critical role of assessing and critiquing engineered ideas and prototypes
- To children as *informants*, suggesting modifications and adjusting the design process throughout its duration
- To children as *equal and fully-empowered design partners*, with the same opportunities to suggest ideas and initiate changes as the designers

Deciding which one of these four roles is the most suitable for a project should be based on the actual needs and goals of the project at hand or on pragmatic restrictions; namely, limitations on resources, time, participants' availability and so on, or should be grounded in more solid theoretical and methodological choices. The most prominent methodological approaches found in the literature include the Participatory and/or Cooperative Design and Informant Design, and the traditions of User-centered and Learner-centered Design. A more elaborate review of these approaches can be found in Nesset & Large (2004).

Based on these theoretical approaches, a number of methods and techniques for the inclusion of children of all age groups in the design process have been developed. Cooperative Inquiry, developed by Druin and her colleagues at the University of Maryland, using a number of techniques inspired by Participatory, Collaborative Design and Contextual Inquiry (Druin, 1999), assigns to children the role of equal design partners. By collecting data from the children's environment, involving them in cooperative prototyping and brainstorming activities, and capturing activity patterns in technology-rich environments, Cooperative Inquiry has been reported, in several publications, as a very efficient and effective approach for working with children. Bonded Design (Large et al., 2006) is another approach which, using design techniques such as needs assessment, evaluation, discussion, brainstorming, prototyping and consensus building, aims at creating low-tech prototypes of information technology products with intergenerational teams of users. The authors of Bonded Design situate the approach somewhere between Cooperative Inquiry and the Informant Design model, *"sharing the former's belief in the ability of children to work as partners in all aspects of the design process, but the latter's reservations about the extent to which full and equal cooperation can be established across the generational divide."* (Large et al., 2006). Mixing Ideas (Guha et al., 2004) is another Cooperative Inquiry technique aiming at establishing an effective collaboration with children within the age-group of 4-6 years. It was used in a research project envisioning the Classroom of the Future in order to *"understand(ing) the unique needs of young children (ages 3-6) in learning environments; develop(ing) new technologies in partnership with children and teachers; and understand(ing) the impact these technologies can have on young children and their early childhood environments"* (Guha et al., 2004). Finally, KidReporter (Bekker et al., 2003) is a method that aims at gathering requirements of children at the age of 9-10 years for the design of interactive and educational projects. The method offers a diverse range and choice of activities to children, allowing them to express their opinions on the design problem, which results in a newspaper containing their ideas and suggestions (Bekker et al., 2003).

Apart from the somewhat obvious benefits of designing more situated and appropriate technology products, the analysis of children's involvement in various case studies resulted in additional positive outcomes both for the children and the designers. The educational benefits of such approaches have been advocated by Roda (2004). Roda elaborates on the idea that a participatory design approach in an interdisciplinary context can serve as a pedagogical tool that supports the exchange of knowledge between participants with diverse academic backgrounds and interests, and allows for the application of constructivist learning to take place (Roda, 2004). Kafai et al. (1997), in discussing the benefits of designing educational multimedia software together with children, mention how both designers and learners can develop a different perspective on the subject-matter. Such reciprocal insights into the ways both the instructional designer and the children cope with the subject-matter can help the two sides develop a deeper understanding of each other's needs. Druin refers to Design-Centered Learning (Druin, 1999) as the most positive side-effect of children's participation in the design process while employing the Cooperative Inquiry method. It is an accumulation of different learning outcomes that emerge during intergenerational design collaboration. Such outcomes may include learning about the design process, learning about respect for other design partners and their ideas, learning about collaboration and communication in a team, acquiring new technology skills and knowledge and, finally, acquiring new domain knowledge (Druin, 1999).

These approaches are not without difficulties and shortcomings however. Depending on their age, children may exhibit difficulty in expressing their ideas (Nesset & Large, 2004). At the same time, they may find it hard to collaborate with other, mostly adult, team members, feeling intimidated by previous established and ubiquitous power relations between them and adults, and between them and teachers (Scaife, 1997; Nesset & Large, 2004). Children may withdraw or become visibly upset if they feel that their ideas are not being listened to (Guha et al., 2005). In addition, they may suggest novel and inspired ideas, which are impossible to realize (Nesset & Large, 2004). They can also be easily influenced by other adults or leading figures in the design team, who undermine their creativity (Bekker, 2003).

In order to overcome such obstacles, it is necessary for any participatory design approach to establish a solid ground for collaboration through the use of the necessary mediating tools and techniques appropriate for the project at hand and the age group it is concerned with. At the same time, it should set up a collaborative environment that respects, motivates, stimulates and eventually rewards children for their contributions (Bekker, 2003). All the methods and approaches previously mentioned aim towards the establishment of these terms with undoubtedly positive results. Inspired by these positive tendencies, we have developed the We!Design methodology (Triantafyllakos et al. 2008a), a student-centered participatory design methodology that aims at involving students in the design of e-learning applications.

THE WE!DESIGN METHODOLOGY

Existing methodological approaches and techniques have demanding requirements concerning time, resources and involvement on the part of the students. Most of the approaches aim at the design of learning tools or domain-specific educational applications, and do not cope with educational software that facilitates common cognitive and learning processes (such as note-taking or assessment). Finally, they do not fully take account of or benefit from the design capabilities of students with advanced computer literacy skills and knowledge. Although many commercial and research applications strive to support and enhance similar processes, they are incapable of taking into account the technological, social and cultural particularities of each educational context, such as its social organization (e.g. power relations, collaboration or schooling strategies), the students' computer knowledge or the technical infrastructure of the learning environment (e.g. computer availability or network infrastructure).

In order to overcome such obstacles, the We!Design methodology (a) sets up a solid ground for collaboration through the use of the appropriate techniques, (b) establishes an environment that respects, motivates, stimulates and rewards all students (with either advanced or limited literacy skills) for their contributions (Bekker, 2003) and, eventually, (c) allows for them and their particular technological, social and cultural needs to become the central focus for both the designers and the design process. The methodology's objective is to enable the design of educational software tools that respond accurately to the distinctive conditions of diverse educational environments. It fits with design circumstances where (a) wide-ranging perspectives on the design problem are essential, (b) time-barriers are restricting and (c) participants' long-term involvement is not feasible. It can become an integral part of the everyday reality of an educational institution, in a way that does not disrupt the students' primary learning objectives and/or activities.

The methodology focuses on the collaboration of software designers with students (ranging from secondary to undergraduate university students, thus aged between 12 and 22 years old), educators and other stakeholders, for the design of e-learning applications that support and enhance typical educational processes such as communication, cooperation, knowledge management, knowledge sharing, course management, and so on. Following the paradigm of a communicative approach to design (Visscher-Voerman & Gustafson, 2004) the methodology assigns students a primary role in the design process, confronting design dilemmas through discussion and democratic decision-making. It differs from other participatory design approaches in its demand for several iterations of the same brief and structured process while employing different students as participants in each repetition.

The Methodology's Phases

Compiled out of a set of techniques, the We!Design methodology consists of two phases: one in which students participating in different design sessions create needs, tasks and user interface prototypes and a second one in which designers analyze and compile the students' suggestions.

Phase 1: Design Sessions with Students

During the first phase, multiple iterations of the same, concise and highly-structured, collaborative design session are conducted with different students. These sessions last for approximately 3 hours and consist of three stages:

a. Initially, students recall and elaborate upon their prior problems and needs concerning the e-learning application and prioritize them (approximately 70 minutes)
b. They work together in order to suggest ways of satisfying those needs in the form of exact sequences of user actions and system responses – we call this the task analysis stage (approximately 80 minutes)
c. They design a low-tech prototype interface, which incorporates those sequences, using a whiteboard, coloured markers and Post-it™ notes (approximately 40 minutes)

Setting, Participants and Coordinators

Each design session requires the participation of three or four students and two coordinators.

Maintaining a small number of participants in a design session helps to minimise the number of possible time-consuming and, sometimes, unproductive conflicts between them and, in addition, reduces the time required for establishing a friendly atmosphere throughout the session. One of the coordinators (the domain expert) must have a deep understanding of the educational process under examination and his responsibility is to ensure that the students' design decisions do not run contrary to commonly-accepted pedagogical norms and educators' and other stakeholders' interests. The other coordinator is a human-computer-interaction (HCI) expert, whose focal interest is to preserve the usability of the prototype designed (Bødker, Greenbaum & Kyng, 1991; Muller, 1991). Both coordinators must ensure that each student has the same chances as everyone else to present his ideas or elaborate on the ideas of others (Guha et al, 2005; Muller, 1991), and that all suggestions are given both careful and equal consideration (Guha et al, 2004; Muller, 1991). While doing that though, the coordinators should be careful not to interfere with the students' decision-making processes. It is important that they take on this helpful but unobtrusive role for themselves and establish a democratic, pleasant and informal atmosphere throughout the design process. The way they dress, talk and behave can greatly help in achieving this goal and thus it is recommended that they be casual and not strict or formal in any way. Furthermore, the use of ice-breakers at the beginning of the session is considered to be a good way to achieve the desired informality.

All participants sit around a table. A whiteboard is used for the design of a low-tech prototype of the application during the last stage of the methodology. A video recorder captures the design surface and provides a detailed documentation of the design process.

Stage 1: Needs Analysis

At the beginning of each session, the coordinators give a concise description of the methodology and try to ensure that all students appreciate the significance of their participation. The domain expert introduces the educational process under consideration and describes circumstances and examples that can stimulate students to recall similar experiences (Nesset & Large, 2004; Svanæs & Seland, 2004). The domain expert then asks the students to build a set of needs either based on their prior experiences, strategies, problems and goals or by envisioning relevant facilities that could be provided by electronic means. He makes clear that the description of the needs should not refer to the way in which the needs will be satisfied (Go & Carroll, 2004) so as to avoid shifting the focus of the discussion to technical issues or immediate solutions. During the time that students recall and record their needs, the coordinators should provide any kind of explanation or support that may be needed. Eventually, when students feel that they are ready (usually after a period of 10 to 15 minutes) they present a first set of about five needs to their fellow students in the form of concise scenarios. During students' presentations of their needs, the coordinators must avoid any corrections or interruptions. If they feel that a student is reluctant to speak, they must encourage them to present their thoughts, while, if the opposite happens i.e. a student takes over the process, they should then try to discretely transpose the focus to the rest of the students. After a student has finished his scenario presentation, the domain expert must restate the proposed scenario with the help of the students in a more detailed manner. By doing that, he helps students become more rapidly acquainted with what is asked of them. He may then ask for clarification of the proposed needs, so as to ensure that they are described without ambiguity, while the rest of the students can elaborate on them, ask questions or suggest relevant needs. After a first round of needs have been suggested and discussed, the same process is repeated for 2 or 3 additional rounds, depending on the duration of the discussions that generate needs and the limitations of time. In order to help students, the coordinators use a number of creative activities and variations of their initial request, such as transferring the educational process under examination in an imagined future setting, assigning dramatic roles to the students and so on. Furthermore, mediation artifacts can be provided in order to better stimulate students' thinking e.g. the provision of printed multiple-choice questions for the design of an assessment application. Finally, the commonly-agreed and accepted needs are recorded and, at the end of the first stage, the students evaluate the importance of each need on a 5-point Likert scale. In this manner, students agree upon the design priorities to be followed in the rest of the design session. A short break follows, while the suggested needs are sorted by the coordinators based on student rankings.

Step 2: Task Analysis

At the second stage, students are asked to describe task sequences i.e. exact sequences of user actions and system responses that can satisfy each previously-stated need. These task sequences should contain an analysis of all the physical and computational objects involved in those interactions. This step aims at familiarizing students with the design space of each need separately, before more specific prototype design moves constrain their intuition and creativity. Concurrently, students explore the process of transforming a need to an abstract solution and then into an interaction model, gradually shifting their focus from requests to technical solutions.

It is very important at the beginning of this stage, that the coordinators should clarify that, from this point on, the students are assigned full control of the process. Conflicts or divergent ideas that occur should be resolved through a consensus-reaching process achieved by the students themselves. They are asked to agree upon one commonly-agreed task sequence for each need through a process of mutual agreement and compromise. If this is not possible, the coordinators can interfere and make the students decide upon the alternatives or else create one joint solution; however, their role is more transparent in this process than in the first step. The second stage ends when all the needs suggested have been examined or when the stage exceeds its predetermined duration. The fact that the agreed needs are ordered according to their importance, ensures that the most significant ones are always considered.

Step 3: Interface Prototyping

In the third and final stage of the design sessions, students design a low-tech prototype application using a process similar to PICTIVE (Muller, 1991). They are asked to portray the interactive objects of each final task sequence upon the whiteboard using colored markers and Post-it™ notes. The design begins with the task sequence of the most important need and goes on from there. Each task sequence is re-evaluated against the interim state of the prototype interface and either new interaction solutions are initiated or previously designed objects are transformed in order for the analyzed tasks to be embedded in the interface prototype. Once again, the domain expert remains impartial and lets the students initiate and advance any design movement. However, if the expert feels that a design decision is ambiguous or vague students are asked to clarify their suggestions, so as to avoid misinterpretations or confusion. On the other hand, the HCI expert actively provides scaffolding for the students in the design of a usable interface prototype by providing alternative interaction objects and observing possible interaction flaws.

Eventually, a walkthrough test is conducted, in which some team members role-play stereotypical students, using the educational application, while others record usability issues and potential revisions. This is the last activity of the design session and the coordinators thank students for their participation and their valuable contributions and the session ends. The resulting prototype is photographed and together with the intermediate products of the session i.e. the list of commonly-agreed needs and their corresponding task sequences, this constitutes the sum of products generated in each session which will eventually be used by the designers to develop the final software product.

Phase 2: Synthesis of the Final Application

In the second phase, the designers gather and analyze the products of the design sessions in order to synthesize one single software product. Initially, the suggested needs are clustered, based on their content, and similar needs are grouped and rewritten so that overlapping is avoided. Each need is re-evaluated in accordance with the number of sessions in which it appeared, and the students' average assessment of its importance. The needs are sorted based on their new rankings, and the most important needs are selected so as to constrain the design space. The designers compile the diverse task sequences of each final need into one task sequence, analyze the students' prototypes in order to detect common interactive objects and workspaces, and progressively build the final application. However, it should be emphasized that the synthesis of the various students' task sequences and prototypes stems from the HCI expert's subjective interpretation of the students' proposals. Although the methodology ensures that different HCI experts would suggest similar features for the final application, it is also probable that they would propose slightly different interfaces for the application. Whichever the case, the final application is once again presented to the participating students for them to evaluate and for them to suggest possible weaknesses or flaws. A schematic summary of the We!Design methodology is presented in Figure 1.

Figure 1. Schematic summary of the We!Design methodology phases and design activities

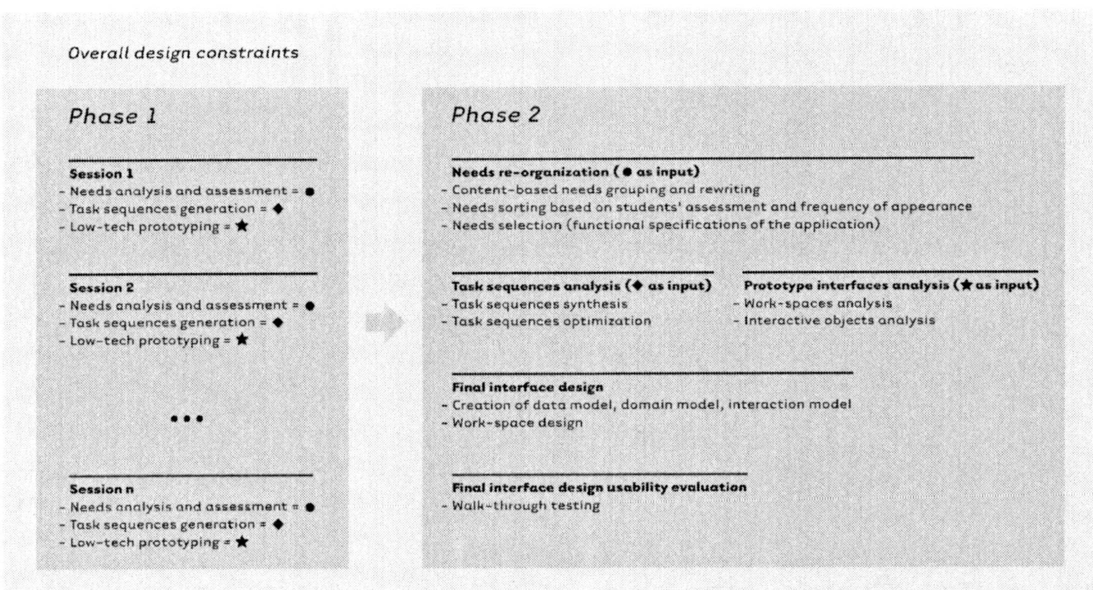

THE DESIGN OF FOUR EDUCATIONAL SOFTWARE TOOLS WITH THE WE!DESIGN METHODOLOGY

During the course of the past 3 years, we have deployed the We!Design methodology with the participation of 168 students and educators in 46 design sessions, for the design of four educational software tools: (a) a web-based e-assessment application for tertiary education, (b) a course web site, and (c) an e-Portfolio application, and (d) a Tablet-PC based e-assessment application for secondary education.

The first 3 projects took place in an Informatics Department with the participation of undergraduate students in the 3rd or 4th year of their studies. All students had limited experience of software engineering and design and, thus, they could be considered as merely experienced computer users. Students' registration in the design sessions was voluntary and was conducted through the use of a web-based registration system; hence, group synthesis was not controlled. For the design of the e-assessment application, we conducted 16 design sessions with the participation of 59 undergraduate students. Twenty-six (26) students were female (44%) and 33 were male (56%). For the design of the course website, we conducted 12 design sessions with another 45 undergraduate students. Twenty-one (21) students were female (46%) and 24 were male (54%). Finally, for the design of the e-Portfolio application, we conducted 9 design sessions with the participation of 33 undergraduate students. Ten (10) students were female (30%) and 23 were male (60%).

The last project was the only one that took place in a high school setting and it was concerned with the development of a Tablet-PC based assessment application for secondary education. This was also the first time that we modified the We!Design methodology in such a way as to place teachers in the students' position. We conducted 9 design sessions with the participation of 15 students in 4 sessions and 16 educators in 5 sessions. Three (3) students were female (20%) and 12 were male (80%), while 8 educators were female (50%) and 8 were male (50%). The age of all students ranged from 12 to 13 years, while none of them had previous experience of software design or engineering. They were selected for participation by their educators based on our demand for students with at least basic skills and knowledge of computer use.

All students and educators participating in the design projects were asked to complete two questionnaires at the end of each session and another one when the design of the final application was completed, as a means of evaluating the methodology and its products. The first two questionnaires aimed at examining their beliefs about the methodology, as well as the perceived usefulness and ease of use of the interface prototype from each session. The last questionnaire, which was also concerned with ease of use and perceived usefulness, was used for the evaluation of the final application interface. All questionnaires contained responses on 5-point Likert scales. Apart from the questionnaires, the researchers examined the video recordings thoroughly in order to perform a qualitative evaluation of the methodology application and identify issues concerning students' problems and/or inefficiencies in the methodology.

Each project lasted for approximately 8–9 weeks; the design sessions were conducted in the first 2 or 3 weeks, while during the remaining weeks the designers analyzed the session products, synthesized the requirements and built the mock-up application. The session questionnaires, intermediate products and the resulting prototype applications of all projects can be found at the URL address: http://ierg.csd.auth.gr/We!Design.

In the following section, we will explore the value of the We!Design methodology by trying to address the main questions that might concern an educational designer before selecting a design methodology: Were the students satisfied with their participation in the design sessions? Was it a pleasant experience? Did the participants confront difficulties when following the design session processes? How have the design products been assessed? Does the methodology manage to take into consideration the particularities of each educational environment? And finally, are the participants willing to contribute to the development of their future tools? We will elaborate on those questions, providing examples from our overall experiences with the methodology for the past 3 years.

Results

Were the Students Satisfied with Their Participation in the Design Sessions? Was It a Pleasant Experience?

A statistical survey concerned with the realization and evaluation of each project is presented in Table 1. Overall, the participants' attitude towards the We!Design methodology was very positive, as can be observed in Table 1, while their engagement with the design projects was intense. Their average satisfaction (Mean = 4.64, Standard Deviation = .28), along with their evaluation of their participation (M = 4.53, S.D. = .28) and their freedom of expression (M = 4.50, S.D. = .29) during the design process of all projects was high. They appreciated the coordinators' role in the process, praising their ability to establish a friendly atmosphere (M = 4.67, S.D. = .31), their preparedness (M = 4.51, S.D. = .30) and the fact that they avoided interfering in the design decisions (M = 4.47, S.D. = .29). Participants felt relatively at ease with our demand to video-record their interactions (M = 4.36, S.D. = .29).

It was evident to the researchers that the cohesion of the methodology stages (since each activity was well-related to the following ones), the progressive exploration of the design space (from needs to independent abstract solutions and to the integration of specific technical proposals) and the managed demand for cooperation (from extracting needs almost alone, to negotiating common task sequences, and to cooperatively designing the prototype) strengthened students' self-confidence and their commitment to the methodology. No significant statistical differences were detected either between males' and females' evaluations or between students' and teachers' assessments. Informal comments at the end of several design sessions such as 'I wish we had more opportunities to participate in such activities', 'It was a stimulating experience', 'It was my best university experience' etc, reaffirmed the interesting, enjoyable and stimulating character of the design sessions.

Hence, the methodology can be appealing per se and attract students and teachers as an intense experience, irrespective of its final product outcome. Participants seemed to enjoy the design experience.

Did the Participants Confront Difficulties When Following the Design Session Processes?

The participants did not have any significant problems in understanding and putting into practice what was asked of them. In the needs analysis stage, initially, they tended to propose technical solutions to address implicit needs and were puzzled about how to recall and state prior problems and desires. They expected that the sessions would focus on the exploration of technical solutions. However, they quickly became acquainted with the demands of the methodology. Inevitably, due to limitations of time, each session focused on a subset of the domain issues and, hence, the multiplicity of the design sessions was a necessity. When participants had experience with the domain and/or similar tools (mostly in the web course project), they proposed refined needs easily, while when the domain was not familiar (as in the e-portfolio project), they were reluctant to recall and elaborate on corresponding issues and needs. The We!Design methodology seemed to

Table 1. Summarizing statistics for each design project

Sessions	Mean Duration				Participants		Average needs per session	Satisfaction with the methodology	Satisfaction with their participation	Satisfaction with the coordinators' role	Usefulness of prototype	Ease of use of prototype	Usefulness of final prototype	Ease of use of final prototype
		N	T	P	F	M								
Project 1: Web-based electronic assessment application for tertiary education														
16	3h 08m	54	74	37	26	33	20.25	4.75 (.27)	4.49 (.38)	4.49 (.22)	4.12 (.39)	4.37 (.27)	3.79 (.27)	4.42 (.20)
Project 2: Course website														
12	2h 55m	58	79	39	21	24	20.7	4.47 (.33)	4.46 (.16)	4.60 (.31)	4.42 (.38)	4.31 (.31)	4.42 (.18)	3.97 (.29)
Project 3: e-Portfolio														
9	2h 54m	50	67	53	10	23	12.7	4.41 (.36)	4.34 (.38)	4.43 (.21)	3.81 (.41)	4.37 (.33)	4.40 (.29)	4.61 (.35)
Project 4: Electronic assessment application for secondary education (e: educators, s: students)														
5 (e)	2h 10m	54	55	21	8	8	18.2	4.91 (.13)	4.89 (.16)	4.83 (.18)	3.95 (.27)	3.91 (.47)	-	-
4 (s)	1h 45m	43	35	26	3	12	19	4.91 (.10)	4.71 (.18)	4.73 (.21)	4.55 (.17)	4.15 (.25)	3.93 (.97)	3.36 (.87)
N: needs stage duration, **T:** task analysis stage duration, **P:** prototyping stage duration (in minutes)														
F: female, **M:** male, **Statistics format:** Mean (Standard Deviation)														

be more suited to improving educational practices (electronic or not) which students had extended experience of. In each session, some general contexts of needs emerged which guided the formation of new needs.

During the task sequences generation stage, the participants managed to cooperate successfully and resolve many conflicts which arose, even though, at times, their arguments were based on intuitive rationale and empirical evaluation rather than formal knowledge of the HCI domain. The coordinators' mediation in such cases was critical in order to help participants decide democratically and continue the procedure. In all projects, participants' computer literacy was a critical prerequisite for the development of the tasks since their prior computer interaction functioned as the main pool of ideas. Task analysis for hypertext interaction (as in the web-course project) seemed unproblematic since they are simple and straightforward, without the involvement of complicated interactive objects.

Eventually, the participants' successful collaboration continued throughout the low-tech prototyping stage. The low-tech prototyping stage was the shorter one on all occasions because it merely represented design decisions already made concerning the application requirements; consequently, it lacked any significant exploration of the design space. However, the participants' prior computer experience, knowledge and skills once again allowed them to come up with interesting and, at times, novel interface design ideas. Due to the limited duration of the prototyping stage and their lack of explicit knowledge of HCI models and theories, the resulting interface prototypes of almost all design sessions were incomplete and suffered from a few usability and consistency problems. That was also something evident to the participants since their evaluations of the ease of use of the prototypes were relatively low. We can claim that participants' competences, in constructing interaction schemes and interface designs that are usable, aesthetically and functionally complete, were limited. This is not unusual when working with low-fidelity prototypes (Rudd et al, 1996) and with non-professional interface designers. However, their contribution, in giving tangible design directions and revealing trends of technology use of specific cultural groups such as students (Satchell, 2008), is certainly appreciated.

Ultimately, the steps in the methodology were easily understood and able to be followed by the participants.

How Have the Design Products Been Assessed?

The two e-assessment applications for tertiary and secondary education were evaluated after their deployment in real conditions. The e-assessment application for tertiary education was evaluated by 60 undergraduate students in their final exams for an Educational Technology course. Their assessment of the usefulness of the application was relatively high (M = 3.79, S.D. = .27) and of its ease of use was very positive (M = 4.42, S.D. = .20). The e-assessment application for secondary education was assessed by 67 students using two different platforms, Tablet-PCs and typical PCs. Its averages for usefulness (M = 3.93, S.D. = .97) and for perceived ease of use (M = 3.36, S.D. = .87) were positive. The course website and the e-Portfolio applications were published online and students were asked to explore and evaluate them in their own time. The results of their evaluation showed that both the usefulness of the application (course website: M = 4.42, S.D. = .18; e-Portfolio: M = 4.40, S.D. = .29) and perceived ease of use (course website: M = 3.97, S.D. = .29; e-Portfolio: M = 4.61, S.D. = .35) were considered adequate.

Although all final applications were evaluated as useful and easy to use, further evaluations need to be conducted in the future in order to appreciate the real value of these applications for educational practice.

Does the Methodology Manage to Take into Consideration the Particularities of Each Educational Environment?

A participatory design methodology should take into consideration issues concerning the technical infrastructure of the educational institution, the work structure, and the cultural predispositions of the members of the educational institution. The We!Design methodology proved to be an effective tool for the incorporation of the aforementioned concerns in the design process.

This can be supported by the comparison of the two assessment applications for secondary and tertiary education (Siozos, 2008). The two applications, even though concerned with the same educational process, had rather distinctive features. For example, process and anxiety management were revealed as a vital part of undergraduate students' experience with assessment processes. Thus, in their application they included sophisticated and innovative schemes for time management (multiple alerts with sliding bells in the time bar, analytical presentation of time-response performance indicators during the test), emergency management features (technical problem alerts, recovery strategies) etc., while the high school students seemed interested in the creation of a complete feedback process. Diversity could be attributed to the particular context of the assessment within higher and secondary education and within Greece. Undergraduate students concentrated on creating the optimum conditions for extracting the best performance. Secondary students paid more attention to exploiting the learning prospects of the assessment process. Another example of differentiation was the level of complexity of the two interfaces. Undergraduate students had designed a composite adaptive display for the presentation of the questions while employing complex navigational objects (such as lists and scrollbars with semantic notations and colors) while the secondary students were more focused on developing a readable and clear presentation of questions and answers.

Overall, the methodology manages to reflect in the designed applications both the differences of the students and of the educational environments.

Are the Students Willing to Contribute to the Development of Their Future Tools?

Students' initial hesitation and uncertainty as to whether they could actually contribute to the design process, weakened and were replaced by feelings of trust and appreciation for their skills and ideas, and confidence that the We!Design methodology can create the necessary conditions for democratic and fruitful collaboration. In addition, at several sessions the participants were critical towards the available educational software or the existing practices. The overwhelming majority of participants asserted that they would rely more on educational software designed using this approach ($M = 4.46$. $S.D. = .30$), thus revealing their willingness to take over responsibility for their learning.

However, the type of educational application being designed can play a major role in participants' attitude towards participation and the resulting products. In the case of the design of the course website, participants seemed to be less intrigued by the project goal, since most of them had used a lot of similar websites in the past. As a result, the participants were rather unsure of their ability to produce something original or more sophisticated. That was also the case in the design of the e-Portfolio, but for the opposite reasons. The fact that the participants did not have extensive previous experience with portfolio management hindered their ability to be able to recall numerous needs (the mean number of needs proposed in each session was the smallest one compared to the rest of the design projects) and diminished their appreciation of the usefulness of the final prototypes (the mean value of the participants' evaluation of the usefulness of the prototype is pretty low). Nonetheless, this did not affect the positive reception of the We!Design methodology per se.

The We!Design methodology seemed more appropriate for the design of applications that support typical educational processes with which students have had extensive experience in the past. Students, in such cases, have a more developed understanding of their problems and needs and consequently can easily capture and elaborate on proposals and solutions. Students can and want to be productive design partners mainly in those cases.

DISCUSSION AND IMPLICATIONS

The We!Design methodology proved an adequate means for successful user needs analysis and educational software design. Both students and teachers were excited by their participation in the design sessions, and they asserted that they would rely more on educational tools designed using this approach. Our results suggest that students want and can assume a more determinating role in inventing their future learning.

Such approaches to designing e-learning applications have three important implications:

- **They promote a decentralized future that empowers locality and diversity:** No mass applications will be imposed on students and teachers, while the cultural integrity of each distinct educational environment can be preserved and further cultivated alongside current technical developments.
- **They promote participation and involvement, and come in opposition to homogenization and passivity:** Students' continuous use, evaluation and enhancement of applications will transform their attitude towards the educational environment from an imposed and external determined reality to a co-created desired prospect that embeds and respects their diversity. We expect that, reciprocally, those elements will strengthen students' educational identity.
- **They promote change management and not abrupt educational interventions:** New e- learning tools provoke significant shifts in students' and learners' practices and participatory design can assure that educational transformation will involve the people rather than them having something imposed upon them. Such approaches do not cancel previous practices but enhance them.

However, it can certainly be argued that those approaches conceal dangers since:

- **They can invoke simplifications and disguise the potentialities:** Students are not experts; they have limited design skills and are incapable of knowing, experiencing and taking advantage of pioneer technologies. Consequently, their contribution, which is guided by experience and intuition, tends to be simplistic and, at times, unoriginal.
- **They may be validated only because of their phenomenal "political correctness" and not assessed in pure educational terms:** Participatory design conveys a sense of social care, of self-determination and confidence, of independence and social justice and sometimes there is the danger that those characteristics can become an end in themselves for its advocates or the evaluators. This remark calls for participatory design advantages to be well verified and measured.
- **They may increase significantly the burden and cost of software development and maintenance:** Contemporary software engineering approaches do not address the demand for many separate and slightly different applications which will

be continuously maintained and updated in different educational environments. Development teams in every university or every school may be required, while component-based architectures could function as a starting point for supporting this diversity. However, further research in software engineering should be conducted so as to transform participatory methodologies to an affordable and realistic alternative approach in wide-scale and long-term educational programs.

There are a number of assumptions that still need to be examined. Although some of the characteristics of the typical learning processes drove the development of our methodology, those processes differed significantly between them. Hence, the methodology's evaluation should involve a more detailed analysis for each of the products designed. Additionally, no information about the students' design rationale and experience were taken into account in our analysis. Even though one could claim that students of an Informatics Department belong to the same community of practice as professional software designers (Bødker & Iversen, 2002) and can thus participate in their advanced language games, it was apparent that the students' contribution was based more on their intuitive experiences than on their knowledge of end-user applications design. Their profile closely resembled that of experienced users, but whether the prospective participants should be novice software designers-developers or just experienced computer users, remains unanswered. The application of the methodology with the participation of diverse types of students (e.g. adult users of e-learning applications) is certainly another interesting course of action for our future research. Furthermore, the success of the final products was not confirmed by novice users. Experienced users externalized their needs and interaction preferences without explicitly adapting them to computer illiterate users. Finally, further examination and testing should take place. The process of employing and analyzing a design methodology and its results (e.g. content analysis) in depth is a difficult and time-consuming one. Thus, we will continue the evaluation of students' designed products so as to gain more insight in the ways the methodology succeeded or not.

Our current and prospective efforts focus on the improvement of the methodology via intensifying the participatory experience. Our main hypothesis is that, since: (a) students' engagement, availability and satisfaction during the We!Design sessions were high, even higher than anticipated, (b) there were even more opportunities for improvements to be made, especially framing students' experience, (c) there were occasions where the facilitators felt that students' familiarization with the process, the locus of attention and engagement in analysis and design activities could be further enhanced, the use of narrative theory could be a means to a more detailed organization of the collaborative design process and thus a way to prescribe a more complete and intense experience for the students (Triantafyllakos, 2008b). We are concerned with the cognitive responses that narrative aesthetics can raise in participants and with the creation of a macro-typology of narrative schemes for each discrete phase of the We!Design methodology.

REFERENCES

Bekker, M., Beusmans, J., Keyson, D., & Lloyd, P. (2003). KidReporter: a user requirements gathering technique for designing with children. *Interacting with Computers, 15*(3), 187–202. doi:10.1016/S0953-5438(03)00007-9

Bødker, S., Greenbaum, J., & Kyng, M. (1991). Setting the stage for design as action. In J. Greenbaum & M. Kyng (Eds.), *Design at work: cooperative design of computer systems* (pp. 139–154). Hillsdale, NJ: Lawrence Erlbaum Associates.

Druin, A. (1999). Cooperative inquiry: developing new technologies for children with children. In *Proceedings of CHI'99,* Pittsburgh, PA, USA, May 15–20 (pp. 592–599). New York: ACM.

Druin, A. (2002). The role of children in the design of new technology. *Behaviour & Information Technology, 21*(1), 1–25.

Ehn, P., & Kyng, M. (1991). Cardboard computers: mocking-it-up or hands-on the future. In J. Greenbaum & M. Kyng (Eds.) *Design at work: cooperative design of computer systems* (pp. 169–195). Hillsdale, NJ: Lawrence Erlbaum Associates.

Go, K., & Carroll, J. M. (2004). Scenario-based task analysis. In D. Diaper & N. Stanton (Eds.), *The Handbook of Task Analysis for Human-Computer Interaction* (pp. 117–134). Hillsdale, NJ: Lawrence Erlbaum Associates.

Guha, M. L., Druin, A., Chipman, G., Fails, J. A., Simms, S., & Farber, A. (2004). Mixing Ideas: A New Technique for Working with Young Children as Design Partners. In *Proceedings of Interaction Design and Children (IDC) 2004 Conference,* ACM, New York, NY (pp. 35–42).

Guha, M. L., Druin, A., Chipman, G., Fails, J. A., Simms, S., & Farber, A. (2005). Working with Young Children as technology design partners. *Communications of the ACM, 48*(1), 39–42. doi:10.1145/1039539.1039567

Iversen, O. S. (2005). *Participatory Design Beyond Work Practices: Designing with Children.* Doctoral Dissertation, Submitted to the Department of Computer Science, University of Aarhus, Denmark.

Kafai, Y. B., Carter-Ching, C., & Marshall, S. (1997). Children as designers of educational multimedia software. *Computers & Education, 29*(2/3), 117–126. doi:10.1016/S0360-1315(97)00036-5

Könings, K. D., van Zundert, M. J., Brand-Gruwel, S., & van Merriënboer, J. J. G. (2007). Participatory design in secondary education: is it a good idea? Students' and teachers' opinions on its desirability and feasibility. *Educational Studies, 33*(4), 445–465. doi:10.1080/03055690701423648

Large, A., Nesset, V., Beheshti, J., & Bowler, L. (2006). Bonded design: A novel approach to intergenerational information technology design. *Library & Information Science Research, 28,* 64–82. doi:10.1016/j.lisr.2005.11.014

Markopoulos, P., & Bekker, M. (2003). Interaction Design and Children. *Interacting with Computers, 15*(2), 141–149. doi:10.1016/S0953-5438(03)00004-3

Muller, M. J. (1991). PICTIVE: Democratizing the dynamics of the design session. In D. Schuler & A. Namioka (Eds.) *Participatory design: principles and practices* (pp. 211–237). Hillsdale, NJ: Lawrence Erlbaum Associates.

Nesset, V., & Large, A. (2004). Children in the information technology design process. *Library & Information Science Research, 26,* 140–161. doi:10.1016/j.lisr.2003.12.002

Roda, C. (2004). Participatory system design as a tool for learning. In *Proceedings of International Conference on Cognition and Exploratory Learning in the Digital Age (CELDA)* (pp. 366–372).

Rudd, J., Stern, K., & Isensee, S. (1996). Low vs. high fidelity prototyping debate. *Interaction, 3*(1), 76–85. doi:10.1145/223500.223514

Satchell, C. (2008). Cultural Theory and Design: Identifying Trends by Looking at the Action in the Periphery. *Interaction, 15*(6), 23–25. doi:10.1145/1409040.1409046

Scaife, M., Rogers, Y., Aldrich, F., & Davies, M. (1997). Designing for or designing with? Informant design for interactive learning environments. In S. Pemberton (Ed.), *Proceedings of the SIGCHI Conference on Human Factors in Computing Systems,* Atlanta, Georgia, United States, March 22–27, 1997 (pp. 343–350). New York: ACM.

Siozos, P., Palaigeorgiou, G., Triantafyllakos, G., & Despotakis, F. (2008). Computer based testing using "digital ink": participatory design of a Tablet PC based assessment application for secondary education. *Computers and Education 52(4), May 2009,* 811-819.

Svanæs, D., & Seland, G. (2004). Putting the users center stage. In *Proceedings of the ACM CHI'04 Human Factors in Computing Systems Conference* (pp. 479–486).

Triantafyllakos, G., Palaigeorgiou, G., & Tsoukalas, I. A. (2008b). Collaborative design as narrative. In *Proceedings of the 10th Participatory Design Conference, PDC08,* 1–4 October 2008, Bloomington, Indiana, USA (pp. 210–213).

Triantafyllakos, G. N., Palaigeorgiou, G. E., & Tsoukalas, I. A. (2008a). We!Design: A student-centred participatory methodology for the design of educational applications. *British Journal of Educational Technology, 39*(1), 125–139.

Visscher-Voerman, I., & Gustafson, K. L. (2004). Paradigms in the theory and practice of education and training design. *Educational Technology Research and Development, 52*(2), 69–89. doi:10.1007/BF02504840

Webb, B. R. (1996). The role of users in interactive systems design: when computers are theatre, do we want the audience to write the script? *Behaviour & Information Technology, 15*(2), 76–83. doi:10.1080/014492996120283

ADDITIONAL READINGS

Bjerknes, G., Ehn, P., & Kyng, M. (Eds.). (1987). *Computers and Democracy: A Scandinavian Challenge*. Aldershot, UK: Avebury.

Greenbaum, J., & Kyng, M. (Eds.). (1991). *Design at Work: Cooperative Design of Computer Systems*. Hillsdale, NJ: Lawrence Erlbaum Associates.

Kyng, M., & Mathiassen, L. (Eds.). (1997). *Computers and Design in Context*. Cambridge, MA: MIT Press.

Schuler, D., & Namioka, A. (Eds.). (1993). *Participatory Design: Principles and Practices*. Lawrence Erlbaum Associates

KEY TERMS AND DEFINITIONS

Participatory Design: A design framework that asks for the active involvement of users in the design process as a means towards the creation of more usable and situated design products.

Design Methodology: A systematic approach to design that contains techniques, actions, events and artefacts in an orderly arrangement.

Educational Software: Computer software whose primary purpose is teaching of self-learning.

E-Learning: Refers to diverse types of technology supported education/learning through the use of computers.

Chapter 8
Orchestrating Ontologies for Courseware Design

Tatiana Gavrilova
Saint-Petersburg State University, Russia

ABSTRACT

This chapter presents an approach aimed at creating teaching strategies for e-learning based on the principles of ontological engineering and cognitive psychology. The proposed framework is important for many reasons. It is targeted at the development of methodologies and related technologies that can scaffold the process of knowledge structuring and orchestrating teaching ontologies for courseware design. The orchestrating procedure is the kernel of ontology development. Ontologies that describe the main concepts of exemplary domains are used both for teaching and assessment techniques. The main stress is put on using visual techniques of mind-mapping and concept mapping as a powerful mind learning tool. Cognitive bias and some results of Gestalt psychology are highlighted as a general guideline. The ideas of balance, clarity, and beauty are applied to the ontology orchestrating procedures. The examples are taken mainly from the course in C-programming, and in the foundations of intelligent systems development.

INTRODUCTION

During the last decade, visual knowledge representation has become one of the key considerations in e-learning methodology and it is heavily associated with ontology design and development. Alongside this, so-called teaching and learning ontologies have arguably come to play a central role in courseware content. These ontologies, which are built on conceptual skeleton of the teaching domain, might serve various purposes such as better understanding, knowledge sharing, and collaborative learning, problem solving, seeking advice, or developing competences by learning from peers. Recently, ontological engineering perspective has gained interest in the domain of computer-aided learning and cognitive psychology involving the study of the structure and patterns of knowledge. These studies

DOI: 10.4018/978-1-60566-940-3.ch008

rely heavily on theory and tools from knowledge engineering analysis that has already a longstanding tradition in the knowledge-based systems domain (Mizoguchi & Bordeau, 2007). The tools and techniques developed in this domain can be applied fruitfully in the field of learning structuring and design (Schreiber, 2000; Knight, Gašević & Richards, 2006), SemanticWeb applications (Davies *et al.*, 2002). The ideas of using ontologies and visual structuring in educational e-learning were discussed in many works (Davies, 20008; Gavrilova et al., 2003) and now are implemented in several software tools. These techniques can be used as the assessment tools also.

Ontological engineering can also be used as an effective research instrument to study how the structure and patterns of the domain knowledge are related to other course content pieces such as hands-on tasks, quizzes, exercises, and slideshows or data repositories. Much of the research so far has focused on a limited number of formal representations that are typically easy to be developed while cognitive and methodological issues are rather underestimated. Furthermore, categorization and laddering as the creative synthesizing activities also did not receive much attention in e-learning while they proofed their importance in socio-technical and management research.

Regardless of how ontological engineering is used, in all cases it is necessary to analyze the design procedure. This is typically done using interviews with the students and teachers which is a labor intensive task. The described ontologies were designed and orchestrated for the courses on knowledge engineering delivered by the author in face-to-face and e-learning formats in Graduate School of Management at Saint-Petersburg State University, the School of Computer Science at St.Petersburg State Polytechnic University (both Russia) and University of Milano (Italy), the ontologies for the C-programming course were developed for the course of Dr. Peter Brusilovsky in School of Information Sciences and Libraries at University of Pittsburgh (USA) together with his PhD students.

This chapter traces the cognitive foundations of educational design using the methods of structured ontological engineering. The purpose of the described methodology is to provide teachers and learners with the distinct recommendations in ontology design and orchestrating for better knowledge transfer and sharing.

BACKGROUND

The idea of using visual structuring of information to improve the quality of student's learning and understanding is not new. For more than twenty years concept mapping (Sowa, 1994; Jonassen, 1998; Conlon, 1997) has been used for providing structures and mental models that support the process of teaching and learning. As such, the visual representation of general domain concepts facilitates and supports student understanding of both substantive and syntactic knowledge. Many teachers, especially those who teach sciences and engineering courses, operate as a knowledge analysts or knowledge engineers by making visible the skeleton of the studied discipline and showing the domain's conceptual structure (Kinchin, 2006). Often this structure is called "ontology".

However, ontology-based approach to knowledge representation in pedagogy is a relatively new development. Ontology is a set of distinctions we make in understanding and viewing the world. There are numerous definitions of this milestone term (Neche et al, 1991; Gruber, 1993; Guarino et al, 1995; Gomez-Peres, 1999). Together, these definitions clarify the ontological approach to knowledge structuring while giving enough freedom to open-ended, creative thinking. So, for example, ontological engineering can provide a clear representation of a course structure, main concepts, approaches, terms and their inter-relationships. Many researchers and practitioners argue about distinctions between ontology and a conceptual model. We suppose that ontology corresponds to the analyst's view

Figure 1. Summarizing the ontology classifications in a mind-map

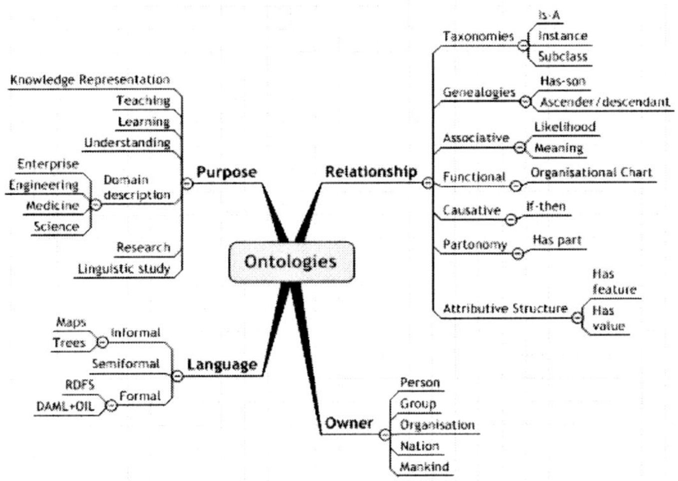

of the conceptual model, but is not de facto the model itself. There are more than one hundred of the techniques and notations that help to define and to visualize the conceptual models. Ontologies now supposed to be the most universal and sharable forms of such modeling.

It originated in knowledge engineering (Boose, 1990; Wielinga, Schreiber, Breuker, 1992), and then it was transferred to knowledge management (Fensel, 2001). Ontologies are useful structuring tools, in that they provide an organizing axis along which every student can mentally mark his vision in the information hyper-space of domain knowledge. Frequently, it is impossible to express the information as a single ontology. Accordingly, subject knowledge storage provides for a set of related ontologies. Some problems may occur when moving from one ontological space to another, but constructing meta-ontologies may help to resolve these problems.

Meta-ontology provides more general description dealing with higher level abstractions. Figure 1 illustrates different ontology classifications in the form of the mind map. Mind-mapping (Buzan, 2005) and concept mapping (Novak & Canas, 2006) are now widely used for visualizing of the ontologies at the design stage.

A mind map is a diagram used to represent words, ideas, tasks, or other items linked to and arranged around a central key word or idea. The central topic sits in the middle with related topics branching out from it. Ideas are further broken down and extended until you've fully explored each branch of your map. Mind maps are used to generate, visualize, structure, and classify ideas, and as an aid in study, organization, and writing. The elements of a given mind map are arranged intuitively according to the importance of the concepts, and are classified into groupings, branches, or areas, with the goal of representing semantic or other connections between portions of information. Some of the earliest examples of mind maps were developed by Porphyry of Tyros, a noted thinker of the 3rd century, as he graphically visualized the concept categories of Aristotle. Philosopher Ramon Lull (1235 - 1315) also used mind maps. British popular psychology author Tony Buzan claims to have invented modern mind mapping. Buzan argues that while 'traditional' outlines force readers to scan left to right and top to bottom, readers actually tend to scan the entire page in a non-linear fashion. Buzan also uses popular assumptions about the cerebral hemispheres in order to promote the exclusive use of mind mapping over other forms of note making.

A concept map is a diagram showing the relationships among concepts. Such maps are graphical tools for organizing and representing knowledge. They include concepts, usually enclosed in circles or boxes of some type, and relationships between concepts indicated by a connecting line linking two concepts. One way to use concept maps for instruction is to have students create maps before and after each instructional activity in a unit. This allows teachers to determine the level of knowledge prior to teaching and to determine whether the desired objectives were met after instruction while allowing students to review their knowledge. Teachers can also discuss and correct any conceptual errors that their students may.

The concept maps represent and clearly name both objects and relations between objects, while mind maps only present objects and the hierarchy of them. The mind map and concept map modelling language involved is based upon a class-based object-oriented language that supports the classification and parameterisation of knowledge entities. As such, it can be applied to developing those tutoring systems where general understanding is more important than factual details. We used such an approach in our teaching of artificial intelligence and cognitive science.

Ontology design also may be used as an assessment procedure where it is used for expressive as opposed to exploratory learning. These are different and complementary modes of learning. Exploratory tools allow learners to investigate models of a given domain which are different from theirs and so examine consequences and conflicts. Expressive tools give the students the opportunity to express their own models about reality and so learn through representing, exploring and reflecting on the consequences of these.

For both formative and summative assessment purposes, students, through creating ontologies and explaining the processes involved, can clearly indicate the extent and nature of their knowledge and understanding. Knowledge entities that represent static knowledge of the domain are stored in the hierarchical order in the knowledge repository and can be reused by others. At the same time those knowledge entities can be also reused in description of the properties or methodological approach as applied in the context of another related knowledge entity.

By static knowledge we mean that the main knowledge patterns don't change at some given period of time. They are supposed to be the same during the substantial period.

ONTOLOGICAL ENGINEERING FOR COURSEWARE DESIGN

Ontological engineering as presented at Figure 2 covers all the issues of ontology development and applications. But it is an unfortunate tradition that technological aspects are much more explored than the methodological ones. Ontology development still faces the knowledge acquisition bottleneck problem, as it was described in the work (Guarino, Giaretta, 1998). The teacher as the ontology developer comes up against the additional problem of not having any sufficiently tested and generalized methodologies recommending what activities to perform and at what stage of the ontology development process these activities should be performed. That is, each ontologist usually follows his/her own set of principles, design criteria, and steps in the ontology development process. Even the last decade when some effective tutorials on ontology development were presented (Noy, 2001; Mizoguchi & Bourdeau, 2000), the absence of structured guidelines and methods hindered the development of shared and consensual ontologies within and between teams; the extension of a given ontology by others; and its reuse in other ontologies and final applications.

Until now, few domain-independent methodological approaches have been reported for building ontologies (Fensel, 2000; Noy, McGuin-

Figure 2. Ontological engineering

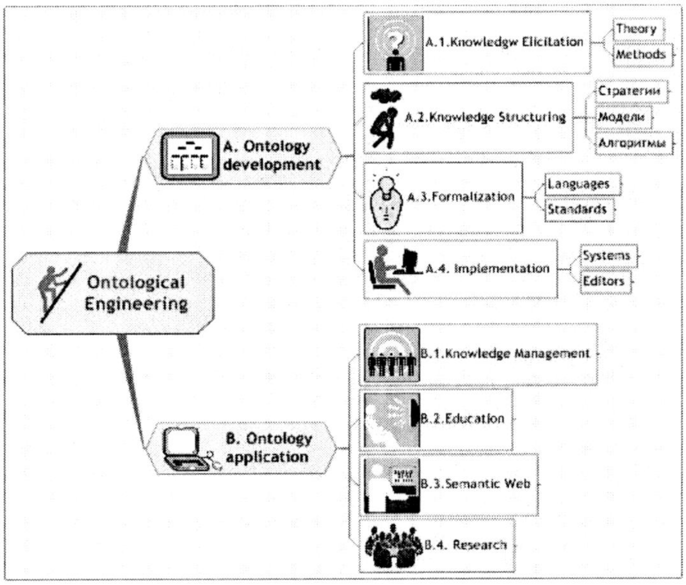

ness, 2001; Dicheva, Aroyo, 2004). These methodologies have in common that they start from the identification of the purpose of the ontology and the need for domain knowledge acquisition. However, having acquired a significant amount of knowledge, major researchers propose a formal language expressing the idea as a set of intermediate representations and then generating the ontology using translators. These representations bridge the gap between how people see a domain and the languages in which ontologies are formalized. The conceptual models are implicit in the implementation codes. A re-engineering process is usually required to make the conceptual models explicit. Ontological commitments and design criteria are implicit in the ontology code.

This chapter proposes a clear, explicit approach to ontology design - to use the visual, iconic representation in a form of a tree or set of tree diagrams/structures. Figures will illustrate the idea how ontology can bridge the gap between the chaos of unstructured data and a clearly mapped representation. However, ontology developers who are unfamiliar with or simply inexperienced in the languages in which ontologies are coded, (e.g. DAML, OIL, RDF) may find it difficult to understand how such ontologies have been created, and, conversely, even how to build a new ontology.

At the basic level of knowledge representation, within the context of everyday heuristics, it is easier for educationalists simply to draw the ontology using conventional "pen and pencil" techniques. It is useful and illuminating to allow learners to create multiple representations (perhaps using different tools) of the same content. However, for more sophisticated and elaborate knowledge representation it is necessary to master appropriate programming and the language involved.

Simple Recipe for Ontology Design

While in major works the emphasis is put on ontology specification (or coding), we would like to elucidate again the essentials of ontology capture in the simplest form as a recipe for "dummies":

A. **Goals, strategy, and boundary identification:** The first step in ontology development should be to identify the purpose of the ontology and the needs for the domain knowledge acquisition. It is important to be clear about what type of the ontology (see Figure 1) is being built (taxonomy, partonomy, genealogy, etc.) and what level of granularity the concepts is. We also need to elucidate the scope or "boundaries" of the ontology, before compiling a glossary. That effort is done at this step, as it affects the following stages of the design.

B. **Glossary development or meta-concept identification:** This time consuming step is devoted to gathering all the information relevant to the learned domain. The main goal of this step is selecting and verbalizing all of the essential objects and concepts in the domain. A battery of knowledge elicitation techniques may be used – from interviews to free association word lists.

C. **Laddering, including categorization and specification:** Having all the essential objects and concepts of the domain in hand, the next step is to define the main levels of abstraction. Consequently, the high level hierarchies among the concepts should be revealed and the hierarchy should be represented visually on the defined levels. This could be done via a top-down strategy by trying to break the high level concept from the root of the previously built hierarchy, by detailing and specifying instance of concepts. Revealing a structured hierarchy is one of the main goals at this stage. Another way is generalization via bottom-up structuring strategy. Associating similar concepts to create meta-concepts from leaves of the aforementioned hierarchy could do this. The main difficulty is forming categories by creating high level concepts and/or breaking them into a set of detailed ones where it is needed. Categorization is one of the higher cognitive activities, and it is a teacher's work to create and label all the main categories, sub-categories, and concepts of the teaching content. The learners may be involved in this process also. The collaborative work in groups sometimes gives positive synergetic effect. Such approach doesn't go against the mainstream constructivist way of university learning. It only puts stress on structuring methodology.

D. **Orchestration:** This term means the harmonious organization (Orchestration, 2008). The final step is devoted to updating the visual ontology structure by excluding any excessiveness, synonymy, and contradictions. The main goal of this final step is to create a beautiful or harmonious ontology.

Beauty is a characteristic of an object, or idea that provides a perceptual experience of pleasure, meaning, or satisfaction [Beauty, 2008]. Beauty is studied as part of aesthetics, sociology, social psychology, and culture. Of course there are cultural differences in perception of beauty. The experience of "beauty" often involves the interpretation of some entity as being in balance and harmony with nature, which may lead to feelings of attraction and emotional well-being. Because this is a subjective experience, it is often said that "beauty is in the eye of the beholder [Martin, 2007]. But in many cases learners and teachers agree at the evidently beautiful structures.

The ideas of "beautification" are well known in basic studies beginning from the search for beautiful formula, model, or result. Beauty was always a very strong criterion of scientific truth. We believe that harmony and clarity are the main properties that make an ontology beautiful.

Visual Ontology Orchestrating

Bearing in mind that teaching ontologies are to be used not only as a knowledge component of the courseware system but also as a mind tool for comprehensiveness and better understanding, we tried to follow the principle of good shape (or beauty) that is not new in basic scientific abstraction and modeling (e.g. physics, chemistry, etc.). It is difficult to give the formal definition of this concept but it features the imprecise sense of harmonious or aesthetically-pleasing proportionality and balance. The most substantial impulse to it was given by the German psychologist Max Wertheimer. His criteria of good Gestalt (image or pattern) (Wertheimer, 1945) we partially transferred to ontological engineering:

- **Law of Pragnanz (the law of good shape):** The organization of any structure in the nature or cognition will be as good as the prevailing conditions allow. 'Good' here means regular, complete, balanced, and/or symmetrical.
- **Law of Parsimony:** The simplest example is the best (the Ockham's razor principle): entities should not be multiplied unnecessarily.

In the case of building ontological hierarchies, we have to keep in mind that a well balanced hierarchy corresponds to a strong and comprehensible representation of the domain knowledge. We enlist below some tips that we consider useful in formulating the idea of "harmony" (Gavrilova, 2003):

- Concepts of one level should be linked to their parent concept by one type of relationships, for example, "is-a", "has part", etc. This means that concepts of one layer have similar nature and level of granularity.
- The ontology tree should be balanced, that is, the depth of the paths in the ontological tree should be more or less equal (±2 nodes). This will also insure that the general layout is symmetrical. Asymmetry means that shorter branch is less investigated or longer one is too detailed (see Figure 3).
- Cross-links should be avoided as much as possible.

Moreover, when building an ontology, which is used for information visualization and browsing, it is important to pay attention to clarity. Minimizing the number of concepts is the best tip according to the Law of Parsimony. The maximal number of branches and the number of levels may follow Miller's "magical number" (7±2), which is related to the human capacity for processing information (Miller, 1956).

"Beautification" bias works as a strong methodological approach that helps find the points (nodes) of "growth", "weak" branches, inconsistence, and excessiveness. But, in fact, specific domain knowledge features may be of higher priority than design principles.

We have produced several simple hints to refine and illuminate the ontology's design stage.

Figure 3. Well-balanced (A) and ill-balanced (B) ontologies

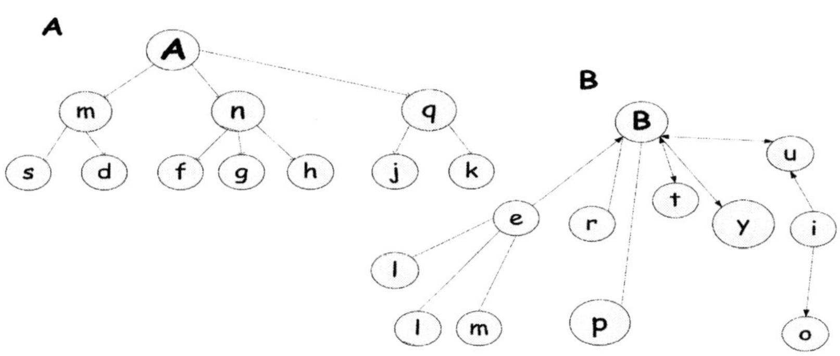

1. Use different font sizes for different levels
2. Use different colors to distinguish particular subsets or branches
3. Use a vertical layout of the tree structure/diagram
4. If needed, use different shapes for different types of node

We have already developed more than 20 teaching ontologies for the "AI"–course and some other courses, e.g. together with Peter Brusilovsky, Sergei Sosnovsky and Rosta Farsan for course on C-programming (Brusilovsky, Gavrilova, Sosnovsky, 2005). They are based on WHAT-knowledge conceptual structures to help students understand and remember the main concepts of the course.

Also several research ontologies were developed to help the research community to generalize their shared understanding – the domains were "user modeling" (with Peter Brusilovsky and Michael Yudelson) (Brusilovsky et al., 2005) and "ontologies in education" (with Darina Dicheva and Sergey Sosnovsky) (Gavrilova et al., 2005). That work is still in progress as the domains are changing very quickly.

As we are speaking about the pre-design stage of creating light-weight ontologies (without formalizing into OWL or other language), the usage of any available graphical editors may be helpful. These editors work as powerful assistants. The best results we received were when using mind mapping and concept mapping tools.

There are many popular tools that have been developed to create Mind Maps. These tools are limited in the sense that they typically cannot produce any other type of graph structure and do not allow for explicit linking terms within or across branches. Mind Maps are often very colorful, so that the best commercial software has sophisticated color and imaging options. The tools are very handy, simple and clear, so these tools' features also enrich the usability as well as impressiveness of representation. Some of these tools have become fairly sophisticated in terms of linking to Internet resources, the addition of notes, and support for collaborative use. The most widely used and developed versions include:

1. *Mind Manager* from MindJet http://www.mindjet.com/index.shtml
2. *Visual Mind*http://www.visual-mind.com/
3. *VisiMap* by CoCo Systems http://www.coco.co.uk./. http://www.coco.co.uk./prodvm.html
4. *Mind Mapper* from SimTech USA http://www.mindmapper.com/
5. *Concept Draw* has a Mind Mapping product, as well as general drawing and diagramming products that integrate with *Visio*. More information may be found at http://www.conceptdraw.com/en/products/CDPMindMap/.

But any effective computer program for ontological engineering should perform the functions described for structuring the stages of a subject domain. Accordingly, it should correspond to the phenomenological nature of the knowledge elicitation involved using different appropriate algorithms. This program must support the knowledge engineer through incorporating "game rules" that are clearing, transparent, and functional. Ideally, the knowledge engineer should be able to tailor the program to his or her specific requirements. Concerning this, each analytical stage may be represented visually and accurately modeling the knowledge domain, an element that has already been realized in some commercial expert system shells.

To achieve these goals, a set of special visual tools were developed and named CAKE-2, VICONT, PORTO, and VITA (together with Tim Geleverya, Alex Voinov, Vitaliy Fertman and Vladimir Gorovoy). They illustrate the idea of knowledge mappability as applied to data extraction, analysis, and structuring for heterogeneous knowledge base design (Gavrilova et al, 2000-2009).

Developing Teaching Ontologies

We have already developed more than 20 teaching ontologies for the courses "Artificial Intelligence" and "Knowledge Engineering" (Gavrilova, Stash, Texier, 2001; Gavrilova, Dicheva, Sosnovsky, Brusilovsky, 2005). They are based on WHAT-knowledge conceptual structures to help students understand and remember the main concepts of the course.

We can propose different types of teaching ontologies which substantially can aid effective learning:

- Main concepts ontology (or conceptual structure)
- Historical ontology (genealogy)
- Partonomy of the discipline, where the main relation between learning objects is "has_part'
- Taxonomy of the theories, methods and techniques, etc.

Figure 4 illustrates the ontology that describes the skeleton of the "knowledge elicitation" problem for expert systems development. It integrates the main theoretical and practical issues of this multi-disciplinary and multi-faceted area. This ontology is rather subjective as it summarizes the author's 20-years experience in working as a knowledge analyst and a tutor. This ontology combines two main types of relations – A_kind_of and A_part_of representing the so-called mixed ontology (mix of partonomy and taxonomy). It took more than 5 years of research and teaching to elaborate this structure.

Ontology-based approach is universal. We used it also for methodological scaffolding of some other courses, e.g. together with Peter Brusilovsky, Sergei Sosnovsky and Rosta Farsan for course on C-programming (Brusilovsky, Gavrilova, Sosnovsky, 2005; Gavrilova, Farzan, Brusilovsky, 2005) at the University of Pittsburgh.

In this section, we describe our attempt to develop ontology for C programming language

Figure 4. Ontology of "Knowledge Elicitation" domain

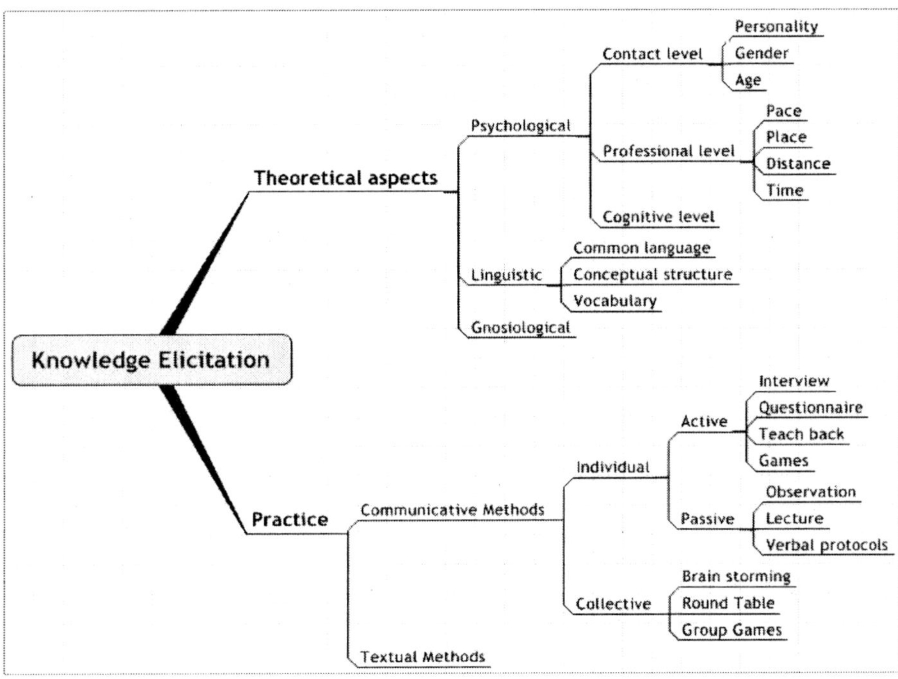

Figure 5. Glossary of the terms for teaching C programming

Data type	While loop	User defined function
Integer	Statement	Parameter passing
Character	Block	By Values
Float	Sequential execution	By reference
Primitive data type	Condition	Kernel command
Expression	Nested if	Function prototype
Data structure	If-else	Pointer & Function
Array	If	Pointer
Array processing	Multiple selections	Computer memory
Data aggregate	Switch	Memory address
String	Complex conditionals	Declaring pointer
Two dimensional arrays	File	Malloc
Declaration of two	Simple file processing	Stack
dimensional arrays	Advanced file processing	Recursion
Variable	IO	Operator
Variable initialization	Input	Pointer operation
Variable assignment	Standard input	Push
Variable declaration	Scanf	Conditional operator
Readable program	Input redirection	Arithmetic operation
Indentation	Standard input	Decrement expression
Understandable program	Output	Pre-decrement
Comments	Printf	Post-decrement
Constant	Printing	Increment expression
Define	Standard output	Post-increment
Literal constant	Output redirection	Pre-increment
Pre-processor	Conversion	Logical operator
Directive	Explicit conversion	OR operator
C compiler	Typecasting operator	Not operator
Loop	Casting	AND operator
Do-while loop	Automatic type conversion	Character operator
Counter controlled loop	Assignment conversion	Relational operator
Sentinel controlled loop	Safe type conversion	Associativity of operators
For loop	Unsafe type conversion	Order of calculation
Nested loop	Function	Precedence of operators
Threshold controlled loop	Function parameter	
	Standard function	

following the aforementioned 4-steps algorithm. We have tried to report the exact practical procedures we followed at each step by including all the visual structures.

Steps A and B: Goals Identification and Glossary Development

As previously mentioned the first steps in building ontology consist of strategic planning and collecting information in the domain. Then the glossary building of terms for the domain is conducted. To build a glossary for teaching introductory C programming course, we collected the terms from two different types of resources: closed-corpus material and open-corpus material.

The closed corpus materials are in the form of lecture notes of Professor Brusilovsky that are specially designed for the course. The open corpus materials include several online tutorials in C programming. We extracted the terms from the lecture notes manually by carefully reviewing the lecture handout. The terms from open-corpus material were extracted automatically (Brusilovsky & Rizzo, 2002). Consequently, we tried to combine the automatically extracted terms with manually extracted terms to build a single glossary. Figure 5 presents the combined unsorted glossary.

Step C: Laddering (Building an Initial Mind Map Structure)

At this step, an initial visual structure of the glossary terms was built and examined. The main goal of this step is to create the sets of preliminary ideas and notions and to categorize those terms into concepts. A mind map can be a useful visual structure for this step. Figure 6 presents the mind map of that initial categorization. Since the categorization in this step was preliminary, some of terms might not fit into any of the initial categorization. We should mention that the categorization in this step was done entirely manually by Rosta Farzan. However, we employed the lecture notes, which were used to build the glossary in the previous step, to build the initial categories as well. We

Figure 6. Trivial categorization

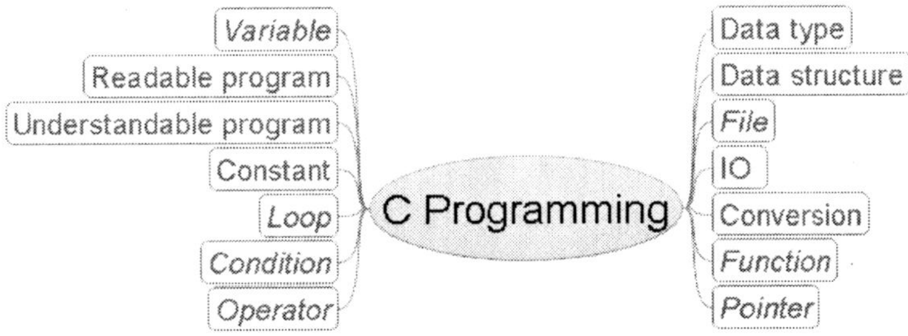

can consider the lecture notes, as expert help, to design the ontology. This is due to the fact that the lecture notes were designed by the expert who taught the course for a couple of years.

Figure 7 represents the details of our initial categorization of the terms into the concept shown in Figure 8. The visual structures presented at this step, illustrates the idea of how an ontology can bridge the gap between the chaos of unstructured data presented in the glossary and be a clear means of showing mapped representations. Another good example of this bridge can be our ontology of Italian artistic schools which is built from chaos of names of great Italian artists (Gavrilova, Kurochkin, Veremiev, 2004). It was made using several guides, books and encyclopedia on Italian art. The ontology presents the genealogy of three schools of painting (Paduan, Florentian and Venetian) in visual form.

Figure 7. Details of first level categorization

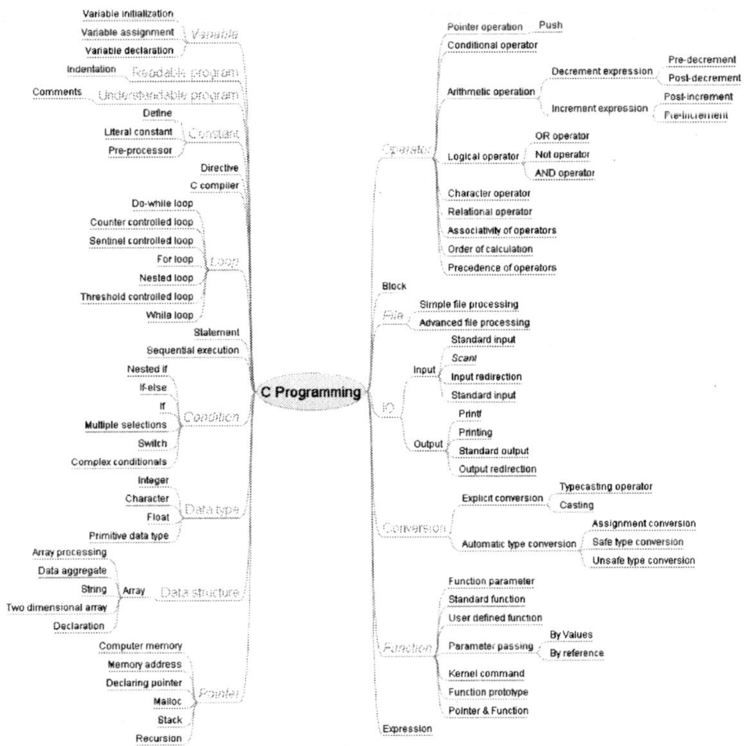

Figure 8. General ontology

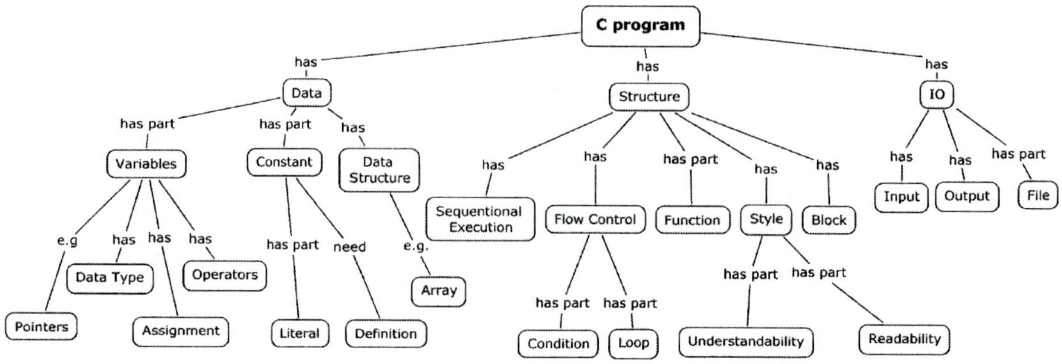

At the same step we composed more precise concepts and hierarchies by analyzing the glossary and previously built visual structure. First we employed the top-down design strategy to create meta-concepts such as "Date", "Structure", and "IO". Then using the bottom-up strategy, we tried to fit the terms and concepts into the meta-concept. Moreover, we created the relationships between the concepts. A concept map is the most useful visual structure for representation of the results of this stage, since it gives the ability of defining the relationship in addition to building the hierarchy. The output of this step is a large and detailed map, which covers the course in a hierarchical way. Because of the huge size of this concept map it is difficult to include it in the chapter. However, since this ontology is designed for teaching purposes it is important to offer the overall picture and a general hierarchy as well.

Therefore, based on the detailed concept map, we built the general ontology shown in Figure 8.

Step D: Orchestration

As described in the algorithm, the final step is devoted to making the ontology beautiful. We used mentioned above practical tips and hints that can harmonize the designing of an ontology.

In addition, we re-built the general ontology while taking into consideration the harmony and clarity factors. Comparing Figures 8 and 9 one can see these changes (e.g. the concept "I/O"- (input/output) was enriched in order to correspond to the level of detailing of the "Data" and "Structure" concept branches). Consequently, we tried to balance the depth of the branches by adding one more level to the "IO" branch. Another feature of harmony is having the same relationship at each

Figure 9. Harmony and clarity in the ontology

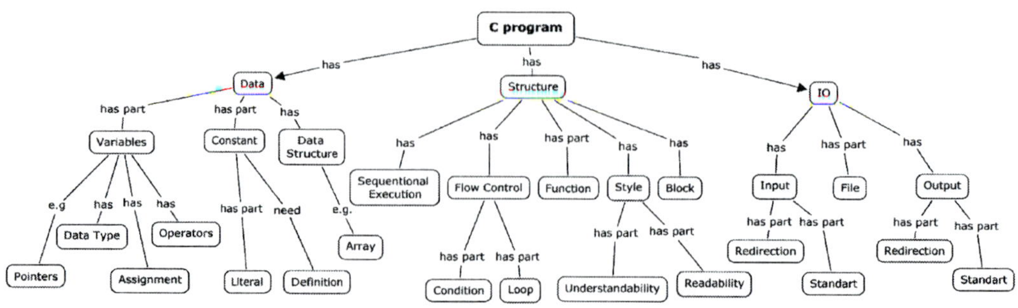

level. Since this is not easy to achieve, we tried to differentiate the level of the nodes based on the relationships in the same depth. For example, all nodes with the "has" relationship are at the same level and all the node with the "has part" relationship are also at the same level. Moreover, to achieve clarity we removed all unnecessary nodes and use the standard relationships that are easy to understand.

And after using the above-mentioned recipe the core ontology of the lecture course by Peter Brusilovsky was developed (see Figure 9).

It is interesting that the similar work done by another post-graduate student Sergey Sosnovsky (see Figure 10) of the same research group leads to the totally different ontology (Sosnovsky, Gavrilova, 2006). This fact proves again the subjective nature of ontology design especially on the upper levels of domain ontologies. While the leaves of the tree may be very resembling the branches could vary both in number and name. It may be explained by the different style and manner of the categorization procedure used by the analysts.

Categorization deals with the creating of classes of objects that share common features. If two analysts see different features they will compose different categorization trees. They both may be correct. However, there is no visible way to assess the quality of those ontologies besides finding of a super-expert who may become the judge.

Several research ontologies were also developed to help the research community to generalize their shared understanding – the domains were "user modeling" (with Peter Brusilovsky and Michael Yudelson, 2004) and "ontologies in education" (with Darina Dicheva, 2005). That work is still in progress as the domains are rapidly changing.

Figure 10. Top levels of the educational ontology of C programming

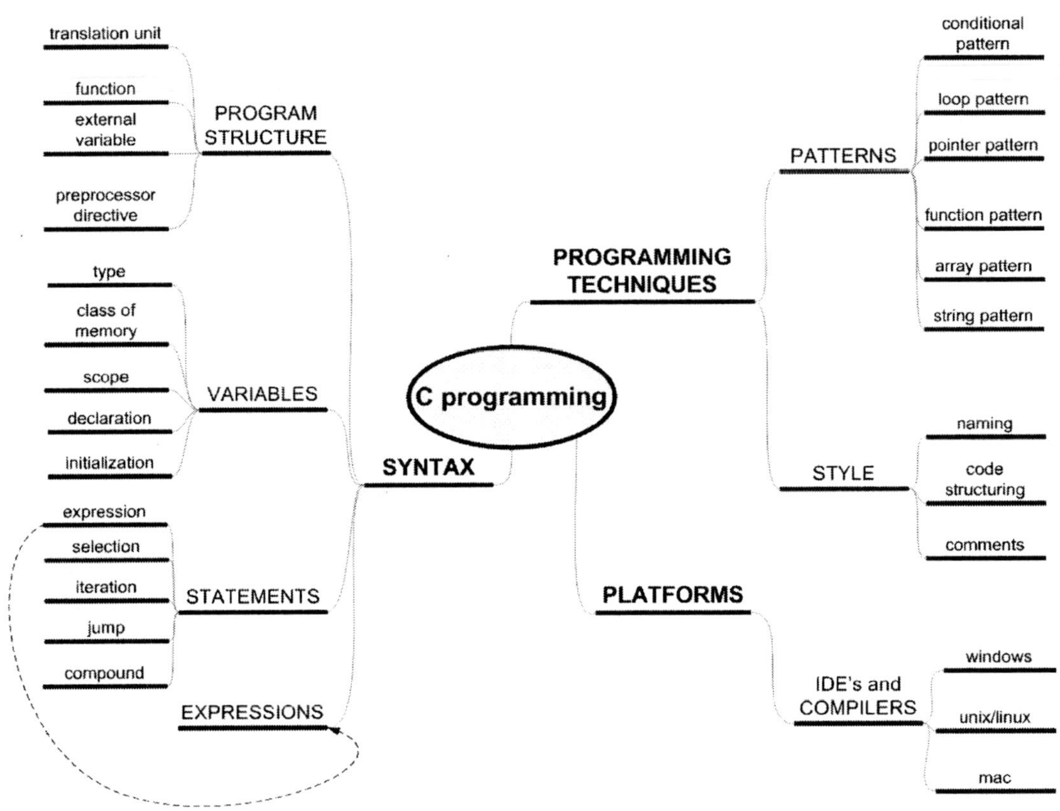

FUTURE RESEARCH DIRECTIONS

All the visual models of knowledge are node-link representations in which ideas are located in nodes and connected to other related ideas through a series of labeled links. The research on knowledge mapping in the last decade has produced a number of consistent and interesting findings (O'Donell *et al.,* 2002; Dicheva, Dichev, 2007). Students recall more central ideas when they learn from mind map or ontology than when they learn from text and those with low verbal ability or low prior knowledge often benefit the most. The use of ontology engineering also appears to amplify the benefits associated with structured approach. Learning from maps is enhanced by active processing strategies such as summarization or annotation and by designing maps according to gestalt principles of organization. Fruitful areas for future research on ontology mapping include examining whether visual representations reduce cognitive load, how map learning is influenced by the structure of the information to be learned, and the possibilities for transfer.

The future research will be devoted to the theoretical and methodological issues of categorizing and laddering processes. It seems to be challenging to study the feasibility of using the suggested approach in the new forms of teaching, e.g. blended education. Visual mapping may be also used in different teaching assignments – as writing research articles or reviewing the books and papers. The great interest in visual approach is seen in many disciplines and the new graphical models become *en vogue*. These models are roadmaps or strategic plans (Alitek Consulting, 2003), knowledge maps (O'Donell *et al.,* 2002) that show where knowledge is stored in companies, topic maps aimed at the representation and interchange of knowledge, with an emphasis on the findability of information (Dicheva, Dichev, 2005) and many other.

Our next projects are devoted to the study of deeper cognitive basics of structuring processes and are aimed at developing of technologies and tools that scaffolds the visual design and representing of the learning ontologies.

CONCLUSION

The described approach and the numerous study of many educationalists (Canas *et al*, 2003) allow us to sketch some patterns of use what to enhance the learning effectiveness of visual models. First, when knowledge mapping is used in a course of instruction, it is better that it be an integral, on-going feature of the learning process, not just some isolated "add-on" at the beginning or end. In this regard, ontology mapping appears to be particularly beneficial when it is used in an on-going way to consolidate or crystallize educational experiences in the classroom, for example, a lecture, demonstration, or laboratory experience. In this mode, learners experience an educational event and then use visual mapping in a reflective way to enhance knowledge acquisition from the event. There is also indication that learning is enhanced when in the course of knowledge engineering learners adopt an active, deep, and questioning process.

Now we can see how many new visual models (roadmaps, knowledge maps, topic maps, etc.) have become popular in the learning process. Some of them have also an ontological base. It seems that in the future visual ontological design will be a must in courseware development.

Second, our research stresses the role of ontology orchestrating for developing ontologies quickly, efficiently and effectively. We follow David Johnassen's idea of "using concept maps as a mind tool". The use of visual paradigm to represent and support the teaching process not only helps a professional tutor to concentrate on the problem rather than on details, but also enables learners and students to process and understand great volumes of information.

The development of beautiful knowledge structures in the form of ontologies provide learning supports and scaffolds that may improve student understanding of substantive and syntactic knowledge. As such, they can play a part in the overall pattern of learning by facilitating for example analysis, comparison, generalization, and transferability of understanding to analogous problems. Therefore, the visual knowledge structure editors provide is a two dimensional, iconic model that represents the teacher's understanding of key elements in the subject.

Third, as an assessment tool, ontologies can be used to visualize and analyze the student's knowledge and understanding. Through visual inspection of the ontology it is possible to detect gaps and misunderstandings in the student's cognitive model of the learnt knowledge. However, there is not much consensus yet about the designing and orchestrating of the courseware structure that should be used. Furthermore, in many cases it is not known what the structure of socially legitimate knowledge pattern looks like and how a particular instance of a knowledge model is deviating from that "ideal" state (e.g. teacher's view). But teachers are individuals, and they may disagree among themselves.

ACKNOWLEDGMENT

Thanks to Piter Brusilovsky, Rosta Farzan and Sergey Sosnovsky for the fruitful discussions and the collaboration on C-language ontology. Special thanks to Joshua Grove for his kind assistance in checking and editing, and Olga Malinovskaya for editing the figures.

This work was partially supported by grants of Russian Foundation for Basic Research and SPbGU.

REFERENCES

Adeli, H. (1994). *Knowledge Engineering*. New York: McGraw-Hill.

Alitek Consulting. (2003). *What is strategic mapping?* Retrieved August 1, 2003, from Beauty. (2009). *Wikipedia*. Retrieved April 2009, from http://en.wikipedia.org/wiki/Beauty

Boose, J. H. (1990). Knowledge Acquisition Tools, Methods and Mediating Representations. In H. Motoda, et al. (Eds.), *Knowledge Acquisition for Knowledge-Based Systems* (pp. 123-168.). Tokyo, Ohinsha Ltd.

Brusilovsky, P., & Rizzo, R. (2002). Map-Based Horizontal Navigation in Educational Hypertext. In *Proceedings of Hypertext*, University Of Maryland, College Park, USA.

Brusilovsky, P., Yudelson, M., & Gavrilova, T. (2005). *Towards User Modeling Meta Ontology*. In L. Ardissono, P. Brna & A. Mitrovic (Eds.), Proceedings of 10th International conference User Modeling (LNAI 3538, pp. 448-452). New York: Springer.

Buzan, T. *Mind Map handbook*. Thorsons, 2005.

Conlon, T. (1997). Towards Diversity: Advancing Knowledge-based Modelling with Knowledge Acquisition. In *Proceedings of 8th International PEG Conference*, Sozopol, Bulgaria (pp. 379-386).

Davies, J., van Harmelen, F., & Fensel, D. (Eds.). (2002). *Towards the Semantic Web: Ontology-Driven Knowledge Management*. New York: John Wiley & Sons, Inc.

Dicheva, D., & Aroyo, L. (2004). Concepts and Ontologies in Web-based Educational Systems. *Int. J. Cont. Engineering Education and Life-long Learning, 14*(3), 187–190.

Dicheva, D., & Dichev, C. (2005). Authoring Educational Topic Maps: Can We Make It Easier? In . *Proceedings of ICALT, 2005*, 216–219.

Dicheva, D., & Dichev, C. (2007). Helping Courseware Authors to Build Ontologies: the Case of TM4L. In *13th Int. Conference on Artificial Intelligence in Education*, July 9-13, 2007, California (pp. 77-84).

Eisenstadt, M., Domingue, J., Rajan, T., & Motta, E. (1990). Visual Knowledge Engineering. *IEEE Transactions on Software Engineering, 16*(10), 1164–1177. doi:10.1109/32.60296

Eleventh Workshop on Knowledge Acquisition. *Modeling and Management*, Banff, Alberta, Canada (pp. 124-129).

Fensel, D. (2001). *Ontologies: A Silver Bullet for Knowledge Management and Electronic Commerce*. New York: Springer.

Gavrilova, T. (2003). Teaching via Using Ontological Engineering. In *Proceedings of XI Int. Conf. Powerful ICT for Teaching and Learning PEG-2003*, St.Petersburg (pp. 23-26).

Gavrilova, T., Brusilovsky, P., Yudelson, M., & Puuronen, S. (2006). Creating Ontology for User Modelling Research. In *Workshop Ubiquitus User Modeling on European Conference on Artificial Intelligence ECAI 2006*, Riva del Garda, Italy (pp. 11-15).

Gavrilova, T., Dicheva, D., Sosnovsky, S., & Brusilovsky, P. (2005). Ontological Web Portal for Educational Ontologies. In *Proc. Of Applications of Semantic Web Technologies for E-Learning Workshop* (SW-EL'05) *in conjunction with 12th Int.Conf. on Artificial Intelligence in Education (AI-ED'05)*, Amsterdam (pp. 19-29).

Gavrilova, T., Farzan, R., & Brusilovsky, P. (2005). One Practical Algorithm of Creating Teaching Ontologies. In http://www.alitek.com.au/strategic-mapping.htm

Gavrilova, T., Kurochkin, M., & Veremiev, V. (2004). Teaching Strategies and Ontologies for E-learning. *Int. Journal Information Theories and Applications, 11*(1), 35–42.

Gavrilova, T., & Laird, D. (2005). Practical Design of Business Enterprise Ontologie. In M. Bramer and V. Terzyan (Eds.), *Industrial Applications of Semantic Web* (pp. 61-81). New York: Springer.

Gavrilova, T., Texier, R., & Stash, N. (2001). VITA: Using PYTHON for Visual Design of Web-based Tutorials// Proc. of the Tenth International PEG Conference *Intelligent Computer and Communications Technology – Learning in On-Line Communities*, Tampere, Finland, 44-50.

Gavrilova, T. A., & Voinov, A. (1996). Visualized Conceptual Structuring for Heterogeneous Knowledge Acquisition. In *Proceedings of International Conference on Educational Multimedia and Hypermedia, EDMEDIA'96*, MIT, Boston, USA (pp. 258-264).

Gómez-Pérez, A., Fernández-López, M., & Corcho, O. (2004). *Ontological Engineering with examples from the areas of Knowledge Management, e-Commerce and the Semantic Web*. London: Springer-Verlag.

Gruber, T. (1993). A translation approach to portable ontology specifications. *Knowledge Acquisition, 5*, 199–220. doi:10.1006/knac.1993.1008

Guarino, N., & Giaretta, P. (1998). Ontologies and Knowledge Bases: Towards a Terminological Clarification. In *Towards Very Large Knowledge Bases: Knowledge Building & Knowledge Sharing* (pp. 25- 32).

http://cmap.ihmc.us/Publications/ResearchPapers/TheoryUnderlyingConceptMaps.pdf

Jonassen, D. H. (1998). Designing constructivist learning environments. In C.M. Reigeluth (Ed.), *Instructional design models and strategies* (2nd ed.). Mahwah, NJ: Lawrence Erlbaum.

Kinchin, I. M., De-Leij, F. A. A. M., & Hay, D. B. (2005). The evolution of a collaborative concept mapping activity for undergraduate microbiology. *Journal of Further and Higher Education, 29*(1), 1–14. doi:10.1080/03098770500037655

Knight, C., Gašević, D., & Richards, G. (2006). An Ontology-Based Framework for Bridging Learning Design and Learning Content. *Educational Technology & Society, 9*(1), 23–3.

Kremer, R. (1998). Visual Languages for Knowledge Representation. In http://www.alitek.com.au/strategic-mapping.htm

Martin, G. (2007). Beauty is in the eye of the beholder. *The Phrase Finder*. Retrieved on December 4, 2007, from http://www.phrases.org.uk/meanings/59100.html

Miller, G. (1956). The Magical Number Seven, Plus or Minus Two: Some Limits on Our Capacity for Processing Information. *Psychological Review, 63*, 81–97. doi:10.1037/h0043158

Mizoguchi, R., & Bourdeau, J. (2000). Using Ontological Engineering to Overcome Common AI-ED Problems. *International Journal of Artificial Intelligence in Education, 11*(2), 107–121.

Neches, (1991). Enabling Technology for Knowledge Sharing. *AI Magazine*, (Winter): 36–56.

Novak, J. D., & Cañas, A. J. (2006). *The Theory Underlying Concept Maps and How to Construct Them*. Technical Report IHMC CmapTools 2006-01, Florida Institute for Human and Machine Cognition, 2006. Retrieved from

Noy, N. & McGuinness, D. (2001). *Ontology Development 101: A Guide to Creating Your First Ontology.* Stanford Knowledge Systems Laboratory Technical Report KSL-01-05 and Stanford Medical Informatics Technical Report SMI-2001-0880, March 2001.

O'Donnell, A., Dansereau, D., & Hall, R. (2002). Knowledge Maps as Scaffolds for Cognitive Processing Educational. *Psychological Review, 14*(1).

Orchestration. (2008). *Merriam-Webster Online Dictionary*. Retrieved November 9, 2008, from http://www.merriam-webster.com/dictionary/orchestration

Schreiber, G. (2000). *Knowledge Engineering and Management: The CommonKADS Methodology*. Cambridge, MA: MIT Press.

Sosnovsky, S., & Gavrilova, T. (2006). One Approach to Development of Educational Ontology for C-Programming. *Int. Journal of Information Theories and Applications, 13*(4), 303–308.

Sowa, J. F. (1984). *Conceptual Structures: Information Processing in Mind and Machine.* Reading, MA: Addison-Wesley.

12*th International Network-Based Education Conference NBE* 2005, Rovaniemi, Finland (pp. 29-37).

Tu, S., Eriksson, H., Gennari, J., Shahar, Y., & Musen, M. (1995). Ontology-Based Configuration of Problem-Solving Methods and Generation of Knowledge-Acquisition Tools. *Artificial Intelligence in Medicine*, (7): 257–289. doi:10.1016/0933-3657(95)00006-R

Vestal, W. (2005). Knowledge Mapping: The Essentials for Success. *APQC*.

Werthheimer, M. (1945). *Productive Thinking*. New York: Harper Collins.

Wielinga, B., Schreiber, G., & Breuker, J. (1992). A Modelling Approach to Knowledge Engineering. *Knowledge Acquisition, 4*(1), 23–39. doi:10.1016/1042-8143(92)90013-Q

ADDITIONAL READING

Baader, F., Horrocks, I., & Sattler, U. (2004). *Handbook on ontologies*. New York: Springer.

Booch, G. (2007). *Object-Oriented Analysis and Design with Applications* (3rd Ed.). Reading, MA: Addison-Wesley Object Technology Series.

Bouguettaya, D. (Ed.). (1999). *Ontologies and Databases*. Amsterdam: Kluwer Academic Publishers.

Brown, J., Collins, A., & Duguid, P. (1989). Situated cognition and the culture of learning. *Educational Researcher, 18*(1), 32–42.

Chang, S. K. (Ed.). (2002). *Handbook of Software Engineering and Knowledge Engineering*. New York: World Scientific Publishing Co., Inc.

Devedšić, V. (2003). Next-generation web-based education. *International Journal of Continuing Engineering Education and Life-long Learning, 13*(3/4), 232–247. doi:10.1504/IJCEELL.2003.003278

Devedzic, V. (2004). Education and the Semantic Web . *Artificial Intelligence in Education, 4*(2), 165–191.

Dicheva, D., & Dichev, C. (2008). Ontological Support for Learning Content Management. *Scientia Journal, 19*(2), 68–76.

Hollsapple, A., & Joshi, K. (2002). A collaborative approach to ontology design. *Communications of the ACM, 45*(2), 42–47. doi:10.1145/503124.503147

Ipsilandis, P. (2001). A structured approach for creating WEB based teaching materials. In *Proceedings 3rd International Conference on New Learning Technologies*, Fribourg, Switzerland.

Rabinowitz, M., Blumberg, F., & Everson, H. (2004). The esign of instruction and evaluation: affordances of using media and technology. London: Routledge.

Sayre, M. (1997). Belief and Knowledge: Mapping the Cognitive Landscape. Lanham, MD: Rowman & Littlefield.

Scott, A., Clayton, J. E., & Gibson, E. L. (1994). *A Practical Guide to Knowledge Acquisition*. Reading, MA: Addison-Wesley.

Sowa, J. (2000). *Knowledge Representation: Logical, Philosophical, and Computational Foundations*. Pacific Grove, CA: Course Technology.

Swartout, B., Patil, R., Knight, K., & Russ, T. (1997). Toward Distributed Use of Large-Scale Ontologies. In *Ontological Engineering, AAAI-97 Spring Symposium Series,* 138-148.

Tazzoli, R., Castagna, P., & Campanini, S. E. (2004). Towards a Semantic Wiki Wiki Web Poster Track. In *3rd International Semantic Web Conference* (ISWC2004), 7-11 November 2004, Hiroshima, Japan.

Wenger, E. (1998). *Communities of practice. Learning, meaning and identity.* New York: Cambridge University Press.

White, D. (Ed.). (2002). *Knowledge Mapping and Management.* Hershey, PA: IRM Press.

Yourdon, E. (1989). *Modern Structured Analysis.* Reading, MA: Prentice-Hall.

KEY TERMS AND DEFINITIONS

Concept Map: Directed graph which nodes present concept and links present relations.

Knowledge Engineering: Science of knowledge acquisition, structuring and formalization.

Laddering: Creating hierarchical structures of concepts.

Mind-Maps: Visual diagrams that represent ideas and information using a combination of words and images using lines to link topics.

Ontology: Conceptual structured vocabulary.

Chapter 9
PAUL:
An Adaptive Electronic Learning Environment to Develop Teacher Expertise and ICT-Related Technological Pedagogical Content Knowledge (ICT-TPCK)

Charoula Angeli
University of Cyprus, Cyprus

George Veletsianos
University of Manchester, UK

ABSTRACT

Adaptive e-learning systems can be extremely valuable tools in developing innovative learner-centered environments in any content domain. One area that can benefit greatly from adaptive e-learning systems is teacher development in the educational uses of computers. In this chapter, we discuss the design of PAUL, an adaptive computer-based learning environment for the development of ICT-related pedagogical content knowledge, a unique body of knowledge that teachers need to develop in order to be able to teach with ICT. PAUL combines two opposing trends in adapting instruction, namely instruction that is both controlled by the learner and the system. We expect the impact of PAUL to be significant as it will provide a venue for effective teacher professional development situating learning in virtual communities of practice and supporting teacher thinking about the educational uses of ICT in teaching and learning.

INTRODUCTION

Over the last ten years, the use of technology in education has exploded. From mobile phones, to MP3 devices, to social networking sites, technology is employed in varied environments in an attempt to enhance not only educational outcomes, but also the nature of instruction and learning. While technology usage for educational purposes in both formal and informal settings has been rapidly expanding, questions about its pedagogical underpinnings and quality remain. The focus of the present chapter is not on technology per se, but on technology-enhanced learning experiences. In particular, the authors aim

DOI: 10.4018/978-1-60566-940-3.ch009

to show how a powerful pedagogical framework (i.e., ICT-TPCK) requires a technological solution to satisfy the needs of teachers, and therefore to exemplify not only the importance of developing powerful e-learning applications, but most importantly the need to provide valuable educational experiences with these tools.

Researchers have noted that many e-learning systems are simply designed in the same way as traditional forms of instruction–that is, they focus on information dissemination and disregard the capabilities of technology for education. As a result, such systems are often ineffective (Kirschner, Strijbos, Kreijns, & Beers, 2004), disconnected from recent developments in instructional design and human cognitive architecture (Sweller, van Merrienboer & Paas, 1998), and entangled in dated debates of whether technology influences learning (Clark, 1994; Kozma, 1994; Tracey & Hasting, 2005). Equally important, numerous courses, learning applications, and educational interventions are dominated by the so-called learning management systems (LMS). Despite the fact that LMS are considered powerful systems that offer multiple possibilities for learning, they are also based on the "one size fits all" notion, highlighting efficiency and template-driven education (Wilson, Parrish, & Veletsianos, 2008). More specifically, all learners enrolled in LMS-based courses receive the same educational materials, and tools regardless of their knowledge, goals, expertise, and interests. As educators and researchers, we are surprised to discover that one of the most important features of effective and engaging teaching – namely personalized, individualized, and adaptive teaching – has been largely disregarded in the e-learning sphere.

While "adaptive e-learning" has been explored by computer scientists, the capabilities and possibilities of adaptive learning environments are not prominently explored in the education, instructional design, and educational technology literatures. While recent research on adaptive e-learning educational systems has sought solutions to the "one size fits all" approach with promising results, various issues still need to be addressed for the field to arrive at a holistic understanding of the instructional and pedagogical design of such systems. A related issue concerns the fact that designers and researchers seem to replicate traditional notions of adaptive instruction. Specifically, obsolete views of adaptive learning focus on how the system can control both the content and the learning process ignoring, for the most part, the learner, even though learner control appears to be an important determinant of success in e-learning (Singhanayok & Hooper, 1998). Approaches to adaptive learning should strive to enable and balance system *and* learner control. Such shared control between the learner and the system enables (a) the system to ensure that the learning process is effective, efficient, and engaging, and (b) the learner to feel empowered and motivated to continue learning.

Adaptive electronic learning environments can be extremely valuable tools in developing engaging learning environments for any content area. One area that can benefit greatly from adaptive e-learning systems is teacher training and development. Educating teachers on how to effectively integrate ICT in classroom practices for the purpose of improving education and reforming curricula has been one of the main goals of national and international school reform efforts in various countries (Kirschner, 2003). A variety of approaches have been adopted over the years to prepare and support teachers in ICT integration, but the results have not always been positive, with technology increasingly been seen as having done little to change the ways students learn and the ways teachers teach (Cuban, 1993, 2001). The failure of teacher development programs to adequately prepare teachers to integrate ICT in teaching and learning can be attributed to various factors. Amongst others, the limited amount of time that is usually devoted for traditional ICT training courses and teachers' different needs, skills, knowledge, expectations, expertise, subject-matter area, and in general readiness, render traditional face to face professional development courses inadequate in effectively preparing teachers in the pedagogical uses of ICT (Angeli & Valanides, 2009; Papanastasiou & Angeli, 2008; Mishra & Koehler, 2006).

In this chapter, we propose that an adaptive electronic learning environment can remedy these weaknesses, and be a valuable tool for educators, teacher trainers, in-service and pre-service teachers, regional teacher training centers, teacher education departments, schools, and informal learning settings. Our team is currently involved with the design, development, and research surrounding PAUL (**P**ersonalized and **AU**thentic **L**earning environment), which is the focus of this chapter. Specifically, this chapter will proceed by (a) examining the issues, controversies, and problems related to training teachers to teach with technology, (b) presenting the notion of ICT-related Technological Pedagogical Content Knowledge (ICT-TPCK), and (c) explaining how adaptive e-learning can assist in eliminating the problems most often associated with training teachers to teach with technology, while at the same time putting forth PAUL as an innovative step towards solving such problems. The chapter concludes by investigating future research prospects for ICT-TPCK, teacher training, and adaptive electronic learning environments.

CHALLENGES IN PREPARING TEACHERS TO TEACH WITH TECHNOLOGY

The preparation of teachers in the educational uses of technology appears to be a key component in almost every improvement plan for education and educational reform programs (Davis & Falba, 2002; Dawson, Pringle, & Adams, 2003; International Society for Technology in Education, 2002; Thomas, 1999; Thompson, Schmidt, & Davis, 2003). Essentially, research evidence shows that in spite of the many efforts that researchers and educators invested over the years in preparing teachers in the educational uses of technology, teachers still lack the skills and knowledge needed to be able to teach with technology successfully (Rodrigues, 2003; Niess, 2005).

The failure to adequately prepare teachers to teach with technology can be attributed to various factors (Cuban, 2001). The emphasis of educational technology courses on skills regarding the use of various computer applications, such as word processing, spreadsheets, email, Internet, and graphics, is one major contributing factor. As Selinger (2001) explained, although basic computing skills constitute the cornerstone of technology literacy, skills-based courses are not enough for preparing teachers how to teach with technology because they are usually taught in isolation from a pedagogical context. Kenny (2002) stated that the lack of a subject specific focus in many technology programs remains an issue, but even in those cases where subject applications are discussed, matters of how technology interacts with the subject matter and subject-specific pedagogy are not sufficiently explored and thus teachers cannot effectively think how to link technology with the teaching of a particular content domain.

Most importantly, the lack of theory and conceptual frameworks to inform and guide research in the area of technology integration in teaching and learning is a major weakness in the educational technology literature (Selfe, 1990; Willis & Mehlinger, 1996; Wilson, 2003; Zhao, 2003; Margerum-Rays & Marx, 2003; Niess, 2005; Angeli & Valanides, 2005; Mishra & Koehler, 2006; Doering, Veletsianos, & Scharber, 2007). In view of recognizing that the knowledge base of the teaching profession is not adequately developed to guide teacher preparation in technology integration, researchers during the last five years initiated systematic research programs for the purpose of developing theory and models to ground research in the area of teacher cognition about technology integration (Margerum-Rays &

Marx, 2003; Niess, 2005; Angeli, 2005; Angeli & Valanides, 2005; Mishra & Koehler, 2006; Koehler & Mishra, 2008). These researchers advocate that teachers need to develop a new body of knowledge that constitutes an extension to Shulmans' (1987) notion of pedagogical content knowledge (PCK) and which results from the interaction among other sources of teacher knowledge such as knowledge about subject matter, pedagogy, learners, context, and ICT. Angeli and Valanides (2009) refer to this body of knowledge as ICT-related technological pedagogical content knowledge (ICT-TPCK).

ICT-TPCK AS A CONCEPTUAL FRAMEWORK FOR TEACHER TRAINING

Scholars unanimously recognize that both subject-matter knowledge and pedagogical knowledge are crucial to good teaching (Shulman, 1986). In addition, Shulman (1986, 1987) suggested that teaching expertise should be described and evaluated in terms of PCK that concerns the manner in which teachers relate their subject matter knowledge to their pedagogical knowledge. For Shulman (1986), PCK:

embodies the aspects of content most germane to its teachability. Within the category of pedagogical content knowledge I include, ... the most powerful analogies, illustrations, examples, explanations, and demonstrations – in a word the ways of representing and formulating the subject that make it comprehensible to others ... [It] also includes an understanding of what makes the learning of specific concepts easy or difficult: the conceptions and preconceptions that students of different ages and backgrounds bring with them to the learning (p. 9).

Other scholars also adopted the key elements of PCK (comprehensible representations of subject matter and understanding of content-related learning difficulties) and extended the concept of PCK by including in it some additional elements. For example, Cochran, DeRuiter, and King (1993) proposed a modification of Shulman's notion of PCK. They defined PCK as "a teacher's integrated understanding of four components, namely, pedagogy, subject matter content, student characteristics, and the environmental context of learning" (p. 266). Moreover, Cochran and colleagues emphasized the integrated nature of PCK and argued that the four components of PCK should not be acquired separately and then put together somehow, but should be developed concurrently. Thus, teacher education programs should promote integration of these components by providing appropriate learning experiences to prospective teachers, so that teachers simultaneously engage with all of the components of PCK and their complex interrelationships.

The steady increase of computers in schools and the numerous applications of technology in teaching and learning make it necessary to expand the construct of PCK to account for the phenomenon of teachers learning how to teach with technology. From this perspective, knowledge of technology becomes another important category of the knowledge base of teaching. In this chapter, we use the term ICT-TPCK from Angeli and Valanides' (2009) work to describe a form of knowledge that constitutes an enhancement or an extension of Shulman's and Cochran et al´s conceptualization of PCK. ICT-TPCK constitutes a special amalgam of several sources of teachers' knowledge base including pedagogical knowledge, subject area knowledge, knowledge of students, knowledge of context, and ICT knowledge. ICT knowledge is defined as knowing how to operate a computer, knowing how to use a multitude of tools/software, and knowing about their capabilities. ICT-TPCK is the form of knowledge that makes a teacher competent to teach with ICT and can be described as the ways knowledge about tools and their capabilities, pedagogy, content, learners, and context are synthesized into an understanding of how particular topics can be taught with ICT, for specific learners, in specific contexts, and in ways that *signify the added value of ICT.* It can thus be defined in terms of five principles related to knowing how to:

1. Identify topics to be taught with ICT in ways that signify the added value of ICT tools, such as topics that students cannot easily comprehend, or teachers face difficulties in teaching them effectively in class
2. Identify representations for transforming the content to be taught into forms that are comprehensible to learners and difficult to be supported by traditional means
3. Identify teaching strategies, which are difficult or impossible to be implemented by traditional means, such as application of ideas into contexts not possible to be experienced in real life, interactive learning, dynamic and context-situated feedback, authentic learning, and adaptive learning to meet the needs of any learner
4. Select ICT tools with inherent features to afford content transformations and support teaching strategies
5. Infuse ICT activities in the classroom

DEVELOPING ICT-TPCK COMPETENCIES WITH PAUL

At the heart of the conceptualization of ICT-TPCK is the view that technology is not a delivery vehicle that simply relays information, but a cognitive partner that transforms instruction while amplifying and augmenting student learning. ICT-TPCK is a body of knowledge that grows continuously with systematic engagement in rich teaching experiences. This means that any program or instructional design model that aims at the development of ICT-TPCK must consider teachers' knowledge and classroom expertise, and use them as the starting point for initiating efforts aiming at the development and/or growth of ICT-TPCK.

This last issue is important, because research on instructional design and teacher education clearly indicates that teachers' instructional thinking and decision making is guided by a unique body of knowledge that is deeply situated in classroom practices (Moallem, 1998). In Moallem´s study, teachers' situated knowledge was considered as a highly contextual and practical complex body of knowledge that teachers acquire through years of experience. This knowledge consists of different forms that interact with one another, such as, epistemological beliefs about teaching and learning, contextual knowledge of school expectations and values, practical classroom knowledge - what works and what does not in a classroom - curriculum, content, pedagogy, and learners. These findings have important implications, because they clearly indicate how teachers' situated knowledge can affect their instructional decisions. Consequently, this implies that any preparation for ICT-TPCK development should take into consideration teachers' contextual and highly practical body of knowledge. In other words, ICT-TPCK cannot be considered as a body of knowledge that exists independently of teachers' beliefs and practical experience.

The development of teachers' ICT-TPCK knowledge is not an easy task. Since teachers differ in their experiences and amount of prior knowledge, when learning how to effectively integrate ICT in classroom practice, it is critical to adjust the difficulty and support level of learning tasks to their ability and current level of performance. Giving teachers control over task selection is an intuitive and appealing instructional method to address these individual differences. In this way, teachers become independent of the system and can match their own real-time requirements to instructional features of the curriculum, enabling them to be decision-makers in their own learning. PAUL represents a solution for the development of teachers' ICT-TPCK by fostering effective task selection in demand driven education by all teachers.

THE NEED FOR DESIGNING PAUL AS AN ADAPTIVE LEARNING ENVIRONMENT

Teaching with technology is a complex task as it demands technological, pedagogical, and content proficiency on the part of teachers, but also encompasses contextual factors (e.g., organizational demands) that make effective and engaging technology integration a formidable task. While educators and researchers have struggled for years to delineate how technology can enhance and transform teaching practices, teachers do not yet appear to be able to use technology in creative ways, such that the capabilities of technology are exploited. To this end, we believe that an adaptive electronic learning environment focused on enhancing teachers' ICT-TPCK offers great potential. While in face-to-face interactions we are able to adapt and, to an extent, individualize instruction based on a number of variables (e.g., learner feedback, learner background), such activity has not yet been successfully implemented in teacher training via electronic means. Even though examples of offline personalization are plentiful, one notable instance of large-scale personalization is presented by Dexter, Doering, and Riedel (2006) who describe a teacher education program that offers content- and cohort-specific technology integration courses. While the authors of this paper did not present their work in terms of personalized instruction, it essentially is a first attempt to personalize teacher experience with respect to teaching with content-specific technologies.

Defining Adaptivity and Personalization in Electronic Learning Settings

Adaptive learning and personalization are two closely interlinked terms. To ensure consistency and clarity when using these two terms, we will define each one. Another reason for defining these two terms here is because we were not able to find a definition in prior literature that focused specifically on technology-enhanced education, teaching, and learning as complex processes mediated by contextual factors and knowledge domains.

Previous definitions of adaptive learning share a concern for flexible and differentiated instruction and learning. Grigoriadou et al. (2006) note that "Adaptive Learning Environments (ALE), designed on the basis of modern learning theories, aim to provide academics with flexible learning tools that fulfill the learning needs of a heterogeneous learning community." (p. 155). While this definition highlights flexibility for diverse learners, Howard, Remenyi, and Pap (2006) emphasize that the focus is on the individual learner: "adaptive learning uses what is known about an individual learner, a priori or through interactions, to dynamically alter the flow or content of learning activities." (p. 3). This parsimonious definition of adaptive learning encompasses many of the characteristics that we believe define adaptive learning and adaptive learning environments, yet it is focused exclusively on learning activities. Finally, Paramythis and Loidl-Reisinger, (2004) propose that "a learning environment is considered adaptive if it is capable of: monitoring the activities of its users; interpreting these on the basis of domain-specific models; inferring user requirements and preferences out of the interpreted activities, appropriately representing these in associated models; and, finally, acting upon the available knowledge on its users and the subject matter at hand, to dynamically facilitate the learning process." (p. 6). While this third definition of adaptive learning sufficiently captures adaptivity, it focuses on the system as the sole source of adaptation, while it is possible that the learner can initiate (system-wide and individual) adaptive behavior (e.g., by choosing to repeat learning activities). Therefore, in this paper, we propose a definition of adaptive e-learning environments that we hope encompasses varied systems while having education at its core:

Adaptive e-learning environments are those virtual environments whose educational, learning and instructional features (e.g., content, activities, assessment) change dynamically to satisfy the user experience, needs, goals, wants, preferences, and requirements of individual and heterogeneous learners and instructors.

This definition encompasses two important components that need to be further identified. First, adaptive behavior can be system-driven or user-driven. Second, while some dynamic adaptations may be superficial in relation to others (e.g., changing background color versus adapting instruction according to prior knowledge), we propose that such differences are delineated in the description of individual systems rather than in the definition of adaptive e-learning environments.

With regards to personalization we have found the following definition, in the context of education, to clearly encompass our ideas, and when we refer to personalization, this grounds our understanding:

Simply stated from one point of view, personalization is about building customer loyalty by building a meaningful one-to-one relationship; by understanding the needs of each individual [learner] and helping satisfy a goal that efficiently and knowledgeably addresses each individual's need in a given context [education]. To extend this point, it is about the mapping and satisfying of a user's/customer's goal in a specific context with a service's/business's goal in its respective context (Riecken, 2000).

Previous Work in the Educational Uses of Adaptive Systems

Individuals are unique and different. Those differences - individual differences - are also evident in the classroom. Students have varied learning preferences, skills, abilities, aptitude, life experiences, interests, and socioeconomic backgrounds (Jonassen & Grabowski, 1993; Boettcher 2007). Such differences not only impact learning and skill acquisition, but also influence the learning environment and the methods and assessments used in the classroom (ibid). While understanding that face-to-face instruction needs to adapt to learners, technology-enhanced education seems to suffer from the one-size-fits-all approach (Brusilovsky & Eklund, 1998), where uniform learning activities, assessments, and, ultimately, learning environments, are presented to heterogeneous and diverse learners.

Despite the fact that the literature is rich with examples of adaptive systems architectures or adaptive systems developed for the purpose of satisfying different learner needs, we were not able to find research that specifically discussed the prospects of using technology-enhanced adaptive learning within the context of in-service teacher training, with the exception of only a few articles (e.g., Bork, 2003; Korres & Garcia-Barriocanal, 2008). Thus, to the best of our knowledge, no adaptive e-learning environment, experimental or otherwise, has been developed to train teachers in the educational uses of computers in the classroom.

While a review of systems, methods, and successes/failures of previous attempts at adaptive e-learning systems is beyond the scope of this chapter, it is important to note that designing and developing adaptive e-learning is a multidisciplinary endeavor, encompassing ideas from diverse, yet complementary fields, such as educational psychology, instructional design, the learning sciences, interaction design, and computer science. Additionally, the specific context of the e-learning environment also matters. In our situation for example, our users involve pre- and in-service teachers who are to be supported to become experts in effective, efficient, and engaging classroom technology integration based on a framework of knowledge acquisition termed ICT-TPCK (Angeli & Valanides, 2009). Reference to prior work with regards to understandings from experimental psychology, instructional design, and interaction design will be employed in the context of the next section of this chapter to explain how such work has informed our design of PAUL.

Design Decisions Guiding PAUL

PAUL is an immersive electronic learning environment intended to support teachers to become experts in using computers in their teaching. While the system consists of four interrelated spaces, or "rooms" as they are referred to in the environment, the focus of this chapter is on the room where the bulk of the adaptation ensues.

Assuming that the learner enters the system for the first time, the learner will be guided through the steps of developing a learner profile. This profile consists of answering demographic questions (for research purposes), embodying oneself by personalizing an avatar (Figure 1), completing a survey collecting data on learners' skills, knowledge, and attitudes (Papanastasiou & Angeli, 2008), and completing a diagnostic assessment aiming at evaluating the learner's domain expertise, and individual and situational interest (c.f. Alexander, 2003).

Depending on the learner's level of expertise as diagnosed when the learner first enters the environment, the first task is presented to the learner. This first task is a simple completion problem with tools supporting the learner towards completing the task. Such tools include information about the content, content-specific pedagogical support, regulating learners' misconceptions, technical knowledge/assistance of how to use the tools, and supports related to the interrelationship between pedagogy, content, and tool capabilities: what Angeli and Valanides (2009) have termed technology mapping - how the capabilities of a tool can be used to transform a content domain and how the pedagogical uses of these transformations can be put into practice.

Once the first task is completed, the student moves to completing new tasks (worked-out examples, semi-completed problems, or new

Figure 1. Embodiment and personalization in PAUL

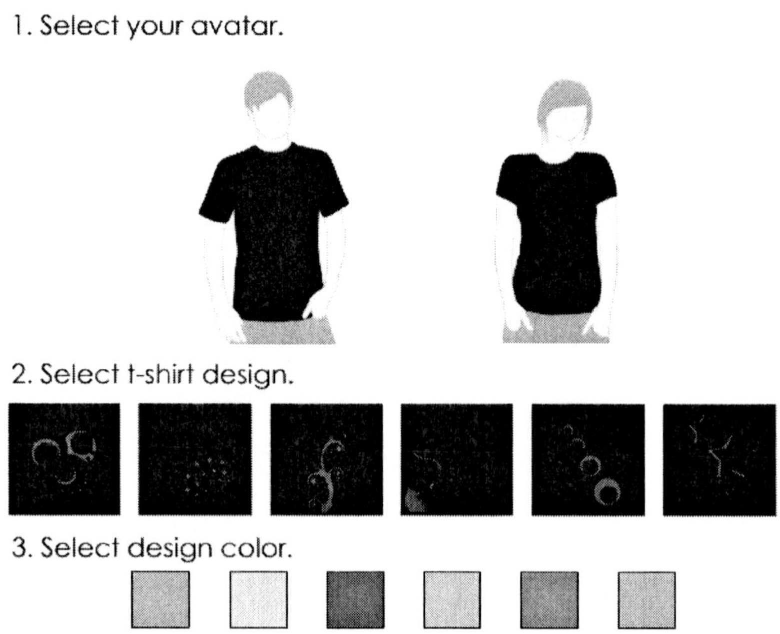

integration problems). The initial task presented to the learner is system selected, but at the end of each task the learner is asked to rate how much cognitive effort s/he is investing into the task (Figure 2). This rating represents a way to measure the learner's cognitive load (Paas, Tuovinen, Tabbers, & Van Gerven, 2003). A high value on this rating implies that the learner found the task complex or difficult and represents a high mental effort on the part of the learner. A low value on this rating means that the learner found the task easy or simple and represents lower levels of mental effort.

Once the rating is executed, there exist two possibilities for action: (a) the learner can give control to the system to select the next task, or (b) the learner can select a task from a set of options chosen according to the cognitive load rating. This is one of the main differences between PAUL and other adaptive learning environments: PAUL includes instances of shared instructional control, where adaptive behavior is controlled both by the learner and the system. System-controlled adaptation includes rules to determine task-selection as mentioned above. Finally, as the learner goes through this experience, learning tasks are sequenced according to the learner's level of expertise, cognitive load, and prior performance.

The instructional design model that drives the design of the e-learning environment is the 4C/ID instructional design model (van Merriënboer, 1997; van Merrinboer & Kirschner, 2007). In accordance with the 4C/ID model which is based upon the premise of presenting learners with meaningful whole-tasks, the methods of case-based and problem-based learning are used for the design of the system. For instance, the 4C/ID model suggests starting a new task-class with learning tasks that provide the learners with a high level of support and then ending with classes of learning tasks in which guidance is not provided. This type of mediation is implemented by starting with case-based learning, continuing with problem-based learning with enough guidance and support and finally working on complex projects with faded supports and a high measure of independence.

Figure 2. Cognitive load rating tool

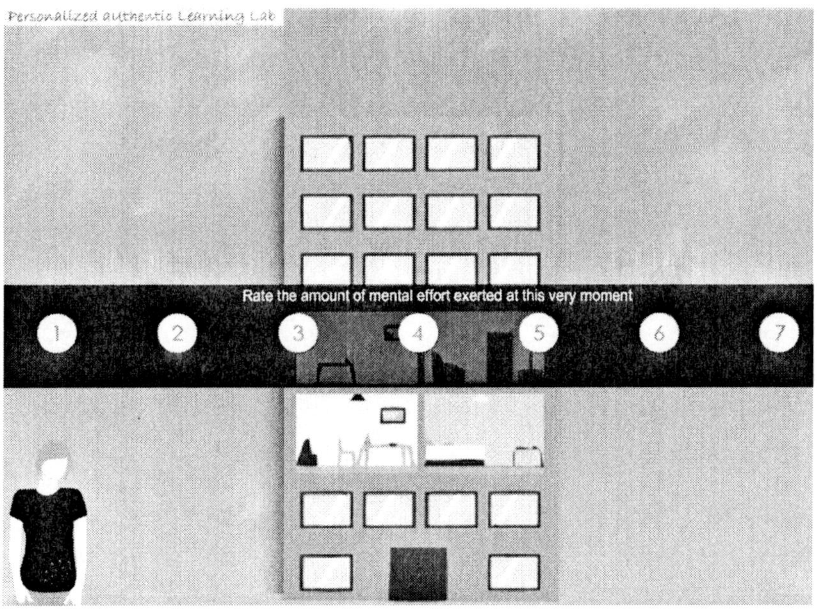

Finally, PAUL also encompasses design aspects and components often disregarded in traditional e-learning development work. These include a focus on aesthetics - both in terms of attractiveness and beauty (Norman, 2004; Lavie & Tractinsky, 2004; Tractinsky, Katz, & Ikar, 2000) and in terms of heightened learning experiences (c.f Wilson, Parrish, & Veletsianos, 2008); a positive outlook of learning as a fun and enjoyable learning experience (c.f. Kirschner & Gerjets, 2006); and engagement as an indicator of powerful learning experiences (Wilson, Parrish, & Veletsianos, 2008).

FUTURE TRENDS AND RESEARCH

While this project is still at its infancy, it is important to highlight the value of empirical research in investigating its objectives and outcomes. Ideally, such research needs to be user-centered, design-based, and multi-paradigmatic. More specifically, when researching adaptive e-learning environments, it is our hope that (a) research, design, and development endeavors will place the learner at the heart of the respective processes rather than treating him/her as a person who merely tests the learning environment, (b) researchers will employ a design-based approach to their work, striving to understand learning in context and within iterative and authentic learning environments that employ "real-world" interventions (Brown, 1992; Collins, 1992; Wang & Hannafin, 2005), and (c) researchers will employ diverse research methods that span research paradigms and epistemologies to holistically evaluate phenomena of interest.

Treating the above issues as the foundation for future research, we believe that the following questions may be worthwhile to explore:

- How do teachers move from novice to expert thinking about technology integration in an online learning environment?
- To what extent is cognitive load adaptation an effective way of individualizing and adapting instruction?
- How do we holistically evaluate adaptive e-learning?
- How do learners experience adaptive e-learning applications?
- What does it mean for the learner to be "engaged" in the learning process in an adaptive learning environment?
- How is engagement sustained in an electronic learning environment in general, and in an adaptive e-learning application in particular?

CONCLUSION

In this chapter, we have presented the notion of ICT-TPCK investigating at the same time the issues, controversies, and problems related to training teachers to teach with technology. Next, we explained how adaptive e-learning can play a role in teacher training and proposed PAUL as an innovative e-learning environment towards training teachers how to teach with technology. We concluded our discussion by proposing future research directions with regards to PAUL, teacher training, and adaptive e-learning.

Technology integration in schools and classrooms internationally has not been as effective as educators have hoped. Yet, recent developments in teacher education, both in the United States and in Europe, present a more optimistic picture of the future. Armed with recent understandings regarding teacher knowledge and multidisciplinary methods of engaging learners in innovative electronic learning environments, we are hopeful of what the near future will bring. Although education as a field is slow (and at times resistant) to change, we see the recent popularity of the ICT-TPCK construct as the impetus required to push the field forward both in research and in practice.

REFERENCES

Alexander, P. A. (2003). The development of expertise: The journey from acclimation to proficiency. *Educational Researcher*, *32*(8), 10–14. doi:10.3102/0013189X032008010

Angeli, C. (2005). Transforming a Teacher Education Method Course through Technology: Effects on Preservice Teachers' Technology Competency. *Computers & Education*, *45*(4), 383–398. doi:10.1016/j.compedu.2004.06.002

Angeli, C., & Valanides, N. (2005). Preservice Teachers as ICT Designers: An Instructional Design Model Based on an Expanded View of Pedagogical Content Knowledge. *Journal of Computer Assisted Learning*, *21*(4), 292–302. doi:10.1111/j.1365-2729.2005.00135.x

Angeli, C., & Valanides, N. (2009). Epistemological and Methodological Issues for the Conceptualization, Development, and Assessment of ICT-TPCK: Advances in Technological Pedagogical Content Knowledge (TPCK). *Computers & Education*, *52*, 154–168. doi:10.1016/j.compedu.2008.07.006

Boettcher, J. (2007). Ten Core Principles for Designing Effective Learning Environments: Insights from Brain Research and Pedagogical Theory. *Innovate, 3*(3). Retrieved on November 2, 2008 from http://www.innovateonline.info/index.php?view=article&id=54

Bork, A. (2003). The dilemma of teacher training. *Contemporary Issues in Technology and Teacher Education, 3*(2). Retrieved on September 28, 2008 from http://www.citejournal.org/vol3/iss2/general/article1.cfm

Brown, A. (1992). Design experiments: Theoretical and methodological challenges in creating complex interventions in classroom settings. *Journal of the Learning Sciences*, *2*(2), 141–178. doi:10.1207/s15327809jls0202_2

Brusilovsky, P., & Eklund, J. (1998). A study of user-model based link annotation in educational hypermedia. *Journal of Universal Computer Science*, *4*(4), 429–448.

Clark, R. E. (1994). Media will Never Influence Learning. *Educational Technology Research and Development*, *42*(2), 21–29. doi:10.1007/BF02299088

Cochran, K. F., Derutier, J. A., & King, R. A. (1993). Pedagogical content knowing: an integrative model for teacher preparation. *Journal of Teacher Education*, *44*, 263–272. doi:10.1177/0022487193044004004

Collins, A. (1992). Towards a design science of education. In E. Scanlon & T. O'Shea (Eds.), *New directions in educational technology* (pp. 15-22). Berlin, Germany: Springer.

Corbalan, G., Kester, L., & Van Merriënboer, J. J. G. (2006). Towards a personalized task selection model with shared instructional control. *Instructional Science*, *34*, 399–422. doi:10.1007/s11251-005-5774-2

Cuban, L. (1993). Computers meet classroom: classroom wins. *Teachers College Record*, *95*(2), 185–210.

Cuban, L. (2001). *Oversold and Underused: Computers in the Classroom*. London: Harvard University Press.

Davis, K. S., & Falba, C. J. (2002). Integrating technology in elementary preservice teacher education: Orchestrating scientific inquiry in meaningful ways. *Journal of Science Teacher Education*, *13*(4), 303–329. doi:10.1023/A:1022535516780

Dawson, K., Pringle, R., & Adams, T. L. (2003). Providing links between technology integration, methods courses, and school-based field experiences: A curriculum-based and technology-enhanced microteaching. *Journal of Computing in Teacher Education*, *20*(1), 41–47.

Dexter, S., Doering, A., & Riedel, E. (2006). Content Area Specific Technology Integration: A Model For Educating Teachers. *Journal of Technology and Teacher Education, 14*(2), 325–345.

Doering, A., Veletsianos, G., & Scharber, C. (2007). Coming of Age: Research and Pedagogy on Geospatial Technologies within K-12 Social Studies Education. In A. J. Milson & M. Alibrandi (Eds.), *Digital Geography: Geo-Spatial Technologies in the Social Studies Classroom* (pp. 213-226). Charlotte, NC: Information Age Publishing

Grigoriadou, M., Papanikolaou, K., Tsaganou, G., Gouli, E., & Gogoulou, A. (2006). eCompetence Skills for Adaptive Learning Environments in Higher Education. In Labhraim et al. (Eds.), *The Challenge of eCompetence in Academic Staff Development* (pp. 155-166). Galway, Ireland: CELT, NUI. Retrieved on October 18, 2008 from http://www.ecompetence.info/uploads/media/ch17.pdf

Howard, L., Remenyi, Z., & Pap, G. (2006). Adaptive Blended Learning Environments. In *Proceedings of the International Conference on Engineering Education*, July 23-28, 2006, San Juan, Puerto Rico. Retrieved on October 20, 2008 from http://w3.isis.vanderbilt.edu/Projects/VaNTH/papers/icee_2006_p1.pdf

International Society for Technology in Education. (2002). *National Educational Technology Standards for Teachers: Preparing Teachers to Use Technology*. Danvers, MA: ISTE.

Jonassen, D. H., & Grabowski, B. L. (1993). *Handbook of Individual Differences, Learning and Instruction*. Hillsdale, NJ: Lawrence Erlbaum Associates.

Kalyuga, S. (2006). Expert-novice differences and design of adaptive multimedia. In G. Ghinea & S. Chen (Eds.), *Digital Multimedia Perception and Design* (pp. 206-223). Hershey, PA: Idea Group Inc.

Kalyuga, S., & Sweller, J. (2005). Rapid dynamic assessment of expertise to optimize the efficiency of e-learning. *Educational Technology Research and Development, 53*(3). doi:10.1007/BF02504800

Kenny, J. (2002). What did we get for our training money? *TES Online*. http://www.tes.co.uk/search/story/?story_id=357732.

Kirschner, P. (Ed.). (2003). Special issue on ICT and Teacher Training. *Technology, Pedagogy and Education, 12*(1).

Kirschner, P., & Gerjets, P. (2006). Instructional design for effective and enjoyable computer-supported learning. *Computers in Human Behavior, 22*(1), 1–8. doi:10.1016/j.chb.2005.01.004

Kirschner, P., Strijbos, J., Kreijns, K., & Beers, P. (2004). Designing Electronic Collaborative Learning Environments. *Educational Technology Research and Development, 52*(3), 47–66. doi:10.1007/BF02504675

Koehler, M. J., & Mishra, P. (2008). Introducing TPCK. In AACTE Committee on Innovation and Technology (Ed.), *Handbook of Technological Pedagogical Content Knowledge (TPCK) for Educators* (pp. 3-29). New York: Routledge.

Koehler, M. J., Mishra, P., & Yahya, K. (2007). Tracing the development of teacher knowledge in a design seminar: Integrating content, pedagogy, and technology. *Computers & Education, 49*, 740–762. doi:10.1016/j.compedu.2005.11.012

Korres, M. P., & Garcia-Barriocanal, E. (2008). Development of personalized learning objects for training adult educators of special groups . *Journal of Knowledge Management, 12*(6), 89–101. doi:10.1108/13673270810913649

Kozma, R. (1994). Will media influence learning? Reframing the debate. *Educational Technology Research and Development, 42*(2), 7–19. doi:10.1007/BF02299087

Lavie, T., & Tractinsky, N. (2004). Assessing dimensions of perceived visual aesthetics of web sites. *International Journal of Human-Computer Studies*, *60*(3), 269–298. doi:10.1016/j.ijhcs.2003.09.002

Margerum-Lays, J., & Marx, R. W. (2003). Teacher knowledge of educational technology: A case study of student/mentor teacher pairs. In Y. Zhao (Ed.), *What Should Teachers Know about Technology? Perspectives and Practices* (pp. 123–159). Greenwich, CO: Information Age Publishing.

Mishra, P., & Koehler, M. J. (2006). Technological Pedagogical Content Knowledge: A framework for teacher knowledge. *Teachers College Record*, *108*(6), 1017–1054. doi:10.1111/j.1467-9620.2006.00684.x

Moallem, M. (1998). An expert teacher's thinking and teaching and instructional design models and principles: An ethnographic study. *Educational Technology Research and Development*, *46*, 37–64. doi:10.1007/BF02299788

Niess, M. L. (2005). Preparing teachers to teach science and mathematics with technology: Developing a technology pedagogical content knowledge. *Teaching and Teacher Education*, *21*(5), 509–523. doi:10.1016/j.tate.2005.03.006

Norman, D. (2004). *Emotional design: Why we love (or hate) everyday things*. New York: Basic Books.

Paas, F., Tuovinen, J., Tabbers, H., & Van Gerven, P. W. M. (2003). Cognitive load measurement as a means to advance cognitive load theory. *Educational Psychologist*, *38*, 63–71. doi:10.1207/S15326985EP3801_8

Papanastasiou, E. C., & Angeli, C. (2008). Evaluating the Use of ICT in Education: Psychometric Properties of the Survey of Factors Affecting Teachers Teaching with Technology (SFA-T3). *Educational Technology & Society*, *11*(1), 69–86.

Paramythis, A., & Loidl-Reisinger, S. (2004). Adaptive learning environments and e-learning standards. *Electronic Journal of eLearning*, 2(1). Retrieved on September 10, 2008 from http://www.ejel.org/volume-2/vol2-issue1/issue1-art11.htm

Riecken, D. (2000). Personalized views of personalization: Introduction. *Communications of the ACM*, *43*(8), 26–28. doi:10.1145/345124.345133

Rodrigues, S. (2003). Experiences from the partnership in primary science project: Teacher professional development involving ICT and science pedagogical content knowledge. *Science Education International*, *14*(2), 2–11.

Selfe, C. (1990). Technology in the English classroom: Computers through the lens of feminist pedagogy. In C. Handa (Ed.), *Computers and community: Teaching composition in the twenty-first century* (pp. 118–139). Portsmouth, NH: Boynton/Cook.

Selinger, M. (2001). Learning Information and Communications Technology skills and the subject context of the learning. *Journal of Information Technology for Teacher Education*, *10*(1-2), 143–154.

Shulman, L. S. (1986). Those who understand: Knowledge growth in teaching. *Educational Researcher*, *15*(2), 4–14.

Shulman, L. S. (1987). Knowledge and teaching: Foundations of the new reform. *Harvard Educational Review*, *57*(1), 1–22.

Singhanayok, C., & Hooper, S. (1998). The effects of cooperative learning and learner control on students' achievement, option selections, and attitudes. *Educational Technology Research and Development*, *46*(2), 17–33. doi:10.1007/BF02299787

Sweller, J. (1988). Cognitive load during problem solving: Effects on learning. *Cognitive Science*, *12*(1), 257–285.

Sweller, J., van Merrienboer, J., & Paas, F. (1998). Cognitive architecture and instructional design. *Educational Psychology Review*, *10*, 251–296. doi:10.1023/A:1022193728205

Thomas, L. H. (1999). *A study of pre-service teachers' integration of technology applications into the elementary classroom*. Unpublished doctoral dissertation, Mississippi State University.

Thompson, A. D., Schmidt, D. A., & Davis, N. E. (2003). Technology collaboratives for simultaneous renewal in teacher education. *Educational Technology Research and Development*, *51*(1), 124–128. doi:10.1007/BF02504519

Tracey, M. W., & Hasting, N. B. (2005). Does media affect learning: Where are we? *TechTrends*, *49*(2), 28–30.

Tractinsky, N., Katz, A., & Ikar, D. (2000). What is beautiful is usable. *Interacting with Computers*, *13*, 127–145. doi:10.1016/S0953-5438(00)00031-X

van Merrinboer, J. J. G. (1997). *Training complex cognitive skills: A four component instructional design model for technical training*. Englewood Cliffs, NJ: Educational Technology Publications.

van Merrinboer, J. J. G., & Kirschner, P. A. (2007). *Ten steps to complex learning: A systematic approach to four-component instructional design*. Mahwah, NJ: Lawrence Erlbaum.

Wang, F., & Hannafin, M. J. (2005). Design-based research and technology-enhanced learning environments. *Educational Technology Research and Development*, *53*(4), 5–23. doi:10.1007/BF02504682

Willis, J. W., & Mehlinger, H. D. (1996). Information technology and teacher education. In J. Sikula (Ed.), *Handbook of Research on Teacher Education* (pp. 978–1029). New York: Macmillan.

Wilson, B., Parrish, P., & Veletsianos, G. (2008). Raising the bar for instructional outcomes: Towards transformative learning experiences. *Educational Technology*, *48*(3), 39–44.

Wilson, E. K. (2003). Preservice secondary social studies teachers and technology integration: what do they think and do in their field experiences. *Journal of Computing in Teacher Education*, *20*(1), 29–39.

Zhao, Y. (Ed.). (2003). *What Should Teachers Know about Technology? Perspectives and Practices*. Greenwich, CO: Information Age Publishing.

Chapter 10
Using E-Learning to Achieve Fluency in Foreign Languages

Michael Zock
LIF, CNRS, France

Stergos Afantenos
LINA, Université de Nantes, France

ABSTRACT

Speaking a language and achieving proficiency in another one is a highly complex process which requires the acquisition of various kinds of knowledge, declarative and procedural (skills), like the learning of words, rules or patterns and their connection to communicative goals (intentions), the usual starting point. In order to help the learner acquire these skills we propose an electronic version of an age old method: pattern drills (henceforth **PD***s). While being highly regarded in the fifties, PDs have become unpopular since then, partially because of their rigidity and lack of contextual and communicative grounding. Despite these shortcomings we do believe in the virtues of this approach, at least with regard to the acquisition of basic linguistic reflexes or skills (automatisms), necessary to produce language at a 'normal' rate. Of course, the method needs improvement, and we will show here how this can be achieved. Unlike tapes or books, computers are open media, allowing for dynamic changes, taking users' performances and preferences into account. Our DT, a small web-application still in its prototype phase, allows for this. It is a free, electronic version of PDs, i.e. an exercise generator, open and accomodatable to the users' ever changing needs.*

1. INTRODUCTION

Spontaneous speech is a cyclic process involving a loosely ordered set of tasks: conceptual preparation, formulation, articulation (Levelt, 1989). Given a goal one has to decide what to say (conceptualization) and how to say it (formulation), making sure that the chosen elements, words, can be integrated into a coherent whole (sentence frame) and do conform to the grammar rules of the language (syntax, morphology). During vocal delivery (articulation), in itself already a quite demanding task, the speaker may decide to initiate the next cycle, namely starting to plan the subsequent ideational fragment.

DOI: 10.4018/978-1-60566-940-3.ch010

Obviously, smooth execution of such a complex task requires not only access to a huge library of ready made fragments in more or less abstract form (expressions/patterns), but also excellent organizational skills. Speed and knowledge are not all; proficient speakers are also flexible, capable to change on the fly incompatible elements (dynamic accommodation). Not everything is necessarily planned in advance, local adjustments may become necessary.

If speaking in one's mother tongue is already a daunting task, to do so in a foreign language can be overwhelming. There are at least three, probably related reasons for this: lack of *knowledge*, lack of *assurance* and lack of *remembrance*. Indeed, learning to speak a new language requires not only learning a stock of new words and rules, but also to have the necessary confidence to dare to speak, which supposes, of course, quick access and remembrance of what has been learned.

To achieve these goals (increase/consolidation of knowledge, boosting of confidence, fixation/memorisation) we have refurbished and enhanced an age-old method, pattern drills, by building an electronic version of it. While the drill tutor is built for learning Japanese, we believe that the method is general enough to be applied to other languages.

PDs are a special kind of exercise based on notions like: analogy, task decomposition (small steps), systematicity, repetition and feedback. Important as they may be, PDs, or exercises in general, are but one of the many tools teachers rely on for teaching a language. Dictionaries, grammars, video and textbooks being supplementary resources. None of them, except the first one will be taken into consideration here. PDs are typically used in audio-oral lessons. Such lessons are generally composed of the following steps:

1. Presentation of a little *story*, where people try to solve a communication problem (hotel reservation, train station, barber shop). The student hears the story and is encouraged to play one of the roles
2. Contrastive presentation of examples to allow *rule induction*
3. Use of pattern drills for *rule fixation*
4. Rule-transposition, i.e. re-use of the learned patterns in a similar but different situation

These four stages fulfill, roughly speaking, the following functions (a) symbol grounding, i.e. illustration of the pragmatic usage of the structure; (b) conceptualization, i.e. explanation/understanding of the rule; (c) memorization/automatization of the patterns,[1] and (d) generalization/transposition/consolidation of the learned material.

Obviously, there are many ways to learn a language, yet, one of them has proven to be quite efficient, at least for survival purposes: PDs.[2] Since PDs are neither a new nor an uncontroversial method, let us show how many, if not most, of their shortcomings can be overcome.

Linguists describe languages in terms of rules, but people hardly ever learn such descriptions, at least not at the initial stages of acquiring a new language. What people do learn though are patterns complying with these rules.[3] This is definitely the case for beginners and this holds both for first and second language acquisition. R. Weir (Weir, 1962) provided evidence for this by showing that children do spontaneously what we do when being asked: rehearse linguistic structures. Recording her daughter at bedtime, she heard her doing spontaneously, what we do in school: drilling patterns. This kind of behavior has been confirmed by other studies. As the learner makes progress, i.e. acquires more knowledge about the language, s/he will see the limitations of the pattern (overgeneralisation), possibly refining it such as to accommodate for the exceptions. Of course, people learn not only patterns, but also the situations (context) in which they occur. The latter can be seen as goals: *introduce oneself* when meeting someone, *ask for a favor* or *offer help*, etc. Seeing a strong correlation between a situation and verbal behavior, the learner realizes that people tend to use over and over the same pattern, though not necessarily always in the same situation. Given this tight connection between means (patterns) and ends (goals), we have decided to integrate this link in our DT: the fact that patterns are indexed in terms of goals allows the user to choose the means (patterns) as a function of the end (goal, input). People are generally little motivated to do something, unless they perceive its use, that is, the end a given action is serving for (means).

PDs are generally practiced by using a tape recoder. The problem with books or audio cassettes is that they are closed media, hence, everything they contain has to be anticipated in all its details prior to their release. Yet anticipation can never be perfect for at least two reasons. Different people have different needs (for example, the specific words someone would like to learn, i.e. with which to drill a given pattern), and people's needs change over time. This being so, we must take individual differences and the users' ever evolving needs into account. Yet this is precisely what is precluded in the case of closed media. They do not accept any change, update or accommodation after the product's release. In addition they ignore user preferences, or personal learning history: the road to "success" (the method offered) is the same for all, forcing the learner into a straightjacket which, technologically speaking, is not justified anymore. Indeed, none of these constraints are very problematic for open media like computers. The *instances* (lexical values) with which to instantiate the patterns' variables can be changed at any moment, so can the *order* of examples, the *speed* of their presentation and the *number* of repetitions. As a result, the same exercise can be used by a much larger group, or over a longer period of time.

2. RELATED WORK

The notion of *pattern* or *schema* is by no means new. It has a long tradition in *philosophy* (Kant 1781), in *sociology* (Goffmann 1974), in *linguistics* (Harris 1951; Fries 1952; Roberts 1962; van Dijk 1977, Fillmore, 1977), in *psychology* (Bartlett 1932; Koffka 1935; Piaget 1970; Bruner 1973; Rumelhart 1975; Mandler 1979; Ausubel 1980, Hill & Arbib, 1984), in *artificial intelligence* (Minsky 1975; Wilks 1975, Schank & Abelson 1977) and in *natural language processing* (Becker, 1975; Hanks & Pustejovsky 2005). After its rejection by generativists and cognitive psychologists, the notion has experienced a true revival in the arena of computational linguistics. The use of patterns spans a wide spectrum, ranging from *knowledge extraction* (Riloff and Jones, 1999; Hearst, 1998) to *machine translation* (Nagao, 1984). By and large, schemata follow a well beaten path, a kind of pattern or normal curve (called the hype-cycle) for technology adoption: after pioneering discovery and enthousiastic reaction, the idea is rejected, to be finally adopted after having evolved towards a mature notion with more realistic expectations. There is no doubt, patterns are a valuable strategy for producing language under real-time constraints, or for learning this skill. Also, given the initial successes of TEXT (McKeown, 1985), a system producing paragraph-length texts on the basis of patterns linked to goals, it is not surprising to see that they have been used so extensively by the 'natural-language-generation' community. For more information you may want to take a look at CLINT (http://www.cs.bgu.ac.il/~elhadad/clint.html/), or the papers presented in a special workshop devoted to this issue (Becker and Busemann, 1999: http://www.dfki.de/service/NLG/KI99-schedule.html/).

3. AN EXAMPLE OF THE PROCESS

Before showing how the resource is built, let us see how it is meant to work and in what respect it differs from conventional PDs used in a language lab. Let's start with the latter, illustrating it with the simplest case, *substitution drills* requiring no morphological changes.

Figure 1. The basic interactions between the DT and the student

A. Goal Tree

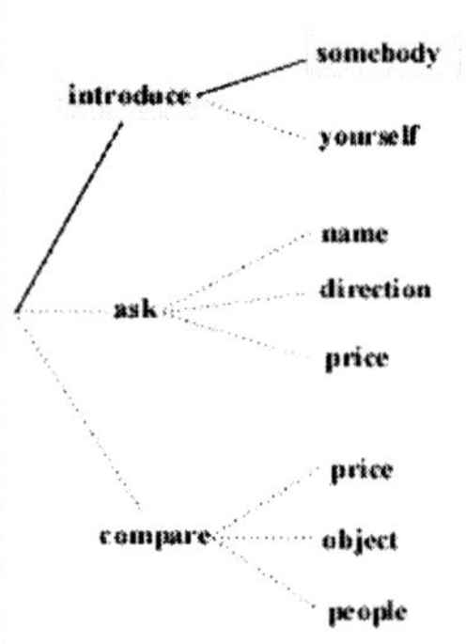

B. Choose one of the patterns

Goal	Possible patterns
Presentation	1. This is <title> <name> Kore wa <name> <title> desu.
	2. This is <title> <name> from <country>. Kono kata wa <origin> no <name> <title> desu.

C. Provide values (words) for the variables

<title>	Mr., Mrs., Dr., Professor
<name>	Matsumoto, Schmidt, Tanaka, Dupont
<country>	Japan, Germany, France

D. Set of possible outputs

1 This is Mr. Schmidt from Germany.
Kono kata wa <doitsu> no <sumisu> <san> desu.
この かた は ドイツ の スミス さん です。

2 This is Prof. Tanaka from Japan.
Kono kata wa <nihon> no <tanaka> <sensei> desu.
この かた は にほん の たなか せんせい です。

The student receives a model, which could be composed of a *question* (let's say, "what is this?"), a *stimulus* ("a pen") and the *answer* ("This is a pen"). From then on, s/he will only be given the stimulus and the feedback concerning her/his answer (the machine producing the correct sentence). Of course, the user has to produce the answer in the first place. [4]

Figure 1 above illustrates the way how the student gets from the starting point, a *goal* (frame A), to its *linguistic realization*, the endpoint (frame D), a well-formed sentence. The process is initiated by the student who chooses a *goal* (frame A, e.g. *introduce somebody*), to which the system responds with the *patterns* it knows for achieving it (frame B). [5] The user chooses one of them (B1° vs. B2°), specifying then (frame C) the specific lexical values he'd like the pattern to be instantiated with (Schmidt vs. Tanaka). Frame D displays the possible outputs on the basis of the users' inputs (goal and lexical values).

Of course, the lexical values could be given by the system as stimulus, and this is actually the way pattern drills work in traditional language labs (see table 1 and table 2), but, as mentionned already, we would like the system to be open, allowing the students to feed the patterns with the words that are of interest for *them*, as this is one of our main goals. Obviously, if the values of the variables <title> <name> <origin> were (Professor, Tanaka, Japan) rather than (Mr, Smith, Germany), then the outputs would vary accordingly (see Table 2).

The system has now basically all the information needed to create the exercise and to some extent enough information to evaluate the student's subsequent response. To this end it will create an output on the basis of the users' inputs (chosen goal, pattern and words), and compare it with the learner's output.[6] The process continues until the student has done all the exercises, or until s/he decides to stop.

Three points might be worth mentioning here:

- Conceptual input is distributed over time, specification taking place in several steps: first by choosing the abstract overall structure or pattern (steps 1 and 2) and then by providing the variables' concrete lexical

Table 1. Model given by the system

Goal:	Introduce Somebody
1a) Pattern in English:	This is **<title>** **<name>** from **<origin>**.
1b) Pattern in Japanese:	Kono kata wa **<origin>** no **<name>** **<title>** desu.
2) Stimuli:	Mr, Schmidt, Germany
3) Instantiated Sentence:	Kono kata wa **doitsu** no **Sumisu san** desu.

Table 2. Interaction with the user during the training session. Variation of the input (stimulus) yielding differences in the output.

System (stimuli)	Professor, Tanaka, Japan
User: (response)	Kono kata wa **nihon** no **Tanaka sensei** desu.
System (verification):	excellent

values: 'Mr, Mrs, Dr', or 'Professor' for the variable <title> (step 4).

- At the moment, we do not rely on any morphological component which obviously limits the system's scope. Any question-answer pair or sentence transformation may require such a component, and we will surely integrate it later on.[7] For the time being, the idea is just to illustrate the system's basic mechanism and the interaction between the system and the student.
- While being similar to classical PDs, our approach is nevertheless quite a bit different. First of all, it is the student who chooses the pattern s/he'd like to work on, as s/he knows (arguably) best what her/his needs are. Next, our patterns are indexed in terms of goals. This is necessary in order to locate or find the pattern one would like to work on. With the system growing, grows the list of patterns. Hence, access becomes an issue. Also, associating patterns with goals allows the student to realize the pattern's communicative function. Third, since we do not have a parser or speech analyzer, we have a problem to evaluate the user's output. Actually, the learner does not type at all his output, s/he only confirms via a keystroke that his/her mentally (or orally produced) answer conforms to the system's output. The reason for this is simple. The focus being on speed (fluency), we would like to avoid slowing down the process by having the input being provided via the keyboard. Fourth, the system's output is given in written form. This can be considered as a disadvantage, yet it can also be turned into a big advantage if, as planned, a speech synthesizer is added. Doing so would allow not only to discover grapheme-phoneme mappings,[8] hence support the learning of reading and writing, but also allow to support memorization by showing intonation curves. In addition this would allow us to control the speed of the vocal output, which leads us to the last point. Unlike books or tapes, computers allow at any moment to change the *speed*; *order* of examples, or the *intervals* of repetitions, that is, the number of repetitions after which an element is taken from the list, to maximize presentation of resisting structures and words (Ebbinghaus,1885; Leitner, 1972).[9]

4. CURRENT STATE OF THE DRILL TUTOR

The work presented here is the result of about one year's work. The DT is a client/server web application, written in PHP and sitting atop an Apache server in a Linux machine. The program is divided into two areas: one reserved for the creation of the tool, the expert area (figure 2a and 2c), the other one being reserved for its use, *exercise area* (figure 2b and 2e-j). The expert area deals mainly with *data acquisition*, i.e the creation of the data-base, that is, the insertion of patterns and their links to goals (see figure 2a and 2c). The other section is reserved for the student to allow him to *customize* the tool and to do the *exercises* (2b and 2e-j). The implemented operations are as follows.

Figure 2. Building (2a, c, d) and using the resource (2b, e-j)

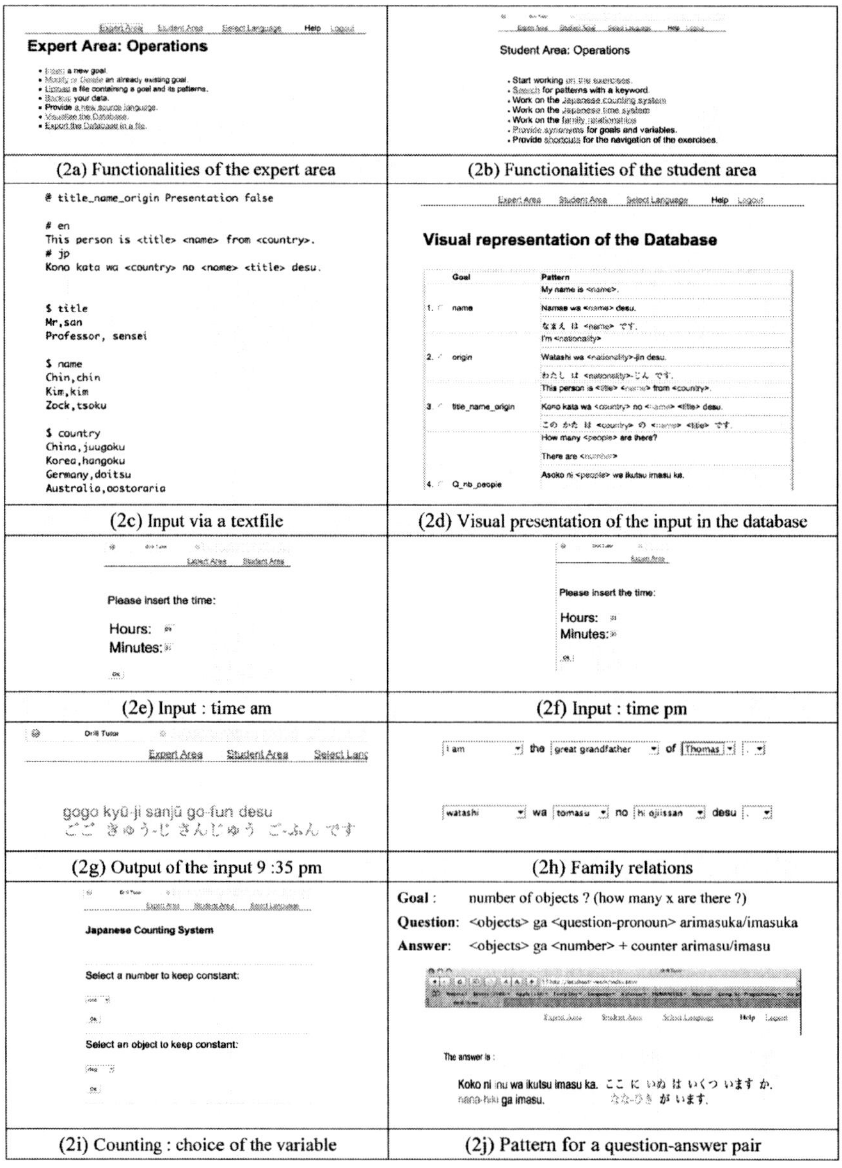

4.1. Expert Area

4.1.1 User Authentication

People entitled to make changes to the database (so called experts) and users (students) have to authenticate themselves via a user name and a password. This is necessary in order to avoid inconsistencies/noise in the database and to ensure that people work on their own data.

4.1.2 Creation of New Patterns and Goals

Currently the system has about 50 patterns and 500 words.[10] To allow for quick access, patterns need to be indexed. This is done here via *goals*. Of course, other criteria (syntactic, semantic) could or should be used. In order to provide new data, typically a new goal and its associated patterns and words, the expert can either use the system's graphical user interface (henceforth GUI), or upload a textfile containing the necessary information (see figure 2c). This implies in the first case (a) to name the *goal* and its parent (see also the next paragraph), (b) to list, in the source and target languages, the *patterns* likely to achieve this goal, and (c) to provide *lexical values* for the variables. After this the expert can either provide the next goal and its associated pattern(s), or ask the system to present all possible sentences computable on the basis of the input, the goal here being to check wellformedness.

A typical input for the goal 'presentation' and its associated subgoals (title, name, origin) can be seen in figure 2c, where the first line specifies the goal and its position in the hierarchy. The next block contains the corresponding pattern(s), i.e. constants and variables, in the source- and target language (here, English and Japanese). The remaining blocks specify the lexical values of the variables mentionned in the pattern, here *title*, *name* and *country*. Figure 2d displays the input in a more graphical way, transliterating the roman caracters into the phonetic japanese correspondants (kana, i.e. hiragana or katakana). The pattern associated with the goal given as input could yield a sentence like the following as output: 'This is Professor Tanaka from Japan' ('kono kata wa nihon no Tanaka sensei desu'), which translates literally into 'this-person-topic-Japan-origin-Tanaka-professor-is'. As this example clearly shows, if ever there was need, it is impossible to speak these languages if one translates one into the other word-by-word, since the order is reversed. By contrast, it is quite easy to switch from one language to the other by instantiating a pattern, since the latter contains basically the sentence plan, that is, the expected (type of) words in the right order.

4.1.3 Organizing Goals into Trees to Allow for Quick Navigation

Learners knowing their needs prefer to make their own choices rather than being told what patterns to work on. To do so, we must give them the means to express their needs, quickly and naturally, which in our case here means 'locate a pattern'. This is done here via an index expressed in terms of goals. Indexing can be done from various points of view (pragmatic, semantic, syntactic). We have chosen the first (pragmatic), leaving syntactic/semantic indexing (i.e. composing the message) for later on. As goals can contain other goals, we have a tree or a hierarchy of goals. Hence, in order to find the wanted pattern, the student has to navigate in such a goal tree (see section A in Figure 1). To enable the system to create this kind of structure, experts have to state with their input where in the hierarchy fits their new goal and its associated pattern(s). This is done via the parent node.

4.1.4 Modification of Goals and Changing the Interface Language

The data given to the system (goals, patterns and lexical values) can be modified at any time. In other words, experts can add, delete or modify the patterns and values for any given goal.

The learning of a new language should be independent of the used interface language, i.e. the language in which the information relevant for teaching/learning takes place. In order to accomplish this, the DT allows the expert to translate the interface and the linguistic data into a chosen target language (usually, the learner's mother tongue). The same holds true for the transliteration table, whose equivalents have to be given in the desired language. This can easily be done via the GUI (graphical user-interface): a -> あ; e -> え, etc...

4.2. The Student Area

At this level there are basically two issues, those concerning the interface (most notably, the interface language) and those related to the DT's usage.

4.2.1 Interface Issues: Tailor the Environment to the Students' Likings

4.2.1.1 Defining the Interface

While not being fundamental with regard to the main goal (achieving fluency), interface issues (color, size and position of letters, icons, - delays between input and output, etc.) can become extremely important, in particular when they run counter the users' expectations and needs. Hence, ideally, this part should be parametrizable. We haven't done this yet, but this is something we shall certainly do so in the near future. Of more immediate concern are issues related to the interface language.

4.2.1.2 Interface Language

As mentioned already in section 4.1, experts have the possibility to provide other interface languages than the default one, which in our case is English. This allows students to receive all relevant information (instructions and feedback) via a language they are familiar with, generally their mother tongue. Hence, in principle, everyone is able to see the menus, scripts (transliterated Hiragana), goals and patterns in their mother tongue. Of course, this information (in general a translation) must be given somewhere, and this is done via the GUI level, hence it is quite straighforward. Depending on the language, the situation can become more complex though for transliterations. For example, vowels are left implicit in arabic, which poses a problem for its direct mapping on a syllabary like the japanese kana script (hiragana or katakana).

4.2.1.3 Baptising: Why Not Have the Students Use Their Own Metalanguage?

Experts and users have to decide at some point how to refer to a given *variable* or *goal*, that is, they have to decide how to call or name them. Any of the following could be used to refer to a given entity, let's say a 'banana': *subject*, *object*, *noun*, *food*. This being so, students may still like none of them. So, why not give them the means to name the object according to *their* liking? After all, what counts is that they can find what 'they' are looking for, and to this end they have to rely on (or navigate by using) concepts that are meaningful to 'them'. Hence, we should give them the means to name things the way they want to, possibly even using several terms. To this end we provide a GUI allowing students to change the names of the variables and goals the way they want. This information is kept in the form of cookies on the learner's side (private space), as it is personal: different people using different terms to refer to a given object.

4.2.2 Working on the Exercises

This is the most important part from the student's point of view. As mentioned already, the students can choose the pattern they'd like to work on. To find the wanted pattern they navigate in the goal hierarchy (frame A in figure 1). Once they have found or chosen the goal they will be presented with all its associated patterns, meaning that they have to choose again, though, this time from a much smaller set (the result is shown in frame B). Of course, they could also choose to work with all of the goals, but this is rather atypical at this stage. While this would add variety to the exercise, hence potentially fight boredom, it would also increase complexity, which is not what is necessarily wanted at the beginning stages. Whatever the user's choice (one vs. several patterns), the process develops as follows. First, students are shown an example sentence (model) in which a single element will be replaced. In the simplest case only one element will be replaced, no morphological changes taking place (substitution drill). Next are given, in random order, the elements (stimulus) to be inserted into the proper slot (frame C). Doing so should help the students not only to memorize words, but also to use (or to produce) them in the proper syntactic context. In other terms, words are not learned in isolation, but in context. Once the student has provided his answer, s/he is given some kind of rudimentary feedback: the system displays the correct sentence both in roman characters as well as in their transliterated Japanese form (for the time being only in Hiragana-see figure 2e and 2j). The process iterates until the student has acquired the patterns or has decided to stop. It should be noted that the transliteration of the Hiragana appears in the interface language chosen by the user. If it were Greek or Russian, then the transliterated sentence would be in the characters of either of these two languages, next to the Hiragana, of course.

The main steps of the process are represented in figure 2 here above. Users are allowed to define keyboard shortcuts, using keystrokes rather than moving the mouse over radio buttons. This increases speed and confort for telling the system that one has been able to produce the expected output, information necessary to decide whether a given combination (pattern + specific word) should be kept on the exercise list.

4.2.3 Exercises for Specific Problems

One of the many problems foreigners have when learning Japanese is their counting system, as the words expressing numerical values depend not only on these values, but also on the *nature* (or certain features) of the counted object. To this end, 'quantifiers' (-bon, -mai, -biki, etc.) are added to the counters. While western languages use the same word, let's say the word 'three' to talk about given number of 'pencils, tickets, or dogs', japanese use a different quantifier for each case: sanbon, san-mai, san-biki, etc. In order to account for this fact, we have created exercises allowing for selective variation of the *number*, the *object* or both. Similarly, we have created specific exercises for learning the expression of *time* or *family relationships* (see figure 2e-h). It should be noted, that object inherent features ('animate/inanimate', 'bottle/cup/paper', etc.) may have an impact not only on the counter and the interrogative pronoun, but also on the verb (see 2j, *imasu* vs. *arimasu*, meaning "to have" or "to be"). Hence, unlike in English, we cannot decide on the precise pattern before having specified the object (animate or inanimate), as it may affect the surface form of any of these categories (verb, counter, interrogative pronoun).

4.2.4 Evaluation, i.e. Feedback

Of course, the whole process would be of limited use if the students were not given some means (feedback) to assess the quality of their work. Actually, the system keeps track of the users' performance (errors made during the training session), allowing thus to devote more time to problematic cases (spaced repetition, i.e. optimization of memorisation schedule).

A problem that remains though is the fact that the user's output is purely quantitative: congruency of his and the system's output. Not having access to the concrete form of the output (since neither the vocal nor the written output are recorded), the system cannot fully interprete it (What went wrong? Why? How to correct the mistake?) and provide explanations.

5. FUTURE WORK

5.1. Manual Creation and Enrichment of the Database

At the moment of writing this paper, we have mainly been concerned with the implementation of the basic infrastructure and the editor. Actually, little effort has been made so far to feed the database with data (goals, patterns and values), yet this is vital information. While there are many sources we can draw upon either manually (Alfonso, 1974; Chino, 2004; Kamiya, 2005) or (semi-)automatically, care must be taken to make the right choices. Increasing the number of patterns is not all, we must also make sure to choose only those that are really useful. In addition, attention needs to be paid to the metalanguage, which ideally should be meaningful even for the linguistically innocent users (see section 5.3.1).

Since the required steps of *data acquisition* (section 4.1.2) and *conceptual input* (in particular the last step of specifying the lexical values) are cumbersome, they should be improved. Indeed, with every new *goal* we have to provide not only its associated *patterns*, but also a list of *lexical items* i.e the variables' values. This puts a lot of work on the experts' or users' shoulders. To alleviate this task we could do several things: (a) integrate a multilingual dictionary, (b) mine or detect automatically patterns in a corpus, i.e. abstract automatically patterns on the basis of concrete input (sentences); (c) find pattern instances, i.e. concrete sentences, in a given corpus, and use them not only to build our data-base, but also to extend the learner's experience in the new language by allowing him to go beyond the precise forms encountered in the initial training set (see below).

5.2. Integration of a Dictionary

Adding a multi-lingual dictionary would definitely be useful. Not only would it cut down on the fatigue, possible typing errors and the time needed to provide input, it would also allow for on-the-fly-translations of words. To do this successfully we need to address though the issue of polysemy or word-sense disambuiguation (bank: *geographical location* vs. *money institution*).

While a dictionary is without any doubt very useful, in our context it is not the main component. Our primary goal is building sentences rather than choosing words, hence we need first to find the pattern into which to insert then the relevant words.

5.3. Automatic Creation of a Pattern Library and the Problem of Conceptual Input

In order to communicate an idea, one must have an idea to begin with. Yet, no one wants to listen to anyone for an hour to find out WHAT this persons wants to say, to tell him then HOW to say it in a given language. In other words, no one is willing to listen to some abstract or obscure metalanguage, no matter how elegant and powerful it may be. People want to hear plain talk, that is concrete words, i.e. natural language. While intermediate languages (concepts, interlingua, semantic networks, conceptual graphs, etc.) are at first sight attractive, in real life they hardly ever work, be it for theoretical reasons (lack of clarity, underspecification, ambiguity) or simply time constraints. This being so, we have thought of another solution, composed of two complementary steps, to be performed automatically: pattern abstraction and mining of pattern-instances.

Table 3. A pattern in English and Japanese

English pattern:	*Japanese pattern*	*Japanese pattern*
A: What is that?	A: Are wa nan desu ka?	A: あれはなんですか
B: That is a <object>.	B: Are wa <object> desu.	B: あれは<object> です.

5.3.1 Guessing Patterns from Concrete Instances, i.e. Sentences

We would like to get the computer to guess somehow the meaning of the user's input and to produce a similar, though not necessarily identical output in the target language. Bear in mind though, that our purpose here is exercising and knowledge expansion, i.e. presentation of similar sentences, rather than finding a perfect translation of a given input. Suppose the latter were "quiero una cerveza" ('I want a/some beer'), then you'd like the system to understand not only literally, that you, John Lennon, would like a beer, but also, more generally, that "there is a *person desiring* a certain kind of *drink*", allowing a search engine to retrieve from a corpus somehow similar sentences like "Obama wants a coke", "the kid wants an ice-cream", etc. Of course, depending on one's inclination, one can start arguing here. And indeed, there are several issues here at stake, some dealing with the relative, semantic proximity of the input and output (can we consider the two examples here above still as reasonably close?), others dealing with technical aspects involved in solving this problem, namely:

- Which parts of the sentence should be replaced by a variable? There are quite a few sentences in which all major lexical categories can be replaced;
- Shall the process be fully automatized, or is it more reasonable to make it semi-automatic (interactive)?
- How shall a given variable be named? This issue becomes relevant if we are to present such patterns to the user, so that he can build then a sentence on this basis. While notions such as *subjects* or *noun-phrase* (NP) are meaningful for a linguist, semantic categories like "people, fruit, means of transportation," etc. are far more natural for "normal" people. In this context, many readers may think of WordNet (Fellbaum, 1998), and indeed this resource could be used. Unfortunately it cannot fully address the issue at hand, as only nouns are systematically linked via hypernymes;
- What sort of information needs to be added (by annotation) and what kind of transformations need to be performed to enable the program to find instances of the abstracted category, variable or word?

5.3.2 Searching in a Corpus for Instances of Patterns

As mentioned already, creating a data-base of patterns, is a tedious task. Consider the following. When providing a pattern, the expert has not only to link it to a goal, he has also to provide a list of *values* with which to fill the pattern's variables. Imagine the following patterns in English and Japanese in response to the question or goal "What is this?" (see Table 3).

Obviously, the list of possible fillers for a general slot like <object> can become extremely long, making it a dreadful and error prone task. In addition, the list is most likely to be incomplete, possibly lacking what the user needs. This being so, we have thought of another solution.

While the database (goals, patterns and slot fillers) could obviously be created by hand, part of it might be created automatically. Here is the underlying rationale. Having linked patterns to goals, we know the pattern as soon as we know the goal. Yet patterns can be used for filtering a corpus, allowing among other things

- The extraction of full sentences, illustrating a given pattern (pattern instances) along with appropriate lexical material for the various slots (words being shown in context)
- The extraction of pattern instances (sentences) in various languages, provided that we have defined the corresponding pattern mappings. This is particularly interesting if we want to specify the input (message) in one language and receive similar sentences (example sentences) in another language, as this might be the case when learning a new language.
- To extract a list of lexical candidats ready to be used for the various pattern slots

Searching for potential lexical values amounts to making a *grep-like* search over a well chosen text (say, the electronic version of a text book, a teaching method, a set of e-mails, etc.), replacing the variables by the values' *wild-card* characters *. For example, a pattern like "the major export good of <COUNTRY-X> is <OBJECT-Y>", might yield *wine* and *cheese* in the case of *France*, and *cigars* and *rhum* in the case of *Cuba*. Search for slot fillers of the pattern given in Table 3b could take the following form: "That is a *", where "*" is a wild-card character.

Obviously, the success of this kind of approach hinges critically on the quality of the corpus and the query. If the query is too specific, i.e. restrictive, we will miss many candidates, eventhough they do exist. If the query is too general, we will get too many hits, which, while being compatible with the pattern, are not really what we are looking for. For example, the pattern here above could yield not only "that is a *house*", which is fine, but also "that is a *QBitmap object*", or "that is a *chair that Louis XIV used to have in one of his bedrooms*", which are probably not the kind of examples we are looking for.

The procedure just described could be useful not only for the expert, but also for the student. Indeed, the same techniques could be used to search for instances of a pattern, i.e."similar" sentences to the one provided as input, but in a *different context*. To this end the system could perform a grep search in a corpus, large enough to yield interesting examples, while being sufficiently accessible to be meaningful for the user. Hence, rather than resorting to the web which contains too much noise, we could use texts the user is familiar with, that is, text composed of sentences encountered before, or text s/he is likely to understand. A tourist guidebook containing survival phrases, or the coursebook used for teaching the language would be good candidates. This process, which we call "push and pull" would not only allow to strengthen the memory traces of already known material (push), but also help expanding the students' experience of the patterns and the language, by illustrating less-known words, or showing well-known words in less-known contexts. Put differently, this might help the students learn news words, or old words in new contexts. In either case it would help building a new or strenghtening an already existing memory trace.

5.4. Evaluation

As mentioned already the DT is so far only a prototype. While it has been tested by various colleagues, it has not received any formal evaluation so far. Yet, this is needed at some point.

A good way to evaluate the performance of a model (or tool) is to embed it into a task and measure the overall gain due to its use. Unfortunately, such end-to-end or extrinsic evaluations are very expensive. This, is why people have defined intrinsic evaluations, which measure the potential gains of a model without confronting it with the concrete situation of use (application). In other words, intrinsic evaluation measures the system in itself by relating it to an ideal, usually some kind of (gold) standard, whereas extrinsic metrics evaluate how a model, system or tool performs with respect to a specific task. (Galliers and Sparck Jones, 1993). While an extensive overview and critique of the various evaluation schemes used in HLT is out of the scope of this paper,[11] we will present here briefly some ideas of how we plan to perform our evaluation.

5.4.1 Intrinsic Evaluation

As mentioned already (section 4.2), once the user has answered a question, he is given some feedback concerning the quality of his output, and statistics are kept concerning the number of correct answers. Since every student has a private space, i.e. separate session, this can be done very easily. The goal is to check how much time the student has spent on the DT and whether its use resulted in any measurable *improvement* (increase of the *speed* and number of *correct* responses). If performance increases proportionally to the time spent using the tool (decrease of errors), then we may well conclude that the DT is a valuable tool for learning the skill we are trying to teach.

5.4.2 Extrinsic Evaluation

Extrinsic evaluation could be done after a longer training period by measuring the users' performance in a setting other than the initial learning environment (in front of the computer). An ideal situation would be to confront the student with a real world situation (a place where this language is actually spoken) and then ask her/him to perform one of the many tasks acquired while using the DT, for example, ask for directions, compare two things, express preferences, etc. Alas, such a scenario requires not only quite an amount of resources (tape recorder, time, etc.), but it also makes it hard to control all the external variables. Yet this is required in a serious evaluation. This is why we plan to run the experiments in a laboratory.

In such a case, the use of a *double blind* procedure is very important. This might imply in our case that we ask some native speakers to start a conversation with some students. The latter can either be students who have used the DT, or people who don't, but who speak the target language. The important point is that the judges don't know who is who, that is, who has learned the language with what tool. If both groups perform reasonably alike, then we may well conclude that the DT is indeed an appropriate platform for the task at hand.

6. DISCUSSION AND CONCLUSION

Becoming fluent in a language requires not only learning words and methods for accessing them quickly, but also learning how to place them and how to make the necessary morphological adjustments. This is not a small feat, considering that all this has to be done fast, and that on top of it, the next conceptual fragment needs be planned and possibly be evaluated. This kind of timesharing is hard to accomplish if not at least part of the component processes are automatized.

The work presented here is the result of 12 months' work. It is implemented in PHP, and the supported languages are English at the interface level and Japanese as the language to be learned. We plan to add other languages, a speech synthesizer and a morphological component. We also plan to combine simple patterns into more complex ones (scripts, discourse patterns), to improve the interface, and, last, but not least, we intend to make the system available on the web by the end of the year.

Having linked patterns to goals should help users to perceive the function of a given structure (i.e which goal(s) can be reached by using a particular pattern). Yet, most importantly, this linkage offers the possibility to get instances of the pattern from a document (corpus). This is interesting not only for *data acquisition* (building the resource by feeding it with lexical entries likely to occur in a given pattern), but also for *remembrance*. In addition, presenting patterns with new material allows expanding the learner's experience of the language. The fact that most goals are associated with multiple patterns allows to extend the range of the exercise, reducing thus boredom. Instead of drilling one single pattern in response to a chosen goal, the system can prompt the user by presenting him various patterns.

Obviously, PDs are not a panacea. They can even be harmful it not used properly (paroting, mindless repetition), but used in the right way, that is, at the right moment, with the right goals and at the right proportion, they can do wonders. Just like a tennis player might want to go back to the court and train his basic strokes, a language learner may feel the need to drill resisting patterns. Whoever has tried to become skillful in a language very different from his own can't but agree with deKeyser (2001) when he writes: "Without automatization no amount of knowledge will ever translate into the levels of skill required for real life use".

Still, true as it may be, we must beware that patterns are but one element of a long chain, i.e one of the many elements of the speaker's toolbox. They need to be learned, but once interiorized they must be placed back into the context where they have come from, an authentic communicative scene. Without this additional experience they will simply fail to produce the wanted effect, that is, help us achieve our communicative goals.

Computers are a medium escaping many of the constraints (rigidity, closedness) other media (tapes or books) are condemned to. They allow for variable order of presentation, dynamic updating of words and much more. Learning a language does not mean memorizing sentences, actually, we tend to forget those sooner or later. What usually remains are ideas, words and patterns, rather than full fledged sentences and rules. Hence, forgetting sentences is not a problem anymore, since we know now how to build them, and this is precisely one of the goals of the tutor described here.

7. REFERENCES

Alfonso, A. (1974). *Japanese language patterns*. Sofia University, Center of Applied Linguistics, Tokyo.

Ausubel, D. (1980). Schemata, Cognitive Structure and Advance Organisers: A Reply to Anderson, Spiro and Anderson. *American Educational Research Journal*, *17*(3), 400–404.

Bartlett, F. (1932). *Remembering*. Cambridge, UK: Cambridge University Press.

Becker, J. (1975). *The Phrasal Lexicon* [BBN Report No. 3081]. Cambridge, MA: Bolt Beranek & Newman.

Becker, T., & Busemann, S. (Eds.). (1999). *"May I Speak Freely?" Between Templates and Free Choice in Natural Language Generation*. D-99-01, DFKI, Saarbrücken.

Belz, A. (2009). That's Nice… What Can You Do With It? *Computational Linguistics*, *35*(1), 111–118. doi:10.1162/coli.2009.35.1.111

Bruner, J. (1973). Beyond the Information Given: Studies in the Psychology of Knowing. New York: W. Norton.

Chastain, K. (1969). The audio-lingual habit learning theory vs. the code-cognitif learning theory. *IRAL*, *7*(2), 97–107. doi:10.1515/iral.1969.7.2.97

Chino, N. (2004). *A Dictionary of Basic Japanese Sentence Patterns*. Kodansha, Tokyo.

Chomsky, N. (1959). A review of B. F. Skinner's Verbal Behavior. *Language*, *31*(1), 26–58. doi:10.2307/411334

deKeyser, R. (2001). *Automaticity and automatization*. In P. Robinson (Ed.), *Cognition and second language instruction* (pp. 125-151). New York: Cambridge University Press.

deKeyser, R. (2007a). *Skill acquisition theory*. In J. Williams & B. VanPatten (Eds.), *Theories in Second Language Acquisition: An introduction* (pp. 97-113). Mahwah, NJ: Erlbaum.

deKeyser, R. (Ed.). (2007b). *Practicing in a second language: Perspectives from applied linguistics and cognitive psychology*. Cambridge, UK: Cambridge University Press

Ebbinghaus, H. (1962). *Memory: A contribution to experimental psychology*. New York: Dover.

Fellbaum, C. (Ed.). (1998). *WordNet: An Electronic Lexical Database and some of its Applications*. Cambridge, MA: MIT Press.

Fillmore, C. (1977). Scenes-and-frames Semantics. In A. Zampolli (Ed.), *Linguistic Structures Processing* (pp. 55-82). Amsterdam: North Holland.

Fitts, P. (1964). Perceptual motor skill learning. In A. Melton (Ed.), *Categories of human learning* (pp. 243–285). New York: Academic press.

Fries, C. (1952). *The Structure of English. An Introduction to the Construction of English Sentences*. New York: Harcourt, Brace.

Garrod, S., & Pickering, M. J. (2007). Automaticity in language production in monologue and dialogue. In A.S. Meyer, L.R. Wheeldon, & A. Krott (Eds.), *Automaticity and control in language processing* (pp. 1-21). Hove: Psychology Press.

Gatbonton, E., & Segalowitz, N. (1988). Creative automatization: Principles for promoting fluency within a communicative framework. *TESOL Quarterly, 22*, 473–492. doi:10.2307/3587290

Gatbonton, E., & Segalowitz, N. (2005). Rethinking communicative language teaching: a focus on access to fluency. *Canadian Modern Language Review, 61*, 325–353.

Goffman, E. (1974). *Frame analysis. An Essay on the Organisation of Experience*. Cambridge, MA: Harper & Row.

Goldberg, A. (1998). *Patterns of experience in patterns of language*. In M. Tomasello (Ed.), *The new psychology of language* (pp. 203-219). Mahwah, NJ: Lawrence Erlbaum.

Guillaume, P. (1973). *La formation des habitudes*. PUF, Paris.

Hanks, P., & Pustejovsky, J. (2005). A Pattern Dictionary for Natural Language Processing. In *Revue Francaise de linguistique appliquée, 10*,2.

Harris, Z. (1951). *Methods in Structural Linguistics*. Chicago: University of Chicago Press.

Hearst, M. (1998). *Automated discovery of WordNet relations*. In C. Fellbaum, (Ed.), *WordNet an electronic lexical database* (pp. 131–152). Cambridge, MA: MIT Press.

Herriot, P. (1971). *Language and Teaching: A Psychological View*. London: Methuen and Co.

Hill, J., & Arbib, M. (1984). Schemas, Computation and Language Acquisition. *Human Development, 27*, 282–296.

Hulstijn, J. H. (2001). Intentional and incidental second-language vocabulary learning: A reappraisal of elaboration, rehearsal and automaticity. In P. Robinson (Ed.), *Cognition and second language instruction* (pp. 258-286). Cambridge, UK: Cambridge University Press.

Jackendoff, R. (1993). *Patterns in the Mind: Language and Human Nature*. London: Harvester-Wheatsheaf.

Kamiya, T. (2005). *Japanese Sentence Patterns for effective communication*. Tokyo, Japan: Kodansha.

Kant, E. (1781). *Critique of Pure Reason*. Garden City, NY: Anchor Books.

Koffka, K. (1935). *The principles of Gestalt psychology*. New York: Harcourt Brace & World.

Krashen, S. (1981). *Second Language Acquisition and Second Language Learning*. Retrieved from http://www.sdkrashen.com/SL_Acquisition_and_Learning/index.html

Lado, R. (1964). *Language Teaching: A Scientific Approach*. New York: McGraw Hill.

Leitner, s. (1972). *So lernt man lernen* [Learning to learn]. Freiburg, Heider.

Leont'ev, A. (1974). *Psycholinguistik und Sprachunterricht*. Stuttgart, Germany: Kohlhammer.

Levelt, W. (1970). Skill theory and language teaching. *Studies in Second Language Acquisition*, *1*(1), 53–70. doi:10.1017/S0272263100000711

Levelt, W. (1989). *Speaking*. Cambridge, MA: MIT Press.

Mandler, J. (1979). Categorial and Schematic Organisation in Memory. In C. Puff (Ed.), *Memory Organisation and Structure* (pp. 259-299). New York: Academic Press.

McKeown, K. (1985). Discourse strategies for generating natural-language text. *Artificial Intelligence*, *27*, 1–42. doi:10.1016/0004-3702(85)90082-7

Minsky, M. (1975). A Framework for Representing Knowledge. In P. Winston (Eds.), *The Psychology of Computer Vision* (pp. 211-277). New York: McGraw Hill.

Nagao, M. (1984). *A framework of a mechanical translation between japanese and english by analogy principle*. In A. Elithorn & R. Banerji (Eds.), *Artificial and Human Intelligence* (pp. 173–180). Amsterdam: Elsevier.

Piaget, J. (1970). Piaget's Theory. In P. Mussen (Ed.), *Carmichael's Manual of Child Psychology* (vol. 1, pp. 318-323). New York: Wiley.

Posner, M., & Snyder, C. (1975). *Facilitation and inhibition in the processing of signal*. In S. Rabbitt& S. Dornic (Eds.), *Attention and performance* (pp. 669–682). New York: Academic Press.

Riloff, E., & Jones, R. (1999). Learning dictionaries for information extraction by multi-level bootstrapping. In *Proc. of the 16th National Conference on Artificial Intelligence* (pp. 474– 479).

Rivers, W. (1964). *The Psychologist and the Foreign Language Teacher*. University of Chicago Press, Chicago.

Rivers, W. (1972). *Speaking in Many Tongues: Essays in Foreign Language Teaching*. Rowley: Newbury House.

Roberts, P. (1962). *English Sentences*. New York: Harcourt Brace & World.

Rumelhart, D. (1975). Notes on a Schema for Stories. In D. Bobrow & A. Collins (Eds.), Representation and Understanding: Studies in Cognitive Science (pp. 211-236). New York: Academic Press.

Savignon, S. (1983). *Communicative Competence: Theory and Classroom Practice*. Reading, MA: Addison-Wesley.

Schank, R., & Abelson, R. (1977). *Scripts, Plans, Goals and Understanding: an Inquiry into Human Knowledge Structures*. Hillsdale, NJ: Erlbaum.

Scott, D. (1999). The Multilingual Generation Game: authoring fluent texts in unfamiliar languages. In *Proceedings of the 16th International Joint Conference on Artificial Intelligence*.

Segalowitz, N. (2000). *Automaticity and attentional skill in fluent performance*. In H. Riggenbach (Ed.), *Perspectives on fluency* (pp. 200-219). Ann Arbor, MI: University of Michigan Press.

Segalowitz, N. (2003). Automaticity and second language learning. In C. Doughty & M. Long (Eds.), *The handbook of second language acquisition* (pp. 382-408). Oxford, UK: Blackwell.

Segalowitz, N. (2007). Access fluidity, attention control, and the acquisition of fluency in a second language. *TESOL Quarterly*, *41*, 181–186.

Segalowitz, N., & Hulstijn, J. (2005). Automaticity in second language learning. In J.F. Kroll & A.M.B. De Groot (Eds.), *Handbook of bilingualism: Psycholinguistic approaches* (pp 371-388). New York: Oxford University Press.

Spärck Jones, K. (1994). Towards better NLP system evaluation. In *Proceedings of the Workshop on Human Language Technology (HLT'94)* (pp. 102–107).

Spolsky, B. (1966). A psycholinguistic critique of programmed foreign language instruction. *IRAL*, 4(2).

Stevens, V. (1989). *A direction for CALL: From behavioristic to humanistic courseware*. In M. Pennington (Ed.), *Teaching Languages with Computers* (pp. 31–43). La Jolla, CA: Athelstan.

van Dijk, T. (1977). Semantic Macro-Structures and Knowledge frames in Discourse Comprehension. In M. A. Just & P. A. Carpenter (Eds.), *Cognitive Processes in Comprehension* (pp. 3-31). Hillsdale, NJ: Lawrence Erlbaum.

Weir, R. (1962). *Language in the Crib*. Mouton, La Haye.

Wong, W., & VanPatten, B. (2003). The Evidence is IN: Drills are Out. *Foreign Language Annals*, *36*(3), 403–423. doi:10.1111/j.1944-9720.2003.tb02123.x

Zock, M. (1991). SWIM or sink: the problem of communicating thought. In M. Swartz & M. Yazdani (Eds.), *Bridge to International Communication: Intelligent Tutoring Systems for Second Language Learning* (pp. 235-247). New York: Springer.

Zock, M. (1997) *Sentence Generation by Pattern Matching: the Problem of Syntactic Choice*. In R. Mitkov & N. Nicolov (Eds.), *Recent Advances in Natural Language Processing. Series: Current Issues in Linguistic Theory* (pp. 317-352).

Zock, M., Sabatier, P., & Jakubiec-Jamet, L. (2007). Who's Next? From Sentence Completion to Conceptually Guided Message Composition. In *Proceedings of the 4th Int. Workshop on Natural Language Processing and Cognitive Science (NLPCS 2007)* (pp. 38-46).

ENDNOTES

1 Psychologists (Posner and Snyder, 1975) draw a clear line between *automatic* and *attentional* processes. The former are fast, parallel, and mandatory. They do not tax memory, neither do they interfere with other tasks or are available to introspection (consciousness). On the other hand, *attentional processes* are slow, serial and they can be observed and controlled, i.e. stopped. They do tax memory, they can interfere with other tasks, and their (intermediate) results can be accessible to our consciousness.

2 After having been very popular for many years, PDs and instrumental conditioning upon which they rely have been discredited by linguists, —see Chomsky's violent criticism (Chomsky, 1959) of Skinner's book *Verbal Behavior*,— and more directly by psychologists (Levelt, 1970, Herriot, 1971; Leont'ev, 1974; Krashen, 1981) and pedagogues (Rivers, 1964, 1972; Spolsky, 1966;

Chastain, 1969; Savignon, 1983; Stevens, 1989, Wong and vanPatten, 2003). While we partially agree with these criticisms when the creative aspects of language production are at stake, we do not share them at all when *habit formation* or the *acquisition of automatisms* are the learning goal, and we do not seem to be the only ones, see for example: deKeyser (2007a, 2007b, 2001), Fitts, (1964), Garrod & Pickering (2007), Gatbonton & Segalowitz (2005, 1988), Guillaume (1973), Hulstijn (2001), Segalowitz (2007, 2003, 2000), Segalowitz and Hulstijn (2005), to name just those. At least partial automatisation of the process is necessary to become fluent in speaking. Automatisms are the speakers' means to buy time, allowing them to focus on another, possibly more demanding component, for example, the next conceptual fragment, i.e. message, to be uttered. In other words, in order to achieve the skill of fluent speaking, that is, fast conversion of ideas into sounds (Zock, 1997), we do believe that well-staged repetitions of stimulus-response patterns in a clear communicative setting, together with feedback are a valuable learning method. Of course, they are not the whole story. Interestingly enough, patterns have been rehabilitated by well-known linguists like Goldberg (1998) and Jackendoff (1993), one of Chomsky's most brilliant students.

3 In our case, a pattern can be seen as the frozen instance of a step in the derivational process. Which particular step we want to focus on depends on the task (describing data, support the language user). The main function patterns serve in this context is to support the speaker at the next step/level in the process, whatever this level may be. Hence, patterns can be produced by a generative grammar, they do exist at various levels, and they may be hybrid.

4 While this is obviously a very simple example, we should not dismiss it too quickly as being completely devoid of interest, as even quite complex dialogues, i.e. question-answer patterns, are composed of such elementary units, and what might look excessively simple for an outsider may still be a challenge for a true beginner. Just try to repeat a 'simple' word in a language you don't speak yet. Also, combining such question-answer pairs provide each sentence with a context which otherwise is often lacking.

5 The latter is basically a hybrid pattern, composed of constants (words) and one or several variables, which need to be lexically instantiated.

6 Of course, at this stage of development, the system has a very limited understanding of what the student really knows, why he fails, or what is needed in order to improve performance. Lacking a user model and a parser, the system has no direct means at all to understand the student's output (see below).

7 Once such a morphological component is added, *conceptual input* would take place in three-steps: at a global level we would choose the pattern via a *goal*, next we would provide *lexical values* for the pattern's variables, to refine then this global message by specifying *morphological values* (number, tense). This approach would be much more economical for storing and accessing patterns, than storing a pattern for every morphological variant. It would also be much faster than navigating through a *lexical* or *conceptual ontology*, as suggested in (Zock, 1991; Zock & coll. 2007 or Scott, 1999).

8 Actually, these mappings can be quite complex. For example, in French, the syllable /vɛ̃/ can be written in many ways,— 'vin, vins, vingt, vain, vint, vaincs',— to mention but those.

9 This is known as *spaced repetition* (http://en.wikipedia.org/wiki/Spaced_repetition), a technique used in basically all of the better flashcards. Spaced repetition has been shown to be an efficient way to study, giving the most recall for the smallest amount of time spent studying. Notes are scheduled at longer and longer intervals until the schedule is completed.

10 Actually, the number of patterns and the size of the vocabulary is not really what counts at this stage, as the focus is on the implementation of an editor designed for building, modifying and using a database. Also, while it would have been easy to copy patterns from one of the many text books, we have refrained from doing so, not only for reasons of copyright, but also for reasons of metalanguage. The terms in which these patterns are defined are neither always consistent, nor very felicitous.

11 The interested reader may take a look at Belz (2009) who provides an interesting overview as well as a critique of the evaluation approaches used in HLT.

Section 4
Multimedia and Virtual Reality in E-Learning

The role of multimedia, hypermedia and virtual reality is the subject of Section 4. Both current trends and future directions of multimedia learning design are examined while the role of Virtual Reality in building an immersive e-learning experience is discussed in depth.

Chapter 11
Key Factors and New Directions of Multimedia Learning Design

Haido Samaras
University of Macedonia, Greece

Thanasis Giouvanakis
University of Macedonia, Greece

Despina Bousiou
University of Macedonia, Greece

Konstantinos Tarabanis
University of Macedonia, Greece

ABSTRACT

This chapter explores specific topics, issues and directions associated with multimedia and hypermedia learning environments. A key aim is to inform researchers, designers, and developers of multimedia learning systems as well as educators who wish to engage students in learning activities rooted in multimedia learning research and design of the critical factors that have had an impact on maximizing learning through multimedia. Strengths and pitfalls of multimedia learning design are discussed through the review of the important conclusions that two generations of multimedia research have contributed to multimedia design. Finally, emerging factors, which are currently formulating a third generation of multimedia design and learning research are presented.

INTRODUCTION

In today's new digital age traditional classroom education or training does not always satisfy all the needs of the new world of flexible, personalized and lifelong learning. A shift is being made toward e-Learning (also known as online training, distributed learning, CBT, and multimedia courses) where the medium of instruction is through computer technology, particularly involving digital technologies. E-Learning affords a lot of opportunities. It is claimed to have the potential to dramatically change the way teachers teach or learners learn, offering learning-on-demand opportunities and reducing learning cost. As e-Learning continues to evolve, it is important to remember how people learn. Developers must consider and understand instructional design and its integration into build-

DOI: 10.4018/978-1-60566-940-3.ch011

ing e-Learning courses. The quality and value of e-Learning applications is dependent on the use of available technology and the design and development of applications (Huffaker, 2004). A variety of enabling technologies such as multimedia technologies can facilitate the design and implementation of e-Learning systems.

The term multimedia has existed in the educational technology field for some time and refers to the use of different media to convey information; text together with audio, graphics and animation, often packaged on CD-ROM or provided through the Internet combining interactivity. Multimedia finds its application in various areas including advertising, art, education, entertainment, engineering, medicine, and business. In the academic sphere, empirical research regarding the impact of multimedia on learning can be traced back several decades before the large-scale invasion of multimedia learning resources (like CD-ROM titles and Internet applications) into the educational field and originated from areas outside the scholastic community. Although the results are not decisive, the existing multimedia research has contributed to establishing factors that influence effective multimedia design.

This chapter aims to provide a theoretical framework associated with multimedia learning research and design. It will provide insight on specific topics, issues and directions associated with multimedia and hypermedia learning environments. In particular, the chapter aims to provide a comprehensive study of the prevalent ideas and the main directions which have made an impact on multimedia research and design until now.

More specifically, the chapter will provide a review of the important conclusions that two generations of multimedia research have contributed to multimedia design, specifying their key theoretical issues and research directions as well as the weaknesses associated with each one of them. Emerging factors, which are currently formulating a third generation of multimedia design and learning research will be discussed.

BACKGROUND

As has been the case in the past with every innovative form of educational technology, such as motion pictures, radio, educational television and computers (Cuban, 1986), the emergence of multimedia educational technology has been accompanied by contradictory views and attitudes. On the one hand there have been high hopes in support of multimedia, which have been based on a range of claims, such as that multimedia systems have the ability to cut down the time of learning while at the same time they increase learning effectiveness. On the other hand, contrary positions have maintained a state of skepticism and disbelief regarding the use of multimedia in education.

Multimedia learning research and in general educational technology research has been characterized by inconsistency until now, failing to draw explicit conclusions with relation to the impact that multimedia and technology have on the learning process or to provide a comprehensive framework of design principles at the micro-level for the optimal integration of multimedia elements within a multimedia learning system (Koumi, 2003). Over three decades of research have not managed to resolve the problem satisfactorily. The literature does not lack studies with statistically significant results in favor of multimedia use from which a collection of factors that influence effective multimedia design may be drawn (Najjar, 1998, 2001). However, at the same time it includes a large body of studies that do not provide strong evidence to warrant for the use of multimedia as an effective alternative to learning (Hede, 2002).

Up until the late 1980s, before the large-scale invasion of multimedia into the educational field, a number of attempts, (viewed in this chapter as the first generation of multimedia research) had been made to comprehend the ways that learners integrate and capitalize on information that is presented to them verbally and visually (Samuels, 1967; Levie & Lentz, 1982). When, in the following years, the rapid progress of technology made it possible for more and more people to start creating and distributing multimedia materials with greater ease and less expensively, an extensive manufacture of educational multimedia content and systems resulted. This large-scale production led to a new and increased interest in the field of cognitive sciences regarding the extent to which these systems contribute to improved learning and more and more empirical studies (a second generation) began to surface.

In this second generation of research, major attention was given to the topics of learning and instruction. Crucial questions were raised regarding whether, under which conditions, and based on which (grounded-in-research) design principles multimedia should be used in education (Reimann, 2003). It was believed at first that multimedia would be capable of facilitating the understanding and learning of complex knowledge domains (such as meteorology, physics, and engineering) by helping a novice learner to distinguish patterns and relationships of the domain (things experts are capable of achieving with ease) (Goldman, 2003). A key issue in this generation was how verbal and visual information should be arranged and presented to the learner to facilitate him/her in "seeing" these patterns and relationships (Mousavi, Low, & Sweller, 1995; Mayer & Anderson, 1991; Mayer & Moreno, 1998, 1999).

However, the relative literature appeared to end up with conflicting results, with some studies connected to educational multimedia providing positive learning results (Liao, 1999) and especially when they were employed to assist the learner in understanding complex knowledge domains (Mayer & Anderson, 1991; Mayer & Moreno, 1998, 1999), and others pointing to insignificant or even negative effects of learning through multimedia (Mousavi et al., 1995; Dillon & Gabbard, 1998). These latter studies reached a significant conclusion: students were not learning through the multimedia systems any better than they were through single media (unimedia)—such as through text—what the multimedia designers had intended for them to learn (Kozma, 1994; Goldman, 2003). This led to the need to examine factors other than the arrangement and presentation of different types of media. More and more a broader range of issues (such as the content itself, the learner's knowledge or style of learning, and others) began to come into view as significant multimedia learning research variables. Currently there is a growing body of studies that are dealing with such topics and are defining a new generation of multimedia research.

This chapter provides a review of the important conclusions that the existing multimedia research has contributed to multimedia design, specifying key theoretical issues and research directions as well as weaknesses and pitfalls. Emerging factors, which are currently formulating a new generation of multimedia design and learning research, are described. Specifically, the following topics are discussed:

- Which conclusions can be drawn from the media effects debate with respect to how we should be designing multimedia systems and conducting research regarding their effectiveness?
- Which governing learning-theory trends have provided a basis for multimedia design and which characteristics and guidelines are highlighted by each of them?
- Which aspects of the human learning system that concern the comprehension and retention of information presented through multimedia has cognitive science dealt with and how can the features of this system be exploited by multimedia in order to lead to improved learning outcomes?
- What role could the factors that differentiate learners play in multimedia learning research?
- Which are the central issues and research directions that govern the two generations of multimedia learning research, which

models are they based on, and which conclusions have they reached?
- Which factors are researchers beginning to focus on and what role could these factors play in facilitating learning through multimedia?

DRAWING A FRAMEWORK FOR MULTIMEDIA DESIGN THROUGH THE REEXAMINATION OF THE MEDIA EFFECTS DEBATE

An issue that has generated many discussions and studies and is closely related to multimedia design and research is the media effects debate. This issue, still largely unresolved today, was whether media in and of itself affects learning. Richard Clark and Robert Kozma were fervent rivals on the two opposite sides of the debate. After reviewing an exhaustive number of meta-analyses and studies carried out from 1912 until the beginning of the 1980s (Lazarsfeld, 1940; Himmelweit, Oppenheim & Vince, 1959) regarding the influence of media on learning, Richard Clark (1983) reached the conclusion that media are mere vehicles that deliver instruction. Clark alleged that media should not be advocated for their ability to increase learning and that it is basically what the teacher does (i.e., the teaching itself), that influences learning. In short, according to Clark, "there are no learning benefits to be gained from employing any specific medium to deliver instruction; regardless of the media used, which can in the end influence only the cost and speed of learning, what actually contributes to a learning improvement is the instructional method that the teacher employs." This argument instigated many counteractions (Kozma, 1991; Bagui, 1998; Hede, 2002) among which, one that has made a great impact is Robert Kozma's article "Learning with Media" published in 1991. Kozma argued that "medium and method have an inseparable relationship and that they both therefore are key components for the design of instruction."

The value of this debate has been challenged by many (Jonassen, Campbell & Davidson, 1994) on the grounds that the question of whether media affects learning is not a fundamental one and that inevitably it leads to a misconception. The point made is that we should not be seeking to determine that one "super-medium," which will result in effective learning (Jonassen, 1996) and that we cannot expect that our students will achieve significant academic improvement just by coming into contact with that medium (Clark, 1983; Kozma, 1991; Simonsen, Clark, Kulik, Tennyson & Winn, 1987). The problem actually lies in the way we perceive instruction.

For example, if our views were in agreement with Clark's (i.e., that instruction comprises the medium and the instructional method but that these are two separate entities), then we would most probably reach the same conclusion as Clark, that is, that the media alone is incapable of influencing learning but that what does affect learning is the instructional method. If, on the other hand, we supported the notion that, although on a theoretical level separate, in teaching practice medium and method make up an inseparable unit, then we would be closer to Kozma's views, that is, that media does undoubtedly influence learning since it constitutes a necessary component of effective instruction (Nathan & Robinson, 2001). It may even be the case that Clark's and Kozma's views are not in complete disagreement. In fact their positions may appear to stand in contrast and to lead to an opposition exactly because of the different way they view instruction (Nathan & Robinson, 2001). Taking the debate a step further we should also point out that there is a growing body of evidence that multiple media (multimedia) can lead to poorly designed instruction that hinders learning (Hede, 2002). Undoubtedly media (and most likely multiple media) is capable of facilitating learning but this can only occur if it is selected, designed, and examined on the basis of a number of significant characteristics, some of which we will be analyzed next.

First, according to Kozma's opinion, instruction should be considered as an integration of media and methods. This viewpoint leads to the need for careful consideration of the media *together with* the instructional methods adopted when we are designing empirical studies on multimedia learning effectiveness. The simultaneous examination of media and methods will ensure that we do not end up with confounding results as many first generation studies did. As Clark reasoned (1983), evidence regarding media effectiveness will not be valid when experiments allow for changes in other characteristics of multimedia material or systems other than the media (such as the instructional method or content) and yet accredit the learning improvement or obstruction exclusively to the media. *Media and instructional methods therefore need to be examined in close association.*

Second, according to Kozma and his advocates (Kozma, 1991; Rieber 2000; Nathan & Robinson, 2001; Hede, 2002), the fundamental question is not whether media affects learning but *how to take advantage of the various media to make instruction and learning more effective*. We must attempt to understand when (in which situations) media facilitates learning, how to design effective media or how (through which instructional methods) to exploit the attributes of media to support the learning goals that we have set to various learning tasks. At the same time we should focus on what kind of content to use with particular learning tasks, instructional methods, and media, and even consider in which cases it is best to avoid the use of media altogether. In fact, Clark appears to be in agreement with this view when he advises researchers to refrain from producing media comparison studies and to focus instead on necessary characteristics of instructional methods and other variables (Clark, 1983). Only the instruction transmitted through the media has the potential and capabilities of influencing learning and not the media itself (Rieber, 2000) but different media have different instructional capabilities and potential for different situations, learning tasks, students, and forms of content knowledge such as narrative, explanation, description, enumeration of facts, and so forth. (Mayer & Moreno, 2003; Lowe, 2003; Schnotz & Bannert, 2003).

For example animation might facilitate understanding and learning for a particular group of students (such as students with insufficient prior knowledge in the material being presented) when a particular form of content is used and a specific learning task is required within a certain learning situation, for example, a scientific explanation of a complex technical system such as a bicycle tire pump or the explanation of how an algorithm works (Shih & Alessi, 1994; Kann, Lindeman, & Heller, 1997; Mayer & Moreno, 2003). It may, on the other hand, impede learning when the students, the form of content, the learning experience or the learning tasks chosen are different, even if they refer to the same subject matter and are connected to the same set of learning goals (Anderssen & Myburg, 1992). There is a need to establish a theoretical framework that will help designers to predict under which conditions the employment of specific media is beneficial for understanding and learning and under which conditions and situations this particular media would most likely have negligible or detrimental effects.

To some extent, but not adequately, second generation research has taken these factors into consideration. Current multimedia learning research should attempt to deal with these matters much more systematically by investigating the influence of task-appropriate and content-appropriate media on learning and by taking into account a broader range of factors such as the particular characteristics of learners (e.g., low vs. high-prior knowledge, learning style, etc.) or the type of learning situation (e.g., more teacher/system-controlled presentation-form learning experiences based on text and pictures vs. more open-ended, user-controlled forms of multimedia learning experiences such as reality-based learning simulations and immersive virtual reality experiences; Lowe, 2003; Kozma, 2003; Schnotz & Bannert, 2003; Stern, Aprea, & Ebner, 2003).

A third aspect that needs to be taken into account is *the fact that learning tasks need to be placed within a specific context of psychological, cognitive, and social processes* (Nathan & Robinson, 2001). A medium used to support a learning task aligned with a constructivist view of learning (where the key factor is to encourage the learner to "construct" his/her own knowledge) will influence learning to the degree that it allows the learner to achieve this procedure (Nathan & Robinson). For example, if a web-based multimedia course or system has been designed within a framework of constructivist learning goals and provides learning tasks and experiences that place learners in the center of the learning process and encourage them to interact with others to "construct" their own knowledge, then the media—in this case the multimedia course—will have succeeded in influencing learning.

Therefore we cannot set out to design multimedia systems or conduct multimedia learning research without taking these factors into serious consideration. In our investigation and summarization of multimedia learning research, we have distinguished a first generation of multimedia research based mainly on the criterion that it lacks association with the issues previously discussed. These issues began to surface more and more during the second generation of research and are currently, as recent studies have revealed, being more methodically dealt with. Multimedia learning material and systems must aim at combining instructional methods and content that exploit the capabilities and attributes of the media to support specific learning tasks and learner characteristics and multimedia learning research needs to point out and closely examine all of the intervening parameters.

In the next section we look at the two governing learning-theory trends that have served as the underlying theoretical basis for multimedia design. We briefly describe the characteristics and guidelines that are highlighted by each of them and relate them to the three generations of multimedia learning research.

MULTIMEDIA DESIGN DIRECTIONS IN LIGHT OF THE UNDERLYING LEARNING THEORIES

Whether we're designing instruction to be delivered the traditional way in the classroom or through an interactive multimedia system, we cannot neglect to take into account one or more learning theories that will serve as the theoretical basis for our instructional design. The systematic and scientific study of how people learn from the 19th century until today has lead to the formation of two dominant theoretical positions, behaviorism and cognitivism. Each makes different assumptions about the way a person learns and remembers knowledge. Behaviorism focuses only on the objectively observable aspects of learning. Cognitive theories look beyond behavior to explain brain-based learning. These two theoretical positions also serve as the governing directions in the field of learning with interactive courseware such as interactive multimedia (Jonassen, 1991; Atkins, 1993; Hannafin, Hannafin, Hooper, Rieber & Kini, 1996; Deubel, 2003).

Behaviorist multimedia design approaches have mostly been associated with the effectiveness of lower-level learning tasks, for example with rapid acquisition of basic concepts, skills, and factual information (Atkins, 1993) (as long as the stimuli and the presentation modes of those stimuli are selected carefully). On the other hand, their positive impact on higher-order learning tasks such as problem solving or transfer has not yet been proven (Deubel, 2003). First generation multimedia research is based on behaviorist design approaches. It is related to lower-level learning processes (such as reading, and remembering information presented through text with or without accompanying pictures) and behaviorist methods

Table 1. Adapted from Deubel, 2003

Behaviorist ID Characteristics	Cognitive ID Strategies
Material is broken down into small, logically discrete instructional steps. Positive examples are provided as reinforcement and negative to establish conceptual boundaries. The sequence and pacing through the material is usually without learner control. The required operation, procedure, or skill is demonstrated and broken down into its parts with appropriate explanation before learners are expected to copy the desired behavior. Performance standards are made explicit. Assessment is done after learning. occurs. Learners build proficiency from frequent review or revision with check tests at strategic points or repeat practice and feedback.	Discovery learning or learning to learn, including the ability to question, evaluate one's strategies, and answer questions in the content domain. Scaffolding or the gradual removal of a tutor's support for the individual to become an independent problem solver. Coaching or instructor-as-coach who may be more knowledgeable and as a mentor may seek to expand the learner's current conceptions. Problem-based Instruction/Learning where learning is organized around problem solving, rather than around the subject matter. Learner control over pacing, sequence, and actual content of information presented. Cooperative learning in which groups work together to solve problems. Assessment embedded within activities.

of measuring knowledge acquisition (Dwyer, 1972, 1978, 1987; Levie & Lentz, 1982).

On the other hand cognitive multimedia design approaches have mostly been connected with higher-order learning experiences on the condition that they fulfill certain requirements that will ensure the quality of processing that occurs while the learner actively engages with the subject matter (Atkins, 1993). The quality of processing might be affected to the degree to which characteristics and strategies such as discovery learning, problem-based instruction/learning, scaffolding, cooperative learning, and so forth, are applied in the instructional design (Deubel, 2003). The implementation and use of such characteristics within educational multimedia material and systems will most likely lead to improved learning. However cognitive multimedia design approaches appear to have a serious problem; there is no easy way to measure their effectiveness as it is extremely difficult to determine what is going on in the learner's mind. This forces evaluators back on measures such as apparent time on task, apparent engagement with the task presented, and subject estimations of its effectiveness (Atkins; Deubel). Second generation and current multimedia research has been associated with both behaviorist and cognitive multimedia design approaches. Table 1 displays a list of behaviorist and cognitive multimedia instructional design characteristics and strategies.

INSTRUCTIONAL DESIGN GUIDELINES DRAWN FROM COGNITIVE RESEARCH

Cognitive research is research that deals with cognitive processes. Cognitive research attempts to explain how people perceive, learn, remember, and think about information. A cognitive scientist might study how people perceive pictures or why they remember certain facts and forget others, how they learn to speak their language or the way they think when they are playing chess or trying to solve daily problems (Sternberg, 1996).

Various issues associated with how learners perceive, remember, and learn information that is presented to them through a multimedia presentation have been studied. For instance, many attempts have been made to understand how a learner integrates and learns multimedia information presented verbally and visually, e.g. through a text enriched with static pictures or through dynamic pictures (animation or video) that are accompanied by narration (Levin & Lesgold,

1978; Dwyer, 1972; 1978; 1987), or to compare the influence of dynamic against static media for the achievement of particular learning goals (Guttormsen Schar, & Krueger, 2001; Lowe, 2003). The results of these studies have played an important role for the field of multimedia technology and have influenced the definition and direction of multimedia design principles.

Well-known cognitive learning researchers have been concerned with the attributes of the human learning system that affect the comprehension and retention of information presented through multimedia and have examined various ways in which those attributes could be exploited by designers of multimedia systems to lead to improved learning outcomes. The next section provides a brief summary of the main characteristics of human cognitive architecture that cognitive researchers have dealt with along with some of the important instructional design guidelines that they have proposed.

The Limitations of Human Working Memory

Limitations of human working memory resources have been identified as a major factor that needs to be considered when instruction is designed. Basing their convictions on cognitive load theory (Sweller, 1989), researchers have suggested that many commonly used instructional procedures are insufficient due to the fact that they require learners to engage in unnecessary cognitive activities that impose a heavy working memory load (Sweller; Sweller & Chandler, 1994). A considerable amount of multimedia material falls under this category. For example we have often witnessed "overloaded" multimedia applications combining an excessive number or inappropriate combination of multimedia elements that result in cognitive overload and impede learning. The basic principle of cognitive load theory is that instructional messages must be designed to keep the cognitive load of learners at a minimum during the learning process, if they are to be effective. Cognitive load theory is best applied in the area of instructional design of cognitively complex or technically challenging material (such as interactive multimedia material dealing with complex knowledge domains) especially for beginners in a given domain. Significant factors associated with efforts to reduce learner cognitive load are prior knowledge, schema formation, automation, and chunking.

The concepts of 'chunking' and 'chunking mechanisms' are important in many processes of perception, learning and cognition in humans. Mental schemata and automation cause less pressure on the working memory and therefore help improve understanding. The formation of schemata is facilitated by the existence of prior knowledge whereas the lack of prior knowledge (i.e., appropriate schemata) leads to excessive processing in the working memory. The concept of prior knowledge is fundamental in cognitive science (Di Vesta, 1987; Shuell, 1986; Tobias, 1987; Rieber 2000). Its importance is probably best summarized by David Ausubel (epigraph): "The most important single factor influencing learning is what the learner already knows. Ascertain this and teach him accordingly." (cited in Rieber, 2000). Therefore our instructional design must exploit the existence of prior knowledge. Appropriately designed multimedia educational material will help learners activate existing schemata making the information provided to them more meaningful and reducing cognitive load. This will allow them to code and store new knowledge in their memory more easily, as well as retrieve it more effectively. Cognitive load theory has led to significant empirical research from which a number of instructional guidelines have been derived. These guidelines are briefly listed in Table 2 and are important to consider when designing educational multimedia systems.

Another theory that has played an important role for the instructional design of multimedia material and has been used to help explain and

Table 2. Instructional design guidelines drawn from research on cognitive load

Carefully analyze the attention demands of instruction. Processing troubles arise when the learner must attend to too many different elements at the same time.
Use single, coherent representations. These should allow the learner to focus attention rather than split attention between two places, for example, between a diagram and the text or even between a diagram with labels not located close to their referents.
Eliminate redundancy. Redundant information between text and diagrams has been shown to decrease learning.
Provide for systematic problem-space exploration instead of conventional repeated practice.
In multimedia instruction, present animation and audio narration (and/ or text descriptions) simultaneously rather than sequentially.
Provide worked examples as alternatives to conventional problem-based instruction.

Adapted from Brent Wilson and Peggy Cole (1996), Cognitive teaching models. In D. H. Jonassen (Ed.), *Handbook of research for educational communications and technology* (pp. 601-621). New York: MacMillan.

ameliorate working memory limitations when verbal and visual information is presented to the learner is dual coding (Paivio, 1971, 1986, 1991). Paivio suggested that there are two cognitive subsystems or channels, one specialized for the representation and processing of nonverbal objects/events (i.e. imagery), and the other specialized for dealing with language. Learning is better when information is processed through these two channels instead of one. Connections can be made only if corresponding nonverbal and verbal information is in working memory at the same time. Information processed through two channels is called referential processing and has an additive effect on recall (Paivio, 1991; Mayer & Anderson, 1991; Shih & Alessi, 1996). This happens because the learner is able to create more cognitive paths that can be followed to retrieve the information. The dual coding theory attempts to give equal weight to verbal and nonverbal processing. This theory has been strongly criticized by cognitive researchers who support propositional theories, that is, the notion that memory is propositional in nature and that it is the relationship among propositions that gives rise to meaning (Kintsch, 1974). Nevertheless, dual coding has served as the basis for the instructional design of a large amount of educational multimedia software and systems as well as for a significant portion of second generation multimedia research (Mousavi, Low, & Sweller, 1995; Mayer & Anderson, 1991; Mayer & Moreno, 1998).

DIFFERENTIATED LEARNING FACTORS AND MULTIMEDIA DESIGN IMPLICATIONS

Admittedly, the closer that instruction and educational content are adapted to the needs of the learner, the more efficient and effective the learning will be. Educational researchers have been concerned about the implications of different learner traits for instruction for many decades (Tobias, 1990; Kolb, 1984; Bruner, 1966; Gagné, 1967).

Thus, one of the key issues in the field of educational technology has been how to design adaptable multimedia environments that are capable of accommodating diverse learner requirements. This means creating systems that are able to provide individualized instruction and designing and distributing the multimedia content through this system according to characteristics such as learning goals, prior knowledge, aptitude, cognitive styles, learning styles, and so forth. Within this framework a new approach called adaptable or personalized learning has emerged. The basis of this approach is the incorporation of alternative procedures and learning strategies that can be selected by learners and the primary criterion for the categorization of such systems is the kind of adaptation. Hence, we refer to macro-adaptable systems, which, generally, attempt to determine learner aptitudes before the commencement of the educational process and micro-adaptable systems that diagnose different learner characteristics throughout the instruction (Brusilovsky, 2003; Park & Lee, 2003).

Macro-adaptable systems are based on a set of personal characteristics most important of which are considered to be: (a) the intellectual ability of the learner, (b) the learner cognitive and learning style, (c) the prior knowledge that the learner has, and (d) the motivation of the learner. In the case of micro-adaptable systems the number and the specific characteristics of the mistakes made by the learner during instruction serve as the adaptation criteria. Consequently, according to these mistakes, the models that perform the micro-adaptations provide for modifications that are related to: (a) the type (specific content, level of difficulty, etc.) and the amount of multimedia content which is going to be presented to the learner in the following stage of instruction, and (b) the presentation sequence of the content. Clearly there is no distinct borderline between these two types of systems given that they both borrow characteristics from one another. Numerous studies have been conducted to clarify and determine the range of different learner characteristics and, in general, to establish factors that might serve as the basis for personalized instruction as well as to agree on the types of adaptations that ought to be the outcome of these differences (Chou & Lin, 1998; Chuang, 1999; Ross & Schulz, 1999; Riding & Rayner, 1998).

To date multimedia learning research has only limitedly focused on factors that differentiate learners. The vast majority of empirical studies that have been carried out consider learners as a unified single set, thus failing to reach statistically significant results when one or another type of multimedia content is used. In other cases the results appear to be statistically significant, but it becomes apparent that for this positive result to be produced, the variable "content" was merged with the medium that provides the multimedia information and possibly even with the learner characteristics (cognitive style, prior knowledge, motivation, etc.). In many cases, some of these factors are, indirectly or directly, detected by researchers (Mayer & Moreno, 1998; Schnotz & Bannert, 2003). Thus, a crucial issue would be to clarify the variables that intervene and result in either statistically or non-statistically significant results. Within this framework researchers have begun to focus their efforts on the emergence, definition, and elaboration of parameters that determine the characteristics and properties of the content and the instruction as well as parameters that describe the learner, and that contribute, more or less, to the effectiveness of the medium. Undoubtedly, the next important step would be to blend these factors together within new theoretical frameworks and models.

In the past, the majority of educational technology systems did not have the capabilities of providing adaptations. In contrast, the current development of educational environments has made a shift towards the use of learning objects that are based on the incorporation of meta-data and consequently permit the "intelligent" treatment of both the content and the learner (IEEE LTSC, IMS, SCORM). Thus, on a technical level, it is now possible to create open environments that offer personalized learning experiences. Third generation multimedia learning research studies have already begun to focus on these issues by introducing and examining concepts such as *computational efficiency*, *learning style*, *cognitive style*, *prior knowledge*, and so forth.

NEW DIRECTIONS IN MULTIMEDIA LEARNING: THE EMERGENCE OF A NEW GENERATION OF RESEARCH AND DESIGN

The examination of a large body of research regarding multimedia learning, has led to the categorization of these studies in terms of two significant periods or, what we have referred to in this chapter as, generations. A third generation that is currently emerging and is moving researchers towards hopeful new directions (Table 4) is also distinguished in this section.

A Shift from How Different Types of Media Influence Learning to How the Arrangement and Presentation of the Particular Media Makes an Impact on Learning

Studies included in first generation research are basically related to *how learners integrate and capitalize on information that is presented to them verbally and visually*. These studies originated from areas outside the educational community for example, psychology, art, motion pictures, advertising, and so forth (Arneim, 1954; Gombrich, 1969) and gradually passed over into that field before computers and multimedia systems began to be used for educational purposes. However, their results have had a significant impact on educational multimedia design and research (Spaulding, 1955; Levin & Lesgold, 1978; Levie & Lentz, 1982). The goal was to examine the influence of different media such as text, sound, and pictures on the human cognitive system. However the studies conducted during this period focused primarily on combinations of texts and pictures. Significant efforts to summarize first generation multimedia research results were made by Levie and Lentz, Dwyer and his associates (1972, 1978, 1987), and Rieber (2000). Researchers tried to comprehend how people learn through this media, how memory operates on it, (e.g., the way memory perceives, stores, and allows for the retrieval of words and pictures) and tried to discover and propose ways of improving these operations. The main conclusion of this research was that text information is remembered better when it is illustrated by pictures than when there is no illustration (Levie & Lentz, 1982; Levin, Anglin, & Carney, 1987). These findings were generally explained with Paivio's dual coding theory (Paivio, 1986). Also Rieber (1990, 2000) and Dwyer and Dwyer (2003) have provided the most exhaustive reviews regarding the impact of dynamic pictures on learning.

The vast majority of first generation research often tried to attribute results only to the media used, ignoring the existence of the underlying instructional method employed and neglecting to place the medium within the broader scope of the learning situation (involving the learning task and its attributes, the learner characteristics, etc.). It, therefore, failed to recognize the existence of the media-method relationship and this is why it very often reached invalid conclusions (Clark, 1983). Studies were based on the behaviorist approach to instruction/learning with an orientation towards lower-order learning tasks and the acquisition of declarative knowledge through prose (i.e. they focused primarily on whether the media could help learners understand and remember information such as facts and ideas presented to them through text or pictures). They did not deal with the issue of whether media could facilitate higher-order learning tasks such as problem solving and they did not examine the outcomes of learning from diverse forms of content such as scientific explanations or descriptions of complex knowledge domains.

Table 3. Principles for the instructional design of multimedia based on the cognitive theory of multimedia learning

The multiple representation principle states that it is better to present an explanation in words and pictures than solely in words.
The contiguity principle is that it is better to present corresponding words and pictures simultaneously rather than separately when giving a multimedia explanation.
The coherence principle is that multimedia explanations are better understood when they include few rather than many extraneous words and sounds.
The modality principle is that it is better to present words as auditory narration than as visual on-screen text.
The redundancy principle is that it is better to present animation and narration than to present animation, narration, and onscreen text.

Table 4. Research progress regarding the impact of multimedia on learning

Central theoretical issues and research directions	Models proposed	Underlying theories	Characteristics
Research related to how learners integrate and capitalize on information that is presented to them verbally and visually.	Information processing model Single-code model Dual-code model Sensory-semantic model	Gestalt theory and other picture processing theories Paivio's dual coding theory Propositional theories	Failure to recognize the existence of the media-method relationship. Studies based mainly on the behaviorist approach to instruction/learning. Orientation towards lower-order learning tasks (i.e. fact learning instead of problem solving).
Attempts to arrange verbal and visual information in ways that facilitate learners to "see" patterns and relationships in the information presented.	Baddeley's expanded view of working memory Mayer's model of multimedia learning	Cognitive load theory Cognitive theory of multimedia learning	Increased interest in the cognitive approach but research focuses more on behaviorist designs failing to take into account more interactive user-controlled environments. Research regarding the combination and arrangement of media yielded important conclusions for multimedia learning design and research. Research does not examine other important factors such as the content itself or the learning style of the learner.
Studies that aim for a deeper understanding of the impact of multiple forms of representation on learning by taking into account learner and content characteristics.	New emergent models		The research is currently examining the suitability of specific instructional designs in relation to the medium and the instructional method. Researchers are experimenting with diverse representations of informationally equivalent content. Factors that differentiate learners (prior knowledge, cognitive/learning style, motivation, etc.) and also the support required by different learners are taken into account. Research is currently examining the potentials of semantic web technology for learning.

Studies included in second generation research are basically related to *the way verbal and visual information should be arranged and presented.* The 1990s brought about an explosion of educational multimedia materials. During this period there was an increased interest in the cognitive approach to instruction/learning, however many second generation studies still focused narrowly on what we would characterize as more passive behaviorist designs for example, the presentation of text with or without accompanying pictures—static or dynamic—that required no behavioral or social activity on the part of the learner (Mousavi, Low & Sweller, 1995) excluding more highly-interactive user-controlled learning environments. However, some of the distinctive researchers of this generation (Mayer & Anderson, 1991; Mayer & Moreno, 1998, 1999) focused on how to design multimedia messages to promote, what they called, meaningful learning. These researchers maintained that although their multimedia designs were passive, they were planned in such a way, so as to foster appropriate cognitive activity (i.e., that they encouraged students to build meaningful mental representations, an instructional approach they labeled as cognitive constructivism). Also, these second generation studies attempted to move away from testing plain fact learning by measuring higher-order learning abilities, such as transfer and problem solving.

The key issue of second-generation multimedia research was on how verbal and visual information should be arranged and presented to learners to facilitate them in recognizing patterns and relationships that distinguish a novice learner from an expert in a given knowledge domain. Researchers attempted to deal with these issues and to propose guidelines that would help learners make the necessary connections efficiently and effectively and techniques that would allow them to overcome the limitations of human working memory resources while trying to make these connections. The work of Richard Mayer and his associates, who elaborated the dual coding theory to provide evidence for why pictures support, under specific conditions, the understanding of physical phenomena or technical systems, is representative of second-generation research efforts. This research concluded that arrangements of verbal and visual information that highlight important relationships, remove irrelevant information, and manage the information so that learners' working memory resources are not overloaded, tend to improve learning. Mayer proposed that there are three processes in which the learner needs to engage in, if meaningful learning is to occur, whether from visual (static or dynamic), verbal information, or both (i.e. to select relevant words and images, to organize them into coherent verbal and visual representations, and to integrate corresponding verbal and visual representations).

Second generation studies have yielded significant theories, models, and principles for designing multimedia such as Baddeley's (1986) expanded view of working memory, Sweller's (1989) cognitive load theory, and Mayer's (2001) model of multimedia learning. Table 3 displays the *five principles of instructional design for fostering multimedia learning* that have been derived and tested from the cognitive theory of multimedia learning (Mayer & Moreno, 2003).

Current Issues and Future Directions of an Emergent Generation of Multimedia Research

A new generation of multimedia research is currently emerging and a shift is being made towards new models and theories that are expected to provide the insights necessary to advance multimedia research in promising new directions. Ideally, this research should lead to a comprehensive framework of principles at the micro-level for the design of effective multimedia learning systems. Some of the topics that multimedia learning research is currently focusing on are: instructional design across all media versus instructional design unique to a particular medium (based on media enabled affordances), computational efficiency, active processing, support for processing, prior knowledge, cognitive load, motivation, cognitive/learning styles and the affordances of semantic web technologies. A number of these topics have been underlined by Goldman (2003). Each will be briefly discussed next:

- **Instructional design across all media:** We have already elaborated on issues connected to the media effects debate and have emphasized the need to examine media and methods mutually. A large number of researchers find that there is a higher value in trying to agree on how to design instructional messages across various media (Van Merrienboer, 1997; Najjar, 1998, 2001; Mayer, 2003) instead of examining the effects of media per se - such as asking whether it is better to learn from a computer than from a book. Referring to the presentation of multimedia educational content through words and pictures, Mayer focused on the issue of *methods across media* and summarized good instructional design across media in four important design principles: (a) adding pictures to words, (b) eliminating extraneous words and pictures,

(c) placing words near corresponding pictures, and (d) using conversational style for words. However, there may be aspects of instructional design that are unique to a particular medium because that medium enables instructional methods that other media cannot make available (e.g., computers enable interactivity to a much greater extent than books). Research will need to focus both on instructional design principles applicable across media as well as on principles connected to particular media because of the particular methods and affordances for information presentation that those media make possible.

- **Computational efficiency:** Certain representations of information may be very well-suited to particular learning tasks while ill-suited for others that require the learner to first transform the information (to match the task demands) before using it, something that would normally place additional processing demands on learners and may even lead to his/her inability to make the necessary transformation. According to some researchers (Schnotz & Bannert, 2003; Kozma, 2003) the ease with which a learner can extract the necessary information from a certain content representation to deal with a particular task has to do with the *computational efficiency* of that specific representation. For example, several informationally equivalent pictures could visualize the same subject matter in different ways. This area of research focuses on determining the effects that the selection of different forms of visualization would have on the structure of the mental representation created during the comprehension process and also focuses on the computational efficiency of these different representations for specific learning tasks.
- **Active processing:** Media environments do not cause learning; active cognitive processing by the learner causes learning. If learners are not actively processing the information in an attempt to make sense of it, then the accurate design of multimedia and the conformity between media affordances and task demands, may not make much of a difference. Multimedia research is currently exploring ways of promoting active cognitive processing. For example, Mayer (2003) proposed instructional design methods that work across media and that foster active processing and Kozma (2003) proposed engaging learners in scientifically authentic discussions around representations as a way of supporting active cognitive processing.
- **Support for processing:** Another line of research is focusing on the need to determine the effect that different forms of help have for different learners. Goldman (2003) called attention to the fact that different forms of support or help encourage different kinds of processing, and that care needs to be taken to make sure that the kind of processing being supported, is consistent with the demands of the outcome task performance. The effectiveness of various kinds of support is mediated both by the kind of task and the knowledge level of the learner. For example, with respect to task, Seufert (2003) found that her help conditions had different effects that were determined by whether the learners had to recall material or answer comprehension questions. She also found that learners with different levels of prior knowledge react differently when help is given.
- **Prior knowledge:** The effects that prior knowledge has on learning though multimedia is a dominant issue in current multimedia research, both in terms of how it is associated to successful active processing as well as on how it should be supported (Kozma, 2003; Lowe, 2003; Stern et al.,

2003). The research clearly portrays the limiting effects of prior knowledge indicating that the problem of overcoming the way that a novice learner treats multimedia content of a complex domain is complicated and is not simply a matter of presenting the appropriate material or instructing the learner to make use of a specific strategy. Novice learners need to be supported in going beyond the surface features and engaging in deeper active processing that will permit them to perceive and distinguish the underlying principles and concepts. For example, Kozma had students engage in discourse about different representations and Lewalter (2003) encouraged students to generate think-aloud protocols to engage them in active processing. Future research will need to indicate effective ways of supporting learners with different levels of prior knowledge when learning through multimedia environments.

- **Manipulating Germane or Intrinsic Cognitive Load:** Until now researchers in the area of cognitive load have focused on how to design instruction so as to decrease extraneous cognitive load and have ignored the possible positive impact of exploiting germane or intrinsic cognitive load. A shift is currently being made towards studies that examine these effects (Kirschner, 2002; Sweller, 1988; van Merriënboer, Schuurman, de Croock & Paas, 2002; Bodermer and Ploetzner, in press). Whereas extraneous load results from information and activities that do not contribute to the process of schema construction and automation, germane load is related to information and activities that foster these processes (e.g. tasks that are relevant to schema acquisition through increased effort and motivation). Therefore, whereas extraneous load hurts learning, germane load facilitates learning. An area of this research is currently focusing on how to design instruction so as to increase germane cognitive load. Another area is currently investigating the possibility of manipulating intrinsic cognitive load. The manipulation of intrinsic cognitive load is an entirely new approach in instructional design and is particularly interesting not only because it has been proposed by the "fathers" of cognitive load but because it contradicts their initial views since the idea presently supported is that it is possible to decrease intrinsic cognitive load, at least artificially (Bannert, 2002). This can be achieved through the appropriate sequencing of the learning material (appropriate information sequencing). For example, Pollock, Chandler and Sweller (2002) examined the manipulation of intrinsic cognitive load of learners dealing with complex knowledge domains by proposing a method they called the "isolated-interacting elements procedure" and concluded that cognitive load had decreased.
- **Motivation:** Another key variable that influences learning through multimedia is motivation. Studies have shown that extrinsic motivation (e.g., grades or external rewards) does not have significant effects on learning and especially for adult learners. On the contrary, there is evidence that intrinsic motivation - which can be increased in a number of ways, e.g. from giving students choices between different assignments, to minimizing adult supervision over group projects, to letting students monitor and evaluate their own progress (Anderman & Midgley, 1998) or by providing them with interesting and challenging content - encourages the learner to become cognitively engaged with the multimedia material and improves learning (Najjar, 1998, 2001).

- **Cognitive and learning styles:** Multimedia learning research has not satisfactorily focused on the impact that particular learning/cognitive style dimensions have on learning and has not managed to identify robust relationships between learning/cognitive styles, instructional methods, and different forms of content. There is a need for further research to determine a framework for designing effective adaptable multimedia learning environments that will be compatible with particular learning preferences, strengths, weaknesses, and behaviors of students, and will lead to efficient and better learning. Obviously new technologies such as learning objects and ontologies used within the semantic web framework will enable a more multidimensional approach, integrating a broader range of variables such as the ones previously discussed. (See Table 4 for summary of the preceding sections.)
- **The affordances of semantic web technologies:** Semantic web technology has the potential to offer solutions to limitations in existing multimedia learning environments by providing enhanced knowledge access based on the exploitation of machine-processable metadata. The semantic web initiative can improve the current state of the web by using semantic descriptions for all web learning resources, thus creating a semantically-rich environment. This kind of environment could support learners in more demanding learning activities (e.g. inquiry-based learning, problem-solving activities, etc.) through web services. For example, IMS Learning Design uses a semantic conceptual model of the learning process as its basis. Every person is assigned to a role in this process, typically a learner or staff role. In this role the learner works towards certain outcomes by performing more or less structured learning and supporting learning activities within an environment. The environment consists of the appropriate learning objects and services to be used during the performance of the activities. Which role gets which activities at what moment in the process, is determined by the learning design method.

CONCLUSION

In the last two decades multimedia as a concept has achieved a high degree of recognition and a large number of multimedia learning studies have been carried out in order to support its application in the educational sector. Despite this widely documented period in the history of multimedia, the studies carried out until recently have ignored important factors that could influence the appropriate selection of media and have thus failed to yield conclusive multimedia design guidelines. In this chapter an attempt has been made to summarize key issues, characteristics, and weaknesses of this research. Multimedia learning research is currently attempting a deeper understanding of how a broader range of parameters could play a positive role in the design of effective multimedia environments. Specific aspects and parameters of this emerging multimedia research were discussed.

REFERENCES

Anderman, L. H., & Midgley, C. (1998). *Motivation and middle school students* [ERIC digest]. Champaign, IL: ERIC Clearinghouse on Elementary and Early Childhood Education. (ERIC Document Reproduction Service No. ED 421 281).

Anderssen, E. C., & Myburgh, C. P. H. (1992). The acquisition of operating systems concepts by computer science students. *Computers & Education, 19*, 309–320. doi:10.1016/0360-1315(92)90125-O

Arnheim, R. (1954). Art and visual perception: A psychology of the creative eye. In D.H. Jonassen (Ed.), *Handbook for research for educational communications and technology* (pp. 755-794). New York: Simon & Schuster Macmillan.

Atkins, M. J. (1993). Theories of learning and multimedia applications: An overview. *Research Papers in Education, 8*(2), 251–271. doi:10.1080/0267152930080207

Baddeley, A. D. (1986). *Working memory*. Oxford, UK: Oxford University Press.

Bagui, S. (1998). Reasons for increased learning using multimedia. *Journal of Educational Multimedia and Hypermedia, 7*(1), 3–18.

Bannert, M. (2002). Managing cognitive load–recent trends in cognitive load theory. *Learning and Instruction, 12*, 139–146. doi:10.1016/S0959-4752(01)00021-4

Bodemer, D., & Ploetzner, R. (in press). Encouraging the active integration of information during learning with multiple and interactive representations. In H. Niegemann, R. Brünken, & D. Leutner (Eds.), *Instructional design for multimedia learning. Proceedings of the EARLI SIG 6 Biannual Workshop2002in Erfurt.* Muenster, Germany: Waxmann.

Bruner, J. S. (1966). *Toward a theory of instruction.* Cambridge, MA: Harvard University Press.

Brusilovsky, P. (2003). Developing adaptive educational hypermedia systems: From design models to authoring tools. In T. Murray, S. Blessing, & S. Ainsworth (Eds.), *Authoring tools for advanced technology learning environment*. Dordrecht, The Netherlands: Kluwer Academic.

Chou, C., & Lin, H. (1998). The effect of navigation map types and cognitive styles on learners' performance in a computer-networked hypertext learning system. *Journal of Educational Multimedia and Hypermedia, 7*(2/3), 151–176.

Chuang, Y. R. (1999). Teaching in a multimedia computer environment: A study of the effects of learning style, gender, and math achievement. *Interactive Multimedia Electronic Journal of Computer-Enhanced Learning.* Retrieved November 4, 2005, from http://imej.wfu.edu/articles/1999/1/10/index.asp

Clark, R. E. (1983). Reconsidering research on learning from media. *Review of Educational Research, 53*(4), 445–459.

Cuban, L. (1986). *Teachers and machines: The classroom use of technology since 1920.* New York: Teachers College Press.

Deubel, P. (2003). An investigation of behaviourist and cognitive approaches to instructional multimedia design. *Journal of Educational Multimedia and Hypermedia, 12*(1), 63–90.

Di Vesta, F. (1987). The cognitive movement and education. In J. Glover & R. Royce (Eds.), *Historical foundations of education psychology* (pp. 203-233). New York: Plenum Press.

Dillon, A., & Gabbard, R. (1998). Hypermedia as an educational technology: A review of the quantitative research literature on learner comprehension, control and style. *Review of Educational Research, 68*(3), 322–349.

Dwyer, F. M. (1972). *A guide for improving visualized instruction*. State College, PA: Learning Services.

Dwyer, F. M. (1978). *Strategies for improving visual learning*. State College, PA: Learning Services.

Dwyer, F. M. (Ed.). (1987). *Enhancing visualized instruction-recommendations for practitioners.* State College, PA: Learning Services.

Dwyer, F. M., & Dwyer, C. (2003). A systematic assessment of the contributions of animation to knowledge acquisition. In *Proceedings of the 2003 Annual ED-MEDIA Conference*, Honolulu, HI (pp. 1112-1117).

Gagné, R. M. (1967). *Learning and individual differences.* Columbus, OH: Charles E. Merrill Books.

Goldman, S. R. (2003). Learning in complex domains: When and why do multiple representations help? *Learning and Instruction*, *13*, 239–244. doi:10.1016/S0959-4752(02)00023-3

Gombrich, E. H. (1969). Art and illusion: A study in the psychology of pictorial representation. In D.H. Jonassen (Ed.), *Handbook for research for educational communications and technology* (pp. 755-794). New York: Simon & Schuster Macmillan.

Guttormsen, S. S., & Krueger, H. (2001). Empirical research on the effect of dynamic media for information presentation. In *Proceedings of ICL2001 - 4th International Workshop on Interactive Computer Aided Learning - Experiences and Visions, 2001.*

Hannafin, M., Hannafin, K., Hooper, S., Rieber, L., & Kini, A. (1996). Research on and research with emerging technologies. In D. H. Jonassen (Ed.), *Handbook for research for educational communications and technology* (pp. 378-402). New York: Simon & Schuster Macmillan.

Hede, A. (2002). An integrated model of multimedia effects on learning. *Journal of Educational Multimedia and Hypermedia*, *11*(2), 177–191.

Himmelweit, H., Oppenheim, A. N., & Vince, P. (1959). *Television and the child: an empirical study of the effects of television on the young.* London: Oxford University Press.

Huffaker, D. (2004). *The e-Learning Design Challenge: Technology, Models and Design Principles* [White Paper]. Washington DC: American Society for Training & Development (ASTD).

IEEE Learning Technology Standards Committee. (n.d.). *IEEE LOM Working Draft 6.1 (IEEE 1484.12.1-2002)*. Retrieved November 4, 2005, from http://ltsc.ieee.org/wg12/index.html

IMS Global Learning Consortium, Inc. (n.d.). *Open specifications for interoperable learning technology*. Retrieved November 4, 2005, from http:// www.imsproject.org

Jonassen, D. H. (1991). Objectivism versus constructivism: Do we need a new philosophical paradigm? *Educational Technology Research and Development*, *39*(3), 5–14. doi:10.1007/BF02296434

Jonassen, D. H. (Ed.). (1996). *Handbook of research for educational communications and technology*. New York: Simon & Schuster Macmillan.

Jonassen, D. H., Campbell, J. P., & Davidson, M. E. (1994). Learning with media: Restructuring the debate. *Educational Technology Research and Development*, *39*(3), 5–14. doi:10.1007/BF02296434

Kann, C., Lindeman, R., & Heller, R. (1997). Integrating algorithm animation into a learning environment. *Computers & Education*, *28*(4), 223–238. doi:10.1016/S0360-1315(97)00015-8

Kintsch, W. (1974). *The representation of meaning in memory.* Hillsdale, NJ: Lawrence Erlbaum.

Kirschner, P. A. (2002). Cognitive load theory: Implications of cognitive load theory on the design of learning. *Learning and Instruction*, *12*(1), 1–10. doi:10.1016/S0959-4752(01)00014-7

Kolb, D. A. (1984). *Experiential learning: Experience as the source of learning and development.* Englewood Cliffs, NJ: Prentice-Hall.

Koumi, J. (2003). Synergy between audio commentary and visuals in multimedia packages. *Journal of Educational Media, 28*(1), 19–34. doi:10.1080/1358165032000156419

Kozma, R. (1991). Learning with media. *Review of Educational Research, 61*(2), 179–211.

Kozma, R. (1994). Will media influence learning? Reframing the debate. *Educational Technology Research and Development, 42*(2), 7–19. doi:10.1007/BF02299087

Kozma, R. (2003). The material features of multiple representations and their cognitive and social affordances for science understanding. *Learning and Instruction, 13*, 205–226. doi:10.1016/S0959-4752(02)00021-X

Lazarsfeld, P. F. (1940). *Radio and the printed page: an introduction to the study of radio and its role in the communication of ideas.* New York: Duell, Sloan & Pierce.

Levie, W. H., & Lentz, R. (1982). Effects of text illustrations: A review of research. *Educational Communication and Technology Journal, 30*(4), 195–232.

Levin, J. R., Anglin, G. J., & Carney, R. N. (1987). On empirically validating functions of pictures in prose. In D.M. Willows & H.A. Houghton (Eds.), *The psychology of illustration*, (Vol. 1, pp. 51-86). New York: Springer.

Levin, J. R., & Lesgold, A. M. (1978). On pictures in prose. *Educational Communication and Technology Journal, 26*, 233–243.

Lewalter, D. (2003). Cognitive strategies for learning from static and dynamic visuals. *Learning and Instruction, 13*, 177–189. doi:10.1016/S0959-4752(02)00019-1

Liao, Y. C. (1999). Effects of hypermedia on students' achievement: A meta-analysis. *Journal of Educational Multimedia and Hypermedia, 8*(3), 255–277.

Lowe, R. K. (2003). Animation and learning: Selective processing of information in dynamic graphics. *Learning and Instruction, 13*(2), 157–176. doi:10.1016/S0959-4752(02)00018-X

Mayer, R. E. (2001). *Multimedia learning.* Cambridge, UK: Cambridge University Press.

Mayer, R. E. (2003). The promise of multimedia learning: Using the same instructional design methods across different media. *Learning and Instruction, 13*, 125–139. doi:10.1016/S0959-4752(02)00016-6

Mayer, R. E., & Anderson, R. B. (1991). Animations need narrations: An experimental test of a dual-coding hypothesis. *Journal of Educational Psychology, 83*(4), 484–490. doi:10.1037/0022-0663.83.4.484

Mayer, R. E., & Moreno, R. (1998). A split-attention effect in multimedia learning: Evidence for dual processing systems in working memory. *Journal of Educational Psychology, 90*(2), 312–320. doi:10.1037/0022-0663.90.2.312

Mayer, R. E., & Moreno, R. (1999). Cognitive principles of multimedia learning: The role of modality and contiguity. *Journal of Educational Psychology, 91*(2), 358–368. doi:10.1037/0022-0663.91.2.358

Mayer, R. E., & Moreno, R. (2000). Meaningful design for meaningful learning: Applying cognitive theory to multimedia explanations. In *Proceedings of the 2000 Annual ED-MEDIA Conference*, Montreal, Quebec, Canada (pp. 747-752).

Mayer, R. E., & Moreno, R. (2003). Meaningful design for meaningful learning: Applying cognitive theory to multimedia explanations. In *Proceedings of ED-MEDIA, 2003,* Honolulu, HI.

Mousavi, S. Y., Low, R., & Sweller, J. (1995). Reducing cognitive load by mixing auditory and visual presentation modes. *Journal of Educational Psychology*, *87*(2), 319–334. doi:10.1037/0022-0663.87.2.319

Najjar, L. J. (1998). Principles of educational multimedia user interface design. *Human Factors*, *40*(2), 311–323. doi:10.1518/001872098779480505

Najjar, L. J. (2001). Principles of educational multimedia user interface design. In R.W. Swezey & D.H. Andrews (Eds.), *Readings in training and simulation: A 30-year perspective* (pp. 146-158). Santa Monica, CA: Human Factors and Ergonomics Society. Retrieved November 7, 2005, from http://lawrence/najjar.com/papers/Principles_of_educational_multimedia_user_interface_design.html

Nathan, M., & Robinson, C. (2001). Considerations of learning and learning research: Revisiting the "media effects" debate. *Journal of Interactive Learning Research*, *12*, 69–88.

Paivio, A. (1971). *Imagery and verbal processes*. New York: Holt, Rinehart & Winston.

Paivio, A. (1986). *Mental representations: A dual coding approach*. Oxford, UK: Oxford University Press.

Paivio, A. (1991). Dual coding theory: Retrospect and current status. *Canadian Journal of Psychology*, *45*, 255–287. doi:10.1037/h0084295

Park, O., & Lee, J. (2003) Adaptive instructional systems. In D.H. Jonassen (Ed.), *Handbook of research for educational communications and technology* (pp. 651-685). Mahwah, NJ: Lawrence Erlbaum.

Pollock, E., Chandler, P., & Sweller, J. (2002). Assimilating complex information. *Learning and Instruction*, *12*, 61–86. doi:10.1016/S0959-4752(01)00016-0

Reimann, P. (2003). Multimedia learning: Beyond modality. *Learning and Instruction*, *13*, 245–252. doi:10.1016/S0959-4752(02)00024-5

Riding, R., & Rayner, S. (1998). *Cognitive styles and learning strategies*. London: David Fulton.

Rieber, L. P. (1990). Animation in computer-based instruction. *Educational Technology Research and Development*, *38*(1), 77–86. doi:10.1007/BF02298250

Rieber, L. P. (2000). *Computers, graphics & learning*. Madison, WI: Brown & Benchmark.

Ross, J., & Schulz, R. (1999). Can computer-aided instruction accommodate all learners equally? *British Journal of Educational Technology*, *30*(1), 5–24. doi:10.1111/1467-8535.00087

Samuels, S. J. (1967). Attentional process in reading: The effect of pictures on the acquisition of reading responses. *Journal of Educational Psychology*, *58*(6), 337–342. doi:10.1037/h0020045

Schnotz, W., & Bannert, M. (2003). Construction and interference in learning from multiple representation. *Learning and Instruction*, *13*, 141–156. doi:10.1016/S0959-4752(02)00017-8

SCORM. *The sharable content object reference model.* (2001). Retrieved November 4, 2005, from http://www.adlnet.org/

Seufert, T. (2003). Supporting coherence formation in learning from multiple representations. *Learning and Instruction*, *13*, 227–237. doi:10.1016/S0959-4752(02)00022-1

Shih, Y., & Alessi, S. M. (1994). Mental models and transfer of learning in computer programming. *Journal of Research on Computing in Education*, *26*, 155–175.

Shih, Y., & Alessi, S. M. (1996). Effects of Text versus Voice on Learning in Multimedia Courseware. *Journal of Educational Multimedia and Hypermedia, 5*(2), 203–218.

Shuell, T. (1986). Cognitive conceptions of learning. *Review of Educational Research, 56*(4), 411–436.

Simonsen, M., Clark, R., Kulik, J., Tennyson, R., & Winn, W. (1987). Mere vehicles: A symposium on the status of research in instructional technology. In *Proceedings of the 1987 Annual Convention of the Association for Educational Communications and Technology*, Atlanta, GA (pp. 1-43).

Spaulding, S. (1955). Research on pictorial illustration. In D.H. Jonassen (Ed.), *Handbook for research for educational communications and technology* (pp. 755-794). New York: Simon & Schuster Macmillan.

Stern, E., Aprea, C., & Ebner, H. (2003). Improving cross-content transfer in text processing by means of active graphical representation. *Learning and Instruction, 13*, 191–203. doi:10.1016/S0959-4752(02)00020-8

Sternberg, R. J. (1996). *Cognitive psychology.* Orlando, FL: Harbourt Bracc.

Sweller, J. (1988). Cognitive load during problem solving: Effects on learning. *Cognitive Science, 12*, 257–285.

Sweller, J. (1989). Cognitive technology: Some procedures for facilitating learning and problem solving in mathematics and science. *Journal of Educational Psychology, 81*(4), 457–466. doi:10.1037/0022-0663.81.4.457

Sweller, J., & Chandler, P. (1994). Why some material is difficult to learn. *Cognition and Instruction, 12*(3), 185–233. doi:10.1207/s1532690xci1203_1

Tobias, S. (1987). Learner characteristics. In R. Gagné (Ed.), *Instructional technology: Foundations* (pp. 207-232). Hillsdale, NJ: Lawrence Erlbaum.

Tobias, S. (1990). *They're not dumb, they're different: Stalking the second tier.* Tucson, AZ: Research Corporation.

Van Merrienboer, J. J. G. (1997). *Training complex cognitive skills.* Englewood Cliffs, NJ: Educational Technology Press.

van Merriënboer, J. J. G., Schuurman, J. G., de Croock, M. B. M., & Paas, F. G. W. C. (2002). Redirecting learners' attention during training: Effects on cognitive load, transfer test performance and training efficiency. *Learning and Instruction, 12*(1), 11–37. doi:10.1016/S0959-4752(01)00020-2

Wilson, B., & Cole, P. (1996). Cognitive teaching models. In D. H. Jonas-sen (Ed.), *Handbook of research for educational communications and technology* (pp. 601-621). New York: MacMillan.

Chapter 12
Virtual Reality in Education

Chris Christou
University of Nicosia, Cyprus

ABSTRACT

Virtual Reality is implemented by a combination of technologies that are used in order to visualize and provide interaction with a virtual environment. These environments often depict three-dimensional space which may be realistic or imaginary, macroscopic or microscopic and based on realistic physical laws of dynamics, or on imaginary dynamics. The multitude of scenarios that VR may be used to depict make it broadly applicable to the many areas in education. A key feature of VR is that it allows multi-sensory interaction with the space being visualized. Here we look at how this combination of multi-sensory visualization and interactivity make VR ideally suited for effective learning and try to explain this effectiveness in terms of the advantages afforded by active learning through experiences. We also consider some of the applications of VR in education and also some of its drawbacks.

INTRODUCTION

Virtual Reality or VR allows a user to interact with a computer generated three-dimensional model or virtual environment. This environment may be realistic, in the sense that it is familiar to us at a macroscopic scale, it may be realistic in the sense that it depicts the physical world as known to science but which is not usually observable, or it may be used to visualize a world that is entirely imaginary. As such, VR is broadly applicable, and has been applied to, many different areas of education including the sciences, archeology, history and architecture. The advantage of VR over conventional methods of description is that the student is given the opportunity to *experience* subject matter that would be difficult, if not impossible, to illustrate or describe with conventional methods. We argue here that this experiential nature of VR together with its other key feature, interactivity, provides a valuable aid to conventional learning paradigms. In this chapter we give a brief description of common

DOI: 10.4018/978-1-60566-940-3.ch012

VR setups to give a feel for how a VR experience is provided. We also consider, from cognitive and sensory psychology points of view why learning may be facilitated by interactive multi-sensory systems and we provide some examples of the use of VR in educational contexts.

Modern education often requires a student to comprehend complex or abstract concepts or appreciate scenarios and situations that no longer exist. To this end, common mechanisms for teaching abstract concepts are the use of metaphor and analogy, especially within the sciences. By using an analogy we describe an event or abstract concept in terms of commonly observable reality. That is, we relate concepts to experience. The experience provides the material for the construction of a mental model of the concept, which in turn leads to the foundation of knowledge (Duffy & Jonassen, 1992). Humans learn by having experiences, by interacting with their environment and using their senses to derive information from the world. Virtual reality is a technology that replaces sensory input derived from the real world with sensory input created by computer simulation. It provides interactivity by responding to movements and the natural behaviors and actions of humans. In this respect VR may prove to be a powerful resource that can help in teaching by providing an environment that allows the student to experience scenarios and situations rather than imagining them. The experiential nature of VR systems derives from three sources: immersion, interactivity and multi-sensory feedback. Immersion means being enveloped or surrounded by the environment. The benefit of immersion is that it ensures a sense of presence or the feeling that one is really in the depicted world (Schuemie et al., 2001). Interactivity is the ability to control events in the simulation by using ones body movements which in turn initiates responses in the simulation as a result of these movements. The multi-sensory nature of VR means that information can be derived from more than one sense and adds to the experience by making it more believable, engaging (adding to the sense of presence) and providing redundancy of information which reduces the potential for ambiguity and confusion. Sensory combination reinforces information from two or more sensory sources. The aim of VR is therefore to replace the real world with a virtual world and to allow the user to behave as if they were in the real world.

The experiential nature of VR supports a constructivist approach to learning (see Winn, 1993). Constructivism is a theory of knowledge acquisition that states that humans construct knowledge by learning from their experiences. As popularized by Jean Piaget the theory states that the learner attempts to assimilate new experiences within their already established world model. If the learner cannot successfully assimilate new detail they change their world view to accommodate the new experience. When we act on the expectation that the world operates according to our world model and it does not then we must accommodate the new experience by reframing our model of the way the world works; we learn from the experience. This implies that learning is a form of active hypothesis testing. This should be contrasted with the view that learning is a passive accumulation or acceptance of facts. VR provides an environment for this active hypothesis testing and thus provides a powerful medium for learning. In general, and as suggested by Bruner (1961), students who actively engage with new material are more likely to retain this material and recall it at a later stage.

Table 1 lists some of the advantages and potential disadvantages of using VR in an educational context. After reading this chapter, the reader will be able to appreciate how these issues impact on learning. We begin by giving a brief description of VR followed by an account of how interactivity and multi-sensory stimulation (key components of VR) provide a basis for learning. We describe how the perceptual and cognitive processes responsible for learning benefit from interactivity and multi-sensory information. This section is

Table 1. Advantages and disadvantages of using VR

Broad areas of application	Can be expensive and time consuming to set up
Provides a more engaging environment for learning	May in some cases result in simulation sickness
Utilizes interactivity & interactive learning	Learners may feel disorientated as first
Engages multiple senses.	Fidelity issues and lack of realism

then followed by a consideration of the building blocks of an operational VR system with details of the important components of a VR simulation and the various technologies that facilitate interaction and engagement. This is followed by a review of several application areas in educational contexts. We finish the chapter with a look at some of the draw-backs and potential problems associated with the use of VR in its present form.

WHAT IS VR?

In a VR simulation a computer simulates and displays an environment through which we can move and interact with objects and simulated people (commonly referred to as 'agents' or avatars). A virtual environment is depicted usually as a three-dimensional world and often virtual worlds try to replicate the real world both in appearance and in the way that objects behave (e.g. the simulation of gravity). It should be noted however, that there is no necessity that this virtual space be similar to the real world. Indeed, one of the virtues of virtual environments is that they can be used to depict entirely unrealistic scenarios. However, for training purposes virtual environments simulate the environment in which the student will eventually operate and provide a safe environment in which to test scenarios that would be either too difficult or dangerous to perform in real life.

There are many types of VR implementations and below we have grouped them into 4 common setups:

1. Desktop VR (Monoscopic or Stereoscopic)
2. Immersive VR (HMD, CAVE, wide screen)
3. Collaborative systems
4. Mixed or augmented reality

Desktop VR, as its name suggests, has the user seated in front of a desktop computer monitor with interaction provided by a controlling device such as a computer mouse. In immersive systems the users' field of view is completely obstructed by the visualization display in the form of a helmet worn on the head. Collaborative systems may be either desktop based or immersive and involve the interaction between two or more avatars controlled by humans. A recent and most successful implementation of a collaborative system is Second Life (www.secondlife.com). Attempts are also being made to harness the power of collaborative systems for research purposes (e.g. The Presenccia Project, www.presenccia.org). Mixed reality systems display a combination of the real world, viewed either directly or through a camera, with overlaid computer generated content. Although relatively new, these systems have potential for training students in engineering and medicine.

MULTI-SENSORY INTERACTION: A BASIS FOR LEARNING

From infancy, a child learns through activity. With little control over its limbs, the process of learning about the world begins through exploration by reaching, touching, looking, smelling, and tasting whatever comes into its proximity. Through a combination of all the senses the child begins to associate different properties with different objects and through memorization is able to form distinct categories and concepts from the seemingly disparate and chaotic signals that it receives from the world. Even in maturity, perception and activity are crucial for learning. In this section we give a brief description of how we derive information through sensory perception and how the connection between perception and action can be exploited by VR technology for educational purposes.

The Senses

The five senses of vision, audition, touch, taste and olfaction provide different information for different purposes. We focus on vision, touch and audition as these senses are the ones primarily exploited in virtual reality. Of all the senses vision is the most versatile providing us with a wide range of information concerning ourselves and our surroundings. It also provides a means of communication and is used for recognition and identification. The visual system makes use of a wide variety of sensory cues. For example, for spatial perception (the perception of distances and shape) it utilizes stereopsis (the ability to fuse images from two eyes) to detect depth. When fused, the retinal images of the two eyes contain disparities or horizontal misalignments that scale with depth and the visual system uses these disparities to encode the relative depth of objects. Relative depth is also detected from motion parallax (images of objects *closer* to us move *faster* across the retina when they, or the head, moves). The visual system also makes use of so called 'pictorial cues' such as occlusion, shading, perspective etc. (Gregory, 1974) to get information regarding shape and relative depth. Under normal circumstances all of these visual cues are combined to allow us to navigate and understand the world.

Audition can also be used for spatial perception as well as for recognition and communication. For spatial perception auditory cues include inter-aural changes in loudness and pitch. For instance, one is able to localize a sound in the horizontal plane by the differences in sound intensity between the sounds reaching the two ears. This works particularly well if the source is less than a meter from the subject. It is also possible to differentiate the location of sound sources in the vertical plane when the source is the same distance from the two ears. The outer portion of the ear (the pinna) is thought to modulate sound frequency according to its location in the vertical plane thus serving as an auditory localization cue. Recent developments in sound simulation have utilized a Head Related Transfer Function (HRTF) which is a mapping of sound properties as a sound source is placed at different positions around a subject's head. HRTFs are different for each individual (they depend on the shape of the head and body as well the shape of the pinna). Despite this, generic maps have been created which provide compelling simulated spatialised sound with localization cues (see Burdea & Coiffet, 1994).

Touch is used to detect the presence of obstacles, as well as the shape of objects and their material properties. The properties of objects may be derived from two sources: cutaneous sensation and kinesthesia. It is customary to use the term haptics instead of touch to refer to the use and study of both of these sources of information. Cutaneous sensation is what we normally think of as touch and derives from receptors in the skin, not just of the hands but across the body. There are many different types of receptors, located at various levels below the surface of the skin, conveying the sensations of temperature, pain and movement/pressure. The latter are known as mechanoreceptors and different kinds of mechanoreceptors detect a range of stimuli from transient vibrations to extended displacement of the skin. Kinesthetic sensation is used to detect force, position, direction and angles of the joints and is facilitated by the movements and tensions within muscles, joints and tendons located throughout the body. Whilst vibrotactile and electrotactile devices are being developed for use in VR systems the most successful devices have so far been kinesthetic devices which provide the user with haptic feedback by moving their finger or hand when it comes into contact with a virtual object (haptic devices are discussed below).

Multisensory Perception and Sensory Integration

There are many sources of perceptual information emanating from our surroundings. The neurophysiologist Sherrington categorized our sensations of the world into three groups:

1. Sensations coming from the outside world (exteroception)
2. Sensations describing the body's posture and action (proprioception)
3. Sensations emanating from within the body itself (interoception)

For our purposes, the first two types of sensation are most relevant and comprise what we shall refer to as the sensorimotor system. Exteroception uses the primary senses of vision, touch, taste, etc. as described above. Proprioception can be separated into two components: kinaesthesia and the vestibular sense (the vestibular system provides the sense of balance). Under normal circumstances these proprioceptive inputs influence, and are influenced by, the exteroceptive senses. Integrating inputs from the exteroceptive senses in particular helps disambiguate external stimuli and can help to speed up our responses.

As an example of sensory cooperation between exteroceptive and proprioceptive inputs, consider the illusion of self motion experienced when sitting on a train at a station. If there is a train next to us and it starts to move we often have the illusion that we are moving. The motion of a large part of the field of view is misinterpreted as self-motion. In some cases there is even an urge to change posture. It is only when the perceived movement of the self is not reinforced by expected proprioceptive inputs (from touch and the sensation of acceleration, for instance) that the illusion breaks down. This coupling between (vestibular and visual) sensory inputs was demonstrated by the experiments of Lee and Aronson (1974) with young children. After acclimatization within a room whose walls could be moved, the infant's balance when the walls were suddenly shifted towards them or away from them was assessed. In many cases the infants fell over in the direction of movement of the walls (compensation for perceived change in sway in the opposite direction) showing that postural (proprioceptive) senses can be overridden by visual (exteroceptive) inputs.

Many other demonstrations of this cooperation between the senses exist. For example, it is commonly known that under noisy conditions the ability to see a speaker's lips while they are talking enhances comprehension of what they are saying. Related to this is the McGurk effect (McGurk & MacDonald, 1976) in which seen lip movements alter the perceived phoneme that is heard (e.g. the sound of 'ba' can be heard as 'da' if the lip movement is that of 'ga'). In this case the two 'signals' (vision and sound) are fused to form a new percept that would not occur when either is presented in isolation. It seems therefore that multi-sensory integration is an important component of perception. A medium that provides multi-sensory stimulation will therefore provide a richer experience than one that delivers information through only one sensory modality. In the absence of multiple sensory sources of information perception and learning may be slower and more prone to ambiguity (Calvert et al., 2004).

Figure 1. The perception-action loop

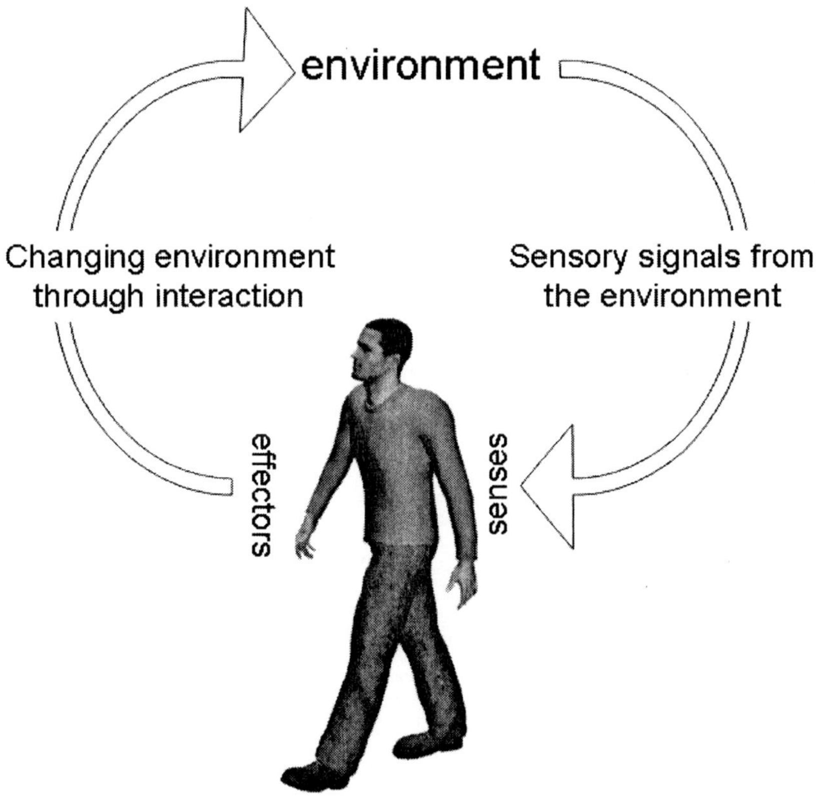

Perception, Action and Active Learning

In everyday situations action is coupled with changes in sensory input in the form of the perception/action loop (Figure 1). Our brains are adapted to exploit this coupling by setting up predictions as to what will happen given a particular input and what responses are appropriate. One evolutionary benefit of this coupling is that it makes responses to quickly changing events faster because it reduces the involvement of cognitive effort, which is relatively slow. Another benefit is that it provides for more concrete concept construction and thus facilitates learning. In this section we consider the theoretical basis of this assertion.

Traditionally it was thought that perception is a passive process. A sensory stimulus, such as the visual sensation from an object, is projected to the retina and conveyed to the brain where it is matched against the contents of memory. Perception in some versions of this view involves a passive registration of sensory stimulation and learning involves becoming attuned to regularities in the environment (for example see Gibson, 1987). Another general view of the perceptual process considers perception as active, not passive. This view casts perception in an active role in which the perceiver performs particular actions in order to acquire the necessary information for perception to take place. As an example, consider an action we all perform when faced with a view of the world that is ambiguous. We usually move our heads from side to side in order to induce the cues of motion parallax that can separate object surfaces at different distances from us. This is a natural response that we rarely think about, but which suggests that we have learned action schemas for assisting and facilitating perception. Perception in this view is a top-down process that is guided by cognition. In cognitive psychology this view is encapsulated by the theories of Neisser (1976, 1987) and Gregory (1974). In particular, Neisser distinguished between seeing and thinking in the perceptual process. In 'seeing' the subject is making use of information in the world (as in Gibson's view) and in 'thinking' the subject is applying top-down information to make sense of the world. This is a constructivist view in which attention, motivation and perceptual processes operate together to make sense of data arriving from all sense modalities but also in which the processes drive the pick-up of information. Neisser's theory sees a perceiver as an active explorer of their environment guided by schemas already laid down in memory and who continually update these schemas based on their experiences. In Gregory's view (e.g. Gregory, 1974) the perceptual process is one of generating and testing hypotheses. When sensory information is limited, the perceiver fills in the gaps with top-down knowledge about the world.

This view of perceptual processing feeds into the constructivist theory of epistemology and learning as propounded by Dewey, Piaget and Vigotsky among others (see Duffy 1992). In constructivism, learning is a personal process of construction of meaning from a multitude of sensory information. In Neisser's terms, the learner constructs their own schemas concerning how the world is and how it works and applies them to new encounters. Piaget saw the learner as one who tries to assimilate new experiences within schemas already laid down. If they cannot, they adjust their current knowledge to accommodate them. In such a theory, learning is facilitated when the learner is allowed to interact with sensory data and allowed to construct their own world view. A number of recent studies in cognitive psychology have investigated the potential benefits of active learning (e.g. Feldman & Acredolo, 1979; Christou & Bülthoff, 1999) and some of these have used VR technology specifically to decouple the various factors that are involved.

These considerations: the interaction between senses, the benefits of sensory integration and a constructivist view of learning, support the use of learning paradigms in which the learner is allowed to form knowledge through context and experience. VR is ideally suited for this. The use of VR provides a multi-sensory, interactive environment that is engaging and that allows learners to construct meaning from experience. For example, in the teaching of complex or abstract ideas it is useful because it provides a means of visualization and allows natural hypothesis making. In teaching historical events it sets these events within a multisensory context. VR provides the possibility of aiding learning by allowing the user to experience subject matter. In the next section we give a description of the inner workings of typical VR systems and of the technology that facilitates interactivity and multi-sensory stimulation.

HOW VR WORKS

Figure 2 is a schematic diagram of the possible components of a virtual reality simulation system and how they relate to each other.

At the core of this system is the control software. This determines when the scene should be drawn on display devices (e.g. the haptic and visual interfaces) and handles communication between the interface layer and the virtual world updating the world appropriately when the user performs some action. The control software may also be used to communicate with the outside world via the internet; a feature that is important for collaborative or multi-user systems. The virtual environment module consists of the actual world model together with a representation of the entities within it. This representation includes not only appearance but also state and position information. These entities may be static objects or dynamic entities such as moving objects or even

Figure 2. A schematic view of a VR system

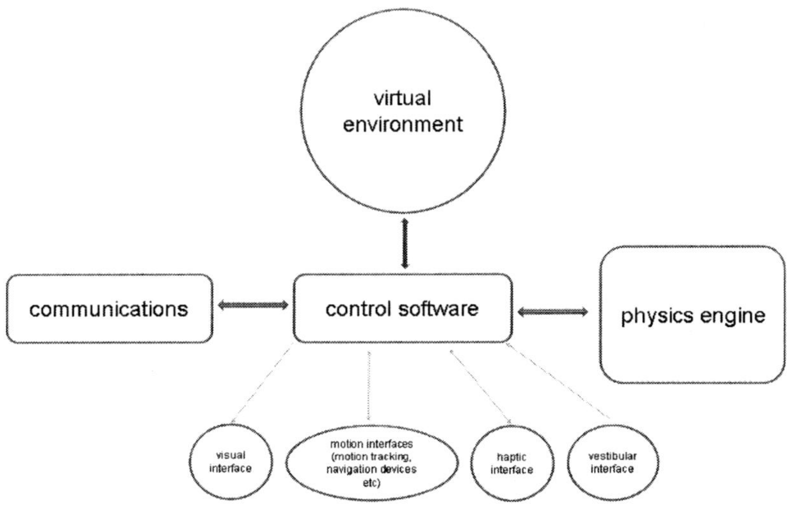

avatars. Dynamic entities must be updated within the virtual environment model on a constant basis. The virtual environment module is a database that stores the form, position and other properties of all constituents of the virtual world.

For realistic simulations a physics engine is a required component (A physics engine is an important requirement to achieve realistic simulations). A physics engine embodies rules that govern the motion and interaction of dynamic objects. Common features of a physics engine include collision detection (calculating when one object intersects with another) and the simulation of the laws of Newtonian mechanics. Using physical laws they implement effects of gravity, friction and motion impulses. The latter effect (impulses) is important in collisions between entities. Collision detection is necessary to detect when two dynamic entities touch and collide with each other. If they do, the physics engine calculates the resulting velocity of both entities according to their simulated 'physical' properties such as their material, mass and velocity.

The sensory interface layer of the system provides input and output to and from the user. It is easily expandable and may include few or many components. Essential components include a visual interface that allows the user to see the world and some form of navigation device. Common visual interfaces include head mounted displays (HMDs) which are used for immersive simulations. HMDs are worn on the head and usually provide a stereoscopic view of the world by projecting a slightly different view of the virtual world to each eye. Other visual interfaces include large screen displays, such as the CAVE developed by the Electronic Visualization Laboratory at the University of Illinois in Chicago and the semi-circular cinema projection screen. The CAVE is a small room in which several people may stand. There are usually 4 projection surfaces (the ground and 3 walls) on which stereo images are projected. The semi-circular screen provides a smooth projection surface with a 180 degree field of view. Both of these require the user to wear stereo shutter glasses. These glasses are synchronized with the refresh of the two images comprising the stereo view of the world and provide a 3D experience.

There are many navigation devices that can be used for VR systems depending on what type of visual input device is used. In the CAVE for example, the user is free to walk around and their position in the virtual space is calculated by a head or body tracker. These trackers are usually electromagnetic devices that detect changes in an electromagnetic field depending on the position of a marker placed on the users' head or limbs. As well as using motion trackers, other common navigation devices include the SpaceMouse which allows 6 degrees of movement (3 for translation, and 3 for rotation) used for desktop systems and the 'data glove' which is a wired glove that tracks movements of the hand.

Additionally, the sensory interface may include a haptics device. Haptic devices allow the user to initiate movements of virtual hands or fingers in the environment (the hand or finger is represented in the environment) and provide haptic feedback to the user when the hand or finger 'touches' an object. Haptic interfaces operate through the use of servo motor combinations similar to those of robot arms used for industrial purposes. A popular haptics interface is the Phantom developed by Sensable Technologies (www.sensable.com) which consists of a stylus or finger thimble. The movement of the finger placed in the thimble is detected and is used to detect collisions between it and the virtual objects represented in the scene. When a collision is detected the motors provide a constraining force to the finger that is appropriate for the shape of the object and its material (hard, soft, liquid etc). Because this process is carried out at up to 1000 times a second it provides a convincing impression of solidity and impedance to motion and is able to simulate a wide range of materials including rubber, ice, glass and liquids as well as a range of dynamics effects such as gravity and other forces. Although haptic interfaces like the Phantom are used in small-scale VR applications (e.g. for desktop systems) large-scale devices have also been developed for use in Cave-like environments (Loscos et al., 2003, Christou et al., 2006).

Advanced virtual environment systems may even include a vestibular interface such as a motion platform. Such devices are often found in flight simulators. They physically respond to events in the simulated world and move the user's seat stimulating their sense of acceleration, orientation and position.

A relative new development in the field of VR is in so called mixed, or augmented, reality. Mixed reality involves both a view of a real-world scenario (such as a desktop, car engine etc) overlaid with 3D virtual detail. In brief, the method works by using a visor through which a user can see a real scene and on which a computer is used to overlay a virtual scene. An initial calibration uses a camera pointed at the real scene to work out the orientation of visible surfaces with respect to the virtual world. If there is a one-to-one mapping between the real and virtual environments then it is possible for data, text, overlays and even virtual characters to be presented interacting with real objects. The usefulness of this for education and training purposes is far reaching because it combines the realism of real world scenarios with the informative detail of computer visualization. Uses include, for example, training for engineers in the functioning of complex mechanisms such jet engines and in medical applications.

APPLICATIONS OF VR IN EDUCATION

The multi-sensory, interactive, nature of VR has made it a popular with many researchers in education, rehabilitation and in cognitive neuroscience. For example, the fact that it can enable a child to interact with a 3D world that can be portrayed in many different forms made it popular with many cognitive psychologists studying how spatial awareness and spatial cognition may be improved in normal students and those with cognitive deficits (e.g. Foreman et al., 2003). This is because the virtual environment is more 'controllable' than the real world. We will restrict our discussion here to application areas within core educational schemes and in training. We give a brief overview of the fields of application of VR in educational contexts but we do not provide a complete listing of specific applications as these are numerous and changing. A thorough description of VR applications in education up to end of the last century is provided by Youngblut (1998). The educational application areas of VR may be categorized into 3 different types:

1. Application in schools and colleges to enhance core curriculum subjects
2. Applications for museums, 'edutainment' and demonstrations
3. Utilization for training

Application in Schools

VR applications in schools and colleges fall into two sub-categories; those in which teachers use pre-developed applications (Cell Biology, Virtual Gorilla Exhibit, MaxwellWorld, Atom World, Newton World, Greek Villa, and those in which students themselves build virtual worlds in order to test hypotheses (Virtual Stage, Wetland Ecology). Pre-developed applications consist of a virtual environment, supporting software and hardware in which students perform a required task. Previous implementations include MaxwellWorld which is part of a suite of three scientific applications called ScienceSpace developed for children aged 9-15 years by Dede and coworkers (Dede, et al., 1996). MaxwellWorld teaches students about electrostatic forces and electric fields by allowing them to position electrical charges and to see and interact with the resultant electromagnetic field. MaxwellWorld is a small-scale VR application occupying a 1 meter cube and with axes used to provide a reference frame. The space is presented in stereo using a HMD and menus are used for interaction. NewtonWorld, also part of ScienceSpace, similarly teaches students about forces in Newtonian Mechanics, and PaulingWorld is used for teaching atomic and molecular structure.

The educational uses of VR is also being investigated by the HITLab at the University of Washington. Previous projects of the HITLab include a HMD stereo system called Atom World which was used to aide teaching of atomic and subatomic particles to Grade 11 students and PhaseWorld used in Chemistry to teach students about state changes in matter and how this depends on volume and ambient temperature and pressure. Current projects of the HITLab are evaluating VR in several teaching areas including visualization in oceanography. Another producer of pre-developed VR systems is Cybernet Systems Corporation which has developed Astronomicon which is a HMD based visualization of the Solar System. Students make changes to planets etc. in order to answer specific questions. They have also developed Virtual Gorilla intended to allow students to reproduce the movements and behaviors of gorillas situated within a gorilla family and within an appropriate habitat.

Other fields where VR techniques are actively being applied for educational purposes are in Cultural Heritage and Archaeology. For example, Learning Sites has developed numerous desktop systems for exploration of Archaeological reconstructions of buildings and sites in Europe and the Middle East. One of these was Attica, Vari House which was developed as a desktop VR system and tested on grade 9 – 12 students. The virtual environment consisted of a reconstructed Hellenic House (modeled using details from excavations). Teaching components included set problem-solving tasks. Another organization that has also been active in the field of cultural heritage is the Institute for the Visualization of History which sells QTVR and VRML models of reconstructed sites such as the Acropolis in Athens. VRML stands for Virtual Reality Modeling Language and was used to quickly set up virtual environment models and the interaction environments in which they could be used. This has now been superseded by X3D which a web based standard that can be used in World Wide Web VR applications.

Museums and 'Edutainment'

A number of research projects have developed VR systems for 'edutainment' in the form of virtual museums. For example, The Exploratorium, which is a public science museum dedicated to teaching science using hands-on exhibits, has recently been ported to Second Life. Second Life (SL) is a large-scale, multiuser, three-dimensional online virtual world. We refer to this as a collaborative environment because multiple users inhabit and interact in the same space and it is displayed as a desktop system using a web browser. You visit this world as an avatar (a representation of oneself) and through the avatar's eyes explore areas and features using navigation controls from a keyboard (www.exploratorium.edu).

More research oriented projects have also built prototype virtual museums for this purpose. The CREATE project (Loscos et al. 2003), an EU funded research project, allowed users to reconstruct an archaeological site. The user's task involved the rebuilding of a temple piece by piece, in order to explore and examine alternative scenarios used in the original construction of the site. The selected site used in CREATE was a location in the ancient city of Messini, founded in 369 BC and located in the South West Peloponnese. Within this site, CREATE focused on the architectural complex of the Doric temple which is located at its centre and although this site is poorly preserved it is well documented, which aided the virtual reconstruction effort.

Training

The final application area of VR in education that we will mention is in training. We might consider training as a separate case of education because it usually entails teaching specific knowledge relating to manual tasks rather than general knowledge. VR training provides a safe environment for training tasks which would otherwise be unfeasible or even dangerous to perform in real life. VR training has been applied to the general fields of transportation, medicine, engineering and military & security. We give a brief overview of these next.

Transportation

Flight simulators were one of the first applications of VR technology. Training pilots to fly using grounded 'simulators' is almost as old as flying itself. Modern VR flight simulators use high resolution computer graphics providing 180 degrees field of view, real instrument panels and motion platforms capable of up to 6 degrees of freedom (translation and rotation). These motion platforms provide the vestibular motion cues which are correlated with auditory and visual events providing highly realistic feedback. Specific simulators are now used for specific aircraft types (e.g. the Airbus A320) allowing commercial pilots to be trained and retrained when transferring from one craft to another and databases of actual airports around the world providing realistic scenarios for take-off and landing. Pilot training is costly both from financial and environmental perspectives, as well as being dangerous. VR simulators therefore provide a commercially viable and safe alternative and can be used to prepare pilots to handling demanding and dangerous situations that would be hard if not impossible to stage in the real world. A leading developer of such systems is Evans & Sutherland (www.es.com); a company that has pioneered developments in computer graphics and VR since 1968.

VR simulators are also being used in other fields of transport. For example driving simulators can be used to train people to drive cars and to handle specific driving conditions including fog and heavy rain. These simulators are similar to flight simulators in that they may be housed on real cars situated on a motion platform to provide vestibular feedback. A number of car manufacturers are adopting this technology. For example, Daimler-Benz has opened its own VR centre for prototyping, ergonomics and for demonstrations.

Medicine

Like pilot training, medical training is an expensive process and involves risk to patients. Conventional medical training therefore required students to use cadavers in initial stages of say surgical training followed by lengthy sessions of overseeing qualified surgeons perform a particular task. Surgical training has benefited the most from developments in haptic feedback devices which provides a realistic sense of control and manipulation of soft body tissue. Most developments of VR in medicine are in training a new range of non-invasive or minimally invasive techniques of endoscopy. Endoscopy has many applications including laparoscopic (operations on the abdomen or pelvic cavity), thoracoscopic (key-hole surgery on the chest) and hysteroscopy (inspection and surgery within the uterine cavity). An endoscope is usually a flexible tube containing a camera and other instruments inserted into the body for visual inspection and for taking biopsies and removing growths and foreign objects. The method involves indirect access to the operation area and therefore causes a lot of disadvantages for the surgeon including restricted vision and difficult hand-eye coordination and handling of instruments with limited mobility. Surgeons require a lot of training and experience to execute an operation successfully and safely. VR endoscopic simulators, such as the Karlsruhe Endoscopic Surgery Trainer (Forschungszentrum Karlsruhe, www.fzk.de), have been developed to reduce the operative risks in training doctors. These systems are usually of the desktop type where real endoscopic equipment is used with a video camera feed being replaced with a computer generated display. The computer display shows simulated regions of the body, tissue membranes, organs etc. New developments include attaching the endoscope arm to a robot arm which provides haptic feedback. The endoscope therefore becomes a haptic end-effector which provides touch feedback when the simulated instrument comes into contact with internal surfaces of the simulated body. Again, this multi-sensory simulation increases the displayable realism and enhances learning by providing interactive control.

Military Training

The last area of application in training is for military purposes; primarily because it allows us to introduce an application of a multi-user 3D environment. These multi-user systems are otherwise known as a distributed interactive simulation (DIS). DIS is a standard for conducting real-time multi-platform war gaming using computers distributed worldwide and is especially used by military organizations. The standard was developed over a series of "DIS Workshops" at the Interactive Networked Simulation for Training symposium, held by the University of Central Florida's Institute for Simulation and Training (IST). The standard was fashioned after the SIMNET distributed interactive simulation protocol, developed in the mid 1980s for Defense Advanced Research Project Agency. SIMNET could potentially handle hundreds of online players and whereas realism, in the form of high fidelity graphics, was not available it was possible to have realistic interaction between 10s or even 100s of participants. For military purposes the benefits here are that users benefit from role playing, planning and operations within a safer environment.

ISSUES RELATING TO THE USE OF VR

Here we consider some of the key problems and drawbacks of using VR as an educational tool. We have identified the following three general and potentially serious drawbacks that have limited or restricted the general application of VR in education:

1. Potentially high financial costs of acquiring a system
2. Lack of realism/fidelity/skill transfer issues
3. Physical effects on end-users

High Costs of Implementing VR Systems

The first of these relates to the high costs involved in developing and/or purchasing a VR system. As we have seen, VR systems consist of software for the control of the visualization, computers for running the software and technology for display and interaction. In the 1990s the relative novelty of the technology meant that relatively few ready-made systems existed and in order to develop a VR setup for an educational application one needed specialist knowledge for acquiring devices and integrating them and for developing control software. Display devices such as a head mounted displays were also expensive with relatively few manufacturers. The continued use of VR however has resulted in the economies of mass production and brought prices of some equipment down. Off-the-shelf educational systems also exist as we have noted and such systems are a cheaper and faster means of utilizing the technology because they do not require development time and development costs. While the technology is relatively new, however, it will remain a relatively expensive alternative to conventional methods of teaching.

Realism

In terms of realism and fidelity the question is how closely the VR simulation resembles the scenario being modeled or visualized. This issue relates both to visual realism and also realism of the dynamics and interaction. Initial visualizations used in VR were indeed rudimentary and lacked such realism. There were two reasons for this. Firstly, the techniques used to generate realistic graphics were quite limited and not fully developed. Secondly, in order to maintain interactivity, graphics display updates should be as high as possible (and certainly above 15 frames per second). However, the greater the realism displayed in the graphics, the greater the processing time required to render them. Most computer graphics methods use shaded polygonal approximations to represent smooth surfaces. To approximate a smooth surface we must therefore use many such polygons otherwise surfaces appear faceted and unrealistic. However, requiring a high polygon count means the computer must do more work and use more memory which in turn slows down the rate at which each frame of the simulation can be rendered. Slow update rates in turn result in sluggish display of movements and slow interactive feedback. Clearly there is a fine balance here between interactivity and realism and the original systems that were developed often sacrificed realism for interactivity.

Realism in visualization is important in as much as it can increase the engagement of the viewer, it can reduce perceptual ambiguity and it can provide redundancy of sensory information, resulting in a richer experience. Much progress has been achieved in the realism obtainable in graphical simulations recently and this is in most part due to the increasing popularity of computer games. The computer games industry has become extremely profitable and this has generated research and development in graphics algorithms and dedicated hardware for rendering graphics and simulating dynamics. This in turn has benefited VR simulations and VR systems. Indeed, while VR systems once required high-end computer support it is now possible to implement rendering, dynamics and interaction control on a single desktop machine. Where additional processing power is required (or the addition of haptics and 3D sound for example) clusters (connected groups) of computer workstations may be used. However, the balancing act between interactivity and realism in many respects still remains.

We believe that viewers can tolerate reduced graphics as long as the simulation is smooth and that there are no delays in interactivity. There are a number of reasons for this. Most importantly, it appears that viewers in a dynamic simulation can make use of dynamics cues (for example head movements) to provide supplementary cues (from motion parallax etc) whenever the depicted scene is ambiguous because of low quality graphics. Original computer games also employed rudimentary graphics and yet the dynamics of the game and absorption into the task made users disregard the low quality graphics. The decision, however, depends on the application. In surgical training, for example, fidelity and realism are of paramount importance. This is counteracted by that fact that the visual environments used in such training are relatively small scale, requiring smaller scenes and are therefore faster to generate and render.

Health Related Issues

Lastly, we consider human factors and physical side effects. These usually manifest themselves in immersive environments and in particular those in which the viewer has to wear a head mounted display. Original HMDs were so heavy that wearers had to be seated to use them. Modern HMDs are much lighter and less invasive and obtrusive although they are significantly heavier than, for example, stereo shutter glasses. HMDs usually consist of two small cathode ray tubes for stereo viewing together with supported optics that magnify the images in front of each eye. Original systems suffered from low resolution as well as heaviness although improvements in resolution are forthcoming. Some of the health related effects of wearing a HMD have been documented by Cobb and coworkers (Cobb et al., 1999). The heaviness of the HMD means that there is the possibility of head shifts within the device itself resulting is misaligned viewing. There is also the potential for fatigue after a user wears the display for a long period of time and, although the lenses in a HMD are close to the eye, there is also a reduced field of view which means that the wearer has to make more head movements than normal. Another issue is that of eye strain resulting from poor adjustments of the optics and other effects such as flicker in the display. Again this is significant only after prolonged usage and the only solution is to limit the amount of time the user spends wearing a HMD.

Another significant health related issue that is not limited to the use of HMD is that of simulator sickness. Simulation sickness, which includes nausea, disorientation and fatigue, usually arises where there is a mismatch between the subject's visual perception and their sense of movement (i.e. derived from the vestibular system). This can occur in wide screen displays as well as with HMDs. Ironically, the better the simulation graphics, the more likely it is that some people will experience simulator sickness. This is because higher quality graphics give a better feeling of movement and thus will be more likely to stimulate the vestibular reflex responses to this perceived movement. Although there is no definitive explanation for simulator sickness, or a remedy for its effects, studies have shown that duration of exposure should be kept to a minimum and that the probability of occurrence is reduced after repeated exposure (Kennedy et al., 2000). Other basic precautions that can be taken include reducing abrupt movements and avoiding changes to the pitch and roll of the visual field.

CONCLUSION

In this chapter we have attempted to convey the usefulness of VR as a technology suitable for education and training purposes. This usefulness is derived from the fact that VR systems are allow the student to experience a wide range of scenarios including those that are physically impossible to set up in the classroom. The range of subject matter that may be taught is enormous; ranging from the sciences and mathematics to history, archaeology and cultural heritage. VR provides the opportunity to visualize the macroscopic world as well as the microscopic world at a human scale thus providing the opportunity to instill an understanding that would be otherwise impossible to achieve using conventional methods.

We have seen that the experiential nature of VR is compatible with a constructivist view of education in which the student is encouraged to explore and experiment in order to form new ideas and concepts and in order to reformulate old ones. VR is a multi-sensory interactive medium which replaces the normal sensory inputs of the subject with artificial sensory signals generated by a computer. These aspects of VR make it ideal for users to initiate similar behaviors in learning as they would in the real world. We have seen that the normal method of deriving information from the world and in forming concepts is multi-sensory in nature with the different senses working together to maximize sensory input and reduce ambiguity. It is increasingly accepted that the provision of multi-sensory inputs allows for disambiguation in real life. Multi-sensory depiction moreover provides a richer environment for the formation of concepts. By using interactive multi-sensory visualization (in the broad sense), complex and abstract concepts may be taught to students. Furthermore, these concepts may be introduced at an even earlier age than is normally possible.

The potential of VR in education is demonstrated by the interest it has generated from researchers and organizations in this field. We have described several examples of the use of VR in educational contexts to give a flavor of the types of application and the subject matter covered. These are not exhaustive with many new applications being currently developed. As well as development of new systems for applied educational purposes, basic research is also being carried out on the effectiveness of using virtual environments and VR on learning and on other cognitive abilities such as memorization, spatial awareness and perception.

As with the introduction of all new technologies, the use of VR has revealed health related issues that have to be addressed. These include adverse effects that can potentially occur with long exposure or continued use. Original systems using HMDs were indeed uncomfortable, especially after continued use. There are also problems regarding simulator sickness. Although the latter occurs infrequently it must be addressed and basic guidelines for reducing its effect are being developed and will be improved in time. Other serious drawbacks include high costs and reduced realism. The former will constrain the general application of VR in schools at least until the technology becomes widespread and thus cheaper. As for realism, there have been many improvements in computer graphics over recent years that will permeate eventually into VR applications. As the technology improves we expect such issues will become less significant and allow for the more general application of this powerful medium.

REFERENCES

Bruner, J. S. (1961). The act of discovery. *Harvard Educational Review*, *31*(1), 21–32.

Burdea, G., & Coiffet, P. (1994). *Virtual reality technology*. New York: Wiley.

Calvert, G. A., Spence, C., & Stein, B. E. (2004). *The Handbook of Multisensory Processing*. Boston: MIT Press.

Christou, C., Angus, C., & Loscos, C. Dettori, A., & Roussou, M. (2006). A versatile large-scale multimodal VR system for cultural heritage visualization. In *VRST '06: Proceedings of the ACM symposium on Virtual reality software and technology*. New York: ACM Press.

Christou, C. G., & Bülthoff, H. H. (1999). View dependence in scene recognition after active learning. *Memory & Cognition*, *27*(6), 996–1007.

Cobb, S., Nichols, S., Ramsey, A., & Wilson, J. R. (1999). Virtual Reality-Induced Symptoms and Effects (VRISE). *Presence (Cambridge, Mass.)*, *8*(2), 169–186. doi:10.1162/105474699566152

Dede, C., Salzman, M. C., & Loftin, R. B. (1996). The development of a virtual world for learning Newtonian mechanics. In P. Brusilovsky, P. Kommers & N. Streitz, (Eds.), *Multimedia, Hypermedia, and Virtual Reality* (pp. 87-106). Berlin, Germany: Springer/Verlag.

Duffy, T. M., & Jonassen, D. H. (1992). *Constructivism and the technology of instruction: A conversation.* Hillsdale, NJ: Lawrence Erlbaum.

Feldman, A., & Acredolo, L. (1979). The effect of active versus passive exploration on memory for spatial location in children. *Child Development*, *50*, 698–704. doi:10.2307/1128935

Foreman, N., Stanton, D., Wilson, P., & Duffy, H. (2003). Spatial knowledge of a real school environment acquired from virtual or physical models by able-bodied children and children with disabilities. *Journal of Experimental Psychology. Applied*, *9*, 67–74. doi:10.1037/1076-898X.9.2.67

Gaunet, F., Vidal, M., Kemeny, A., & Berthoz, A. (2001). Active, passive and snapshot exploration in a virtual environment: influence on scene memory, reorientation and path memory. *Brain Research. Cognitive Brain Research*, *11*(3), 409–420. doi:10.1016/S0926-6410(01)00013-1

Gibson, J. J. (1987). *The Ecological Approach to Visual Perception.* Hillsdale, NJ: Lawrence Erlbaum Associates.

Gregory, R. L. (1974). *Concepts and Mechanisms of Perception.* London: Duckworth.

Kennedy, R. S., Stanney, K. M., & Dunlap, W. P. (2000). Duration and exposure to virtual environments: Sickness curves during and across sessions. *Presence (Cambridge, Mass.)*, *9*(5), 463–472. doi:10.1162/105474600566952

Lee, D. N., & Aronson, E. (1974). Visual proprioceptive control of standing in human infants. *Perception & Psychophysics*, *15*, 529–532.

Loscos, C., Widenfeld, H., & Roussou, M. Meyer, A., Tecchia, F., Drettakis, G., Gallo, E., Martinez, A. R., Tsingos, N., Chrysanthou, Y., Robert, L., Bergamasco, M., Dettori, A., & Soubra, S. (2003). The CREATE Project: Mixed Reality for Design, Education, and Cultural Heritage with a Constructivist Approach. In *ISMAR 03, The Second IEEE and ACM International Symposium on Mixed and Augmented Reality*, The National Center of Sciences, Tokyo, Japan, Oct. 7 - Oct. 10.

McGurk, H., & MacDonald, J. (1976). Hearing lips and seeing voices. *Nature*, *264*(5588), 746–748. doi:10.1038/264746a0

Neisser, U. (1976). *Cognition and reality: principles and implications of cognitive psychology.* New York: W. H. Freeman.

Neisser, U. (1987). *Concepts and conceptual development: ecological and intellectual factors in categorization.* Cambridge, U.K.: Cambridge University Press.

Schuemie, M. J., Van der Straaten, P., Krijn, M., & Van Der Mast, C. (2001). Research on presence in virtual reality. *Cyberpsychology & Behavior*, *4*(2), 183–201. doi:10.1089/109493101300117884

Winn, W. D. (2003). Learning in artificial environments: Embodiment, embeddedness and dynamic adaptation. *Technology, Instruction . Cognition and Learning*, *1*, 87–114.

Chapter 13

From Usability to User Experience:

Evaluating the Educational and Motivational Value of an Augmented Reality Learning Scenario

Costin Pribeanu
National Institute for Research and Development in Informatics, Romania

Dragoş Daniel Iordache
National Institute for Research and Development in Informatics, Romania

ABSTRACT

Augmented Reality (AR) is merging real and virtual environments within a single interaction space. This tight integration of computer technologies into a real environment is creating new opportunities and challenges for the designers of e-learning systems as well as a new kind of user experience (UX) for the learner. More recently, AR-based educational systems were developed that are implementing learning scenarios for primary and secondary schools. An important goal of these novel teaching platforms is to enhance the students' motivation to learn. This chapter reports on the perceived educational and motivational value of an AR-based learning scenario for chemistry based on the results of a user-centered formative usability evaluation. Quantitative and qualitative data were collected during two experiments with students from secondary schools. While the comparison between the two types of measure increases confidence in the evaluation results, the qualitative measures also provide a detailed description of the user learning experience.

INTRODUCTION

The integration of real and virtual environments within a single interaction space is challenging the designers in many application domains such as medicine, education, entertainment and industry. While the configurations based on head mounted displays (HMD) are integrating specific AR devices into a real life environment, the desktop AR configurations are bringing real life objects into a computing environment. The choice of the viewing configuration depends on several conditions such as

DOI: 10.4018/978-1-60566-940-3.ch013

cost, task requirements or maintenance problems (Shim & Kim, 2006).

The user experience with a specific technology depends on how the designers take advantage from the opportunities created by a particular application domain. More recently, AR-based educational systems were developed that are implementing learning scenarios for primary and secondary schools. The increasing interest in using these technologies for the development of e-learning systems is mainly due to their suitability to support new learning paradigms, such as active and collaborative learning.

On another hand, bringing various real life objects into a computing environment is increasing the complexity of the human-computer interaction and requires the development of suitable interaction techniques. In order to prevent usability problems, the interaction components of the AR system have to be tested with users early in the development process. The earlier these problems are identified the less expensive is the development effort to fix them.

According to Theofanos & Quesenbery (2005), formative usability testing is performed in an iterative development cycle and aims at finding and fixing usability problems as early as possible. This kind of usability evaluation is called "formative" in order to distinguish it from "summative" evaluation which is usually performed after a system or some component was developed (Scriven, 1991). Formative usability evaluation can be carried on by conducting an expert-based usability evaluation (sometimes termed as heuristic evaluation) and / or by conducting user testing with a small number of users. In this last case, the evaluation is said to be user-centered, as opposite to expert-based formative evaluation.

This work is based on results from a user-centered formative usability evaluation of an AR-based learning scenario for chemistry which has been developed in the framework of the ARiSE (Augmented Reality for School Environments) research project. The main objective of the ARiSE project is to test the pedagogical effectiveness of introducing AR in primary and secondary schools and creating remote collaboration between classes around AR display systems. An important research goal is to investigate the extent to which each learning scenario is enhancing the students' motivation to learn.

The project is carried on in a consortium of five research partners and two school partners. ARiSE developed a new technology, the Augmented Reality Teaching Platform (ARTP) in three stages thus resulting three research prototypes. In order to get a fast feedback from both teachers and students, each prototype is tested with users during an ARiSE Summer School which is held yearly. The second prototype implemented a chemistry scenario and was tested during the 2nd ARiSE Summer School in Bucharest.

The usability results were useful and revealed several strengths and weaknesses of the implemented scenario (Balog & Pribeanu, 2008). The motivational value of the learning scenario was also analyzed and reported in a previous work (Pribeanu & Iordache, 2008). The results were interesting from both the quantitative and qualitative data but the confidence in our findings is low due to the small number of users and the special context created by the summer school. Therefore we repeated the user testing with a relatively larger number of more representative users.

The basic idea of our approach was to conduct user testing during the summer school in order to get a fast feedback from students having good knowledge in chemistry and to repeat the user testing in different conditions and with a relatively larger number of representative users. The purpose of this chapter is to present, analyze and compare the results of both experiments from the perspective of educational and motivational value. In this respect, we will broaden the scope of traditional usability evaluation to address issues related to perceived utility and attitude towards the system and we will focus on the positive aspects mentioned by students that are describing their learning experience with the teaching platform. The rest of this paper is organized as follows. In the next section we will briefly describe some related work with a focus on UX and constructivist learning approaches. In section 3 we will describe the evaluation set-up. Then we will present and compare the quantitative and qualitative evaluation results that are related to the educational and motivational value of the learning scenario. The paper ends with conclusion and future work in section 5.

BACKGROUND AND RELATED WORK

Usability and User Experience Issues

The ISO/IEC standard 9126 (2001) defined usability as the capability of a software system to be understood, learned, used, and liked by the user when used under specified conditions.

As AR technologies become more widespread, there is an increasing interest in their usability. Designing for usability is not an easy task in the AR field, given the lack of specific user-centered design knowledge and usability data (Bach & Scapin, 2004; Bowman, Gabbard and Hix, 2002; Gabbard et al., 2004; Nielsen & Johansson, 2007). A survey of user-based experimentation elaborated four years ago by Swan & Gabbard (2005) revealed that only 38 out of 1104 articles (published in four main AR publications during 1992-2004) addressed some aspect of HCI and only 21 (~2%) described a user testing experiment. Although the situation changed over the last years there is still little usability data available for the design of specific AR-based applications.

Therefore, a user-centered formative approach is of particular interest for the usability evaluation of AR-based learning systems. Not only it helps to identify usability problems, but it also gives an early feedback on the user experience with the system. On another hand, assessing the learning user experience requires to go beyond the traditional usability approaches.

According to Law et al. (2008) as UX is an emerging research topic in the area of HCI there is neither a consensus on its definition nor a mature methodology for evaluation. In his approach to UX modeling, Marc Hassenzahl (2005) is distinguishing between two kinds of attributes that are giving a product character: pragmatic (related to utility and usability) and hedonic (associated with well being and pleasure). Typical hedonic attributes are attractive, exciting and interesting. Gilbert Cockton (2006) takes a more pragmatic approach on the evaluation of user experience and advocates for grounding UX in some form of intended value. A given context of use brings in front specific values of the application domain. Therefore, measures should be interpreted according to the achieved value that attempt to assess.

According to Sun & Zang (2006) understanding of various factors that influence the users' acceptance of a new technology is crucial. They distinguish between utilitarian and hedonic aspects. Like Hassenzahl, they argue that the character of a system (i.e. predominant utilitarian or hedonic) is perceived by the user according to the tasks it is used for.

The user acceptance is a research direction that emerged two decades ago with the Technology Acceptance Model (TAM) developed by Davis et al. (1989). In this model, the perceived usefulness and perceived enjoyment play an important role in the users' decision to use a given information system. As Dillon & Morris (1996) pointed out, TAM provides with early and useful insights on whether users will or will not accept a new technology. According to Venkatesh et al. (2007), TAM is widely used as an information technology acceptance model able to explain or predict behavioral intention on a variety of information technologies and systems.

Constructivist Approaches to E-Learning and Motivational Issues

Traditionally, there are two main approaches regarding the instructional process: the curriculum-centered approach and the constructivism. The second approach provides with a valid and reliable basis for a theory in various e-learning environments where the challenge for designers is to implement an active, collaborative and authentic learning (Karagiorgi & Symeou, 2005). Therefore, a challenge for the modern education is to integrate traditional and constructive learning approaches.

Social constructivism is viewing each learner as a unique individual with unique needs and backgrounds and is encouraging the learner to arrive at her (his) own version of the truth, influenced by the background, culture or embedded world view. In this respect, learning takes place when the student is able to build conceptual models that are consistent with both what she / he already understands and with the new content. In order to ensure successful adaptation of old knowledge to a new learning experience, a flexible learning direction should be provided (Mantovani, 2001) as well a possibility to put learners in control of the knowledge transfer process (Stary & Tooter, 2006).

A crucial assumption regarding the nature of the learner concerns the level and source of motivation for learning. Motivation is an important factor in education and is appreciated that a high level of motivation is often a prerequisite for success. Conversely, there is a high probability that learning will not be successful if there is a lack of motivation (Holzinger et al., 2006). A way to increase learners' motivation is to integrate educational games that are making the learning process more approachable and enjoyable (Ebner & Holzinger, 2007; Costabile et al., 2008).

A set of heuristics for designing enjoyable user interfaces: challenge, fantasy and curiosity were identified by Malone (1982). These features were also considered as essential characteristics for good educational software by Holzinger et al. (2006). Based on a learner-centered design approach, they extracted a comprehensive list of demands for designing motivating e-learning systems. The main characteristics of the user experience with such a system are: attraction, fun, challenge, fantasy, curiosity, interaction, multi-modality, and ease of use.

AR Technologies and E-Learning

AR-based technologies have a great potential to support new learning paradigms. As pointed out by Chen & Wang (2008), AR can bridge the gap between the theoretical knowledge acquired through analytical activities (such as reading textbooks and listening to lectures) and the practical experience learned from constructive activities.

Traditionally, most of AR-based educational systems targeted students from higher education. A possible reason for this situation is the prohibitive cost of specific AR hardware such as projectors, head-mounted displays and 3D input devices. More recently hardware solutions became less expensive thus allowing the use of novel AR technologies in secondary schools.

Chen (2006) highlighted several benefits for using AR in a constructivist approach to chemistry education: drawing people's attention, enabling students to discover knowledge by themselves, providing a sense of spatial feeling, allowing users to use hands in a direct manipulation with real objects. He reports on an experiment with four undergraduate university students that revealed the advantages of direct 3D manipulation of real objects as compared to a mouse-based interaction in traditional e-learning.

Liu et al. (2007) shown that the AR technology is suitable for the new learning paradigms due to its specific characteristics, such as: enables experiential learning, social or collaborative learning, gives a sense of presence and is interactive. Their approach was grounded in the TAM theory and aimed at exploring the perceived usefulness and perceived enjoyment. They found a positive attitude towards the system which was perceived by students as engaging, interesting and enjoyable (intrinsic motivation) as well as useful for learning process (extrinsic motivation).

According to Manches, O'Malley & Benford (2009), in order to design AR technologies that are effective in supporting the learning process it is important to understand the advantages and limitations afforded by psychical manipulation. They also highlighted the benefits of interacting with physical objects that provide a wealth of visual and tactile information. Users can manipulate individual objects as well as spatial arrangements of objects.

EVALUATION SET-UP

Formative Evaluation Approach

In order to get a fast feedback from both teachers and students, each prototype is tested with users during the ARiSE Summer School which is held yearly. Five schools have been invited to participate at the 2nd ARiSE Summer School that has been held in Bucharest on 24-28 October 2007. From each school, one teacher and 4 students participated that were selected by the teacher based on their communication skills including English language speaking, and knowledge in the target discipline. As such, they are not so representative for the user population.

Then we repeated the evaluation with a relatively larger number of representative users. Two full classes from different schools from Bucharest participated to the user testing on 1-15 November 2007. The basic idea of our approach was to conduct user testing during the summer school in order to get a fast feedback from users having good knowledge in chemistry and then to repeat the user testing in different conditions and with a relatively larger number of representative users. This actually means to perform formative evaluation in two stages and to analyze and compare the results.

Equipment

ARTP is a "seated" AR environment featuring a desktop viewing configuration: users are looking to a see-through screen where computer generated images are superimposed over the perceived image of the real objects which are placed on the table (Wind, Riege & Bogen, 2007). The platform has been registered by Fraunhofer IAIS under the trade mark Spinnstube®.

User testing was conducted on the ARTP of ICI Bucharest which is equipped with 4 AR modules organized around a table, as illustrated in Figure 1. A remote controller Wii Nintendo has been used as interaction tool for selecting a menu item.

The real objects integrated into the chemistry scenario are a periodic table of chemical elements and a set of colored balls (4 colors) symbolizing atoms.

The periodic table has two sides: part A, with full notation of chemical elements and part B, with numbered groups and periods. Part B is used to test how students understand the internal structure of atoms. Each workplace has its own periodic table. Once a ball is placed over a chemical element it could be further used as an atom of that element to form molecules. Further on, molecules placed on the tables could be used to simulate chemical reactions.

Figure 1 illustrates how two students participating at the summer school are placing a ball onto their periodic table.

Participants and Tasks

Two groups of students and two teachers from the partner schools and three groups of students accompanied by a total of 4 teachers from 3 general schools in Bucharest were invited to participate at the 2nd ARiSE Summer School. A total of 20

Figure 1. Students testing the chemistry scenario during the Summer School

students from which 10 boys and 10 girls tested the ARTP. 12 students were from 8th class (13-14 years old), 4 from 9th class (14-15 years old) and 4 from 10th class (15-16 years old). Students have different ages because of the differences related to the chemistry curricula in each country. None of them was familiar with the AR technology.

During the summer school, the participants were assigned 14 tasks: an introduction and 13 exercises related to three lessons. The first lesson is about the chemical structure of the atoms and has 2 exercises. The second lesson is about forming molecules and has 8 simple exercises. The third lesson is about chemical reactions and has 3 exercises.

After the summer school, two full classes of students (8th class), each from a different general school in Bucharest participated at user testing in the period 1-15 November 2007. The total number of participants was 42 students from which 19 boys and 23 girls. None of the students was familiar with the AR technology. Students came in groups of 6-8 accompanied by a teacher, so testing has been organized in 2 sessions.

The students have been assigned only 8 tasks: an introduction, both exercises of the 1st lesson, 4 exercises (from 8) of the second lesson and 1 exercise (from 3) of the third lesson. The number of tasks was reduced because of time limitations: both scenarios were tested in the same day, before or after class hours. Nevertheless, all tasks have been tested and each student tested a representative set of tasks. After finishing the assigned exercises, students were free to perform other exercises or to repeat exercises already performed.

The Evaluation Instrument

In this project we took a broader view on usability evaluation by grounding our work in the technology acceptance model. According to our knowledge, there is no TAM model available for AR-based educational systems. Therefore, a usability questionnaire was developed in this project that is targeting several dimensions such as: the general ergonomics of the ARTP, the usability of the target e-learning application, the perceived utility, the attitude towards the system, and the intention to use (Pribeanu, Balog

& Iordache, 2008). The questionnaire provides with both quantitative and qualitative measures of the educational and motivational values of a new learning scenario. This evaluation instrument has 28 closed items (quantitative measures) and 2 open questions, asking users to describe the most 3 positive and most 3 negative aspects (qualitative measures) regarding their interaction with the system. The closed items are presented in Table 1.

Table 1. The usability evaluation instrument

No.	Item
1	Adjusting the "see-through" screen is easy
2	Adjusting the stereo glasses is easy
3	Adjusting the headphones is easy
4	The work place is comfortable
5	Observing through the screen is clear
6	Understanding how to operate with ARTP is easy
7	The superposition between projection and the real object is clear
8	Learning to operate with ARTP is easy
9	Remembering how to operate with ARTP is easy
10	Understanding the vocal explanations is easy
11	Reading the information on the screen is easy
12	Selecting a menu item is easy
13	Correcting the mistakes is easy
14	Collaborating with colleagues is easy
15	Using ARTP helps to understand the lesson more quickly
16	After using ARTP I will get better results at tests
17	After using ARTP I will know more on this topic
18	The system makes learning more interesting
19	Working in group with colleagues is stimulating
20	I like interacting with real objects
21	Performing the exercises is captivating
22	I would like to have this system in school
23	I intend to use this system for learning
24	I will recommend to other colleagues to use ARTP
25	Overall, I find the system easy to use
26	Overall, I find the system useful for learning
27	Overall, I enjoy learning with the system
28	Overall, I find the system exciting

The first 24 closed items are targeting various dimensions such as ergonomics of the AR platform (items 1-5), usability of the application (items 6-14), perceived utility (items 15-17), attitude towards the system (items 18-21) and intention to use (items 22-24). The remainder four items are to assess how the students overall perceived the platform as being easy to use, useful for learning, enjoyable to learn with and exciting.

Procedure

Before testing, a brief introduction to the AR technology and ARiSE project had been done for all students. Each group of students tested ARTP in a session during 75 min at summer school and 60 min. afterwards. During testing, effectiveness (binary task completion and number of errors) and efficiency (time on task) measures were collected in a log file. Measures were collected for all exercises performed. After testing, the students were asked to answer the usability questionnaire by rating the items on a 5-point Likert scale (1-strongly disagree, 2-disagree, 3-neutral, 4-agree, and 5-strongly agree). Prior to the summer school, the questionnaire was translated in the native language of students.

EVALUATION RESULTS

Quantitative Data Analysis

Reliability of the scale (Cronbach's Alpha) was 0.93 for the first sample respectively 0.94 for the second, which is acceptable.

Overall, the items associated with the perceived utility, attitude and intention to use dimensions were better rated in both samples than the items associated with the usability of the ARTP. The lowest mean values got the items related with the clarity of visual perception (1, 5 and 7).

From an educational and motivational point of view, most interesting are the mean values for

Figure 2. Answers to the questionnaire (items 15-24, 26-28) – mean values

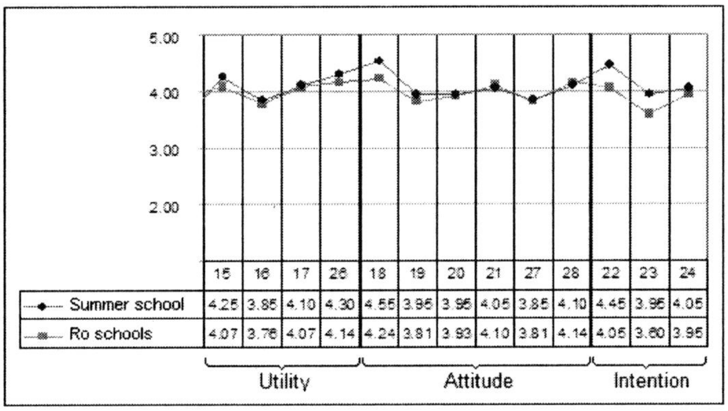

the items 15-24 and 26-28 which are presented in Figure 2, grouped onto the three dimensions.

The mean values of these items were higher (general mean of 4.10 vs. 3.97) for the participants to the summer school. A t-test for independent samples revealed no statistical significant difference between means.

Seven items have mean values over 4.00 for both samples showing that ARTP helps to understand the lesson more quickly (item 15), the students will know more on this topic (item (17), overall ARTP is useful for learning (item 26) and makes learning more interesting (item 18), exercises are captivating (item 21), overall ARTP is exciting (item 28), and the students would like to have it in school (item 22).

A comparative analysis of quantitative measures is revealing two interesting aspects. For the item 18 we have the highest difference between the mean values (0.31) which means that for the participants to the summer school ARTP makes learning much more interesting. For the item 28, we have a higher mean value in the second sample (although the general mean is lower) which means that the students found the system very exciting.

In order to investigate in more detail the educational and motivational value of the ARTP we will compare the answers to items 15-21, and 26-28 with the positive aspects mentioned by students in their answers to the open questions.

Qualitative Data Analysis

The answers to the open questions were analyzed in order to extract key words (attributes). Some students only described one or two aspects while others mentioned several aspects in one sentence

Table 2. Main categories of most positive aspects

Category	(1) Summer school		(2) Romanian schools		Total	
	Frequency	Percent	Frequency	Percent	Frequency	Percent
Educational support	20	28.57	26	27.37	46	27.88
Exciting and motivating	25	35.71	41	43.16	66	40.61
AR visualization & user guidance	17	24.29	10	10.53	27	16.97
Easy to use and other	8	11.43	18	18.95	26	14.55
Total	70		95		165	

Table 3. Categories of positive aspects related to educational support

Item	Aspect (attribute)	(1) Summer school			(2) Romanian schools		
		Frequency	Total	Percent	Frequency	Total	Percent
15	Faster understanding	3	10	50%	2	12	46.15%
	Better understanding	7			5		
	Easier understanding				1		
	Faster learning				1		
	Easier learning				3		
16	Learning more	2	2	10%	-	3	11.54%
	Lesson explanation				3		
17	Good for remembering	2	7	35%	-	5	19.23%
	Better learning	1			4		
	Good for testing	1			-		
	Exercises	3			1		
26	Useful for learning	1	1	5%	3	6	23.08%
	Helps learning	-			2		
	Educative technology	-			1		
	Total	20	20		26	26	

thus yielding a total number of 70 attributes from the summer school participants and 95 from the Romanian students testing the platform after the summer school. Then the attributes were grouped into four main categories which are summarized in Table 2.

The second evaluation confirmed the results from the summer school. In both cases, most of the positive aspects mentioned by students were related to the motivational value. The weight of this category is higher for the second sample (43.16% vs. 35.71%) showing that the need for a more enjoyable learning is stronger for the average student. Overall, the number of positive aspects related to the educational and motivational value collected from both samples account for 68.49% from the total.

Students liked the 3D visualization ("*the 3D visualization of atoms was very well*", "*The creation of molecules and other chemical processes are visualized very nice and demonstrative*" as well as the multimodal interface providing with vocal user guidance throughout the interaction process ("*Explanation complete and easy to understand because of images*", "*The system is telling me if I am performing well or not*"). The total of 27 positive aspects mentioned by students is suggesting the idea that the AR technology is a good facilitator for learning. On total, 50 of the positive aspects (27.88%) are related to the educational value of the ARTP. In Table 3 a detailed grouping of these aspects is presented. The related closed item is specified in the left column.

Most of the aspects are related to item 15 which got a mean of 4.25 in the first sample and 4.07 in the second. Students appreciated that the system provides support for a better understanding ("*Everything is more clear now*", "*I understand better with this system*"), easier understanding ("*I understood the lesson easier than in school*") and easier learning ("*The system make learning more easy*").

The small number of positive aspects related to the gain in new knowledge is consistent with the relatively low rating of item 16 which got the lowest mean value in both sample. This is someway

Table 4. Categories of positive aspects related to motivation

Item	Aspect (attribute)	(1) Summer school			(2) Romanian schools		
		Frequency	Total	Percent	Frequency	Total	Percent
18	Interesting learning	2	10	40%	2	10	24.39%
	Interesting tasks	3			1		
	Interesting atom combination	-			4		
	Interesting experience	-			1		
	Interesting technology	4			2		
	Less boring	1			-		
19	Stimulating team work	1	1	4%	2	6	14.39%
	Good for team work	-			2		
	Collaborating with colleagues	-			2		
20	Mastering the learning process	4	5	20%	-		
	AR interaction	1			-		
21	Captivating exercises	2	2	8%	2	5	12.20%
	Nice exercises	-			2		
	Doing exercises	-			1		
27	Pleasant	-	6	24%	1	10	24.39%
	Attractive learning	3			2		
	Funny	3			7		
28	Novel	1	1	4%	1	10	24.39%
	Unique experience	-			1		
	Fascinating technology	-			2		
	Stimulating	-			1		
	Exciting	-			3		
	Captivating	-			2		
	Total	25	25		41	41	

normal since the AR technology is not intended to support an extensive coverage of the topic.

Students found the scenario good for testing their knowledge and improving their performance on tests. Participants at the summer school mentioned that ARTP helps to better remember the lesson and provides with useful exercises. Also, students from the two Romanian schools found that explanations given before performing the exercises are very useful ("*Explanations before exercises were welcomed*").

A total number of 66 the positive aspects (40.61%) are related to the motivational value of the ARTP. A detailed grouping of these aspects is presented in Table 4. Essentially, these are the hedonic attributes of the ARTP as perceived by students.

Most of the aspects (10) are related to item 18 which got the highest rating in both samples (4.55 respectively 4.24) and clearly shows that the system makes learning more interesting. The difference in the mean values is also consistent with the different number of positive aspects mentioned by each sample for this sub-category (40% vs. 24.39%).

Two students found this learning scenario more interesting than a traditional one: "*The lessons will be more interesting by using a device like this*".

Three students found the tasks (i.e. exercises) very interesting: "*It was very interesting to fill in all periodic table*"; "*The tasks are very interesting. Especially the third one*". Four students mentioned in a more or less specific way that it was interesting ("*It was very interesting*", "*It is interesting to work and interact*", "*The system is interesting*"). One student mentioned that learning with the ARTP is less boring ("*Less boring than the teachers*").

This last aspect also reveals a students' preference to work individually which is consistent with the lower rating of item 19 (3.95/3.81).

The lower rating of the item 20 (3.95/3.93) is closely related with some usability problems. Students complained that it was difficult to distinguish the real balls through the screen because of the augmentation and the superposition of the real and virtual objects.

Nevertheless, the positive aspects mentioned by students participating at the summer school are revealing an interesting facet of a user learning experience: mastering of a chemical process. Students were attracted by the interaction in the AR environment which is giving the students the possibility to build something by their own: "*I was surprised that I was able to interact with balls, to move them whatever where you want. It was like my direct influence to something*", "*You can feel your direct influence. It is great.*", and "*You can feel that something can be created by yourself, not by teachers*". These comments are expressing the students' preference for a learning experience based on learning by doing instead of learning by reading.

Students found the exercises captivating which shows an intrinsic motivation created by the AR technology and the added value of exploiting the need to play, predominant to the age of students in primary and secondary school.

Students liked the idea of learning with ARTP which is both enjoyable and exciting. The attributes extracted from the positive aspects related to the items 27 and 28 are very diverse and express a good user experience. The students found the scenario as being attractive (*"It is very attractive to produce atoms and molecules"*), novel (*"It is something new"*), funny (*"It is funny to touch and move the atoms", "The different colors make learning more funny"*).

For the students in the second sample, most of the positive aspects related to motivation correspond to items 18, 27 and 28 (24.39% each).

Age and Gender Analysis of Aspects Related to Motivation

A grouping by age and gender of the positive aspects which are related to the hedonic attributes of the ARTP is presented in Table 5.

Table 5. Positive aspects by age and gender

Category	(1) Summer school				(2) Romanian schools		Total	
	13-14 years		15-16 years		13-14 years			
	Girls	Boys	Girls	Boys	Girls	Boys	Girls	Boys
Interesting, novel	1	3	5	2	9	2	15	7
Stimulating	1	1	2	2	4	3	7	6
Captivating, fascinating	2	-	-	-	2	5	4	5
Funny	1	1	-	1	3	4	4	6
Attractive, pleasant, nice	-	2	-	1	3	3	3	6
Exciting	-	-	-	-	3	-	3	-
Total	5	7	7	6	24	17	36	30

At summer school, the 8 students from the 9th and 10th classes mentioned a total of 13 positive aspects while the 12 students from the 8th class only mentioned 12 positive aspects that are related to the hedonic function of the ARTP. Older students found the learning scenario more interesting and appreciated the possibility to master the learning process.

The boys found learning with the ARTP more enjoyable and novel than girls. On the other hand, the girls mentioned a greater number of positive aspects related to the interesting and captivating character of the chemistry scenario.

After the summer school the girls mentioned more positive aspects than the boys (24 vs. 17). Like the girls participating to the summer school, they mentioned more aspects related to the interesting character of the chemistry scenario than the boys. On the other hand, the boys found it more funny and captivating.

CONCLUSION AND FUTURE WORK

In this chapter we briefly discussed the quantitative and qualitative data and we mainly focused on the measures related to the educational and motivational value. However, students also mentioned 65 negative aspects in the first evaluation and 116 in the second. These aspects are describing usability problems which are consistent with the relatively low ratings of the items 1-14 and the general item 25, such as lack of superposition accuracy, selection difficulties, and visualization issues. Therefore a future research direction is to investigate to which extent the learning experience is negatively affected by specific usability problems.

The evaluation results provided with an early feedback on the usability of the implemented scenario. The formative evaluation approach was useful and the results from both experiments provided with useful insights on how students perceive an AR-based learning system. The results of this research are showing that measuring the educational and motivational values is providing with useful UX measures. Nevertheless, there are some inherent limitations since it was difficult to relate some aspects to a specific closed item. In order to get more useful results, some more items might be needed. The qualitative data could also gain in accuracy by interviewing students after filling in the questionnaire.

ARTP was perceived by students as a useful teaching aid able to answer the increasing demands of a modern education. The AR-based chemistry scenario is featuring 3D visualization of abstract chemical processes and multimodal user guidance throughout the learning process. The basic idea of this scenario based on the semantic relation between two categories of real objects (balls and periodic table) was perceived by young learners as both useful and enjoyable. Assigning semantics to a colored ball by placing it onto the periodic table is something new and makes learning more interesting. The students liked the idea of "learning by doing" which provides them with a better understanding of the chemical reactions.

Qualitative data results are showing that in both samples most of the positive aspects related to the educational value are pointing to the support for easier and better understanding of the lesson. This suggests that AR-based learning scenarios for primary and secondary schools should focus on topics that are by their nature more difficult to understand.

While item 26 (usefulness for learning) received the highest rating among the general items at the first evaluation (4.30), most of the positive aspects mentioned by the students participating to the summer school were related to motivation. From the one hand, the quantitative data results suggest that they mainly perceived the chemistry lesson as a useful *learning experience*. From another hand, the qualitative data results are revealing the importance of the motivational value for the learning process.

After repeating the evaluation with all students from two classes, item 28 received the highest rating (4.14) among the general items and the quantitative measure is consistent with the number of positive aspects related to motivation. These facts clearly show that the motivational value of e-learning systems is important for the young learners since they are sometimes getting bored in the traditional learning environments.

Overall, a detailed analysis of educational and motivational benefits of an AR-based educational system proved to be useful since it highlighted what the students like in terms of a learning experience. In this respect, it complemented the traditional formative usability evaluation by providing an early feedback on the intended value of the system. This way, the results from a formative usability evaluation help designers to establish priorities not only to fix usability problems but also to enhance the user learning experience.

ACKNOWLEDGMENT

We gratefully acknowledge the support of the ARiSE research project, funded under FP6-023039.

REFERENCES

Bach, C., & Scapin, D. (2004). Obstacles and perspectives for evaluating mixed reality systems usability. In *Proceedings of Mixer Workshop - IUI-CADUI 2004*, Funchal (pp. 72-79).

Balog, A., & Pribeanu, C. (2008). A comparative usability evaluation of two augmented reality learning scenarios. In *Proceedings of SIGMAP 2008 –International Conference on Signal Processing and Multimedia Applications*, 26-29 July (pp. 370-375).

Bowman, D., Gabbard, J., & Hix, D. (2002). A Survey of Usability Evaluation in Virtual Environments: Classification and Comparison of Methods. *Presence (Cambridge, Mass.)*, *11*(4), 404–424. doi:10.1162/105474602760204309

Chen, R. (2006). A study of comparing the use of augmented reality and physical models in chemistry education. *Proceedings of the 2006 ACM international conference on Virtual reality continuum and its applications,* 369-372. New York: ACM Press.

Chen, R., & Wang, X. (2008). An empirical study on tangible augmented reality learning space for design skill transfer. *Tsinghua Science and Technology*, *13*(S1), 13–18. doi:10.1016/S1007-0214(08)70120-2

Cockton, G. (2006). Valuing User Experience. In [Oslo: ACM Press.]. *Proceedings of UX Workshop NordiCHI, 2006*, 100–105.

Costabile, M. F., De Angeli, A., Lanzilotti, R., Ardito, C., Buono, P., & Pederson, T. (2008). Explore! Possibilities and Challenges of Mobile Learning. In *Proceedings of CHI 2008* (pp. 145-154). New York: ACM Press.

Davis, F. D., Bagozzi, R. P., & Warshaw, P. R. (1989). User Acceptance of Computer Technology: A Comparison of Two Theoretical Models. *Management Science*, *35*(8), 982–1003. doi:10.1287/mnsc.35.8.982

Dillon, A., & Morris, M. (1996). User acceptance of new information technology: theories and models. In M. Williams (Ed.), *Annual Review of Information Science and Technology* (Vol. 31, pp. 3-32). Medford, NJ: Information Today.

Ebner, M., & Holzinger, A. (2007). Successful implementation of user-centered game based learning in higher education: An example from civil engineering. *Computers & Education*, *49*(3), 873–890. doi:10.1016/j.compedu.2005.11.026

Gabbard, J., Hix, D., Swan, E., Livingston, M., Herer, T., Julier, S., et al. (2004). A cost-effective usability evaluation progression for novel interactive systems. In *Proceedings of Hawaii International. Conference on Systems Sciences* (pp. 90276c). Washington, DC: IEEE.

Hassenzahl, M. (2005). The thing and I: understanding the relationship between user and product. In M. Blythe, K. Overbeeke, A. Monk, & P. Wright (Eds.), *Funology: from usability to enjoyment* (pp. 31-42). New York: Springer.

Holzinger, A., Pichler, A., & Maurer, H. (2006). Multi Media eLearning Software TRIANGLE Case-Study: Experimental Results and Lessons Learned. *Journal of Universal Science and Technology of Learning*, *0*(0), 61–92.

ISO 9126-4:2001. (n.d.). *Software Engineering - Software product quality. Part 1: Quality model.*

Jeon, S., Shim, H., & Kim, G. (2006). Viewpoint Usability for Desktop Augmented Reality. *The International Journal of Virtual Reality*, *5*(3), 33–39.

Karagiorgi, Y., & Symeou, L. (2005). Translating Constructivism into Instructional Design: Potential and Limitations. *Educational Technology & Society*, *8*(1), 17–27.

Law, E., Bevan, N., Gristou, G., Springett, M., & Larusdottir, M. (2008). *Meaningful measures: valid useful user experience measurement - VUUM Workshop*, Reykjavik. COST Action 294 – MAUSE.

Liu, W., Cheok, A. D., Mei-Ling, C. L., & Theng, Y.-L. (2007). Mixed reality classroom: learning from entertainment. In *Proceedings of the 2nd international conference on Digital interactive media in entertainment and arts* (pp. 65-72). New York: ACM Press.

Malone, T. W. (1982). Heuristics for Designing Enjoyable User Interfaces: Lessons from Computer Games. In *Proceedings of the 1982 conference on Human factors in computing systems*, Gaithersburg, MD, United States (pp. 63–68).

Manches, A., O'Malley, C., & Benford, S. (2009). Physical manipulation: evaluating the potential for tangible designs. In *Proceedings of the 3rd International Conference on Tangible and Embedded Interaction* (pp. 77-84). New York: ACM Press.

Mantovani, F. (2001). VR Learning: Potential and Challenges for the Use of 3D Environments in Education and Training. In G. Riva & C. Galimberti (Eds.), *Towards CyberPsychology: Mind, Cognitions and Society in the Internet.* Amsterdam: IOS Press.

Nielsen, S., & Johansson, B. (2007). Fun and Usable: Augmented Reality Instruction in a Hospital Setting. In [New York: ACM Press.]. *Proceedings of OzCHI*, *2007*, 123–130. doi:10.1145/1324892.1324915

Pribeanu, C., & Iordache, D. D. (2008). Evaluating the motivational value of an augmented reality system for learning chemistry. In A. Holzinger (Ed.), *Proceedings of USAB 2008* (LNCS 5298, pp. 31-42). New York: Springer.

Price, S., & Rogers, I. (2004). Let's get physical: the learning benefits of interacting in digitally augmented physiscal spaces. *Computers & Education*, *43*, 137–151. doi:10.1016/j.compedu.2003.12.009

Scriven, M. (1991). *Evaluation thesaurus* (4th ed). Newbury Park, CA: Sage Publications.

Stary, C., & Tooter, A. (2006). On Learner Control in e-Learning. In *Proceedings of ECCE 06 – Trust and Control in complex Socio-technical Systems* (pp. 41-48). New York: ACM Press.

Sun, H., & Zhang, P. (2006). Causal Relationships between Perceived Enjoyment and perceived Ease of Use: An Alternative Approach. *Journal of the Association for Information Systems*, *7*(9), 618–645.

Swann, J. E., II, & Gabbard, J. (2005). Survey of User-Based Experimentation in Augmented Reality. In *Proceedings of 1st International Conference on Virtual Reality*, July 22-27, Las Vegas, Nevada.

Theofanos, M., & Quesenbery, W. (2005). Towards the Design of Effective Formative Test Reports. *Journal of Usability Studies*, *1*(1), 27–45.

Venkatesh, V., Davis, F. D., & Morris, M. G. (2007). Dead or Alive? The development, trajectory and future of technology adoption research. *Journal of the Association for Information Systems*, *8*(4), 267–286.

Wind, J., Riege, K., & Bogen, M. (2007). Spinnstube®: A Seated Augmented Reality Display System. In *Virtual Environments, IPT-EGVE – EG/ACM Symposium Proceedings* (pp. 17-23).

Section 5
Affective Computing in E-Learning Environments

Section 5 examines some interesting ideas of affective computing and their utilization in e-learning systems. Although automatic emotion recognition is not yet as effective as one may expect adding emotion expressivity in technology enhanced learning is feasible and it is presented throughout this section.

Chapter 14

The Potential of Affective Computing in E-Learning: The Journey from Theory to Practice in the "Myself" Project

Fabrizia Mantovani
University of Milan-Bicocca, Italy

Linda Confalonieri
University of Milan-Bicocca, Italy

Marcello Mortillaro
Swiss Center for Affective Sciences, Switzerland

Olivia Realdon
University of Milan-Bicocca, Italy

Valentino Zurloni
University of Milan-Bicocca, Italy

Luigi Anolli
University of Milan-Bicocca, Italy

ABSTRACT

The main goal of this chapter is to discuss the potential of affective computing for improving the e-learning experience, both from a theoretical and a practical perspective. First, we focus on the important role emotions play in the (e-)learning process and on the rationale to include affect in e-learning design . Second, we briefly present three trends in the affective computing domain which represent the core features of the EU-funded project on technology-enhanced learning "Myself": the use of affective Embodied Conversational Agents as virtual tutors; the possibility of automatic recognition of - and adaptation to- the emotional and motivational state of the learner; the use of 3D simulations for web-based training of emotional competence. Finally, focusing on the feature of automatic recognition and adaptation, we present an account of the approach developed within the project and use it as a framework for discussing the main benefits and current limitations to the complex process of integration of affective computing features into e-learning systems.

DOI: 10.4018/978-1-60566-940-3.ch014

INTRODUCTION

The design and implementation of personalized e-learning solutions, tailored to learners' and trainees' characteristics currently represents one of the most relevant challenges to better leverage the opportunities offered by technology-enhanced learning.

Together with the effort of adapting to individual preferences, levels of knowledge, and learning styles, some recent advances in research on the use of adaptive media for learning have highlighted the importance of including users' mental states (affective and cognitive), as a key element in the design of personalized **e-learning** systems (D'Mello, Picard, & Graesser, 2007; Prendinger, Mori, & Ishikuza, 2005).

The underlying assumption is that a technology-enhanced learning system which is able to identify and respond to the dynamic changes in emotional, attentional, and cognitive states of the learner (which are strongly intertwined with the ongoing learning process), would highly empower the effectiveness and efficacy of the process, increase users' satisfaction, as well as significantly reduce drop-outs, offering therefore benefits at both individual and organizational level.

In particular, the role **emotions** play in learning processes is more and more acknowledged both in educational and cognitive sciences research literature (Gardner, 1999; Kinard, 2001; LeDoux, 1998; Schutz & Pekrun, 2007).

In academic and educational contexts, emotions were found to be significantly related to student motivation, learning strategies, cognitive resources and achievement (Pekrun, Goetz, Titz, & Perry, 2002). As stated by Barrett and Salovey (2002), affect in learning facilitates the development of persistence and interest in a topic; also, emotions can influence learning through information processing activity and organization of recall (Pekrun et al., 2002). Our learning, therefore, is heavily dependent on the emotional state we are in (LeDoux, 1998), and on the dynamic pattern of positive and negative emotions occurring in a given time period within a learning context (Sansone & Thoman, 2005).

In particular, studies in cognitive sciences pointed out how positive and negative emotions can trigger different neural activity patterns and thinking styles (Damasio, Grabowski, Bechara, Damasio, Ponto, Parvizi, & Hichwa, 2000; Isen, 1999; Lane, Reiman, Ahern, Schwartz, & Davidson, 1997): on the one hand, the presence of a positive emotional state can foster a thinking style characterized by higher creativity and flexibility in problem-solving, by more articulated information processing and higher efficacy in decision-making (Isen, 1999; Picard, Papert, Bender, Blumberg, Breazeal, Cavallo, Machover, Resnick, Roy, & Strohecker, 2004); on the other hand, negative emotions, such as fear, sadness and anger, can influence the blood inflow to different brain areas, making learning more difficult (Damasio et al., 2000; Lane et al., 1997).

Moreover, emotions are intrinsically related to the learner's ongoing evaluation of the experience, since they are linked to control- and value-related appraisals within a learning environment (Gläser-Zikuda & Mayring, 2003): their expression by the learner can therefore represent an important source of information to a teacher or a tutor in order to tune and adapt rhythm, contents and strategies. For instance, positive emotions generally indicate that successful task-control and interest have been experienced, as well as negative emotions such as frustration, puzzlement and confusion can suggest that some form of feedback might be opportune.

When the learning process takes place in e-learning settings, some specific features can make the affective issue more difficult to deal with but at the same time even more relevant. On the one hand, in fact, the reduced social presence experienced, due to both the longer time spent in self-directed, individual learning and to the reduced communication cues (in particular nonverbal) available when interacting with teachers/tutors and peers, can make it harder to infer the learners' emotional and motivational state along the path and to consistently adapt to it. On the other hand, the interaction with technology and with e-learning contents can pose some additional challenges to the affective quality of the learning experience, due both to the possible technical and usability problems directly related to the technology (e.g. network delays, unsatisfying ergonomics, etc.) and to the features of the e-learning contents and formats, which, despite many efforts and advances, still consist mainly of text-based materials organized in a quite rigid way.

In order to effectively support the learning process, it is therefore of extreme importance to address this need for systematically considering affect both in the design and delivery of the e-learning experience.

Traditionally, this need is addressed in a number of ways, going from an increase in the quantity and quality of forms of collaborative learning and blended learning, as well as with providing higher support to the learner through online tutoring.

More recently, the emergence of the affective computing domain, within Human-Computer Interaction, has suggested that these technologies might represent a valid tool to integrate in order to deal with emotional aspects in the learning process (Picard et al., 2004).

Affective Computing is a field of research dealing with the computational processing of **emotions** in human-computer interaction (Picard, 1997). More specifically, it can be defined as "computing that relates to, arises from, or deliberately influences, emotion" (Picard, 1997) and it aims to endow computer systems with the ability to express, model, communicate, and respond to emotion (Picard, 2003).

In the last five-ten years, a number of projects and research studies have investigated the possible role of affective computing in technology-enhanced learning (among others, D'Mello, Picard, & Graesser, 2007; Kapoor, Mota & Picard, 2001; Kort, & Reilly, 2001; Prendinger, Mori, & Ishikuza, 2005; Zhou & Conati, 2004). In particular, it is possible to identify three trends in affective computing which hold a potential for enhancing the e-learning experience: first, the use of Animated Pedagogical Agents with affective features as virtual tutors; second, the possibility of automatic recognition of (and adaptation to) learner's emotional and motivational state; third, the use of 3D **simulations** and immersive environments for web-based training of emotional competence.

First, ensuring adequate levels of social presence in individual e-learning settings entails more than providing a learning environment with the mere visual presence of virtual agents playing the role of tutors. In order to create, maintain and modify suitable relationships with the users, agents need both to be designed according to consistent pedagogical models and to be appropriately endowed with communicative and emotional competence. The achievement of this goal requires integration between the work carried out in the domains of Animated Pedagogical Agents (APAs) and Embodied Conversational Agents (ECAs). Animated Pedagogical Agents are autonomous personal agents characterized by a visible presence in the user interface, designed to facilitate learning in computer-based environments (Moreno, 2005; Baylor, 1999). Indeed, from the late nineties, research on human-like agents and Embodied Conversational Agents has shown that agent anthropomorphism is not a benefit in itself, unless it is coupled with adequate expressive, conversational and interactive abilities (Cassell, Sullivan, Prevost, & Churchill, 2000). In current research, ECAs are defined as a kind of software agent, that use speech, gaze, gesture, intonation and other signalling systems similarly to humans in the communication process (Cassell, 2000; De Rosis, Pelachaud, Poggi, Carofiglio, & De Carolis, 2003; Bickmore & Picard, 2004). An ECA with affective (expressive and adaptive) features is typically able to express **emotions**, both verbally and nonverbally, and it is also endowed with a cognitive and affective architecture. Within the learning process, the affective tutor is not only intended to create a friendly and engaging learning environment. It is also expected to assist the learner increase his metacognitive awareness and improve his emotion regulation abilities in coping with difficulties encountered during learning.

Second, when discussing the adaptive features of e-learning systems, an important opportunity for **affective computing** to enhance instructional technology is the possibility to provide the system with the ability to infer user's **emotions** (based on multimodal user signals) and react to them by adapting the learning path and experience. We will present and discuss this feature in more depth in the central part of this chapter.

A third emerging trend in affective computing aims at responding to the up-to-now limited focus on soft skills in elearning, with an emphasis on experiential learning. To succeed in today's economy, organizations need to develop core competencies in responding to, and even thriving on, change. These competencies depend not only on professionals' ability to think critically, to solve problems, and to anticipate new possibilities, but also on their ability to manage relationships. Social, emotional and communicative skills have traditionally been considered as typical face-to-face/classroom learning topics. The learning of these capabilities is rooted in real and social experience, since they require a number of (verbal and nonverbal) cues that are managed hic et nunc in the flow of the communicative exchange. So far, few opportunities exist to learn by experience in an e-learning environment that can combine user trial-and-error with an adequate scaffolding structure, affording the learner both the opportunity to fail and the opportunity to make sense of her mistakes and experience. Despite this view, some recent work on computer-based interactive **simulations** and embodied agents (Aldrich, 2003; Enz, Zoll, Vannini, Schneider, Hall, Paiva, & Aylett, 2007; Paiva, Dias, Sobral, Aylett, Sobreperez, Woods, Zoll, & Hall, 2004), as well as on modelling of emotional intra- and interpersonal dynamics, offers new opportunities for training in communication and emotional competence in a variety of professional contexts.

The EU-funded **MYSELF project** (Anolli et al., 2008) recently tried to integrate these three levels of **affective computing** in an e-learning system. Myself (short title for "Multimodal e-learning System based on Simulations, Role-Playing, Automatic Coaching and Voice Recognition interaction for Affective Profiling"; web-site: http://www.myself-proj.it) is a 'CRAFT' project (Cooperative Research within Support Measures to Small and Medium Enterprises-SMEs), funded by the European Commission under the 6th Framework Programme. It involved fourteen partners, from six different EU countries, including universities and research labs, as well as large companies and SMEs from the educational and IT sectors.

The main goal of the project was the design and development of a web-based platform with affective computing capabilities for individual and collaborative learning **simulations**. The focus of the Myself platform was to provide training in soft skills for two different professional settings: banking and health-care. The platform was designed and validated for web use, and tried to use affective computing for the enrichment of the e-learning experience through the integration of a **virtual tutor** named Linda, a module for automatic inference of user's emotional state from multimodal signals, and a set of 3D interactive simulations for the training of communication and emotional skills. The specific features of the call under which Myself project was funded, aiming at significantly fostering the partner SMEs' innovation power and position on the market resulted in a concrete focus on the implementation of all the three affective computing features into a marketable solution. This required to face (and partially solve) questions and challenges relevant for the actual implementation and diffusion of affective computing solutions in e-learning systems.

In order to provide a systematic account of the main design issues and problems, as well as of the experienced solutions and envisaged recommendations, in the central and main part of this chapter, we will focus only on the feature of automatic recognition and adaptation. After discussing some of the most important questions and choices driving the design of this feature, we present an account of the approach developed within the project and use it as a framework for discussing the main benefits and current limitations to the complex process of integration of affective computing features into e-learning systems.

RECOGNIZING AND REACTING TO THE EMOTIONAL AND MOTIVATIONAL STATE OF THE USER: ISSUES, CONTROVERSIES, AND PROBLEMS

Designing an emotional recognition and adaptation feature to be used within an e-learning system entails using technology, within a sound pedagogical framework, in order to make an automatic inference about the emotional state of the user, and subsequently to consistently and dynamically adapt the learning process according to it.

The implementation of this feature requires therefore a cognitive architecture and an inferential engine with two main components:

a. **Recognition:** Operating the automatic recognition (or better, inference) of the user's emotional state
b. **Dynamic adaptation:** Triggering consistent reactions of the system according to the detected emotional state

In order to achieve this goal, a number of important theoretical and design issues need to be faced, leading to *choices* and trade-offs along the design and implementation process:

- Which **emotions** do we want the system to recognize? What are the relevant emotional states to consider in learning? Under which theoretical paradigm should we build our model?
- From which input and sources are we going to gain information about the emotional state of the learner? Which dynamic signals, which users' and tasks' profile information to use as an input? And more, as there are further specific questions underlying each of these inputs: how are these data acquired and processed? Which algorithms to use to fuse them together within a reliable inferential engine?
- When should the emotion recognition feature be active? When shall we proceed to the inference (that is, at which stages in the learning process should the system be emotionally aware? Continuous monitoring and/or in specific points?)
- Which forms of adaptation and reactions should the system display as a function of the user's emotional state? What kind of actions and changes can/should it perform? How to effectively map these reaction categories onto emotional states?

Of course all of these questions have many further underlying levels of questions to solve but our goal in this section, due to length limitations, is to provide a general discussion of these issues to set up a preliminary framework for the design of an affect recognition device and its functional integration into the e-learning system.

Moreover, all of them are clearly intertwined and need to be framed in (and answered within) a unique and consistent pedagogical framework but in this case we will analyze them separately to provide a more systematic account.

Which Emotions to Consider?

A first issue concerns the question about which are the emotional states that should be considered and that we would like our system to be able to infer. This is far from being a trivial question, since there is currently no agreement within the scientific community about what an emotion actually is and whether emotional states are better understood and described in terms of discrete/categorical vs continuous/dimensional approaches (see Kagan, 2007, for a systematic account of these debates). Despite the lack of a shared definition, "the extent to which emotional upsets can interfere with mental life is no news to teachers. Students who are anxious, angry or depressed don't learn; people who are caught in these states do not take information efficiently or deal with it very well" (Goleman, 1995). Although the relationship between learning and emotions is far from being that simple and linear, it is now recognized that positive and negative affect states trigger different kinds of thinking, and this may have important implications for perspectives on education and training.

A range of emotions occur naturally in a real learning process, from positive ones (e.g. joy, satisfaction, elation, etc. in the case of successful achievement), to negative ones (e.g. frustration, sadness, confusion as a result, for instance, of failure and lack of understanding), to emotions more related to interest, curiosity and surprise elicited by a new topic (Kort & Reilly, 2001; Mostafa Al Masum & Ishizuka, 2005). An effective regulation of one's own emotions along the learning cycle is also very important to ensure the focusing of cognitive resources and attention.

Which Inputs to Use in the Inferential Engine?

Starting from the assumption that emotions are multidimensional processes (including physiological reactions, cognitive evaluations, verbal and nonverbal expressions through voice, face, body, subjective feelings, action tendencies), different modalities to detect **emotions** have been proposed (see Pantic & Rothkrantz, 2003, for a review): self-report measures (questionnaires, text and or picture-based); verbal speech (uttered and/or typed); observational **nonverbal measures**, including vocal parameters (time, intensity, frequency, etc.), facial expressions, posture and gestures; psychophysiological measures (biosensor analysis) such as heart rate, blood pressure, breathing rhythm, GSR (galvanic skin response), oximetry, electromyiography (EMG), as well as neural activity indicators.

On the whole, each of these measures has specific characteristics and requirements for data acquisition and processing. In particular, for example, nonverbal behavioural and physiological measures need a device to capture the signals related to the behavioural component of interest (e.g. microphone, webcam, physiological sensors), a processing procedure of these signals in order to extract relevant features, and the application of different algorithms for emotional classifications and clustering (see Oudeyer, 2003, for a review and critical analysis).

All of the mentioned potential input sources present their strengths and limits in terms of different criteria: reliability, need for data acquisition hardware, intrusiveness, costs, etc, (see Zurloni, Mantovani, Mortillaro, Vescovo, & Anolli, 2007, for a review).

Each of them alone is generally insufficient to correctly infer a user's emotional state, and the possibility of a full understanding and sense-making of the ongoing emotional process requires both bottom-up (real-time signals from the user) and top-down (data about user characteristics, learning tasks and context) information (see Zeng, Pantic, Roisman, & Huang, 2009, for an updated account of state of the art and challenges in affect recognition methods). Therefore, a sound approach to emotional automatic inference should consider on the one hand the adoption of a multimodal approach; on the other hand, the integration (in the inferential engine) of the bottom-up, real-time information about the user with information coming from individual characteristics (e.g. personality characteristics, level of knowledge, assessed at the very beginning, etc.) and from task information (topic, level of difficulty, multimedia format etc.) in a comprehensive cognitive architecture.

When Should the Detection of Emotion Be Performed?

With regard to the timing issue, emotion recognition processes may be activated in three different periods vis-à-vis the learning path: measurement immediately before and/or after the learning process; measurement during the learning process; and stimulated recall measurement of emotions after the learning process (Wosnitza & Volet, 2005).

Measuring **emotions** just before or after the learning process, on the one hand does not interrupt the learning experience but, on the other, requires specific pre-scripted moments to be integrated that may irritate the user and may lose efficacy due to the delay between the emotional experience and the emotional assessment. The delay factor also impairs the effectiveness of the "emotional coping" that the system should ideally carry out. Similar, but amplified, drawbacks apply to stimulated recall measurement.

Emotion recognition during the learning process may be a better solution. This involves real-time emotion assessment, with the potential to be time-effective when an emotionally relevant modification occurs. On the other hand, real-time emotion automatic recognition faces greater technical challenges than the other possible timing options, and furthermore needs to be as truly automatic as possible in order to minimize the risk of disrupting the learning process. In consequence, a balanced recommendation is for real-time emotion recognition to take place in specific and critical learning moments; moreover, it is clear that the answer cannot be independent of the learning material and activities, the context and the target users, and still requires careful and grounded pedagogical design.

Which Forms of Adaptation and Which Reactions Should the System Display?

Once an inference on the emotional state of the learner has been made, the next challenge is how to make the most out of these recognition capabilities to optimize and enhance the learning experience. In fact, to be pedagogically effective, the system should include a cognitive architecture modelling together affective states and learning process, allowing the system to consistently personalize the learning path according to the user's affective profile and to provide relevant responses to changes in user motivational and affective states during the training experience (adapting path order, level of difficulty, conversational interventions by tutor, specific activities, etc.). The issue here is not only at a technical level, but is also and mainly at a conceptual one. As to the design of the set of reactions and kind of adaptive responses that the system should provide, two different broad categories of action might be envisaged: one aimed to actively and directly impact on the learning materials and activities (change in the structure of the path, level of difficulty, suggestion of a support theoretical tutorial, changes in the format, etc.); another focused on supporting an effective self-regulation of potentially dysfunctional emotional states through the intervention of a virtual (an APA and/or a human) tutor, who may provide *ad hoc* suggestions and specific activities.

DESIGN AND IMPLEMENTATION OF EMOTION RECOGNITION IN THE MYSELF SYSTEM: THE FIRST PROTOTYPE

Within this section, we will briefly describe the process and specific choices which lead to the development of the fist prototype of the emotion recognition module in the Myself project.

First of all, a preliminary research phase was carried out to build a multimodal database, focusing on several emotional states most pertinent to the training process (including interest, frustration, joy/satisfaction, boredom, etc.). This work provided useful indications for the implementation of the user emotion recognition system and constituted vital groundwork for the training and testing of algorithms and decision systems (Anolli, Mantovani, Mortillaro, Vescovo, Agliati, Confalonieri, Realdon, Zurloni, & Sacchi, 2005). Importantly, this preliminary study also served to evaluate the feasibility of implementing the different channels/modalities in prospective e-learning applications, across several key parameters such as technical requirements, costs, reliability, intrusiveness, which all need to be considered carefully when defining the final solution. The degree of intrusiveness of the different devices for our target users had to be assessed, since the final aim of Myself is the implementation of a concrete e-learning platform to be used in everyday working contexts. For example, having a hand blocked by physiological sensors while interacting with a computer can be very irritating. Cost was another fundamental issue, since the commercial application of the Myself platform is a further objective of the project. Technical difficulties had likewise to be addressed, especially going forward to the next stages of Myself involving the provision of personalized feedback by the system in reaction to the emotional and motivational state of the user.

Within this framework, and according to the output of the phase of database building and analysis, we excluded from the first version of the prototype the physiological correlates and nonverbal behavior meant as facial expression and posture, for a number of reasons. First of all, the real-time measurement and processing of physiological correlates proved in our case to have limited accuracy, especially when done in natural contexts (like for example, in offices) since the measures could vary quite broadly for contingent reasons. Moreover, this measurement was perceived by our participants as overly intrusive, artificial and "cumbersome". As far as facial nonverbal behavior is concerned, technical difficulties were even higher in natural contexts, where continuous illumination levels variations, presence of glasses in a significant numbers of our participants were more than exceptions. Also, costs and development time envisaged at time of the prototype design (started in early 2006) for real-time stable solutions not requiring human intervention were still very high.

On the other hand, since the Myself e-learning system was already endowed with **speech recognition** capabilities, and the user browsing and interaction with the system is mostly voice- and dialogue- based, the use of verbal and vocal non-verbal cues appeared as feasible and relatively unobtrusive.

Therefore, the first version of the **Myself** prototype included in the platform a module for automatic emotion recognition based on three input modalities: verbal speech, self-report questionnaires, and vocal non verbal features.

The prototype integrated the module for affective recognition and adaptation in the more general architecture of the e-learning system, being more specifically a component of the virtual autonomous tutor LINDA (*Learning INtelligent Dynamic Agent*). LINDA represents the guide and partner for the learner along the whole learning path, and has also the function of interface for the affective aspects.

What follows is a synthetic description of how and when the automatic recognition device comes into play along the interaction of the learner with the Myself system.

At the beginning, the user goes through "start-up" phase consisting of three different moments. First, she is presented a traditional tutorial to start using the general Myself system (what she needs to do in order to browse the different activities and contents present in the e-learning platform, such as the interactive simulations, the tutorials, the exercises, etc.).

Second, in order to build an individual vocal database to train the system to the automatic participant's speech recognition, the participant is asked to utter a predefined set of words that will be then recognized by the system on a phonetic basis.

Third, an explanation is provided to the participant about how to manage the voice-based interaction with the system.

Fourth, the user is told about the multimodal emotion recognition device and is presented the instruments for the self-report of affective states.

In particular, the participant is explained that there will be specific moments along the path where her emotional and motivational state will be monitored, partially unobtrusively and partially not, and that the **virtual tutor** will ask her a feedback on her affective state during the experience; this request is explicitly motivated to the learner as a way to gather useful information to define how to carry on in the learning activities in a interesting and effective way. Presenting this information and explanation at the very beginning of the experience is crucial in order to overcome potential skepticisms and obstacles concerning the use of an emotional recognition system. It also allows for a better acceptance of the more automatic part of the process of emotion recognition, giving the feeling that the output of the process (in terms of the inferences done according to the information acquired by the system) would somehow be kept within the control of the learner and would work in the direction of supporting her learning path. Both our preliminary user needs analysis and the following pilot validation study, in fact, highlighted the importance of involving the learner and considering her as an active participant in the process of identification and regulation of the emotions experienced during the learning process.

As far as *verbal speech* is concerned, the participant is invited to communicate to the system her affective state through a number of adjectives as clearly as possible, avoiding interjections, full pauses and other elements that might result in a "disturbance" for the system. The proprietary **speech recognition** engine (called "Dialogo Attivo") is able to manage, beyond more conventional interaction commands (such as "open", "close", "pause", etc.), also a relatively broad number of affective terms. This emotional lexicon, built *ad hoc* for our prototype, consists of about 130 adjectives (in both masculine and feminine version) which were identified through an extensive review of studies carried out on emotions (both in Italian and foreign languages) (Gius, Cozzi, & Spagnotto, 1992; Omondi, 1997; Ortony, Clore, & Collins, 1988).

As to *self-report instruments*, we used a pictorial interface: the participants expressed their emotional state by choosing two figures within two sets, one referring to the hedonic dimension of the emotional state, the other to activation. The reference model for building this instrument was the Self Assessment Manikin (Bradley & Lang, 1994).

As far as *vocal nonverbal analysis* is concerned, we built a large database of vocal stimuli referring to the specific emotions considered. This database has been validated and used for the training of the emotional clustering algorithms according to a number of acoustic features (related to pitch, intensity, rhythm, etc.). In order to reach this objective the technical development partners in the project developed a dedicated, proprietary acoustic analysis software, integrated in the Myself platform. As to the clustering algorithms, the team used and integrated in the platform the open-source software WEKA (http://www.cs.waikato.ac.nz/ml/weka/). Several clustering algorithms were tested and compared, including k-nearest neighbor,

Decision tree, bayesian networks, reaching in the final steps an average success classification rate of 70%. These results, although encouraging, indicate a need for further work on database development and testing, including a better individual user acoustic profiling and the possibility to implement forms of genetic algorithms.

On the whole, the above described recognition modalities are triggered by the system in a series of specific moments of user interaction. The identification of these moments follows three criteria: a) as little as possible interruption of the learning activity; b) presence of relevant transition points in user-system interaction; c) consideration of contextual aspects. Examples of these moments are the end of an interactive simulation, the conclusion of a training exercise, and so on.

The information coming from the three different input sources converges in the inferential system and undergoes a decision process according to which a certain emotional state is attributed to her.

This attribution is useful to the system to decide how to proceed in the interaction (e.g. whether to make a pause, to propose a new learning activity, to introduce interludes to lower tension, to introduce a tutorial to better explain some complex contents of the simulations, to modify the level of difficulty, etc.).

In synthesis, the first version of the prototype under development includes three input modalities (self-report questionnaires, verbal speech and vocal nonverbal features) as well as some elements of the context modeling. In the next developments, in order to empower the emotional and motivational state recognition process as well as the adaptation one, we envisage: to integrate the current prototype with the other input modalities (see comments on recommendations and future trends in the next section); to proceed to a more complex modeling of context, task, and user profiles; and to achieve a more comprehensive modeling and implementation of reaction strategies.

LIMITATIONS, RECOMMENDATIONS AND FUTURE TRENDS

As a general consideration on the *limitations of our first prototype*, we have to acknowledge that time, costs, technical feasibility and know-how, skill leverage, cultural acceptance and privacy issues, surely represented significant *complexities when going down from theory to practice*.

When looking back from the actual achievement to the original and initial vision, at moments a sense of frustration and disappointment emerged, due to the many *trade-offs* that were necessary to get to the first working prototype. The limited number of modalities included (with the exclusion of facial expression, gestures/posture, and physiological signals), as well as the still simple level of individual and contextual modeling, and of reactions and adaptations designed, appear to us as an oversimplification and therefore represent only a starting point for a more mature development.

At the same time, these very trade-offs were at this stage somehow necessary in order to have a manageable and fully working prototype, realistically fitting in the context of use, and consistent with the requirements of this specific kind of funded projects (i.e. developing a readily usable and near-to-market solution). Moreover, they required us to focus, face (and partially solve) questions and challenges relevant for the concrete integration of affective computing solutions in **e-learning**.

In particular, this (not always successful) effort allowed us to get some important insights and to envisage a number of recommendations and future directions for developments in this field.

First of all, it is clear that a *stronger agreement on theoretical models of emotions* is an important issue: although it is probably not possible to get to a full convergence or a strong choice in this domain (which is still subject of passionate debate within the scientific community), it is necessary a more explicit theory-laden design. Many design and implementation choices are shaped by (more or less explicit) theoretical assumptions on the emotional process and on the relationships between emotion and learning, and without a clear account of them by designers and developers of such systems it will be extremely difficult to work and debate around shared questions.

Second, as far as the *multimodal inferential engine* is concerned, a key issue for the actual implementation of such a device into e-learning system is represented by a *shift of focus* from design and development of all the required components (including lower-level components) to adopting and integrating a number of already developed solutions within the broader **affective computing** community (the situation and availability of such solutions in the last 3 years has strongly increased, thanks also to the systematic efforts of the Network of Excellence HUMAINE (http://emotion-research.net). The possibility not to spend too much time and money to develop low-level components would allow to focusing on the more general pedagogical and technological integration framework (which is a hard work by itself). Of course, this approach will prove viable only if the affective computing community will work more and more in the direction of defining *standards* (e.g. see work on Emotional Mark-up Language in Schröder, Devillers, Karpouzis, Martin, Pelachaud, Peter, Pirker, Schuller, Tao, & Wilson, 2007) and shared formal ontologies related to the different aspects of emotional expression, recognition and modeling. Also, its adoption would be facilitated by the availability and use of *open-source software solutions*, both for input signal processing (e.g. PRAAT for acoustic voice analysis, Boersma & Weenink, 2008) and inferential and clustering algorithms (e.g. WEKA, Witten & Frank, 2005). As to the inclusion of specific modalities, for example psycho-physiological features, the progress in the domain of wearable computing (Peter, Schultz, Voskamp, Urban, Nowack, Janik, Kraft, Göcke, 2007) will be critical to reduce the intrusiveness of physiological sensors and therefore to improve user acceptance.

Third, in order to validate the adaptation module it would be important to extend the work on a broader set of learning contents and formats than the ones developed within the project, and to develop a meta-tagging system compliant with AICC and SCORM standards.

Fourth, it is advisable to improve the user acceptance of the idea of automatic recognition of emotions, by involving users both in the design and implementation process and by improving our dealing with ethical and privacy issues (Reynolds & Picard, 2004) in personal data processing.

Finally, concerning the design process, the experienced gained in the project lead us to an approach characterized by these features: a more extensive use of preliminary testing and user-evaluations based on Wizard-of-Oz methodology (Dahlbäck, Jönsson, & Ahrenberg,1993; when design and development time/cost efforts are high like in this case, this allows to perform a pre-selection of the most important and reliable features to implement and to get an evaluation of temptative solutions before actually fully developing them); a systematic user-centred and situated design, with a focus on solutions which are effectively tailored to the target users and the contexts of use. On the whole, we should probably abandon the goal of a universal affective computing device, "one-size-fits-all" kind of -, and move to the idea of a situated device, where the general skeleton based on extensively open-source solutions can be flexibly customized.

CONCLUSION

Taking into account the emotional aspects of the learning process is fundamental to ensure an effective e-learning experience. The research domain of affective computing (modelling and implementing emotional processes, at various levels, through technology) might be a (part of the) answer to this need. In particular, in this chapter we discussed the potential and limitations for the design of an automatic emotion recognition feature to be integrated within e-learning systems. The possibility to automatically infer the emotional and motivational state of the learner has, in fact, a number of interesting applications in e-learning systems: on the one hand it could be used in individual e-learning activities for a more tailored and personalized learning, providing dynamic and automatic adaptation of the learning path; on the other hand, it could be useful as a support to an online (human) tutor to better monitor the emotional climate of the virtual classroom.

As described in the previous sections of this chapter, *going from theory to practice* in the process of design and implementation of affective computing features in e-learning systems is a tough *challenge*, currently entailing the acceptance of significant compromises and trade-offs.

At the same time, it is a very insightful step. First, all the modelling efforts involved in the design of affective computing features has the positive side-effect of pushing forward theoretical reflection and understanding: many gaps, unsatisfying operationalizations of constructs, underspecified concepts or relationships between them in the theoretical model of reference are immediately evident and require an answer before proceeding further. Before actually facing the challenge of developing a working prototype it is very difficult to get a full awareness of the many questions underlying successful design: many of them arise or acquire growing importance along the way. Second, all the technological limitations (both in terms of technical feasibility and costs) constantly challenge initial functional requirements and specifications, forcing designers to keep an eye on whether an "appealing" feature really makes sense from a pedagogical point of view and/or is worth time and money.

In general, the possibility to fully exploit the potential of affective computing for enhancing the e-learning experience depends on the ability to achieve a good (though) complex balance between pedagogical and technological design issues and on the cyclical back-and-forth between the long-term vision of basic research and the short-term requirements of implementation.

REFERENCES

Aldrich, C. (2003). *Simulations and the future of learning: An innovative (and perhaps revolutionary) approach to e-learning*. San Francisco, CA: Jossey-Bass/Pfeiffer.

Anolli, L., Mantovani, F., Balestra, M., Kommers, P., Robotti, O., Salamin, A. D., et al. (2008). Experiential learning and affective computing for training soft-skills: Myself project. In T. Kidd & H. Song (Eds.), *Handbook of research on instructional systems and technology* (Vol.1, pp. 360-372). Hershey, PA: Information Science Reference.

Anolli, L., Mantovani, F., Mortillaro, M., Vescovo, A., Agliati, A., Confalonieri, L., et al. (2005). A Multimodal Database as a Background for Emotional Synthesis, Recognition and Training in E-Learning Systems. In J. Tao, T. Tan, & R. W. Picard (Eds.), *Affective Computing and Intelligent Interaction: First International Conference, ACII 2005*, Beijing, China, October 22-24, 2005, (LNCS 3784, pp. 566 – 573).

Barrett, L., & Salovey, P. (Eds.). (2002). *The wisdom in feeling: Psychological processes in emotional intelligence*. New York: Guilford Press.

Baylor, A. (1999). Intelligent agents as cognitive tools for education. *Educational Technology, 39*(2), 36–40.

Bickmore, T., & Picard, R. W. (2004). Towards Caring Machines. In *CHI Extended Abstracts* (pp. 1489-1492).

Boersma, P., & Weenink, D. (2008). *Praat: doing phonetics by computer (Version 4.3.14)* [Computer program]. Retrieved November 14, 2008, from http://www.praat.org/

Bradley, M. M., & Lang, P. J. (1994). Measuring emotion: The self-assessment manikin and the semantic differential. *Journal of Behavior Therapy and Experimental Psychiatry, 25*, 49–59. doi:10.1016/0005-7916(94)90063-9

Cassell, J. (2000). More than just another pretty face: Embodied Conversational Agents. *Communications of the ACM, 43*(4), 70–78. doi:10.1145/332051.332075

Cassell, J., Sullivan, J., Prevost, S., & Churchill, E. (2000). *Embodied Conversational Agents.* Cambridge MA: The MIT Press.

D'Mello, S. K., Picard, R. W., & Graesser, A. C. (2007). Towards an Affect-Sensitive AutoTutor. *Special issue on Intelligent Educational Systems – . IEEE Intelligent Systems, 22*(4), 53–61. doi:10.1109/MIS.2007.79

Dahlbäck, N., Jönsson, A., & Ahrenberg, L. (1993). Wizard of Oz studies: why and how. *In Proceedings of the 1st international conference on Intelligent user interfaces*, January 04-07, 1993, Orlando, Florida, United States (pp. 193-200).

Damasio, A. R., Grabowski, T. J., Bechara, A., Damasio, H., Ponto, L. L. B., Parvizi, J., & Hichwa, R. D. (2000). Subcortical and cortical brain activity during the feeling of self-generated emotions. *Nature Neuroscience, 3*, 1049–1056. doi:10.1038/79871

De Rosis, F., Pelachaud, C., Poggi, I., Carofiglio, V., & De Carolis, B. (2003). From Greta's mind to her face: modelling the dynamics of affective states in a conversational Embodied Agent. *International Journal of Human-Computer Studies, 59*, 81–118. doi:10.1016/S1071-5819(03)00020-X

Enz, S., Zoll, C., Vannini, N., Schneider, W., Hall, L., Paiva, A., & Aylett, R. (2007). Emotional Learning in Primary Schools: FearNot! An Anti-bullying intervention based on Virtual Role Play with Intelligent Synthetic Characters, *6th European Conference on e-Learning (ECEL)*, Copenhagen, Denmark, 4-5 October, 2007.

Gardner, H. (1999). *The disciplined mind: What all students should understand.* New York: Simon & Schuster.

Gius, E., Cozzi, A., & Spagnotto, D. (1992). Il linguaggio delle emozioni. Studio sull'origine delle parole che comunicano stati emotivi. *Giornale Italiano di Psicologia, 19*, 563–584.

Gläser-Zikuda, M., & Mayring, P. (2003). A qualitative oriented approach to learning emotions at school. In P. Mayring & C. von Rhöneck (Eds.), *Learning Emotions. The influence of Affective Factors on Classroom Learning* (pp. 103-126). New York, NY: Lang.

Goleman, D. (1995). *Emotional intelligence.* New York: Bantam Books.

Isen, A. M. (1999). Positive affect and decision making. In Lewis M., Haviland J.M. (Eds.), *Handbook of emotions* (pp. 417-435). New York: The Guilford Press.

Kagan, J. (2007). *What is emotion? History, measures and meanings.* New York: Yale University Press.

Kapoor, A., Mota, S., & Picard, R. W. (2001). Towards a learning companion that recognizes affect. In *AAAI Fall Symposium 2001*, North Falmouth, MA.

Kinard, E. M. (2001). Perceived and actual academic competence in maltreated children. *Child Abuse & Neglect, 25*(1), 33–45. doi:10.1016/S0145-2134(00)00219-2

Kort, B., & Reilly, R. (2001). *Analytical Models of Emotions, Learning and Relationships: Towards an Affect-sensitive Cognitive Machine.* MIT Media Lab Tech, Report No 548.

Lane, R., Reiman, E. M., Ahern, G. L., Schwartz, G. E., & Davidson, R. J. (1997). Neuroanatomical correlates of happiness, sadness and disgust. *The American Journal of Psychiatry*, *154*, 926–933.

LeDoux, J. (1998). *The emotional brain: The mysterious underpinnings of emotional life*. London: Weidenfeld & Nicholson.

Moreno, R. (2005). Multimedia learning with animated pedagogical agents. In R. Mayer (Ed.), *Cambridge Handbook of Multimedia Learning* (pp. 507-524). New York: Cambridge University Press.

Mostafa Al Masum, S., & Ishikuza, M. (2005). An Affective Role Model of Software Agent for Effective Agent-based E-Learning by Interplaying between Emotions and Learning. In *Proceedings of the 1st International Conference on Web Information Systems and Technologies (WEBIST 2005)*, Miami, Florida, USA, 449-456.

Omondi, L. (1997). Dholuo emotional language: An overview. In S. Niemeier & R. Dirven (Eds.), *The language of emotions* (pp. 87-110). Amsterdam: John Benjamins Publishing.

Ortony, A., Clore, G. L., & Collins, A. (1988). *The cognitive structure of emotions.* Cambridge, UK: University Press.

Oudeyer, P. Y. (2003). The production and recognition of emotions in speech: features and algorithms. *International Journal of Human-Computer Studies*, *59*(1-2), 157–183. doi:10.1016/S1071-5819(02)00141-6

Paiva, A., Dias, J., Sobral, D., Aylett, R., Sobreperez, P., Woods, S., et al. (2004). Caring for agents and agents that care: Building empathic relations with synthetic agents. In *Proceedings of the International Conference on Autonomous Agents and Multiagent Systems* (pp. 194–201). New York: ACM Press.

Pantic, M., & Rothkrantz, L. J. M. (2003). Toward an affect sensitive multimodal human-computer interaction. *Proceedings of the IEEE*, *91*(9), 1370–1390. doi:10.1109/JPROC.2003.817122

Pekrun, R., Goetz, T., Titz, W., & Perry, R. P. (2002). Academic emotions in students' self-regulated learning and achievement: a program of qualitative and quantitative research. *Educational Psychologist*, *37*(2), 91–105. doi:10.1207/S15326985EP3702_4

Peter, C., Schultz, R., Voskamp, J., Urban, B., Nowack, N., Janik, H., et al. (2007). EREC-II in Use – Studies on Usability and Suitability of a Sensor System for Affect Detection and Human Performance Monitoring. In J. Jacko (Ed.): *Human-Computer Interaction, Part III, HCII 2007* (LNCS 4552, pp. 465–474).

Picard, R. W. (1997). *Affective computing*. Cambridge, MA: The MIT Press.

Picard, R. W. (2003). Affective Computing: Challenges. *International Journal of Human-Computer Studies*, *59*(1-2), 55–64. doi:10.1016/S1071-5819(03)00052-1

Picard, R. W., Papert, S., Bender, W., Blumberg, B., Breazeal, C., & Cavallo, D. (2004). Affective learning - A manifesto. *BT Technology Journal*, *22*(4), 253–269. doi:10.1023/B:BTTJ.0000047603.37042.33

Prendinger, H., Mori, J., & Ishizuka, M. (2005). Using human physiology to evaluate subtle expressivity of a virtual quizmaster in a mathematical game. *International Journal of Human-Computer Studies*, *62*, 231–245. doi:10.1016/j.ijhcs.2004.11.009

Reynolds, C., & Picard, R. W. (2004). Affective Sensors, Privacy, and Ethical Contracts. In *Proceedings of CHI*, Vienna, April 2004.

Sansone, C., & Thoman, D. B. (2005). Does what we feel affect what we learn? Some answers and new questions. *Learning and Instruction*, *15*(5), 507–515. doi:10.1016/j.learninstruc.2005.07.015

Schröder, M., Devillers, L., Karpouzis, K., Martin, J., Pelachaud, C., Peter, C., et al. (2007). What should a generic emotion markup language be able to represent? In Paiva A. et al. (Ed.), *Affective Computing and Intelligent Interaction, Second International Conference, ACII 2007*, September 12-14, Lisbon, Portugal, (LNCS 4738, pp. 440-451). Berlin-Heidelberg, Germany: Springer.

Schutz, P. A., & Pekrun, R. (2007). *Emotions in education*. San Diego CA: Elsevier Inc.

Witten, I. H., & Frank, E. (2005). *Data Mining: Practical Machine Learning Tools and Techniques*. San Francisco: Morgan Kaufmann.

Wosnitza, M., & Volet, S. (2005). Origin, direction and impact of emotions in social online learning. *Learning and Instruction*, *15*(5), 449–464. doi:10.1016/j.learninstruc.2005.07.009

Zeng, Z., Pantic, M., Roisman, G. I., & Huang, T. H. (2009). A survey of affect recognition methods: Audio, visual, and spontaneous expressions. *IEEE Transactions on Pattern Analysis and Machine Intelligence*, *31*(1), 39–58. doi:10.1109/TPAMI.2008.52

Zhou, X., & Conati, C. (2002). Modeling students' emotions from cognitive appraisal in educational games. In S. A. Cem, G. Gouarderes, & F. Paraguacu (Eds.), *Intelligent Tutoring Systems 2002, Biarritz, France. Lecture Notes in Computer Science, 2363* (pp. 944-954). Berlin, Germany: Springer Verlag.

Zurloni, V., Mantovani, F., Mortillaro, M., Vescovo, A., & Anolli, L. (2008). Addressing emotions within e-learning systems. In T. Kidd & H. Song (Eds.), *Handbook of research on instructional systems and technology* (Vol.2, pp. 803-816). Hershey, PA: Information Science Reference.

Chapter 15
Affective E-Learning System: Analysis of Learners' State

G. Caridakis
Image, Video and Multimedia Systems Laboratory, Greece

P. Tzouveli
Image, Video and Multimedia Systems Laboratory, Greece

L. Malatesta
Image, Video and Multimedia Systems Laboratory, Greece

A. Raouzaiou
Image, Video and Multimedia Systems Laboratory, Greece

K. Karpouzis
Image, Video and Multimedia Systems Laboratory, Greece

S. Kollias
Image, Video and Multimedia Systems Laboratory, Greece

ABSTRACT

Learning systems provide adaptation to the learners' preferences without taking under consideration the learners' current status. The more a learning system exchanges relevant fragments of information about the learner's affective status the more it adapts to it. Following this direction, we propose an integrated learning system taking under consideration learners' emotional state in order to provide a personalized e-learning system. An extended version of the IEEE Reference Model (WG) LTSA (IEEE 2003) is used for this purpose. The proposed approach is based on the automatic analysis of the learners' emotional state providing different learners' profiles which are built and maintained by "observing" each learner behavior. As a learner is strongly positively affected to the learning procedure in the presence of an agent, the proposed system has adopted an expressive ECA (Embodied Conversational Agent) which is adapted to the learner's emotional states in the duration of the learning procedure.

DOI: 10.4018/978-1-60566-940-3.ch015

INTRODUCTION

Nowadays, it is widely accepted that information technology improves the learning experience. Learning methods are becoming more and more portable, flexible, and adaptive. The WWW has been broadly adopted as a medium for network-enabled transfer of skills, information and knowledge and plays a significant role in all fields of education (Commission of European Communities, 2000). Web-oriented applications try to satisfy current educational needs, closing the gap between traditional educational techniques and future trends in technology-blended education. Towards this goal, various e-learning systems have been developed missing functionalities like educational multimedia environments, personalized capabilities and tracking of learners' input and relevance feedback (Karagiannidis, 2002). Though, tracking and grasping user behavior in real time remains the most challenging task to retrieve an appropriate and fine-grained user profile as well as to provide personalized learning content.

In this direction, we have adopted the IEEE Reference Model (WG) of the Learning Technology Standards Committee and especially an extension of it. In particular, this extension includes an analysis of learners' state as well as a profiling procedure. Moreover, concerning learner's emotional state, human computer interaction techniques are being employed. Sometimes, a simple facial expression or hand gesture, such as placing a person's hands over his ears, can pass on the message that he has had enough of what he is hearing; this is conveyed more expressively than with any other spoken phrase.

On one hand, application design must take into account the ability of humans to provide multimodal input to computers, thus moving away from the monolithic window-mouse-pointer interface paradigm and utilizing more intuitive concepts, closer to human niches (Jaimes, 2006; Petland, 2005). A large part of this naturalistic interaction concept is expressivity (Picard, 2000), both in terms of interpreting the reaction of the user to a particular event or taking into account their emotional state and adapting learning procedure to it, even for less technology-savvy users.

Since the early 1970s, Paul Ekman and his colleagues have performed extensive studies of human facial expressions. They found evidence to support universality in facial expressions. These "universal facial expressions" are those representing happiness, sadness, anger, fear, surprise, and disgust. They studied facial expressions in different cultures, including preliterate cultures, and found much commonality in the expression and recognition of emotions on the face. However, they observed differences in expressions as well, and proposed that facial expressions are governed by "display rules" in different social contexts. Additionally, the vocal aspect of a communicative message carries various kinds of information. If we disregard the manner in which the message was spoken and consider the verbal part (e.g., words) only, we might miss the important aspects of the pertinent utterance and we might even completely misunderstand what was the meaning of the message. Nevertheless, in contrast to spoken language processing, which has recently witnessed significant advances, the processing of emotional speech has not been widely explored. Finally, emotion consists of more than outward physical expression; it also consists of internal feelings and thoughts, as well as other internal processes of which the person having the emotion may not be aware. Still, these physiological processes can be naturally recognized by people. A stranger shaking your hand can feel its clamminess (related to skin conductivity); a friend leaning next to you may sense your heart pounding, etc.

On the other hand, the captivating presence of the agents can motivate learners to interact more frequently with agent-based educational software (Raouzaiou, 2002). To design the most effective agent-based learning environment, it is essential to understand how students perceive an animated pedagogical agent with regard to affective dimensions such as encouragement, utility, credibility, and clarity. In (Karpouzis et al, 2007), a study of the affective impact of animated pedagogical agents on learning experiences is presented. This study revealed the persona effect, which mentioned that the presence of a lifelike expressive character in an interactive learning environment can have a strong positive effect on student's perception of their learning experience. The study also demonstrates the interesting effect of multiple types of explanatory behaviors on both affective perception and learning performance.

Consequently, the ability of virtual agents to provide expressive feedback to a learner is an important aspect to support their naturalness. In this framework, the proposed system provides learners' states analysis and an ECA-synthesis of multimodal cues constitutes an important part of an e-learning system.

The structure of the chapter is as follows: Section 2 discusses related work, related both to ECAs and ECA enhanced integrated e-learning environments while Section 3 presents the overall system architecture as well as how the IEEE LTSA is extended in order to provide an adaptive learning system. Section 4, describes in detail the recording of the learners' state and more specifically the facial expression analysis, the hand detection and tracking and the gesture expressivity features extraction process. Finally, Section 5 concludes this work by summarizing the article, discussing the presented work and proposing future directions.

RELATED WORK

E-Learning, Affective Computing and Embodied Conversational Agents are extremely active research areas and in recent times several attempts have been made to integrate them in a unified context. These research areas benefit much more than merely discovering application areas in one another but new, extremely interesting problems, issues and points arise from such a constructive fusion.

ECAs

Embodied Conversational Agents (ECAs) are anthropomorphic virtual agents that have a human-like look and can interact with the user. Interactions can range from a textual input field and textual output for chatting with the agent to speech, gesture and even emotion-recognition and generation.

A student can learn interacting with one or more ECAs, who may provide information or encouragement, share knowledge, or collaborate with the student (Morishima, 2006; Baylor & Kim, 2005; Erickson, 1997). Agents can help overcome some constraints of conventional e- learning. Students exposed to an environment with an agent presented deeper learning and higher motivation than students without one (Mulken, 1998).

There are many examples of "teaching" agents: AutoTutor plays the role of tutor (Moreno, 2001), the agents Steve and Adele developed by CARTE are experts in naval training tasks (Graesser, 2001) while the agents developed by Baylor and Kim (Morishima, 2004) served distinct instructional purposes as an expert, a motivator, and a mentor. There is also the approach of learning companion (Johnson, 2000; Chan, 1990;0 Chou, 2003; Goodman, 1998; Hietala, 1998; Kapoor, 2005; Kim, 2003).

One of the issues in using ECAs as tutors is the ability to perceive and realistically express emotions during the interaction with the student. Social interaction is "the process by which we act and react to those around us" (Ryokai, 2003; Lang, 1995) and consists of verbal and non-verbal communication. Non-verbal communication is performed via communication channels like body language, gesture and mimics (see Ryokai, 2003). As these communication channels all have to do with body movement the body has to look and behave human-like. Humans need believable and human-like behavior to trust such a virtual agent. For mimics good simulation of emotion is crucial to social interaction as showing emotions is part of our mimics (see Giddens, 2003; Ekman,1993).

Emotional models have increasingly become the center of interest in agent research over the last decade. This is attributable to the fact that one's own emotions play a crucial role in decision making (see e.g. Ekman, 1999), and that emotional information can easily be expressed by facial expressions. Moreover, it has become feasible to register the user's emotional state and integrate it in the agent's decision making process (see Bates 1994).

One approach that has proven successful and that is widely used for implementing an agent's emotional behavior is the OCC-model (Picard, 1997). A different approach that is widely employed makes use of a dimensional model of emotions (Ortony, 1988). Such a model is widely used for emotion recognition as well as emotion generation (Lang, 1995; Prendinger, 2004). Typically, emotions are defined by the two dimensions of arousal and valence.

Another important part for a credible virtual agent, especially in e-learning application, is how the virtual agents feel in a particular situation, how they react, while the transition between the different emotional situations (e.g. if they feel understood, accepted or not they get more friendly/satisfied or angry) is also important.

Agents capable enhanced with the above mentioned features have successfully been tested in small-scale teaching scenarios. Agents in learning environments do not only allow for realistic communicative behaviors, but also for creating a sense of emotional involvement.

Pelachaud et al. (2002) focus on realistic facial and dialogue behaviors in an embodied conversational agent interacting with the user.

Hall and colleagues (2005) describe a virtual learning environment for children that makes use of autonomous agents. The agent's actions are triggered by an affective agent architecture that is used to appraise a situation and to suggest suitable ways of action depending on the agent's emotional state. By instructing an agent what to do next, the user is able to influence the enfolding story.

Hubal and colleagues (2000; 2003) developed a training software for law enforcement personnel that has to be able to recognize different behavioral signs (gestures, verbal cues) of mental illnesses like schizophrenia or paranoia.

Marsella and colleagues (2003) present an interactive pedagogical drama featuring a virtual character to teach problem solving skills to mothers of pediatric cancer patients. The agent is in the same situation as the mother and by interacting with the agent, the user is presented with some guidance on typical problems.

A number of different ways have been adopted by these systems to reconcile the ability of the agent to make choices about its next action and the requirement for a coherent narrative. In some cases, a branching approach is chosen, where user interaction follows one of a small number of finite paths. A more flexible approach adopted by Hall et al. (2005) is that of a Story Facilitator that shapes the story by selecting the initial conditions for episodes and using triggers to cause events within them (Aylett, 2006). An extension of this approach (Louchart, 2007) gives agents themselves the ability to evaluate the possible impact on others of their actions and select accordingly. Finally, the story-telling guide (Lim, 2007) constructs narrative from story-fragments and adds its own point of view as a commentary upon it.

Most of the above mentioned systems can be classified as proof of concept, where a small part of a domain is modeled. All include some kind of emotional modeling - either for realistically displaying the agent or for affective reasoning processes and have shown the importance of including such a model in critical training applications. User interactions are mostly restrained to simple speech input and/or mouse interactions.

ECA Enhanced Integrated E-Learning Systems

Jung et al. (2005) developed an e-learning system enhanced with the presence of a virtual agent and focus more on the always sensitive situation of hospitalized children. Haptek virtual technology was employed and the affective virtual patient was multimodal in the sense that both highly emotional facial expression and lip-synchronized speech were controlled by the XML based modeling language used as the control system.

McQuiggan et al.(2008) study the possibilities of affective reasoning in a train/test scenario (CARE) where a trainer guides a virtual agent through a series of problem-solving tasks and then empathy models are used to drive runtime situation-appropriate empathetic behaviors by selecting suitable parallel or reactive empathetic expressions. Parallel empathy refers to mere replication of another's affective state, whereas reactive empathy exhibits greater cognitive awareness and may lead to incongruent emotional responses.

Virtual European School (VES) project (Bouras, 2001) also incorporates a communicative character of the multiuser distributed virtual environment that allows students and staff to meet in social shared spaces and engage in on-line real-time seminars and tutorials. This collaborative learning system that incorporates agents equipped with social intelligence is also presented by Morishima et al (2004). The effectiveness of the application was supported by a content quiz, according to which participants to the two co-learner conditions (Social Model and No Social Model) attained higher scores of correct answers than those in the no-agent condition. Interestingly enough the social model co-learner situation participants scored higher than the ones that participated a session where the agent had no social model associated with its behavior.

Fernandez-Caballero (2003) present Intelligent Tutoring System an application for enhancing e-learning / e-teaching. ITS consists of three components: the Student, Model and the Pedagogical Model. VBroker is presented by Laufer et al (2004) which is actually an E-learning curriculum and a virtual stock exchange game. Emphasis is given on the emotional model enabling the tutoring agent to provide proper emotional feedback and humorous behavior to achieve edutainment.

Finally, a collaborative affective virtual environment system is introduced by Neji & Ammar (2007). This technology offers the possibility of interlocutors to express themselves emotionally in an efficient and effective way, an animated virtual head, in the framework of EMASPEL (Emotional Multi-Agents System for Peer to peer E-Learning).

OVERALL ARCHITECTURE OF THE SYSTEM

In this section, the architecture of the proposed e-learning system is described. The proposed system includes three individual components which are considered as standalone entities, while, at the same time, collaborate with each other. The main entity, Learner, includes learners, participating in the learning process as individuals or in groups. The entity Experts includes experts in the e-learning field and computer engineers. The goal of that group is the design and continuous improvement of the system, with respect to computational integrity and educational efficiency. The Experts' Group is responsible for determining the learning topics that the e-learning schema can provide to the learners' group to which is addressed. The last entity is formed by the Server System, including all system hardware and software. Each subcomponent of this entity can be part of a centralized computer system or rely on separate hardware units scattered around the network. The internal architecture, in which the software of the proposed system has been based and developed, is considered as an extension of the IEEE Reference Model (WG) of the Learning Technology

Figure 1. Extension of LTSA IEEE learning system

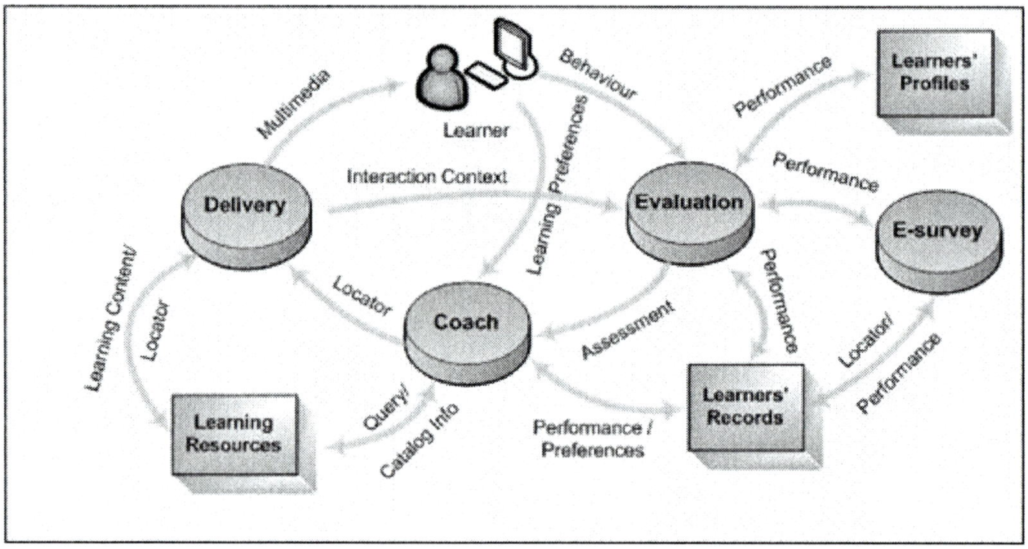

Standards Committee (LTSA). The IEEE LTSA (2001) contains three types of entities: processes (oval), process the information received from the stores entities via flows, stores (rectangles) implement an inactive system component used as an information repository and flows (vectors), denotes the transfer of information (control or data) from one entity to another. In the generic approach to e-learning systems outlined in the LTSA Draft Standard, system's ability to adapt its operation to the learner is not defined, although an evaluation process exists.

To handle this issue, we introduce in Figure 1 an extension of the IEEE LTSA enriching behavior flow (Mylonas et al, 2007) and all process modules with new functionalities, on the purpose of achieving effective collaboration between them. In the following, let us examine the role and the behavior of the different components in the proposed framework. Firstly, the group of experts defines the learning content in a specific learning subject which is accompanied with an affective Embodied Conversational Agent (ECA). The learner content together with the ECA is illustrated to the learners through multimedia flow (Figure 1) on their first access to the system. The user can choose if the learning content will be provided to her through the usual interface or by the ECA. The ECA is capable to present the content-it reads the text, shows the images in a more affective and stimulating way, by performing gestures and facial expressions.

While a learning resource is presented to the learners, both behavior and reactions are observed. The behavior information, when a learner uses it for the first time, includes the recording of learner's reaction by a web camera which is placed in front of him. The learner entity's observable behavior and is given as input to the evaluation process which produces assessment information about the learner situation and sends it to the coach process. In addition, the evaluation process creates performance information flow stored in the learner records. Performance information can come from both the evaluation process (e.g. video recordings, learners' profile, answer to the questionnaire, grades on lessons) and the coach process (e.g. certifications). The learner records store hold information about the past (e.g. historical learner records), the present (e.g. current assessments for suspending and resuming sessions, current behavior) and the future (e.g. presentation rate, pedagogy, learner).

In order to extract learner profiles, the evaluation process takes into consideration the learner behavior and the learners' profile store. After that, the learner's level of knowledge in specific subject is computed, classifying the learner's profile, which is then stored in the learner records. In addition, we design a new store, i.e. learner profiles, which contain the current profiles of the e-learning system. Thus, once a learner is assigned to a learner profile, the coach uses information in order to locate the learning material from the learning resources store that best matches learner' profile and an appropriated agent is displayed to him according to his learning ability. Change of learners' profiles can be performed during their training, updating the learner records store.

The entity coach can receive performance information from the learner records at any time. Performance information, such as assessment information, certifications and preferences are stored in the learner records by the coach process. Based on this information, the coach requests the appropriate learning materials for each learner from the learning resources. Finally the delivery process transforms these materials via learning content store into a presentation which is accompanied with expressive ECA which is adapted to the learner emotional states.

RECORDING LEARNERS' STATE

A very important part of an educational system should be both recording and analysis of learner's state. The system becomes more efficient when it can be adjusted to every user. All learners don't concentrate for the same period of time or lose their interest when the rate of learning material is not very fast. On this section we analyze the way that the learner state is captured, intending to include this information to the learners' profile providing to the learner the proper learning material and in a proper learning rate.

Active or passive, engaged or not, hyperactive or not active at all, positive or negative are some of possibly detected learner's states. Learner's state is extracted using face and hands gestures analysis together with body posture and motion. The detection of the learner's face and hands in the captured images is based on detection and evaluation of either skin segments or blobs that the captured images contain. For this purpose, the position and shape of mouth, eyes and eyelids are detected and features related to them are extracted.

Once the learner's state is recognized, the presentation of the learning content is tailored to the profile of each learner, while the system supports on-line adaptation to the learner's state through this multimodal analysis, being adapted to short term changes of the learner's state. Adaptation of the learner interface will be performed by getting relevant information from the current learner's profile and the current learner's state.

Facial Expression Analysis

Facial analysis includes a number of processing steps which attempt to detect or track the face, to locate characteristic facial regions such as eyes, mouth and nose on it, to extract and follow the movement of facial features, such as characteristic points in these regions, or model facial gestures using anatomic information about the face (Karpouzis et al, 2007).

Facial analysis includes a number of processing steps which attempt to detect or track the face, to locate characteristic facial regions such as eyes, mouth and nose on it, to extract and follow the movement of facial features, such as characteristic points in these regions, or model facial gestures using anatomic information about the face. Although FAPs provide all the necessary elements for MPEG-4 compatible animation, we cannot use them for the analysis of expressions from video scenes, due to the absence of a clear quantitative definition framework. In order to measure FAPs in real image sequences,

Figure 2. (a) Eyebrow-candidates, (b) selected eyebrow mask

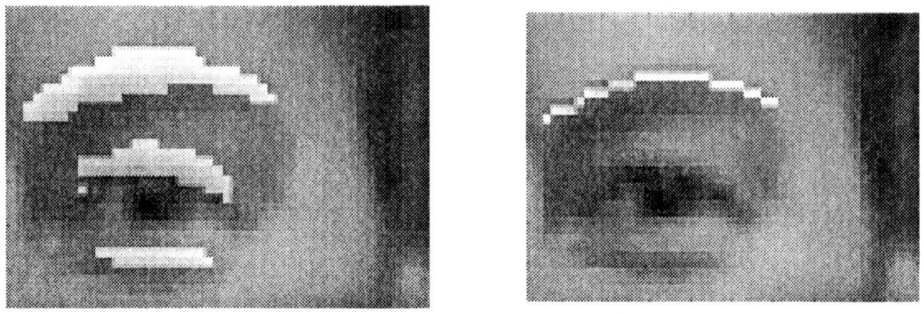

Figure 3. Eye masks

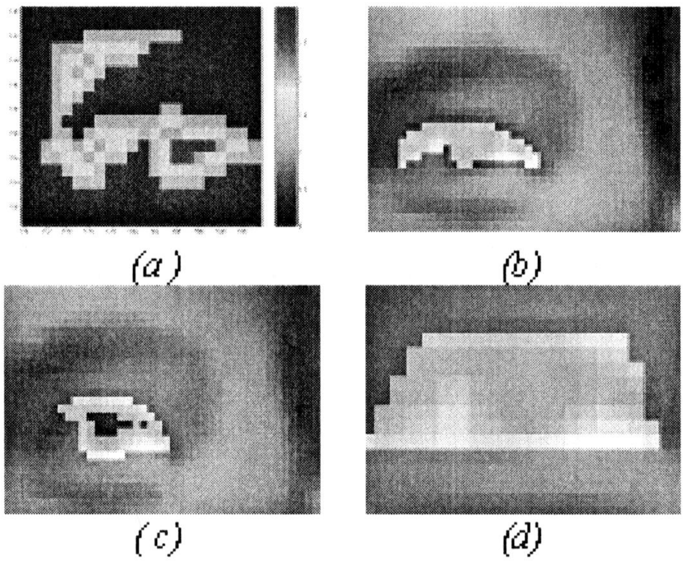

we have to define a mapping between them and the movement of specific facial definition parameters (FDPs) feature points (FPs), which correspond to salient points on the human face.

The face is first located, so that approximate facial feature locations can be estimated from the head position and rotation. Face roll rotation is estimated and corrected and the head is segmented focusing on the following facial areas: left eye/eyebrow, right eye/eyebrow, nose and mouth. Each of those areas, called feature-candidate areas, contains the features whose boundaries need to be extracted for our purposes. Inside the corresponding feature-candidate areas precise feature extraction is performed for each facial feature, i.e. eyebrows (Figure 2), eyes (Figure 3), mouth and nose, using a multi-cue approach, generating a small number of intermediate feature masks. Feature masks generated for each facial feature are fused together to produce the final mask for that feature. The mask fusion process uses anthropometric criteria to perform validation and weight assignment on each intermediate mask; each feature's weighted masks are then fused to produce a final mask along with confidence level estimation. The edges of the final masks are considered to be the extracted feature points as can be seen in Figure 2 (a).

Measurement of FAPs requires the availability of a frame where the subject's expression is found to be

Figure 4. Williams' Index distribution, eyes/mouth

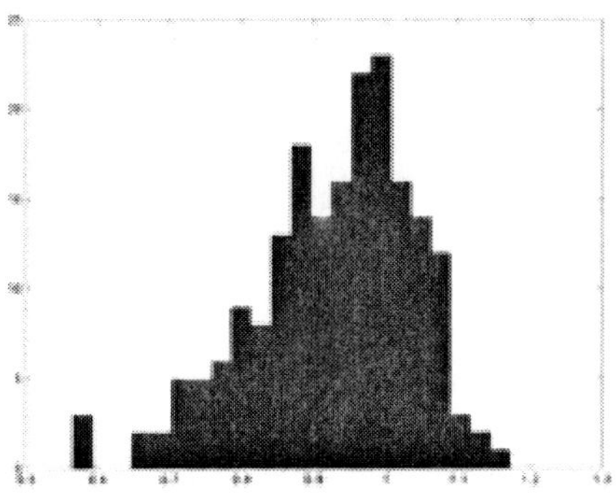

Figure 5. Williams' Index distribution, eyebrows

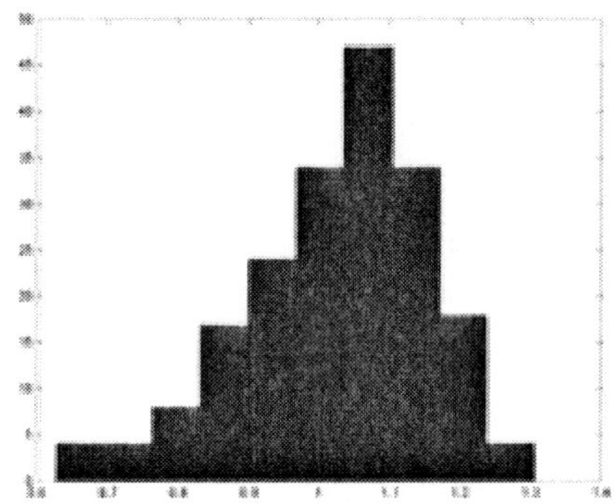

neutral. This frame will be called the neutral frame and is manually selected from video sequences to be analyzed or interactively provided to the system when initially brought into a specific user's ownership. The final feature masks are used to extract 19 Feature Points (FPs); Feature Points obtained from each frame are compared to FPs obtained from the neutral frame to estimate facial deformations and produce the Facial Animation Parameters (FAPs). Confidence levels on FAP estimation are derived from the equivalent feature point confidence levels. The FAPs are used along with their confidence levels to provide the facial expression estimation.

Concerning the robustness of the proposed algorithm we had a subset of the available dataset manually annotated by a number of reviewers and compared this annotation versus the automatic one obtained by the described system. As a metric for robustness evaluation we incorporated a modified Williams' Index where the results of automatic feature extraction are considered as one of the reviewers. When WI is larger than 1, the computer generated mask disagrees less with the observers than the observers disagree with each other. Figure 4 and Figure 5 show the distribution of WI for eyes/mouth and eyebrows regions respectively. These results indicate that the described algorithm is efficient given the image is of acceptable quality, the head pose is quite frontal so that feature occlusion does not occur.

In terms of affective state recognition a dynamic approach was adopted (Cowie et al, 2008), where a recurrent neural network, whose short term memory and approximation capabilities cater for modeling dynamic events and classifying input patterns to emotional states. In order to consider the dynamics of displayed expressions a classification model that is able to model and learn dynamics is employed. Whereas conventional neural networks deal with static patterns the first layer of an Elman network has a recurrent connection adding a delay which stores values from the previous time step which can be used in the current time step, thus providing the element of memory. Finally the combination of facial expressions with other modalities would allows us to capture the users' emotional state (Figure 6), relying on the best performing modality in cases where one modality suffers from noise or bad sensing conditions (Castellano et al., 2007).

Head and Hand Tracking

Several approaches have been reviewed for the head-hand tracking module. The major factors taken under consideration are computational cost and robustness, resulting in an accurate near real-time skin detection and tracking module. The general process involves the creation

Figure 6. Facial feature points on one of the subjects

of moving skin masks, namely skin color areas that are tracked between subsequent frames. By tracking the centroid of those skin masks, we produce an estimate of the learner's movements. A priori knowledge concerning the human body and the circumstances when filming the gestures was incorporated into the module indicating the different body parts (head, right hand, left hand). Subsequently we expect to locate the head in the middle area of the upper half of the frame and the hand segments near the respective lower corners. The upper and lower segments of the hands are not detected or tracked.

The general process involves the creation of moving skin masks, namely skin color areas that are tracked between subsequent frames. By tracking the centroid of those skin masks, we produce an estimate of the user's movements. A priori knowledge concerning the human body and the circumstances when filming the gestures was incorporated into the module indicating the different body parts (head, right hand, left hand). For each frame a skin color probability matrix is computed by calculating the joint probability of the Cr/Cb image values. The skin color mask is then obtained from the skin probability matrix using thresholding. Possible moving areas are found by thresholding the pixels' difference between the current frame and the next, resulting in the possible-motion mask. This mask does not contain information about the direction or the magnitude of the movement, but is only indicative of the motion and is used to accelerate the algorithm by concentrating tracking only in moving image areas. Both color and motion masks contain a large number of small objects due to the presence of noise and objects with color similar to the skin. To overcome this, morphological filtering is employed on both masks to remove small objects. All described morphological operations are carried out with a disk-structuring element with a radius of 1% of the image width. The distance transform of the color mask is first calculated and only objects above the desired size are retained. These objects are used as markers for the morphological reconstruction of the initial color mask. The color mask is then closed to provide better centroid calculation. For the next frame, a new moving skin mask is created, and a one-to-one object correspondence is performed. Object correspondence between two frames is performed on the color mask and is based on object centroid distance for objects of similar (at least 50%) area. In the case of hand object merging and splitting, e.g., in the case of clapping, we establish a new matching of the left-most candidate object to the user's right hand and the right-most object to the left hand. The Sagittal plane information of the gesture was ignored since it would require depth information from the video stream and it would make the performance of the proposed algorithm very poor or would require a side camera and parallel processing of the two streams. The described algorithm is lightweight, allowing a rate of around 12 fps on a usual PC during our experiments, which is enough for continuous gesture tracking. The object correspondence heuristic makes it possible to individually track the hand segments correctly, at least during usual meaningful gesture sequences. In addition, the fusion of color and motion information eliminates any background noise or artifacts, thus reinforcing the robustness of the proposed approach.

The tracking algorithm is responsible for classifying the skin regions in the image sequence of the examined gesture based on the skin regions extracted from the described method. Skin region size, distance with reference to the previous classified position of the region, flow alignment and spatial constraints. These criteria ensure that the next region selected to replace the current one is approximately the same size, close to the last position and moves along the same direction as the previous one as long as the instantaneous speed is above a certain threshold. As a result each candidate region is being awarded a bonus for satisfying these criteria or is being penalized for failing to comply with the restrictions applied. The winner region is appointed as the reference region for the next frame (figure 7).

Figure 7. Key steps in hand detection and tracking (a) skin probability, (b) thresholding and morphology operators, (c) distance transformation, (d) frame difference

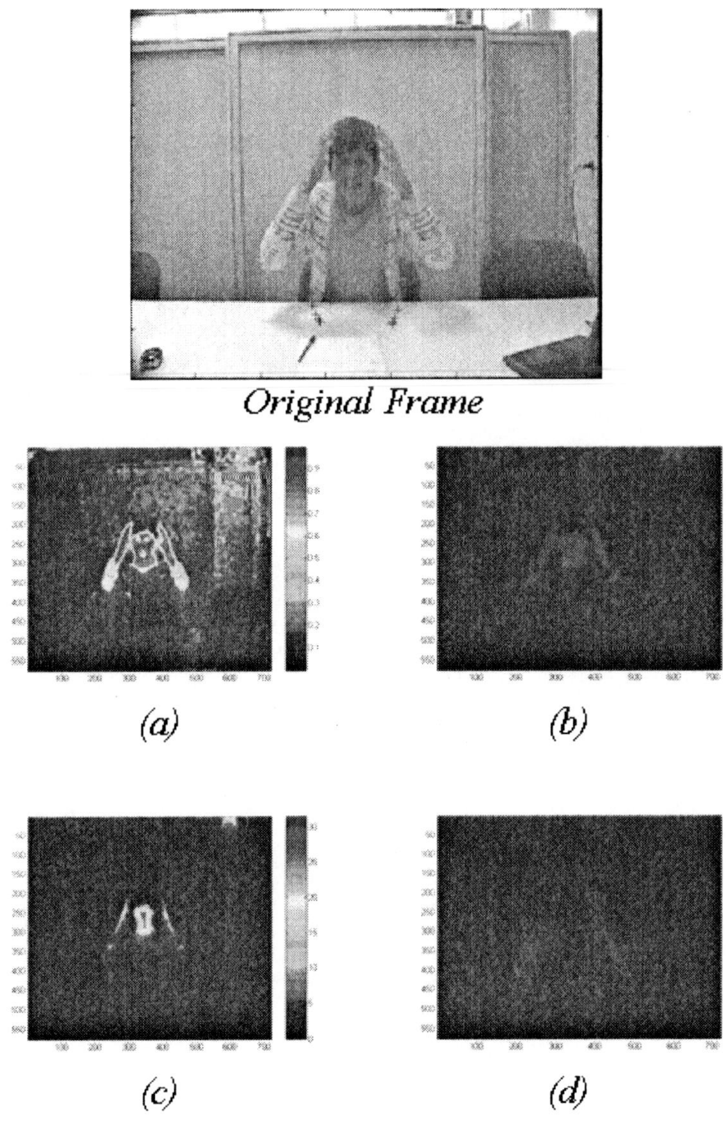

The criteria don't have an eliminating effect, meaning that if a region fails to satisfy one of them is not being excluded from the process, and the bonus or penalty given to the region is relative to the score achieved in every criterion test. The finally selected region's score is thresholded so that poor scoring winning regions are excluded. In this case the position of the body part is unchanged with reference to that in the previous frame. This feature is especially useful in occlusion cases when the position of the body part remains the same as just before occlusion occurs. After a certain number of frames the whole process is reinitialized so that a possible misclassification is not propagated. Head and head occlusion is tackled with the following simplistic yet efficient method. Suppose occlusion occurs at frame n and ceases to exist at frame k. The position of the hand during the occlusion phase (frames n-k) is considered to be the position of the hand at frame n-1. After frame k the detection and tracking algorithm for the specific hand continues normally.

Gesture Expressivity Features Extraction

Expressivity of behavior is an integral part of the communication process as it can provide information on the current emotional state, mood, and personality of a person (Wallbott & Scherer, 1986). Many researchers have investigated human motion characteristics and encoded them into dual categories such as slow/fast, small/expansive, weak/energetic, small/large, unpleasant/pleasant. To model expressivity, in our work, we use the six dimensions of behavior described by Hartmann et al., (2005), as a more accomplished way to describe the expressivity, since it tackles all the parameters of expression of emotion. Five parameters modeling behavior expressivity have been defined at the analysis level, as a subset of the above-mentioned six dimensions of behavior (see also next Section):

Overall activation
Spatial extent
Temporal
Fluidity
Power

Overall activation is considered as the quantity of movement during a conversational turn. In our case it is computed as the sum of the motion vectors' norm:

$$A = \sum_{i=1}^{N} \left|r\right|^2 + \left|1\right|^2$$

Spatial extent is modeled by expanding or condensing the entire space in front of the agent that is used for gesturing and is calculated as the maximum Euclidean distance of the position of the two hands: . The average spatial extent is also calculated for normalization reasons. The temporal expressivity parameter of the gesture signifies the duration of the movement while the speed expressivity parameter refers to the arm movement during the gesture's stroke phase (e.g., quick versus sustained actions). Gestures have three phases: preparation, stroke and retraction. The real message is in the stroke, whilst the preparation and retraction elements consist of moving the arms to and from the rest position, to and from the start and end of the stroke. Fluidity differentiates smooth/graceful from sudden/jerky ones. This concept seeks to capture the continuity between movements, as such, it seems appropriate to modify the continuity of the arms' trajectory paths as well as the acceleration and deceleration of the limbs. To extract this feature from the input image sequences we calculate the sum of the variance of the norms of the motion vectors. Power actually is identical with the first derivative of the motion vectors calculated in the first steps.

Expressive Synthesis

Communicative capabilities of conversational agents could be significantly improved if they could also convey the expressive component of physical behavior. Starting from the results reported in [Wallbott, 1986], we have defined and implemented [Hartmann, 2005a] a set of five parameters that affect the quality of the agent's behavior, that is the movement's spatial volume (SPC), speed (TMP), energy (PWR), fluidity (FLT) and repetitivity (REP). Thus, the same gestures or facial expressions are performed by the agent in a qualitatively different way depending on this set of parameters. The Spatial Extent (SPC) parameter modulates the amplitude of the movement of arms, wrists (involved in the animation of a gesture), head and eyebrows (involved in the animation of a facial expression); it influences how wide or narrow their displacement will be during the final animation. For example let us consider the eyebrows raising in the expression of surprise: if the value of the Spatial Extent parameter is very high the final position of the eyebrows will be very high in the forehead (i.e. the eyebrows move under a strong of muscular contraction). The Temporal Extent (TMP) parameter shortens or lengthens the motion of the preparation and retraction phases of the gesture as well as the onset and offset duration for facial expression. On of the effect on the face is to speed up or slow down the rising/lowering of the eyebrows. The agent animation is generated by defining some key frames and computing the interpolation curves passing through these frames. The Fluidity (FLT) and Power (PWR) parameters act on the interpolation curves. Fluidity increases/reduces the continuity of the curves allowing the system to generate more/less smooth animations. Let us consider its effect on the head: if the value of the Fluidity parameter is very low the resulting curve of the head movement will appear as generated through linear interpolation. Thus, during its final animation the head will have a jerky movement. Power introduces a gesture/expression overshooting, that is a little lapse of time in which the body part involved by the gesture reaches a point in space further than the final one. For example the frown displayed in the expression of anger will be stronger for a short period of time, and then the eyebrows will reach the final position. The last parameter, Repetition (REP), exerts an influence on gestures and head movements. It increases the number of stroke of gestures to obtain repetition of the gestures themselves in the final animation. Let us consider the gesture "wrists going up and down in front of the body with open hands and palms up", a high value of the Repetition parameter will increase the number of the up and down movements. On the other hand this parameter decreases the time period of head nods and head shakes to obtain more nods and shakes in the same lapse of time.

ARCHITECTURE EVALUATION

A formative evaluation of the so far implemented system is judged of crucial importance in order to decipher how the synthesized behavior is perceived and thus identify ways to improve the current output produced. Feedback on expressivity makes sense both within and out of context [Hartmann et al., 2005b]. At this point we are going to present a scheme on ways we propose in order to evaluate current work. Due to strict time limitations the results of this ongoing evaluation scheme will be made available in future publications.

Evaluation Scheme

There are various questions worth answering, through rating tests, regarding the perception of synthesized emotional expressions in order to continue an in depth analysis of the parameters just mentioned. In our case, a first question is the perception and classification of the synthesized output by human viewers. We plan to conduct a rating test where twenty postgraduate students will be asked to rate a sequence of videos – one at a time. They will be presented a questionnaire comprised of scale questions regarding the percent of each class they believe the video snippet they just watched belongs to. The choice of classes is dictated by the natural language scenarios given to the actors of the original videos.

Participants will be asked how synthesised animations are perceived both in and out of the originating actor context by viewing the videos of the behavior mimicry scenarios. Thus, they will be divided into two groups, and will be randomly assigned to two conditions; the first group will be presented with the synthesised videos whereas the second group will be presented with both acted videos and their synthesised equivalents. The playback order of each set of videos will be chosen randomly so as to avoid ordering effects. In each group we plan to include a neutral condition of Greta simply blinking and looking straight ahead with a neutral expression as our conceptual baseline.

Questionnaires will also be used to collect participant feedback on which emotion they identified in each of the sequences they viewed. Their replies will be constrained with labels. Participants' confidence shall again be measured indirectly by asking them questions about the intensity of the perceived emotion.

Results from this first rating test can provide useful data on the perception and recognition of the synthesised expressions, as well as information on the effect of context (acted video sequences) in affective state perception of synthesized mimicked versions. Confidence measures will help draw conclusions on the role of the expressivity parameters and further refined manipulation of these parameters in conjunction with new rating tests can help decipher the role of these parameters in the perception of synthesized expressions.

Preliminary Results

Although a formal evaluation of the overall architecture is not yet implemented, evaluating intermediate components has been carried out. We investigated the correlation of the automatic analysis results with the participants' results for each expressivity parameter (Table 1). Fist we took into account all 16 sets of ratings for each participant. Then we also calculated correlation coefficients when only taking into account ratings for the last 12 videos that each user viewed based on the idea that users had a by then developed a clearer idea of what they were doing. In both cases we correlated both the average of users' scores for each expressivity parameter of each video (rows marked as 'Avg' in Table 1 for 16 and 12 videos respectively), as well as their median scores (rows marked as 'Median' in Table 1 for 16 and 12 videos respectively).

From these results it is apparent that there is no significant variance between the different data views investigated. We measured significant correlation only in the case of the special extent feature. Power and speed also correlated relatively well. The low values for overall activation and the negative correlation for the case of fluidity show that user's did not conceive these parameters correctly. These values might also be caused by the fact that the videos were of particularly short duration.

Table 1. Correlation coefficients of users' expressivity parameters against machine extracted values

	Ov.Act.	Sp.Ext	Speed	Fluid	Power
Avg/16	0.38	0.78	0.53	-0.20	0.57
Median/16	0.38	0.76	0.50	-0.21	0.61
Avg/12	0.36	0.74	0.50	-0.22	0.52
Median/12	0.38	076	0.48	-0.18	0.55

FUTURE RESEARCH DIRECTIONS

Future work includes the integration of a pedagogical module which will cater the reasoning of the ECA's behavior according to the cues received from the user and processed by the proposed system. Such a process will ensure that the ECA's behavior complies with widely accepted pedagogical methods and goes beyond an expressive agent.

The evaluation study should be continued for the proposed system. User feedback and systematic monitoring of the students' curriculum performance will be collected through questionnaires and student grades respectively for different tutoring scenarios. The implemented scenarios will include traditional e-learning tutoring system, ECA enhanced tutoring system and finally the affective ECA tutoring system. Thus the system's efficiency will be evaluated and appropriate redesign adjustments will be carried out.

CONCLUSION

Present work introduces an affective approach to an e-learning system adaptive to the learner's emotional state bringing together established and emerging research areas such as e-Learning, Affective Computing and Embodied Conversational Agents. Extending the IEEE Reference Model (WG) LTSA, by enriching behavior flow and modules with new functionalities, with the purpose of achieving effective collaboration between them, the proposed system is enriched with emotional awareness and by taking under consideration the learners' emotional state provides a personalized e-learning system both in terms of content and presentation. Affective awareness is achieved via facial expression recognition and extraction of gesture expressivity features while the ECA, shouldering the role of the teacher, attempts to adapt its behavior accordingly. The persona effect is then maximized since the learning procedure in the presence of an agent especially an expressive and life-like one. In this framework, the proposed system provides learners' states analysis and an ECA-synthesis of multimodal cues constitutes an important part of an e-learning system.

REFERENCES

P1484. *1 Architecture and Reference Model.* (n.d.). IEEE Learning Techonology Standards Committee. Retrieved July 2003, from http://ltsc.ieee.org/index.html

Aylett, R. S., Figuieredo, R., Louchart, S., Dias, J., & Paiva, A. (2006). Making it up as you go along – improvising stories for pedagogical purposes. In J. Gratch, M. Young, R. Aylett, D. Ballin & P. Olivier (Eds.), *6th International Conference, IVA* (LNAI 4133, pp. 307-315). New York: Springer.

Bates, J. (1994). The role of emotion in believable agents. *Communications of the ACM, 37*(7), 122–125. doi:10.1145/176789.176803

Baylor, A. L., & Kim, Y. (2005). Simulating instructional roles through pedagogical agents. *International Journal of Artificial Intelligence in Education, 15*(2), 95–115.

Bouras, C., Philopoulos, A., & Tsiatsos, T. (2001). e-Learning through distributed virtual environments. *Journal of Network and Computer Applications, 24*(3), 175–199. doi:10.1006/jnca.2001.0131

Castellano, G., Kessous, L., & Caridakis, G. (2007). Multimodal emotion recognition from expressive faces, body gestures and speech. In C. Peter & R. Beale (Eds.), *Affect and Emotion in Human-Computer Interaction, Lecture Notes in Computer Science*. Berlin, Germany: Springer.

Chan, T. W., & Baskin, A. B. (1990). Learning companion systems. In C. Frasson & G. Gauthier (Eds.), *Intelligent tutoring systems at the crossroads of artificial intelligence and education* (pp. 7–33). NJ: Ablex Publishing Corporation.

Chou, C. Y., Chan, T. W., & Lin, C. J. (2003). Redefining the learning companion: The past, present, and future of educational agents. *Computers & Education*, *40*, 255–269. doi:10.1016/S0360-1315(02)00130-6

Commission of European Communities. (2000). *Communication from the Commission: e-Learning – Designing Tomorrow's Education*. Brussels, Belgium.

Cowie, R., Douglas-Cowie, E., Karpouzis, K., Caridakis, G., Wallace, M., & Kollias, S. (2008). Recognition of Emotional States in Natural Human-Computer Interaction. In D. Tzovaras (Ed.), *Multimodal User Interfaces* (pp. 119-153). Berlin Heidelberg, Germany: Springer.

Damasio, A. R. (1994). *Descartes' Error: Emotion, Reason, and the Human Brain*. New York: Harper.

Ekman, P. (1993). Facial Expressions and Emotion. *The American Psychologist*, *48*(4), 384–392. doi:10.1037/0003-066X.48.4.384

Ekman, P. (1999). *Basic Emotions*. In T. Dalgleish & T. Power (Eds.), *The Handbook of Cognition and Emotion* (pp. 45-60). Hoboken, NJ: John Wiley and Sons.

Erickson, T. (1997). Designing agents as if people mattered. In J. M. Bradshaw (Ed.), *Software agents* (pp. 79–96). Menlo Park, CA: MIT Press.

Fernandez-Caballero, A., Lopez-Jaquero, V., Montero, F., & Gonzalez, P. (2003). Adaptive Interaction Multi-agent Systems in E-learning/E-teaching on the Web. In *Lecture Notes In Computer Science*, (pp.144-153). New York: Springer.

Giddens, A., Duneier, M., & Appelbaum, R. P. (2003) Introduction to Sociology. 4th edition.

Goodman, B., Soller, A., Linton, F., & Gaimari, R. (1998). Encouraging student reflection and articulartion using a learning companion. Paper presented at the 8th International Conference on Artificial Intelligence in Education, Kobe, Japan.

Graesser, A. C., Person, N. K., Harter, D., & Group, T. R. (2001). Teaching tactics and dialog in autotutor. *International Journal of Artificial Intelligence in Education*, *12*, 257–279.

Hall, L., Woods, S., & Aylett, R. Newall, L. & Paiva, A. (2005). Achieving empathic engagement through affective interaction with synthetic characters. Affective computing and intelligent interaction, Springer.

Hartmann, B., Mancini, M., Buisine, S., & Pelachaud, C. (2005b). Design and evaluation of expressive gesture synthesis for embodied conversational agents. AAMAS'05. Utretch.

Hietala, P., & Niemirepo, T. (1998). The competence of learning companion agents. *International Journal of Artificial Intelligence in Education*, *9*, 178–192.

Hubal, R. C., Frank, G. A., & Guin, C. (2003). Lessons Learned in Modeling Schizophrenic and Depressed Responsive Virtual Humans for Training. Proceedings of International Conference on Intelligent User Interfaces (pp. 85 – 92), ACM

Hubal, R. C., Kizakevich, P. N., Guinn, C. I., Merino, K. D., & West, S. L. (2000). The Virtual Standardized Patient – Simulated Patient-Practitioner Dialog for Patient Interview Training. In Envisioning Healing: Interactive Technology and the Patient-Practitioner Dialogue, (pp.133-138) IOS Press: Amsterdam.

Jaimes, A. (2006). Human-Centered Multimedia: Culture, Deployment, and Access, IEEE Multimedia Magazine, Vol. 13, No.1.

Johnson, W. L., Rickel, J. W., & Lester, J. C. (2000). Animated pedagogical agents: Faceto- face interaction in interactive learning environments. *International Journal of Artificial Intelligence in Education*, *11*, 47–78.

Jung, B., Ahad, A., & Weber, M. (2005). The Affective Virtual Patient: An E-Learning Tool for Social Interaction Training within the Medical Field Proceedings of International Conference TESI-Training Education & Education. IEEE standard for learning technology-learning technology systems architecture (LTSA) (2003), IEEE Std 1484.1-2003 Volume, Issue, Page(s): 0_1 – 97

Kapoor, A., & Picard, R. W. (2005). Multimodal affect recognition in learning environments. Proceedings of the 13th annual ACM international conference on Multimedia, (pp.677-682), ACM New York, NY, USA

Karagiannidis, C., Sampson, D.G., & Cardinali, F.(2002). An architecture for Web-based e-Learning promoting reusable adaptive educational e-content, Educational Technology & Society, 5(4).

Karpouzis, K., Caridakis, G., Kessous, L., Amir, N., Raouzaiou, A., Malatesta, L., & Kollias, S. (2006). Modeling naturalistic affective states via facial, vocal, and bodily expressions recognition. In T. Huang, A. Nijholt, M. Pantic, A. Pentland (eds.), Lecture Notes in Artificial Intelligence, Special Volume on AI for Human Computing, pp. 91-112, Springer.

Kim, J., André, E., Rehm, M., Vogt, T., & Wagner, J. (2005). Integrating Information from Speech and Physiological Signals to Achieve Emotional Sensitivity, in: Proceedings of Interspeech/Eurospeech, 2005.

Kim, Y. (2003). An agent as a learning companion: What it matters. Paper presented at the Annual Conference of Association for Educational Communications and Technology, Anaheim, CA.

Lang, P. J. (1995). The Emotion Probe: Studies of Motivation and Attention . *The American Psychologist*, *50*(5), 372–385. doi:10.1037/0003-066X.50.5.372

Laufer, L., & Tatai, G. (2004). Learn, Chat & Play-An ECA Supported Stock Markets E-Learning Curricula'. Proceedings of the IASTED International Conference on Web-Based Education (pp.16-18) ACTA Press.

Lester, J. C., Converse, S. A., Kahler, S. E., Barlow, S. T., Stone, B. A., & Bhogal, R. S. (1997). The persona effect: affective impact of animated pedagogical agents, Proceedings of the SIGCHI conference on Human factors in computing systems, (pp.359-366), ACM New York, NY, USA

Lim, M. Y., & Aylett, R. S. (2007). Feel the difference: A Guide with Attitude! In C. Pelachaud et al. (Eds.) Intelligent virtual agents, (pp. 317-330), Springer-Verlag Berlin Heidelberg

Louchart, S., & Aylett, R. (2007). From Synthetic Characters to Virtual Actors. Proceedings of International Conference in Artificial Intelligence for Interactive Digital Entertainment (pp. 88-91)

Marsella, S., Johnson, W. L., & La Bore, C. M. (2003). Interactive Pedagogical Drama for Health Interventions, 11th International Conference on Artificial Intelligence in Education Australia

McQuiggan, S., Robison, J., Phillips, R., & Lester, J. (2008). Modeling parallel and reactive empathy in virtual agents: An inductive approach. In *International Joint Conference on Autonomous Agents and Multi-Agent Systems*, Portugal.

Moreno, R., Mayer, R. E., Spires, H. A., & Lester, J. C. (2001). The case for social agency in computer-based teaching: Do students learn more deeply when they interact with animated pedagogical agents? *Cognition and Instruction, 19*(2), 177–213. doi:10.1207/S1532690XCI1902_02

Morishima, Y., Nakajima, H., Brave, S., Yamada, R., Maldonado, H., Nass, C., & Kawaji, S. (2004). The Role of Affect and Sociality in the Agent-Based Collaborative Learning System.In *Lecture Notes in Computer Science* (pp. 265-275).

Mulken, S. V., Andre, E., & Muller, J. (1998). *The persona effect: How substantial is it?* Paper presented at the HCI-98, Berlin.

Mylonas, Ph., Tzouveli, P., & Kollias, S. (2007). E-learning and intelligent content adaptation: an integrated approach. *International Journal of Continuing Engineering Education and Life-long Learning, 17*(4/5), 273–293. doi:10.1504/IJCEELL.2007.015043

Neji, M., & Ammar, M. (2007). Agent-based Collaborative Affective e-Learning Framework. *Electronic Journal of e-Learning, 5*, 123-134.

Ortony, A., Clore, G. L., & Collins, A. (1988). The Cognitive Structure of Emotions. Cambridge, UK: Cambridge University Press.

Paliouras, G., Papatheodorou, C., & Spyropoulos, C. D. (2002). Discovering Learner Communities on the Internet Using Unsupervised Machine Learning Techniques. *Interacting with Computers . Journal of Interacting with Computers, 14*(6), 761–791. doi:10.1016/S0953-5438(02)00015-2

Pelachaud, C., Carofiglio, V., Poggi, I., De Carolis, B., & De Rosis, F. (2002). Embodied Contextual Agent in Information Delivering Application. Proceedings of the First international Joint Conference on Autonomous Agents and Multiagent Systems: Part 2, (pp. 758-765), ACM Press.

Pentland, A. S. (2005). Socially Aware Computation and Communication. *Computer, 38*(3), 33–40. doi:10.1109/MC.2005.104

Picard, R. (1997). *Affective Computing*. Cambridge, MA: MIT Press.

Picard, R. W. (2000). Towards computers that recognize and respond to user emotion. *IBM Systems Journal, 39*(3), 705–719.

Prendinger, H., Dohi, H., Wang, H., Mayer, S., & Ishizuka, M. (2004). Empathic embodied interfaces: Addressing users' affective state. *Lecture Notes in Computer Science, 3068*, 53–64.

Raouzaiou, A., Tsapatsoulis, N., Karpouzis, K., & Kollias, S. (2002). Parameterized facial expression synthesis based on MPEG-4. *EURASIP Journal on Applied Signal Processing*, (10): 1021–1038. doi:10.1155/S1110865702206149

Ryokai, K., Vaucelle, C., & Cassell, J. (2003). Virtual peers as partners in storytelling and literacy learning. *Journal of Computer Assisted Learning, 19*(2), 195–208. doi:10.1046/j.0266-4909.2003.00020.x

ADDITIONAL READING

Aylett, R. S., Figuieredo, R., Louchart, S., Dias, J., & Paiva, A. (2006). Making it up as you go along – improvising stories for pedagogical purposes. In: J. Gratch, M. Young, R. Aylett, D. Ballin, & P. Olivier (Eds.), *6th International Conference, IVA*, (LNAI 4133, pp. 307-315).

Castellano, G., Kessous, L., & Caridakis, G. (2007). Multimodal emotion recognition from expressive faces, body gestures and speech. In C. Peter & R. Beale (Eds.), *Affect and Emotion in Human-Computer Interaction, Lecture Notes in Computer Science*.

Cowie, R., Douglas-Cowie, E., Karpouzis, K., Caridakis, G., Wallace, M., & Kollias, S. (2008). Recognition of Emotional States in Natural Human-Computer Interaction. In D. Tzovaras (Ed.), *Multimodal User Interfaces* (pp. 119-153). Berlin Heidelberg: Springer.

Ekman, P. (1999). Basic Emotions. In T. Dalgleish & T. Power (Eds.), *The Handbook of Cognition and Emotion* (pp. 45-60). Hoboken, NJ: John Wiley and Sons.

Hartmann, B., Mancini, M., Buisine, S., & Pelachaud, C. (2005b). Design and evaluation of expressive gesture synthesis for embodied conversational agents. In *AAMAS'05*, Utretch.

IEEE standard for learning technology-learning technology systems architecture (LTSA). (2003). *IEEE Std 1484.1-2003*, 1 – 97.

Jaimes, A. (2006). Human-Centered Multimedia: Culture, Deployment, and Access. *IEEE Multimedia Magazine, 13*(1).

Johnson, W. L., Rickel, J. W., & Lester, J. C. (2000). Animated pedagogical agents: Face-to- face interaction in interactive learning environments. *International Journal of Artificial Intelligence in Education, 11*, 47–78.

Karpouzis, K., Caridakis, G., Kessous, L., Amir, N., Raouzaiou, A., Malatesta, L., & Kollias, S. (2006). Modeling naturalistic affective states via facial, vocal, and bodily expressions recognition. In T. Huang, A. Nijholt, M. Pantic & A. Pentland (Eds.), *Lecture Notes in Artificial Intelligence, Special Volume on AI for Human Computing* (pp. 91-112). Berlin, Germany: Springer.

Lim, M. Y., & Aylett, R. S. (2007). Feel the difference: A Guide with Attitude! In C. Pelachaud et al. (Eds.) *Intelligent virtual agents* (pp. 317-330). Berlin Heidelberg, Germany: Springer-Verlag.

Louchart, S., & Aylett, R. (2007). From Synthetic Characters to Virtual Actors. In *Proceedings of International Conference in Artificial Intelligence for Interactive Digital Entertainment* (pp. 88-91)

Marsella, S., Johnson, W. L., & La Bore, C. M. (2003). Interactive Pedagogical Drama for Health Interventions.In *11th International Conference on Artificial Intelligence in Education*, Australia.

Moreno, R., Mayer, R. E., Spires, H. A., & Lester, J. C. (2001). The case for social agency in computer-based teaching: Do students learn more deeply when they interact with animated pedagogical agents? *Cognition and Instruction, 19*(2), 177–213. doi:10.1207/S1532690XCI1902_02

Ortony, A., Clore, G. L., & Collins, A. (1988). The Cognitive Structure of Emotions. Cambridge, UK: Cambridge University Press.

Pelachaud, C., Carofiglio, V., Poggi, I., De Carolis, B., & De Rosis, F. (2002). Embodied Contextual Agent in Information Delivering Application. In *Proceedings of the First international Joint Conference on Autonomous Agents and Multiagent Systems: Part 2*, (pp. 758-765). New York: ACM Press.

Pentland, A. S. (2005). Socially Aware Computation and Communication. *Computer, 38*(3), 33–40. doi:10.1109/MC.2005.104

Picard, R. (1997). Affective Computing. Cambridge, MA: MIT Press.

Picard, R. W. (2000). Towards computers that recognize and respond to user emotion. *IBM Systems Journal, 39*(3), 705–719.

Prendinger, H., Dohi, H., Wang, H., Mayer, S., & Ishizuka, M. (2004). Empathic embodied interfaces: Addressing users' affective state. []. New York: Springer.]. *Lecture Notes in Computer Science, 3068*, 53–64.

Raouzaiou, A., Tsapatsoulis, N., Karpouzis, K., & Kollias, S. (2002). Parameterized facial expression synthesis based on MPEG-4. *EURASIP Journal on Applied Signal Processing*, (10): 1021–1038. doi:10.1155/S1110865702206149

KEY TERMS AND DEFINITIONS

Decision Making: Scientific methodology to help understand, predict, or control marketing situations or problems.

Knowledge Utilization: The study of how individuals and teams acquire, construct, synthesize, share, and apply knowledge.

Emotion: Mental and physiological state associated with a wide variety of feelings, thoughts, and behavior.

Neural Networks: Systems used for solving artificial intelligence problems without necessarily creating a model of a real biological system.

Expressivity: Term used in genetics that refers to variations of a phenotype in individuals carrying a particular genotype. The term can be used to qualitatively or quantitatively characterize the extent of the phenotype variation given a particular genotype.

Electronic Learning (E-Learning): All types of technology-enhanced learning, where technology is used to support the learning process.

Motion Estimation: Process of determining motion vectors that describe the transformation from one 2D image to another; usually from adjacent frames in a video sequence.

Compilation of References

12th International Network-Based Education Conference NBE 2005, Rovaniemi, Finland (pp. 29-37).

Ackerman, M., & Starr, B. (1995). Social activity indicators: interface components for CSCW systems. In *8th annual ACM symposium on User interface and software technology*, Pittsburgh, Pennsylvania, United States.

Ackoff, R. L. (1989). From Data to Wisdom. *Journal of Applies Systems Analysis, 16*, 3–9.

Adeli, H. (1994). *Knowledge Engineering.* New York: McGraw-Hill.

Akkoyunlu, A., & Yılmaz-Soylu, M. (2008)... *The Internet and Higher Education, 11*, 26–32. doi:10.1016/j.iheduc.2007.12.006

Ala-Mutka, K., & Punie, Y. (2007). Aging Societies, Learning and ICT, *eLearning Papers,* 6 (November), http://www.elearningeuropa.info/files/media/media-14198.pdf

Alben, L. (1996). Quality of Experience. *Interaction, 13*(5), 12–15.

Alborzi, H., et al. (2000). Designing StoryRooms: Interactive Storytelling Spaces for Children. In *Proc. DIS'00.* New York: ACM Press.

Aldrich, C. (2003). *Simulations and the future of learning: An innovative (and perhaps revolutionary) approach to e-learning.* San Francisco, CA: Jossey-Bass/Pfeiffer.

Alexander, B. (2006). Web 2.0. A new wave of innovation for teaching and learning? *EDUCAUSE Review, 41*(2), 32–44.

Alexander, C. (1979). *The Timeless Way of Building.* New York: Oxford University Press.

Alexander, C. (2001). *A Just So Story. How patternlanguage.com got its name.* Retrieved July 22, 2006, from http://www.patternlanguage.com/leveltwo/patterns-frame.htm?/leveltwo/./ history/ajustsostory6.htm

Alexander, C., Ishikawa, S., Silverstein, M., & Jacobson, M. Fiksdahl-King, & Angel, S. (1977). *A Pattern Language.* New York: Oxford University Press.

Alexander, P. A. (2003). The development of expertise: The journey from acclimation to proficiency. *Educational Researcher, 32*(8), 10–14. doi:10.3102/0013189X032008010

Alfonso, A. (1974). *Japanese language patterns.* Sofia University, Center of Applied Linguistics, Tokyo.

Alitek Consulting. (2003). *What is strategic mapping?* Retrieved August 1, 2003, from Beauty. (2009). *Wikipedia.* Retrieved April 2009, from http://en.wikipedia.org/wiki/Beauty

Allen, I. E., Seaman, J., & Garrett, R. (2007). *Blending in. The extent and promise of blended education in the United States.* Retrieved on November 5, 2008, from http://www.blendedteaching.org/system/files/Blending_In.pdf

Anderman, L. H., & Midgley, C. (1998). *Motivation and middle school students* [ERIC digest]. Champaign, IL: ERIC Clearinghouse on Elementary and Early Childhood Education. (ERIC Document Reproduction Service No. ED 421 281).

Anderson, T. (2003a). Getting the mix right again: An updated and theoretical rationale for Interaction. *International Review of Research in Open and Distance Learning, 4*(2).

Anderson, T. (2003b). Modes of interaction in distance education: Recent developments and research questions. In M. Moore (Ed.), *Handbook of Distance Education* (pp. 129-144). Mahwah, NJ: Erlbaum.

Anderssen, E. C., & Myburgh, C. P. H. (1992). The acquisition of operating systems concepts by computer science students. *Computers & Education, 19*, 309–320. doi:10.1016/0360-1315(92)90125-O

Angeli, C. (2005). Transforming a Teacher Education Method Course through Technology: Effects on Preservice Teachers' Technology Competency. *Computers & Education, 45*(4), 383–398. doi:10.1016/j.compedu.2004.06.002

Angeli, C., & Valanides, N. (2005). Preservice Teachers as ICT Designers: An Instructional Design Model Based on an Expanded View of Pedagogical Content Knowledge. *Journal of Computer Assisted Learning, 21*(4), 292–302. doi:10.1111/j.1365-2729.2005.00135.x

Angeli, C., & Valanides, N. (2009). Epistemological and Methodological Issues for the Conceptualization, Development, and Assessment of ICT-TPCK: Advances in Technological Pedagogical Content Knowledge (TPCK). *Computers & Education, 52*, 154–168. doi:10.1016/j.compedu.2008.07.006

Anolli, L., Mantovani, F., Balestra, M., Kommers, P., Robotti, O., Salamin, A. D., et al. (2008). Experiential learning and affective computing for training soft-skills: Myself project. In T. Kidd & H. Song (Eds.), *Handbook of research on instructional systems and technology* (Vol.1, pp. 360-372). Hershey, PA: Information Science Reference.

Anolli, L., Mantovani, F., Mortillaro, M., Vescovo, A., Agliati, A., Confalonieri, L., et al. (2005). A Multimodal Database as a Background for Emotional Synthesis, Recognition and Training in E-Learning Systems. In J. Tao, T. Tan, & R. W. Picard (Eds.), *Affective Computing and Intelligent Interaction: First International Conference, ACII 2005*, Beijing, China, October 22-24, 2005, (LNCS 3784, pp. 566 – 573).

Antle, A. (2003). *Case Study:The Design of CB4Kids' Story Builder.* Proc. IDC 2003, Preston, UK, ACM Press, 59-67.

Antoniou, P., Delidou, E., Aggeioplasti, K., & Kaldoudi, E. (2008). Astronomy Education for the Public via Web 2.0 technologies. In *Proceeding of ICERI2008 – International Conference of Education, Research and Innovation,* Madrid, Spain.

Argyle, M. (1967). *The Psychology of Interpersonal Relations.* London: Penguin Books.

Argyle, M. (1975). *Bodily Communication.* New York: International Universities Press.

Argyle, M. (1976). *Social Interaction.* London: Tavistock.

Armstrong, K., & Retterer, O. (2008). Blogging as L2 writing: A case study. *Association for the Advancement of Computing in Education Journal, 16*(3), 233–251.

Arnheim, R. (1954). Art and visual perception: A psychology of the creative eye. In D.H. Jonassen (Ed.), *Handbook for research for educational communications and technology* (pp. 755-794). New York: Simon & Schuster Macmillan.

Atkins, M. J. (1993). Theories of learning and multimedia applications: An overview. *Research Papers in Education, 8*(2), 251–271. doi:10.1080/0267152930080207

Atwell, G. (2007, January). Personal Learning Environments – the Future of eLearning? *eLearning Papers*, 2. Retrieved from http://www.elearningeuropa.info/files/media/media- 11561.pdf

Augar, N., Raitman, R., & Zhou, W. (2004). Teaching and learning online with wikis. In R. Atkinson, C. McBeath, D. Jonas-Dwyer & R. Phillips (Eds.), *Beyond the comfort zone: Proceedings of the 21st ASCILITE Conference,* Perth, Australia (pp. 95-104).

Austin, H. (2000). Design for What? Six Dimensions of Activity. *Interaction*, 17–22.

Ausubel, D. (1980). Schemata, Cognitive Structure and Advance Organisers: A Reply to Anderson, Spiro and Anderson. *American Educational Research Journal*, *17*(3), 400–404.

Aviram, A., Ronen, Y., Somekh, S., Winer, A., & Sarid, A. (2008, July). Self-Regulated Personalised Learning (SRPL): Developing iClass Pedagogical Model. *eLearning Papers*, 4. Retrieved from http://www.elearningeuropa.info/files/media/media15974.pdf

Aycock, A., Garnham, C., & Kaleta, R. (2002). Lessons learned from the hybrid course project. *Teaching with Technology Today, 8*(6). Retrieved November 5, 2008, from http://www.uwsa.edu/ttt/articles/garnham2.htm

Aylett, R. S., Figuieredo, R., Louchart, S., Dias, J., & Paiva, A. (2006). Making it up as you go along – improvising stories for pedagogical purposes. In J. Gratch, M. Young, R. Aylett, D. Ballin & P. Olivier (Eds.), *6th International Conference, IVA* (LNAI 4133, pp. 307-315). New York: Springer.

Bach, C., & Scapin, D. (2004). Obstacles and perspectives for evaluating mixed reality systems usability. In *Proceedings of Mixer Workshop - IUI-CADUI 2004*, Funchal (pp. 72-79).

Baddeley, A. D. (1986). *Working memory*. Oxford, UK: Oxford University Press.

Bagui, S. (1998). Reasons for increased learning using multimedia. *Journal of Educational Multimedia and Hypermedia*, *7*(1), 3–18.

Balog, A., & Pribeanu, C. (2008). A comparative usability evaluation of two augmented reality learning scenarios. In *Proceedings of SIGMAP 2008 – International Conference on Signal Processing and Multimedia Applications*, 26-29 July (pp. 370-375).

Bamidis, P. D., & Pappas, C. (2008). *Medical Informatics and the Internet in Contemporary Healthcare Services*. Authority of the 3rd Health Region, Thessaloniki, Greece.

Bamidis, P. D., Constantinidis, S., Kaldoudi, E., Maglaveras, N., & Pappas, C. (2008). The use of Web 2.0 in teaching Medical Informatics to postgraduate medical students: first experiences. In G. Eysenbach (Ed.), *Medicine 2.0: Social Networking, Collaboration, Participation, Apomediation, and Openness. J Med Internet Res, 10*(3). Retrieved from http://www.jmir.org/2008/3/e22/

Bannert, M. (2002). Managing cognitive load–recent trends in cognitive load theory. *Learning and Instruction*, *12*, 139–146. doi:10.1016/S0959-4752(01)00021-4

Banyard, P., & Underwood, J. (2008). Understanding the Learning Space. *eLearning Papers*, 4. Retrieved from http://www.elearningeuropa.info/files/media/media15970.pdf

Barab, S. A., & Duffy, T. (2000). From practice fields to communities of practice. In D. Johassen & S. M. Land (Eds.), *Theoretical Foundations of Learning Environments* (pp. 25-56). Mahwah, NJ: Erlbaum.

Barab, S. A., Kling, A., & Gray, J. H. (2004). *Designing for Virtual Communities in the Service of Learning*. Cambridge, UK: Cambridge University Press.

Barbieri, T. (2000). Networked Virtual Environments for the Web: The WebTalk-I and WebTalk-II Architectures. In *IEEE Computer Multimedia & Expo 2000 (ICME)*, New York, NY.

Barbieri, T., & Paolini, P. (2000). Cooperative Visits to WWW Museum Sites a Year Later: Evaluating the effect. In *Proceeding Museums&Web2000*, Minneapolis, USA.

Barrett, L., & Salovey, P. (Eds.). (2002). *The wisdom in feeling: Psychological processes in emotional intelligence*. New York: Guilford Press.

Barrows, H. (1999). *Problem based learning initiative: Generic problem-based learning essentials*. Retrieved November 5, 2008 from http://www.pbli.org/pbl/generic_pbl.htm

Bartlett, F. (1932). *Remembering*. Cambridge, UK: Cambridge University Press.

Barton, D., & Tusting, K. (2005). *Beyond Communities of Practice. Language, Power and Social Context*. Cambridge, UK: Cambridge University Press.

Bates, A. W. (2005). *Technology, E-Learning and Distance Education*. London: Routledge.

Bates, J. (1994). The role of emotion in believable agents. *Communications of the ACM, 37*(7), 122–125. doi:10.1145/176789.176803

Bates, M. (2005). Fundamental Forms of Information. *Journal of the American Society for Information and Technology*. Retrieved November 5, 2008, from http://www.gseis.ucla.edu/ faculty/bates/articles/NatRep_info_11m_050514.html

Baylor, A. (1999). Intelligent agents as cognitive tools for education. *Educational Technology, 39*(2), 36–40.

Baylor, A. L., & Kim, Y. (2005). Simulating instructional roles through pedagogical agents. *International Journal of Artificial Intelligence in Education, 15*(2), 95–115.

Beach, V. (2002). *The E-Learning Industry – Retrospect and Prospect*. Retrieved from http://www.learningcircuits.org/2002/sep2002/beach.html

Beard, C., Wilson, J. P., & McCaster, R. (2007). Towards a Theory of e-Learning: Experimental e-Learning. *Journal of Hospitality, Leisure . Sport and Tourism Education, 6*(2), 3–15.

Becker, B., Dawson, P., Devine, K., Hannum, C., Hill, S., Leydens, J., et al. (2005). *Case Studies*. Writing@CSU, Colorado State University Department of English. Retrieved November 5, 2008, from http://writing.colostate.edu/ guides/research/casestudy/ com4a3.cfm/

Becker, H. S. (2003). The Politics of Presentation: Goffman and Total Institutions. *Caliber. Symbolic Interaction, 26*(4), 659–669. doi:10.1525/si.2003.26.4.659

Becker, J. (1975). *The Phrasal Lexicon* [BBN Report No. 3081]. Cambridge, MA: Bolt Beranek & Newman.

Becker, T., & Busemann, S. (Eds.). (1999). *"May I Speak Freely?" Between Templates and Free Choice in Natural Language Generation*. D-99-01, DFKI, Saarbrücken.

Bekker, M., Beusmans, J., Keyson, D., & Lloyd, P. (2003). KidReporter: a user requirements gathering technique for designing with children. *Interacting with Computers, 15*(3), 187–202. doi:10.1016/S0953-5438(03)00007-9

Belanger, Y. (2005). *Duke University iPod first year experience final evaluation report*. Durham, NC: Duke University. Retrieved November 14, 2008, from http://www.duke.edu/ddi/ipodfye.html

Bell, D. (1980). The Social Framework of the Information Society. In T. Forester (Ed.), *The Microelectronics Revolution*. Cambridge, MA: The MIT Press.

Bell, J., Bush, T., Fox, A., Goodey, J., & Goulding, S. (1984). *Conducting Small-Scale Investigations on Educational Management*. London: Paul Chapman Publishing.

Belz, A. (2009). That's Nice... What Can You Do With It? *Computational Linguistics, 35*(1), 111–118. doi:10.1162/coli.2009.35.1.111

Benford, S., et al. (2000). Designing Storytelling Technologies to Encourage Collaboration Between Young Children. In *Proc. CHI 2000*, The Hague, Netherlands (pp. 236-245).

Benigno, V., Bocconi, S., & Ott, M. (2007, November). Inclusive education: Helping Teachers to Choose ICT Resources and to Use Them Effectively. *eLearning Papers*, 6. Retrieved from http://www.elearningeuropa.info/files/media/media14199.pdf

Berliner, D., & Calfee, R. (Eds.). (1996). *Handbook of educational psychology*. New York: Macmillan.

Berners-Lee, T., Hendler, J., & Lassila, O. (2001). The semantic web. *Scientific American, 184*(5), 34–43. doi:10.1038/scientificamerican0501-34

Bickmore, T., & Picard, R. W. (2004). Towards Caring Machines. In *CHI Extended Abstracts* (pp. 1489-1492).

Bickmore, T., Consolvo, S., & Intille, S. (2009). Engagement by Design. In *CHI 2009 Extended Abstracts*.

Biocca, F. (1997). The cyborg's dilemma: progressive embodiment in virtual environments. *Journal of Computer-Mediated Communication, 3*(2).

Biocca, F., Burgoon, J., Harm, C., & Stoner, M. (2001). *Criteria and scope conditions for a theory and measure of social presence*. Retrieved March 29, 2007, from http://www.temple.edu/ispr/prev_conferences/proceedings/2001/Bioccal.pdf

Bliuc, A.-M., Goodyear, P., & Ellis, R. A. (2007)... *The Internet and Higher Education, 10*, 231–244. doi:10.1016/j.iheduc.2007.08.001

Bloom, B. S. (Ed.). (1956). *Taxonomy of Educational Objectives: The Classification of Educational Goals*. New York: Susan Fauer Company.

Bloom, B. S., Mesia, B. B., & Krathwohl, D. R. (1964). *Taxonomy of Educational Objectives*. New York: David McKay.

Blythe, M., Hassenzahl, M., & Wright, P. (2004). More funology. A special issue. *Interaction, 11*(5).

Bodemer, D., & Ploetzner, R. (in press). Encouraging the active integration of information during learning with multiple and interactive representations. In H. Niegemann, R. Brünken, & D. Leutner (Eds.), *Instructional design for multimedia learning. Proceedings of the EARLI SIG 6 Biannual Workshop2002in Erfurt*. Muenster, Germany: Waxmann.

Bødker, S., Greenbaum, J., & Kyng, M. (1991). Setting the stage for design as action. In J. Greenbaum & M. Kyng (Eds.), *Design at work: cooperative design of computer systems* (pp. 139–154). Hillsdale, NJ: Lawrence Erlbaum Associates.

Boersma, P., & Weenink, D. (2008). *Praat: doing phonetics by computer (Version 4.3.14)* [Computer program]. Retrieved November 14, 2008, from http://www.praat.org/

Boettcher, J. (2007). Ten Core Principles for Designing Effective Learning Environments: Insights from Brain Research and Pedagogical Theory. *Innovate, 3*(3). Retrieved on November 2, 2008 from http://www.innovateonline.info/index.php?view=article&id=54

Bolchini, D., & Garzotto, F. (2008). Success Factors for Hypermedia Tools in Education. In *Proc. ACM Hypertext 2008*, June 2008, Pittsburgh, USA.

Bonwell, C., & Eison, J. (1991). *Active Learning: Creating Excitement in the Classroom. AEHE-ERIC Higher Education Report No.1*. Washington, DC.

Boon, J., Ramasundram, V., Van der Klink, M., & Tattersall, C. (2005). Developing a Critical View on e-Learning Trend Reports: Trend Watching or Trend Setting? *International Journal of Training and Development, 9*(3), 205–211. doi:10.1111/j.1468-2419.2005.00229.x

Boose, J. H. (1990). Knowledge Acquisition Tools, Methods and Mediating Representations. In H. Motoda, et al. (Eds.), *Knowledge Acquisition for Knowledge-Based Systems* (pp. 123-168.). Tokyo, Ohinsha Ltd.

Borger, R., & Seaborne, A. E. M. (1966). *The Psychology of Learning*. London: Pelican Books.

Bork, A. (2003). The dilemma of teacher training. *Contemporary Issues in Technology and Teacher Education, 3*(2). Retrieved on September 28, 2008 from http://www.citejournal.org/vol3/iss2/general/article1.cfm

Botturi, L. (2008). E2ML: A Tool for Sketching Instructional Designs. In L. Botturi & T. Stubbs (eds.), *Handbook of Visual Languages in Instructional Design: Theories and Practices* (pp. 112-132). Hershey, PA: Informing Science Reference.

Botturi, L., Inglese, T., & Rozalèn, S. (2003). Design and Trust as Key Factor in E-learning. In *AACE, SITE 2003*, Albuquerque, New Mexico (pp. 1379-1382).

Boulos, M. K. (2007). *Healthcare on Web 2.0*. Healthcare Information and Management Systems Society. Retrieved on 30 Dec 2007 from http://emea.himss.org/news/expertviews_archive.asp

Boulos, M., Maramba, I., & Wheeler, S. (2006). Wikis, blogs and podcasts: A new generation of web-based tools for virtual collaborative clinical practice and education. *BMC Medical Education, 6*(41).

Bouras, C., Philopoulos, A., & Tsiatsos, T. (2001). e-Learning through distributed virtual environments. *Journal of Network and Computer Applications, 24*(3), 175–199. doi:10.1006/jnca.2001.0131

Bouthillier, F., & Shearer, K. (2002, October). Understanding Knowledge Management and Information Management: the Need for an Empirical Perspective. *Information Research*, 8(1).

Bowman, D., Gabbard, J., & Hix, D. (2002). A Survey of Usability Evaluation in Virtual Environments: Classification and Comparison of Methods. *Presence (Cambridge, Mass.)*, *11*(4), 404–424. doi:10.1162/105474602760204309

Boyle, E., & Crosland, A. (1976). *The Politics of Education (Conversations with M. Kogan) (2nd Ed.)*. Harmondsworth, UK: Penguin Books.

Bradley, M. M., & Lang, P. J. (1994). Measuring emotion: The self-assessment manikin and the semantic differential. *Journal of Behavior Therapy and Experimental Psychiatry*, *25*, 49–59. doi:10.1016/0005-7916(94)90063-9

Bramble, W. J. (2008). *Economics of Distance and Online Learning: Theory, Practice and Research*. London & New York: Routledge.

Brandon, B. (Ed.). (2008). *Handbook of e-Learning*. Retrieved from http://www.elearningguild.com/showfile.cfm?id=2509

Brandsford, J. D., Brown, A. L., & Cocking, R. R. (Eds.). (2000). *How People Learn: Brain, Mind, Experience and School*. Washington, DC: National Academies Press.

Bratsas, C., Bamidis, P. D., Kaimakamis, E., & Maglaveras, N. (2008). Usage of Semantic Web Technologies (Web-3.0) Aiming to Facilitate the Utilisation of Computerized Algorithmic Medicine in Clinical Practice. In G. Eysenbach (Ed.), *Medicine 2.0: Social Networking, Collaboration, Participation, Apomediation, and Openness. J Med Internet Res, 10*(3). Retrieved from http://www.jmir.org/2008/3/e22/

Bray, M. (2007). The Shadow Education System: Private Tutoring and its Implication for Planners. *Fundamentals of Educational Planning, 61.*

Breakwell, G. M., Hammond, S., & Fife-Schaw, C. (2000). *Research methods in psychology* (2nd Ed.). London: Sage Publications.

Brenner, J. (2005). Knowledge as system: A logic of epistemology. In *6ème Congrès de l'Union européenne de systémique,* Paris, 19-22 September 2005. Retrieved November 5, 2008, from http://www.autogenesis.ch/brenner.html

Brown, A. (1992). Design experiments: Theoretical and methodological challenges in creating complex interventions in classroom settings. *Journal of the Learning Sciences*, *2*(2), 141–178. doi:10.1207/s15327809jls0202_2

Brown, J. S., Collins, A., & Duguid, P. (1989). Situated cognition and the culture of learning. *Educational Researcher*, *18*(1), 32–42.

Bruner, J. (1973). Beyond the Information Given: Studies in the Psychology of Knowing. New York: W. Norton.

Bruner, J. S. (1961). The act of discovery. *Harvard Educational Review*, *31*(1), 21–32.

Bruner, J. S. (1966). *Toward a theory of instruction.* Cambridge, MA: Harvard University Press.

Brusilovsky, P. (2003). Developing adaptive educational hypermedia systems: From design models to authoring tools. In T. Murray, S. Blessing, & S. Ainsworth (Eds.), *Authoring tools for advanced technology learning environment*. Dordrecht, The Netherlands: Kluwer Academic.

Brusilovsky, P., & Eklund, J. (1998). A study of user-model based link annotation in educational hypermedia. *Journal of Universal Computer Science*, *4*(4), 429–448.

Brusilovsky, P., & Rizzo, R. (2002). Map-Based Horizontal Navigation in Educational Hypertext. In *Proceedings of Hypertext*, University Of Maryland, College Park, USA.

Brusilovsky, P., Yudelson, M., & Gavrilova, T. (2005). *Towards User Modeling Meta Ontology*. In L. Ardissono, P. Brna & A. Mitrovic (Eds.), Proceedings of 10th International conference User Modeling (LNAI 3538, pp. 448-452). New York: Springer.

Burdea, G., & Coiffet, P. (1994). *Virtual reality technology.* New York: Wiley.

Buzan, T. *Mind Map handbook*. Thorsons, 2005.

Byrne, R. M. J. (2007). *The Rational Imagination: How People Create Alternatives to Reality*. Cambridge, MA: MIT.

Calvert, G. A., Spence, C., & Stein, B. E. (2004). *The Handbook of Multisensory Processing*. Boston: MIT Press.

Capuano, N., Marsella, M., & Salerno, S. (2000). ABITS: An agent based intelligent tutoring system for distance learning. In C. Peylo, (Ed.), *Proceedings of the International Workshop on Adaptive and Intelligent Web- Based Educational Systems* (pp. 17–28).

Carliner, S., & Shank, P. (Eds.). (2008). *The e-Learning Handbook: Past Promises, Present Challenges*. San Francisco: Pfeiffer.

Carwile, J. (2007). A Constructivist Approach to Online Teaching and Learning. *Inquiry*, *12*(1), 68–73.

Casacuberta, D. (2007, November). Digital Inclusion: Best Practices from eLearning. *eLearning Papers*, 6. Retrieved from http://www.elearningeuropa.info/files/media/media-14197.pdf

Cassel, J., & Ryokoiai, K. (2001). Making space for Voice: Technologies to support Children Fantasy and Storytelling. *Personal and Ubiquitous Computing, 5*(3). Clayton, L., Brand, C., Cherry, G., & Rader, C. (98). Adapting User Interface Design Methods to the Design of Educational Activities. In *Proc. CHI 98*, Los Angeles, CA, USA (pp. 619-628).

Cassell, J. (2000). More than just another pretty face: Embodied Conversational Agents. *Communications of the ACM, 43*(4), 70–78. doi:10.1145/332051.332075

Cassell, J., Sullivan, J., Prevost, S., & Churchill, E. (2000). *Embodied Conversational Agents*. Cambridge MA: The MIT Press.

Castellano, G., Kessous, L., & Caridakis, G. (2007). Multimodal emotion recognition from expressive faces, body gestures and speech. In C. Peter & R. Beale (Eds.), *Affect and Emotion in Human-Computer Interaction, Lecture Notes in Computer Science*. Berlin, Germany: Springer.

Castillo, D., & Sjöberg, M. (2008). A Theoretical Framework for the Economics of E-Learning in Castillo, D. (ed.), *The Economics of E-Learning*, Monograph, *Revista de Univesidad y Sociedad del Conocimiento*, Vol. 5, No. 1, pp. 1-11, Universitat Oberta de Catalunya, http://www.uoc.edu/rusc/5/1/dt/eng/monograph.pdf

CEC - Commission of European Communities. (2008). *Towards More Knowledge-Based Policy and Practice in Education and Training*, Commission Staff Working Document, http://www.eenee.de/portal/page/portal/EENEEContent/_IMPORT-_TELECENTRUM/DOCS/Commission_eductrain.PDF

Centre for Educational Research and Innovation (CERI). OECD (2003). *New Challenges for Educational Research*. Paris, OECD

Centre for Educational Research and Innovation (CERI). OECD/ (2007) *Evidence in Education: Linking Research and Policy*, Paris, OECD

CESifo. (2007). World Economic Survey, Volume 6, N. 1

Champion, R. (2001). Planning for action, step by step. *Journal of Staff Development*. [NSDC]. *National Staff Development Council, 22*(4), 62–63.

Chan, T. W., & Baskin, A. B. (1990). Learning companion systems. In C. Frasson & G. Gauthier (Eds.), *Intelligent tutoring systems at the crossroads of artificial intelligence and education* (pp. 7–33). NJ: Ablex Publishing Corporation.

Chastain, K. (1969). The audio-lingual habit learning theory vs. the code-cognitif learning theory. *IRAL, 7*(2), 97–107. doi:10.1515/iral.1969.7.2.97

Chen, C. (1999). *Information visualisation and virtual environments*. London: Springer.

Chen, R. (2006). A study of comparing the use of augmented reality and physical models in chemistry education. *Proceedings of the 2006 ACM international conference on Virtual reality continuum and its applications,* 369-372. New York: ACM Press.

Chen, R. S., & Hsiang, C. (2006). A study on the critical success factors for corporations embarking on knowledge community-based e-learning. *Information Sciences, 177,* 570–586. doi:10.1016/j.ins.2006.06.005

Chen, R., & Wang, X. (2008). An empirical study on tangible augmented reality learning space for design skill transfer. *Tsinghua Science and Technology, 13*(S1), 13–18. doi:10.1016/S1007-0214(08)70120-2

Chino, N. (2004). *A Dictionary of Basic Japanese Sentence Patterns.* Kodansha, Tokyo.

Chomsky, N. (1959). A review of B. F. Skinner's Verbal Behavior. *Language, 31*(1), 26–58. doi:10.2307/411334

Chou, C. Y., Chan, T. W., & Lin, C. J. (2003). Redefining the learning companion: The past, present, and future of educational agents. *Computers & Education, 40,* 255–269. doi:10.1016/S0360-1315(02)00130-6

Chou, C., & Lin, H. (1998). The effect of navigation map types and cognitive styles on learners' performance in a computer-networked hypertext learning system. *Journal of Educational Multimedia and Hypermedia, 7*(2/3), 151–176.

Christou, C. G., & Bülthoff, H. H. (1999). View dependence in scene recognition after active learning. *Memory & Cognition, 27*(6), 996–1007.

Christou, C., Angus, C., & Loscos, C. Dettori, A., & Roussou, M. (2006). A versatile large-scale multimodal VR system for cultural heritage visualization. In *VRST '06: Proceedings of the ACM symposium on Virtual reality software and technology.* New York: ACM Press.

Chuang, Y. R. (1999). Teaching in a multimedia computer environment: A study of the effects of learning style, gender, and math achievement. *Interactive Multimedia Electronic Journal of Computer-Enhanced Learning.* Retrieved November 4, 2005, from http://imej.wfu.edu/arti-cles/1999/1/10/index.asp

Clark, R. C., & Mayer, R. E. (2002). *E-Learning and the Science of Instruction: Proven Guidelines for Consumers and Designers of Multimedia Learning.* San Francisco: Pfeiffer.

Clark, R. E. (1983). Reconsidering research on learning from media. *Review of Educational Research, 53*(4), 445–459.

Clark, R. E. (1994). Media will Never Influence Learning. *Educational Technology Research and Development, 42*(2), 21–29. doi:10.1007/BF02299088

Cobb, C. W. (1992). *Responsive Schools, Renewed Communities.* San Francisco: Institute for Contemporary Studies.

Cobb, P. (2003). Design Experiments in Educational Research. *Educational Researcher, 32*(1), 9–13. doi:10.3102/0013189X032001009

Cobb, S., Nichols, S., Ramsey, A., & Wilson, J. R. (1999). Virtual Reality-Induced Symptoms and Effects (VRISE). *Presence (Cambridge, Mass.), 8*(2), 169–186. doi:10.1162/105474699566152

Cochran, K. F., Derutier, J. A., & King, R. A. (1993). Pedagogical content knowing: an integrative model for teacher preparation. *Journal of Teacher Education, 44,* 263–272. doi:10.1177/0022487193044004004

Cockton, G. (2006). Valuing User Experience. In [Oslo: ACM Press.]. *Proceedings of UX Workshop NordiCHI, 2006,* 100–105.

Coffield, F., Moseley, D., Hall, E., & Ecclestone, K. (2004). *Learning styles and pedagogy in post-16 learning. A systematic and critical review.* London: Learning and Skills Research Centre.

Collins, A. (1992). Towards a design science of education. In E. Scanlon & T. O'Shea (Eds.), *New directions in educational technology* (pp. 15-22). Berlin, Germany: Springer.

Collins, A., & Ferguson, W. (2003). Epistemic forms and epistemic games: Structures and strategies to guide inquiry. *Educational Psychologist, 28*(1), 25–42. doi:10.1207/s15326985ep2801_3

Commission of European Communities. (2000). *Communication from the Commission: e-Learning – Designing Tomorrow's Education*. Brussels, Belgium.

Conlon, T. (1997). Towards Diversity: Advancing Knowledge-based Modelling with Knowledge Acquisition. In *Proceedings of 8th International PEG Conference*, Sozopol, Bulgaria (pp. 379-386).

Contreras-Castillo, J., Favela, J., Perez-Fragoso, C., & Santamaria-del-Angel, E. (2003). Informal interaction and their implications for online courses. *Computers & Education, 42*, 149–168. doi:10.1016/S0360-1315(03)00069-1

Cook, P. (2002). *Knowledge Economics. Clusters, Learning and Cooperative Advantage*. London: Rutledge.

Coplien, J. O. (2005). *A Pattern Definition. Software Patterns*. Retrieved November 5, 2008, from http://hillside.net/patterns/definition.html

Corbalan, G., Kester, L., & Van Merriënboer, J. J. G. (2006). Towards a personalized task selection model with shared instructional control. *Instructional Science, 34*, 399–422. doi:10.1007/s11251-005-5774-2

Cosin, B. R. (Ed.). (1972). *Education: Structure and Society*. Hamondsworth, UK: Penguin Books.

Costabile, M. F., De Angeli, A., Lanzilotti, R., Ardito, C., Buono, P., & Pederson, T. (2008). Explore! Possibilities and Challenges of Mobile Learning. In *Proceedings of CHI 2008* (pp. 145-154). New York: ACM Press.

Cowie, R., Douglas-Cowie, E., Karpouzis, K., Caridakis, G., Wallace, M., & Kollias, S. (2008). Recognition of Emotional States in Natural Human-Computer Interaction. In D. Tzovaras (Ed.), *Multimodal User Interfaces* (pp. 119-153). Berlin Heidelberg, Germany: Springer.

Cronje, J. C. (2001). Metaphors and models in internet-based learning. *Computers & Education, 37*(3-4), 241–256. doi:10.1016/S0360-1315(01)00049-5

Csikszentmihalyi, M. (1991). *Flow: The Psychology of Optimal Experience*. New York: Harper Perennial.

Cuban, L. (1986). *Teachers and machines: The classroom use of technology since 1920*. New York: Teachers College Press.

Cuban, L. (1993). Computers meet classroom: classroom wins. *Teachers College Record, 95*(2), 185–210.

Cuban, L. (2001). *Oversold and Underused: Computers in the Classroom*. London: Harvard University Press.

D'Mello, S. K., Picard, R. W., & Graesser, A. C. (2007). Towards an Affect-Sensitive AutoTutor. *Special issue on Intelligent Educational Systems – . IEEE Intelligent Systems, 22*(4), 53–61. doi:10.1109/MIS.2007.79

Dahlbäck, N., Jönsson, A., & Ahrenberg, L. (1993). Wizard of Oz studies: why and how. *In Proceedings of the 1st international conference on Intelligent user interfaces*, January 04-07, 1993, Orlando, Florida, United States (pp. 193-200).

Dalsgård, P., & Halskov, K. (2006). Real Life Experiences with Experience Design. In *Proc. NordiCHI 2006*, (pp. 331-340).

Damasio, A. R. (1994). *Descartes' Error: Emotion, Reason, and the Human Brain*. New York: Harper.

Damasio, A. R. (2003). *Spinoza avait raison: Joie et tristesse, le cerveau des émotions*. Paris: Odile Jacob.

Damasio, A. R., Grabowski, T. J., Bechara, A., Damasio, H., Ponto, L. L. B., Parvizi, J., & Hichwa, R. D. (2000). Subcortical and cortical brain activity during the feeling of self-generated emotions. *Nature Neuroscience, 3*, 1049–1056. doi:10.1038/79871

Daradoumis, T., Martinez-Monés, A., & Xhafa, F. (2004). An integrated approach for analysing and assessing the performance of virtual learning groups. In *Lecture Notes in Computer Science*. Springer Berlin/Heidelberg

Davenport, T., & Prusak, L. (1998). *Working knowledge: how organizations manage what they know*. Cambridge, MA: Harvard Business School Press.

Davey, P. (2007, January). Can Technologies Offer Intelligence in Tutoring? An Interview with Prof. Ulrich Hoppe. *eLearning Papers*, 2. Retrieved from http://www.elearningeuropa.info/files/media/media11562.pdf

Davies, C. (1989, June). Goffman's concept of the total institution: Criticisms and revisions. *Human Studies*, *12*(1-2), 77–95. doi:10.1007/BF00142840

Davies, J., van Harmelen, F., & Fensel, D. (Eds.). (2002). *Towards the Semantic Web: Ontology-Driven Knowledge Management*. New York: John Wiley & Sons, Inc.

Davis, F. D., Bagozzi, R. P., & Warshaw, P. R. (1989). User Acceptance of Computer Technology: A Comparison of Two Theoretical Models. *Management Science*, *35*(8), 982–1003. doi:10.1287/mnsc.35.8.982

Davis, K. S., & Falba, C. J. (2002). Integrating technology in elementary preservice teacher education: Orchestrating scientific inquiry in meaningful ways. *Journal of Science Teacher Education*, *13*(4), 303–329. doi:10.1023/A:1022535516780

Dawson, K., Pringle, R., & Adams, T. L. (2003). Providing links between technology integration, methods courses, and school-based field experiences: A curriculum-based and technology-enhanced microteaching. *Journal of Computing in Teacher Education*, *20*(1), 41–47.

De Lucia, A., Francese, R., Passero, I., & Tortora, G. (2009). Development and evaluation of a virtual campus on Second Life: The case of SecondDMI. *Computers & Education*, *52*(1), 220–233. doi:10.1016/j.compedu.2008.08.001

De Rosis, F., Pelachaud, C., Poggi, I., Carofiglio, V., & De Carolis, B. (2003). From Greta's mind to her face: modelling the dynamics of affective states in a conversational Embodied Agent. *International Journal of Human-Computer Studies*, *59*, 81–118. doi:10.1016/S1071-5819(03)00020-X

Dede, C., Salzman, M. C., & Loftin, R. B. (1996). The development of a virtual world for learning Newtonian mechanics. In P. Brusilovsky, P. Kommers & N. Streitz, (Eds.), *Multimedia, Hypermedia, and Virtual Reality* (pp. 87-106). Berlin, Germany: Springer/Verlag.

deKeyser, R. (2001). *Automaticity and automatization*. In P. Robinson (Ed.), *Cognition and second language instruction* (pp. 125-151). New York: Cambridge University Press.

deKeyser, R. (2007a). *Skill acquisition theory*. In J. Williams & B. VanPatten (Eds.), *Theories in Second Language Acquisition: An introduction* (pp. 97-113). Mahwah, NJ: Erlbaum.

deKeyser, R. (Ed.). (2007b). *Practicing in a second language: Perspectives from applied linguistics and cognitive psychology*. Cambridge, UK: Cambridge University Press

Delrio, C., & Fischer, T. (2007, May). HELIOS: Redefining e-Learning Territories. *eLearning Papers*, 4. Retrieved from http://www.elearningeuropa.info/files/media/media12725.pdf

Deproost, P.-A. (1998). *L'héritage latin. Une culture de l'universel*. Research seminar on L'Europe et la culture des cultures, Council of Europe project EUxIN. University of Louvain, Belgium. Retrieved July 22, 2006 from www.areopage.net/heritage.htm

Dertouzos, M. (1997). *What will be*. London: Judy Piatkus Ltd.

Desmet, P. M. A. (2008). *Pleasant emotions in product experience*. In P.M.A. Desmet, M.A. Karlsson, & J. van Erp (Eds.), *Design & Emotion Moves*. Cambridge, UK: Cambridge Scholars Publishing.

Desurvire, H., Maplan, M., & Toth, J. A. (2004). Using heuristics to evaluate the playability of games. In *Extended Abstracts of CHI 2004* (pp. 1509-1512).

Deubel, P. (2003). An investigation of behaviourist and cognitive approaches to instructional multimedia design. *Journal of Educational Multimedia and Hypermedia*, *12*(1), 63–90.

Devlin, K. (2000). *The Math Gene: How Mathematical Thinking Evolved and Why Numbers Are Like Gossip*. New York: Basic Books.

Dexter, S., Doering, A., & Riedel, E. (2006). Content Area Specific Technology Integration: A Model For Educating Teachers. *Journal of Technology and Teacher Education*, *14*(2), 325–345.

Di Blas, N., & Poggi, C. (2006). 3D for Cultural Heritage and Education: Evaluating the Impact. In D. Bearman

& J. Trant (Eds.), *Selected Papers from Museums and the Web'06*. Albuquerque, NM: Archives and Museum Informatics.

Di Blas, N., Paolini, P., & Poggi, C. (2005). Educational benefits: testing and evaluation of a collaborative 3d world. In *Proc. ED-MEDIA 2005* (pp. 1002-1011).

Di Blas, N., Paolini, P., Poggi, C., & Torrebruno, A. (2008). 3D Worlds for Learning and Play: 6 years of Experience. In *Proc. E-Learn 2008*, AACE.

Di Blas, N., Poggi, C., & Reeves, T. (2006). Collaborative Learning in a 3D Virtual Environment: Design Factors and Evaluation Results. In *Proc. 7th International Conference of the Learning Sciences (ICLS)*, Indiana University, Bloomington, IN (Vol. 1, pp. 127-133).

Di Vesta, F. (1987). The cognitive movement and education. In J. Glover & R. Royce (Eds.), *Historical foundations of education psychology* (pp. 203-233). New York: Plenum Press.

Dichenz, H. (2001). *E-Learning, A Linguistic, Psychological and Pedagogical Analysis of A Misleading Term.* A Paper Presented at the 20th ICDE World Conference, Düsseldorf, Germany.

Dicheva, D., & Aroyo, L. (2004). Concepts and Ontologies in Web-based Educational Systems. *Int. J. Cont. Engineering Education and Life-long Learning, 14*(3), 187–190.

Dicheva, D., & Dichev, C. (2005). Authoring Educational Topic Maps: Can We Make It Easier? In . *Proceedings of ICALT, 2005*, 216–219.

Dicheva, D., & Dichev, C. (2007). Helping Courseware Authors to Build Ontologies: the Case of TM4L. In *13th Int. Conference on Artificial Intelligence in Education*, July 9-13, 2007, California (pp. 77-84).

Dillon, A., & Gabbard, R. (1998). Hypermedia as an educational technology: A review of the quantitative research literature on learner comprehension, control and style. *Review of Educational Research, 68*(3), 322–349.

Dillon, A., & Morris, M. (1996). User acceptance of new information technology: theories and models. In M. Williams (Ed.), *Annual Review of Information Science and Technology* (Vol. 31, pp. 3-32). Medford, NJ: Information Today.

Dindler, C., et al. (2005), *Mission from Mars-A Method for Exploring User Requirements for Children in a Narrative Space*. In *Proc. IDC 2005*, Boulder, USA.

DiSessa, A. (2001). *Changing minds: computer, learning, and literacy.* Cambridge, MA: MIT Press.

Doering, A., Veletsianos, G., & Scharber, C. (2007). Coming of Age: Research and Pedagogy on Geospatial Technologies within K-12 Social Studies Education. In A. J. Milson & M. Alibrandi (Eds.), *Digital Geography: Geo-Spatial Technologies in the Social Studies Classroom* (pp. 213-226). Charlotte, NC: Information Age Publishing

Dondis, D. A. (1973). *A primer of visual literacy* (7th Ed.). London: The MIT Press.

Downes, S. (2005). *The Economy of E-Learning.* Retrieved from http://www.downes.ca/cgi-bin/page.cgi?post=5

Drucker, P. (2001). *Management Challenges for the 21st Century.* New York: Harper Business Press.

Druin, A. (1999). Cooperative inquiry: developing new technologies for children with children. In *Proceedings of CHI'99*, Pittsburgh, PA, USA, May 15–20 (pp. 592–599). New York: ACM.

Druin, A. (2002). The Child as Learner, Critic, Inventor, and Technology Design Partner. *International Journal of Technology and Design Education, 12*, 189–213. doi:10.1023/A:1020255806645

Druin, A. (2002). The role of children in the design of new technology. *Behaviour & Information Technology, 21*(1), 1–25.

Druin, A. (Ed.). (1999). *The Design of Children's Technology.* San Francisco, CA: Morgan Kaufmann.

Druin, A., et al. (1997). KidPad: A Design Collaboration Between Children, Technologists, and Educators. In *Proc. CHI' 97*, Atlanta, GA, USA.

Druin, A., et al. (2001). Designing a Digital Library for Young Children: An Intergenerational Partnership. In *Proc. JCDL'01*, Roanoke, Virginia, USA (pp. 398-405).

Ducheneaut, N., Yee, N., Nickel, E., & Moore, R. (2006). Alone Together: Exploring the social dynamics of massively multiplayer online games. In *Proc. CHI2006*, (pp. 407-416).

Duffy, T. M., & Jonassen, D. H. (1992). *Constructivism and the technology of instruction: A conversation.* Hillsdale, NJ: Lawrence Erlbaum.

Dwyer, F. M. (1972). *A guide for improving visualized instruction.* State College, PA: Learning Services.

Dwyer, F. M. (1978). *Strategies for improving visual learning.* State College, PA: Learning Services.

Dwyer, F. M. (Ed.). (1987). *Enhancing visualized instruction-recommendations for practitioners.* State College, PA: Learning Services.

Dwyer, F. M., & Dwyer, C. (2003). A systematic assessment of the contributions of animation to knowledge acquisition. In *Proceedings of the 2003 Annual ED-MEDIA Conference*, Honolulu, HI (pp. 1112-1117).

Ebbinghaus, H. (1962). *Memory: A contribution to experimental psychology.* New York: Dover.

Ebner, M., & Holzinger, A. (2007). Successful implementation of user-centered game based learning in higher education: An example from civil engineering. *Computers & Education*, *49*(3), 873–890. doi:10.1016/j.compedu.2005.11.026

Ebner, M., Holzinger, A., & Maurer, H. (2007). Web 2.0 Technology: Future Interfaces for Technology Enhanced Learning. In C. Stephanidis (Ed.), *Universal Access in HCI, Part III, HCII 2007* (LNCS 4556, pp. 559–568). Berlin: Springer-Verlag. Ehlers, U. (2007). The new pathway for e-learning: From distribution to collaboration and competence in e-learning. *Association for the Advancement of Computing in Education Journal*, 16(2), 187-20.

ECP. (2000, May 24). *EC Policy Document on e-Learning.*

Eggins, S. (1997). *Analysing casual conversation.* London: Cassell.

Ehlers, U. D. (2007, January). The 'E' – Empowering Learners: Myths and Realities in Learner-Oriented eLearning Quality. *eLearning Papers,* 2. Retrieved from http://www.elearningeuropa.info/files/media/media11560.pdf

Ehn, P., & Kyng, M. (1991). Cardboard computers: mocking-it-up or hands-on the future. In J. Greenbaum & M. Kyng (Eds.) *Design at work: cooperative design of computer systems* (pp. 169–195). Hillsdale, NJ: Lawrence Erlbaum Associates.

Eisenstadt, M., Domingue, J., Rajan, T., & Motta, E. (1990). Visual Knowledge Engineering. *IEEE Transactions on Software Engineering, 16*(10), 1164–1177. doi:10.1109/32.60296

Ekman, P. (1993). Facial Expressions and Emotion. *The American Psychologist, 48*(4), 384–392. doi:10.1037/0003-066X.48.4.384

Ekman, P. (1999). *Basic Emotions.* In T. Dalgleish & T. Power (Eds.), *The Handbook of Cognition and Emotion* (pp. 45-60). Hoboken, NJ: John Wiley and Sons.

Eleventh Workshop on Knowledge Acquisition. *Modeling and Management*, Banff, Alberta, Canada (pp. 124-129).

Engeström, R. Miettinen, & R. Punamaki (Eds.), *Perspectives on Activity theory.* New York: Cambridge University Press.

Engeström, Y. (1987). *Learning by expanding: An activity-theoretical approach to developmental research,* Helsinki: Orienta-Konstultit.

Engeström, Y. (1999). Activity theory and individual and social transformation. In Y.

Engeström, Y. (1999). Expansive visibilization of work: An activity-theoretical perspective. In *Computer Supported Collaborative Work (CSCW).* Vol 8, Nos 1 and 2). pp 63-93.

Ennew, C. T., & Fernandez-Young, A. (2006). Weapons of mass instruction? The rhetoric and reality of online learning. *Marketing Intelligence & Planning, 24*(2), 148–157. doi:10.1108/02634500610654008

Enz, S., Zoll, C., Vannini, N., Schneider, W., Hall, L., Paiva, A., & Aylett, R. (2007). Emotional Learning in Primary Schools: FearNot! An Anti-bullying intervention based on Virtual Role Play with Intelligent Synthetic Characters, *6th European Conference on e-Learning (ECEL)*, Copenhagen, Denmark, 4-5 October, 2007.

Equal. (2004). *Mainstreaming and Creating Impact – A Guide for Development Partnerships.* Sharing Practice from the Equal Programme. Birmingham, UK: Equal Support Unit. Retrieved July 13, 2008 from http://www.equal.ecotec.co.uk/resources/gpg/ gpg/down_doc.asp?file=gpg_mainstreaming.doc

Erickson, T. (1997). Designing agents as if people mattered. In J. M. Bradshaw (Ed.), *Software agents* (pp. 79–96). Menlo Park, CA: MIT Press.

Erickson, T., & Kellogg, W. A. (2000). Social translucence: an approach to designing systems that support social processes. *ACM Transactions on Computer-Human Interaction, 7*(1), 59–83. doi:10.1145/344949.345004

EU. (2001, September). *2001 – Where is e-Learning Headed?* Fallon, C., & Brown, S. (2008). *e-Learning Standards.* Boca Raton, FL: Sage & St. Lucie Press.

European Council. (2000). *Employment, economic reforms and social cohesion - towards a Europe based on innovation and knowledge.* Document submitted to Lisbon European Council, official number 5256/00. Lisbon, Portugal: European Council. Retrieved November 4, 2008, from http://ue.eu.int/ueDocs/cms_Data/docs/pressdata/en/misc/05256.en0.html

Evans, C. (2008). The effectiveness of m-learning in the form of podcast revision lectures in higher education. *Computers & Education, 50*(2), 491–498. doi:10.1016/j.compedu.2007.09.016

Eysenbach, G. (2007). From intermediation to disintermediation and apomediation: new models for consumers to access and assess the credibility of health information in the age of Web2.0. *Studies in Health Technology and Informatics, 129*(Pt 1), 162–166.

Fadel, L. M., & Dyson, M. C. (2006a). Comparing a text- and visual-based interface presenting social information in an online environment. In *IEEE Symposium on Visual Languages and Human-Centric Computing,* Brighton, UK.

Fadel, L. M., & Dyson, M. C. (2006b). The effect of interface design on the enhancement of social presence in online courses. In *ICL2006*, Villach, Austria.

Fadel, L. M., & Dyson, M. C. (2006c). A Comparison of the perception of social information in text and visual-based interfaces. In *12th International Conference on Technology Supported Learning & Training - Online Educa Berlin*, Berlin, Germany.

Fadel, L. M., & Dyson, M. C. (2007). Enhancing interactivity in an e-learning environment. In *Interact 07 - Socially responsible interaction*, Rio de Janeiro, Brazil.

Feldman, A., & Acredolo, L. (1979). The effect of active versus passive exploration on memory for spatial location in children. *Child Development, 50*, 698–704. doi:10.2307/1128935

Fellbaum, C. (Ed.). (1998). *WordNet: An Electronic Lexical Database and some of its Applications.* Cambridge, MA: MIT Press.

Fensel, D. (2001). *Ontologies: A Silver Bullet for Knowledge Management and Electronic Commerce*. New York: Springer.

Fernandez-Caballero, A., Lopez-Jaquero, V., Montero, F., & Gonzalez, P. (2003). Adaptive Interaction Multi-agent Systems in E-learning/E-teaching on the Web. In *Lecture Notes In Computer Science*, (pp.144-153). New York: Springer.

Fillmore, C. (1977). Scenes-and-frames Semantics. In A. Zampolli (Ed.), *Linguistic Structures Processing* (pp. 55-82). Amsterdam: North Holland.

Fincher, S. (1999). Analysis of design: an exploration of patterns and pattern languages for pedagogy. *Journal of Computers in Mathematics and Science Teaching, 18*(3), 331–348.

Fincher, S., & Utting, I. (2002). Pedagogical patterns: their place in the genre. In *Proceedings of the 7th annual conference, Innovation and technology in computer science education* (pp.199-202). Denmark: Aarhus.

Fisch, M. S. (2005). Making Educational Computer Games "Educational." In *Proc. IDC'05*, Boulder, CO, June 2005.

Fiske, E. B., & Ladd, H. F. (2000). *When Schools Compete: A Cautionary Tale*. Washington, DC: Brookings Institution Press.

Fitts, P. (1964). Perceptual motor skill learning. In A. Melton (Ed.), *Categories of human learning* (pp. 243–285). New York: Academic press.

Foray, D. (2004). *Economics of Knowledge*. Cambridge, MA: MIT Press.

Foreman, N., Stanton, D., Wilson, P., & Duffy, H. (2003). Spatial knowledge of a real school environment acquired from virtual or physical models by able-bodied children and children with disabilities. *Journal of Experimental Psychology. Applied, 9*, 67–74. doi:10.1037/1076-898X.9.2.67

Forlizzi, J., & Battarbee, K. (2004). Understanding Experience in Interactive Systems. In *Proc. DIS2004*, Cambridge, MA, USA (pp. 261-68).

Foucault, M. (2001). Le Sujet du pouvoir. In D. Defert & F. Ewald (Eds.), *Michel Foucault. Dits et Ecrits II* (pp. 1041-1062). Paris: Gallimard.

Freire, P. (1985). *The Politics of Education - Culture, Power, and Liberation*. (D. Macedo, Trans.). New York: Bergin & Garvey.

Freire, P. (1987). *Pedagogy of the Oppressed*. (M. Bergman Ramos, Trans.). New York: The Continuum Publishing Corporation.

Friedman, B., & Kahn, P. H., Jr. (2003). Human values, ethics, and design. In J. A. Jacko & A. Sears (Eds.), *The human-computer interaction handbook* (pp. 1177-1201). Mahwah, NJ: Lawrence Erlbaum Associates.

Friedman, K. (2003). Theory construction in design research: criteria: approaches, and methods. *Design Studies, 24*, 507–522. doi:10.1016/S0142-694X(03)00039-5

Fries, C. (1952). *The Structure of English. An Introduction to the Construction of English Sentences*. New York: Harcourt, Brace.

Furlong, J., & Oancea, A. (2005). *Assessing Quality in Applied and Practice-based Educational Research, A Framework for Discussion*. Oxford, UK, The University Department of Educational Studies.

Fyrenious, A. (2005). Lectures in problem-based learning—Why, when and how? An example of interactive lecturing that stimulates meaningful learning. *Medical Teacher, 27*(1), 61–65. doi:10.1080/01421590400016365

Gabbard, J., Hix, D., Swan, E., Livingston, M., Herer, T., Julier, S., et al. (2004). A cost-effective usability evaluation progression for novel interactive systems. In *Proceedings of Hawaii International. Conference on Systems Sciences* (pp. 90276c). Washington, DC: IEEE.

Gagné, R. M. (1967). *Learning and individual differences*. Columbus, OH: Charles E. Merrill Books.

Gagné, R., Briggs, R., & Wager, W. (1992). *Principles of Instructional Design*. Houston, TX: HBJ College Publishers.

Gajos, K. Z., Everitt, K., Tan, D. S., Czerwinski, M., & Weld, D. S. (2008). Predictability and Accuracy in Adaptive User Interfaces. In *SIGCHI Conference on Human Factors in Computing Systems* (pp. 1271-1274). ACM Press: Florence, Italy.

Gamma, E. (1991). *Object-oriented software development based on ET++: Design patterns, class library, tools*. Unpublished Doctoral thesis, University of Zurich, Institut für Informatik.

Gamma, E., Helm, R., Johnson, R., & Vlissides, J. (1995). *Design patterns: elements of reusable object-oriented software*. Boston, MA: Addison-Wesley Longman Publishing.

Gardner, H. (1999). *The disciplined mind: What all students should understand*. New York: Simon & Schuster.

Garramone, G. M., Harris, A. C., & Anderson, R. (1986). Uses of political computer bulletin boards. *Journal of Broadcasting & Electronic Media*, *30*(3), 325–339.

Garrett, J. J. (2002). The Elements of User Experience: User-Centered Design for the Web. New York: New Riders Publishing.

Garrison, D. R., & Kanuka, H. (2004)... *The Internet and Higher Education*, *7*, 95–105. doi:10.1016/j.iheduc.2004.02.001

Garrison, D. R., Anderson, T., & Archer, W. (2000). *Critical inquiry in a text-based environment: Computer conferencing in higher education*. Unpublished manuscript, Edmonton, CA.

Garrod, S., & Pickering, M. J. (2007). Automaticity in language production in monologue and dialogue. In A.S. Meyer, L.R. Wheeldon, & A. Krott (Eds.), *Automaticity and control in language processing* (pp. 1-21). Hove: Psychology Press.

Garzotto, F. (2007). Investigating the Educational Effectiveness of Multiplayer Online Games for Children. In *Proc. IDC 2007 (Interaction Design and Children)*, June 2007 (pp. 56-59).

Garzotto, F. (2007). Was Vygotsky Right? Evaluating Learning Effects of Social Interaction in Children Internet Games. In *Proc. INTERACT 2007*, Rio de Janeiro (Brazil), Sept. 2007 (pp. 147-151).

Garzotto, F. (2008, June). Broadening Children's Involvement as Design Partners: From Technology to Experience. In *Proc. ACM IDC 2008 - Interaction Design and Children 2008*, Chicago, USA.

Garzotto, F., & Forfori, M. (2006). Hyperstories and Social Interaction in 2D and 3D Edutainment Spaces for Children. In *Proc. ACM Hypertext '06*, Odense, Denmark (pp. 46-55).

Garzotto, F., & Poggi, C. (2009). Design Patterns for Collaborative Learning in Shared Virtual Worlds. In P. Goodyear & S. Retalis (Eds.), *Technology-enhanced learning: design patterns and pattern languages*. Hershey, PA: IGI Global.

Garzotto, F., & Rizzo, F. (2005). Interactive Storytelling, Cooperative e-Learning, and Kids: a Field Study. In *Proc. IDC'05*, Boulder, USA (pp. 121-123).

Garzotto, F., & Schelhowe, H. (2008). Marginalized Young People: Inclusion Through ICT. In *Proc. ACM IDC 2008 - Interaction Design and Children 2008*, Chicago, USA.

Gatbonton, E., & Segalowitz, N. (1988). Creative automatization: Principles for promoting fluency within a communicative framework. *TESOL Quarterly*, *22*, 473–492. doi:10.2307/3587290

Gatbonton, E., & Segalowitz, N. (2005). Rethinking communicative language teaching: a focus on access to fluency. *Canadian Modern Language Review*, *61*, 325–353.

Gaunet, F., Vidal, M., Kemeny, A., & Berthoz, A. (2001). Active, passive and snapshot exploration in a virtual environment: influence on scene memory, reorientation and path memory. *Brain Research. Cognitive Brain Research*, *11*(3), 409–420. doi:10.1016/S0926-6410(01)00013-1

Gavrilova, T. (2003). Teaching via Using Ontological Engineering. In *Proceedings of XI Int. Conf. Powerful ICT for Teaching and Learning PEG-2003*, St.Petersburg (pp. 23-26).

Gavrilova, T. A., & Voinov, A. (1996). Visualized Conceptual Structuring for Heterogeneous Knowledge Acquisition. In *Proceedings of International Conference on Educational Multimedia and Hypermedia, EDMEDIA'96*, MIT, Boston, USA (pp. 258-264).

Gavrilova, T., & Laird, D. (2005). Practical Design of Business Enterprise Ontologie. In M. Bramer and V. Terzyan (Eds.), *Industrial Applications of Semantic Web* (pp. 61-81). New York: Springer.

Gavrilova, T., Brusilovsky, P., Yudelson, M., & Puuronen, S. (2006). Creating Ontology for User Modelling Research. In *Workshop Ubiquitus User Modeling on European Conference on Artificial Intelligence ECAI 2006*, Riva del Garda, Italy (pp. 11-15).

Gavrilova, T., Dicheva, D., Sosnovsky, S., & Brusilovsky, P. (2005). Ontological Web Portal for Educational Ontologies. In *Proc. Of Applications of Semantic Web Technologies for E-Learning Workshop* (SW-EL'05) *in conjunction with 12th Int.Conf. on Artificial Intelligence in Education (AI-ED'05)*, Amsterdam (pp. 19-29).

Gavrilova, T., Farzan, R., & Brusilovsky, P. (2005). One Practical Algorithm of Creating Teaching Ontologies. In http://www.alitek.com.au/strategic-mapping.htm

Gavrilova, T., Kurochkin, M., & Veremiev, V. (2004). Teaching Strategies and Ontologies for E-learning. *Int. Journal Information Theories and Applications, 11*(1), 35–42.

Gavrilova, T., Texier, R., & Stash, N. (2001). VITA: Using PYTHON for Visual Design of Web-based Tutorials// Proc. of the Tenth International PEG Conference *Intelligent Computer and Communications Technology – Learning in On-Line Communities*, Tampere, Finland, 44-50.

Gibson, J. J. (1987). *The Ecological Approach to Visual Perception*. Hillsdale, NJ: Lawrence Erlbaum Associates.

Giddens, A., Duneier, M., & Appelbaum, R. P. (2003) Introduction to Sociology. 4th edition.

Gilbert, L., & Gale, V. (2008). *Principles of e-Learning Systems Engineering*. Cambridge, UK: Chandos.

Girgensohn, A., & Lee, A. (2002, November). Making web sites be places for social interaction. In *CSCW'02*, New Orleans.

Gius, E., Cozzi, A., & Spagnotto, D. (1992). Il linguaggio delle emozioni. Studio sull'origine delle parole che comunicano stati emotivi. *Giornale Italiano di Psicologia, 19*, 563–584.

Gjøvik, Ø. (2009). Connections between Learning Theory and e-Learning Theory. *Scrib*. Retrieved from http://www.scribd.com/doc/2932693

Gläser-Zikuda, M., & Mayring, P. (2003). A qualitative oriented approach to learning emotions at school. In P. Mayring & C. von Rhöneck (Eds.), *Learning Emotions. The influence of Affective Factors on Classroom Learning* (pp. 103-126). New York, NY: Lang.

Go, K., & Carroll, J. M. (2004). Scenario-based task analysis. In D. Diaper & N. Stanton (Eds.), *The Handbook of Task Analysis for Human-Computer Interaction* (pp. 117–134). Hillsdale, NJ: Lawrence Erlbaum Associates.

Godejord, P. A. (2007, November). Perspectives on Project Based Teaching and 'Blended Learning' to Develop Ethical Awareness in Students. *eLearning Papers*, 6. Retrieved from http://www.elearningeuropa.info/files/media/media14200.pdf

Goffman, E. (1957). Characteristics of Total Institutions. In *Symposium on Preventative and Social Psychiatry*, Washington, DC (pp. 43-93).

Goffman, E. (1974). *Frame analysis. An Essay on the Organisation of Experience*. Cambridge, MA: Harper & Row.

Goffman, E. (1991). *Les cadres de l'expérience*. Paris: Editions de Minuit.

Golafshani, N. (2003). Understanding reliability and validity in questionnaire research. *Qualitative Report, 8*(4), 597–607.

Goldberg, A. (1998). *Patterns of experience in patterns of language*. In M. Tomasello (Ed.), *The new psychology of language* (pp. 203-219). Mahwah, NJ: Lawrence Erlbaum.

Goldman, S. R. (2003). Learning in complex domains: When and why do multiple representations help? *Learning and Instruction, 13*, 239–244. doi:10.1016/S0959-4752(02)00023-3

Goleman, D. (1995). *Emotional intelligence*. New York: Bantam Books.

Goleman, D., Boyatzis, R., & McKee, A. (2002). *L'intelligence émotionnelle au travail*. Paris: Editions Village Mondial.

Gombrich, E. H. (1969). Art and illusion: A study in the psychology of pictorial representation. In D.H. Jonassen

(Ed.), *Handbook for research for educational communications and technology* (pp. 755-794). New York: Simon & Schuster Macmillan.

Gómez-Pérez, A., Fernández-López, M., & Corcho, O. (2004). *Ontological Engineering with examples from the areas of Knowledge Management, e-Commerce and the Semantic Web.* London: Springer-Verlag.

Gonella, L., & Panto, E. (2008, July). Didactic Architecture and Organisation Models: a Process of Mutual Adaptation. *eLearning Papers, 9*. Retrieved from http://www.elearningeuropa.info/files/media/media15973.pdf

Goodman, B., Soller, A., Linton, F., & Gaimari, R. (1998). Encouraging student reflection and articulartion using a learning companion. Paper presented at the 8th International Conference on Artificial Intelligence in Education, Kobe, Japan.

Gordon, C. (2002). *Contributions of Cultural Anthropology and Social Capital Theory to Understandings of Knowledge Management.* Unpublished Doctoral Thesis, Ontario Institute for Studies in Education, University of Toronto.

Graesser, A. C., Person, N. K., Harter, D., & Group, T. R. (2001). Teaching tactics and dialog in autotutor. *International Journal of Artificial Intelligence in Education, 12*, 257–279.

Gregory, R. L. (1974). *Concepts and Mechanisms of Perception.* London: Duckworth.

Grigoriadou, M., Papanikolaou, K., Tsaganou, G., Gouli, E., & Gogoulou, A. (2006). eCompetence Skills for Adaptive Learning Environments in Higher Education. In Labhraim et al. (Eds.), *The Challenge of eCompetence in Academic Staff Development* (pp. 155-166). Galway, Ireland: CELT, NUI. Retrieved on October 18, 2008 from http://www.ecompetence.info/uploads/media/ch17.pdf

Gruber, T. (1993). A translation approach to portable ontology specifications. *Knowledge Acquisition, 5*, 199–220. doi:10.1006/knac.1993.1008

Guarino, N., & Giaretta, P. (1998). Ontologies and Knowledge Bases: Towards a Terminological Clarification. In *Towards Very Large Knowledge Bases: Knowledge Building & Knowledge Sharing* (pp. 25- 32).

Guha M. et al. (2005). *Working with Young Children as Technology Design Partners*, CACM Jan. 2005/Vol. 48, No. 1 39, 39-42

Guha, M. L., Druin, A., Chipman, G., Fails, J. A., Simms, S., & Farber, A. (2004). Mixing Ideas: A New Technique for Working with Young Children as Design Partners. In *Proceedings of Interaction Design and Children (IDC) 2004 Conference*, ACM, New York, NY (pp. 35–42).

Guha, M. L., Druin, A., Chipman, G., Fails, J. A., Simms, S., & Farber, A. (2005). Working with Young Children as technology design partners. *Communications of the ACM, 48*(1), 39–42. doi:10.1145/1039539.1039567

Guha, M., et al. (2004). Mixing Ideas: A New Technique for Working with Young Children as Design Partners. In *Proc. IDC 2004*, College Park, MD, USA (pp. 35-42).

Guillaume, P. (1973). *La formation des habitudes.* PUF, Paris.

Gunawardena, C. N. (1995). Social presence theory and implications for interactions and collaborative learning in computer conferences. *International Journal of Educational Telecommunications, 1*(2/3), 147–166.

Gunawardena, C. N., & Zittle, F. J. (1997). Social presence as a predictor of satisfaction within a computer-mediated conferencing environment. *American Journal of Distance Education, 11*(3), 8–26. doi:10.1080/08923649709526970

Gustafson, K. L., & Branch, R. M. (1997). Revisioning Models of Instructional Development. *Educational Technology Research and Development, 45*(3), 73–89. doi:10.1007/BF02299731

Guttormsen, S. S., & Krueger, H. (2001). Empirical research on the effect of dynamic media for information presentation. In *Proceedings of ICL2001 - 4th International Workshop on Interactive Computer Aided Learning - Experiences and Visions, 2001.*

Hall, L., Woods, S., & Aylett, R. Newall, L. & Paiva, A. (2005). Achieving empathic engagement through affective interaction with synthetic characters. Affective computing and intelligent interaction, Springer.

Halsey, A. H. (1979). Social Mobility and Education, pp. 57-78 in Rubinstein (1979)

Hammond, M. (2006). Blogging within formal and informal learning contexts: Where are the opportunities and constraints? In *Proceedings of the International Research Conference on Networked Learning 2006*, Lancaster, UK.

Hanks, P., & Pustejovsky, J. (2005). A Pattern Dictionary for Natural Language Processing. In *Revue Francaise de linguistique appliquée, 10*,2.

Hanna, L., Neapolitan, D., & Risden, K. (2004). *Evaluating Computer Game Concepts with Children.* In *Proc. IDC 2004*, College Park, Maryland, USA (pp. 49-47).

Hannafin, M., Hannafin, K., Hooper, S., Rieber, L., & Kini, A. (1996). Research on and research with emerging technologies. In D. H. Jonassen (Ed.), *Handbook for research for educational communications and technology* (pp. 378-402). New York: Simon & Schuster Macmillan.

Harel, I., & Papert, S. (1991). *Constructionism.* New York: Ablex Publishing Corporation.

Hargreaves, D. H. (2000). The production, Mediation and Use of Professional Knowledge among Teachers and Doctors: a Comparative Analysis. In *CERI 2000.*

Harris, Z. (1951). *Methods in Structural Linguistics.* Chicago: University of Chicago Press.

Hartman, H. J. (2001). *Metacognition in Learning and Instruction: Theory, Research and Practice.* Dordrecht, Netherlands: Kluwer Academic Publishers.

Hartmann, B., Mancini, M., Buisine, S., & Pelachaud, C. (2005b). Design and evaluation of expressive gesture synthesis for embodied conversational agents. In *AAMAS'05*, Utretch.

Hassenzahl, M. (2005). The thing and I: understanding the relationship between user and product. In M. Blythe, K. Overbeeke, A. Monk, & P. Wright (Eds.), *Funology: from usability to enjoyment* (pp. 31-42). New York: Springer.

Hearst, M. (1998). *Automated discovery of Word-Net relations.* In C. Fellbaum, (Ed.), *WordNet an electronic lexical database* (pp. 131–152). Cambridge, MA: MIT Press.

Hebb, D. (1949). *The Organization of Behavior.* New York: Wiley.

Hede, A. (2002). An integrated model of multimedia effects on learning. *Journal of Educational Multimedia and Hypermedia, 11*(2), 177–191.

Hegarty, M., Carpenter, P. A., & Just, M. A. (1991). Diagrams in the comprehension of scientific text. In R. Barr, M. L. Kamil, P. B. Mosenthal & P. D. Pearson (Eds.), *Handbook of reading research* (Vol. 2, pp. 641-668). New York: Longman.

Hein, G. E. (1991). Constructivist Learning Theory, the Museum and the Needs of People. In *CECA (International Committee of Museum Educators) Conference*, Jerusalem, Israel, Institute of Inquiry. Retrieved from http://www.exploratorium.edu/ifi/resources/constructivistlearning.html

Heinrich, R., Molenda, M., & Russell, J. (1983). *Instructional Media and new Technologies.* New York: Macmillan.

Henig, J. R. (1994). *Rethinking School Choice: Limits of the Market Metaphor.* Princeton, NJ: Princeton University Press

Herriot, P. (1971). *Language and Teaching: A Psychological View.* London: Methuen and Co.

Hietala, P., & Niemirepo, T. (1998). The competence of learning companion agents. *International Journal of Artificial Intelligence in Education, 9*, 178–192.

Hildreth, P., & Kimble, C. (2004). *Knowledge Networks: Innovation through Communities of Practice.* Hershey, PA: Idea Group Publishing.

Hill, J., & Arbib, M. (1984). Schemas, Computation and Language Acquisition. *Human Development, 27*, 282–296.

Himmelweit, H., Oppenheim, A. N., & Vince, P. (1959). *Television and the child: an empirical study of the effects of television on the young.* London: Oxford University Press.

Holmes, B., & Gardner, J. (2006). *E-Learning, Concepts and Practice.* Thousand Oaks, CA: Page Publications.

Holzinger, A., Pichler, A., & Maurer, H. (2006). Multi Media eLearning Software TRIANGLE Case-Study: Experimental Results and Lessons Learned. *Journal of Universal Science and Technology of Learning, 0*(0), 61–92.

Hourcade, J. P. (2006). *Design for Children.* In G. Salvendy (Ed.), *Handbook of Human Factors and Ergonomics* (3rd ed.) (pp. 1446-1458). New York: Wiley.

Houssaye, J. (1992). *Théorie et pratiques de l'éducation scolaire I: Le triangle pédagogique.* Berne, Switzerland: Peter Lang.

Howard, L., Remenyi, Z., & Pap, G. (2006). Adaptive Blended Learning Environments. In *Proceedings of the International Conference on Engineering Education,* July 23-28, 2006, San Juan, Puerto Rico. Retrieved on October 20, 2008 from http://w3.isis.vanderbilt.edu/Projects/VaNTH/papers/icee_2006_p1.pdf

http://cmap.ihmc.us/Publications/ResearchPapers/TheoryUnderlyingConceptMaps.pdf

Hubal, R. C., Frank, G. A., & Guin, C. (2003). Lessons Learned in Modeling Schizophrenic and Depressed Responsive Virtual Humans for Training. Proceedings of International Conference on Intelligent User Interfaces (pp. 85 – 92), ACM

Hubal, R. C., Kizakevich, P. N., Guinn, C. I., Merino, K. D., & West, S. L. (2000). The Virtual Standardized Patient – Simulated Patient-Practitioner Dialog for Patient Interview Training. In Envisioning Healing: Interactive Technology and the Patient-Practitioner Dialogue, (pp.133-138) IOS Press: Amsterdam.

Huffaker, D. (2004). *The e-Learning Design Challenge: Technology, Models and Design Principles* [White Paper]. Washington DC: American Society for Training & Development (ASTD).

Hulstijn, J. H. (2001). Intentional and incidental second-language vocabulary learning: A reappraisal of elaboration, rehearsal and automaticity. In P. Robinson (Ed.), *Cognition and second language instruction* (pp. 258-286). Cambridge, UK: Cambridge University Press.

IEEE Learning Technology Standards Committee. (n.d.). *IEEE LOM Working Draft 6.1 (IEEE 1484.12.1-2002).* Retrieved November 4, 2005, from http://ltsc.ieee.org/wg12/index.html

IEEE standard for learning technology-learning technology systems architecture (LTSA). (2003). *IEEE Std 1484.1-2003,* 1 – 97.

IMS Global Learning Consortium, Inc. (n.d.). *Open specifications for interoperable learning technology.* Retrieved November 4, 2005, from http:// www.imsproject.org

International Society for Technology in Education. (2002). *National Educational Technology Standards for Teachers: Preparing Teachers to Use Technology.* Danvers, MA: ISTE.

Isen, A. M. (1999). Positive affect and decision making. In Lewis M., Haviland J.M. (Eds.), *Handbook of emotions* (pp. 417-435). New York: The Guilford Press.

ISO 9126-4:2001. (n.d.). *Software Engineering - Software product quality. Part 1: Quality model.*

Iversen, O. S. (2005). *Participatory Design Beyond Work Practices: Designing with Children.* Doctoral Dissertation, Submitted to the Department of Computer Science, University of Aarhus, Denmark.

Jackendoff, R. (1993). *Patterns in the Mind: Language and Human Nature.* London: Harvester-Wheatsheaf.

Jackson, B., & Marsden, D. (1962). *Education and the Working Class.* Harmondworth, UK: Penguin Books.

Jaimes, A. (2006). Human-Centered Multimedia: Culture, Deployment, and Access. *IEEE Multimedia Magazine, 13*(1).

Jensen, J., & Skov, M. (2005). A Review of Research methods in Children's Technology Design. In *Proc. IDC 05,* Boulder, USA.

Jeon, S., Shim, H., & Kim, G. (2006). Viewpoint Usability for Desktop Augmented Reality. *The International Journal of Virtual Reality*, *5*(3), 33–39.

Johansson, G. (1973). Visual perception of biological motion and a model for its analysis. *Perception & Psychophysics*, *14*(2), 201–211.

Johnson, W. L., Rickel, J. W., & Lester, J. C. (2000). Animated pedagogical agents: Face-to- face interaction in interactive learning environments. *International Journal of Artificial Intelligence in Education*, *11*, 47–78.

Jonassen, D. H. (1991). Objectivism versus constructivism: Do we need a new philosophical paradigm? *Educational Technology Research and Development*, *39*(3), 5–14. doi:10.1007/BF02296434

Jonassen, D. H. (1998). Designing constructivist learning environments. In C.M. Reigeluth (Ed.), *Instructional design models and strategies* (2nd ed.). Mahwah, NJ: Lawrence Erlbaum.

Jonassen, D. H. (Ed.). (1996). *Handbook of research for educational communications and technology*. New York: Simon & Schuster Macmillan.

Jonassen, D. H., & Grabowski, B. L. (1993). *Handbook of Individual Differences, Learning and Instruction*. Hillsdale, NJ: Lawrence Erlbaum Associates.

Jonassen, D. H., Campbell, J. P., & Davidson, M. E. (1994). Learning with media: Restructuring the debate. *Educational Technology Research and Development*, *39*(3), 5–14. doi:10.1007/BF02296434

Jones, R., Higgs, R., de Angelis, C., & Prideaux, D. (2001). Changing face of medical curricula. *Lancet*, *357*(9257), 699–703. doi:10.1016/S0140-6736(00)04134-9

Jung, B., Ahad, A., & Weber, M. (2005). The Affective Virtual Patient: An E-Learning Tool for Social Interaction Training within the Medical Field Proceedings of International Conference TESI-Training Education & Education. IEEE standard for learning technology-learning technology systems architecture (LTSA) (2003), IEEE Std 1484.1-2003 Volume, Issue, Page(s): 0_1 – 97

Jung, Y., & Lee, A. (2000). Design of social interaction environment for electronic marketplaces. In *DIS'00 - Designing Interactive Systems: Processes, Practices, Methods, Techniques*, New York.

Junge, K., & Hadjivassiliou, K. (2007, November). What are the EU and Member States Doing to Address Digital Literacy? *eLearning Papers,* 6. Retrieved from http://www.elearningeuropa.info/files/media/media14196.pdf

Kafai, Y. B., Carter-Ching, C., & Marshall, S. (1997). Children as designers of educational multimedia software. *Computers & Education*, *29*(2/3), 117–126. doi:10.1016/S0360-1315(97)00036-5

Kagan, J. (2007). *What is emotion? History, measures and meanings.* New York: Yale University Press.

Kaldoudi, E., Bamidis, P. D., Papaioakeim, M., & Vargemezis, V. (2008). Problem-based learning via Web 2.0 technologies. In *Proceedings of CBMS2008: The 21th IEEE International Symposium on Computer-Based Medical Systems, Special Track: Technology Enhanced Learning in Medical Education* (pp. 391-396). Jyväskylä, Finland: IEEE Computer Society.

Kaldoudi, E., Papaioakeim, M., Bamidis, P. M., & Vargemezis, V. (2008). Towards expert content sharing in medical education. In *Proceedings of INTED2008: International Technology, Education and Development Conference*. Valencia, Spain: IATED.

Kalyuga, S. (2006). Expert-novice differences and design of adaptive multimedia. In G. Ghinea & S. Chen (Eds.), *Digital Multimedia Perception and Design* (pp. 206-223). Hershey, PA: Idea Group Inc.

Kalyuga, S., & Sweller, J. (2005). Rapid dynamic assessment of expertise to optimize the efficiency of e-learning. *Educational Technology Research and Development*, *53*(3). doi:10.1007/BF02504800

Kamiya, T. (2005). *Japanese Sentence Patterns for effective communication.* Tokyo, Japan: Kodansha.

Kann, C., Lindeman, R., & Heller, R. (1997). Integrating algorithm animation into a learning environment.

Computers & Education, *28*(4), 223–238. doi:10.1016/S0360-1315(97)00015-8

Kant, E. (1781). *Critique of Pure Reason.* Garden City, NY: Anchor Books.

Kapoor, A., & Picard, R. W. (2005). Multimodal affect recognition in learning environments. Proceedings of the 13th annual ACM international conference on Multimedia, (pp.677-682), ACM New York, NY, USA

Kapoor, A., Mota, S., & Picard, R. W. (2001). Towards a learning companion that recognizes affect. In *AAAI Fall Symposium 2001*, North Falmouth, MA.

Kaptelinin, V., Nardi, B., & Macaulay, C. (1999). The Activity Checklist: A Tool for Representing the "Space" of Context. *Interaction*, 27–30. doi:10.1145/306412.306431

Karagiannidis, C., Sampson, D.G., & Cardinali, F.(2002). An architecture for Web-based e-Learning promoting reusable adaptive educational e-content, Educational Technology & Society, 5(4).

Karagiorgi, Y., & Symeou, L. (2005). Translating Constructivism into Instructional Design: Potential and Limitations. *Educational Technology & Society*, *8*(1), 17–27.

Karagiorgi, Y., & Symeou, L. (2005). Translating Constructivism into Instructional Design: Potential and Limitations. *Educational Technology & Society*, *8*(1), 17–27.

Karpouzis, K., Caridakis, G., Kessous, L., Amir, N., Raouzaiou, A., Malatesta, L., & Kollias, S. (2006). Modeling naturalistic affective states via facial, vocal, and bodily expressions recognition. In T. Huang, A. Nijholt, M. Pantic, A. Pentland (eds.), Lecture Notes in Artificial Intelligence, Special Volume on AI for Human Computing, pp. 91-112, Springer.

Karpouzis, K., Caridakis, G., Kessous, L., Amir, N., Raouzaiou, A., Malatesta, L., & Kollias, S. (2006). Modeling naturalistic affective states via facial, vocal, and bodily expressions recognition. In T. Huang, A. Nijholt, M. Pantic & A. Pentland (Eds.), *Lecture Notes in Artificial Intelligence, Special Volume on AI for Human Computing* (pp. 91-112). Berlin, Germany: Springer.

Kastis, N. (2007, May). Observing the e-Learning Phenomenon: the Case of School Education. Analysing the Transformative Innovation of e-Learning. *eLearning Papers,* 4. Retrieved from http://www.elearningeuropa.info/files/media/media12729.pdf

Keegan, D. (2002). *The Future of learning: from e-Learning to m-learning.* Institute for Research into Distance Education, Fein University (Hagen, Germany).

Kelly, S. R., et al. (2006). Bluebells: A Design Method for Child-Centred Product Development. In *Proc. NordiCHI 2006* (pp. 362-369)

Kelton, A. J. (2008). Virtual worlds: Outlook good. *EDUCAUSE Review*, *43*(5), 5–22.

Kennedy, R. S., Stanney, K. M., & Dunlap, W. P. (2000). Duration and exposure to virtual environments: Sickness curves during and across sessions. *Presence (Cambridge, Mass.)*, *9*(5), 463–472. doi:10.1162/105474600566952

Kenny, J. (2002). What did we get for our training money? *TES Online.* http://www.tes.co.uk/search/story/?story_id=357732.

Kim, H. N. (2008). The phenomenon of blogs and theoretical model of blog use in educational contexts. *Computers & Education*, *51*(3), 1342–1352. doi:10.1016/j.compedu.2007.12.005

Kim, J., André, E., Rehm, M., Vogt, T., & Wagner, J. (2005). Integrating Information from Speech and Physiological Signals to Achieve Emotional Sensitivity, in: Proceedings of Interspeech/Eurospeech, 2005.

Kim, K. J., Bonk, C. J., & Zeng, T. T. (2005, June). Surveying the Future of Workplace e-Learning: the Rise of Blending, Interactivity, and Authentic Learning. *e-Learn Magazine*, 2005(6).

Kim, Y. (2003). An agent as a learning companion: What it matters. Paper presented at the Annual Conference of Association for Educational Communications and Technology, Anaheim, CA.

Kinard, E. M. (2001). Perceived and actual academic competence in maltreated children. *Child Abuse & Neglect*, *25*(1), 33–45. doi:10.1016/S0145-2134(00)00219-2

Kinchin, I. M., De-Leij, F. A. A. M., & Hay, D. B. (2005). The evolution of a collaborative concept mapping activity for undergraduate microbiology. *Journal of Further and Higher Education*, *29*(1), 1–14. doi:10.1080/03098770500037655

Kintsch, W. (1974). *The representation of meaning in memory.* Hillsdale, NJ: Lawrence Erlbaum.

Kirschner, P. (Ed.). (2003). Special issue on ICT and Teacher Training. *Technology, Pedagogy and Education*, *12*(1).

Kirschner, P. A. (2002). Cognitive load theory: Implications of cognitive load theory on the design of learning. *Learning and Instruction*, *12*(1), 1–10. doi:10.1016/S0959-4752(01)00014-7

Kirschner, P., & Gerjets, P. (2006). Instructional design for effective and enjoyable computer-supported learning. *Computers in Human Behavior*, *22*(1), 1–8. doi:10.1016/j.chb.2005.01.004

Kirschner, P., Strijbos, J., Kreijns, K., & Beers, P. (2004). Designing Electronic Collaborative Learning Environments. *Educational Technology Research and Development*, *52*(3), 47–66. doi:10.1007/BF02504675

Knight, C., Gašević, D., & Richards, G. (2006). An Ontology-Based Framework for Bridging Learning Design and Learning Content. *Educational Technology & Society*, *9*(1), 23–3.

Knowles, M. S. (1975). *Self-Directed Learning, a Guide for Learners and Teachers*, Englewood Cliffs, Prentice Hall/ Cambridge

Knuth, R. A., & Cunningham, D. J. (1993). Tools for Constructivism. In T. M. Duffy, J. Lowyck & D. H. Jonassen (Eds.), *Designing Environment for Constructive Learning* (pp. 163-188). Berlin, Germany: Springer.

Koehler, M. J., & Mishra, P. (2008). Introducing TPCK. In AACTE Committee on Innovation and Technology (Ed.), *Handbook of Technological Pedagogical Content Knowledge (TPCK) for Educators* (pp. 3-29). New York: Routledge.

Koehler, M. J., Mishra, P., & Yahya, K. (2007). Tracing the development of teacher knowledge in a design seminar: Integrating content, pedagogy, and technology. *Computers & Education*, *49*, 740–762. doi:10.1016/j.compedu.2005.11.012

Koffka, K. (1935). *The principles of Gestalt psychology.* New York: Harcourt Brace & World.

Kolb, D. A. (1984). *Experiential learning: Experience as the source of learning and development.* Englewood Cliffs, NJ: Prentice-Hall.

Kollock, P. (1996). *Design principles for online communities.* Harvard Conference on the Internet and Society.

Kolski, C. (1997). *Interfaces homme-machine, application aux systèmes industriels complexes.* Paris: Hermes Science Publishers.

Kolski, C., Sagar, M., & Loslever, P. (2004a). Experiment based on participative ergonomics and performed as part of a supervision engineers' training course. In *Proceedings HAAMAHA'2004. Human and Organisational Issues in the Digital Enterprise*, Galway, Ireland.

Kolski, C., Sagar, M., & Loslever, P. (2004b). Spécification d'IHM dans les systèmes critiques: retour d'expérience sur une pratique en enseignement de l'IHM. In *Proceedings IHM'2004, Interaction Homme-Machine*, Namur, Belgium.

Könings, K. D., van Zundert, M. J., Brand-Gruwel, S., & van Merriënboer, J. J. G. (2007). Participatory design in secondary education: is it a good idea? Students' and teachers' opinions on its desirability and feasibility. *Educational Studies*, *33*(4), 445–465. doi:10.1080/03055690701423648

Korres, M. P., & Garcia-Barriocanal, E. (2008). Development of personalized learning objects for training adult educators of special groups. *Journal of Knowledge Management*, *12*(6), 89–101. doi:10.1108/13673270810913649

Kort, B., & Reilly, R. (2001). *Analytical Models of Emotions, Learning and Relationships: Towards an*

Affect-sensitive Cognitive Machine. MIT Media Lab Tech, Report No 548.

Korte, W. B., & Hüsing, T. (2006, January). Benchmarking Access and Use of ICT in European Schools 2006: Results from Head Teacher and a Classroom Teacher Surveys in 27 European countries. *eLearning Papers, 2*. Retrieved from http://www.elearningeuropa.info/files/media/media11563.pdf

Koumi, J. (2003). Synergy between audio commentary and visuals in multimedia packages. *Journal of Educational Media, 28*(1), 19–34. doi:10.1080/1358165032000156419

Kozma, R. (1991). Learning with media. *Review of Educational Research, 61*(2), 179–211.

Kozma, R. (1994). Will media influence learning? Reframing the debate. *Educational Technology Research and Development, 42*(2), 7–19. doi:10.1007/BF02299087

Kozma, R. (2003). The material features of multiple representations and their cognitive and social affordances for science understanding. *Learning and Instruction, 13*, 205–226. doi:10.1016/S0959-4752(02)00021-X

Krashen, S. (1981). *Second Language Acquisition and Second Language Learning.* Retrieved from http://www.sdkrashen.com/SL_Acquisition_and_Learning/index.html

Krech, D., Crutchfield, R. S., & Ballachey, E. L. (1962). *Individual in Society.* New York: McGraw Hill.

Kreijns, K., Kirschner, P. A., & Jochems, W. (2002). The sociability of computer-supported collaborative learning environments. *Educational Technology & Society, 5*(1), 1–19.

Kremer, R. (1998). Visual Languages for Knowledge Representation. In http://www.alitek.com.au/strategic-mapping.htm

Kurtz, B., Fenwick, J., & Ellsworth, C. (2007). Using podcasts and tablet PCs in computer science. In *Proceedings of 45th ACM South East Conference* (pp. 484 - 489). Winston Salem, NC: ACM.

Kvale, S. (1996). *InterViews. An Introduction to Qualitative Research Interviewing.* Thousand Oaks, CA: Sage Publications.

Labour, M. (1998). *Que pense l'apprenant de l'apprentissage guidé de l'anglais ? Un*

Labour, M. (2002). Integrating ICT and learning profiles in an EFL training course for primary school teachers. In *Australian Computers in Education Conference 2002, Linking learners*, Hobart, Australia.

Labour, M. (2006). Recomposer les métiers du multimédia: quel espace pour un *empowerment* coopératif? Cinquième Colloque international. *Formation, Recherche et Métiers des Technologies de l'Information et de la Communication (TIC).* Invited paper, University Antonine.

Labour, M., Useille, P., & Crévits, I. (2006). Evaluation formative et TIC: quelle résolution d'une problématique interdisciplinaire? In *8e Biennale de l'éducation et de la formation, Débats sur les recherches et les innovations,* Lyon, France. Retrieved June 2, 2006, from http://ateliers.inrp.fr/Biennale/Ateliers/Atelier-2/travaux/DIGOR_Biennale2006.doc

Lado, R. (1964). *Language Teaching: A Scientific Approach.* New York: McGraw Hill.

Lane, R., Reiman, E. M., Ahern, G. L., Schwartz, G. E., & Davidson, R. J. (1997). Neuroanatomical correlates of happiness, sadness and disgust. *The American Journal of Psychiatry, 154*, 926–933.

Lang, P. J. (1995). The Emotion Probe: Studies of Motivation and Attention. *The American Psychologist, 50*(5), 372–385. doi:10.1037/0003-066X.50.5.372

Large, A., Beheshti, J., Breuleux, A., & Renaud, A. (1994). Multimedia and comprehension: a cognitive study. *Journal of the American Society for Information Science American Society for Information Science, 45*(7), 515–528. doi:10.1002/(SICI)1097-4571(199408)45:7<515::AID-ASI6>3.0.CO;2-3

Large, A., Beheshti, J., Breuleux, A., & Renaud, A. (1995). Multimedia and comprehension: the relationship among text, animation, and captions. *Journal of the American Society for Information Science American Society for Information Science*, *46*(5), 340–347. doi:10.1002/(SICI)1097-4571(199506)46:5<340::AID-ASI5>3.0.CO;2-S

Large, A., Beheshti, J., Breuleux, A., & Renaud, A. (1996). Effect of animation in enhancing descriptive and procedural texts in a multimedia learning environment. *Journal of the American Society for Information Science American Society for Information Science*, *47*(6), 437–448. doi:10.1002/(SICI)1097-4571(199606)47:6<437::AID-ASI4>3.0.CO;2-W

Large, A., Nesset, V., Beheshti, J., & Bowler, L. (2006). Bonded design: A novel approach to intergenerational information technology design. *Library & Information Science Research*, *28*, 64–82. doi:10.1016/j.lisr.2005.11.014

Laufer, L., & Tatai, G. (2004). Learn, Chat & Play-An ECA Supported Stock Markets E-Learning Curricula'. Proceedings of the IASTED International Conference on Web-Based Education (pp.16-18) ACTA Press.

Lavie, T., & Tractinsky, N. (2004). Assessing dimensions of perceived visual aesthetics of web sites. *International Journal of Human-Computer Studies*, *60*(3), 269–298. doi:10.1016/j.ijhcs.2003.09.002

Law, E., Bevan, N., Gristou, G., Springett, M., & Larusdottir, M. (2008). *Meaningful measures: valid useful user experience measurement - VUUM Workshop*, Reykjavik. COST Action 294 – MAUSE.

Lazarsfeld, P. F. (1940). *Radio and the printed page: an introduction to the study of radio and its role in the communication of ideas.* New York: Duell, Sloan & Pierce.

LeDoux, J. (1998). *The emotional brain: The mysterious underpinnings of emotional life*. London: Weidenfeld & Nicholson.

Lee, A., Danis, C., Miller, T., & Jung, Y. (2001). Fostering social interaction in online spaces. In *INTERACT 2001*, Amsterdam.

Lee, D. N., & Aronson, E. (1974). Visual proprioceptive control of standing in human infants. *Perception & Psychophysics*, *15*, 529–532.

Lee, K. M., & Nass, C. (2003, April). Designing social presence of social actors in human computer interaction. In *CHI 2003*, Ft. Lauderdale.

Lee, S. H., & Boling, E. (1999). Screen design guidelines for motivation in interactive multimedia instruction: A survey and framework for designers. *Educational Technology*, *39*, 19–26.

Leitner, s. (1972). *So lernt man lernen* [Learning to learn]. Freiburg, Heider.

Leont'ev, A. (1974). *Psycholinguistik und Sprachunterricht.* Stuttgart, Germany: Kohlhammer.

Leont'ev, A. N. (1978). *Activity, consciousness and personality.* Englewood Cliffs, NJ: Prentice Hall.

Leont'ev, A. N. (1981). *Problems of the development of mind.* Moscow: Progress Press.

Lester, J. C., Converse, S. A., Kahler, S. E., Barlow, S. T., Stone, B. A., & Bhogal, R. S. (1997). The persona effect: affective impact of animated pedagogical agents, Proceedings of the SIGCHI conference on Human factors in computing systems, (pp.359-366), ACM New York, NY, USA

Levelt, W. (1970). Skill theory and language teaching. *Studies in Second Language Acquisition*, *1*(1), 53–70. doi:10.1017/S0272263100000711

Levelt, W. (1989). *Speaking.* Cambridge, MA: MIT Press.

Levie, W. H., & Lentz, R. (1982). Effects of text illustrations: A review of research. *Educational Communication and Technology Journal*, *30*(4), 195–232.

Levin, J. R., & Lesgold, A. M. (1978). On pictures in prose. *Educational Communication and Technology Journal*, *26*, 233–243.

Levin, J. R., Anglin, G. J., & Carney, R. N. (1987). On empirically validating functions of pictures in prose. In

D.M. Willows & H.A. Houghton (Eds.), *The psychology of illustration*, (Vol. 1, pp. 51-86). New York: Springer.

Levy, Y. (2006). The top 10 most valuable online learning activities for graduate MS students. *International Journal of Information and Communication Technology Education, 2*(3), 27–44.

Levy, Y. (2008). An empirical development of critical value factors (CVF) of online learning activities: An application of activity theory and cognitive value theory. *Computers & Education, 51*, 1664–1675. doi:10.1016/j.compedu.2008.04.003

Lewalter, D. (2003). Cognitive strategies for learning from static and dynamic visuals. *Learning and Instruction, 13*, 177–189. doi:10.1016/S0959-4752(02)00019-1

Li, J., et al. (2007). Comicboarding: Using Comics as Proxies for Participatory Design with Children. In *Proc. CHI 2007*, San Jose, CA (pp. 1371-1375).

Liao, Y. C. (1999). Effects of hypermedia on students' achievement: A meta-analysis. *Journal of Educational Multimedia and Hypermedia, 8*(3), 255–277.

Lim, C. C., Yu, M. H., & Jin, J. J. (2005). Generic e-Learning Data Structure and Web Teaching. In *Proceedings of IEEE 2005 the International Conference on e-Technology, e-Commerce and e-Service* (pp. 564-569).

Lim, M. Y., & Aylett, R. S. (2007). Feel the difference: A Guide with Attitude! In C. Pelachaud et al. (Eds.) *Intelligent virtual agents* (pp. 317-330). Berlin Heidelberg, Germany: Springer-Verlag.

Limoges, S., Ware, C., & Knight, W. (1989, June). Displaying correlations using position, motion, point size or point colour. In *Graphics Interface*, London, Ontario.

Litwin, M. S. (1995). *How to Measure Survey Reliability and Validity*. London: Sage Publications.

Liu, W., Cheok, A. D., Mei-Ling, C. L., & Theng, Y.-L. (2007). Mixed reality classroom: learning from entertainment. In *Proceedings of the 2nd international conference on Digital interactive media in entertainment and arts* (pp. 65-72). New York: ACM Press.

Lohr, L. L. (2003). *Creating graphics for learning and performance: Lessons in visual literacy*. Columbus, Ohio: Merrill Prentice Hall.

Lombard, M., & Ditton, T. (1997). At the heart of it all: The concept of presence. *Journal of Computer-Mediated Communication, 3*(2), 1–43.

Loscos, C., Widenfeld, H., & Roussou, M. Meyer, A., Tecchia, F., Drettakis, G., Gallo, E., Martinez, A. R., Tsingos, N., Chrysanthou, Y., Robert, L., Bergamasco, M., Dettori, A., & Soubra, S. (2003). The CREATE Project: Mixed Reality for Design, Education, and Cultural Heritage with a Constructivist Approach. In *ISMAR 03, The Second IEEE and ACM International Symposium on Mixed and Augmented Reality*, The National Center of Sciences, Tokyo, Japan, Oct. 7 - Oct. 10.

Louchart, S., & Aylett, R. (2007). From Synthetic Characters to Virtual Actors. In *Proceedings of International Conference in Artificial Intelligence for Interactive Digital Entertainment* (pp. 88-91)

Lowe, R. K. (2003). Animation and learning: Selective processing of information in dynamic graphics. *Learning and Instruction, 13*(2), 157–176. doi:10.1016/S0959-4752(02)00018-X

Lyons, J. (2001). *Paulo Freire's Educational Theory*. New Foundations. Retrieved from http://www.newfoundations.com/GALLERY/Freire.html

Mace, C. A. (1932). *The Psychology of Study*. London: Pelican Books.

Malone, T. W. (1982). Heuristics for Designing Enjoyable User Interfaces: Lessons from Computer Games. In *Proceedings of the 1982 conference on Human factors in computing systems*, Gaithersburg, MD, United States (pp. 63–68).

Manches, A., O'Malley, C., & Benford, S. (2009). Physical manipulation: evaluating the potential for tangible designs. In *Proceedings of the 3rd International Conference on Tangible and Embedded Interaction* (pp. 77-84). New York: ACM Press.

Mandler, J. (1979). Categorial and Schematic Organisation in Memory. In C. Puff (Ed.), *Memory Organisation and Structure* (pp. 259-299). New York: Academic Press.

Mantovani, F. (2001). VR Learning: Potential and Challenges for the Use of 3D Environments in Education and Training. In G. Riva & C. Galimberti (Eds.), *Towards CyberPsychology: Mind, Cognitions and Society in the Internet.* Amsterdam: IOS Press.

Marcus, A. (2002). The Challenge of User Experience Design. *Interaction*, 29–35.

Margerum-Lays, J., & Marx, R. W. (2003). Teacher knowledge of educational technology: A case study of student/mentor teacher pairs. In Y. Zhao (Ed.), *What Should Teachers Know about Technology? Perspectives and Practices* (pp. 123–159). Greenwich, CO: Information Age Publishing.

Markopoulos, P., & Bekker, M. (2003). Interaction Design and Children. *Interacting with Computers, 15*(2), 141–149. doi:10.1016/S0953-5438(03)00004-3

Marriott, R. de C. V., & Torres, P. L. (Eds.). (2008). *Handbook of Research on e-Learning Methodologies for Language Acquisition.* Hershey, PA: Information Science Reference.

Marsella, S., Johnson, W. L., & La Bore, C. M. (2003). Interactive Pedagogical Drama for Health Interventions. In *11th International Conference on Artificial Intelligence in Education*, Australia.

Martin, G. (2007). Beauty is in the eye of the beholder. *The Phrase Finder.* Retrieved on December 4, 2007, from http://www.phrases.org.uk/meanings/59100.html

Marton, F., Dahlgren, L.-O., Svensson, L., & Saljo, R. (1977). *Inlarning och omvarldsuppfattning.* Stockholm, Sweden: Almqvist och Wiksell forlag AB.

Mayer, R. E. (2001). *Multimedia learning.* Cambridge, UK: Cambridge University Press.

Mayer, R. E. (2003). The promise of multimedia learning: Using the same instructional design methods across different media. *Learning and Instruction, 13*, 125–139. doi:10.1016/S0959-4752(02)00016-6

Mayer, R. E., & Anderson, R. B. (1991). Animations need narrations: An experimental test of a dual-coding hypothesis. *Journal of Educational Psychology, 83*(4), 484–490. doi:10.1037/0022-0663.83.4.484

Mayer, R. E., & Moreno, R. (1998). A split-attention effect in multimedia learning: Evidence for dual processing systems in working memory. *Journal of Educational Psychology, 90*(2), 312–320. doi:10.1037/0022-0663.90.2.312

Mayer, R. E., & Moreno, R. (1999). Cognitive principles of multimedia learning: The role of modality and contiguity. *Journal of Educational Psychology, 91*(2), 358–368. doi:10.1037/0022-0663.91.2.358

Mayer, R. E., & Moreno, R. (2000). Meaningful design for meaningful learning: Applying cognitive theory to multimedia explanations. In *Proceedings of the 2000 Annual ED-MEDIA Conference*, Montreal, Quebec, Canada (pp. 747-752).

Mayer, R. E., & Moreno, R. (2003). Meaningful design for meaningful learning: Applying cognitive theory to multimedia explanations. In *Proceedings of ED-MEDIA, 2003,* Honolulu, HI.

McAfee, A. (2006). Enterprise 2.0: The dawn of emergent collaboration. *MIT Sloan Management Review, 47*(3), 21–28.

McClellan, I. (2005). User Experience' Design - A new form of design practice takes shape. In *Proc. CHI'05*, Portland, Oregon, April 2005 (pp. 1097-1097)

McCloskey, D. N. (1985). *The Rhetoric of Economics.* Madison, WI: University of Wisconsin Press.

McGurk, H., & MacDonald, J. (1976). Hearing lips and seeing voices. *Nature, 264*(5588), 746–748. doi:10.1038/264746a0

McInnerney, J. M., & Roberts, T. S. (2004). E-learning: Social interaction and the creation of a sense of community. *Educational Technology & Society, 7*(3), 73–81.

McKeown, K. (1985). Discourse strategies for generating natural-language text. *Artificial Intelligence, 27,* 1–42. doi:10.1016/0004-3702(85)90082-7

McLuhan, M. (1964). *Understanding Media: The Extensions of Man*. New York: Mentor.

McQuiggan, S., Robison, J., Phillips, R., & Lester, J. (2008). Modeling parallel and reactive empathy in virtual agents: An inductive approach. In *International Joint Conference on Autonomous Agents and Multi-Agent Systems*, Portugal.

Meadow, C. T., Boyce, B. R., & Kraft, D. H. (2000). *Text information retrieval systems* (2nd ed.). San Diego, CA: Academic Press.

Merriam-Webster Online. (2005). Retrieved November 5, 2008, from http://www.m-w.com/

Miller, G. (1956). The Magical Number Seven, Plus or Minus Two: Some Limits on Our Capacity for Processing Information. *Psychological Review*, *63*, 81–97. doi:10.1037/h0043158

Miller, G. A. (1967). *The Psychology of Communication*. London: Penguin Books.

Minsky, M. (1975). A Framework for Representing Knowledge. In P. Winston (Eds.), *The Psychology of Computer Vision* (pp. 211-277). New York: McGraw Hill.

Mishra, P., & Koehler, M. J. (2006). Technological Pedagogical Content Knowledge: A framework for teacher knowledge. *Teachers College Record*, *108*(6), 1017–1054. doi:10.1111/j.1467-9620.2006.00684.x

Mitchell, K. D. (2000). Knowledge management: the Next Big Thing. *Public Management*, *29*(2), 57–60.

Mizoguchi, R., & Bourdeau, J. (2000). Using Ontological Engineering to Overcome Common AI-ED Problems. *International Journal of Artificial Intelligence in Education*, *11*(2), 107–121.

Moallem, M. (1998). An expert teacher's thinking and teaching and instructional design models and principles: An ethnographic study. *Educational Technology Research and Development*, *46*, 37–64. doi:10.1007/BF02299788

Monk, A., Hassenzahl, M., Blythe, M., & Reed, D. (2002). *Funology: designing enjoyment*. In *Proc. CHI'02*, (pp. 2135-145).

Moreno, R. (2005). Multimedia learning with animated pedagogical agents. In R. Mayer (Ed.), *Cambridge Handbook of Multimedia Learning* (pp. 507-524). New York: Cambridge University Press.

Moreno, R., Mayer, R. E., Spires, H. A., & Lester, J. C. (2001). The case for social agency in computer-based teaching: Do students learn more deeply when they interact with animated pedagogical agents? *Cognition and Instruction*, *19*(2), 177–213. doi:10.1207/S1532690XCI1902_02

Morishima, Y., Nakajima, H., Brave, S., Yamada, R., Maldonado, H., Nass, C., & Kawaji, S. (2004). The Role of Affect and Sociality in the Agent-Based Collaborative Learning System.In *Lecture Notes in Computer Science* (pp. 265-275).

Mostafa Al Masum, S., & Ishikuza, M. (2005). An Affective Role Model of Software Agent for Effective Agent-based E-Learning by Interplaying between Emotions and Learning. In *Proceedings of the 1st International Conference on Web Information Systems and Technologies (WEBIST 2005)*, Miami, Florida, USA, 449-456.

Mousavi, S. Y., Low, R., & Sweller, J. (1995). Reducing cognitive load by mixing auditory and visual presentation modes. *Journal of Educational Psychology*, *87*(2), 319–334. doi:10.1037/0022-0663.87.2.319

Mudur, S. P. (2005). e-Learning: Prospects and Challenges. *Elel Tech India*. Retrieved from http://elearn.cdac.in/eSikshak/eleltechIndia05/PDF/00-E-Learning%20Prospects%20and%20Challenges-%20SP%20Mudur-00.pdf

Mulken, S. V., Andre, E., & Muller, J. (1998). *The persona effect: How substantial is it?* Paper presented at the HCI-98, Berlin.

Muller, M. J. (1991). PICTIVE: Democratizing the dynamics of the design session. In D. Schuler & A. Namioka (Eds.) *Participatory design: principles and practices* (pp. 211–237). Hillsdale, NJ: Lawrence Erlbaum Associates.

Mullet, K., & Sano, D. (1995). *Designing visual interfaces.* Mountain View: SunSoft Press.

Mylonas, Ph., Tzouveli, P., & Kollias, S. (2007). E-learning and intelligent content adaptation: an integrated approach. *International Journal of Continuing Engineering Education and Lifelong Learning, 17*(4/5), 273–293. doi:10.1504/IJCEELL.2007.015043

Nagao, M. (1984). *A framework of a mechanical translation between japanese and english by analogy principle.* In A. Elithorn & R. Banerji (Eds.), *Artificial and Human Intelligence* (pp. 173–180). Amsterdam: Elsevier.

Najjar, L. J. (2001). Principles of educational multimedia user interface design. In R.W. Swezey & D.H. Andrews (Eds.), *Readings in training and simulation: A 30-year perspective* (pp. 146-158). Santa Monica, CA: Human Factors and Ergonomics Society. Retrieved November 7, 2005, from http://lawrence/najjar.com/papers/Principles_of_educational_multimedia_user_interface_design.html

Nathan, M., & Robinson, C. (2001). Considerations of learning and learning research: Revisiting the "media effects" debate. *Journal of Interactive Learning Research, 12*, 69–88.

National Research Council. (1999). *How people learn.* Washington, DC: National Academy Press.

Neches, (1991). Enabling Technology for Knowledge Sharing. *AI Magazine*, (Winter): 36–56.

Neisser, U. (1967). *Cognitive Psychology.* New York: Appleton-Century-Crofts.

Neisser, U. (1976). *Cognition and reality: principles and implications of cognitive psychology.* New York: W. H. Freeman.

Neisser, U. (1987). *Concepts and conceptual development: ecological and intellectual factors in categorization.* Cambridge, U.K.: Cambridge University Press.

Neji, M., & Ammar, M. (2007). Agent-based Collaborative Affective e-Learning Framework. *Electronic Journal of e-Learning, 5*, 123-134.

Nesset, V., & Large, A. (2004). Children in the information technology design process. *Library & Information Science Research, 26*, 140–161. doi:10.1016/j.lisr.2003.12.002

Nichols, M. (2003a). Formal Discussion: A Theory for e-Learning. In *International Forum of Educational Technology and Society, March.* Retrieved from http://ifntcs.ieee.org/discussions/discuss_march 2003.html

Nicohls, M. (2003). A Theory for e-Learning. *Educational Technology and Society, 6*(2), 1–10.

Nicolescu, B. (2000). Transdisciplinarity and Complexity: Levels of Reality as Source of Indeterminacy. *Bulletin Interactif du Centre International de Recherches et Études transdisciplinaires* n° 15. Centre International de Recherches et Études Transdisciplinaires.

Nielsen, S., & Johansson, B. (2007). Fun and Usable: Augmented Reality Instruction in a Hospital Setting. In [New York: ACM Press.]. *Proceedings of OzCHI, 2007*, 123–130. doi:10.1145/1324892.1324915

Niess, M. L. (2005). Preparing teachers to teach science and mathematics with technology: Developing a technology pedagogical content knowledge. *Teaching and Teacher Education, 21*(5), 509–523. doi:10.1016/j.tate.2005.03.006

Nonaka, I., & Takeuchi, H. (1995). *The knowledge creating company: how Japanese companies create the dynamics of innovation.* New York: Oxford University Press.

Norman, D. (2004). *Emotional design: Why we love (or hate) everyday things.* New York: Basic Books.

Novak, J. D., & Cañas, A. J. (2006). *The Theory Underlying Concept Maps and How to Construct Them.* Technical Report IHMC CmapTools 2006-01, Florida Institute for Human and Machine Cognition, 2006. Retrieved from

Noy, N. & McGuinness, D. (2001). *Ontology Development 101: A Guide to Creating Your First Ontology.* Stanford Knowledge Systems Laboratory Technical Report KSL-01-05 and Stanford Medical Informatics Technical Report SMI-2001-0880, March 2001.

O'Donnell, A., Dansereau, D., & Hall, R. (2002). Knowledge Maps as Scaffolds for Cognitive Processing Educational. *Psychological Review*, *14*(1).

O'Reilly, T. (2005). *What is Web 2.0: Design patterns and business models for the next generation of software.* Retrieved February 1, 2008, from http://www.oreillynet.com/pub/a/oreilly/tim/news/2005/09/30/what-is-web-20.html

Ohler, J. (2008). The semantic web in education. *EDUCAUSE Quarterly*, *31*(4), 7–9.

Oliver, M., & Trigwell, K. (2005). Can "blended learning" be redeemed. *E-Learning, 2*(1). Retrieved September 2, 2006 from http://www.wwwords.co.uk/pdf/viewpdf.asp?j=elea&vol =2&issue=1&year= 2005&article=3_Oliver_ELEA_2_1_web&id=86.215.192.54

Omondi, L. (1997). Dholuo emotional language: An overview. In S. Niemeier & R. Dirven (Eds.), *The language of emotions* (pp. 87-110). Amsterdam: John Benjamins Publishing.

Orchestration. (2008). *Merriam-Webster Online Dictionary.* Retrieved November 9, 2008, from http://www.merriam-webster.com/dictionary/orchestration

Ornstein, R. E. (1972). *The Psychology of Consciousness.* London: Pelican Books.

Ortony, A., Clore, G. L., & Collins, A. (1988). *The cognitive structure of emotions.* Cambridge, UK: University Press.

Oudeyer, P. Y. (2003). The production and recognition of emotions in speech: features and algorithms. *International Journal of Human-Computer Studies*, *59*(1-2), 157–183. doi:10.1016/S1071-5819(02)00141-6

P1484. *1 Architecture and Reference Model.* (n.d.). IEEE Learning Techonology Standards Committee. Retrieved July 2003, from http://ltsc.ieee.org/index.html

Paas, F., Tuovinen, J., Tabbers, H., & Van Gerven, P. W. M. (2003). Cognitive load measurement as a means to advance cognitive load theory. *Educational Psychologist*, *38*, 63–71. doi:10.1207/S15326985EP3801_8

Paiva, A., Dias, J., Sobral, D., Aylett, R., Sobreperez, P., Woods, S., et al. (2004). Caring for agents and agents that care: Building empathic relations with synthetic agents. In *Proceedings of the International Conference on Autonomous Agents and Multiagent Systems* (pp. 194–201). New York: ACM Press.

Paivio, A. (1971). *Imagery and verbal processes.* New York: Holt, Rinehart & Winston.

Paivio, A. (1979). *Imagery and verbal processes.* Hillsdale, NJ: Lawrence Erlbaum.

Paivio, A. (1986). *Mental representations: A dual coding approach.* Oxford, UK: Oxford University Press.

Paivio, A. (1991). Dual coding theory: Retrospect and current status. *Canadian Journal of Psychology*, *45*, 255–287. doi:10.1037/h0084295

Paliouras, G., Papatheodorou, C., & Spyropoulos, C. D. (2002). Discovering Learner Communities on the Internet Using Unsupervised Machine Learning Techniques. *Interacting with Computers . Journal of Interacting with Computers*, *14*(6), 761–791. doi:10.1016/S0953-5438(02)00015-2

Pallant, J. (2005). *SPSS Survival Manual.* Maidenhead, UK: Open University Press.

Panorama des représentations des adultes en formation continue. Unpublished doctoral Thesis, Université de Technologie de Compiègne, France.

Pantic, M., & Rothkrantz, L. J. M. (2003). Toward an affect sensitive multimodal human-computer interaction. *Proceedings of the IEEE*, *91*(9), 1370–1390. doi:10.1109/JPROC.2003.817122

Paolini, P., & Di Blas, N. (2006). Multi-User Virtual Environments for Education: A European Experience. In *Proc. E-Learn 06 Conference*, Honolulu, HI (pp. 1383-1394).

Papaioakeim, M., Kaldoudi, E., Vargemezis, V., & Simopoulos, K. (2006). Confronting the problem of ever expanding core knowledge and the necessity of handling overspecialized disciplines in medical education. In *Proceedings of ITAB 2006: IEEE International Special Topic*

Conference on Information Technology in Biomedicine. Ioannina, Greece: IEEE.

Papanastasiou, E. C., & Angeli, C. (2008). Evaluating the Use of ICT in Education: Psychometric Properties of the Survey of Factors Affecting Teachers Teaching with Technology (SFA-T3). *Educational Technology & Society, 11*(1), 69–86.

Paramythis, A., & Loidl-Reisinger, S. (2004). Adaptive learning environments and e-learning standards. *Electronic Journal of eLearning,* 2(1). Retrieved on September 10, 2008 from http://www.ejel.org/volume-2/vol2-issue1/issue1-art11.htm

Park, O., & Lee, J. (2003) Adaptive instructional systems. In D.H. Jonassen (Ed.), *Handbook of research for educational communications and technology* (pp. 651-685). Mahwah, NJ: Lawrence Erlbaum.

Parker, K. R., & Chao, J. T. (2007). Wiki as a teaching tool. *Interdisciplinary Journal of Knowledge and Learning Objects, 3,* 57–72.

Paula, R. D., Ding, X., Dourish, P., Nies, K., Pillet, B., Redmiles, D., et al. (2005, July 6-8). Two experience designing for effective security. In *Symposium On Usable Privacy and Security (SOUPS)*, Pittsburgh, PA.

Pedagogical Patterns Project. (2001). Retrieved November 5, 2008, from http://www.pedagogicalpatterns.org/

Peeck, J. (1987). The role of illustrations in processing and remembering illustrated text. *The Psychology of Illustration, 1,* 115–151.

Pekrun, R., Goetz, T., Titz, W., & Perry, R. P. (2002). Academic emotions in students' self-regulated learning and achievement: a program of qualitative and quantitative research. *Educational Psychologist, 37*(2), 91–105. doi:10.1207/S15326985EP3702_4

Pelachaud, C., Carofiglio, V., Poggi, I., De Carolis, B., & De Rosis, F. (2002). Embodied Contextual Agent in Information Delivering Application. In *Proceedings of the First international Joint Conference on Autonomous Agents and Multiagent Systems: Part 2*, (pp. 758-765). New York: ACM Press.

Pénao, S., Noumon, R. C., Kitaev, I., & Oulai, D. (1997). Financing and Financial Management of Education. In *Pan African Seminar*, Dakar, Senegal, (pp. 12-14).

Pentland, A. S. (2005). Socially Aware Computation and Communication. *Computer, 38*(3), 33–40. doi:10.1109/MC.2005.104

Perse, E., Burton, P., Kovner, E., Lears, M., & Sen, R. (1992). Predicting computer-mediated communication in a college class. *Communication Research Reports, 9*(2), 161–170. doi:10.1080/08824099209359908

Peter, C., Schultz, R., Voskamp, J., Urban, B., Nowack, N., Janik, H., et al. (2007). EREC-II in Use – Studies on Usability and Suitability of a Sensor System for Affect Detection and Human Performance Monitoring. In J. Jacko (Ed.): *Human-Computer Interaction, Part III, HCII 2007* (LNCS 4552, pp. 465–474).

Peters, M. A. (2006). Higher Education, Development and the Learning Economy. *Policy Futures in Education, 4*(3), 279–291. doi:10.2304/pfie.2006.4.3.279

Pharmaceutical Research and Manufacturers Association (PhRMA). (2001). *The Value of Medicines.* Washington, DC.

Phipps, R., & Merisotis, R. (1999). *What's the difference? A review of contemporary research on the effectiveness of distance learning in higher education.* The Institute for Higher Education Policy, Washington, DC.

Piaget, J. (1970). Piaget's Theory. In P. Mussen (Ed.), *Carmichael's Manual of Child Psychology* (vol. 1, pp. 318-323). New York: Wiley.

Picard, R. (1997). *Affective Computing.* Cambridge, MA: MIT Press.

Picard, R. W. (2000). Towards computers that recognize and respond to user emotion. *IBM Systems Journal, 39*(3), 705–719.

Picard, R. W. (2003). Affective Computing: Challenges. *International Journal of Human-Computer Studies, 59*(1-2), 55–64. doi:10.1016/S1071-5819(03)00052-1

Picard, R. W., Papert, S., Bender, W., Blumberg, B., Breazeal, C., & Cavallo, D. (2004). Affective learning - A manifesto. *BT Technology Journal, 22*(4), 253–269. doi:10.1023/B:BTTJ.0000047603.37042.33

Picciano, A. G. (2002). Beyond student perceptions: issues of interaction, presence, and performance in an online course. *JALN, 6*(1), 21–40.

Poggi, C., & Torrebruno, A. (2007). From the Dead Sea Scrolls to Social Sports, passing through European History: an Effective Pedagogical Format Based on 3D Worlds. In *Proceedings of ED-Media 07*, Chesapeake, VA (pp. 4240-4248).

Pollock, E., Chandler, P., & Sweller, J. (2002). Assimilating complex information. *Learning and Instruction, 12*, 61–86. doi:10.1016/S0959-4752(01)00016-0

Posner, M., & Snyder, C. (1975). *Facilitation and inhibition in the processing of signal*. In S. Rabbitt& S. Dornic (Eds.), *Attention and performance* (pp. 669–682). New York: Academic Press.

Prendinger, H., Dohi, H., Wang, H., Mayer, S., & Ishizuka, M. (2004). Empathic embodied interfaces: Addressing users' affective state. *Lecture Notes in Computer Science, 3068*, 53–64.

Prendinger, H., Dohi, H., Wang, H., Mayer, S., & Ishizuka, M. (2004). Empathic embodied interfaces: Addressing users' affective state. [). New York: Springer.]. *Lecture Notes in Computer Science, 3068*, 53–64.

Prendinger, H., Mori, J., & Ishizuka, M. (2005). Using human physiology to evaluate subtle expressivity of a virtual quizmaster in a mathematical game. *International Journal of Human-Computer Studies, 62*, 231–245. doi:10.1016/j.ijhcs.2004.11.009

Prensky, M. (2001). *Digital Game-Based Learning*. New York: McGraw-Hill.

Pribeanu, C., & Iordache, D. D. (2008). Evaluating the motivational value of an augmented reality system for learning chemistry. In A. Holzinger (Ed.), *Proceedings of USAB 2008* (LNCS 5298, pp. 31-42). New York: Springer.

Price, S., & Rogers, I. (2004). Let's get physical: the learning benefits of interacting in digitally augmented physiscal spaces. *Computers & Education, 43*, 137–151. doi:10.1016/j.compedu.2003.12.009

Probst, G., et al. (2002). *Gestão do conhecimento- os elementos construtivos do sucesso* [Knowledge management-the constructive elements of success]. Porto Alegre, Brasil: Bookman.

Pulichind, J. (2006). *The e-Learning Guild Research: Future Directions in e-Learning*. Retrieved from http://www.elearningguild.com/showfile.cfm?id=1685.

Quah, D. (2003). *Digital Goods and the New Economy*. Centre for Economic Performance, LSE. Retrieved from http://cep. lse.ac.uk/pubs/download/dp0563.pdf

Ramachandran, V. S., & Anstis, S. M. (1986). The perception of apparent motion. *Scientific American, 254*(6), 80–87.

Randell, C., Phelps, T., & Rogers, Y. (2003). Ambient Wood: Demonstration of a digitally enhanced field trip for school children. In *Adjunct Proceedings of UbiComp 2003*, Seattle, USA (pp. 100-104).

Raouzaiou, A., Tsapatsoulis, N., Karpouzis, K., & Kollias, S. (2002). Parameterized facial expression synthesis based on MPEG-4. *EURASIP Journal on Applied Signal Processing*, (10): 1021–1038. doi:10.1155/S1110865702206149

Rasmussen, J. (1986). *Information processing and human-machine interaction, an approach to cognitive engineering*. Amsterdam: Elsevier Science Publishing.

Ravenscorft, A. (2001). Designing e-Learning Interactions in the 21st Century: Revisiting and Rethinking the Role of Theory. *European Journal of Education, 36*(2), 133–156. doi:10.1111/1467-3435.00056

Read, J. C., Gregory, P., MacFarlane, S. J., McManus, B., Gray, P., & Patel, R. (2002). An Investigation of Participatory Design with Children - Informant, Balanced and Facilitated Design. In *Proc. IDC 2002*, Eindhoven, Netherlands (pp. 56-64).

Reimann, P. (2003). Multimedia learning: Beyond modality. *Learning and Instruction, 13*, 245–252. doi:10.1016/S0959-4752(02)00024-5

Reiser, R. (2001). A History of Instructional Design and Technology. Part 1: A History of Instructional Media. *Educational Technology Research and Development, 49*(1), 53–64. doi:10.1007/BF02504506

Retalis, S., Papasalouros, A., & Skordalakis, M. (2002). Towards a Generic Conceptual Design Meta-Model for Web-Based Educational Applications. In *Proc. 2nd IWWOST*, Malaga, Spain.

Retrieved from November 5, 2008 http://nicol.club.fr/ciret/bulletin /b15/b15c4.htm.

Revelle, G. (2003). Educating via Entertainment Media: the Sesame Workshop approach. In *ACM Computer and Entertainment, 1*(1), 1-9.

Reynolds, C., & Picard, R. W. (2004). Affective Sensors, Privacy, and Ethical Contracts. In *Proceedings of CHI*, Vienna, April 2004.

Richards, L., & Richards, T. (1994). From filing cabinet to computer. In Bryman, A. & Burgess, R.G. (eds.) *Qualitative Data*. 1994. (pp.146-172). New York: Routledge.

Richardson, J. C., & Swan, K. (2003). Examining social presence in online courses in relation to students' perceived learning and satisfaction. *JALN, 7*(1), 68–88.

Riding, R., & Rayner, S. (1998). *Cognitive styles and learning strategies*. London: David Fulton.

Rieber, L. (1990a). Animation in computer-based instruction. *Educational Technology Research and Development, 38*(1), 77–86. doi:10.1007/BF02298250

Rieber, L. (1990b). Using computer animated graphics in science instruction with children. *Journal of Educational Psychology, 82*, 135–140. doi:10.1037/0022-0663.82.1.135

Rieber, L. P. (1990). Animation in computer-based instruction. *Educational Technology Research and Development, 38*(1), 77–86. doi:10.1007/BF02298250

Rieber, L. P. (2000). *Computers, graphics & learning*. Madison, WI: Brown & Benchmark.

Riecken, D. (2000). Personalized views of personalization: Introduction. *Communications of the ACM, 43*(8), 26–28. doi:10.1145/345124.345133

Riloff, E., & Jones, R. (1999). Learning dictionaries for information extraction by multi-level bootstrapping. In *Proc. of the 16th National Conference on Artificial Intelligence* (pp. 474– 479).

Rivers, W. (1964). *The Psychologist and the Foreign Language Teacher*. University of Chicago Press, Chicago.

Rivers, W. (1972). *Speaking in Many Tongues: Essays in Foreign Language Teaching*. Rowley: Newbury House.

Roberts, P. (1962). *English Sentences*. New York: Harcourt Brace & World.

Roda, C. (2004). Participatory system design as a tool for learning. In *Proceedings of International Conference on Cognition and Exploratory Learning in the Digital Age (CELDA)* (pp. 366–372).

Rodrigues, S. (2003). Experiences from the partnership in primary science project: Teacher professional development involving ICT and science pedagogical content knowledge. *Science Education International, 14*(2), 2–11.

Rogoff, T. (1990). *Apprenticeship in Thinking: Cognitive development in social context*. Oxford, UK: Oxford University Press.

Ross, J., & Schulz, R. (1999). Can computer-aided instruction accommodate all learners equally? *British Journal of Educational Technology, 30*(1), 5–24. doi:10.1111/1467-8535.00087

Roussou, M., Kavalieratou, E., & Doulgeridis, M. (2007). Children Designers in the Museum: Applying Participatory Design for the Development of an Art Education Program. In *Proc. IDC '07*, Aalborg, Denmark (pp. 77-80).

Rubinstein, D. (1979). *Education & Equality*. Harmondsworth, UK: Penguin Books.

Rudd, J., Stern, K., & Isensee, S. (1996). Low vs. high fidelity prototyping debate. *Interaction, 3*(1), 76–85. doi:10.1145/223500.223514

Rumelhart, D. (1975). Notes on a Schema for Stories. In D. Bobrow & A. Collins (Eds.), Representation and Understanding: Studies in Cognitive Science (pp. 211-236). New York: Academic Press.

Russell, T. L. (2001). *The no significant difference phenomenon*. Montgomery, USA: IDECC.

Ryle, G. (1949). *The Concept of the Mind*. Chicago: The University Press.

Ryokai, K., Vaucelle, C., & Cassell, J. (2003). Virtual peers as partners in storytelling and literacy learning. *Journal of Computer Assisted Learning, 19*(2), 195–208. doi:10.1046/j.0266-4909.2003.00020.x

Saint-Onge, H. (2002). *Linking Knowledge to Strategy*. Presentation at the Strategic Planning for KM Conference, Toronto, May 28-29.

Samuels, S. J. (1967). Attentional process in reading: The effect of pictures on the acquisition of reading responses. *Journal of Educational Psychology, 58*(6), 337–342. doi:10.1037/h0020045

Sansone, C., & Thoman, D. B. (2005). Does what we feel affect what we learn? Some answers and new questions. *Learning and Instruction, 15*(5), 507–515. doi:10.1016/j.learninstruc.2005.07.015

Sasha, A. B., & Plucker, J. A. (2002). Smart People or Smart Contexts? Cognition, Ability, and Talent Development in an Age of Situated Approaches to Knowing and Learning. *Educational Psychologist, 37*(3), 165–182. doi:10.1207/S15326985EP3703_3

Satchell, C. (2008). Cultural Theory and Design: Identifying Trends by Looking at the Action in the Periphery. *Interaction, 15*(6), 23–25. doi:10.1145/1409040.1409046

Saunders, M., Lewis, P., & Thornhill, A. (2007). *Research Methods for Business Students*. Harlow, UK: Financial Times Prentice Hall.

Savignon, S. (1983). *Communicative Competence: Theory and Classroom Practice*. Reading, MA: Addison-Wesley.

Scaife, M., Rogers, Y., Aldrich, F., & Davies, M. (1997). Designing for or designing with? Informant design for interactive learning environments. In S. Pemberton (Ed.), *Proceedings of the SIGCHI Conference on Human Factors in Computing Systems,* Atlanta, Georgia, United States, March 22–27, 1997 (pp. 343–350). New York: ACM.

Schaeffer, J.-M. (1999). *Pourquoi la fiction?* Paris: Seuil.

Schaffert, S., & Hilzensauer, W. (2008). On the Way towards Personal Learning Environments: Seven Crucial Aspects. *E-Learning Papers*. Retrieved from http://www.elearningpapers.eu

Schaffert, S., Bischof, D., Buerger, T., Gruber, A., Hilzensauer, W., & Schaffert, S. (2006). Learning with semantic wikis. In *Proceedings of the First Workshop on Semantic Wikis – From Wiki To Semantics (SemWiki2006)*, Budva, Montenegro(pp.109-123).

Schank, R., & Abelson, R. (1977). *Scripts, Plans, Goals and Understanding: an Inquiry into Human Knowledge Structures*. Hillsdale, NJ: Erlbaum.

Schnotz, W., & Bannert, M. (2003). Construction and interference in learning from multiple representation. *Learning and Instruction, 13*, 141–156. doi:10.1016/S0959-4752(02)00017-8

Schreiber, G. (2000). *Knowledge Engineering and Management: The CommonKADS Methodology*. Cambridge, MA: MIT Press.

Schriver, K. A. (1997). *Dynamics in document design: creating text for readers*. New York: Wiley.

Schröder, M., Devillers, L., Karpouzis, K., Martin, J., Pelachaud, C., Peter, C., et al. (2007). What should a generic emotion markup language be able to represent? In Paiva A. et al. (Ed.), *Affective Computing and Intelligent Interaction, Second International Conference, ACII 2007*, September 12-14, Lisbon, Portugal, (LNCS 4738, pp. 440-451). Berlin-Heidelberg, Germany: Springer.

Schuable, L., & Glaser, R. (Eds.). (1996). *Innovations in learning.* New Jersey, NY: Mahwah.

Schubert, T., Regenbrecht, H., & Friedman, F. (2002). Real and illusory interaction enhance presence in virtual environments. *Presence: teleoperators and virtual environment, 11*(4), 425-434.

Schuemie, M. J., Van der Straaten, P., Krijn, M., & Van Der Mast, C. (2001). Research on presence in virtual reality. *Cyberpsychology & Behavior, 4*(2), 183–201. doi:10.1089/109493101300117884

Schutz, P. A., & Pekrun, R. (2007). *Emotions in education.* San Diego CA: Elsevier Inc.

SCORM. *The sharable content object reference model.* (2001). Retrieved November 4, 2005, from http://www.adlnet.org/

Scott, D. (1999). The Multilingual Generation Game: authoring fluent texts in unfamiliar languages. In *Proceedings of the 16th International Joint Conference on Artificial Intelligence.*

Scriven, M. (1991). *Evaluation thesaurus* (4th ed). Newbury Park, CA: Sage Publications.

Segalowitz, N. (2000). *Automaticity and attentional skill in fluent performance.* In H. Riggenbach (Ed.), *Perspectives on fluency* (pp. 200-219). Ann Arbor, MI: University of Michigan Press.

Segalowitz, N. (2003). Automaticity and second language learning. In C. Doughty & M. Long (Eds.), *The handbook of second language acquisition* (pp. 382-408). Oxford, UK: Blackwell.

Segalowitz, N. (2007). Access fluidity, attention control, and the acquisition of fluency in a second language. *TESOL Quarterly, 41,* 181–186.

Segalowitz, N., & Hulstijn, J. (2005). Automaticity in second language learning. In J.F. Kroll & A.M.B. De Groot (Eds.), *Handbook of bilingualism: Psycholinguistic approaches* (pp 371-388). New York: Oxford University Press.

Selfe, C. (1990). Technology in the English classroom: Computers through the lens of feminist pedagogy. In C. Handa (Ed.), *Computers and community: Teaching composition in the twenty-first century* (pp. 118–139). Portsmouth, NH: Boynton/Cook.

Selinger, M. (2001). Learning Information and Communications Technology skills and the subject context of the learning. *Journal of Information Technology for Teacher Education, 10*(1-2), 143–154.

Sengers, P., Boehner, K., Davod, S., & Kaye, J. (2005). Reflective Design. In *Proc. Critical Computing'05,* (pp. 49 – 58).

Seufert, T. (2003). Supporting coherence formation in learning from multiple representations. *Learning and Instruction, 13,* 227–237. doi:10.1016/S0959-4752(02)00022-1

Shepard, R. N. (1967). Recognition memory for words, sentences and pictures. *Journal of Verbal Learning and Verbal Behavior, 6,* 156–163. doi:10.1016/S0022-5371(67)80067-7

Shih, Y., & Alessi, S. M. (1994). Mental models and transfer of learning in computer programming. *Journal of Research on Computing in Education, 26,* 155–175.

Shih, Y., & Alessi, S. M. (1996). Effects of Text versus Voice on Learning in Multimedia Courseware. *Journal of Educational Multimedia and Hypermedia, 5*(2), 203–218.

Short, J., Williams, E., & Christie, B. (1976). *The social psychology of telecommunications.* London: John Wiley & Sons.

Shuell, T. (1986). Cognitive conceptions of learning. *Review of Educational Research, 56*(4), 411–436.

Shulman, L. S. (1986). Those who understand: Knowledge growth in teaching. *Educational Researcher, 15*(2), 4–14.

Shulman, L. S. (1987). Knowledge and teaching: Foundations of the new reform. *Harvard Educational Review, 57*(1), 1–22.

Siebert, H. (1998). Konstruktivismus. Konsequenzen für Bildungsmanagement und. Seminargestaltung. In *Deutsches Institut für Erwachsenenbildung*, Bonn, Germany. Retrieved from http://www.die-bonn.de/esprid/dokumente/doc-1998/siebert98_01.pdf

Siemens, G. (2004). *Learning management systems: The wrong place to start learning.* Retrieved December, 26, 2006, from http://Elearnespace.org.

Simonsen, M., Clark, R., Kulik, J., Tennyson, R., & Winn, W. (1987). Mere vehicles: A symposium on the status of research in instructional technology. In *Proceedings of the 1987 Annual Convention of the Association for Educational Communications and Technology*, Atlanta, GA (pp. 1-43).

Singhanayok, C., & Hooper, S. (1998). The effects of cooperative learning and learner control on students' achievement, option selections, and attitudes. *Educational Technology Research and Development, 46*(2), 17–33. doi:10.1007/BF02299787

Siozos, P., Palaigeorgiou, G., Triantafyllakos, G., & Despotakis, F. (2008). Computer based testing using "digital ink": participatory design of a Tablet PC based assessment application for secondary education. *Computers and Education 52(4), May 2009,* 811-819.

Slavin, R. E. (1990). *Cooperative learning: Theory, research and practice*. London: Allyn and Bacon.

Smith, G. (Ed.). (1999). *Goffman and Social Organisation: Studies in a Sociological Legacy.* London: Routledge.

Software Survey. (2001, April 14). The Beast of Complexity. *The Economist.*

Sosnovsky, S., & Gavrilova, T. (2006). One Approach to Development of Educational Ontology for C-Programming. *Int. Journal of Information Theories and Applications, 13*(4), 303–308.

Sowa, J. F. (1984). *Conceptual Structures: Information Processing in Mind and Machine.* Reading, MA: Addison-Wesley.

Spärck Jones, K. (1994). Towards better NLP system evaluation. In *Proceedings of the Workshop on Human Language Technology (HLT'94)* (pp. 102–107).

Spaulding, S. (1955). Research on pictorial illustration. In D.H. Jonassen (Ed.), *Handbook for research for educational communications and technology* (pp. 755-794). New York: Simon & Schuster Macmillan.

Spolsky, B. (1966). A psycholinguistic critique of programmed foreign language instruction. *IRAL*, 4(2).

Stahl, G. (2006). *Group Cognition. Computer Support for Building Collaborative Knowledge*. Cambridge, MA: MIT Press.

Stanton, D., et al. (2001). Classroom Collaboration in the Design of Tangible Interfaces for Storytelling. In *Proc. CHI 2001*, Seattle, USA (pp. 482-489)

Stary, C., & Tooter, A. (2006). On Learner Control in e-Learning. In *Proceedings of ECCE 06 – Trust and Control in complex Socio-technical Systems* (pp. 41-48). New York: ACM Press.

Steen, H. L. (2008). Effective elearning design. *MERLOT Journal of Online Learning and Teaching, 4*(4), 526-532. Retrieved March 27, 2009, from http://jolt.merlot.org/vol4no4/steen_1208.pdf

Steen, L. A. (1988). The science of patterns. *Science, 240,* 611–616. doi:10.1126/science.240.4852.611

Steiner, B., Kaplan, N., & Moulthrop, S. (2006). When play works: Turning game-playing into learning. In *Proc. IDC'2006*, Tampere, Finland.

Stern, E., Aprea, C., & Ebner, H. (2003). Improving cross-content transfer in text processing by means of active graphical representation. *Learning and Instruction, 13,* 191–203. doi:10.1016/S0959-4752(02)00020-8

Sternberg, R. J. (1996). *Cognitive psychology.* Orlando, FL: Harbourt Brace.

Stevens, V. (1989). *A direction for CALL: From behavioristic to humanistic courseware.* In M. Pennington (Ed.), *Teaching Languages with Computers* (pp. 31–43). La Jolla, CA: Athelstan.

Stevenson, H. W., Lee, S. Y., & Graham, T. (1993). Chinese and Japanese kindergartens: case study in comparative research. In B. Spodek (Ed.), *Handbook of research on the education of young children* (pp. 519–535). New York: Macmillan.

Straub, D., Boudreau, M., & Gefen, D. (2004). Validation guidelines for IS positivist research. *Communications of the Association for Information Systems*, *13*, 380–427.

Sun, H., & Zhang, P. (2006). Causal Relationships between Perceived Enjoyment and perceived Ease of Use: An Alternative Approach. *Journal of the Association for Information Systems*, *7*(9), 618–645.

Svanæs, D., & Seland, G. (2004). Putting the users center stage. In *Proceedings of the ACM CHI '04 Human Factors in Computing Systems Conference* (pp. 479–486).

Swann, J. E., II, & Gabbard, J. (2005). Survey of User-Based Experimentation in Augmented Reality. In *Proceedings of 1st International Conference on Virtual Reality*, July 22-27, Las Vegas, Nevada.

Sweetser, P., & Wyeth, P. (2005). Game Flow: A Model for Evaluating Player Enjoyment in Games. *ACM Computer and Entertainment*, *3*(3), 1–23. doi:10.1145/1077246.1077248

Sweller, J. (1988). Cognitive load during problem solving: Effects on learning. *Cognitive Science*, *12*(1), 257–285.

Sweller, J. (1989). Cognitive technology: Some procedures for facilitating learning and problem solving in mathematics and science. *Journal of Educational Psychology*, *81*(4), 457–466. doi:10.1037/0022-0663.81.4.457

Sweller, J., & Chandler, P. (1994). Why some material is difficult to learn. *Cognition and Instruction*, *12*(3), 185–233. doi:10.1207/s1532690xci1203_1

Sweller, J., van Merrienboer, J., & Paas, F. (1998). Cognitive architecture and instructional design. *Educational Psychology Review*, *10*, 251–296. doi:10.1023/A:1022193728205

Szabo, M., & Kanuka, H. (1999). Effects of violating screen design principles of balance, unity, and focus on recall learning, study, time, and completion rates. *Journal of Educational Multimedia and Hypermedia*, *8*(1), 23–42.

Tai, L. (2008). *Corporate e-Learning: an Inside View of IBM's Solutions*. Oxford, UK: The University Press.

Tams, S. (2008). Self-directed social learning: the role of individual differences. *Journal of Management Development*, *27*(2), 196–213. doi:10.1108/02621710810849335

Theofanos, M., & Quesenbery, W. (2005). Towards the Design of Effective Formative Test Reports. *Journal of Usability Studies*, *1*(1), 27–45.

Thomas, L. H. (1999). *A study of pre-service teachers' integration of technology applications into the elementary classroom*. Unpublished doctoral dissertation, Mississippi State University.

Thompson, A. D., Schmidt, D. A., & Davis, N. E. (2003). Technology collaboratives for simultaneous renewal in teacher education. *Educational Technology Research and Development*, *51*(1), 124–128. doi:10.1007/BF02504519

Thompson, T. L., Colla, T., & MacDonald, J. (2005). Community building, emergent design and expecting the unexpected: Creating a quality e-learning experience. *The Internet and Higher Education*, *8*, 233–249. doi:10.1016/j.iheduc.2005.06.004

Thorndike, E. L. (1931). *Human Learning*. Cambridge, MA: MIT Press.

Tobias, S. (1987). Learner characteristics. In R. Gagné (Ed.), *Instructional technology: Foundations* (pp. 207-232). Hillsdale, NJ: Lawrence Erlbaum.

Tobias, S. (1990). *They're not dumb, they're different: Stalking the second tier*. Tucson, AZ: Research Corporation.

Tolman, E. C. (1948). Cognitive Maps in Rats and Man. *Psychological Review*, *55*, 189–208. doi:10.1037/h0061626

Tolman, E. C. (1967). *Purposive Behavior in Animals and Men*. New York: Appleton-Century-Crofts.

Tonkin, E. (2005). Making the case for a wiki. *Ariadne*, 42. Retrieved November 14, 2008, from http://www.ariadne.ac.uk/issue42/tonkin/

Tracey, M. W., & Hasting, N. B. (2005). Does media affect learning: Where are we? *TechTrends*, *49*(2), 28–30.

Tractinsky, N., Katz, A., & Ikar, D. (2000). What is beautiful is usable. *Interacting with Computers*, *13*, 127–145. doi:10.1016/S0953-5438(00)00031-X

Triantafyllakos, G. N., Palaigeorgiou, G. E., & Tsoukalas, I. A. (2008a). We!Design: A student-centred participatory methodology for the design of educational applications. *British Journal of Educational Technology*, *39*(1), 125–139.

Triantafyllakos, G., Palaigeorgiou, G., & Tsoukalas, I. A. (2008b). Collaborative design as narrative. In *Proceedings of the 10th Participatory Design Conference, PDC08,* 1–4 October 2008, Bloomington, Indiana, USA (pp. 210–213).

Tsui, M.-J. (2009). The Model of Strategic e-Learning: Understanding and Evaluating Student e-Learning from Meta-cognitive Perspectives. *Journal of Educational Technology & Society*, *12*(1), 34–38.

Tu, C.-H. (2002). The impacts of text-based CMC on online social presence. *Journal of Interactive E-learning*, *1*(2), 1–24.

Tu, S., Eriksson, H., Gennari, J., Shahar, Y., & Musen, M. (1995). Ontology-Based Configuration of Problem Solving Methods and Generation of Knowledge-Acquisition Tools. *Artificial Intelligence in Medicine*, (7): 257–289. doi:10.1016/0933-3657(95)00006-R

Tüker, M. A., & Zingel, S. (2008, July). Formative Interfaces for Scaffolding Self-Regulated Learning in PLEs. *eLearning Papers,* 4. Retrieved from http://www.elearningeuropa.info/files/media/media15975.pdf

Tuparova, D., & Tuparov, G. (2007 May). e-Learning in Bulgaria. *eLearning Papers,* 4. Retrieved from http://www.elearningeuropa.info/files/media/media12735.pdf

Underhill, J. W. (2001). *Meaning, language, and mind: an interview with Mark Turner –Interview.* Northern Illinois University: Gale Group. Retrieved November 5, 2008, from http://findarticles.com/p/articles/mi_m2342/is_4_36/ai_98167920/print?tag= artBody;col1

Useille, P. (2007). *Une approche informationnelle du Document: vers l'émergence du sens formatif.* Unpublished doctoral thesis, University of Valenciennes and Hainaut-Cambrèsis, France.

Usoro, A., & Abid, A. (2008). A conceptual view of quality e-learning in higher education. *E-Learning*, *5*(1), 79–90. doi:10.2304/elea.2008.5.1.75

Usoro, A., Sharratt, M. W., Tsui, E., & Shekhar, S. (2007). Trust as an antecedent to knowledge sharing in virtual communities of practice. *Knowledge Management Research and Practice*, *5*, 199–212. doi:10.1057/palgrave.kmrp.8500143

van Dijk, T. (1977). Semantic Macro-Structures and Knowledge frames in Discourse Comprehension. In M. A. Just & P. A. Carpenter (Eds.), *Cognitive Processes in Comprehension* (pp. 3-31). Hillsdale, NJ: Lawrence Erlbaum.

Van Merrienboer, J. J. G. (1997). *Training complex cognitive skills.* Englewood Cliffs, NJ: Educational Technology Press.

van Merriënboer, J. J. G., Schuurman, J. G., de Croock, M. B. M., & Paas, F. G. W. C. (2002). Redirecting learners' attention during training: Effects on cognitive load, transfer test performance and training efficiency. *Learning and Instruction*, *12*(1), 11–37. doi:10.1016/S0959-4752(01)00020-2

van Merrinboer, J. J. G. (1997). *Training complex cognitive skills: A four component instructional design model for technical training.* Englewood Cliffs, NJ: Educational Technology Publications.

van Merrinboer, J. J. G., & Kirschner, P. A. (2007). *Ten steps to complex learning: A systematic approach to four-component instructional design.* Mahwah, NJ: Lawrence Erlbaum.

Venkatesh, V., Davis, F. D., & Morris, M. G. (2007). Dead or Alive? The development, trajectory and future of technology adoption research. *Journal of the Association for Information Systems*, *8*(4), 267–286.

Verclytte, L. (2002). Vers des documents sur mesure au moment opportun. Application au document d'apprentissage. In *Journées doctorales de la Société Française des Sciences de l'Information de la Communication (SFSIC)*, Paris.

Verhaegh, J., et al. (2006). On the design of Camelot, an outdoor game for children. In *Proc. IDC '06,* Tampere, Finland (pp. 9-17).

Vestal, W. (2005). Knowledge Mapping: The Essentials for Success. *APQC.*

Viegas, F. B., & Donath, J. S. (1999, 15-20 May). Chat circles. In *CHI 99*, Pittsburgh, PA.

Visscher-Voerman, I., & Gustafson, K. L. (2004). Paradigms in the theory and practice of education and training design. *Educational Technology Research and Development, 52*(2), 69–89. doi:10.1007/BF02504840

Vitari, C., & Revarini, A. (2006). Validation of IS positivist research: an application and discussion of the Straub, Boudreau and Gefen's guidelines. In *itAIS Conference*, Venice, Italy.

Vorderer, P., Hartmann, T., & Klimmt, C. (2003). Explaining the enjoyment of playing video games: The role of competition. In *Proc. of the 2nd International Conference on Computer Games*, Pittsburgh, PA.

Vygotsky, L. S. (1931). *Mind and society.* Cambridge, MA: MIT Press.

Vygotsky, L. S. (1978). *Mind and Society: The development of higher psychological Process* (M. Cole, V. John Steiner, S. Scribner, & E. Souberman, Eds.). Cambridge, MA: Harvard University Press.

Vygotsky, L. S. (1984). *A formação social da mente - O desenvolvimento dos processos psicológicos superiores* (6th Ed.). São Paulo: Martins Fontes.

Wade, S. J. (2002). The application of pedagogical design patterns to the development of distance learning materials. *Distance Learning Colloquium.* Organised by LTSN-ICS University of York, UK.

Wagner, E. D. (1994). In support of a functional definition of interaction. *American Journal of Distance Education, 8*(2), 6–29. doi:10.1080/08923649409526852

Walberg, H. J., & Bast, J. L. (Eds.). (2003). *Education and Capitalism: How Overcoming Our Fear of Markets and Economics Can Improve America's Schools.* New York: The Hoover Press.

Wallace, M. J. (1998). *Action Research for Language Teachers.* Cambridge, UK: Cambridge University Press

Watzlawick, P., Beavin J., & Jackson D. (1967/1972). *Une logique de la communication.* Paris: Seuil.

Wang, F., & Hannafin, M. J. (2005). Design-based research and technology-enhanced learning environments. *Educational Technology Research and Development, 53*(4), 5–23. doi:10.1007/BF02504682

Wang, K. T., Huang, Y.-M., Jeng, Y.-L., & Wang, T.-I. (2008). A blog-based dynamic learning map. *Computers & Education, 51*(1), 262–278. doi:10.1016/j.compedu.2007.06.005

Wasonga, T. A. (2007). Using technology to enhance collaborative learning. *International Journal of Educational Management, 21*(7), 585–592. doi:10.1108/09513540710822184

Webb, B. R. (1996). The role of users in interactive systems design: when computers are theatre, do we want the audience to write the script? *Behaviour & Information Technology, 15*(2), 76–83. doi:10.1080/014492996120283

Weir, R. (1962). *Language in the Crib.* Mouton, La Haye.

Wenger, E. (1998). *Communities of Practice, Learning, Meaning, and Identity.* Cambridge, UK: Cambridge University Press.

Wenger, E. (1998). Communities of practice. Learning as a social systems. *Systems Thinker, 9*(5).

Wenger, E. (2000). Communities of practice and social learning systems. *Organization, 7*(2), 225–246. doi:10.1177/135050840072002

Wenger, E., McDermott, R., & Snyder, W. (2002). *Cultivating Communities of Practice, a Guide to Managing Knowledge.* Cambridge, MA: Harvard Business School Press.

Werger, E. (1999). *Communities of Practice, Learning, Meaning, and Identity.* Cambridge, UK: University Cambridge Press

Werthheimer, M. (1945). *Productive Thinking.* New York: Harper Collins.

Wheeler, S. (2005). *Creating social presence in digital learning environments: A presence of mind?* TAFE, Queensland, Australia.

Wielinga, B., Schreiber, G., & Breuker, J. (1992). A Modelling Approach to Knowledge Engineering. *Knowledge Acquisition, 4*(1), 23–39. doi:10.1016/1042-8143(92)90013-Q

Wiig, K. M. (1999). Introducing knowledge management into the Enterprise. In J. Liebowitz (Ed.), *Knowledge Management Handbook.* New York: CRC Press

Wild, F., Mödritscher, F., & Sigurdarson, S. (2008, July). Designing for Change: Mash-up Personal Learning Environment. *eLearning Papers,* 9. Retrieved from http://www.elearningeuropa.info/files/media/media15972.pdf

Williams, T. R. (1993). What's so different about visuals? *Journal of the Society for Technical Communication, 40,* 669–676.

Willig, C. (2008). Introducing Qualitative Research in *Psychology.* Maidenhead, UK: Open University Press.

Willis, J. W., & Mehlinger, H. D. (1996). Information technology and teacher education. In J. Sikula (Ed.), *Handbook of Research on Teacher Education* (pp. 978–1029). New York: Macmillan.

Wilson, B., & Cole, P. (1996). Cognitive teaching models. In D. H. Jonas-sen (Ed.), *Handbook of research for educational communications and technology* (pp. 601-621). New York: MacMillan.

Wilson, B., Parrish, P., & Veletsianos, G. (2008). Raising the bar for instructional outcomes: Towards transformative learning experiences. *Educational Technology, 48*(3), 39–44.

Wilson, E. K. (2003). Preservice secondary social studies teachers and technology integration: what do they think and do in their field experiences. *Journal of Computing in Teacher Education, 20*(1), 29–39.

Wind, J., Riege, K., & Bogen, M. (2007). Spinnstube®: A Seated Augmented Reality Display System. In *Virtual Environments, IPT-EGVE – EG/ACM Symposium Proceedings* (pp. 17-23).

Winn, W. D. (2003). Learning in artificial environments: Embodiment, embeddedness and dynamic adaptation. *Technology, Instruction . Cognition and Learning, 1,* 87–114.

Witten, I. H., & Frank, E. (2005). *Data Mining: Practical Machine Learning Tools and Techniques.* San Francisco: Morgan Kaufmann.

Wong, W., & VanPatten, B. (2003). The Evidence is IN: Drills are Out. *Foreign Language Annals, 36*(3), 403–423. doi:10.1111/j.1944-9720.2003.tb02123.x

Wosnitza, M., & Volet, S. (2005). Origin, direction and impact of emotions in social online learning. *Learning and Instruction, 15*(5), 449–464. doi:10.1016/j.learninstruc.2005.07.009

Zeng, Z., Pantic, M., Roisman, G. I., & Huang, T. H. (2009). A survey of affect recognition methods: Audio, visual, and spontaneous expressions. *IEEE Transactions on Pattern Analysis and Machine Intelligence, 31*(1), 39–58. doi:10.1109/TPAMI.2008.52

Zhao, Y. (Ed.). (2003). *What Should Teachers Know about Technology? Perspectives and Practices.* Greenwich, CO: Information Age Publishing.

Zhou, X., & Conati, C. (2002). Modeling students' emotions from cognitive appraisal in educational games. In S. A. Cem, G. Gouarderes, & F. Paraguacu (Eds.), *Intelligent Tutoring Systems 2002, Biarritz, France. Lecture Notes in Computer Science, 2363* (pp. 944-954). Berlin, Germany: Springer Verlag.

Zock, M. (1991). SWIM or sink: the problem of communicating thought. In M. Swartz & M. Yazdani (Eds.), *Bridge to International Communication: Intelligent*

Tutoring Systems for Second Language Learning (pp. 235-247). New York: Springer.

Zock, M. (1997) *Sentence Generation by Pattern Matching: the Problem of Syntactic Choice*. In R. Mitkov & N. Nicolov (Eds.), *Recent Advances in Natural Language Processing. Series: Current Issues in Linguistic Theory* (pp. 317-352).

Zock, M., Sabatier, P., & Jakubiec-Jamet, L. (2007). Who's Next? From Sentence Completion to Conceptually Guided Message Composition. In *Proceedings of the 4th Int. Workshop on Natural Language Processing and Cognitive Science (NLPCS 2007)* (pp. 38-46).

Zurloni, V., Mantovani, F., Mortillaro, M., Vescovo, A., & Anolli, L. (2008). Addressing emotions within e-learning systems. In T. Kidd & H. Song (Eds.), *Handbook of research on instructional systems and technology* (Vol.2, pp. 803-816). Hershey, PA: Information Science Reference.

About the Contributors

Aimilia Tzanavari is Associate Professor at the Department of Design and Multimedia, University of Nicosia, Cyprus. She holds a Ph.D. in Human Computer Interaction from the University of Bristol, United Kingdom. She has worked as a Special Scientist (2006-2008) and a Visiting Lecturer (2002-2004 and 2005) at the Department of Computer Science, University of Cyprus, Cyprus and as a Visiting Assistant Professor (2001-2002) at Miami University, OH, USA. She conducts research and publishes in the areas of human-computer interaction and e-learning and has served as program committee member and reviewer in various European and International workshops and conferences. She has participated in numerous research projects supported by the European Commission holding research and management positions.

Nicolas Tsapatsoulis graduated from the School of Electrical and Computer Engineering (ECE), the National Technical University of Athens (NTUA) in 1994 and received his Ph.D degree, in Image Analysis and Synthesis, in 2000 from the same University. He has worked at the School of Electrical and Computer Eng. of the National Technical University of Athens (2000-2002) as a Research Assistant, being responsible for the project "ORESTEIA" IST-2000-26091, and at the Institute of Communications and Computer Systems (ICCS), Athens, Greece, being a Class C' Researcher (2002-2003). During the academic period 2003-2004 he was with the Computer Science department (CS-UCY). of the University of Cyprus (UCY) being a Visiting Lecturer. The academic period 2004 - 2005 he served as a Visiting Assistant Professor at the same department. During the period September 2005 - January 2008 he worked at the University of Peloponnese (UOP), Department of Telecommunications Science and Technology (TST) as an adjunct (PD407 / 80) Lecturer (2005-2006) and Assistant Professor (2006-2008). The same period he was also a Collaborating Researcher in the Computational Intelligence Laboratory (CIL), at the Institute of Informatics and Telecommunications (IIT), of the National Center for Scientific Research ("DEMOKRITOS"), working for the European project BOEMIE, Bootstrapping Ontology Evolution with Multimedia Information Extraction. Since January 2008 is an Assistant Professor at the department of Communication Science and Technology (CIS) of the Cyprus University of Technology (CUT). He is a member of the Technical Chambers of Greece and Cyprus and a member of IEEE Signal Processing and Communication societies. He has published more than 85 papers in international journals, book chapters and proceedings of international conferences. His research has been recognized by the international research community through more than 330 independent citations (Scholar Google).

* * *

Stergos D. Afantenos earned his PhD in December 2006 from the University of Athens, Greece. His doctorate research was on the issue of Multi-document Summarization for events that evolve through time. During the period from January to December 2007 Dr Afantenos joined the Laboratoire d'Informatique Fondamentale in Marseille, France where he collaborated with Dr Michael Zock for the creation of the «Drill Tutor», a platform whose goal is to help someone learn a new language. During the period from January 2008 to August 2009 he joined the team TALN of the LINA laboratory of the University of Nantes, France where he worked on the issue of identifying instances of text reuse or plagiarism. During his stay at LINA, he and his collaborators were awarded with the IBM UIMA award. Dr Afantenos from September 2009 will be joining the IRIT team in Toulouse, France where he will collaborate with Dr Nicholas Asher in order to extract rhetorical relations (based on RST or SDRT) using machine learning techniques.

Charoula Angeli is Assistant Professor of Instructional Technology in the Department of Education at the University of Cyprus. She has undergraduate and graduate studies at Indiana University-Bloomington, USA (BS in Computer Science, 1991, MS in Computer Science, 1993, and Ph.D. in Instructional Systems Technology, 1999). Her research interests include the utilization of educational technologies in K-12, the design of computer-enhanced curricula, educational software design, teacher training, teaching methodology, online learning, computers as cognitive tools and distributed cognition. Dr. Angeli has published in many scientific referred journals and has presented her work in international conferences extensively. She serves on the editorial review boards of several journals in her field.

Luigi Anolli is Full Professor of Cultural Psychology at the University of Milan-Bicocca (Italy). He is also the director of the Centre for Studies in Communication Sciences (CESCOM), and oversees the Ph.D. Program of the Humanities and Social Sciences Department at the same University. He was formerly the director of the Centre for Studies and research in Communication Psychology of the Catholic University in Milan (founded in 1993). He is a member of the international research network on "Methodology for the Analysis of Social Interaction" (MASI) and was involved in several research projects at national and international level. He was co-responsible for the coordination of the University of Milan-Bicocca team in the European project Myself. His main research interests are in psychology of emotions, communication psychology, and cultural psychology, includine such topics as cross-cultural comparisons of emotional and communicative processes, and application of affective computing and serious gaming in learning and training settings.

Panagiotis D. Bamidis is an Assistant Professor of Medical Education Informatics at the Medical School of Aristotle University of Thessaloniki, Greece. He is a permanent member of the International Committee of the iSHIMR conferences, Editorial Board member of the Health Informatics Journal and the Hippokratia Journal, and a reviewer of the IEEE Transactions on Information Technology in BioMedicine, Computer Methods and Programs in BioMedicine, Personal and Ubiquitous Computing and others. His research interests are within Affective and Physiological Computing and HCI, affective and assistive technologies for the disabled and the elderly, technology enhanced learning in medical education, collaborative learning and content sharing and social educational networks, areas in which he has published over 80 papers in various journals and conference proceedings. He has been the Scientific Co-ordinator of 8 national and international grants, while he is currently the project director for the CIP-PSP Long Lasting Memories/LLM project and the eContentPlus2008 project mEducator.

Zohar Ben-Asher was educated in Israel, USA and UK where he also held senior academic position for many years in the areas of Strategic Planning and Management, Education & Teacher Training and China Studies. Prof. Ben-Asher has also taught at institutions of high learning in various countries in Europe, Asia and America. Zohar has served as a consultant on educational system planning and educational policies to local, national and regional governments and has designed a teacher training system for which he has won an international education planning prize. In addition, Prof. Ben-Asher has been involved in designing and management of EU grant supported projects in various FP programmes, including ICT-related projects. Prof. Ben-Asher is the Chairman and Academic Director of the London based ABC Consultants which offers strategic planning services and heads European Research & Financing which offers preparation, management and co-ordination of EU funded R&D projects.

Leonard Bloom has taught and researched Psychology in the USA, the UK and in Southern and West Africa. His most recent position was as Visiting Professor of Psychology at the University of Botswana at Gaborone, where he was responsible for teaching Psychopathology, Developmental Psychology and gave seminars on, broadly, Individual Development in rapidly changing societies. He is currently working on psychological aspects of bilingualism. He has published some 65 professional papers and three books that thematically deal with identity development despite socio-economic and political pressures for conformity. His most recent book is entitled Identity and Ethnic Relations in Africa (1998), a selection of nine of his professional papers.

George Caridakis graduated from the Department of Informatics and Telecommunications from the School of Sciences of the National and Kapodistrian University of Athens in 2004 and received his Ph.D. degree in 2009 from the the Department of Electrical and Computer Engineering, of the National Technical University of Athens. His current research interests lie in the areas of human computer interaction, artificial intelligence, neural networks, image and video processing, 3D computer animation, gesture and sign language recognition, sign language synthesis and virtual reality. He has published more than 15 papers in international journals and proceedings of international conferences. Since 2004 he has participated in 6 research projects at the Greek and European levels.

Chris Christou is Associate Professor in Applied Multimedia at the University of Nicosia, Cyprus. He has a first degree in Philosophy and Cognitive Studies from the University of Sussex, UK, a Master's degree in Knowledge Based Systems from Heriot-Watt University, Edinburgh and a DPhil from Oxford University, UK. His doctoral work utilized photorealistic computer generated 3D graphics to investigate higher-level human vision in shape perception, cue-combination and cue-disambiguation. Subsequent, post-doctoral work concentrated on using interactive 3D virtual environments in perceptual and human spatial memory tasks. Most of this research was carried out at the Max Planck Institute for Biological Cybernetics, one of the leading institutions for VR research in the world. He has also been involved in industrial applications of VR for consumer testing with Unilever Research, UK, and has acted as a consultant in the field of psychophysical testing for Unilever, USA.

Linda Confalonieri received a MS in Psychology from the Catholic University of Milan (Italy) and a Ph.D. in "Subjective well-being, health and cross cultural communication" from the University of Milan-Bicocca. She carries out research activity at the Centre for Studies in Communication Psychology (CESCOM) of the University of Milan-Bicocca. She has active scientific collaboration with Emory

University (GA, USA), where she was visiting student in 2006/07. Her research addresses the communication processes between humans and virtual agents, especially in e-learning environments.

Mary Dyson is a Senior Lecturer in the Department of Typography & Graphic Communication at the University of Reading, UK. She has a background in psychology which has influenced her work within typography and graphic communication in a number of ways. Appointed to teach and research within an area once known as Electronic Publishing, she has focused on users and their interactions with documents, not the technology. One of her primary research interests is empirical investigations of how changes in the design of documents affect performance. In particular, Mary has done experiments with screen-based material and published this work alongside reviews of other research in this area. She has developed various e-learning materials to support her own teaching and supervised PhD students working on the interface design of Virtual Learning Environments, of which Luciane Maria Fadel was one.

Luciane Maria Fadel is a Senior Lecturer and course developer in the Department of Design at the Unoesc Videira, Brazil. Having a background in visual communication and computer engineering has been a strong influence in her area of research which is multi faceted computer interface design combined with human factor interaction. Exploring the human factor interaction within the e-learning environment was the enhanced area of research undertaken during her PhD study within the United Kingdom. Returning to Brazil she has progressed further her ideas for the Unoesc Videira within this emerging and complex area of technology as a means delivering effective e-learning solutions. Recognising the combination of e-learning with an emotional and cultural sensitivity is an emerging and accelerating trend in education service delivery not only in Brazil but in other universities around the world.

Franca Garzotto is Associate Professor of Computer Engineering at Politecnico di Milano - Department of Electronics and Information. She has a Master in Mathematics from University of Padova (Italy) and a Ph.D in Computer Engineering from Politecnico di Milano. Her research topics include: usability engineering, web design models, user requirements, multichannel web applications, design patterns, tangible interaction, mainly in the domains of e-learning and e-culture. She is (co-) author of over 100 publications in international conference proceedings, journals, and books. She served as Co-Chair of several international workshops and conferences, including ICHIM (International Cultural Heritage Informatics Meeting) in 2001 and ACM-SIGCHI IDC (Interaction Design and Children Conference) in 2009. She was European chair of ACM SIG-WEB (Special Interest Group on Hypermedia & Web) from 1997 to 1999. Since 1988, she has been involved in many EC funded research projects, including INDOC, SUPERDOC, MINER, HYTEA, HYPERTOUR, SITMOON, UWA, OPENDRAMA, VNET5, HELP, MINERVA, EPOCH, TELL, ADAPT, ELEN, EDUCOMICS.

Tatiana Gavrilova is a Head of Information Technologies in Management Department at Graduate School of Management in St.Petersburg State University. In 1986 she got PhD in Computer Science at St. Petersburg State Technical University, and in 1996 was awarded a Doctor of Science Diploma (habilitation) in the same university. She is Head of St. Petersburg Division of Russian Association for Artificial Intelligence (RAAI) and a member of Petersburg Scientific Union. Dr. Gavrilova has published over 100 journal articles and conference papers (more than 60 in English), she is the author of 5 books and text books (in Russian) For her research she received first prize for fundamental studies in 1994 from

RAAI. Dr. Gavrilova is lecturing in English at the Universities in Finland, Italy, Poland and Estonia. In 1998 and 2004 she has been Fulbright Visiting Senior Research Scholar and Lecturer in Pennsylvania State University and University of Pittsburgh (USA).

Athanasios V. Giouvanakis has received a PhD from the University of Macedonia, Thessaloniki, Greece on "Designing and developing adaptive e-learning systems in a semantic web environment". He also has received a Master in Information Systems, University of Macedonia, Thessaloniki, Greece and a Diploma in Physics from the Aristotelian University, Thessaloniki, Greece. His research interests include E-learning methodologies, the Semantic web, software design and development platforms and Multimedia applications. Since 1999 he is a Researcher in the Information Systems Laboratory at the University of Macedonia, Greece. He has led the e-Learning project IRIS – An Integrated E-Learning Environment on Business Processes Administration and International Accounting Standards and he has participated in many other Research and Development projects. He has taught introductory and specialized courses at the University of Western Macedonia, the University of Macedonia and the Technological Educational Institute of Serres and his research work has been awarded for its excellence by the AACE (Association for the Advancement of Computing in Education).

Dragoş Daniel Iordache is currently a psychologist at the National Institute for Research and Development in Informatics – ICI Bucharest. Previously he was a pedagogical adviser at "Gheorghe Asachi" High School in Bucharest. He received a BSc degree in Sociology-Psychology from "Spiru Haret" University, Bucharest in 2003, a BSc degree in Educational sciences from University of Bucharest in 2004 and an MSc degree in Educational counselling from University of Bucharest in 2006. He is currently a PhD student in educational Sciences University of Bucharest. His research interests include usability and pedagogical evaluation of educational systems. He is a RoCHI (ACM SIGCHI Romania) member and served as reviewer for the RoCHI 2008 conference.

Eleni Kaldoudi is an Assistant Professor of Physics of Medical Imaging and Telemedicine at the School of Medicine, Democritus University of Thrace, Greece. Her research interests are within medical informatics and telematics, with emphasis on technologies supporting medical education, home care telematics, medical image management, and magnetic resonance imaging, areas in which she has published one book and over 50 papers in various journals and conference proceedings. She is currently acting as an expert in the EU FP7 Programme "Capacities: Regions of Knowledge, Research Potential and Coherent Development of Policies", and has been an Associate Editor in the field of "eLearning" for the journal of IEEE Transactions on Information Technology in Biomedicine. She has been a reviewer in a number of scientific journals and a member of the scientific committee for a number of international conferences in the field of medical informatics and telematics, and a scientific/technical coordinator in 6 national and EU grants.

Kostas Karpouzis graduated from the Department of Electrical and Computer Engineering from the National Technical University of Athens in 1998 and received his Ph.D. degree in 2001 from the same University. His current research interests lie in the areas of human computer interaction, artificial intelligence, neural networks, image and video processing, 3D computer animation, sign language synthesis and virtual reality. Dr. Karpouzis has published more than 70 papers in international journals and in proceedings of international conferences. He is a member of the technical committee of the

International Conference on Image Processing (ICIP) and a reviewer in many international journals. Since 1995 he has participated in more than 10 research projects at the Greek and European levels. Dr. Karpouzis is an associate researcher at the Institute of Communication and Computer Systems (ICCS) and holds an adjunct lecturer position in the University of Piraeus, teaching Medical Informatics and Image Processing. He is also a national representative in IFIPWorking Groups 12.5 'Artificial Intelligence Applications' and 3.2 'Informatics and ICT in Higher Education'.

Stefanos Kollias was born in Athens, Greece, in 1956. He received his Diploma in electrical and computer engineering from the National Technical University of Athens (NTUA), Athens, Greece, in 1979, his M.Sc. degree in communication engineering in 1980 from the University of Manchester Institute of Science and Technology, Manchester, UK, and his Ph.D. degree in signal processing from the Computer Science Division, NTUA. He has been with the Electrical Engineering Department, NTUA, since 1986, where he currently serves as a Professor. Since 1990, he has been the Director of the Image, Video, and Multimedia Systems Laboratory, NTUA. His current research interests lie in the areas of image and video processing, analysis, coding, storage, retrieval, multimedia systems, computer graphics and virtual reality, artificial intelligence, neural networks, human computer interaction, and medical imaging. He has published more than 120 papers, 50 of which in international journals. He has been a member of the technical or advisory committee or invited speaker in 40 international conferences. He is a reviewer of ten IEEE Transactions and of ten other journals. Ten graduate students have completed their doctorate under his supervision, while another ten are currently performing their Ph.D. thesis. He and his team have been participating in 38 European and national projects.

Christophe Kolski obtained his Ph.D in 1989 and his post-doctoral degree (*Habilitation à Diriger des Recherches*) in 1995. He is specialized in human-computer interaction, software engineering for interactive systems and intelligent systems design. He is professor in Computer Science at the University of Valenciennes and Hainaut-Cambrésis (France) and head of the "Automated Reasoning and Human-Computer Interaction" research group in the LAMIH. He is author, editor or co-editor of a great number of books, book chapters, articles in scientific journals and international congresses, and final research reports in relation with industry in different application domains. He was the president of the organization committee of the CADUI'2002 conference and co-president of the scientific committee of the IHM'2003 and ERGO-IA'2006 conferences.

Stathis Konstantinidis has received a Bachelor Degree in Computer Science, University of Crete, Greece, and an MSc in Medical Informatics, Aristotle University of Thessaloniki, Greece. He is currently a PhD Candidate in Medical Education Informatics, Aristotle University of Thessaloniki, Greece, and he is also working as research associate at the Laboratory of Medical Informatics of Medical School of Aristotle University of Thessaloniki and teaching at Technological Educational Institute of West Macedonia, Kozani, Greece.

Michel Labour obtained his Ph.d in 1998 by studying the relationship between empowerment and learning preferences of adults. His present research focuses on the emotional and social conditions and the manner in which individuals make sense of informational-linked saliencies in the appropriative process. This involves looking at the "bleed-through" effect between online virtual worlds and face-to-face realities, and more generally, the empowering use of technology to breach cultural and social divides. He is also a specialist in adult education and training, and in charge of promoting Information & Communication Technologies in continuing education at the University of Valenciennes and Hainaut-Cambrésis (France). He is a reviewer of a number of impact-factor rated scientific journals, and international scientific conferences, as well as being on organising committees of H2PTM'01, H2PTM'09, and "Complexité 2010".

Grzegorz Majewski obtained his MSc in Information Systems and Quantitative Techniques from the Warsaw School of Economics in 2005. His MSc was on workflow-based e-learning. He has also obtained an MSc in Computer System Development from the University of the West of Scotland (UWS) in 2007. Currently he is a research student at the UWS where he is specialising in knowledge sharing, e-learning, organizational knowledge and their implications for business and modern organizations. He was also active on professional basis in financial and telecommunications industry. His papers were presented during the following conferences: The 9th European Conference on Knowledge Management, Southampton 2008, Conference on Information Technology and Economic Development, Nigeria 2008, ISOneWorld, Las Vegas 2009, IADIS Web Communities, and Portugal 2009.

Despina Makridou - Bousiou is a Professor of Applied Informatics at the University of Macedonia, Greece. Dr. Makridou - Bousiou teaches principles of economics, teaching methods, teaching techniques for economists and teaching techniques for political sciences. Her academic interests are in the field of teaching economics with new technologies and e-learning models. She uses a variety of electronic tools to design, prepare and deliver her instruction. In return she expects her students to make use of these tools as a component of their learning experience. Dr. Makridou - Bousiou has participated as a speaker at numerous national and international meetings and conferences.

Lori Malatesta graduated from the Department of Electrical and Computer Engineering in the National Technical University of Athens in 2000. She was awarded a Master of Science degree with distinction on Cognitive Science and Natural Language Processing from the University of Edinburgh in 2001. During the next three years she was occupied as a junior computer engineer in the Education Technology Sector of the Research Academic Computer Technology Institute in Greece. She is currently pursuing her Ph.D. degree on Affective Computing at the Image, Video and Multimedia Systems Laboratory in the National Technical University of Athens. Her research interests include computational modelling of affective phenomena, synthesis and analysis of non-verbal human expressivity, and affective interface adaptation. She participated in the NoE HUMAINE (IST-2002-2.3.1.6 Multimodal Interfaces) as well as in several European and National R&D projects.

Fabrizia Mantovani received her PhD in Communication Psychology from the Catholic University of Milan (Italy). She is Research Professor of General Psychology (tenured position) at the University of Milan-Bicocca, where she carries out research at the Centre for Studies in Communication Sciences (CESCOM). She teaches "Communication Psychology" in the Faculty of Education and is a member of the Teaching Committee of the Ph.D. in "Sciences of Education and Communication". Member of the international research network on "Methodology for the Analysis of Social Interaction" (MASI) and of the Editorial Board of the Open Communication Journal, she serves as a reviewer for several international journals and conferences. Since 2000 she has been involved as team manager in several research projects on Information and Communication Technologies funded by the European Commission. Her research interests include: affective computing and e-learning; serious games; nonverbal communication; virtual reality applications for therapy and training; embodied conversational agents.

Marcello Mortillaro received a bachelor's degree in Psychology from the Catholic University of Milan (Italy) and a Ph.D. in Communication Psychology from the same University. He is currently a Post-Doc researcher at the Swiss Centre for Affective Sciences of Genere (Switzerland). His research addresses the multimodal expression of emotion and the synchronization among the different modalities, within the framework of the Component Process Model, as well as the application of the multimodal approach to the emotional expression in music and to the emotional communication occurring within natural settings.

George E. Palaigeorgiou holds a PhD in Students-Computers Interactions from the Informatics Department of the Aristotle University of Thessaloniki. He has several publications in scientific journals such as Journal of Computer Assisted Learning, Computers & Education, etc. and he has participated in many funded research projects. His research interests include learning about computers, participatory design, computer attitudes, cognitive tools and computer ethics.

Costin Pribeanu is currently a Senior Researcher at the National Institute for Research and Development in Informatics – ICI Bucharest. He received a BSc degree in Planning and Economic Cybernetics in 1982 and a PhD degree in Economic Informatics in 1997 from the Academy of Economic Studies in Bucharest, Romania. His research interests include usability evaluation and design of interactive systems, with a focus on task analysis, task-based design of user interfaces, design patterns, and guidelines-based evaluation. He is the author of several scientific papers on user interface design and evaluation. He is an editorial board member for HCI Book Series published by Springer and served as program committee member / reviewer for several major conferences in the domain. He has been chair of TAMODIA 2002 and co-chair of CADUI 2006. Costin Pribeanu chaired RoCHI (ACM SIGCHI Romania) from April 2001 to June 2009. He is ACM Senior Member since 2009.

Amaryllis Raouzaiou is a senior researcher at the Image, Video and Multimedia Systems Laboratory of ICCS-NTUA. She received her PhD in Human-Computer Interaction from the Department of Electrical and Computer Engineering, the National Technical University of Athens in 2006. Her current research interests lie in the areas of human-computer interaction, synthesis and recognition of expressions and non-verbal communication. She is a member of the Technical Chamber of Greece. She participated to the NoE HUMAINE (IST-2002-2.3.1.6 Multimodal Interfaces.) and she has been involved in several European and National R&D projects and has published journal articles and conference papers in the above fields. She is currently participating to the IP CALLAS and METABO and the STREP Feelix-Growing.

Olivia Realdon graduated in Philosophy at the Catholic University of Milan in 1990 and since 2000 has been serving as a Lecturer for the course of Communication Psychology in several Italian universities (University of Urbino, Catholic University of Milan, Free University of Bozen, and the University of Milan-Bicocca). Member of the international research network on "Methodology for the Analysis of Social Interaction" (MASI), she carries out research activity at the "Centre for Studies in Communication Sciences" (CESCOM) of the University of Milan-Bicocca, where she was involved in the European FP6 project "MYSELF"- SME-2003-1-508259. Her research interests include psychology of emotion, positive psychology with a focus on optimism, nonverbal communication and cross-cultural communication. The scientific study of emotions also finds expression in research activities in the affective computing domain and in the use of interactive simulations and serious games for the training of emotional and communication skills.

Haido A. Samaras has received a PhD from the University of Macedonia, Thessaloniki, Greece on "Modelling and developing adaptive multimedia e-learning systems based on learning objects within a Web environment". She has also received a Master in Information Systems from the University of Macedonia, Thessaloniki, Greece, a Bachelors Degree in Mathematics and a Bachelors Degree in English Literature from the Aristotelian University, Thessaloniki, Greece. Her research interests include E-learning methodologies, Multimedia Learning Environments, Learning Objects and the Semantic Web. From 1999-2002 she worked as a Researcher in the Information Systems Laboratory at the University of Macedonia, Greece. She has participated in multiple EU-funded research projects such as TELEMATHOS and PENED. She is currently Deputy Dean at the Anatolia American College in Thessaloniki, Greece. She is also a coordinator for the Network of Innovative Schools, a privately funded project for Greek secondary school teachers under the auspices of the Greek Ministry of Education. Her research work has been awarded for its excellence by the AACE (Association for the Advancement of Computing in Education).

Peter B. Sloep: After graduating as a (theoretical) biologist (1978) at the Free University of Amsterdam (Vrije Universiteit, VU), Peter Sloep completed a PhD in theoretical biology at the State University of Groningen, Netherlands (1983). After post-docs at Arizona State University (USA), the University of Guelph (Canada) and the University of Groningen, he became assistent professor, later associate professor at the Science Faculty of the Open University of the Netherlands (OUNL) in 1986. While working there, he spent a year as a Research Fellow at the University of Bielefeld's Zentrum für Interdiziplinärforschung working a project that sought the bridge the gap between the social and biological sciences. In 1999 he switched departments at the OUNL and became assistent professor at the Educational Expertise Centre (OTEC). From 2003 to 2007 Sloep also fulfilled a part-time position of associate professor ('lector') in Educational Functions of ICT at the Fontys University of Applied Sciences, where he led a research group ('kenniskring") which investigated the use and application of ICT for learning at the secondary school level. In 2008, he became full professor in Technology Enhanced Learning at OTEC, OUNL, and programme director of its R&D programme on Learning Networks. In addition to this, het heads one of the programme lines of the OUNL's laboratory for lifelong Learning (NeLLL) and is the acting director of NeLLL as of May 2009. From its inception in 2001, Sloep has chaired the Technical Committee Learning Technology of the Dutch Standards Organisation (NEN). He serves on the Editorial Board of ALT-J, on the Consulting Board of *Computers in Human Behaviour*, frequently reviews papers for various other journals and conferences in the e-learning field, and has reviewed proposals for the Canadian, US and Dutch research bodies. He supervises several doctoral students. During his stay at the Open University, Sloep has worked for about 10 years as a developer of distance teaching courses, mainly in the areas of biology and its theoretical underpinnings, writing and editing courses on such diverse subjects as *Evolutionary Biology, Mathematical Models for the Life Sciences, Understanding Scientific Reasoning*, and *Environmental Policy.* Over the years his work ever more turned towards matters educational. Examples of educational innovation projects he was involved in are a project sponsored by one of the early European Framework programmes on erecting a network of European Study centres for distance learning, and the Virtual Company - a simulated company in which groups of students carry out authentic assignments. This prompted his move to the then research and development programme of the OUNL's Educational Expertise Centre (OTEC). This programme is still reknown for its development of the Educational Modelling Language EML, which underlies the IMS Learning Design specification. Since the beginning of 2008, Sloep coordinates this programma, which has changed both name (R & D on Learning Networks) and focus. Its current topic is Competence Development, specifically in the context of Learning Networks, online social networks that are designed to support non-formal (informal) learning. This programme has received several research funds, notably through the TENCompetence Integrated Project by the EU's 6th Framework Programma. Currently, Sloep also coordinates an EU funded so-called STREP on collaborative, innovative product design (idSpace).

Konstantinos A. Tarabanis is a professor at the Department of Business Administration of the University of Macedonia, Greece. He received an Engineering Diploma from the National Technical University of Athens (1983), an M.S. degree in Engineering and Computer Science (1984 and 1988 respectively) and a Ph.D. degree in Computer Science (1991) at Columbia University, New York. He was Research Staff Member at the IBM T.J. Watson Research Center where he worked on e-manufacturing techniques. His current research interests include conceptual modeling of information systems, service models and architectures, as well as the domains of e-government, e-learning, e-participation and e-business. He has authored several research publications in the areas of software modeling and development for information systems in the domains of e-government, e-business, e-learning and e-manufacturing. He has received best paper awards from IEEE in the area of e-manufacturing, the European Conference on Information Systems for his work in e-government and the International Academy of e-business for his work in e-business.

George N. Triantafyllakos is a doctoral student in the Informatics Department of Aristotle University in Thessaloniki. His scientific area of interest is Participatory Software Design and HCI. He has presented and published his academic work in several international conferences and scientific journals. He is also freelancing as a graphic and web designer, and his design work has been exhibited in various local and international exhibitions.

Ioannis A. Tsoukalas is a professor-emeritus in the Informatics Department of Aristotle University of Thessaloniki. His interests include information society technologies, educational technology and international R&D policies.

Paraskevi Tzouveli graduated from the School of Electrical and Computer Engineering of National Technical University of Athens in 2001 and received her Ph.D. degree in 2009 at the Image, Video, and Multimedia Systems Laboratory at the same University. Her current research interests lie in the areas of image and video analysis, information retrieval, knowledge manipulation and e-learning systems. She is a member of the Technical Chamber of Greece. She has been involved in several European and National R&D projects and has published journal articles and conference papers in the above fields. Contact her at tpar@image.ntua.gr

Abel Usoro, BSc(Hons), MSc, PhD, MBCS, lectures in the School of Computing, University of the West of Scotland, United Kingdom. His research interest is information systems, including e-learning and knowledge management. He has widely published in refereed journals, such as *Knowledge Management Research and Practice*, and books, for example, *Advanced Topics in Global Information Management: 1*, edited by Felix Tan (IGI Publishing, 2002). He is a member of the British Computer Society, among others. He has chaired, organised and served on the scientific committees of many international conferences. His research and teaching has taken him to many countries in North and South America, Europe, Africa and Asia. His consultancy and teaching includes technical aspects of information systems such as Oracle database design and PL SQL with the Oracle IT Academy. *Correspondence*: Dr Abel Usoro, School of Computing, University of the West of Scotland, Paisley PA1 2BE, UK (abel.usoro@uws.ac.uk). *Url: http://cis.paisley.ac.uk/usor-ci0*

George Veletsianos holds a PhD in Learning Technologies from the University of Minnesota, USA and is Lecturer of Digital Technologies, Communication & Education at the University of Manchester, UK. He has had in excess of 50 studies presented in Europe, Latin America, and the United States and in excess of 30 articles and manuscripts published in academic journals, books, and conference proceedings. George's teaching and research expertise lies on the design, development, and evaluation of pedagogical agents, adventure learning, and electronic learning environments, with special focus on the learner experience. His research crosses disciplinary lines and has appeared in international journals such as the *Journal of Computer Assisted Learning, Journal of Educational Computing Research*, and *Journal of Research on Technology in Education.*

Michael Zock was born in Germany where lived until the age of twenty. Ever since then he has been living in France where he got his PhD 1980 in experimental psychology (psycholinguistics). He entered the CNRS 1989, working at Limsi, an AI lab close to Paris (Orsay). 2003 he has been promoted to become research director, and 2005 he has joined the NLP group of the *Laboratoire d'Informatique Fondamentale* (LIF) at Luminy, Marseille. His research interests are geared towards *language production* by people and machines, with a special emphasis on the simulation of the process and the building of tools to help people to perform this task or to acquire the needed skills. His current research foci comprise *lexical access, acquisition of verbal fluency*, ontology-driven *message-* and *outline planning.*

Valentino Zurloni is Assistant Professor of General Psychology (tenured position) at the University of Milan-Bicocca and member of the Teaching Committe of the Ph.D. in "Sciences of Education and Communication" at the same university. He teaches "Cross-cultural Communication Psychology" in the Faculty of Education at University of Milan Bicocca, and "General psychology" at Free University of Bolzen. He is member of the international research network on "Methodology for the Analysis of Social Interaction" (MASI). He carries out research activity at the "Centre for Studies in Communication Sciences" (CESCOM) of the University of Milan-Bicocca. During his research studies, Zurloni has been concerned with different psychological fields, with a special focus on communication psychology. In particular, he has closely examined persuasive and deceptive communication in their different aspects. Other research interests focus on verbal and nonverbal communication, psychology of emotion, cultural and cross-cultural psychology, and affective computing.

Index

B

C

D

E

M

N

O

P

Q

R

S

U

V

W

X